Critical

Social Issues

in American

Education

Critical

TOWARD

Social Issues

THE 21ST

in American

CENTURY

Education

Edited by

H. Svi Shapiro
University of North Carolina at Greensboro

David E. Purpel
University of North Carolina at Greensboro

Longman
New York & London

**Critical Social Issues in American
Education: Toward the Twenty-first Century**

Longman, 10 Bank Street, White Plains, N.Y. 10606

Associated companies:
Longman Group Ltd., London
Longman Cheshire Pty., Melbourne
Longman Paul Pty., Auckland
Copp Clark Pitman, Toronto

Acquisitions editor: Kenneth Clinton
Sponsoring editor: Naomi Silverman
Development editor: Virginia L. Blanford
Production editor: Victoria Mifsud
Cover design: Michelle Szabo
Text art: Pencil Point Studio
Production supervisor: Anne Armeny

Library of Congress Cataloging-in-Publication Data

Critical social issues in American education : toward the twenty-first
    century / edited by H. Svi Shapiro and David E. Purpel.
        p.   cm.
    Includes bibliographical references.
    ISBN 0-8013-0950-6
        1. Critical pedagogy—United States.   2. Education—Social
    aspects—United States.   3. Education—Political aspects—United
    States.   I. Shapiro, H. Svi.   II. Purpel, David E.
    LC196.5.U6C75   1993
    370.19′0973—dc20   92-5504
                                                            CIP

1 2 3 4 5 6 7 8 9 10–MA–9695949392

For my father,
Sydney Shapiro,
who taught me the importance of the news;
and my mother,
Rebecca Shapiro,
who showed me what it means to have faith in hard times

Contents

Foreword

Robert N. Bellah and his colleagues begin their new book, *The Good Society* (New York: Knopf, 1991), by pointing to the need on the part of people who work in institutions to exert themselves to make sense of the larger world around them. Aware of the complexity of that world, they caution their readers that complexity "should not be a cover beneath which undemocratic managers and experts can hide." Some of the reasons to welcome this text are that it decodes, demystifies, and uncovers. Its contributors not only provide a variegated context for an enriched understanding of education today, they also offer a range of sense-making opportunities from the vantage points of a diversity of disciplines. Whether the discipline is sociology, economics, ethnography, educational theory, black studies, women's studies, or ecology on a global scale, each one becomes a remarkable lens through which a reader can gain a fresh view of the changing, pulsating reality of American public schools in a moment of crisis. Certain of the problems confronted seem overwhelming at first look. Certain of the consequences of the decline recounted here seem catastrophic. But there are voices here that open spaces for promise and for possibility: personal voices, prophetic voices, poetic voices, political voices. The book challenges its readers, therefore, to take positions, to refuse determinism, to choose themselves as agents of change.

It must be said that the writers here, all distinguished in their own fields, have succeeded in avoiding clichés and stereotypes. Moreover, all—in their own fashion—have stressed dissonances, contradictions, and dialectical connections in such a way as to indicate that the involvement of schools with the forces around is not to be seen as seamless or totalized. Granting the pressures of hierarchy, corporate interests, and military and technological concerns, the writers here recognize the democratizing powers of the schools. In various idioms, they present the inevitable contest between the role of the schools in reproduction and maintenance of the old capitalist workplace and their role in promoting equality and mobility, not to speak of democratic values. Few professionals have not felt the strain of such a conflict; and, if nothing else, the chapters to come will enable them to name its sources, articulate its meanings for teachers and for students, and perhaps do something to transform.

The accounts of recent conservatism in what is called the "welfare-educational state" highlight still further that conflict in its most contemporary form. When more details are offered with regard to the New Right, and the question is raised with reference to left-wing and liberal responses, professionals and publics are again challenged to reject old categories and definitions and, as Christopher Lasch writes, to redefine "the terms of political debate." One of the fundamental intentions of this book comes even clearer: the editors and the writers are admonishing their readers to develop a significant critique, an appropriate language, and a newly reflective mode of action on the world.

The chapters on social injustice, the strivings for equality and decency, the effects of tracking: all these lead to a serious challenge to present conceptions of reform. They end, in the unique spirit of this book, with some sharp-edged images of driven mothers, suffering poor children, alienated members of minority groups. There are thought-provoking accounts of the relation between racial identity (and what Signithia Fordham calls "racelessness") and school success, as there are enlightening things to be read about what is meant by excellence in what the editors call our "fractured community."

The last few chapters are, in some measure, symphonic. They extend the arguments to relate them to new kinds of emergent sensibility, to new modes of liberation from what exists and what is taken for granted, to global interdependence. Then the prophetic voices are tapped to speak about the moral and spiritual crisis as it affects education: the despair, the estrangements, the self-deceptions, and the instances of hope and quests for meaning. The reader is continually reminded that education is never neutral, that it is political; and in these chapters, the meeting of the personal and the political (and the opening of spaces in between), sheds a particularly clarifying light on what might be done and on what can be done if alternative pedagogies can be developed. As one of the editors writes, such a pedagogy must be joined to a pedagogy of vision. "The critical spirit underpinning such an education is not one of sheer negativity but is one of a coin whose reverse face is concerned with reconstructive possibilities." There are unlikely to be such possibilities without understanding of complex contexts, without namings of the lived world. This book makes this far more likely for readers willing to be awakened to ask the probing questions, to enter into the restless dialogue.

Maxine Greene
Teachers College, Columbia University

Acknowledgments

This book is the fruit of our teaching and as such could not have been developed without the passionate involvement, dialogue, interest, and critical judgments of our students. Their engagement in the question of how education might truly connect to the making of a more democratic, just, and compassionate world has nourished this project. My friend and colleague David E. Purpel has, as always, pushed me into distinguishing academic vanities from those intellectual qualities that might truly contribute to realizing our deepest moral and social commitments. For this and much else in developing this volume, I am appreciative.

I wish to thank, in particular, Naomi Silverman, whose interest, insight, and imagination were crucial in the genesis of this book. In addition, I want to thank Susan Books for her invaluable help in editing this work and Jeannette Dean for her secretarial assistance and constant good cheer.

H. Svi Shapiro

Introduction

In this book our goal is to provide a focus for thinking about education in the context of a society that, as it enters the final decade of this millennium, is faced with a range of critical, sometimes catastrophic, issues and problems such as poverty and growing social injustice, racism and sexism, and other forms of exclusion; the depersonalization of social and political life; the moral and spiritual decay of the culture; and the ecological deterioration of the planet. Our concern is not only American society (although this is the emphasis) but also the larger global community.

We start from the conviction that as both citizens and educators we dare not ignore these issues and problems. We believe that educational discourse in both professional and public circles has become narrow and trivial, and we offer this book as part of our continuing efforts to resist and transform the assumptions and concerns of such discourse. For education to become a humanly vital, ethically responsible endeavor, infused with a serious commitment to democratic values, we must understand its connection to the urgent and pressing issues laid out in this book. These issues represent what we believe to be the most critical issues that we and our children face as we move into the twenty-first century.

This book is intended to work on two levels. First, we are concerned with developing an awareness concerning how education is connected to the wider structures of social, cultural, political, and economic life. Any attempt to apprehend the nature and purpose of education in the United States requires us to grasp the interrelatedness between schooling and the larger culture. The readings were selected to heighten understanding of these linkages. For example, some of the chapters examine how educational reform has been a response to popular movements concerned with equality and social justice. Others explore how changes in education are connected to the restructuring of American labor and the decline of U.S. manufacturing. Further readings discuss ways in which the process of schooling legitimizes the hierarchies of social class, race, and gender and transmits the dominant ideology.

It is important to add here that we have come to appreciate the debilitating and demoralizing effects on students of critical analyses that *only* criticize. Empowering human beings for the purpose of social change requires, we believe, not merely brilliantly insightful criticism but also the vision of alternatives that can be positively embraced and, ultimately, worked for. Such descriptions helps us to re-image the future and to make in Maxine Greene's words, "the strange familiar."[1]

Thus, on a second level, our goal in this book is to encourage not only a critical examination of our present social reality but also a serious discussion of alternatives—of what a transformed society and educational process might look like—through what Henry Giroux calls a "language of possibility."[2] Thus, this book provides elements of what might be termed a new paradigm for conceiving of our social, cultural, economic, political, and moral world.

The major theme of this book—that education is intimately connected to the major social concerns and issues of our times—challenges the conventional shallow terms of educational discourse. What is perhaps unusual about the collection is that we have included not only chapters specifically about education but also those that provide a broader social perspective. In this way we hope to maintain a dialectic between the issues and problems of education and those of the larger society. The book includes pieces by authors who are influential both inside and outside the field of educational studies.

This collection is intended to focus on issues we believe to be crucial aspects of a growing world crisis. And in this context a word is in order about what this book *is not*. The readings are not offered as a contribution to the preparation of impartial social scientists. Nor are they meant to titillate detached, aloof, uninvolved voyeurs of a catastrophic global condition filled, as it is, with human suffering of enormous proportions. What we *do* intend in presenting these readings is to challenge educators increasingly to define education as a political and ethical activity explicitly connected to the making of a world where such suffering is reduced, if not eliminated. Indeed, the fact that professional and theoretical discourse about education is not centered on the immense problems confronting humanity indicates the degree to which it has been trivialized. This discourse is concerned with such issues as merit pay, achievement test scores, homework, and the like—rather than with the looming issues confronting all of humankind today.

Some people concerned with teacher education would argue that the primary value of teaching educators about social issues is to make them more "well rounded." But our view is quite different. We believe that as educators and future educators, we must understand what is happening around us (and as a consequence, in us and to us) because these larger issues are the ones we must actively address in our work. In a world in which 40,000 children die each day from starvation—over 500,000 a year[3]—any other kind of education represents a failure of our deepest human responsibilities.

Many of the students we have taught find disturbing, even shocking, our efforts to connect deliberately the work of teachers to an ethically committed, politically charged pedagogy. This linkage flies in the face of many teachers' best liberal instincts about the moral neutrality of what is taught and the impartial role of teachers. Our primary response to those teachers is to point to the substantial literature about schools that clearly demonstrates education is a human practice that always has been and always will be a moral and political practice. We believe that education is always and everywhere about the business of legitimizing and reproducing existing social relations, values, and ways of life—*or* about working to oppose them. Richard Shaull has expressed it well:

> There is no such thing as a *neutral* educational process. Education either functions as an instrument which is used to facilitate the integration of the younger generation into the logic of the present system and bring about conformity to it, or it becomes "the practice of freedom," the means by which men and women deal critically and creatively with reality and discover how to participate in the transformation of their world.[4]

Our book is specifically organized to raise awareness of what is at stake in this country and in the world as we move into the twenty-first century. More than this, however, we hope that it cries out for the need for us to act, as citizens and as educators, to address the pain, the dilemmas, and the crises that pervade our national life and the life of the planet. Through consideration of the issues addressed in this book, we hope to contribute to increased awareness and greater human commitment. We are not suggesting that simple, easy answers are always available, nor are we arguing that policy choices can be merely "read off" from ethical commitments. But this is not to say that there are *no* responses or solutions to the problems and crises discussed in this book. We believe that there are. The most honest stance we can take—one that is neither simplistically hopeful nor bleakly hopeless—is to alert our readers to the often contradictory demands and pulls of the modern (or perhaps more accurately, postmodern) condition. Thus, one consideration guiding the selection of the readings in this volume is what we perceive to be some of the most difficult dilemmas of our time: the free-market economy versus democratic and egalitarian values; the assertion of cultural differences versus community; social justice and responsibility versus individual freedom; moral commitment versus the uncertainty of truth or knowledge; full-employment versus the end of the work-oriented culture.

The issues raised in this book have shaped and will shape the present and future condition of all our lives—our hopes, fears, anxieties, and dreams. Addressing these issues is not simply a matter of referring and *de*ferring to the "experts," for we all know a great deal, even if, as Michael Polanyi notes, we frequently know "more than we can say."[5] Antonio Gramsci, the Italian Marxist, taught us to recognize that in the often-maligned (especially in academic circles) common sense of the people, there are penetrating insights into the nature and workings of our social reality.[6] Gramsci and those influenced by him tell us that in dealing with our lived world we are *all*, unavoidably, philosophers and social scientists. This world in crisis is the world in which all of us struggle to survive, produce meaning, and derive joy. The crises we are concerned with are not just faraway events depicted on the television evening news but also are mirrored in our family life, sexual relations, the quality of life in our neighborhoods and communities, and nature of our work experiences. It must be added, however, that although we all know about and have something to say about these matters, in the classroom students often choose not to speak up. Many voices are never heard. Such silence, as those who espouse critical pedagogy or study the lives of the disempowered have made abundantly clear, is also an important dimension of the crisis. It is the consequence of a world—especially schooling—that systematically devalues and excludes the voices of many individuals. Paulo Freire powerfully summarizes this process as the "banking method" of teaching:

> The teacher teaches and the students are taught.
> The teacher knows everything and the students know nothing.
> The teacher thinks and the students are thought about.
> The teacher talks and the students listen meekly.
> The teacher chooses and enforces a choice, and the students comply.
> The teacher is the subject of the learning process, while the pupils are mere objects.[7]

Of course, taking seriously the voices of students certainly undermines the teacher's possibility of "covering" the curriculum. But this is a problem that does not worry us too much because covering a prescribed number of text pages or topics or sequencing the topics in the right order are problems more relevant to bureaucrats than to teachers. Our concerns for the readers of this book are of a different type. Through these chapters we hope that students will confront the truly critical issues that face us as individual human beings, as citizens of U.S. society, and as members of a global community—and will consider what are, or ought to be, the consequences of these issues for education. We have tried to assemble here more than just another reader in the social foundations of education. Our goal is to offer a set of readings that demands a critical encounter between the reader and education's social and cultural function at a point that we believe is a crucial historical juncture.

This book developed out of our work as teachers in the social foundations of education. Specifically, it reflects themes and concerns that have formed an important focus of the work in a course for graduate students entitled Critical Social Issues in American Education. Although students come to the class for a variety of reasons and with diverse emotions, by the end most admit that it represented a significant and influential departure in the way they had learned to think about and approach their work in the field of education. Quite apart from the idiosyncratic qualities of the course and the teacher, it is clear that the changes students taking it experience point to important issues in the nature and discourse of educational studies—issues that in turn raise fundamental questions about the relevance or adequacy of these studies to the extraordinary conditions that we and our children face today as members of both a national and a global community.

The language of educational studies frequently is devoid of any serious or sustained engagement with the concept of society. Such studies are a stunning example of what Russell Jacoby has so aptly termed "social amnesia."[8] The focus in these studies of the educational process, it appears, are individuals abstracted from their positions within a historically constituted culture, human beings unrealistically stripped of the results of their lifelong immersion in a socially constructed world. The amnesia that Jacoby refers to is "forgetting" that we come to be who we are through a process in which our very subjectivity is shaped in the structures of our social world. We are gendered, speak a language, are situated as members of a social class and race, and assume the characteristics of a national or other cultural community. None of these aspects can be separated from the relational or social nature of human existence.

Indeed, the very predilection to see our individuality apart from its social context is an important manifestation of our social consciousness. It is part of a national ideology that mystifies and distorts the nature of human life and is an aspect of a social consciousness that denies its own existence. This predilection is spawned by a national culture that has historically demanded personal self-sufficiency; promoted an aggressive individualism; and celebrated those who, in search of better things, could appear to tear up their historic ties and communal dependencies.

Our apparently asocial consciousness, however, is not merely intellectually bogus. More important, it is politically crippling. It denies us full awareness of the way in which all of our lives are embedded in social relationships structured through and around conditions of power. From the bedroom to the classroom, office, or factory, social relationships imply political relationships. And it should be added, in our particular world, these relationships are generally hierarchical, implying the systematic control of some human beings by others.

What kind of an educational discourse ignores, denies, or forgets the social and political nature of human existence? It is, in fact, one that most students in the United States are exposed to. It is one that puts overwhelming emphasis on psychological perspectives and explanations—for example, in the study of learning theories, human development, instructional methodologies, or curriculum planning. Such discourse focuses on the individual student or on the student in interaction with the teacher or the texts and materials that form the curriculum. The theoretical discourse most likely will acknowledge a sphere of influence on the student that includes the family and the school as an institution. But little is said about the wider circles of influence that shape human lives, constitute the very conditions and meanings of educational practice, and form our understanding of what school is meant to accomplish in this culture at this particular moment in history.

The limited, circumscribed, nonsociological perspective of most educational theorizing reifies our school world. It teaches us to accept as given most of what appears essential in the construction of this world. Notions of childhood and adolescence, the roles of student and teacher, the kinds of knowledge considered valid and valuable— all the areas that constitute the educational world—become unquestionable facts of life, not social practices that can be challenged or even transformed.

Not to locate schooling in the larger culture or society is to attempt to grapple with educational issues with one arm tied behind one's back. It is a fraudulent intellectual endeavor that disables those whose business is education and who study education so that they might in some way apprehend the real universe in which they work. Semester after semester we are confronted by individuals whose often considerable time spent as students in a university department of education has made them social amnesiacs—individuals whose studies in education have excluded any substantial intellectual encounter with their society or culture. Such students are seriously disempowered by a professional discourse that disconnects them from any critical interrogation of the culture that shapes their existence as well as the existence of the young people they will teach. Although restoring this truncated discourse necessitates some development of sociological imagination, any expectation that educators can truly address their human and ethical responsibilities requires an understanding of the unprecedented, indeed cataclysmic, social forces transforming our world.

Our book is predicated on these assumptions. Educators must see their work as being in the eye of a vast social storm. Education and teaching are inseparably linked to the crises of the social order—cultural, moral, political, economic, ecological, and spiritual. It is impossible to make sense of what is happening educationally if what is happening is not placed in the context of the stresses, strains, and contradictions of both our national and our global society. Issues such as: the growing administrative control over teachers' lives; allegations about the mediocrity of American schools; the crisis of funding and concern about what is called "excellence"; the impoverishment of increasing numbers of children and adolescents; fears about moral degeneration; bitter contention over the nature of curriculum and of school knowledge; and widening disparities in educational achievement among ethnic and racial groups—all must be seen, at the same time, as both critical issues in American education and as metaphors for our larger human and societal situation. This awareness is what we have tried to convey in this book. What happens in school, or as part of the educational experience, is only a part of a larger process—a process that raises profound questions about the direction and nature of the society we inhabit as we enter the final decade of the twentieth century.

In Section I ("The Future of Capitalism: Contradiction and Crisis"), our goal is to locate education in the dynamics of the capitalist economy. The readings seek to make clear how educational policies and the nature of contemporary public discourse about education reflect the crises and dislocations generated in this economy. In the deskilling of labor, the process of deindustrialization, the fiscal crisis of the state, and the erosion of communal stability and undermining of traditional moral values, the economic system produces conflicts and contradictions to which education must respond.

However, as our readings also make clear, education should not be viewed only as a means of ameliorating such problems and crises. It should also be seen as an important force in raising demands concerning the unmet promises of American economic and political life. Schools reproduce the unequal, hierarchical relations of the capitalist workplace *and* function as a primary force for expanding economic opportunity for subordinate groups and for extending democratic rights. Schools, the readings emphasize, are pervaded by conflicts and contradictions that stem from serving both the needs of capital and the democratic imperatives to which public institutions must respond. Schools, it is shown, through the expansion of educational opportunities and rights, have played an important role in invigorating the demand for popular entitlements. The readings demonstrate how much politics, from the 1960s through the 1980s, focused on the rights of citizenship—in particular, to what degree these rights should be extended from a purely political and legal character to ones that empower the mass of people in their social and economic lives.

Section II ("Social Justice: Promises and Despair") focuses on the way in which the massive inequities of American life are reconciled with its egalitarian public discourse. How are we to understand the paradox of powerful movements of disadvantaged people demanding redress for the unmet promises of society, given the continual, indeed intensifying, injustices produced by the divisions of class, race, and gender as well as other social distinctions? The chapters make it clear that the United

States is moving with alarming speed into an era marked by growing disparities of income and conditions of life.

Beyond presenting the harsh reality of social injustice in contemporary America, the readings raise two related questions. The first concerns how this situation has developed: What are the social, economic, and political dynamics of inequality in this country? What are the conditions that produce disproportionate degrees of poverty among women, children, and people of color? The second concerns the nature of the ideology that legitimizes inequality and hierarchy in the context of a (formally) democratic culture. As the readings make clear, the role of public schooling has been and continues to be critical. It is the key institution in the process of social differentiation and selection and central to the ideological process through which inequality is made to appear legitimate. The chapters also contrast the essential metaphors and ways of understanding that govern patriarchal, capitalist societies with those necessary to a society in which the well-being of all is ensured. Thus the readings provide a powerful countervision and rejoinder to those for whom the present competitive and individualistic society seems fixed and unalterable.

Section III ("Marginality and Difference: The Fractured Community") focuses on the failure of our national community to come to terms with its own diversity and complexity. Through a succession of readings we witness the way in which the most public of institutions—the public schools—continues to measure and validate the competence and worth of students by the imposition of restrictive cultural and intellectual standards. The results, the readings demonstrate, include the devastation of human dignity, the effacement of communal traditions and histories, the marginalization of sensibilities and outlooks not in the "mainstream," and the disempowerment of a wide variety of individuals and groups. Some of the chapters in this section are phenomenological or ethnographic. They emphasize the lived experience of students in schools (and illustrate the growing importance of new methodological approaches to educational research). In particular they describe the experience of individuals marginalized or excluded from the dominant culture because they are designated handicapped, are persons of color, or are victims of gender discrimination. Overall the section poses powerful questions about the relationship of education to human empowerment, individual dignity, and the meaning of community in a democratic society. Running throughout is the call for and vision of a transformed notion of community— one that honors human and culture differences and simultaneously celebrates the shared, interdependent quality of human existence.

In Section IV ("Curriculum and Teaching: Dangers and Dreams"), we move toward a consideration of what is ostensibly the heart of the educational process. The readings here are concerned with the struggle being waged over the purpose of education, that is, with the human and social vision expressed in conflicting notions of the school curriculum. The chapters make it clear that decisions about curriculum are inextricable from cultural, ideological, and moral choices. Discussions of what schools need to teach are ultimately inseparable from much larger questions of how we should value human life and what kinds of community or social relationships we should envision and encourage. The readings illustrate that movements to define curriculum around, for example, "basic skills" or "minimal competencies" or "cultural literacy" express tensions arising from declining opportunities for social mobility, the moral and spiritual disintegration of the culture, and the crisis of authority concerning matters of knowledge and truth. The readings in this section convey some of the roots of the increasingly fierce conflicts over curriculum, and also provide new visions of curricular purposes that speak to the need for redefining the public discourse about education. Such visions attempt to locate issues of curriculum in the struggle for a freer, more democratic, socially just and compassionate public world.

We are concerned in this section, too, with how we should think about the work of teachers. The chapters attempt to characterize the increasingly problematic nature of teaching, as teacher's work more and more is defined as a deintellectualized activity remote from moral or political concerns. The work of teachers, it is shown, increasingly is defined in purely technical and instrumental terms. The infiltration of bureaucratic values ensures that teachers are measured by the criteria of effectiveness and efficiency and by their willingness to submit to performance-oriented, behavioral measures of success. In the process, teachers become further and further removed from any kind of transformative or prophetic role as agents of social, cultural, and political change. Readings that offer a countervision of teachers' work provide a very different notion of their role, one that radically changes their relationship to knowledge and to those they teach. It provides a sharp contrast to dominant notions of pedagogy that emphasize the "transmission" of information and the "time-on-task" classroom. Such alternative and contrasting visions of teaching do, of course, reflect deep divisions over how we are to conceive of human practices and social relationships: whether we wish to develop individuals suited to a passive and uncritical role in a hierarchical and reified world or individuals who, acting on deep ethical commitments, are ready and able to question and challenge their world.

The final section ("Toward the Twenty-first Century: Global Catastrophe or Social Transformation?") addresses the larger question of human consciousness and how we think in an imperiled world. The readings in this section are not centered on school as such but are concerned with issues of education in its broadest sense. They raise questions, for example, about the obsession with the growth and expansion of production that appears to characterize all nations. The modern obsession with work, discipline, and technology characterizes all so-called advanced societies. The young in such societies must be socialized to revere work, discipline, and technology to the detriment of such things as joy, freedom, and aesthetic and sensual development. Of course, the modernist impulse in all such societies leads to what Max Weber calls the "disenchantment of the world."[9] The will to power brings with it an anthropocentric perspective in which the organic relation between humans and their environment is sundered. Nature becomes a commodity to be plundered and exploited. In this context, argue writers in this section, nothing less than a fundamental transformation in humankind's sensibilities and outlook is demanded. We need a new consciousness to replace the dominant rationalistic and positivist worldview. The growing spiritual impoverishment of human life, the erosion and depletion of the planet's life-support system, and the threat of nuclear annihilation require a new integration of human capacities—a wider, more expansive employment of reason along with a renewed reverence for the universe. The readings make clear that any education that does not address itself to the dangerous and extraordinary conditions we face is irresponsible and irrelevant. Moreover, the readings offer new and exciting visions and possibilities for education.

We have attempted to organize the readings in a thematically meaningful structure. The five sections in the book—on the state and politics, social justice, marginality and difference, curriculum and the role of teachers, and the global crisis—offer one useful way to make sense of the crises and concerns that confront us. Each section is preceded by a brief essay in which we describe our reasons for selecting and structuring the readings. Still, the organization must be viewed as only a heuristic measure. In the real world, issues do not come neatly and conveniently packaged or compartmentalized. One problem or crisis flows out of and into another, forming interrelated aspects of a social totality. Whether one aspect of this totality ought to be seen as fundamental, as in some way determining all others, is the subject of much theorizing. Those who assert that the key is found in capitalism, patriarchy, modernism, or elsewhere dispute where the lion's share of the blame must go. Reflections of this debate can be found in the pages of this book.

The readings in this collection represent, we believe, important, sometimes seminal, statements on critical social and educational issues. They offer a perspective on both the long-range and the more immediate problems and issues we face as a national and global community, and they provide a consideration of these concerns at both an applied and a theoretical level. We hope the reader will experience the disjunction between readings that deal explicitly with education and those whose concerns are broader, not as a juxtaposition, but as connected moments of a dialectic—a vehicle for moving between the distinct but very related aspects of a single social world. Most of all, however, we hope readers will feel they have gained something by giving up a trivializing, narrow discourse that dominates so much of professional education for one that is broader in its sweep, even though this broader vision is also sometimes thoroughly dispiriting. It is hard to dispute that the pages of this volume are filled with a terrible commentary on the human condition. Yet as we have often found, attempting to connect the field of education to the most serious and pressing concerns of humankind as we shape our future, however overwhelming this task may appear, ultimately elevates and ennobles the perception that educators have of their work. We hope this conviction will be borne out of those who make use of this text.

NOTES

1. See Maxine Greene, "The Humanities and Emancipatory Possibility," *Journal of Education* 163, no. 4 (Fall 1981): 287–305; quote from p. 289.
2. Henry A. Giroux and Stanley Aronowitz, "Curriculum Theory and the Language of Possibility," in *Education under Siege* (South Hadley, MA: Bergin & Garvey, 1985).
3. Report of the United Nations Children and Education Fund, 1988.
4. Richard Shaull, Introduction, in Paulo Freire, *Pedagogy of the Oppressed* (New York: Continuum, 1988), p. 15.
5. Michael Polanyi, *The Tacit Dimension* (Garden City, NY: Doubleday, 1966).
6. See Joseph Femia, *Gramsci's Political Thought* (Oxford, England: Clarendon Press, 1981).
7. Freire, *Pedagogy of the Oppressed*, p. 59.
8. Russell Jacoby, *Social Amnesia* (Boston: Beacon Press, 1975).
9. See Stanislav Andreski, ed., *Max Weber on Capitalism, Bureaucracy, and Religion* (Boston: Allen & Unwin, 1983).

SECTION I

The Future of Capitalism: Contradiction and Crisis

A peculiar feature of American society is that relatively few people, including educators, are willing or able to name the social and economic system within which they live. Whether we choose euphemisms (e.g., "the free enterprise system") or names that avoid the issue of economics altogether ("democratic society"), we shy away from the term *capitalism*. Yet any attempt to understand or grasp the nature of our world that does not situate our lives within a capitalist society is doomed to irrelevance. It is, after all, within capitalist institutions that most of us spend our hours at work; it is through the market that most of the resources that enable us to survive or flourish are allocated; our national and global life is increasingly dominated by the investment decisions of transnational corporations; and our cultural values and belief systems, in no small measure, serve and legitimize capitalist social relations and practices. Consider, for example, the pervasive effects of advertising, whose subtext is always the need to buy or consume more in order to address such fundamental human concerns as sociability, sexuality, security, femininity and masculinity, or physical well-being. No attempt to address present and future issues in education can be successful if schooling is not related to capitalism. Sociologists of education in recent years have documented how schools in the United States (and elsewhere) reproduce the unequal, hierarchical, and competitive structures of capitalist institutions, especially those of the workplace. Schooling simply cannot be understood unless its relationship to capitalist society is recognized. Schools, in the language of critical sociology,

1

are "cultural sites" that attempt to socialize children into the reigning values, beliefs, meanings, and knowledge required to live and work in this kind of society. Schools are important vehicles for shaping subjectivities compatible with the demands of the corporate and bureaucratic world. Of course, schools are not the only avenue for socialization. The mass media, for example, also clearly exert enormous influence. Nonetheless, the powerful role of schools in transmitting capitalist values (such as the emphasis on personal achievement and success, competitive individualism, and the distinctions between work and play) is undeniable.

Although schools are shaped by and encoded with the imperatives of the wider social and economic system, this is not a fully synchronized process. Schools and other institutions do not work together as a well-oiled machine, each part serving and supporting every other part. On the contrary, American society contains explosive conflicts and contradictions. We contend, along with the other authors in this section, that we have entered a period of profound instability and crisis and that our economic, political, and cultural crises deeply affect education. Indeed, whether in the direction of educational policies or in the substance of public discourse about schools, the crises and dislocations generated by the system have already begun to show themselves. The readings point to how the intensifying de-skilling of labor, the dismantling of the traditional manufacturing base of the economy, the fiscal crisis of the state, the erosion of communal stability, and the undermining of traditional moral values create points of pressure that education is frequently called on to relieve. However, as the readings also make clear, education is far from being only a means to paper over cracks in the system. It also is and has been an important force in raising demands concerning the unmet promises of American economic and political life. Indeed, as two of the chapters show, public schools exist at the intersection of the conflicting demands of the social system and increasingly will be subject to the strains and stresses of contradictory social pressures.

Martin Carnoy and Henry Levin note that schools, on the one hand, reproduce the unequal, hierarchical relations of the capitalist workplace and, on the other, function as a primary force for expanding economic opportunity for subordinate groups and extending democratic rights. Schools, say these authors, are pervaded by conflicts and contradictions that come from serving American capitalist expansion as well as democratic imperatives. Of course, these conflicting dynamics in the schools mirror the larger social conflicts outside the schools. Carnoy and Levin look at how these conflicts are revealed in the tensions plaguing public education. The political struggle over resources for schooling, for example, pits the state's commitment to enhance the profitability of capital against the commitments of reform movements to increase the social mobility of subordinate groups in society. It also includes the contradiction between preparing students to fit into the authoritarian and hierarchial division of labor in the workplace and providing an education that equips a future citizen for democratic public life. Finally, it includes the way that schools, as they have come to correspond structurally to the workplace, mirror the alienation, conflicts, and resistance that accompany class, race, and gender hierarchies and divisions.

H. Svi Shapiro provides a parallel framework of analysis in his discussion of the meaning of conservative social and educational policies in the 1980s. Such policies, he argues, need to be understood in the context of the way in which the state in capitalist society has become increasingly Janus-faced. The state is called upon, on one side, to support and facilitate capital accumulation and the profitability of big business and, on the other, to respond to social movements that have demanded the expansion of personal rights and entitlements. Under pressure from capital and with the support of a tax-burdened middle class, the politics of the 1980s have attempted to turn back the effects of popular movements that have sought to ameliorate the harsh or damaging effects of the market on working and living in American society. Despite the ferocity of the attack on the social and educational programs of the state, it is clear, argues Shapiro, that the expansion of social rights and economic entitlements represents an extension of the rights of citizenship that will not easily be revoked. But, he says, the conflict between a socially responsive and compassionate state and corporate demands for unlimited profitability will remain at the center of public policy struggles in the coming decade. Like Carnoy and Levin, Shapiro asserts that an adequate understanding of education in this society requires one to see that it not only reproduces capitalist social relations but also historically has invigorated the demands for popular entitlements through the expansion of educational opportunities and rights. Education mirrors the political contest between democratic rights and the rights of property in a capitalist society.

Christopher Lasch eloquently describes how the obsessive consumerism of contemporary society undermines and destroys what might be called "traditional values." Enduring commitments, responsibility, continuity, and rootedness are incompatible with the "logic of consumerism," which ceaselessly propagandizes for the benefits of endless novelty and unlimited possibility. Drugs, says Lasch, are merely the most obvious form of addiction to commodities that alleviate boredom and satisfy the socially stimulated desire for variety and excitement. For Lasch, the tragedy of conservatism is that whereas it articulates and focuses the moral and spiritual anguish brought on by the economy, it says nothing about how to change things for the better. Indeed, it constitutes a refusal to confront the forces in modern life that engender progressively more social disorder and existential crisis. Although this piece contains no explicit reference to schools, its message is clear. A right-wing moral agenda for schools that seeks to censor texts, to mandate prayer or the pledge of allegiance, or to impose severe behavioral rules constitutes a popular response to the cultural crisis Lasch describes. However, this is what Lasch calls an ideology of denial because it refuses to confront the values of modern capitalism.

The final reading in this section offers a social vision in which some of the contradictions of capitalist society we have looked at might be resolved. In this vision—what the authors Samuel Bowles and Herbert Gintis call post-liberal democracy—the central moral and political concern is the creation of a new social order in which people are more nearly the authors of their own individual and collective histories. This is a radically more democratic picture of life in America, in which economic inequality is significantly attenuated and economic and social institutions are made accountable through both representative and participatory forms of governance. For Bowles and Gintis, democracy is not simply a means toward greater social justice. It also has *educational* significance. Commitment to democracy entails the advocacy of institutions that promote rather than impede human development. Because learning and human development are central and lifelong social activities, Bowles and Gintis argue, those places that regulate learning—schools, families, neighborhoods, and workplaces—ought to be gauged by the degree to which they reduce the power of unaccountable authority and facilitate personal choice and autonomy. The vision depicted by these authors, while certainly implying a profound transformation of the society, is at the same time rooted in the promises of democracy and liberty—ideas that continue to exert a powerful influence on public discourse in America.

All the writing in this section rejects the widespread assumption that education and schools can be understood as phenomena separate from the social and economic milieu. Although professional studies in education continue to emphasize the psychological or developmental life of students or the internal organizational structure of schools, they fail egregiously to come to grips with education as a part of the social totality. Such studies offer little to the struggle for a public discourse that consciously attempts to discern how education could or should address itself to the critical social, economic, or political concerns that beset the nation (and the world). The writings we have selected here reflect the development of a powerful set of analyses that *do* attempt to explicate education's connection to the institutions of capitalism and the state. We hope this work will encourage educators to begin to define the nature and purposes of their practice in ways that confront its political character.

Contradiction in Education

Martin Carnoy and Henry Levin

Education, we have argued, is set in the context of social conflict and is an integral part of such conflict. Public schools in America are an institution of the State, and like other State institutions are subject to the pull of two conflicting forces over their control, purpose, and operation. On the one hand, schools reproduce the unequal, hierarchical relations of the capitalist workplace; on the other, schooling represents the primary force in the United States for expanding economic opportunity for subordinate groups and the extension of democratic rights.

These forces are in structural opposition, creating contradictions—i.e. conflicts and internal incompatibilities—in education that result in a continuing struggle over direction. Although at any given time one of the forces may appear to dominate and achieve hegemony, the existence of underlying contradiction means that the struggle continues in various latent forms. Contradiction is at the heart of educational change by generating a series of continuing conflicts and accommodations that transform the shape of the schooling process. Changes generated by educational contradictions also induce changes in the workplace.

Schools are characterized by contradiction and conflict through their very function of serving American capitalist expansion and the democratic political system. These democratic and class-reproductive dynamics are conditioned by the larger social conflict outside the schools. To the extent that the democratic dynamic gains ground, the educational system diverges in certain respects from the structural exigencies of reproducing capitalist relations of production and the division of labor. This divergence, in turn, is capable of exacerbating or changing the character of social conflict. It is therefore not only conflict in production that can lead to crises in capitalist development, but also contradictions in reproduction. In the latter case, crisis

Reprinted from *Schooling and Work in the Democratic State* by Martin Carnoy and Henry M. Levin with the permission of the publishers, Stanford University Press. © 1985 by the Board of Trustees of the Leland Stanford Junior University.

5

emerges from the failure of one of the more important institutions of reproduction to reproduce properly the labor skills, the division of labor, and the social relations of production.

This chapter discusses contradictions in education. We argue that there are three types of contradictions associated with schooling, all of which result directly or indirectly from the tension that arises between the democratic thrust of schools and their role in reproducing the class and work structure. The first type of contradiction manifests itself in the political struggle over resources for schooling. Since schooling is "public," it has been the object of social and reform movements committed to increasing the social mobility of subordinate groups. These movements have usually sought to increase the resources going to schooling for school expansion generally and for the education of working-class and minority groups in particular. But such resource demands may reduce the capacity of the State to enhance the profitability of capital, with the result that conflict will occur over school expansion between capital and labor in times of declining or stagnant profits, slow economic growth, and declining real wages—as in the 1970's and early 1980's.

A second type of contradiction is internal to the educational process. The reproductive dynamic creates pressures in schools to produce a labor force with skills, attitudes, and values that fit into the hierarchical division of labor and to reproduce capitalist relations of production. At the same time, the democratic dynamic emphasizes individual liberty and democratic participation as well as equality of opportunity and occupational mobility through education. The student must be prepared to participate in an authoritarian and hierarchical system of work, but also be prepared to benefit from and contribute to a system of egalitarian democratic practices. To a large degree, establishing a curriculum, teaching process, and educational structure that support one set of requirements must be done at the expense of the other. As we will show below, one consequence of this type of contradiction is the development of workers who are overeducated for the types of jobs that will be available to them.

A third type of contradiction is imported into the educational process through the fact that the schools correspond with the workplace. Contradictions of this type arise out of the correspondence process itself. As the features of the workplace are embodied in schools, so are the contradictions of the workplace embodied in schooling practices. Especially important is the educational manifestation of the contradiction between capital and labor.

CONTRADICTIONS IN RESOURCE ALLOCATION

As we have stressed, the democratic capitalist State faces competing demands upon its resources. On one side are demands to use the resources of the State to increase the profitability of capital. On the other side are demands for greater opportunity and the expansion of democratic rights. Though some educational funding is clearly used to support the first of these objectives, considerable portions are also allocated to improve the opportunities of disadvantaged groups, including students from low-income families, the handicapped, minorities, and those from bilingual and immigrant backgrounds. Much of the growth of educational funding during the 1960's and 1970's was specifically devoted to these groups, especially in the form of the expansion of public higher education to accommodate the quest for social mobility of these and other "nontraditional" students.

But funding used to improve educational opportunities for subordinate groups may put a drain on the rate of capital accumulation by increasing taxes and reducing the types of assistance that benefit capital more directly. At a time of economic stagnation, the expansion of educational opportunities is particularly resisted by the representatives of capital, just as it is advanced by the advocates of labor. Additional resources for education must come either from increased taxation or from reduced services in other domains, including services to businesses.

There are also conflicts within capital and labor about school expansion. Some fractions of the capitalist class have an interest in a better-trained labor force, even when public resources are limited. These fractions line up with fractions of the working class that also want school expansion even if it means more taxes. Yet there are other fractions of the working class that resist school expansion during a fiscal crisis because they do not want to bear the tax burden of such an expansion. As it is external to school organization, it can be generalized to the social struggle within the State as a whole, rather than just within schools. The particular nature of the current crisis is that social spending, which had traditionally expanded during recessions, is now resisted politically. The State's capacity to undertake deficit financing or increased taxation is limited by political resistance to inflation and to higher taxes. Growth in resources for the next wave of economic expansion is required during a recession. However, in the recent (1981–82) crisis the expansion of social spending by the State was severely constrained. The struggle over schooling resources became accentuated as unemployment and the competition for available jobs increased.

And though some employers may support the expansion of educational spending, their vision focuses on the resulting production of certain skills pertinent to their industries. For example, the high technology industry is pushing for increasing science and math education, but its demands do not discuss who is to get such training, how widespread the training should be, or how science and math should be taught. Middle-class-oriented science and math programs may be totally inconsistent with the needs of the poor for high-quality mass primary and secondary scientific education. . . .

CONTRADICTIONS INTRINSIC TO THE EDUCATIONAL PROCESS

Schools must produce workers who meet the needs of capitalist production. This means developing workers with appropriate cognitive and vocational skills for existing jobs or on-the-job training and with behaviors, habits, and values predisposing them to the organization of capitalist production. It also means establishing a system of socialization and certification for work roles according to class, race, and gender that systematically legitimates differences in life chances among those groups. Finally, it means promoting an ideology among youth that portrays capitalism as the embodiment of individual liberty and democracy and inculcates political loyalty to it as a system.

However, at the same time the schools are charged with producing citizens who know and care about democratic rights and equal opportunity and who are able to participate fully in the economic, social, and political life of society. The result is that schools generate a range of functions that contradict the efficient reproduction of capitalist workers. We have identified five of these functions that support the democratic side of schooling: (1) democratic participation; (2) social equality; (3) social mobility; (4) cultural development; and (5) independence of the educational bureaucracy. Each serves to divert the schools from the preparation of properly socialized workers by inculcating in students various traits that are in conflict with work requirements.

1. Democratic Participation

Since schools must prepare the young for democratic political participation, students are provided with considerable rights in the educational system that are absent in the work context. For example, students have wide latitude with respect to freedom of expression within the school—something that is neither guaranteed nor commonly found in the workplace (Kemerer & Deutsch 1979: Chap. 3). A student's constitutional rights to free speech are protected in virtually all schooling activities as long as he does not materially and substantially interfere with the operations of the school or the rights of others. Whereas workers can be fired at will unless they are able to negotiate contracts with other provisions, students cannot be summarily suspended from school (Kemerer & Deutsch 1979: Chaps. 5 & 6). The constitutional right to an education places far more stringent due process requirements on schools in expelling or suspending students than on the workplace in dismissing workers.

Even though schools are hierarchical and share many features with the workplace, there are far more opportunities for students to influence the educational process than for workers to influence the work process. These opportunities stem not only from the greater protections and guarantees of due process just mentioned but also from the fact that there are a range of educational decisions in which students and their families can have influence. For example, the student can participate in the choice of courses, teachers, and schedules, and family members can confer with school or school district authorities about particular educational needs or a child or group of children. School boards are usually elected, so educational decisions can be influenced through electoral politics as well. It is difficult to find any counterpart to these mechanisms for democratic participation in the workplace.

This is not to argue that the schools are always responsive to parent and student concerns. . . . Participation by parents differs according to the occupational role of the parents, and some schools are more responsive to participation than others. Nevertheless, the very possibility of community control allows for greater democratic participation in decisions affecting schooling practices. Universities also allow for student and faculty influence over decision-making in areas such as investment and curriculum policy and hiring and firing. In both schools and universities, this participation is a source of contradiction. Participation can interfere with the reproduction of the relations of production; community, student, or faculty control can exacerbate contradictions in production rather than smooth the reproduction of social relations.

Yet, these outcomes must be within the realm of possibility, since the schools—like other state apparatuses—are supposed to represent the will of the people and to reflect their needs in democratic societies.

Finally, an important part of the school curriculum is devoted to political socialization of the young. Students are introduced to the fact that we are a nation of laws with considerable rights and obligations. They are indoctrinated with the sense of justice built into a representative government with checks and balances. They are also provided a version of their history which stresses the fight against injustice (e.g. taxation without representation, slavery, prejudice, tyranny, and aggression). Yet the political rights and responsibilities of citizens and their constitutional protections—so heavily stressed in the schools—are largely absent from the work relation. Thus, an important part of the educational process challenges directly the very premises on which the employment relation is based.

2. Social Equality

In contrast to the ideology of the workplace, that of schooling has placed great emphasis on social equality. Historically, it was assumed that access to a uniform system of compulsory schooling would provide, in itself, equality of educational opportunity. But recent years have seen the interpretation of educational equality as turning more toward a quest for equal resources, equal educational processes, and equal educational results (Coleman 1968). Where inequalities are promoted, they are inequalities favoring those who need additional educational resources the most to compensate for some "undeserved" educational deficiency (Rawls 1971: 100–101). Examples of the quest for equal educational opportunity abound. Since the *Brown* decision of the U.S. Supreme Court in 1954 there have been numerous challenges to racial segregation in the schools. Inequalities arising from state systems of educational finance that have channeled more money to wealthy school districts than to poor ones have also been challenged and overturned (J. Pincus ed. 1974). Federal and state laws providing special programs for handicapped, low-income, and bilingual children also respond to this issue.

Attempts to provide greater equality of educational opportunity impart a dynamic to the school quite different from that of the workplace. There is an implicit tension between what schools are expected to do for the poor and discriminated against and what the economy is supposed to do for them. These expectations have been galvanized into the social movements that have challenged educational inequalities associated with race, gender, and family income, as well as other sources of what has been perceived as unequal treatment. These movements have pressured schools to pursue egalitarian outcomes, even when they are not consistent with the priorities of the workplace or of taxpayers. For example, testing and tracking patterns are constantly being challenged in the courts and by parent groups. Federal attempts to provide compensatory resources for low-income children have had to counter the attempts of local educational authorities to use such assistance to replace funding that would have otherwise been provided for the poor out of state and local sources.

Not all of these practices have created more equal educational outcomes, but they have raised expectations of more nearly evenhanded educational practices. For example, there is evidence of only modest improvements in the relative test scores of children from low-income backgrounds, despite almost two decades of compensatory programs (Levin 1977; Burton & Jones 1982); this suggests that the schools alone cannot compensate for substantial economic and other disadvantages. The evidence on the effects of school integration is also ambiguous. In fact, the previous chapter suggests that social class-related reproduction is sometimes subtle and independent of resource availability, and that certain forms of reproduction cannot be easily altered by educational policies. But the expectations of greater equality in the schools and the use of social movements and the courts to obtain it have contributed to a dynamic for the schools that undermines the strict preparation of workers.

3. Social Mobility

A related aspect of the drive for social equality in schooling is the quest for social mobility. Schools today are the most important institution for families seeking social mobility for their children, and their importance has grown over time as the availability of other routes has lessened. For example, the great decline in opportunities to enter or establish small businesses as large corporations have increasingly dominated the economy has left over 90 percent of the labor force consisting of employees working for wages and salaries. In most jobs, educational credentials are required for consideration for employment; and the higher the level of occupation and income, the greater the educational attainment required. Although the precise reasons for this relation are hotly debated (see Becker 1964; Berg 1970; Thurow 1975), the close relation between education and occupational opportunities is not.

The role of education in enabling individuals to improve their social position is not new. Even in colonial times, when status could be readily achieved through the amassing of property, education "was, together with wealth, essential for achieving the highest social rank" (Main 1965: 251). And as education began to be a requirement for industrial jobs in the latter part of the nineteenth century, there was a direct tie between a worker's level of education and his job. In fact, an important motivation for taking schooling was the improvement in vocational opportunities afforded to those with more education. The role of compulsory attendance laws in increasing school enrollments has probably been exaggerated, given the high economic returns to pursuing schooling from the late nineteenth century on (Landes & Solmon 1972).

Making education in effect a requirement for mobility creates contradictions in the workplace if the growth of skilled jobs does not keep pace with school expansion. As long as the economy grows rapidly and the demand for skilled labor increases, it is possible for the labor market to absorb the increases in educated labor. This has been the case in the United States until recently. The shift to manufacturing from agriculture established an initial demand for educated workers, and then the expansion of the work hierarchy required higher levels of education for managers and technical specialists. Following this transition there was a shift from manufacturing to services, with an attendant increase in the demand for white-collar workers, managers, and professionals. The expansion of the government sector in the postwar period also contributed to this increase.

But the ability of the economy to absorb educated workers has broken down in recent years. The expectation that education would lead to social mobility generated an expansion of educational enrollments and attainments that has exceeded the available number of jobs requiring those credentials (Berg 1970; Rumberger 1981). This has led to a serious underutilization of educated workers, a situation that may be creating a major force for change in the workplace as frustrated and overeducated workers behave in ways that are counterproductive to the requirements of existing work organizations. This phenomenon will be evaluated more fully later in this chapter.

4. Cultural Development

The popular view of school is that it addresses the cultural preparation of youth as well as their vocational preparation. This derives from the classical notion of education, with its emphasis on the humanities and liberal arts. Today's typical elementary school curriculum provides exposure to music, fine arts, literature, drama, and physical education, all in the interest of the full development of the young child. The standard fare at the secondary level includes these as well as even heavier doses of languages, history, and literature. In addition, there are optional or extracurricular activities in drama, chorus, and varsity sports. At the university level, it is possible to find cultural studies even farther removed from the concrete cognitive skills required in job markets.

This aspect of the school is relatively independent of the influence of the workplace, although it competes for school resources with more vocationally oriented programs. Certainly schools could prepare workers more efficiently for corporate production if cultural aspects were eliminated, but such an action would conflict directly with the social demand for such activities, especially by the middle class; moreover, the prominence of schooling in preparing people for the workplace would then no longer be hidden behind a patina of culture and citizenship.

Not only does the cultural aspect reduce the capacity of schools to develop workplace skills, but it may even create values and norms inconsistent with capitalist relations of production. The values that underlie the humanities, and literary and artistic criticism, create a critical approach to the acceptance of social institutions and customs. That this dynamic of the school is in conflict with the school's class-reproductive role is reflected in the relatively marginal nature of such subjects. During times of budgetary stringencies, the cultural courses are often referred to as "frills"— a term that makes them highly susceptible to cutting. Further, liberal arts graduates suffer most from poor economic conditions, since they cannot claim a specific job skill. Thus, the cultural autonomy of the school is monitored by the periodic downturns in the economy, and the long-run expansion of the educational system tends to emphasize the inculcation of vocational rather than cultural skills, as shown by the rise of community colleges and by the increasingly job-related nature of curricula in higher education. The cultural component in the curriculum has become less important as each level of schooling has become characterized by mass participation.

5. Independence of the Educational Bureaucracy

The fifth source of contradiction emerging from the schools' internal dynamics is the independence of the educational bureaucracy from the direct control of capitalist firms. There are limits to this independence, since the business community and its supporters can exert considerable influence, politically, on curriculum and schooling practices. Yet within those limits, educational personnel are not directly answerable to capitalist firms. Most educators have the protection of lifetime contracts that enable them to withstand obvious pressures by outside interests. Educators and their organizations can also pursue their own professional goals with relative impunity. Teacher organizations and other groups of educational professionals have developed effective political representation through their ability and willingness to contribute substantial sums to those candidates who support their goals. It should come as no surprise that much of the legislation governing the schools at both the federal and the state levels has been heavily influenced by organizations of professional educators.

Furthermore, through collective-bargaining agreements educational employees are able to exert pressures on educational practices in the directions of their own preferences, some of which may conflict with efficient preparation of the young for the workplace. For example, educators have generally been highly supportive of the democratic role of schooling. In addition, teachers are guaranteed broad latitude in their freedom of expression, and they are protected from arbitrary dismissal (D. Rubin 1972). The result is that educational professionals have substantial independence to address their own visions of schooling, rather than being highly accountable to a narrow set of vocational criteria. This relative independence on the part of the educational bureaucracy means that they may oppose many of the values and practices associated with a strict preparation of the young for jobs in existing work organizations.

CONTRADICTIONS FROM THE REPRODUCTIVE PROCESS

Another level of contradiction emerges from the very nature of schooling in a democratic capitalist society. As schools have come to correspond structurally to the workplace, they have also taken on many of the internal contradictions of the workplace. By corresponding to the relations of production and division of labor based on class, gender, and race, schools bring into the education process the key elements of the social conflict itself, so we find pupils alienated from their learning, and teachers fighting over pay and working conditions rather than over educational issues. There is often resistance by the working class or by minorities to a class- or race-biased curriculum and a schooling process that is blatantly dead-end for these groups. Thus we can identify three sources of contradiction associated with the correspondence of school functions to the needs of a class-, race-, and gender-structured workplace. These can be summarized under the headings of students as alienated labor; teachers as alienated labor; and class resistance to the school agenda.

1. Students as Alienated Labor

Just as most of the structure and content of the work process is set out by forces external to the worker, so there is a parallel situation facing the student. Although the student has greater freedom of expression than the worker and somewhat more choice in his or her activities, the overall educational agenda consists of course requirements and teaching methods formulated on the basis of state requirements and implemented by local school authorities. In this respect, students have little influence over the shape of their own educational activities, since they must work within a structure imposed without their influence or participation. Thus students pursue their schooling because it is compulsory and may lead to improved status and career prospects, not because it consists of activities that are freely chosen and intrinsically satisfying. In this context, schooling activities are undertaken by students in order to obtain external rewards—grades, promotions, and educational credentials. But this arrangement means that students are primarily interested in obtaining certification rather than knowledge, just as school authorities expect that students will learn what the institution is certifying at each level and for each type of education. Students therefore have an incentive to take shortcuts to credentials through short-term memorizing, giving the answers they think particular instructors want, and turning in work performed by others. It is little wonder that cheating is considered to be common in schools and that an entire "term paper industry" has developed around colleges and universities.

When students seek credentials rather than knowledge and skills, the role of schooling as a producer of trained labor will actually be undermined over time. That is, the schools will tend to provide workers whose actual skill levels are lower than their educational credentials imply. Since student effort is motivated by external payoffs such as the exchange value of those credentials in the marketplace, the content of the credentials will be further undermined by a fall in their value. For example, as the returns to college education have fallen (Freeman 1976; Rumberger 1981), students have begun taking fewer difficult courses (U.S. Dep't of Ed. 1981) and have done more poorly on test scores (Harnischfeger & Wiley 1975; Wirtz et al. 1977). The attempt by schools to reproduce capitalist relations of production creates an alienating experience for students, and the learning content of schooling diminishes over time for any particular credential—with the consequence for the firm being falling worker productivity.

The alienated student also affects school discipline. Many students are in school only because attendance is compulsory and future employment is tied to an educational credential, not because they are intrinsically involved in the educational process. Such students represent a constant potential for disruption. To the degree that they do comply with school authorities, it is from fear of punishment rather than from satisfaction with school activities. In this respect, students and workers are in a similar quandary. However, given students' greater constitutional rights to free expression and due process protections against expulsion, sanctions are much less effective against them than against workers. Accordingly, school discipline problems and disruption are inevitable, placing continual obstacles in the path of a smooth and ongoing process of educational reproduction. As youth unemployment has risen precipitously and remained at high levels (Levin 1983b)—especially for minority youth—the returns to compliance with the school regimen have fallen and discipline problems have increased.

2. Teachers as Alienated Labor

Although teachers are viewed as professionals, they do not have the autonomy of other professions. Teachers are charged with implementing educational laws and school policies without participating in the formulation or evaluation of such policies. In this respect, both the process and the outcomes of their activities are controlled by external forces, so that teachers are alienated like other workers. They lack the power to influence or control significant aspects of their working lives, since they operate within the detailed conditions of their jobs set out by school authorities (Levin 1980). Although they may aspire to greater control over their activities, they are dependent for employment on State schools that are based upon a restrictive work environment. In this respect, schools are largely characterized by capitalist relations of production, somewhat altered by particular characteristics of State employment in a capitalist society (Carnoy, Girling & Rumberger 1976). Thus, the fact that schools are employers—with relations of production between teachers and administrators that correspond roughly to those in capitalist private enterprises—means that labor conflicts in the schools will occur and will take approximately the same form as in the private sector.

Teachers have organized into unions that negotiate contracts with their government employers. If the negotiations are not successful, the teachers strike. In collective bargaining and teacher strikes, however, a community composed of families and their pupils—the raw material of the production process—indirectly employs the teachers, at least in theory. If the schools are viewed as *the* legitimate institution for preparing youth for both their work and their social obligations, their continued operation is vital to the community. The teachers negotiate and strike both against their immediate adversaries—State administrators—and against the community that they serve. Since parents pay teachers through taxes, it is against parents' interests to have higher teacher salaries or cuts in teacher services. Yet teachers work in a capitalist production unit and therefore behave like exploited workers. The fact that their service is vital to the community only makes their bargaining power greater.

In a sense, teachers have little choice, given the lack of alternatives for influencing the educational process and their own working conditions. They have to conduct their struggle for fundamental occupational rights as though they were private-sector workers in basic conflict with their employer. But demands for higher teacher wages create a dilemma for the State. If parents pay higher taxes, the dilemma is solved; but if, as is now the case, there is resistance to paying more, schooling services must be cut, with obvious implications for the capability of the schools to deliver properly prepared and socialized youth to the workplace.[1]

Teacher negotiations and strikes also affect the process of student ideological formation. School administrators take an active role in turning community sentiment—especially parent and pupil sentiment—against negotiating teachers with threats that students will sacrifice learning and potential employment and college eligibility if the strike is prolonged. Antiteacher sentiments may be further reinforced by an anti-union bias, which has been promoted by business interests and has become more prominent in recent years. Teachers are characterized as selfish and greedy rather than "pulling together" on behalf of the community as workers are supposed to do on behalf of the corporation. Demanding higher wages and striking against *the community* is characterized as "typical union activity." Yet even this antilabor sentiment contains contradictions, for these are the same teachers who are responsible for judging pupil performance and for inculcating pupils with values and skills once the negotiations and strikes are over. How can the teacher be at once selfish and also a source of inspiration for learning and dedication to knowledge?

3. Class Resistance to the School Agenda

Several major works on the schools in America (Sennett & Cobb 1972; Giroux 1981; Apple 1982a), in England (Willis 1977), and in France (Baudelot & Establet 1971) have discussed the school as a place of resistance by working-class youth to class domination. Since the school is a class-based institution, it must treat working-class children differently from those of managers and professionals, not to mention those of the capitalist class, even if these differences are less pronounced in schools than elsewhere. We have already suggested that this differential treatment starts early, and consists of signaling to lower-class children that they will not do well in school and that expectations for them are minimal. Sennett and Cobb show that this generates responses of overt defiance among some adolescents—those who seek to gain esteem and leadership among peers by acting out against authority. Doing well in school among lower-class youth may be considered as "giving in" or cooperating, particularly because it is so unusual for them to do well. They appear to be selected by the teacher for special consideration. Most adolescents, however, simply "drop out" in the classroom, resisting passively by not listening even though required to be in school until the age of sixteen.

Baudelot and Establet stress collective resistance. Schools are defaced and youth rebel openly in the classroom, even attacking teachers. The school is just one more dominating institution that has to be overthrown, a continuation of the class struggle in the workplace. Yet Baudelot and Establet stress that the struggle in the school is not the same as in the workplace. Students are not workers; they do not produce, and there is no surplus extraction on the part of schools. Thus the nature of the struggle is totally different: it is resistance to incorporation into production in a particular way, and resistance to the values and norms being pressed onto working-class youth— values that are alien and designed to dominate (Willis 1977).

For both Sennett and Cobb and Baudelot and Establet resistance is generated by the incorporation of class conflicts into the schools. The reproduction of the social structure generates resistance on the part of those who will occupy the lowest rungs in that structure—those designated to fail in school and therefore to fail in life. The fact that many pupils must do poorly (or just not well) in school to fill the ranks of subordinate labor markets creates the possibility of resistance to class-structured education. It is the reproduction of capitalist social relations and of racial divisions, therefore, that is the source of resistance; conflicts inherent in capitalist society, though different in nature from those of the schools, are carried over into the schools.

Social conflict is thus also carried over into the educational system, even though its form may be different from that in the workplace and other social institutions.

Giroux (1981) and Apple (1982a) call on Gramsci's dialectical concept of hegemony and counterhegemony in arguing that schools reproduce class but that the practices of schooling—in attempting to expand and deepen capitalist hegemony—are resisted by counterhegemonic tendencies in working-class youth, young women, and minorities. However, counterhegemony as Gramsci defined it is necessarily rooted in social and political movements, as in 1968 in France and Mexico or in 1970 in the United States. The relation between movements and resistance to the hegemonic "hidden curriculum" in schools is not spelled out by Apple and Giroux. . . . The constant struggle to expand democratic rights, both political and economic, also takes place within education, expanding the role of schools in the process of social mobility and in the more equitable treatment of subordinate groups. Therefore, social conflict shapes educational change over time. Resistance to ideologically based curricula and other schooling practices has to be set in the context of this conflict. Such resistance is not independent of the struggle going on outside the schools.

This interpretation is not meant to depreciate the contribution made by Apple, Giroux, and others writing about school practices from the ideological perspective. Their work is important to a fuller understanding of what takes in schools and why. Yet we consider that resistance to schooling practices is a secondary rather than a primary contradiction. We agree that counterhegemony is often manifested as indirect resistance by pupils to the ideology imposed upon them by the schools. But we think that more important forms of counterhegemony inherent in social movements have historically influenced the very ideology that schools imposed. Thus, dominant ideology as reflected in schooling is continually shaped by social conflict both outside and inside the schools.

THE DIVERGENCE OF EDUCATION AND JOBS

Now that we have reviewed the tension within an educational system charged both with reproducing a work force segmented along lines of class, race, and gender and with expanding social mobility, equity, and human rights, we turn to a specific example of one of the contradictions produced by this tension: the "overexpansion" of the educational system relative to the availability of "suitable" jobs in the labor market.

When the educational system begins to diverge from reproducing capitalist relations of production in a direction that results in failure to prepare labor skills corresponding to the needs of capitalist development, there will be pressures on the educational system to change. Changes in the workplace may also ensue to accommodate the problems created by the new labor force, and such work reforms may have educational consequences. In order to understand this process, it is useful to explore further the dynamic of educational expansion and its relationship to the expansion of appropriate job opportunities. Individuals and families demand schooling largely for social mobility. Higher levels of educational attainment are associated with better occupational opportunities and incomes, and the expectations of a better job and income are important factors that motivate students to obtain additional schooling.

In periods of rapid economic growth, a shortage of skilled labor creates pressure on firms to train and upgrade existing workers and labor-market entrants to fill needed positions for which there are not enough candidates with appropriate education and training. This is a relatively easy challenge to meet. But when economic growth is slow and creates relatively few positions for educated workers relative to their supply, the potential for conflict rises. Workers who pursued education to attain higher occupational positions will find their quest for social mobility frustrated by a lack of appropriate jobs. As we will argue below, such workers are likely to create problems for a smooth process of production and capital accumulation. This is the problem of overeducation or the underutilization of educated labor.

The "Overeducation" Phenomenon

Overeducation refers to the situation in which workers possess more education than can be utilized in available jobs. The reproduction of educated workers means that at each educational level appropriate skills, attitudes, behaviors, and expectations are inculcated that correspond to a particular level of occupations. Normally, workers expect to obtain jobs at a level commensurate with their educational attainments. We believe that a natural consequence of the democratic dynamic of the schools will be a tendency to produce far more people with higher educational attainments than can be absorbed by jobs requiring those credentials.

What, then, is the relationship between the jobs available for educated people and the numbers of people who are educated? This question can be divided into two parts. The first involves an analysis of historical increases in jobs that require educated workers, particularly those with a college degree. The second involves an analysis of the nature of increases in the number of people who have received college training. Taking the two parts together, we can compare the availability of appropriate opportunities for college graduates with the number of college graduates that are likely to be produced by the educational system.

Changes in Jobs for College Graduates

College training has been required mainly for professional and managerial positions. Three principal factors have determined the availability of such positions (Welch 1970). First, the overall growth of the economy has provided additional employment opportunities for graduates at all levels, including the college level. Second, changes in production technology have tended to increase the relative need for college graduates. And third, structural shifts in production from agriculture to manufacturing and from manufacturing to services have created increases in the number of positions requiring college-level skills. All these factors are responsible for the historical increases in career openings for college graduates, especially in managerial and professional positions.

Since the turn of the century, the United States has experienced relatively high levels of economic growth (Denison 1962). As the economy has expanded, so have openings for people with college-level training. After the Second World War, the annual real growth of the economy averaged 4 percent. This could have increased the size of real Gross National Product half again each decade if it could have been sustained, but by the 1970's real growth declined to only 2 percent annually.

The accord between capital, labor, and the State that had been struck during the Roosevelt Administration disintegrated in the late 1960's. Business investment patterns had changed from investing in increased labor productivity to investing in processes to reduce costs of energy and labor. The late 1970's were characterized by declines in real wages and profits, chronic inflation, *and* high unemployment (Carnoy, Shearer & Rumberger 1983). The economy has entered a new phase in which projections of growth and of new occupational positions for college graduates are much lower.[2]

A shift of the economy in the postwar period toward production demanding an increasingly educated labor force has also had substantial effects on increasing opportunities for college graduates. As noted above, the United States has experienced profound shifts from agriculture to manufacturing and in more recent years from manufacturing to services (Fuchs 1968). These shifts have been accompanied by occupational movements from farmwork to blue-collar work, and then from blue-collar to white-collar work, with an expanding managerial and professional component in the labor force. In 1900, about 10 percent of both the male and female labor force were found in managerial and professional occupations (M. Gordon 1974: 28). These proportions had risen to 14 percent for males and 16 percent for females by 1940 (Fuchs 1968) and to 30 percent and 24 percent, respectively, by 1980 (U.S. Dep't of Commerce, *Statistical Abstract 1982–83*: 386).

However, since 1970 the increases in these ratios have slowed down. As Richard Freeman (1976: 64–69) has noted, the future growth of industries that utilize college-educated people will be especially sluggish in comparison with the unusually high-growth period of the 1960's. Such education-intensive activities include the educational sector itself, research and development, and government employment. All of these have fallen on hard times as the school population has stabilized or declined— and as fiscal crisis has hit the government, in turn reducing social welfare spending and university-based research. There will actually be declines in employment in some fields, notably in public education (M. Gordon 1974: 37).

Increasing Numbers of College Graduates

It is interesting to compare the pattern of changes in professional and managerial opportunities with the increases in the numbers of college graduates. The college-age population and college attendance burgeoned following the Second World War. From 1950 to 1977 the number of 17-year-olds doubled from about 2 million to over 4 million, and the number of high school graduates increased from about 1.2 million to over 3 million (Dearman & Plisko eds. 1982: 65). Whereas only about one-fourth of those 18 to 24 were enrolling in colleges in 1963, the proportion had reached over 40 percent by 1981 (*ibid*.: 92). In 1950 about 500,000 students enrolled for the first time in institutions of higher education, but by 1980 the figure had reached almost 2.6 million (Grant & Eiden 1982: 130). During the same period the numbers of bachelor's degrees awarded rose from 400,000 to 929,000 (U.S. Dep't of HEW 1976: 197; Dearman & Plisko eds. 1982: 116). The number of master's degrees awarded increased fivefold from 1950 to 1980, and doctoral as well as first professional degrees showed similar increases (U.S. Dep't of HEW 1976: 198; Dearman & Plisko eds. 1982: 116, 118). In 1967–74 alone, the number of bachelor's degrees awarded rose from 558,000 to 946,000.

Future increases in the number of college graduates will depend upon the rate of growth of the eligible population and their enrollment rates in higher educational institutions. We believe that projected declines in the growth rate of college-age youth (Cartter 1976: 45) will be offset by increasing enrollment rates and completion rates for college. Between 1970 and 1980 the proportion of 18- to 24-year-olds enrolled in college rose from about 35 percent to almost 42 percent (Grant & Eiden 1982: 92). As college graduates compete for jobs in a tight labor market, they will reduce the options available to high school graduates and increase the incentives to enroll in college. The most reasonable forecast seems to be for a more rapid increase in the number of college graduates than the modest rise in the population of 18-year-olds.

Evidence of Overeducation

This contrasting pattern of growth between job opportunities and the increase of college graduates suggests that in recent years there have not been enough positions requiring college-level skills and expectations to employ the available graduates. According to the Carnegie Commission on Higher Education (1973a), there have been three phases in college demand. Prior to 1950, opportunities for college graduates seem to have kept pace with the supply except in periods of severe economic dislocation, such as the Depression and the Second World War. From 1950 to the mid-1960's, the expansion of opportunities outpaced the increase in college graduates. This represented a golden age for college graduates—their salaries rose more rapidly than those for other groups in the population (Welch 1970; Freeman 1976). But since the late 1960's, the number of college-educated people has increased much more rapidly than the number of appropriate jobs.

There is general agreement among many analysts—despite their use of different assessment techniques—that from about 1968 there have been and in the foreseeable future there will be an inadequate number of jobs requiring college-level skills and training and challenging enough to be consonant with the expectations of college graduates (Berg 1970; Rumberger 1981a, 1983, 1984). This "oversupply" means that college graduates must settle increasingly for positions that have not required college training in the past, or that could be filled satisfactorily by persons with high school training or less.

Evidence of this trend is found in recent data on the educational attainments of workers in different occupations. Table 1 shows the percentage of employed graduates by occupational grouping, broken down into experienced and inexperienced workers. From 1960 to 1970 the proportion of experienced college graduates employed in professional and managerial occupations increased, whereas the proportion in other occupations decreased. From 1970 to 1980 this trend was generally reversed, except for employment in managerial occupations. For young, inexperienced workers, the decline in employment opportunities during the 1970's—especially in professional areas—was even more severe: in 1970 more than two-thirds of all young college graduates found jobs in professional occupations, whereas in 1980 less than half did. The decline was especially hard on women, who are more dependent on public-sector expansion for employment opportunities (primarily in teaching). By 1980, one-fifth of all inexperienced white female graduates were employed in clerical occupations, almost twice the proportion in 1970 (Rumberger 1984: Table 5).

TABLE 1 Major Occupational Groups of Experienced and Inexperienced College Graduates, 1960, 1970, and 1980

	1960	1970	1980[a]
Experienced workers (25–64)			
Professional and technical	61.9%	66.6%	56.8%
Managerial	14.3	18.0	19.9
Sales	6.7	5.3	6.7
Clerical	7.2	5.4	8.0
Other occupations	9.9	4.7	8.6
Total	100.0%	100.0%	100.0%
Inexperienced workers (under 27)[b]			
Professional and technical	66.3%	70.0%	47.5%
Managerial	4.8	5.9	14.4
Sales	9.9	6.2	7.8
Clerical	12.5	10.6	15.1
Other occupations	6.5	7.3	15.2
Total	100.0%	100.0%	100.0%

SOURCE: U.S. Dep't of Commerce, Bureau of the Census. *Educational Attainment in the United States: 1979 and 1978*, Current Population Reports, Series P-20. No. 356 (Washington, D.C.: G.P.O. 1980). Table 12; Russell Rumberger. "The Job Market and College Graduates, 1960–1990," *Journal of Higher Education*, 55, no. 4 (July–Aug. 1984). Tables 4, 6.
[a]Based on 1979 data.
[b]Workers with less than five years of labor market experience.

Are Jobs Changing?

One obvious possibility is that occupational titles do not adequately reflect changing educational requirements, and that the same occupations have come to require higher skill levels over time. Another possibility is that a more educated person will be more productive in virtually any job, because of his or her higher skill level. It is conceivable that the increasing number of college graduates who are relegated to jobs not previously requiring this level of education might not be "overeducated" for their jobs; rather, the attribution of overeducation would result from our not adjusting the data on occupations for other relevant factors.

Neoclassical human capital analysis argues that productivity is higher for people with more education within each job classification. There are two bases for this assertion. The first is that the more educated worker is able to be more productive within the narrow occupational role itself—higher sales for the clerk, more accurate and abundant paperwork processed for the clerical worker, and so on. But data indicate that workers with an "inappropriately high" level of education show no higher or lower productivity than "appropriately educated" workers (Berg 1970). The second basis for assuming that a higher level of education improves worker productivity within an occupation is that workers with more education are able to adjust to change or to situations of disequilibrium better and to make better allocative decisions in the use of their time and other resources.[3] Although such arguments have been made for the labor market as a whole, their empirical support is limited to data from small farms in less-developed societies (Jamison & Lau 1982). The contention therefore requires a heroic extrapolation to such highly industrialized societies as the United States, where only 4 percent of the labor force is in agriculture and many of these workers are employed on large corporate farms. Indeed, both the theory (Alchian & Demsetz 1972; Williamson 1975) and the reality (Braverman 1974; Edwards 1979) underlying modern corporate production techniques require that the vast majority of workers have well-defined and highly routinized jobs that can be easily supervised and that do not permit a large amount of discretion or decision-making on the part of the worker.

A more formidable argument against our assertation of overeducation is that the same occupational classifications require greater education and skills needs over time to accommodate new technologies. According to this view, clerical and sales workers, as well as workers in manufacturing and other occupations, have faced an increasingly complex set of job demands that have required successively higher levels of formal education. There are two methods of examining this hypothesis. The first is to review the nature of change in job content for particular occupations; the second is to examine the actual educational requirements of jobs at the present time and to compare these requirements with the educational attributes of jobholders.

Some of the most extensive studies of changing skill requirements associated with increased automation were carried out by James Bright (1958, 1966). Bright explored the implications of automating the production of both goods and services on an industry-by-industry basis. He found that in most cases the changes were in the direction of *reducing* the skills and training required of workers through increasing the routinization of tasks and decreasing the decision-making components. Braverman's (1974: Chaps. 15 & 20) historical analysis of office work and Greenbaum's (1979) study of data processing also suggest that the increasingly capital-intensive nature of clerical work has tended to reduce the scope of decision making and the complexity of skills necessary to perform in those jobs. The conclusions of these case studies are also supported by a recent analysis of changes in the skill requirements of jobs throughout the economy between 1960 and 1976 (Rumberger 1981b). Rumberger found little change in aggregate skill levels required.

The comparison of educational requirements for particular jobs and the educational characteristics of jobholders also supports the view that the rising educational attainments of workers cannot be linked to ostensible increases in job complexity. For example, Rawlins and Ulman (1974) have compared the educational requirements of jobs as determined by the U.S. Employment Service with the educational qualifications of jobholders. An analysis of 38 professional and technical occupations in the 1950–60 period showed that "much of the growth of education in the postwar period cannot be explained by job-related demand for academic skills" (p. 208). In independent studies using more recent data from the U.S. Employment Service's *Dictionary of Occupational Titles*, Miller (1971), Lucas (1972), and Rumberger (1981a) made detailed comparisons of educational requirements for jobs and the educational attainments of workers holding those jobs. They concluded that most jobs in the U.S. occupational structure require considerably less education than the average attainments of workers actually in those positions.

Our overeducation analysis is also reflected in the experiences of recent graduates themselves, especially those who were unable to attain entry to professional and technical occupations. A survey by the U.S. Department of Labor of recent college graduates in the fall of 1972 found that whereas almost 88 percent of those employed in professional and technical jobs indicated that their work was related to their field of study, only 39 percent so indicated among those employed as managers, sales work-ers, and clerical workers, and 32 percent among those in all other occupations (U.S. Dep't of Labor, Bureau of Labor Statistics 1974). A 1974 survey of graduates who had entered college in 1961 found that only a minority felt that their skills were fully utilized in their work (Bisconti & Solomon 1976: 7). Job satisfaction was particularly low for those in occupations that are not traditionally associated with college training, such as clerical and other nonprofessional work (*ibid.*: 8).

On balance, it appears that a large number of recent college graduates have found themselves in occupational positions for which they are overeducated. It is unlikely that the situation will improve in the foreseeable future. The college-eligible popula-tion is leveling off, but high unemployment and falling returns to high school educa-tion are stimulating an ever greater proportion of that population to obtain degrees. And in a period of relatively stagnant demand, each new graduate is competing with a large backlog of graduates from the recent past for each appropriate opening.[4]

The longer-run outlook for economic growth is not only relatively gloomy, but the single most important employer of college graduates—the government—is likely to *reduce* significantly the number of new hirings in the 1980's. Further, the effects of high technologies on most existing jobs appear to be reducing the skill demands of such jobs rather than increasing them (Levin & Rumberger 1983a, 1983b). In particu-lar, there has been and will continue to be a loss of autonomy in the professions. Health-care personnel, lawyers, accountants, and others increasingly find that their career options are primarily in corporate and government enterprises. The tradition of being one's own boss and choosing one's specialty and hours of work is becoming increasingly circumscribed. Many professionals will find themselves relegated to rela-tively repetitive, specialized roles in large organizations (U.S. Dep't of HEW 1973: 20–23).

Overeducation and Unfulfilled Expectations

Overall, then, the long-run picture is one in which college graduates are likely to have greater expectations than the labor market can fulfill. In the past, obtaining a certain level of education usually meant attaining an occupation that was consonant with that level of education—and such expectations still seem to characterize young people. A comparison of the occupational aspirations of a national sample of 1972 high school graduates with the labor force's occupational pattern in 1972 and 1985 supports this view. Even two and a half years after leaving high school, having been either in the labor market or in college or both, about one-half the respondents aspired to professional and technical careers. But such occupations accounted for only about 14 percent of positions in the labor force in 1972 and were projected to be about 17 percent by 1985. By contrast, far fewer respondents aspired to the lower-level occupa-tions, although there were relatively more positions in these areas (U.S. Dep't of HEW, Nat'l Center for Ed. Statistics, *Nat'l Longitudinal Study of the High School Class of 1972*, prelim. data; U.S. Dep't of HEW 1976: 245).

With additional years of schooling, people increasingly expect that the jobs they obtain will correspond to their higher educational status. Not only are there prestige differences in terms of occupations that have required traditionally more education

(Duncan, Featherman & Duncan 1972), but there are substantial income differences among occupations (Sewell & Hauser 1975) and in fringe benefits, employment stability, working conditions, and independence (Duncan 1976).

What will the consequences be if such expectations are left unfulfilled? Before discussing this question, it is important to note the context in which the job dissatisfaction of the young, overeducated worker takes place. In the past, economic insecurity was a dominant factor in workers' adapting to jobs that were below their expectations or were intrinsically distasteful. The possibility of future upward mobility gave at least some hope that things might become substantially better through conscientiousness and hard work. But recent surveys show distinct breaks from these past patterns, largely owing to youth's higher educational levels and to the social gains by labor in the New Deal and after—unemployment insurance, food stamps, and other kinds of economic cushions. A survey of college seniors suggests that they see themselves as being far less concerned than their fathers with earnings and security and much more concerned with the altruistic and intrinsic aspects of the job.[5] Comparing youth opinion polls in 1967 and 1973, Yankelovich (1974: 37) found that:

Today's generation of young people is less fearful of economic insecurity than generations in the past. They want interesting and challenging work, but they assume that their employers cannot—or will not—provide it. By their own say-so, they are inclined to take "less crap" than older workers. They are not as automatically loyal to the organization as their fathers, and they are far more cognizant of their own needs and rights. Nor are they as awed by organizational and hierarchical authority. Being less fearful of "discipline" and the threat of losing their jobs, they feel free to express their discontent in myriad ways, from fooling around on the job to sabotage. They are better educated than their parents, even without a college degree. They want more freedom and opportunity and will struggle harder to achieve it.

These attitudes have probably changed again since the early 1970's, especially in the last two years of severe recession and reduction of social-welfare spending. There is undoubtedly more fear among young workers today than ten years ago, but the underlying divergence from earlier generations' attitudes toward authority on the job and aspirations for greater freedom and intrinsically more interesting jobs have probably remained.

In summary, the prospect of job dissatisfaction and its possible deleterious consequences for productivity seems to be increasingly related to the disparity between rising expectations for better jobs and the available job opportunities. Education has been found to be related to job dissatisfaction in a number of studies, the most thorough being one by Quinn and Baldi De Mandilovitch (1975). Using the extensive data from the 1973 Quality of Employment Survey as well as sophisticated statistical techniques to attempt to isolate the relations between education and job satisfaction, they found that "the most dissatisfied workers were those who were too highly educated for their jobs" (p. vii). In a related study, Kalleberg and Sorensen (1973) found that workers whose educational levels exceeded the estimated educational requirements for jobs showed higher levels of job dissatisfaction. The evidence points consistently to the probability that as the discrepancy grows between the job expectations of increasingly educated entrants to the labor force and the actual jobs available, the dissatisfaction of this group will increase.

JOB DISSATISFACTION AND IMPLICATIONS FOR PRODUCTION

Job dissatisfaction is a rising function of the discrepancy between the educational requirements of existing jobs and the rising levels of educational attainments and job expectations of the young. But what are the implications of such dissatisfaction for work organizations? There are few accurate indices on the extent to which such factors as employee turnover, alcoholism, absenteeism, drug problems, sabotage and related problems of quality control, or wildcat strikes have changed over time, and virtually no information on such changes for those occupations and industries whose labor force is characterized by increased percentages of young and overeducated workers.[6] It is therefore difficult to relate rises in overeducation to such costly problems as work stoppages, deterioration in quality control, and employee turnover or absenteeism (Henle 1974; Flanagan et al. 1974).

The problem of linking changes in the proportion of overeducated workers to longer-term changes in worker behavior is further compounded by the effects of the business cycle. During periods of recession, high rates of unemployment tend to discipline the work force. The lack of alternative employment tends to reduce worker disruption, turnover, and absenteeism. Whereas employee absentee rates rose from 1967 to 1970, they seem to have leveled off or even fallen during the recession of 1974–75 (Hedges 1973, 1975). For the overeducation issue, it is the longer-run changes that are interesting. A related problem is the lack of consistency in both concepts and operationalization of such terms as "employee turnover," "absenteeism," or other measures of worker dissatisfaction and behavior. Different studies on the subject have viewed the phenomenon and its measurement in different ways, and statistical studies that have looked for *relationships* have varied considerably in their rigor (Lyons 1972; Katzell & Yankelovitch 1975; Hedges 1973, 1975; Bureau of Nat'l Affairs 1970).

However, there is considerable support for the view that job dissatisfaction is directly related to both absenteeism and turnover (see, e.g., White 1960; Newman 1974; and Schneider & Snyder 1975). The view is intuitively compelling, although the relationship is probably a complex one that requires an improved understanding of both the psychosociological dynamics of the workplace and the research operationalization of those concepts (Brayfield & Crockett 1955; Srivastva et al. 1975).

More direct ties between overeducation and indices of employee productivity, such as employee turnover, have been reviewed by Berg (1970). He concludes that overeducation may have deleterious consequences for production. The most ambitious study that explored the connection between hiring standards and actual job requirements (Diamond & Bedrosian 1970) was carried out for ten major "entry and near-entry" jobs in each of five white-collar and four blue-collar occupations as well as one service occupation for 20 groups of firms. The authors found that hiring requirements were unrelated to job performance across cities, industries, or firms. In 17 of the 20 samples, there was little or no difference in job performance associated with the level of educational attainment of the worker. But the differences between the hiring standards and the actual requirements needed for the jobs "appeared to be an important cause of costly turnover in a major segment of virtually all of the 20 groups" (p. 7).

Other survey results suggest a relationship between job dissatisfaction and both industrial sabotage and drug use within the workplace. Quinn et al. (1973) investigated these linkages with data from the Quality of Employment Survey. They found that workers' reports of industrial sabotage were most common among dissatisfied workers, young workers, and men (p. 40; see also Quinn & Shepard 1974).

These findings are also consistent with the few case studies of work organizations characterized by rising numbers of young and more highly educated workers. Perhaps the most poignant of these is the experience of General Motors with its new Vega plant in Lordstown, Ohio. The relatively well educated and young work force responded to management's attempts to tighten worker discipline and increase production levels with wildcat strikes, sabotage, high absenteeism, drugs, and other disruptive activities (Aronowitz 1973: Chap. 1). Kremen (1972) describes a similar situation in a steel mill, and the *Work in America* report (U.S. Dep't of HEW 1973) indicates more generally the high potential losses in productivity for both business and government from the increasing disparity between worker aspirations and the reality of work organization.

We suggest, then, that rising levels of overeducation for the available jobs in conjunction with relatively high levels of material affluence are tending to create increasing problems for the production of goods and services in the United States. The higher levels of youth education are creating enhanced expectations for jobs that will confer high status, income, and responsibility. But the expansion of such occupational positions is falling far short of the increase of college-educated youth, and there also appears to be a tendency for existing professional and managerial jobs to become more routinized or proletarianized over time. We expect that these contradictory dynamics will create increasing dissatisfaction in the workplace, which will threaten productivity by increasing the level of disruptive behavior among workers.[7]

IMPLICATIONS FOR REFORM OF EDUCATON AND WORK

We have already emphasized that the tension between the democratic and class-reproductive dynamics of the educational system has implications for changing both work and education. As the educational system tends in a variety of ways to become a democratizing institution, it may exacerbate rather than mediate contradictions in production. The expansion of the system of education to satisfy the ideology of social mobility through educational mobility is an important example of a phenomenon that will disrupt production if permitted to continue. Of course, as the threats to productivity and the symptoms of worker unrest increase, there will be attempts to stem the potential disruptive effects of education's democratic dynamic through the reform of both the workplace and education. The most evident efforts to reorganize the conditions of work are the efforts by the federal government in the 1980's to reduce public assistance and other social expenditures, to pursue policies that have resulted in higher unemployment rates (in which 7 percent unemployment is tacitly defined as full employment), and to encourage anti-union policies. All of these efforts serve to make workers less choosy in terms of jobs and wages out of desperation. But there are also attempts by employers to humanize work and to increase worker participation at the various organizational levels to assimilate the "new" worker. On the educational side, the federal government has reduced its support for programs for improving the opportunities of disadvantaged, bilingual, and handicapped students and those in segregated schools. The generosity of appropriations for student loans and grants at the college level is also being reduced, and there are attempts to change educational patterns by getting young people into the labor force at an earlier age. In the following chapters we review these reforms in the context of the larger social conflict in American society.

NOTES

1. O'Connor deals specifically with State workers' unions in the context of the "fiscal crisis of the State" (1974: 146–51).
2. Of course a number of unforeseen factors may upset these forecasts, e.g. a major war. For an excellent exposition of forecasting long-run economic growth and a comparison of alternative forecasting models, see G. Fromm 1976.
3. See particularly Schultz (1975) and Welch (1970). There is a wishful quality about this argument for anyone who has visited a large office or production complex where the timing of work and resource allocation are often set out on the basis of rigid rules.
4. The U.S. Department of Labor already estimated in 1976 that in 1985 there would be one million more college graduates than jobs requiring a four-year-college degree (U.S. Dep't of Labor 1976: 20). Of course, even these estimates do not take account of the extent to which the *content* of future jobs requiring four years of college will utilize the skills of these graduates.
5. U.S. Dep't of Labor 1974: 4. See the model of Flanagan et al. (1974) that attempts to illustrate the relationship between economic growth and the quest for nonpecuniary job rewards (p. 101).
6. Berg (1976) has argued that the poor quality of such data is an indicator of the low priority that workers are given by managers; it may also reflect the fact that such information may be interpreted as a criticism of poor management. In the latter case there is a disincentive for collecting and reporting accurate time series on the symptoms of worker dissatisfaction. See also Herrick (1975) for a discussion of these data and their formulation.
7. For an analysis of this phenomenon within the overall framework of contemporary U.S. monopoly capitalism, see Wyco (1975). Herrick (1975) discusses ten aspects of counterproductive labor activity and suggests methods for estimating their magnitudes.

REFERENCES

Alchian, A., and H. Demsetz. 1972. "Production, Information Costs, and Economic Organization," *American Economic Review*, 62, no. 5 (Dec.), pp. 777–95.

Apple, Michael W. 1982a. *Cultural and Economic Reproduction in Education*. London: Routledge and Kegan Paul.

Aronowitz, Stanley. 1973. *False Promises*. New York: McGraw-Hill.

Baudelot, Christian, and Roger Establet. 1971. *L'Ecole capitaliste en France*. Paris: Maspero.

Becker, Gary S. 1964. *Human Capital*. New York: Columbia U.P.

Berg, Ivar. 1970. *Education and Jobs: The Great Training Robbery*. New York: Praeger.

Bisconti, Ann S., and Lewis C. Solomon. 1976. *College Education on the Job: The Graduates' Viewpoint*. Bethlehem, Penn.: The CPC Foundation.

Braverman, Harry. 1974. *Labor and Monopoly Capital*. New York: Monthly Review Press.

Brayfield, Arthur H., and Walter H. Crockett. 1955. "Employee Attitudes and Employee Performance," *Psychological Bulletin*, 52, pp. 396–424.

Bright, James. 1958. "Does Automation Raise Skill Requirements?," *Harvard Business Review*, 36, no. 4 (July/Aug.), pp. 85–98.

————. 1966. "The Relationship of Increasing Automation and Skill Requirements," in *The Employment Impact of Technological Change* (Washington, D.C.: G.P.O.), pp. 207–21. The Report of the National Commission on Technology, Automation, and Economic Progress, Appendix Vol. 2.

Bureau of National Affairs, Inc. 1970. *Turnover and Job Satisfaction*. Personnel Policies Forum, Survey No. 91. Washington, D.C.

Burton, Nancy W., and Lyle V. Jones, 1982. "Recent Trends in Achievement Levels of Black and White Youth," *Education Researcher*, 11, no. 4 (Apr.), pp. 10–14.

Carnegie Commission on Higher Education. 1973a. *College Graduates and Jobs*. New York: McGraw-Hill.

————. 1973b. *Higher Education: Who Pays? Who Benefits? Who Should Pay?* New York: McGraw-Hill.

————. 1973c. *Toward a Learning Society: Alternative Channels to Life, Work and Service*, New York: McGraw-Hill.

Carnoy, Martin, Robert Girling, and Russell W. Rumberger. 1976. *Education and Public Sector Employment*. Palo Alto, Calif.: Center for Economic Studies.

Carnoy, Martin, Derek Shearer, and Russell Rumberger. 1983. *A New Social Contract: The Economy and Government After Reagan*. New York: Harper and Row.

Cartter, Allan M. 1976. *Ph.D.'s and the Academic Labor Market*. New York: McGraw-Hill.

Coleman, James S. 1968. "The Concept of Equality of Educational Opportunity," *Harvard Educational Review*, 38, no. 1, pp. 7–22.

Dearman, Nancy B., and Valena White Plisko, eds. 1982. *The Condition of Education: 1982 Edition*. Washington, D.C.: Nat'l Center for Ed. Statistics.

Denison, Edward, 1962. *The Sources of Economic Growth in the United States and the Alternatives Before Us*. New York: Committee for Economic Development.

Diamond, Daniel, and Hrach Bedrosian. 1970. *Hiring Standards and Job Performance*. U.S. Department of Labor, Manpower Research Monograph no. 18. Washington, D.C.: G.P.O.

Duncan, Greg, 1976. "Earnings Functions and Nonpecuniary Benefits," *Journal of Human Resources*, 11 (Fall), pp. 462–83.

Duncan, Otis Dudley, David L. Featherman, and Beverly Duncan. 1972. *Socioeconomic Background and Achievement*. New York: Seminar.

Edwards, Richard C. 1979. *Contested Terrain: The Transformation of the Workplace in the 20th Century*. New York: Basic.

Flanagan, Robert J., *et al.* 1974. "Worker Discontent and Workplace Behavior," Berkeley, Calif.: Inst. of Indus. Relations, U.C. reprint 388.

Freeman, Richard B. 1976. *The Over-Educated American*. New York: Academic.

Fuchs, Victor R. 1968. *The Service Economy*. New York: Nat'l Bureau of Econ. Research.

Giroux, Henry A. 1981. *Ideology, Culture, and the Process of Schooling*. Philadelphia: Temple U.P.

Gordon, M.S. 1974. "The Changing Labor Market for College Graduates," in M. Gordon, ed., *Higher Education and the Labor Market* (New York: McGraw-Hill), Chap. 2.

Grant, W. Vance, and Leo J. Eiden. 1982. *Digest of Education Statistics*. National Center for Education Statistics. Washington, D.C.: G.P.O.

Greenbaum, Joan M. 1979. *In the Name of Efficiency*. Philadelphia, Penn.: Temple U.P.

Harnischfeger, A., and D. E. Wiley, 1975. "Achievement Test Score Decline: Do We Need to Worry?" Chicago: ML-Group for Policy Studies in Education, CEMREL, Inc.

Hedges, Janice. 1973. "Absence from Work—A Look at Some National Data," *Monthly Labor Review* (July), pp. 24–30.

————. 1975. "Unscheduled Absence from Work—An Update," *Monthly Labor Review* (Aug.), pp. 36–39.

Henle, Peter. 1974. "Economic Effects: Reviewing the Evidence," in J.M. Rosow, ed., *The Worker and the Job* (Englewood Cliffs, N.J.: Prentice-Hall), pp. 119–44.

Herrick, Neal Q. 1975. *The Quality of Work and Its Outcomes: Estimating Potential Increases in Labor Productivity*. Columbus, Ohio: Academy for Contemporary Problems.

Jamison, Dean T., and Lawrence J. Lau. 1982. *Farmer Education and Farm Efficiency*. Baltimore, Md.: Johns Hopkins U.P.

Kalleberg, Arne, and Aage Sorensen. 1973. "The Measurement of the Effects of Overtraining on Job Attitudes," *Sociological Methods and Research*, 2, no. 2 (Nov.), pp. 215–38.

Katzell, Raymond A., and Daniel Yankelovich. 1975. *Work, Productivity, and Job Satisfaction*. New York: Psychological Corp.

Kemerer, Frank R., and Kenneth L. Deutsch. 1979. *Constitutional Rights and Student Life*. St. Paul, Minn.: West.

Kremen, Bennett. 1972. "No Pride in This Dust," *Dissent* (Winter), pp. 21–28.

Landes, William W., and Lewis C. Solmon. 1972. "Compulsory Schooling Legislation: An Economic Analysis of Law and Social Change in the Nineteenth Century," *The Journal of Economic History*, 32, no. 1 (Mar.), pp. 54–91.

Levin, Henry M. 1977. "A Decade of Policy Development in Improving Education and Training of Low Income Populations," in R. Haveman, ed., *A Decade of Federal Antipoverty Programs: Achievements, Failures and Lessons* (New York: Academic), Chap. 4.

————. 1980. "Educational Production Theory and Teacher Inputs," in Charles Bidwell and Douglas Windham, eds., *The Analysis of Educational Productivity: Issues in Macroanalysis* (Cambridge, Mass.: Ballinger), vol. 2, Chap. 5.

————. 1983b. "Youth Unemployment and Its Educational Consequences," *Educational Evaluation and Policy Analysis*, 2, no. 2 (Summer), pp. 231–47.

Lucas, R. 1972, "Working Conditions, Wage Rates and Human Capital: A Hedonic Study," Ph.D. Diss., MIT.

Lyons, Thomas F. 1972. "Turnover and Absenteeism: A Review of Relationship and Shared Correlates," *Personnel Psychology*, 25, no. 2, pp. 271–81.

Main, Jackson T. 1965. *The Social Structure of Revolutionary America*. Princeton, N.J.: Princeton U.P.

Miller, Anne R. 1971. "Occupations of the Labor Force According to the Dictionary of Occupational Titles." Philadelphia, Penn.: Population Studies Center.

Newman, John E. 1974. "Predicting Absenteeism and Turnover: A Field Comparison of Fishbein's Model and Traditional Job Attitude Measures," *Journal of Applied Psychology*, 59, no. 5, pp. 610–15.

Pincus, John, ed. 1974. *School Finance in Transition*. Cambridge, Mass.: Ballinger.

Quinn, Robert P., *et al.* 1973. "Evaluating Working Conditions in America," *Monthly Labor Review*, 96 (Nov.), pp. 32–41.

Quinn, Robert P., and Linda J. Shepard. 1974. *The 1972–73 Quality of Employment Survey: Descriptive Statistics, with Comparison Data from the 1967–70 Survey of Working Conditions*. Ann Arbor, Mich.: Univ. of Mich., Institute for Social Research.

Quinn, Robert P., and Martha S. Baldi DeMandilovitch. 1975. "Education and Job Satisfaction: A Questionable Payoff." Ann Arbor, Mich.: Univ. of Mich. Survey Research Center.

Rawlins, V. Lane, and Lloyd Ulman. 1974. "The Utilization of College-Trained Manpower in the United States," in Margaret S. Gordon, ed., *Higher Education and the Labor Market* (New York: McGraw-Hill), pp. 195–236.

Rawls, John. 1971. *A Theory of Justice*. Cambridge, Mass.: Belknap.

Rubin, David. 1972. *The Rights of Teachers*. New York: Avon.

Rumberger, Russell W. 1981a. *Overeducation in the U.S. Labor Market*. New York: Praeger.

————. 1981b. "The Changing Skill Requirements of Jobs in the U.S. Economy," *Industrial and Labor Relations Review*, 34, no. 4 (July), pp. 578–90.

————. 1983. "Dropping Out of High School: The Influence of Race, Sex, and Family Background," *American Educational Research Journal*, 20, no. 2 (Summer), pp. 199–220.

————. 1984. "The Job Market for College Graduates, 1960–1990," *Journal of Higher Education*, 55, no. 4 (July/Aug.), pp. 433–54.

Schneider, Benjamin, and Robert A. Snyder. 1975. "Some Relationships Between Job Satisfaction and Organizational Climate," *Journal of Applied Psychology*, 60, no. 3, pp. 318–28.

Sennett, Richard, and Jonathan Cobb. 1972. *Hidden Injuries of Class*. New York: Knopf.

Sewell, William H., and Robert M. Hauser. 1975. *Education, Occupation and Earnings: Achievement in the Early Career*. New York: Academic.

Srivastva, S., *et al.* 1975. *Job Satisfaction and Productivity*. Cleveland, Ohio: Case Western Univ., Dep't of Organizational Behavior.

Thurow, Lester. 1975. *Generating Inequality*. New York: Basic.

U.S. Department of Commerce, Bureau of the Census. 1978. *Historical Statistics of the United States, Colonial Period to 1970, Part I*. Washington, D.C.

U.S. Department of Commerce. 1982. *Statistical Abstract of the United States: 1982–83*. 103d ed. Washington, D.C.: G.P.O.

U.S. Department of Education, National Center for Educational Statistics. 1981. *High School and Beyond, A Capsule Description of High School Students*. Review Edition. Washington, D.C.: G.P.O.

U.S. Department of Health, Education, and Welfare. 1973. *Work in America*. Cambridge, Mass.: MIT Press.

————. 1976. *The Condition of Education*. National Center for Educational Statistics, NCES 7a6-400. Washington, D.C.: G.P.O.

U.S. Department of Labor, Bureau of Labor Statistics. 1974. "Employment of Recent College Graduates, October 1972." Special Labor Force Report 169. Washington, D.C.: G.P.O.

Welch, Finis. 1970. "Education in Production," *Journal of Political Economy*, 78, no. 1 (Jan./ Feb.), pp. 35–59.

White, B. L. 1960. "Job Attitudes, Absence From Work and Labour Turnover," *Personnel Practice Bulletin*, 16, no. 4 (Dec.), pp. 18–23.

Willis, Paul. 1977. *Learning to Labor*. Lexington, Mass.: Heath.

Wirtz, Willard, *et al.* 1977. *On Further Examination: Report of the Advisory Panel on the Scholastic Aptitude Test Score Decline*. New York: College Entrance Examination Board.

Wyko, Bill. 1975. "The Work Shortage: Class Struggle and Capital Reproduction," *Review of Radical Political Economics*, 7, no. 2 (Summer), pp. 11–26.

Yankelovich, Daniel. 1974. *The New Morality: A Profile of American Youth in the 70's*. New York: McGraw-Hill.

Crisis and Hope:
The Dialectic of the
Welfare-Educational State, II

H. Svi Shapiro

In ways that have been typical of right-wing movements, the conservative politics of the 1980s in America may be seen as the alliance of two distinct social forces: on the one hand are the concerns of economically threatened corporate interests and, on the other hand, the concerns of a beleaguered middle class.[1] While the former has sought to alleviate its position through government policies aimed at enhancing profitability and the income of upper-level social groups, the latter has sought to right a world that appeared to be turning upside-down, by the pursuit of legislation that would restore traditional values and a prior social order. Against the cultural anxieties (catalyzed as they are by economic concerns) of the middle class, the goals of the corporate element in the conservative movement have been far more direct and explicit. Its aims, put simply, have been to raise the profitability of big business in America. Arguing that a capital shortage was the cause of declining productivity in American industry, businessmen and their political and intellectual allies have sought to hold down or cut back social and educational programs, restrain wages and, hence, increase the return to capital. Such policies have amounted to a redistribution of the social product in favor of business and away from the welfare state and the New Frontier and Great Society programs of the 1960s. Whatever else might be said of such policies, it is clear that the profitability of United States business has declined as it has met stiffer competition from capitalist rivals in Japan, West Germany and elsewhere in Europe, and as small Third World nations have begun to resist United States political and economic domination. In addition, the problem has been compounded by the extended period of "stagflation" that has followed the domestic boom of the late '60s, during which time the American economic pie began to shrink and the real incomes of both working people and capitalists stagnated or declined.

There can be little doubt that in terms of the government measures proposed to meet this situation corporate interests had remarkable success.[2] There was, indeed, a significant redistribution of wealth to upper-income groups (who, it was argued, would use the increased income to fund the national economy). The sharp decline in the relative weight of the taxation in the national economy carried by big business is vividly illustrated by the fact that corporate taxes now represent just 7 percent of the total taxes levied (in 1948 it stood at 23 percent). Since corporate wealth is distributed disproportionately among a very small group of individuals at the top of the income ladder, this only confirms the sharply redistributive effects of recent tax policies in favor of the rich. The Congressional Budget Office estimated that the 1981 Reagan tax plan gave 162,000 people who made over $200,000 a year $22,000 in tax cuts per capita, while 32 million people earning $15,000 or less got just $92.00. The net effect on annual family income of the 1981 tax and benefit cuts ranged from an additional income of $15,000 for those earning $80,000 and above, to an added $810 for those receiving between $20,000 and $40,000, down to a low of $240 for those earning less than $10,000. The Reagan tax plan of 1985, despite its lowering of the tax rate for low-income earners, continued the trend towards a less progressive income tax. The real beneficiaries of Reagan's second tax reform were those with the highest incomes whose tax rates fell to 35 percent (from 70 percent in 1979) and whose capital gains taxes were reduced from 20 percent to 17.5 percent.

In effecting such a redistribution of income the impact on social and educational programs can be little doubted. In North Carolina, for example, reductions in federal aid included the following results: the major education block grant lost 33 percent of its funding; child nutrition programs lost 96 percent of the Special Milk Program, 15.3 percent of the School Breakfast Program, and 9.4 percent of the Child Care Food Program; infant aid was cut by 47.6 percent; and Appalachian regional education aid by 86 percent. In other areas, the Primary Health Care Block grant was cut by 13 percent, the Health Prevention and Health Service block grant by 29 percent, Maternal and Child Health grants by 17 percent, and immunization of infants and preschool children by 48 percent. The Alcohol, Drug Abuse and Mental Health Services block grant lost 30 percent, and the Social Services (Title XX) block grant was reduced by 18.5 percent.[3]

At the ideological core of these very significant cutbacks was the attempt to restrain, curtail, and even revoke the expansion of social rights, economic expectations, and entitlement that have accompanied the enlargement of the state (in which the notion of educational rights has played an important role). Thus in the pursuit of raised profitability for the corporate sector, the attack on social and educational rights (as those are embodied in the programs and outlays of the state) was a central policy concern. While there can be little doubt as to unparalleled influence of corporate interests in the policies of the Reagan administration, it is also important to note the limitations that emerged around such policies. The dominant role of the big business in the formation of government policies—whatever its obvious and massive influence—must also be viewed in terms of the countervailing power that such policies evoked. Despite its wide and clear successes, capital does indeed face barriers to the implementation of its programs. For those concerned with education, for example, any review of the policies of the Reagan administration will reveal two outstanding features. First were the massive and unparalleled attacks on the programs that constitute the federal role in education in this country. The second, paradoxically, has been the emergence of countervailing pressures on the pursuit or implementation of such policies. Whatever the extent of the butchery committed by the Reagan administration in the field of education, its goals fell significantly short of what was anticipated. Despite the ferocity of the attack on the social-educational state, it is now clear that the expansion of social rights and economic entitlements represent an expansion of the political rights of citizenship that will not easily be revoked. The expansion of political rights into an increasing number of social, economic and cultural rights forms a formidable barrier to the pursuit of corporate goals.

These barriers represent, according to Richard Cloward and Frances Fox Piven, a profound change, especially during the last fifty years, in the perceptions that ordinary people have of the relationship between politics and economics.[4] There has been a fundamental erosion, they argue, of the idea that democratic rights do not enable ordinary people to act upon the most urgent economic problems of their lives. There has been an erosion of the doctrine of *laissez-faire* which holds that economic relationships are determined by "natural" laws in which neither the state, nor the majorities that come to participate in the state, should interfere. In the nineteenth century:

> Political rights were thus separated from economic rights, and the economic experiences of ordinary people were made to have little bearing on their ideas about politics. . . . The world of the market was in effect shielded from the world of politics to which common people had gained some access.[5]

During the course of the twentieth century, however, the doctrine of separation has weakened. Grievances against property and the effects of the market increasingly took the form of protests directed against the state:

> The broad movement by common people to exercise political rights in behalf of economic rights culminated in the great popular struggles of the 1930s and 1960s— in mass protests by the unemployed, industrial workers, the aged, blacks and women. Politics and economics fused in the granting of federal emergency relief to the masses of unemployed, in collective bargaining legislation, in wage-and-hour laws, in unemployment insurance, in pensions for the aged and disabled, in the enactment of public welfare subsidies for unemployable, in occupational health and safety standards, in medical and housing programs, in civil rights legislation and affirmative action programs, and in a spate of general environmental protection.[6]

The process by which the doctrine of separation collapsed and political rights expanded to a place where they could be used by ordinary people to act on the most pressing issues of their lives, meant that the state became the major area of class conflict. More and more, the poor, working-class and middle-income Americans have expected or demanded that the state protect them against the vicissitudes of the market, the inequities of a class society, the injustices of racism and sexism, and the effects of uncontrolled industrial growth. Increasingly, unemployment, inflation, the availability of credit, the questions of adequate health care or nutrition, the effects of disability or retirement, the quality of consumer products and the environment, and access to schooling have become the subject of popular demands and democratic expectations.

As Cloward and Piven point out, the rising tide of expectations and entitlements that have accompanied the emergence of the welfare state is part of the wider process of the politicization of our economic system. While the distinctive American political institutions of the nineteenth century shielded the various ways in which the state served capital from public view (and thus gave the ideology of *laissez-faire* a certain credibility), by the twentieth century the penetration of the economy by the state on behalf of business had so expanded that the hypocrisy of *laissez-faire* became more transparently evident. It was no longer possible, they assert, to sustain a doctrine prescribing the separation of economy and polity because it was so at odds with the reality.

All of this has contributed to the demystification of *laissez-faire* ideas and made clear the way in which the interests of capital depend on the state. Such developments have, in turn, led to pressures for new kinds of state interventions into the economy—ones which have involved demands that arise from the bottom end of the social structure rather than from the top. The movements which embodied these demands wrought fundamental changes in both the perceptions of social reality, and in the reality itself. The movements of the 1930s and of the 1960s, though they have subsided, left in their wake a profound transformation:

> The new programs of the 1930s and 1960s produced pervasive new linkages between the state and democratic publics that paralleled older linkages between the state and business. . . . The agencies established to administer new benefit programs, services, and regulations represent another set of linkages, not with business but with the unemployed and the poor, women and blacks, the elderly and the disabled, and unions and environmental groups. By incorporating so wide a range of an enfranchised population, the state itself has become partially democratized.[7]

The process of democratization has meant an expanding array of laws and regulations which have embodied the popular ideology of the twentieth century—the notion that political rights are also social and economic rights. It has meant accelerating popular demands for political interventions that ameliorate the effects of industrial change, redress inequities caused by the market, and protect the casualties of the economic cycle and the process of capital accumulation. Not surprisingly, such a democratization of the state has had deleterious consequences for big business. The politicization of economic life—the notion that more and more aspects of the lives of ordinary people become matters of public policy and areas of popular entitlement—has weakened the bargaining power of capital, and has placed increasing restrictions around the operation and effects of the market in capitalist society. It is precisely this that corporate support of the campaign against "big government" has sought to address. Cloward and Piven argue that the concern with big government is really a concern with the expansion of the welfare state. It is an issue of resisting and disassembling the interventions of the state around matters of equity or social and occupational responsibility. They note:

> The Reagan administration may rail against interference in the economy by "big business," but what it actually means to condemn and eliminate is government interference on behalf of ordinary people, not government interference on behalf of business.[8]

Indeed far from a reduction in the costs or obligations of government, the policies of the Reagan administration involved a massive expansion of support for corporate interests and their high income beneficiaries. The campaign against big government meant a *shifting* of government support, far more than any contraction. The reduction in support of social and educational programs, the restructuring of tax policies, the curtailment of regulative activity, and the huge enlargement of defense outlays, made government policies enormously favorable to the interest of capital. The unprecedented levels of unemployment coupled with reductions in the levels of subsistence benefits have been important forces weakening the bargaining power of working people. The result has been a lowering of the rate of inflation through a reduction in the incomes of working and middle class Americans.

The campaign against government was an attempt to revitalize *laissez-faire* ideology so that the economic process would be disconnected from popular pressures and political rights. Whether around the question of jobs, educational opportunities, clean air, the provisions of health care, nutrition, or safe working conditions, the campaign has sought to convince Americans that their interests are best served if the state is required to respond less to the "clamor of popular demands." It has sought to reassert the idea that the market, not the government, ought to be the mechanism that regulates the conditions of our social and economic lives.

Despite the apparently contradictory election results of the 1980s, there is now mounting evidence that there has been no real abandonment of the notion that the state must intervene to ameliorate or redress the effects of the market and that the state is compelled to protect the livelihoods and opportunities of ordinary people. Certainly the election of Ronald Reagan and the emergence of the policies of "supply-side" economics did not signify a massive embrace of *laissez-faire* ideology or an abandonment of the idea that political rights are also economic rights.[9] The present government, no less than any other since 1932, was directed by a popular mandate to resolve the problems facing working people, especially inflation and unemployment. Indeed, as Cloward and Piven note, unless these problems are resolved, worsening economic conditions will likely once again bring to power national administrations committed to resolve popular economic grievances by rebuilding the welfare state, and even adding to its power.

THE POLITICS OF RESISTANCE IN THE 1980s

Despite some profound changes that have occurred in recent years, there are limits to the implementation of conservative policies in education and in other areas connected to the welfare or social state in the United States. Such limits on reform are not simply consequences of the particular acumen, skill, or statecraft of politicians on the Right (of which there certainly is no lack) but, more substantially, reflect deepening structural restraints in the alignments and dynamics typically associated with conservative social and educational policy making.

From the earliest days of its ascent to power the Reagan administration showed itself to be, both in its choice of functionaries and in its programmatic emphases, aligned far more closely with the concerns and goals of capital, rather than with the social agenda of the New Right which had not a single successful act of substantial legislation pass in the 97th Congress. In the field of education the New Right was unable to pass legislation that would allow prayer in public schools, or amendments limiting the jurisdiction of the court in matters of school busing, or legislation supporting tax credits for private school attendance.

While failure at the congressional level represents an important political phenomenon, this does not reflect the sum total of New Right achievements. Activities at the local and state levels—censorship of school materials, reinstatement of more severe (traditional) behavioral standards, and exclusion of unwanted teachers—represent a shift in the politics and ideology of schooling in the United States that predate the Reagan presidency but are certainly buoyed by the events of the 1980s. Our concern, however, is with the relationship of such grassroots influences on the priorities of those wielding national power. The last few years reveal a pattern in which middle-class interests have achieved little significant power. While these grassroots groups have played an indispensable role in mobilizing public opinion and electoral support for right wing politicians, their influence in the formation of national policies has been more illusory than real. Capital, through its alliance with reactionary groups that express the fears and anxieties of the middle class, has been able to construct a political battering ram for the achievement of its own profit-oriented ends.

Still, the economic reforms of the Right have been considerably more radical in their effects. At the same time, there has indeed been significant, at times aggressive, resistance to policies that have attempted to reduce the scope of social and economic rights. In struggles around environmental issues, social security, and questions of educational opportunity, there have been widespread mobilizations to stop attempts to reduce the protections, safeguards, and opportunities hitherto guaranteed by the state. While clearly not forestalling the Reagan budget axe, popular pressures over educational issues significantly impacted proposed cuts. Popular resistance to such cuts has, at least in some areas, stayed the hand of the executioner. Evidence of this is found in a recent report of the Congressional Research Service. The report notes that the 97th Congress generally supported education assistance programs in the face of the Administration's efforts to reduce sharply federal funding and influence in education. It continued:

> The Congress reduced the funding for some programs in FY 1982, but the total amount was increased over FY 1980 funding levels. Additional reductions were made to some elementary and secondary education programs in FY 1982 but large increases in some of the higher education student assistance programs nearly maintained the overall funding levels. Efforts by the Administration to make further reduction in FY 1982 funding by means of rescissions to enacted appropriations have been rejected.[10]

We may assume that such action was motivated, at least in part, by popular and democratic pressures unleashed by the harshness of the administration's proposals.[11]

The area of student loans provides probably the most dramatic evidence of the connection between political rights and economic rights (mediated through the opportunity for higher education). Cuts in student loans were opposed by a broad coalition of groups that stretched from the minority poor to sections of the white middle class. (Far larger cuts in many other areas were implemented in programs that touched smaller and more vulnerable segments of the population.) The breadth of the mobilization in this case makes clear the extent to which the state in America has politicized the hopes and aspirations of a larger and larger proportion of the population. It is precisely the size of this population that stands as a barrier to any simple return to the ideology of an unhindered economic marketplace. Nor, despite the ballyhoo about electoral realignments, is there much evidence that the majority of the electorate wants such a return. Neither in electoral results nor opinion surveys is there evidence of a fundamental shift in ideology. The latter, for example, continually underline the salience of the kind of complex consciousness suggested by Antonio Gramsci. Whatever support there is at the level of "formal" beliefs for smaller government, unrestricted free enterprise, and leaving it to the market, at the level of "practical" consciousness a majority of the people want continued interventions into the market and social interventions, to ensure a cleaner environment, access to schooling, protection as a result of age, disability, and unemployment, safe working conditions, regulation of consumer quality standards, and more. Indeed, there is reason to believe that there are sizable majorities in favor of an expanded social state (concerned, for example, with universal health care or affordable day care). Electoral results in 1980, 1982, and 1984 show more than anything else the class-skewed nature of voter-turnout.[12] The slightly more than half of the eligible electorate that turned out in the presidential elections was disproportionately represented by more affluent voters who know well how their class interests are best served. While more than a third of all Democratic support comes now from low-income voters, the remaining working-class and middle-class voters showed a frequent disposition toward split voting—supporting a popular president who was, at the same time, clearly identified with the interests of the wealthy, as well as electing Democratic congressional candidates who are perceived as more likely to protect social security, student loans, medicare, and the environment. As Thomas Edsall makes so clear in his study, the real problems for the Democratic Party among middle-class and working-class voters is the tendency to see the party as beneficent to the poor (and especially minorities) without responding adequately to these voters' interest—indeed to perceive the Democratic Party as siding with those groups against the middle class.[13] There is a political vacuum which cannot, ultimately, be filled by a Republican Party that is so strongly the representative of the wealthy and the powerful.

These prevarications at the electoral level are certainly reflected in subsequent budget discussions and decisions. The limits of economic conservatism were made very clear when, even with the nearly unprecedented scale of the 1984 presidential victory, the president's budget-cutting proposals could not safely be accepted by politicians. While Reagan's extraordinary success in the passage of the 1982 budget was not unrelated to the fact that about 40 percent of the Federal savings resulted from changes in benefit programs affecting households with incomes of less than $10,000, and another 30 percent from those with incomes between $10,000 and

$20,000—certainly the most vulnerable strata of the population—larger budget pro-
posals attempted to undermine or dismantle the social state of the middle class.[14] It is
at this point that we see the extent to which the social state in America has politicized
the expectations and aspirations of an increasingly larger proportion of the population.
They are now strongly invested in the expansion of social rights and antipathetic to, in
anything but the most abstract sense, reductions in those rights.

Notwithstanding the rootedness among broad sections of the population of social
and economic rights that have politicized so many of the areas of our lives that were
previously left to the market, this is, in no sense, meant to diminish what have been
the accomplishments of the Reagan years. While the politicization of our access to
schooling, environmental quality, work conditions, the inability to work for a living,
means the emergence of a powerful ideological and political bulwark against too much
budget-cutting, the damage to the social state has, nonetheless, been extensive. Measured in human suffering—poverty, hunger, infant mortality, joblessness—the effects
are incalculable. The results are only just beginning to be seen and felt. Most
importantly, this "golden age" of conservatism has been able to alter the boundaries
of political debate. It has upset the political consensus surrounding the welfare state,
reconstructing the political agenda so that a series of hitherto long-fought for civil
rights or entitlements can no longer be assumed or taken for granted. To whatever
extend these entitlements were diminished as a result of the Reagan budgetary initiatives, the more serious consequence is that their fundamental assuredness as a result
of previous social and political struggles can no longer be relied upon. The balance of
ideological and political power that has constituted the particular form of hegemonic
domination until this time has reformed on terms that are distinctively less advanta-
geous to those in the middle and lower end of the social order.

Yet the social and political agenda of this era has its ideological limits. Such
limits are reinforced by a number of effects noted by Alan Wolfe. He says that
conservative economic programs are based on an explosive combination of pain and
hope:

> Accept pain now, the right wing suggests, and with faith your life will improve.
> Cutbacks in social services, higher tax burdens for those least able to afford them
> and increasing rates of unemployment are, it is claimed, the necessary price to pay
> for reindustrialization and eventual prosperity.[15]

Yet, says Wolfe, such behavior runs directly counter to the taste for immediate
gratification so powerfully nurtured by modern capitalism:

> Right-wing governments ask for patience, but capitalism finds patience intolerable. It
> expects quick results, immediate consumption, instant pleasure. The political time
> needed for conservative programs to work is negated by every television commercial
> and money market fund. Conservatives are done in by the very rhetoric that brings
> them to power.[16]

The austerity and deprivation imposed on unprecedented numbers during this time
stand in ever sharper relief against the accentuated privileges available to the rich.

These developments have given rise to one of the most startling and hopeful phenomena in American politics—the Jackson candidacy and the Rainbow Coalition—the first significant popularly based social democratic movement in fifty years. In addition to the resulting heightening of class awareness and class antagonism, the transfer of wealth into a massive build-up of America's nuclear arsenal generated, within a relatively short space of time, a mass movement in favor of a weapons freeze and arms limitation agreements. The moral dimensions of a politics that deprive individuals of basic human resources, like housing, while funding, at unprecedented levels, the programs of the military-industrial complex, become increasingly unpalatable to a significant segment of the American population.

Interestingly, however, the limits on economic conservatism that could prove most decisive in the long run may not be the ones that "surge from the bottom up." Within the corporate sector itself and among a growing band of economists there is an accelerating recognition that modern organized bureaucratic capitalism demands policies quite different from those conservative remedies that emphasize a nostalgic return to the free, unregulated market. For those opposing such policies, the critical issues facing America in the area of industrial investment and productivity can be met only through enhanced levels of state planning and coordinated interventions into the economic market. One of the most prominent spokesmen for this renewed role of the national state is Lester C. Thurow, professor of economics at M.I.T. He writes:

> If current policies do not restore economic growth, then it will be obviously true that salvation does not lie in the direction of "getting the government off the backs of the people." Debates about less government will die out and be replaced with debates not about more government but about what government should do to promote economic growth.[17]

Thurow and others favor government interventions in the market to enhance the competitiveness of American industry *vis-à-vis* other industrial nations.[18] Through the development of a formal industrial-planning policy (as in France or Japan) it would be possible to "develop an integrated strategy that treats public investment, private investment and investment in human capital as part of one policy."[19] Its purpose would be to encourage the fast-growth sector of the economy (the so-called sunrise industries), administer re-industrialization of America's basic industries, and renovate the disintegrating economic infrastructure (roads, bridges, and tunnels).

In all such alternatives for enhancing the competitiveness of the corporate sector, policies concerned with "investments in human capital" are strongly emphasized. Such policies speak to the need for a renewed funding of America's educational system as the means to ensure a workforce equipped with an adequate level of technical or other skills. Indeed, as I have argued previously, it is precisely those concerns that are the cornerstone of the most influential of the recent reports on the crisis in our system of education.[20] As the antigovernment politics of Reagan's conservatism runs its course without really enhancing the productivity of American industry, a new politics is likely to emerge—one that will emphasize a renewed role for the state in the revitalization of the corporate sector. While the renewed federal commitment to the educational system that is likely to follow will certainly proclaim an end to the policies of neglect, inequity, and the unfulfilled opportunities of the Reagan era, those concerned about education may, however, find renewed cause for concern. In the brave new world of corporate-state-school cooperation, education becomes ever more widely defined as technical training, the means to ensure industrial harmony, and the mechanism for assuring individuals well-adjusted to the demands of the bureaucratic world. In this "human capital" view of education, the ideals of a critically intelligent, liberally educated, and humane citizenry is likely to be a subordinate goal. Transcending the limits of conservative policy in education may spell more money and more resources for the hard-pressed domain of schooling. It is unlikely, however, to mean any fundamental reorientation in the nature of the school experience itself. Such an experience is likely to become ever more suffused with the positivist and hierarchical values of bureaucratic capitalism.

CONCLUSION: THE DIALECTIC
OF THE WELFARE-EDUCATIONAL STATE

Above all else, this chapter and the ones preceding it have attempted to refute interpretations of schooling in which it is perceived only in terms of its social control functions. Education, and especially public education, does far more than ensure a passive, compliant, or submissive population. While studies of the hidden curriculum and other critically oriented work have made clear the relationship of schooling to the socialization of a workforce differentiated and adapted to the values, norms, and beliefs of a bureaucratically organized capitalist economy, this is only a partial description of the effects of education in the United States. Such partiality has drawn our attention away from the total process—the dialectic of schooling in this country. In ways that are analogous to the effects of the welfare state as a whole, education must be seen as both regulating and invigorating popular concerns. Education not only cools out social and economic demands, it also infuses them with greater energy and assertiveness.[21] The important expansion of social and economic rights over the last fifty years has been buttressed by the expansion of educational opportunities and educational rights. There has been an enlargement of the realm in which democratic rights, rather than the criteria of the marketplace, have become the arbiter of the distribution of services, benefits, and resources; in which jobs and the economy need to be responsive to the popular will; and the dissemination of cultural meanings need to be submitted to public scrutiny. Education has been a leading force in reducing the autonomy of the market and the unresponsiveness of capital; it has been an important catalyst in the increasing politicization of social and economic life. Even Reaganomics, which purported to stand for an end to government "interference" in the economy, and a return to *laissez-faire* economics, was not so much predicated on the natural right of capital to pursue its goals unhindered by collective concerns, but as an alternative means to ensure fulfillment of popular economic demands. The 1980 and 1984 elections were little different from any other since 1932 which have "featured claims and counter-claims, promises and counterpromises, intended to appease popular economic discontent."[22]

By placing education within the broader structures of the welfare state, which has caused increasing areas of our social and economic lives to be subjected to democratic demands arising from citizenship rather than the marketplace, the nature of recent administrations' policies towards education are most clearly understood. The unprecedented cuts in student loans, for example, can be seen as part of the wider strategy by which popular expectations of the economy and wider demands for economic opportunity are lowered; changes in the regulations concerning the education of the handicapped reduce the scope and extent of citizens' social rights; and support of vouchers for private schooling expands the field in which market criteria are utilized to decide the distribution of resources, opportunity and experience. In all of these ways (and many more) the attack on public education becomes an assault on the realm of social and economic rights won in the struggles of the past fifty years.

Education, paradoxically, is also uniquely placed in attempts to reinvigorate the ideology of the marketplace in American society. It clearly expresses in its practices the individualistic and competitive values which are at the center of the ideology. Attempts to legitimate policies that weaken the social-educational state are able to exploit precisely this ideology in order to support such goals. In particular, through reductions in federal educational interventions, it appears that middle-class anxieties concerning the oversupply of educated manpower can be assuaged. Such interventions, it is suggested, have weakened educational standards, opening up the possibilities of educational success to a far greater (and, it is argued, far less qualified) population. Changes in curriculum and teaching methods have weakened the competitive structure of American education, contributing, so conservatives charge, to reduce standards of ability or achievement. Whatever the truth in these assertions, changes in education, especially in the late 1960s and early '70s, did indeed open up the possibilities of educational success to a far broader population of students. The elimination of liberal educational reforms and the interventions of the federal government are desired so far as to return education to the pre-existing forms of competition and selectivity in which the cultural inheritance of the middle and upper middle classes imbues their offspring with overwhelming educational advantages. Typical of such forms of political mobilization, middle-class support rests on the fears and anxiety that are the product of declining economic circumstances—the increasing competition with other groups for the shrinking number of middle-class jobs. While improving educational standards is the ostensible claim of conservative rhetoric, its real effect is to reinforce the selective and competitive nature of schooling, by pitting the middle class against the poor, blacks against whites, men against women.

The complex and contradictory nature of education presented here facilitates both challenges and adaptation to the structures of power and opportunity in American society. It mirrors the fluid and unresolved nature of the struggle to achieve social and political change in the United States. Thus, as Cloward and Piven argue, despite the powerful assault on the welfare state there is no assuredness that it will, in the long run, be successful. The popular ideology of the twentieth century (the view that citizenship includes not only political rights but also economic rights) is deeply rooted in, and continually confirmed by, twentieth-century experience, they argue. Such experience is rooted in the structural changes that have transformed American society over the past century:

> Neither the decentralization of a few popularly oriented programs nor the restruc-
> turing of the regulatory agencies will suffice to obscure the change of interdependen-

cies between state and economy. . . the scale and obviousness of the state's penetration of the economy will continue to nourish popular convictions that government
has a great deal to do with the economic circumstances of people . . . [and] the
democratic right to participate is likely to continue to produce demands that government enact policies of economic reform.[23]

It will require, they argue, more than propaganda and the still relatively minor
structural changes to restore the nineteenth-century doctrine that economic activities
are regulated by the law of the market rather than the law of the state, and to
persuade people that the government is not the proper arbiter from which to seek
solutions to their social and economic troubles.

Such belief must be a tempered one. In the present and continuing economic
crisis more fundamental change can, in no way, be discounted. The lessons of history
in this century must alert us to the catastrophic possibilities that may emerge in
moments of such crisis. What must be affirmed here, both in connection to the study
of education and in terms of the wider society, is the relatively open and undeter-
mined nature of change. While the structural situation rules out certain possibilities
and makes others more likely, this is the most that can be said. Such situations
represent no more than the parameters of the terrain on which the struggle for change
is able to occur. It is finally the situation itself that must be acted upon—and for this,
the conscious intentionality of human involvement is indispensable. The institutions of
the welfare-education state offer a terrain on which the interest and ideology of those
who are most powerful in society may be contested, defined in alternative ways, and
sometimes, transformed. The history of public institutions must be understood as
testimony to such possibilities.

NOTES

1. For a fuller discussion, see H. Svi Shapiro, "The Making of Conservative Educational
   Policy," *Urban Education* 17 (July 1982): 233–52.
2. See, for example, Judis, "To the Wealthy," p. 3.
3. *Federal Budget Cuts in North Carolina, Part II* (Raleigh, N. C.: The North Carolina
   Center for Public Policy Research, 1982).
4. Piven and Cloward, *The New Class War*. New York: Pantheon, 1982.
5. *Ibid.*, p. 42.
6. *Ibid.*, p. 43.
7. *Ibid.*, pp. 118–19.
8. *Ibid.*, p. 44.
9. While opinion surveys have certainly noted the public's desire for smaller, less expensive
   government, they also paradoxically emphasize strong and continued support for the specified categories of social spending—whether in environmental protection, social security,
   medical care, educational aid, or housing.
10. *Impact of Budget Changes in Major Education Programs, Both Enacted and Proposed,
    During the 97th Congress* (Washington, D.C.: Congressional Research Service, The Li-
    brary of Congress, IP199E, September 25, 1982).
11. Dramatic, if surprising, testimony to this is provided by arch-conservative David Stock-
    man, who described Reagan's "failed revolution" in his book, *The Triumph of Politics*
    (New York: Harper and Row, 1986).

12. See Thomas B. Edsall, *The New Politics of Inequality* (New York: Norton, 1984), chapter 5.

13. *Ibid.*

14. See, for example, *Major Legislative Changes in Human Resources Programs since January 1981*. Staff Memorandum from the Congressional Budget Office (August 1983).

15. Alan Wolfe, "The Retreat of the Right," *Nation*, October 23, 1982, p. 400.

16. *Ibid.*

17. Lester C. Thurow, "How to Rescue a Drowning Economy," *The New York Review of Books* 29 (April 1, 1982).

18. Prominent among these are Felix Rohatyn, Barry Bosworth, James Galbraith, Barry Bluestone, Bennett Harrison, and David A. Smith.

19. Quotes in "The New Liberal Economists," *Newsweek*, November 8, 1982.

20. H. Svi Shapiro, "Capitalism at Risk: The Political Economy of the Education Reports of 1982," *Educational Theory* 35 (Winter 1985): 57–72.

21. Piven and Cloward, *The New Class War*, p. 125. New York: Pantheon, 1982.

22. More recent critical education theory has begun to orient us towards the democratic and citizenship traditions in American schooling as a springboard for transforming schools into public spaces where forms of self and social empowerment might be fostered. See for example, Henry A. Giroux and Peter McLaren, "Teacher Education and the Politics of Engagement: The Case for Democratic Schooling," *Harvard Educational Review*, 56 (August 1986); also Martin Carnoy and Henry M. Levin, *Schooling and Work in the Democratic State* (Stanford, Calif.: Stanford University Press, 1985). See also the work of the Public Education Information Network.

23. Piven and Cloward, *The New Class War*, p. 135. New York: Pantheon, 1982.

What's Wrong with the Right

Christopher Lasch

In order to understand what's wrong with the right, we must first understand the basis of its appeal. The conservative revival cannot be dismissed as a "simple political reaction," as Michael Miles wrote some time ago, "whose point is to suppress a radical movement which by its nature poses a threat to the *status quo* distribution of power and wealth." Contemporary conservatism has a strong populist flavor, having identified itself with the aspirations of ordinary Americans and appropriated many of the symbols of popular democracy. It is because conservatives have managed to occupy so much of the ground formerly claimed by the left that they have made themselves an important force in American politics. They say with considerable justification that they speak for the great American middle class: hard-working men and women eager to better themselves, who reject government handouts and ask only a fair chance to prove themselves. Conservatism owes its growing strength to its unembarrassed defense of patriotism, ambition, competition, and common sense, long ridiculed by cosmopolitan sophisticates, and to its demand for a return to basics: to "principles that once proved sound and methods that once shepherded the nation through earlier troubled times," as Burton Pines puts it in his "traditionalist" manifesto, *Back to Basics*.

Far from defending the existing distribution of power, many conservatives, especially those who stress so-called social issues, deplore the excessive influence allegedly exercised by educated elites and see themselves as embattled defenders of values that run counter to the dominant values. They attribute most of the country's ills to the rise of a "highly educated, relatively affluent group which benefits more from America's riches than its less educated fellow countrymen" yet condemns the "values and institutions responsible for producing these riches." Members of this new class, according to Jeanne Kirkpatrick, "shape debate, determine agendas, define standards,

---

and propose and evaluate policies." It is they who allegedly advocate unlimited abortion, attack religion and the family, criticize capitalism, destroy general education in the name of unlimited freedom of choice, replace basic subjects in the lower schools with sex education and values clarification, and promote a new ethic of hedonism and self-exploration. From a conservative point of view, a return to basics demands a democratic movement against entrenched interests, in the course of which traditionalists will have to master techniques of "sustained activism" formerly monop-olized by the left.

Even if it could be shown that conservatives misunderstand American society, exaggerate the power of the so-called new class, underestimate the power of the business class, and ignore the undemocratic implications of their own positions, it would still be important to understand how they can see themselves as underdogs in the struggle for the American future. The left, which until recently has regarded itself as the voice of the "forgotten man," has lost the common touch. Failing to create a popular consensus in favor of its policies, the left has relied on the courts, the federal bureaucracy, and the media to achieve its goals of racial integration, affirmative action, and economic equality. Ever since World War II, it has used essentially undemocratic means to achieve democratic ends, and it has paid the price for this evasive strategy in the loss of public confidence and support. Increasingly isolated from popular opinion, liberals and social democrats attempt to explain away opposi-tion to economic equality as "working-class authoritarianism," status anxiety, *resenti-ment*, "white racism," male chauvinism, and proto-fascism. The left sees nothing but bigotry and superstition in the popular defense of the family or in popular attitudes regarding abortion, crime, busing, and the school curriculum. The left no longer stands for common sense, as it did in the days of Tom Paine. It has come to regard common sense—the traditional wisdom and folkways of the community—as an obstacle to progress and enlightenment. Because it equates tradition with prejudice, it finds itself increasingly unable to converse with ordinary people in their common language. Increasingly it speaks its own jargon, the therapeutic jargon of social science and the service professions that seems to serve mostly to deny what every-body knows.

Progressive rhetoric has the effect of concealing social crisis and moral break-down by presenting them "dialectically" as the birth pangs of a new order. The left dismisses talk about the collapse of family life and talks instead about the emergence of "alternative life-styles" and the growing new diversity of family types. Betty Friedan expresses the enlightened consensus when she says that Americans have to reject the "obsolete image of the family," to "acknowledge the diversity of the families people live in now," and to understand that a family, after all—in the words of the American Home Economics Association—consists simply of "two or more persons who share values and goals, and have commitments to one another over time." This anaemic, euphemistic definition of the family reminds us of the validity of George Orwell's contention that it is a sure sign of trouble when things can no longer be called by their right names and described in plain, forthright speech. The plain fact of the matter—and this is borne out by the very statistics cited to prove the expanding array of "lifestyles" from which people can now choose—is that most of these alternative arrangements, so-called, arise out of the ruins of marriages, not as an improvement of old-fashioned marriage. "Blended" or "reconstituted" families result from divorce, as do "single-parent families." As for the other "alternative" forms of the family, so highly touted by liberals—single "families," gay "marriages," and so on—it makes no sense to consider them as families and would still make no sense if they were important statistically, as they are not. They may be perfectly legitimate living arrangements, but they are arrangements chosen by people who prefer not to live in families at all, with all the unavoidable constraints that families place on individual freedom. The attempt to redefine the family as a purely voluntary arrangement (one among many "alternative" living arrangements) grows out of the modern delusion that people can keep all their options open all the time, avoiding any constraints or demands as long as they don't make any demands of their own or "impose their own values" on others. The left's redefinition of the family encourages the illusion that it is possible to avoid the "trap" of involuntary association and to enjoy its advantages at the same time.

The question of the family, which now divides our society so deeply that the opposing sides cannot even agree on a definition of the institution they are arguing about, illustrates and supports the contention that the left has lost touch with popular opinion, thereby making it possible for the right to present itself as the party of common sense. The presumption behind the older definition of the family is that ties of kinship and even of marriage and adoption are likely to be more demanding than ties of friendship and proximity. This is precisely why many people continue to value them. For most Americans, even for those who are disenchanted with their own marriages, family life continues to represent a stabilizing influence and a source of personal discipline in a world where personal disintegration remains always an imminent danger. A growing awareness of the depth of popular attachment to the family has led some liberals, rather belatedly, to concede that "'family' is not just a buzz word for reaction," as Betty Friedan puts it. But since these same liberals subscribe to the new flexible, pluralistic definition of the family, their defense of families carries no conviction. They ask people to believe, moreover, that there is no conflict between feminism and the family. Most women, according to Friedan, want both feminism and the family and reject categorization as pro-family or anti-family, pro-feminist or anti-feminist. Most women are pragmatists, in other words, who have allowed "extremists" on the left and right to manipulate the family issue for their own purposes and to create a "political polarization between feminism and the family." Her suspicion of ideology and her belief that it is possible to have things both ways—even in a crippled economy—place Friedan's argument squarely in the liberal tradition, the very tradition that needs to be rethought and outgrown.

But if the family issue illustrates characteristic weaknesses of American liberalism, which have been effectively exploited by the right, it also illustrates why the right-wing defense of "traditional values" proves equally unsatisfactory. Consider Rita Kramer's book, *In Defense of the Family*. Although this book contains much good sense about childrearing, its explanation of the plight of the family is completely inadequate. Kramer blames the plight of the family on interfering experts, on liberal intellectuals pushing their own permissive morality as scientific truth, on the mass media, and on the bureaucratic welfare state. She exonerates industrial capitalism, "which gets a bum rap on this issue," and she becomes absolutely lyrical whenever she touches on the subject of industrial technology. She speaks scornfully of those who want to "throw out all the machines and go back to pre-industrial ways of arranging our lives." She insists that we can resist the "numbing and all-pervasive media" and still enjoy the "undeniable blessings of technology." Her position seems to be that the nuclear family is so far superior to any other form of childrearing that its persistence can be taken for granted—if only the experts would go away and leave it alone.

This argument takes no account of the evidence that most people no longer live in nuclear families at all. It takes no account of the likelihood that women have entered the work force because they have no other choice, not because they are besotted by feminist ideology and believe there is no other way to fulfill themselves. The last three decades have seen the collapse of the family wage system, under which American enterprise, in effect, invested in the single-income family as the best way of domesticating the working class and forestalling labor militancy. This development is one more that signals the arrival of a two-tiered society. Today it is no longer an unwritten law of American capitalism that industry will attempt to maintain wages at a level that allows a single wage to support a family. By 1976, only 40% of all jobs paid enough to support a family. This trend reflects, among other things, a radical de-skilling of the work force, the substitution of machinery for skilled labor, and a vast increase in the number of low-paying unskilled jobs, many of which, of course, are now filled by women. These are among the "blessings of technology"—not considered by Rita Kramer. Meanwhile the consumer ethic has spread to men, as Barbara Ehrenreich points out in her study, *The Hearts of Men.* For thirty years, publications like *Playboy* have been urging men to define themselves not as breadwinners but as sybarites, lovers, connoisseurs of sex and style—in short as playboys. The idea that a man has an obligation to support a wife and family has come under attack not by feminist intellectuals or government bureaucrats but by Hugh Hefner and other promoters of a consumerist way of life.

It is the logic of consumerism that undermines the values of loyalty and permanence and promotes a different set of values that is destructive of family life—and much else besides. Kramer argues that the old bourgeois virtues should be "given a long, hard look before we discard them in the name either of greater self-fulfillment or greater altruism." But these values are being discarded precisely because they no longer serve the needs of a system of production based on advanced technology, unskilled labor, and mass consumption.

The therapeutic ethic, which has replaced the 19th-century utilitarian ethic, does not serve the "class interest" of professionals alone, as Daniel Moynihan and other critics of the "new class" have argued; it serves the needs of advanced capitalism as a whole. Moynihan points out that by emphasizing impulse rather than calculation as the determinant of human conduct, and by holding society responsible for the problems confronting individuals, a "government-oriented" professional class has attempted to create a demand for its own services. Professionals, he observes, have a vested interest in discontent, because discontented people turn to professional devices for relief. But the same principle underlies modern capitalism in general, which continually tries to create new demands and new discontents that can be assuaged only by the consumption of commodities. Professional self-aggrandizement grew up side by side with the advertising industry and the whole machinery of demand-creation. The same historical development that turned the citizen into a client transformed the worker from a producer into a consumer. Thus the medical and psychiatric assault on the family as a technologically backward sector of society went hand in hand with the advertising industry's drive to convince people that store-bought goods are superior to homemade goods.

The right insists that the "new class" controls the mass media and uses this control to wage a "class struggle" against business, as Irving Kristol puts it. Since the mass media are financed by advertising revenues, however, it is hard to take this contention seriously. It is advertising and the logic of consumerism, not anti-capitalist ideology, that governs the depiction of reality in the mass media. Conservatives complain that television mocks "free enterprise" and presents businessmen as "greedy, malevolent, and corrupt," like J.R. Ewing. To see anti-capitalist propaganda in a program like *Dallas*, however, requires a suspension not merely of critical judgment but of ordinary faculties of observation. Images of luxury, romance, and excitement dominate such programs, as they dominate the advertisements that surround and engulf them. *Dallas* is itself an advertisement for the good life, like almost everything on television—that is, for the good life conceived as endless novelty, change, and excitement, as the titillation of the senses by every available stimulant, as unlimited possibility. "Make it new" is the message not just of modern art but of modern consumerism, of which modern art, indeed—even when it claims to side with the social revolution—is largely a mirror image. We are all revolutionaries now, addicts of change. The modern capitalist economy rests on the techniques of mass production pioneered by Henry Ford but also, no less solidly, on the principle of planned obsolescence introduced by Alfred E. Sloane when he instituted the annual model change. Relentless "improvement" of the product and upgrading of consumer tastes are the heart of mass merchandising, and these imperatives are built into the mass media at every level. Even the reporting of news has to be understood not as propaganda for any particular ideology, liberal or conservative, but as propaganda for commodities—for the replacement of things by commodities, use values by exchange values, and events by images. The very concept of news celebrates newness. The value of news, like that of any other commodity, consists primarily of its novelty, only secondarily of its informational value. As Waldo Frank pointed out many years ago, the news appeals to the same jaded appetite that makes a child tire of a toy as soon as it becomes familiar and demand a new one in its place. As Frank also pointed out (in *The Re-discovery of America,* published in 1930), the social expectations that stimulate a child's appetite for new toys appeal to the desire for ownership and appropriation: the appeal of toys comes to lie not in their use but in their status as possessions. "A fresh plaything renews the child's opportunity to say: this is mine." A child who seldom gets a new toy, Frank says, "prizes it as part of himself." But if "toys become more frequent, value is gradually transferred from the toy to the toy's novelty . . . The Arrival of the toy, not the toy itself, becomes the event." The news, then, has to be seen as the "plaything of a child whose hunger for toys has been stimulated shrewdly." We can carry this analysis one step further by pointing out that the model of ownership, in a society organized around mass consumption, is addiction. The need for novelty and fresh stimulation become ever more intense, intervening interludes of boredom increasingly intolerable. It is with good reason that William Burroughs refers to the modern consumer as an "image junkie."

Conservatives sense a link between television and drugs, but they do not grasp the nature of this connection any more than they grasp the important fact about news: that it represents another form of advertising, not liberal propaganda. Propaganda in the ordinary sense of the term plays a less and less important part in a consumer society, where people greet all official pronouncements with suspicion. Mass media themselves contribute to the prevailing skepticism; one of their main effects is to undermine trust in authority, devalue heroism and charismatic leadership, and reduce everything to the same dimensions. The effect of the mass media is not to elicit belief but to maintain the apparatus of addiction. Drugs are merely the most obvious form of addiction in our society. It is true that drug addiction is one of the things that undermines "traditional values," but the need for drugs—that is, for commodities that alleviate boredom and satisfy the socially stimulated desire for novelty and excitement—grows out of the very nature of a consumerist economy.

The intellectual debility of contemporary conservatism is indicated by its silence on all these important matters. Neoclassical economics takes no account of the importance of advertising. It extols the "sovereign consumer" and insists that advertising cannot force consumers to buy anything they don't already want to buy. This argument misses the point. The point isn't that advertising manipulates the consumer or directly influences consumer choices. The point is that it makes the consumer an addict, unable to live without increasingly sizeable doses of externally provided stimulation and excitement. Conservatives argue that television erodes the capacity for sustained attention in children. They complain that young people now expect education, for example, to be easy and exciting. This argument is correct as far as it goes. Here again, however, conservatives incorrectly attribute these artificially excited expectations to liberal propaganda—in this case, to theories of permissive childrearing and "creative pedagogy." They ignore the deeper source of the expectations that undermine education, destroy the child's curiosity, and encourage passivity. Ideologies, however appealing and powerful, cannot shape the whole structure of perceptions and conduct unless they are embedded in daily experiences that appear to confirm them. In our society, daily experience teaches the individual to want and need a never-ending supply of new toys and drugs. A defense of "free enterprise" hardly supplies a corrective to these expectations.

Conservatives conceive the capitalist economy as it was in the time of Adam Smith, when property was still distributed fairly widely, businesses were individually owned, and commodities still retained something of the character of useful objects. Their notion of free enterprise takes no account of the forces that have transformed capitalism from within: the rise of the corporation, the bureaucratization of business, the increasing insignificance of private property, and the shift from a work ethic to a consumption ethic. Insofar as conservatives take any note of these developments at all, they attribute them solely to government interference and regulation. They deplore bureaucracy but see only its public face, missing the prevalence of bureaucracy in the private sector. They betray no acquaintance with the rich historical scholarship which shows that the expansion of the public sector came about, in part, in response to pressure from the corporations themselves.

Conservatives assume that deregulation and a return to the free market will solve everything, promoting a revival of the work ethic and a resurgence of "traditional values." Not only do they provide an inadequate explanation of the destruction of those values but they unwittingly side with the social forces that have contributed to their destruction, for example in their advocacy of unlimited growth. The poverty of contemporary conservatism reveals itself most fully in this championship of economic growth—the underlying premise of the consumer culture the by-products of which conservatives deplore. A vital conservatism would identify itself with the demand for limits not only on economic growth but on the conquest of space, the technological conquest of the environment, and the human ambition to acquire godlike powers over nature. A vital conservatism would see in the environmental movement the quintessential conservative cause, since environmentalism opposes reckless innovation and makes conservation the central order of business. Instead of taking environmentalism away from the left, however, conservatives condemn it as a counsel of doom. "Free enterprisers," says Pines, "insist that the economy can indeed expand and as it does so, all society's members can . . . increase their wealth." One of the cardinal tenets of liberalism, the limitlessness of economic growth, now undergirds the so-called conservatism that presents itself as a corrective and alternative to liberalism.

Not only do conservatives have no understanding of modern capitalism, they have a distorted understanding of the "traditional values" they claim to defend. The virtues they want to revive are the pioneer virtues: rugged individualism, boosterism, rapacity, a sentimental deference to women, and a willingness to resort to force. These values are "traditional" only in the sense that they are celebrated in the traditional myth of the Wild West and embodied in the Western hero, the prototypical American lurking in the background, often in the very foreground, of conservative ideology. In their implications and inner meaning, these individualist values are themselves profoundly anti-traditional. They are the values of the man on the make, in flight from his ancestors, from the family claim, from everything that ties him down and limits his freedom of movement. What is traditional about the rejection of tradition, continuity, and rootedness? A conservatism that sides with the forces of restless mobility is a false conservatism. So is the conservatism false that puts on a smiling face, denounces "doomsayers," and refuses to worry about the future. Conservatism appeals to a pervasive and legitimate desire in contemporary society for order, continuity, responsibility, and discipline; but it contains nothing with which to satisfy these desires. It pays lip service to "traditional values," but the policies with which it is associated promise more change, more innovation, more growth, more technology, more weapons, more addictive drugs. Instead of confronting the forces in modern life that make for disorder, it proposes merely to make Americans feel good about themselves. Ostensibly rigorous and realistic, contemporary conservatism is an ideology of denial. Its slogan is the slogan of Alfred E. Neumann: "What? Me worry?" Its symbol is a smile button: that empty round face devoid of features except for two tiny eyes, eyes too small to see anything clearly, and a big smile: the smile of someone who is determined to keep smiling through thick and thin.

Conservatives stress the importance of religion, but their religion is the familiar American blend of flag-waving and personal morality. It centers on the trivial issues of swearing, neatness, gambling, sportsmanship, sexual hygiene, and school prayers.

Adherents of the new religious right correctly reject the separation of politics and religion, but they bring no spiritual insights to politics. They campaign for political reforms designed to discourage homosexuality and pornography, say, but they have nothing to tell us about the connection between pornography and the larger consumerist structure of addiction-maintenance. Their idea of the proper relation between politics and religion is to invoke religious sanctions for specific political positions, as when they declaim that budget deficits, progressive taxation, and the presence of women in the armed forces are "anti-biblical." As in their economic views, conservatives advance views of religion and of the political implications of religion that derive from the tradition of liberal individualism. Liberalism, as a Lutheran critic of the religious right points out, "means straining scripture to mandate specific positions on social justice issues, . . . bending the word of God to fit your political ideas." The religiosity of the American right is self-righteous and idolatrous. It perceives no virtue in its opponents and magnifies its own. In the words of a pamphlet published by the United Methodist Church, "The 'New Religious Right' has . . . made the same mistake committed by the social gospeler earlier in the century. They exaggerate the sins of their opponent and negate any original sin of their own. They have become victims of what Reinhold Niebuhr called 'easy conscience,' or what the New Testament describes as the self-righteousness of the Pharisees." The most offensive and dangerous form of this self-righteousness is the attempt to invoke divine sanction for the national self-aggrandizement of the United States in its global struggle against "godless communism, as if American imperialism were any less godless than Soviet imperialism. In the words of Paul Simmons, a professor at Southern Baptist Theological Seminary, "Identifying the Judeo-Christian posture with American nationalism is to lose the transcendent and absolute nature of the Christian faith. For Christians and Jews, loyalty to God must transcend any earthly loyalties."

The proper reply to right-wing religiosity is not to insist that "politics and religion don't mix." This is the stock response of the left, which has been caught off guard by the right and remains baffled by the revival of religious concerns and by the insistence—by no means confined to the religious right—that a politics without religion is no proper politics at all. Bewildered by the sudden interest in "social issues," the left would like either to get them off the political agenda or, failing that, to redefine them as economic issues. When liberals finally grasped the strength of popular feeling about the family, they tried to appropriate the rhetoric and symbolism of "family values" for their own purposes, while arguing that the only way to strengthen the family is to make it economically viable. There is truth in this contention, of course, but the economic dimension of the family issue can't be separated so easily from the cultural dimension. Nor can bigger welfare budgets make the family economically viable. The economic basis of the family—the family wage—has been eroded by the same developments that have promoted consumerism as a way of life. The family is threatened not only by economic pressures but by an ideology that devalues motherhood, equates personal development with participation in the labor market, and defines freedom as individual freedom of choice—freedom from binding commitments.

The problem isn't how to keep religion out of politics but how to subject political life to spiritual criticism without losing sight of the tension between the political and the spiritual realm. Because politics rests on an irreducible measure of coercion, it can never become a perfect realm of perfect love and justice. But neither can it be dismissed as the work of the devil (as Jacques Ellul maintains in his recent writings). A complete separation of religion and politics, whether it arises out of religious indifference or out of its opposite, the religious passion of Ellul, condemns the political realm to "perpetual warfare," as Niebuhr argued in *Moral Man and Immoral Society*. "If social cohesion is impossible without coercion, and coercion is impossible without the creation of social injustice, and the destruction of injustice is impossible without the use of further coercion, are we not in an endless cycle of social conflict? . . . If power is needed to destroy power, . . . an uneasy balance of power would seem to become the highest goal to which society could aspire." The only way to break the cycle is to subject oneself and one's political friends to the same rigorous moral standards to which one subjects one's opponents and to invoke spiritual standards, moreover, not merely to condemn one's opponents but also to understand and forgive them. An uneasy balance of power—now enshrined as the highest form of politics in the theory of interest-group liberalism—can be ended only by a politics of "angerless wisdom," a politics of nonviolent coercion that seeks to resolve the endless argument about means and ends by making nonviolent means, openness, and truth-telling political ends in their own right.

Needless to say, this is not a task either for the new right, for interest-group liberals, or for those on the left who still cling to the messianic hope of social revolution. Faced with the unexpected growth of the new right, the left has asked itself how it can recover its former strength and momentum. Some call for a vigorous counterattack, a reassertion of the left-wing gospel in all its purity and messianic fervor. Others wait passively for another turn of the political cycle, another age of reform. More thoughtful people on the left have begun, however reluctantly, to acknowledge the legitimacy of some of the concerns that underlie the growth of contemporary conservatism. But even this last response is inadequate if it issues simply in a call for the left to appropriate conservative issues and then to give them a liberal twist. The hope of a new politics does not lie in formulating a left-wing reply to the right. It lies in rejecting conventional political categories and redefining the terms of political debate. The idea of a "left" has outlived its historical time and needs to be decently buried, along with the false conservatism that merely clothes an older liberal tradition in conservative rhetoric. The old labels have no meaning anymore. They can only confuse debate instead of clarifying it. They are products of an earlier era, the age of steam and steel, and are wholly inadequate to the age of electronics, totalitarianism, and mass culture. Let us say good-bye to these old friends, fondly but firmly, and look elsewhere for guidance and moral support.

Preface to the Political Economy of a Postliberal Democracy

Samuel Bowles and Herbert Gintis

Although the neo-Hobbesian and global liberal models may provide the outlines for a new—perhaps hybrid—accommodation between capitalism and liberal democracy, each in its own way consolidating capitalism while eroding democracy, postliberal democracy departs so significantly from both capitalism and liberal democracy that one can hardly consider it a new form of accommodation. It is more accurately described as a process leading to a new social order.

The analysis in the preceding chapters has committed us to a particular vision of how the economic structure of a postliberal democratic social order might look, and to a conception of the historical process by which such a society might come about and survive.

Our vision of a postliberal democracy is based on the following propositions, each derived from the reasoning of earlier chapters. First, the capitalist economy—and indeed virtually any feasible alternative—is a public arena whose structure regulates the distributional, appropriative, political, cultural, and other projects of various social actors. No coherent conception of democracy can escape the conclusion that the powers thus conferred on individual and collective actors in the economy ought to be subject to democratic accountability.

Second, lack of secure access to one's livelihood is a form of dependency, one that confers power on those who control the means of life. Economic dependency—whether in the form of the financial dependence of women on men, unemployment induced deliberately by macroeconomic policy to discipline the labor force, or the instrumental use of the threat of capital flight—arbitrarily limits individual choices and erodes democratic accountability even where it is formally secured. Economic dependency is thus antithetical to both liberty and popular sovereignty.

Third, the economy, the state, and the family produce people. The lifelong development of the capacities, preferences, sentiments, and identities of individuals results from an interaction between genetic potential and structured social practices. The impact of social structure on human development ranges from the relationship between the sexual division of labor and what Nancy Chodorow calls "feminine personality,"[41] to the connection between the hierarchical structure of work and the value that parents place on obedience in their children, and to the effect of the decline of residential neighborhoods on civic orientations. Because the growth and effectiveness of democratic institutions depend on the strength of democratic capacities, a commitment to democracy entails the advocacy of institutions that promote rather than impede the development of a democratic culture. Further, because learning, or more broadly, human development, is a central and lifelong social activity of people, there is no coherent reason for exempting the structures that regulate learning—whether they be schools, families, neighborhoods, or workplaces—from the criteria of democratic accountability and liberty.

Fourth, the power of unaccountable authority and the limitations of personal choice in liberal democratic capitalist societies derive in part from the manner in which our personal identities are intimately bound up with unaccountable collectivities, whether they be the nation-state, the patriarchal family, or the modern corporation. The near-monopoly exercised by these institutions on our sense of social identity is rivaled only by equally antidemocratic invidious distinctions of class, race, and gender. But the modern ideal of universalist values, by leaving the autonomous individual face-to-face with the abstract state, is more likely to exacerbate than to solve the problem. Both liberty and popular sovereignty would be served by the vitality of democratic communities standing between the individual and the state, and by the related possibility of a proliferation of noninvidious distinctions among people.

One cannot derive specific institutional prescriptions from these four quite general propositions. But they do point unmistakably toward the democratization of the economy, the attenuation of economic inequality, the democratization of the learning process, and the promotion of what Hannah Arendt calls "new public spaces for freedom."[42] On balance, these objectives are complementary, yet none is without its dilemmas and contradictions.

The main imperatives of the democratization of the economy are clear—workplace democracy, democratic economic planning, and community access to capital—but as we shall see, the relationships among them are complex at best and possibly contradictory. The logic of the democratic workplace is that democratic decision making in production units will replace unaccountable hierarchy with democratic participation and commitment. One might hope thereby to contribute to a more effective system of production through the reduction in enforcement costs, as well as to support a participatory learning environment and an autonomous democratic community.[43]

By democratic economic planning we mean the socially accountable determination of the broad outlines of the pattern of economic structure and its evolution. Accountability entails the collective deliberation and control over investment decisions, for as we have seen, it is the concentrated control over the accumulation process that places the present and future technological, spatial, environmental, sectoral, and other aspects of economic evolution beyond the realm of popular sovereignty.

Although the central position of democratic control of investment is clear, the instruments by which the overall accountability of the economy might be achieved most effectively cannot be prejudged in advance or in general. The debate on the merits of centralized planning and direct allocation of resources relative to the use of markets is a practical matter to be decided by study of the associated costs in particular cases. Our analysis does not favor one over the other, but rather poses new criteria for the evaluation of each: the evaluation of apparently specialized economic institutions such as markets or systems of economic planning must balance the claims of democratic and other valued forms of human development against the more traditional claims based on the alleviation of scarcity, the enhancement of liberty, and the like. Similarly, the question of public or private ownership of the means of production may be variously answered under differing particular conditions, according to the norms of liberty and democratic accountability.

A generation ago R. H. Tawney observed that a society in which some have more than they need while many do not have enough to get by may possibly claim many virtues, but liberty cannot be among them.[44] Nor, we might add, will popular sovereignty flourish under these circumstances. Our concern with democracy has lead us, like Tawney, to a political critique of economic inequality. We propose that democrats ought to regard the access to a socially acceptable standard of living as a right; depriving people of their livelihood would thus be as contrary to social norms and legality as depriving people of their liberty or violating their physical person. The reasoning of the preceding pages provides ample support for such a notion. We will touch on a perhaps overlooked argument in favor of this egalitarian commitment—what Michael Walzer calls "provision for the sake of community"—and then turn to a problem raised by this argument.

A society that regularly, and as a necessary part of its ordinary functioning, allows a significant fraction of its members to live in conditions of financial insecurity and material distress expresses a degree of indifference or callousness toward its members which both exhibits and fortifies social division and invidious comparison rather than community. If, as Marshall Sahlins says, gifts make friends, it may also be said that ignoring the plight of one's fellow people makes strangers if not enemies. Michael Walzer observes,

> The idea of distributive justice presupposes a bounded world within which distributions take place: a group of people committed to dividing, exchanging, and sharing social goods, first of all among themselves. That world . . . is the political community.

Walzer continues,

> Membership is important because of those things the members of a political community owe to one another and to no one else, or to no one in the same degree. And the first thing they owe is the communal provision of security and welfare. This claim might be reversed: communal provision is important because it teaches us the

value of membership. If we did not provide for one another, if we recognized no distinctions between members and strangers, we would have no reason to form and maintain political communities.[45]

A mutual commitment to securing each person's conditions of life builds the respect and communal identification upon which a democratic culture must rest, but it also raises economic problems. We have emphasized the problem of inducing people to work and stressed the manner in which capitalist societies rely heavily on economic insecurity as a major if often implicit disciplinary and motivational device. Although capitalist society and the hierarchical workplace in particular probably exacerbate the underlying problem, we doubt that any society will dispense with the need to motivate work. If the postliberal social order is to guarantee economic security it must simultaneously alter the meaning of work so that it no longer appears to so many as an alien imposition.

Our commitment to the right to a livelihood does not mean, of course, that good work cannot be rewarded, only that the stakes should not be so high and that the penalties ought not to include deprivation of an acceptable living standard. More important, democratic work groups in an environment of economic security will be pressed to develop means of eliciting good work from their members; participation in decision making and the equitable sharing of the net revenues of the production unit would undoubtedly be augmented by a wide range of recognitions and sanctions, drawing more heavily on work-team members' capacity for pride and shame than on their economic insecurity.

The attenuation of economic inequality and the democratization of the economy would represent a major step toward a more democratic society. They would also contribute significantly to the democratization of the process of human development, or more concretely, to the systematic application of the norms of both democratic accountability and liberty to the manifold institutions of learning and personal transformation. Economic necessity is today one of the most binding constraints on educational choices over the course of one's life; the guarantee of an acceptable livelihood would open up a more ample array of educational choices by eliminating the threat of personal economic calamity as a possible consequence of a wrong choice. More obviously, the democratization of the economy would itself constitute a major step toward accountability and liberty in a major learning environment.

As with the other economic structural characteristics of a postliberal democratic society, the democratization of learning is not without its problems. Any philosophically self-conscious viewpoint must grapple with the difficult issues of choice, authority, and social ends that are necessarily bound up in the analysis of learning. But the apparent intractability of these issues within the liberal framework may stem more from the characteristics of liberal thought than from the peculiar difficulties to which the educational encounter gives rise. Amy Gutmann identifies the key contradiction of both major strands of modern liberalism as educational philosophies in this way:

> Utilitarians and . . . rights theorists . . . agree on one point about the education of children: at least in principle they both are committed to providing an education that is neutral among substantive conceptions of the good life.[46]

We do not share this liberal neutrality concerning the good life. Nor, we suspect, do many liberals in their daily activities as parents, teachers, friends, and citizens.

Our commitment to democracy is both to a means and to an end, although in both cases the commitment is an admittedly minimal and insufficient basis for a fully articulated philosophy of education. Our commitment implies that people ought to learn what they choose to learn when they make choices in a general environment of liberty and popular sovereignty. We do not know what people would choose to become under these conditions: our moral and political commitment is to try and see. Many, indeed most, educational choices are not now made under these conditions. But to the extent that some are made under conditions approximating liberty and accountability we see the possibility of a democratic learning dynamic, one that would inhabit the imperfect realms of democracy and choice in our society and progressively transform ever-wider circles of social life toward democratic ends.

The economic institutions and commitments required to make good the promise of postliberal democracy—the displacement of profit-driven capital markets by the democratically accountable planning of investment and resource allocation, the organization of workplaces and other communities by means of representative and participatory institutions, and the attenuation of economic inequality—are all familiar objectives of democratic socialist movements over the past century. We have chosen to term our visionary-historical alternative postliberal democracy rather than socialism simply because we regard those time-honored commitments of socialists not as ends in themselves but as means toward securing an expanded conception of liberty and popular sovereignty. Our treatment of socialism—and the elimination of class exploitation—as means toward the achievement of democracy in no way diminishes our commitment to these objectives, though it does express our rejection of the not uncommon tendency of socialists to relegate democracy to the status of a means, however indispensable, for the achievement of classlessness.

Our insistence on the priority of the terms "democracy" and its constituent elements—"popular sovereignty" and "liberty"—over more traditional economic phrases of the socialist lexicon, such as the "abolition of exploitation" and "public ownership of the means of production," thus expresses our conception of the political nature of economic concerns, not their unimportance. For example, we have addressed the central issue of economic inequality not primarily from the standpoint of distributive justice but rather as a form of dependency that limits personal freedom. And we have advocated social control over investment not primarily to achieve a more efficient allocation of resources but as a necessary means toward securing popular sovereignty in the face of the threat of capital strike.

Our choice of terms reflects a recognition of both the hegemony of liberal democratic discourse as the virtually exclusive medium of political communication in the advanced capitalist nations and the profoundly contradictory, malleable, and potentially radical nature of this discourse. No less important, the privileged status of democracy in our discourse reflects our central moral commitment and political project: to the creation of a new social order in which people—individuals and communities—are more nearly the authors of their own individual and collective histories.

DEMOCRACY, AGENCY, AND HISTORY

Among the consolations of modern life is the widespread faith that history is on the side of freedom. Whether rooted in the indomitable human spirit, the growth of Reason, or the civilizing character of science and technology, the idea that time is on the side of liberty and equality is deeply ingrained in modern culture. It appears in the liberal notion of modernization as a passage toward affluence, tolerance, and the pluralist commonwealth, and in the Marxian vision of communism as the first society in which the freedom of each is the prerequisite for the freedom of all. It appears as well in our calm belief in the inevitability of Hitler's failure, in the irreparable economic backwardness of authoritarian state socialism, and in the impossibility that relocation camps, napalm, wholesale torture, murder, and the rest of the U.S. coercive state repertoire could be turned against capitalism's "internal enemies."

It will not come as a surprise to the reader that no such faith comforts us. The indomitable human spirit can be broken. Reason is a cruel master. And modern science ever refines the tools for dominating not just nature, but people as well. Not the inevitability of freedom, but rather its existence against great odds, is the true monument to the human spirit.

History, Leon Trotsky wrote, is the natural selection of accidents. Democracy may be, quite simply, an accident of history—an exotic social variety heady with possibilities but with questionable survival capacity. The question the democrat must face is simply this: what conditions contribute to democracy's survival power, and how may our understanding of these conditions allow us to extend and deepen democratic culture and institutions?

Our answer is that the historical viability of a commitment to democracy flows from the dominance of the discourse of rights in the context of a set of rules of the game promoting representative government and individual liberty. At first glance this answer appears to condone a defensive strategy of opposing social innovation in the interest of preserving liberal democratic institutions. However, we have also seen that these very rules of the game involve the joint expansionary logic of personal and property rights, and hence a continuing clash of rights. The further expansion of capitalist property relations seems likely to come at the expense of democratic institutions. And because it is currently capitalism that puts people to work and places food on their tables, it is democracy that will be forced to cede in any confrontation in which democrats shrink from offering alternative economic policies. But the lesson of capital strike in the global economy is that minimum and timid democratic initiatives will probably be either ineffective or quickly defeated by capital's freedom to move. A defensive strategy for the protection of democracy is consequently untenable in the long run. Democracy can only survive by expanding to cover areas of social life now dominated by prerogatives of capitalist property.

But why should economic democracy provide a viable alternative to traditional capitalist institutions? The answer was long ago given by Tocqueville who noted,

> Democracy . . . spreads through the body social a restless activity, superabundant force, and energy never found elsewhere, which, however little favored by circumstance, can do wonders. Those are its true advantages.[47]

There is a huge logical gap in the economic theory that defends the capitalist economy. This theory can justify the importance of markets in reducing information costs associated with the allocation of resources; it can point to the value of competition in promoting innovation and cost reduction. But it cannot solve or even address the problem of agency.

For the capitalist economy to work well workers must somehow be induced to work hard enough at low enough wages so that a surplus flows into the hands of their employers. And their employers, in turn, must somehow be persuaded to invest this surplus in a manner that maintains or improves the functioning of the economy. Yet the defenders of capitalism cannot logically explain why workers would be committed to the success of the enterprise for whom they work, or why those who control the surplus would invest in ways productive of higher living standards in the country in question. These issues loom especially large in an increasingly global economy, and in one marked by the emergence of needs that will be met by goods and services whose measurement and supervision are increasingly costly.

It is here that the economic benefits of democracy come in: economic democracy, by providing an alternative to unaccountable hierarchical authority in investment and production, can promote loyalty, commitment, and accountability on the part of workers and those who control investable resources.

Democracy's first successes were precisely of this nature. People think the lamb is cute, but they are really impressed by the lion. Liberty, equality, and fraternity meant little to the despots of Europe until the rallying cries of the French Revolution were turned into the impressive power of Napoleon's army of untrained but loyal peasants. The American democratic temper that so impressed Tocqueville fired the energies of European democrats in part because it vanquished an imperial enemy and fashioned a viable economic system from the doctrines of free men, free trade, and free soil. The perhaps temporary extension of the welfare state in recent decades was consolidated not so much by a higher level of egalitarian social consciousness, but rather by the evident capacity of the Keynesian accommodation to deliver the goods.

Capitalism could, of course, turn the economic advantages of workplace democracy to its own ends, with owners exercising the power of the purse but no longer directing production. Indeed a hybrid accommodation of globally mobile finance capital and democratically organized workplaces might appear to be a possible outcome of the present period of institutional innovation. Were the power of the purse to remain secure, of course, these arrangements would not achieve the accountability of the power of capital. On the contrary, they would contribute to its invisibility by eliminating its most obvious face-to-face aspect: the relation of boss to worker.

But why should not the workers who have won control of their workplaces also want to make good the promise of democracy writ large? Would the capacities and sentiments fostered in the democratic workplace not seek to range more widely and more effectively over the terrains of finance and investment? Our reading of the history of the expansion of personal rights suggests that a global finance capital/ workplace democracy accommodation might be quite unstable.

The position of capital would be considerably weakened by its increasingly obvious rentier status. The lesson of the demise of feudal power is instructive in this respect. In the late medieval period, feudal lords began their long march toward extinction by withdrawing from production and taking their sustenance from rents and taxes. Marc Bloch described this situation by saying that

> the lord had abdicated from his position as head of a large agrarian and semi-industrial undertaking. . . . Politically speaking, the lord was still a leader to his men, he remained their military commander, their judge, their born protector. But his economic leadership had gone—and all the rest could easily follow. He had become a "stockholder" in the soil.[48]

Like the feudal lords before them, capitalists might be superannuated. They would then be readily transformed in political discourse from their representation today as a bearer of a particular conception of the common interest to just another claimant on income, and not a particularly deserving or productive one at that. Writing in the 1940s, Joseph Schumpeter did not share our confidence that a democracy would revolutionize the capitalist economy. But he understood well the political implications of the reduction of the capitalist class to mere income claimants:

> The capitalist process, by substituting a mere parcel of shares for the walls of . . . a factory, takes the life out of the idea of property. . . . It loosens the grip that was once so strong . . . the holder of the title loses the will to fight, economically, physically, politically, for "his" factory and his control over it, to die if necessary on its steps. And this evaporation of what we may term the material substance of property . . . affects not only the attitude of holders but also that of the workmen and of the public in general. . . . Eventually there will be *nobody* left who really cares to stand for it—nobody within and nobody without the precincts of the big concerns.[49]

Whether the optimistic scenario of a no doubt tumultuous encroachment by economic democracy on the economic prerogatives and ideological hegemony of capital will come to pass will depend in large measure on the ability of democrats first to understand, and then to effectively pursue, the historic project of the expansion and deepening of democratic personal rights in the face of the tenacious and no less expansionary claims of property.

NOTES

41. Nancy Chodorow, *The Reproduction of Mothering* (Berkeley: University California Press, 1978).
42. Quoted in Michael Sandel, *Liberalism and the Limits of Justice* (New York: Cambridge University Press, 1982), 240.
43. Although we believe these expectations—and those discussed later—are supported by much available evidence and are well within the realm of possibility, it seems pointless to review the relevant empirical studies, for the applicability of current experience to social experimentation under quite different social circumstances is somewhat problematic.
44. R. H. Tawney, *Equality* (London: Allen, 1931).
45. Michael Walzer, *Spheres of Justice: A Defense of Pluralism and Equality* (New York: Basic

Books, 1983), 31, 64–65; Sahlins, *Stone Age Economics* (Chicago: Aldine Press, 1972), 186.

46. Amy Gutmann, "What's the Use of Going to School?" in Amartya Sen and Bernard Williams, eds., *Utilitarianism and Beyond* (New York: Cambridge University Press, 1982), 261.

47. Alexis de Tocqueville, *Democracy in America* (Garden City, N.Y.: Doubleday, 1969), 244.

48. Marc Bloch, *French Rural History* (Berkeley: University of California Press, 1973), 100–101.

49. Joseph Schumpeter, *Capitalism, Socialism, and Democracy* (New York: Harper & Row, 1942), 142.

SECTION **II**

Social Justice:
Promises and Despair

Despite the relative quiescence of the 1980s, it is hard to doubt the continuing importance of egalitarian issues in the lives and consciousness of Americans. In a recent major survey of the American electorate, social justice loomed larger than any other single value.[1] Although over the past 200 years it is possible to pick out moments of visible and intense struggle, we must also be aware of the continuing, though less obvious, ways in which people press for a greater measure of justice in their lives. The latter occurs in the daily grind of work, school, and home life as people struggle to resist the processes of dehumanization and subordination. In a variety of ways people continually fight for more dignity, more control over their lives, and more resources with which to live. They do so as workers; consumers; students; members of minority groups; women; oppressed sexual groups; people marginalized by virtue of age, disability, or illness; and so on. As the slogan of the women's movement—"the personal is political"—has taken hold, the struggle for more equality has involved increasing dimensions of the self, moving into areas of life hitherto unimaginable.

Although the struggles ebb and flow, that there is historical continuity should come as no surprise. Our egalitarian faith is, after all, an inescapable component of the republican discourse of the nation, deeply rooted in both the naturalistic social philosophies and the Judeo-Christian values that structure our culture's official language. What ought to be considered more surprising is, perhaps, not the impulse toward greater equality but the way in which this impulse is tempered, or accommodated, to the existing hierarchical social relations. This phenomenon represents an important dimension of the readings in this section. In contrast to conventional educational discourse, which emphasizes the way in which schooling facilitates upward social mobility, our concern is with the way in which egalitarian discourse is reconciled with the massive inequities of our social, economic, and political lives. How does it come to be accepted, for example, that (according to 1988 figures) the poorest 40.0 percent of U.S. families received just 15.7 percent of the national income, whereas the top 40.0 percent received 67.3 percent of this income— the highest percentage ever recorded.[2] Along with the continual, indeed intensifying, injustices produced by the divisions of class, race, and gender, as well as other social distinctions, we need to recognize the coexistence of powerful movements of the disadvantaged who demand redress for the unmet promises of society. As all of the authors in this section make clear, these unmet promises are more than moral or philosophical abstractions. The United States is moving with alarming speed into an era marked by grotesque disparities of income and conditions of life. It becomes harder and harder to escape an awareness of the millions of our fellow citizens (including an unprecedented number of children) who are without adequate shelter, food, or other basic provisions of life such as medical insurance. And the fact that this condition continues despite what was claimed to be the longest peace-time economic recovery indicates that the massive poverty is no aberration but a deeply structured, enduring aspect of our social reality.

Beyond presenting the harsh reality of social injustice in contemporary America we wish to pursue two related questions. The first concerns how this situation has arisen: What are the social, economic, and political dynamics of inequality in this country? We will look at the conditions that produce disproportionate degrees of poverty among women and children as well as among people of color. We are concerned with the nature of an ideology that manages to reconcile quite spectacular levels of inequality with the value of a (formally) democratic culture. (In these questions there is, of course, a clear overlap with the issues and questions raised in the previous section.) The role of public schooling has been, and continues to be, central. It is the key institution in the practical process of social differentiation and selection and the heart of the ideological process though which inequality is made to seem legitimate.

Ann Bastian and her coauthors take up these issues. The new directions in American education, they assert, are aimed toward discrediting the egalitarian impulses of the last two decades. These impulses, it is claimed, have undermined the traditional model of school success, which in turn has contributed to the decline in the country's economic productivity and competitiveness. This argument is flawed, say the authors. It constructs a mythological golden past of American education that vastly exaggerates the contribution of schooling to the process of economic, cultural, and political change. It also inflates the effects of educational reform during the 1960s. Although these reforms represented a powerful democratizing force on public schools, the authors argue, they merely widened access to a system whose fundamental competitive and hierarchical qualities remained unchanged. In actuality the driving force behind the increasingly competitive, test-driven, and quantifiable curriculum in schools is the restructuring of labor in the American economy. This restructuring will bring a vast increase in the proportion of low-skilled, low-paid jobs that are dead ends and unreliable. That these declining economic opportunities are a result of declining school performance, which can be put right with the help of high standards and more discipline, is fake logic. What, in fact, labor market trends tell us, say the authors, is that schools in coming years will become sites of more intense contradictions. Access to rewarding jobs will require greater educational attainment and proficiency, but there will be fewer chances of success even with the most extensive schooling.

This debate reflects persistent and deeply rooted assumptions about human abilities and the role of schools in providing equal opportunity—which is made clear by Jeannie Oakes. Whether the political pendulum swings to the left or right, schools remain organized around the differentiation of educational experiences according to the belief that children possess quite fixed individual abilities. Schools, it has long been assumed, can decide fairly and without bias which students have the capacity for achieving excellence. As a result, and despite the inequalities of American society, equal educational opportunity appears as both a possible and valid means through which to stage the competition for adult positions in the social and economic hierarchy. Despite the many data that show clearly how educational success favors the already privileged, a complex ideology that merges democratic sentiments with meritocratic notions makes schooling appear to be politically and ethically legitimate. For the most part educational reforms that have sought more equality of educational opportunity have remained at the level of changing or "remediating" individual students rather than challenging the assumptions about ability or success built into the process of schooling. Present school reforms focused on the drive for "excellence," says Oakes, serve only to intensify such assumptions. The practices of "excellent" schooling, she says, clearly reflect the "Anglo-conformist" values that historically have discriminated against children who are poor or members of ethnic minorities. The failure of disadvantaged children continues to be seen as a matter of their own deficiencies—social, economic, educational, and linguistic—not of the schools' inadequate response to them. Children, says Oakes, continue to be seen as entrants into an equal, fair, and neutral competitive process.

The absurdity of any such assumptions about the fairness of the competitive process is powerfully underlined by Harold Hodgkinson. He provides a plethora of devastating statistics on the plight of children in the United States in the 1990s. He notes that about one-third of all preschool children in this country are destined for school failure because of poverty, neglect, sickness, handicapping conditions, and lack of adult protection or nurturance. Since 1987 one-fourth of all preschool children in the United States have been living in poverty. On any given night, between 50,000 and 200,000 children have no home. Under such conditions, notions of educational reform (like those enunciated by President Bush and the nation's governors) can have no real credibility. More than one-third of American children have the "deck stacked against them long before they enter school." Any meaningful concern with the fate of education in the United States would have to appreciate that schools cannot do their job in a social vacuum: "Until job opportunities, health care, housing, transportation, and personal security improve in the inner cities, it is impossible to ask schools to get better." Hodgkinson makes clear that educational improvement is inseparable from larger questions of social justice and equity. Economic and social disadvantage on a massive and increasing scale means that those concerned about the education of children will have to demand changes not simply in schools but also across a wide range of social policies. Educational reform and fundamental social, economic, and political change are two sides of the same coin. Reading Hodgkinson, we can no longer doubt that responding to the scope of poverty requires not more emphasis on individual achievement but a commitment to the collective well-being of the society. Nothing short of a fundamental rethinking of our moral, economic, and social commitments is likely to suffice in making such a change.

This is exactly the point of Matthew Fox's argument. Fox contrasts the root metaphors that govern patriarchal, capitalist societies with those necessary to a society in which the well-being of all is ensured. For Fox this goal requires nothing less than a fundamental transformation of how we conceive and organize the relations between human beings. Social justice requires that we give up what he calls the "ladder," or hierarchical economics, which inevitably leads to dualistic, compassionless relations between people. What must be abandoned, he argues, is the "sacralizing of upness"—the obsession with producing "power over/power under" relationships, which permeate all institutions from the church and school to the factory in Western societies. Fox suggests a radically different vision of society, which might make possible the age-old dream of just and compassionate living. His "economics of interdependence" draws on feminist, Christian, and ecological images. It is foreshadowed by those who refuse to be victims, by those who reject the "ladder and its implications that some of us need to be down and victimized." The author provides a powerful countervision and rejoinder to those for whom the present competitive and individualistic society seems fixed and unalterable. And of course, it implies a radically different vision of education—one that teaches just and loving relations between human beings. Such a vision suggests that we need to begin to think differently about how education is connected to human equality. We need to move away from our obsessive focus on success and achievement in schools and from the idea that social justice means establishing conditions through which individual students might fairly "get ahead" of their peers.

Like those found in the previous section, the readings here reflect a critical social account of the purpose of schooling in the United States. The authors insist that the real nature and purposes of education can be grasped only if we view schools as cultural and political sites that give legitimacy to the way social relations are organized in this society. From this perspective, all our talk about education's connection to the realization of human potential is a denial or avoidance of the real work of schools, which is inseparable from the economic, cultural, and social differentiation of students.

NOTES

1. N. Ornstein et al., *The People, The Press, and Politics* (Reading, MA: Addison-Wesley, 1988).
2. Report of the Joint Economic Committee, U.S. Congress, 1988.

Three Myths of School Performance

Ann Bastian, Norm Fruchter, Marilyn Gittell, Colin Greer, and Kenneth Haskins

The democratic purpose of American public education may be far from realized, but it is at least an ideal that most Americans value. Nearly every strategy for school change therefore claims to have universal application and benefit. In the current wave of reform, that claim to universality rests on the promise of reversing economic decline by restoring educational productivity. The idea has great appeal for a wide range of people, both middle and working class, who see a dramatic shrinkage of jobs, incomes, and chances for upward mobility and who feel increasingly powerless to control their occupational destiny or improve the quality of life for their children.

However, attaching this insecurity to a program for more punitive, restrictive, competitive schooling requires several leaps of logic. Education's neo-conservatives have constructed their argument by asserting that economic performance is closely linked to school performance. They have asserted that there is a pervasive drop in academic achievement of recent origins, which impairs our national standing in a technologically driven world economy. They have presumed that a basic cause of this decline is permissive schooling and a dilution of quality, engendered by the misguided egalitarian reforms of the '60s and '70s. And they have characterized these reforms as undermining an education system that previously provided Americans with a rigorous foundation of skills and knowledge and, in doing so, advanced the nation to the forefront of economic productivity and well-being. In their view, the United States was on top because our schools worked well; now we are falling behind because we devalued education with corrosive or utopian social demands.

It is a tidy package, powerful in its simplicity, straightforward in its formula for change, and echoed in nearly every arena of national politics. Social conditions amplify the message: rightfully or not, competition is the order of the day and no one can afford to stand aside, or set their children apart, from the scramble for dwindling

---

opportunities. So the assumptions of the new elitists find multiple points of resonance and their construction of school history becomes the standard text.

Challenging the elitist framework requires an alternative explanation of how the crisis in education emerged: What model for success does traditional schooling really offer? What was the impact of equity reforms in the '60s and '70s? What connection does schooling have to our economic status? Defining a democratic mission for schooling requires that we set our history straight, exposing what have become the great myths of school performance.

1. THE MYTH OF A GOLDEN AGE

Today's school problems are continuously presented by way of contrast with the notion that our schools used to work well. We hear about the *loss* of authority, the *rise* of mediocrity, the *watering down* of curricula, the *lowering* of standards, the *decline* of achievement. The exact location of past school success seems to vary according to the particular remedy proposed. But whatever the specific reference, a common image emerges.

The image of the "golden age" suggests that there were once public schools that provided the masses of American children with solid basic skills and sound work and study habits. The image suggests that these schools were the basis for a disciplined, motivated, and highly productive workforce, which made possible an unprecedented degree of economic development and mobility. Universal public education is especially credited with the advance of immigrant groups. Further, it is suggested that our schools have been a key to social integration, effectively drawing diverse peoples into the mainstream of American civic culture, forming the bedrock of democratic pluralism. Had such a school system ever existed, with such astonishing social returns, the condition of schooling today would indeed represent a catastrophic loss—and might well have captured national attention sooner than 1983.

But today's schools do not function in ways radically different from their predecessors, although important changes have occurred in school populations, in the duration of schooling, and in the social and economic context within which schools operate. It is, in fact, the failure of schools to adapt to these external changes by redefining their mission that is part of the problem. While we cannot recount the complex evolution of schooling here, we can present a very different reading of the character of the "golden age" and the legacy it has left.

The traditional school system prior to World War II was a rigidly two-tiered system, with separate and unequal schools. This system had two distinct missions: to provide a rising professional middle class with academic proficiency and preparation for mobility, and to provide the poor and working class with custody and preparation for the low-wage industrial labor market. The public schools of the privileged were decent and well-endowed institutions—they were the models that today's myths universalize to prove past school success. The schools of the masses, however, were little more than holding pens, promoting high failure rates among the children of the lower strata. Many children remained outside the system, shut out by child labor, by the lack of classroom space, by language and cultural barriers, by schools that were distant or seasonal.

Mass education in its first half-century does not make today's failures look exceptional. Drop-out figures cited in urban school surveys conducted in the early 1900s are nearly identical to the figures cited in the 1979-83 Chicago survey, although the incidence of failure was more likely to be at the elementary school level; some estimates project that in the 1930s two-thirds of American students did not finish high school.[1] Descriptions of traditional mass schooling present the familiar features of educational inequality: intense overcrowding, overworked and underpaid staff, grim and decaying facilities, insufficient and arcane textbooks, ethnic and racial hostility, vast disparities in funding. The socialization that occurred was not a lesson in democratic values, but a convincing exposure to the hard realities of competition and social stigma. Repeatedly, the concept of meritocracy served to bridge the gap between elitist practice and democratic promise, by justifying the application of double standards, by presuming that the disadvantaged were deficient rather than underserved.

There were, of course, intense battles waged by the disenfranchised to gain more widespread inclusion in the promise of education. There was also concern among civic reformers that the abysmal conditions in mass schooling would contribute to social division and unrest. But in opening up the schools between 1900 and 1940, the basic two-tier structure was never challenged. Schools remained instruments of socioeconomic competition, even as the number of competitors expanded. The most significant change of the period was the introduction of free public high schools, a reform largely stimulated by the middle class need to acquire secondary education and to defray its growing costs through the public treasury. High schools, and certainly academic high school programs, were not widely accessible to working class and poor students. Elementary school preparation was poor and high school entrance was selective. In effect, the high school diploma upped the educational ante, with the result that elementary education became more truly universal and, at the same time, more devalued.

Expanding the Hirerarchy

This pattern of school reform has held for eighty years: the pressure for inclusion has been accommodated by gradually increasing access to established levels of schooling, while elite status has been preserved by adding new layers that only the middle classes could widely attain. In the process, the lower levels are universalized and devalued, both in terms of the range of instruction and in terms of the labor market value of educational attainment. In addition, the extension of public schooling has always been accompanied by rigorous sorting mechanisms within each level. Sharp differentials were maintained in the quality of individual schools and in the vocational tracks to which children were assigned on the basis of their class, ethnicity, race, sex, physical and cultural attributes. What the real history of the "golden age" tells us is not surprising: public education has never transcended social or economic stratification; it has merely reproduced it. There were democratic gains, but they extended only the narrowest forms of equal opportunity and did not outpace or overcome the elitist dynamic of school institutions.

What, then, of the immigrant children who rose from rags to at least Middle American comfort? The myth celebrates the rise of the immigrants as the triumph of public education. But a closer look at this history also tells a different story. In the industrial age, until mid-century, only a select group of immigrant children reached the professional or corporate elite and usually *after* their parents had acquired middle class status within the ethnic community, if not beyond it. In the more exceptional cases, when ethnic children made it up the educational ladder without economic security, they were likely to have come from backgrounds where literacy was well-established. As happens today, schools confirmed pre-existing advantages, but did not generally succeed where those advantages were absent. Among the ethnic working class, mobility has been more a factor of jobs and income, of unionization or political patronage, than a reflection of the value of their schooling.[2]

The inequities and devaluation of mass education were not so apparent, however, during periods of economic growth and, particularly, during the 1945-65 boom that absorbed the schoolchildren of the '30s. Economic expansion extended the layers of schooling and pushed the general base of attainment and duration of schooling upward. Job growth helped to mask and mitigate school failure by assimilating drop outs and displaced workers into blue-collar and service employment, which afforded training and promotional opportunities on the job. With the significant exception of marginal workers, minorities, and women, who remained firmly fixed on the bottom, prosperity did raise absolute living standards and income mobility, with only minimal relation to the educational credentials of the workforce.

The historic irony is that as minorities and the poor began to fight successfully for access to secondary and advanced education in the late '60s, prolonged economic expansion gave way to prolonged stagnation. But the myth of education as a springboard for economic advance and a catalyst for economic growth was not thereby dispelled. Instead, it is now assumed that what is wrong with the schools is what is new about them—the influx of disadvantaged minorities and their demands for egalitarian reform. What has been the historic failure of mass education is most readily attributed to its latest victims.

2. THE MYTH OF EGALITARIAN REFORM

We have argued that the traditional school system, as it entered the reform era of the 1960s, had proven far more effective in imposing its two-tier model on an enlarged system of public education than it was in generalizing excellence. The 1960s school reform movement constituted a direct challenge to that legacy, not only a battle for access to all layers of public education but also a battle to make equality of result the standard for school performance.

What was and was not achieved by this thrust toward democratic reform in the '60s and '70s is at the heart of the school debate in the 1980s. The new elite theorists of education have centered much of their argument on discrediting the egalitarian impulses of the last two decades. They have propagated the notion that '60s reforms have undermined the model of traditional school success, are either responsible for the present crisis or make no real contribution toward solving it. Curiously, this perspective generates two different interpretations of the impact of the '60s school change movement. In one version, equity demands were translated into powerful reforms, determining the context in which schooling is presently conducted. The result, in this view, has been the dilution of quality and the reduction of competency standards. In another version, equity demands produced reforms that had negligible impact on eradicating educational disadvantage. The conclusion is that equity reforms are not worth pursuing and, further, that the problems of unequal education are not within the province of schools to remedy.

Neither conclusion is correct. Nonetheless, many progressives feel trapped in the uncomfortable bind of defending previous reforms as hard-won responses to egalitarian demands, when those reforms were, for the most part, limited compromises. Moreover, even these minimal reforms have been continuously eroded in the past ten years by inadequate implementation or outright subversion. Advocates for more, not less, democratic education have been caught in a complicated middle between the failures of the old liberalism and the dangers of the new conservatism.

To move outside these two poles, we need to recognize the value of the gains that were made and the limitations of the compromises that were accepted. The reforms of the '60s and early '70s were positive in that they moved us a few steps beyond the bleak "golden age" of exclusive meritocracy, a few steps toward a more democratic mission for schooling. These reforms brought new populations into the system, enlarged expectations for equality, introduced federal relief funds, and established several models for more effective education. These same reforms proved deficient in that they did not go far enough to make a fundamental difference in the tiered nature of the system, nor far enough to resist a conservative retrenchment. Unfortunately, they made few substantial inroads on the rates of school failure. The record does not tell us that equality in education is a doomed cause, but that we have yet to try in a fully committed and comprehensive way.

To understand this dual character of liberal school reform, we offer an alternative reading of recent school history. Following World War II, there was a broad consensus in corporate, government, and public opinion that secondary education and, to some extent, higher education should become more widely accessible. The post-war expansion was moving into a new frontier of global and technological production, the government sector was mushrooming, the consumer economy called for a more developed service sector. These trends promoted a vast expansion of schooling and raised social minimums for literacy and for school duration. The high school diploma became the mass standard for school performance, serving both to elevate the general level of skill in the workforce and to ease job pressures by delaying the entry of youth into the labor market. Junior colleges and public universities proliferated; the GI Bill was the opening wedge of the modern school mission.

The upward mobility of organized workers and of the new white-collar middle strata also produced grassroots social pressure to broaden educational enfranchisement. Adequate schooling became as symbolic of the American Dream as the tract house in the suburbs; although not a root cause of the rising standard of living, educational attainment was one of its measures, a prized reward. The democratic and economic missions of schooling were indeed coinciding, and appeared to be converging. Significantly, the 1954 *Brown v. Board of Education* decision marked, for the first time, a formal commitment to include blacks in the promise of mobility.

Egalitarian Demands

Through the 1960s, educational opportunities were greatly extended, particularly for the children of white workers in the primary labor force. But opportunities were still negligible, both in access and in resources, for the poor, for the marginal working class, and for minorities. The upsurge of the civil rights movement, reinforced by a mobilized student movement and by the progressive education tradition, raised challenges to these barriers. Demands for universal access to public education centered on the struggle for racial desegregation, but also called for the improvement of inner-city high schools, the expansion of community colleges, and admission to selective institutions. Resources to overcome social and educational disadvantages were demanded as well, including pre-school services, nutrition and social services, remediation, enrichment, and vocational programs.

From these initial struggles, a new vision of democratic education emerged, embryonic to be sure, but distinctly different from prior battles for inclusion. The reform movement questioned the basic construction of the school institution, its educational content, its classroom structures, and its forms of governance. From urban ghettoes to college campuses, the school reform movement sought more options and social relevance in the curriculum, alternative learning methods and environments, citizenship and empowerment skills, respect for cultural diversity. The movement sought schools that did not function as socioeconomic sorting mechanisms and did not assume that children failed because of individual or family deficits. The movement sought schools that operated with the expectation that all children could learn, given appropriate resources and flexible approaches. Integral to this call to transform the classroom was the vision of community control of decentralized school institutions, of parent advocacy and intervention, of student participation. The vision of democratic education was based neither on meritocracy nor on the lowest common denominator, but on a recognition that quality and equality must be measured by each other, that democracy must be taught by example.

It is easy, in these times, to underestimate the intensity of the egalitarian school reform movement of the '60s and early '70s. It should be recalled, however, that the school movement did not exist in isolation from other pressing social issues; it was a central part of the ferment for social justice that defined the political and cultural climate of that decade. The school movement drew on and developed within the activism of youth, minorities, women, the urban and rural poor. It was set in the context of confrontation in the Jim Crow South, of urban riots, of an unjust war, of Third World independence and women's liberation—a tide of social change and a moment of new expectations. And while the sharpest demands came from the angry poor and alienated young, there was a parallel impetus for more, if not different, educational opportunities among the ethnic working and middle classes.

The pressure exerted on schools, as central social institutions, did produce an unprecedented series of landmark legislation: the Vocational Education Act of 1963, and subsequent amendments, targeting low-income, handicapped, and female students; the Civil Rights Act of 1964, extending federal jurisdiction over equal opportunity; the Economic Opportunities Act of 1964, establishing the basis for community-based education and training programs; the Elementary and Secondary Education Act of 1965, the first broad federal support for public education, including Title I funding for compensatory education; the Bilingual Education Act of 1968 (ESEA Title VII), providing aid for bilingual programs; the Education Amendments Act of 1972 (ESEA Title IX), the federal bar on sex discrimination in school services; the Equal Educational Opportunity Act of 1974, mandating schools to redress language barriers; the Women's Educational Equity Act of 1974, funding women's studies; the Family Educational Rights and Privacy Act of 1974, assuring access to school records by parents and students; Public Law 94-142, the Education of All Handicapped Children Act of 1975, mandating a free, appropriate education to all handicapped children.

The period also produced significant court decisions, including *Mills v. D.C. Board of Education* (1972), establishing the access rights of handicapped children, and *Lau v. Nichols* (1974), mandating access rights for students with limited English proficiency. Desegregation plans were ordered; the right of undocumented immigrant children to public education was upheld; students' civil liberties were expanded; affirmative action was applied to school personnel. In addition, some school systems, particularly in urban areas, experimented with new approaches, introducing more socially relevant curricula, scrutinizing sex and race bias students at risk. A large number of community colleges experimented with open admissions. Early childhood education programs were greatly extended in low-income communities, spearheaded by Head Start's pre-school program and the Follow Through program in primary grades.

Although the list of new government and school policies is impressively long, the reforms enacted still fell far short of the egalitarian demands that prompted them. These limitations stem both from flawed construction and from disabling implementation. The most important advance was enlarging access to public education for those previously disenfranchised, but inclusion was not matched by improvements in the quality of education provided to new entrants. Schools were indeed given new demands to meet, but these demands were not accompanied by either the level of resources or the institutional changes necessary to the task. Enrollments were broadened, but the educational ante was again raised, and the high school diploma or junior college certificate was devalued. Taken as a whole, the reforms of the '60s and '70s were cast in the classic pattern of extending inclusion while maintaining meritocratic structures of achievement.

The most significant potential challenge to the predictable outcome, school failure for the lower strata, was the enactment of categorical federal entitlement programs. The entitlement programs—Title I compensatory education, bilingual education, and special education for the handicapped—did represent more than legal access. They acknowledged that added resources were needed and that empowerment was an issue; each of the major entitlements originally included unprecedented mandates for parent advisory councils and intervention rights in the programs.

Yet in their basic design, the entitlement programs were generally based on deficit assumptions about the inadequacies of minority students, rather than an assumption that the schools themselves were inadequate to an egalitarian mission. The models adopted were add-on programs, separate from rather than integrated with a reconstruction of mainstream schooling. The entitlements injected some urgently needed funding into distressed school systems; in many areas, they produced measurable gains for disadvantaged students. Where parent involvement was well developed, the entitlements have also produced a legacy of activism that remains influential well beyond school politics. But at the same time, the entitlement programs have worked within a tiered system to reinforce the segregation of students with special needs. Structurally, compensatory programs have established yet another basis for tracking, labeling, and lowered expectations.

If the reform design was a compromise, the implementation process has been a betrayal of egalitarian school demands, a record of unkept promises. Each of the major entitlements has been grossly underfunded, given the magnitude of services required to meet the needs of all children. In systems that face declining revenues and cutbacks in aid for regular programs, entitlement funds have frequently been treated as discretionary monies, and have been diverted from their original purposes. Many local school authorities have resisted responsibility for children who do not readily survive in the existing system, and have subverted mandates for parent involvement and approval. Non-compliance has not been systematically challenged by state and federal monitors. Often there are not enough qualified teachers, given low levels of compensation and poor training, to operate adequate programs.

In 1980, only 57% of the approximately 9 million students eligible for Title I were provided compensatory services, even though recent studies indicate the program has produced measurable gains for recipients. By 1982, it was estimated that Title I reductions had cut 900,000 children out of the program. In 1980, 77% of Hispanic children with limited English proficiency were not receiving any form of special programming responsive to their linguistic needs; only 10% were in bilingual programs. Special education students remain substantially underserved and overwhelmingly segregated. Vocational programs continue to practice wholesale sex discrimination, and the 30% cuts in federal funds for vocational education are a major setback for sex equity efforts. Even the most successful of all '60s programs, Head Start, which operates independently and innovatively with a record of unparalleled benefit for low-income children and their communities, today reaches only 18% of all eligible children.[3]

The history of desegregation offers an even more shameful example of rights denied through token policy commitments, feeble administration, and retreat in the face of regressive resistance. Although there are some laudable instances of successful desegregation—the NEA cites school systems in Seattle, Houston, and Charlotte-Mecklenburg[4]—the overall results thirty years after *Brown v. Board of Education* are deplorable. As of 1980, 63% of black children were attending predominantly minority schools.[5]

Jennifer Hochschild points out that most of the advances toward desegregation were achieved between 1968 and 1972, with no lessening of segregation since 1976.[6] Throughout much of the rural South, desegregation was accompanied by lowering the tax base for public schools, granting local and state tax exemptions for segregation academies, and imposing what a Mississippi activist has called "martial law" by local school boards.[7] Yet Hochschild reminds us that the southern and border states have made the greatest advances toward desegregation. "Racial isolation has increased considerably in the Northeast and is accelerating. As a consequence, almost one-half of northern black students now attend all-minority schools, compared to only one-quarter of southern black students. . . . [Moreover] resegregation or second-generation discrimination within desegregated schools is considerable."[8] In many areas of the country, desegregation has coincided with cutbacks in school funding, opportunistic polarizations of deprived whites and deprived minorities, and the failure to raise school quality overall. The desegregation of districts has not necessarily produced desegregation in local schools, in tracked programs within schools, or in classroom placements. Today, our nation's schooling remains, to a great extent, separate and unequal.

A large number of democratic demands have been abandoned altogether. Open admissions to public colleges lasted less than five years, with little time, funding, or administrative support to establish viable transition programs. High schools and colleges are increasingly dismantling their minority, ethnic, and women's studies programs. Decentralization of school governance was never achieved on any appreciable scale; trends continue to favor the consolidation of school districts, with even less influence by parents and communities over local school policies and priorities. In addition, we have recently witnessed a growing divestiture of federal and local taxpayer responsibility for public education, through cutbacks and tax revolts such as Proposition 13 and Proposition 2¹/₂. A recent study sponsored by the National Institute of Education (NIE) found that, with the consolidation of federal categorical funding under Chapter 2 block grants, there has been reduced assistance to urban schools, particularly those previously receiving desegregation aid, while federal aid to private schools has grown.[9]

What conservatives attack as corrosive egalitarianism never took place and is not the root cause of persistent school failure. The best of the '60s reforms have had marginal influence on school practice. The implementation process has been a shadow of the legislative intent, which was itself a shadow of popular demands for school equality. While conservatives justify the reversal of such reforms by claiming the programs did not work, they ignore the pervasive failure to make them work and the underlying social forces that have blocked a genuine commitment to progressive school change. Perhaps the most decisive factor has been prolonged economic stagnation, the pattern of recurring recession over the past fifteen years that has shifted national priorities away from social spending and equality goals.

In this climate of fiscal retrenchment, influential sectors of liberal opinion have retreated from their earlier alignment with social movements. In turn, those social movements have suffered serious setbacks and have become increasingly isolated, reducing the grassroots pressure on government. Another disabling factor has been the rising influence of school bureaucrats and professional organizations, which developed parallel to but increasingly apart from the grassroots mobilization for school change. These professional groups have tended to define their interests in opposition to community demands, seeking narrow control over the school institution and its traditional functions, frequently blocking the impetus for school reconstruction in order to maintain their own turf.

Each of these developments has opened the door for resurgent conservatism in school politics and for the reformulation of school goals along elitist lines. But to say that the egalitarian reforms of the 60s and '70s were denied the means to succeed is not to say that the attempt was not worth making. It is to say that the battle was far from won—we are still confronting the conflict between political democracy and economic elitism, between education as a tool of universal empowerment and education as a tool of selective mobility. We are still in a contest over extending the democratic potential of schooling or imposing the standard mold of meritocracy on new conditions.

What was gained by a decade of social activism was essentially a shift from exclusive meritocracy to inclusive meritocracy. Inclusion is not nothing, but it is not enough—and today, even formal access is eroding. Measures that recognized compensatory needs and addressed exclusion and segregation were real victories, but victories because they represented first steps toward more thorough institutional transformation. In the past ten years, those first steps have become inadequate and precarious. The task is now to match the inclusion of new populations in the schools with a new fully democratic mission for public education. Progressives won the first round and lost the second, but the vision that the '60s movement created survives to be built upon.

3. THE MYTH OF THE ECONOMIC IMPERATIVE

Before turning to the instructional and institutional approaches that serve a renewed vision of democratic education, it is important to examine a third myth that underpins the new elitism. This is the myth that we face an economic imperative to adopt get-tough prescriptions and competitive standards. The myth is based on the assumption that declining school performance is a major factor in declining economic performance. A corollary claim is that the restoration of high standards and discipline will help restore economic productivity, competitive advantage, and job creation. The elitism of the new regime is thus justified by the claim that universal economic benefits will result.

We have argued that the fundamental crisis of education is not new, either in regard to massive failure to serve the bottom tiers or in regard to narrow concepts of achievement. This crisis does not correlate chronologically or causally with periods of economic decline. Furthermore, our reading of school history suggests that school performance has not been the motive force for economic growth. In fact, we find precisely the reverse dynamic at work: economic development has directed school change; economic status has determined school achievement; economic mobility has extended school opportunity. School functions have been largely subordinated to economic trends and, at most, play a supportive, not decisive role in the economy. And if schools have not shaped the economy in the past, they are even less likely to do so given current economic trends.

The Economic Hourglass

For the past fifteen years, we have lived in an economy marked by stagnation, recurring recession, and the loss of international predominance. In the past five years, this economy has also gone through a period of dramatic restructuring, gearing up for a new round of global integration and intense competition. These conditions of prolonged contraction and structural change have accelerated the displacement of labor, so that today we face a shortage of jobs in a wide range of skill levels, not a shortage of qualified and motivated workers.

In October 1984, at the peak of a two-year "recovery" period, unemployment stood at 7.4%, or 8.5 million workers, a level that would have been considered recessionary twenty years ago. In addition, the index of "distressed workers"—which counts the discouraged who no longer look for work, the employed who remain in poverty, and involuntary part-time workers—stood at 14.2%, or 16.4 million people.[10] The figures for youth and for minorities are much worse. The jobless rate for black teenagers averages five times the national rate and today stands at well over 50%. Nearly 40% of the unemployed are under twenty-five years of age; nearly 20% are teenagers, who, in the recent upturn, garnered only 3% of all new jobs. Long-term trends indicate that the labor market will continue to contract relative to the workforce: the average jobless rate has risen steadily in each decade, from 4.2% in the 1950s, to 4.8% in the 1960s, to 6.2% in the 1970s, to 8.5% in the first four years of the 1980s.[11]

Structural shifts have also produced a sharper polarization of the workforce, a widening gap between skilled professionals and unskilled, low-wage service workers. We are witnessing the destruction of what for thirty years has been considered the primary workforce. The heart of that primary workforce has been blue-collar operatives in the leading industrial sectors—basic manufacturing, transportation, communications, construction. In general, these workers were unionized and received compensation tied to the rising productivity and the market advantages of their firms. Through the post-war period, this segment of the workforce set a pattern for wages, hours, and benefits, fair labor practices, and job security that became the pivotal standard for all American workers. Primary sector jobs were often semi-skilled and skilled, but educational attainment was not a major condition of job entry, training, or promotion.

These jobs are fast disappearing—over 5 million have been lost since 1980.[12] A once gradual erosion has become rapid and permanent displacement, due to several converging factors: the new wave of electronic automation, rising foreign competition, the flight of capital and production to cheap labor havens overseas, and the rise in non-productive investment. Job conditions are also worsening because of government deregulation of major industries (transportation, banking) and de facto deregulation of industrial standards (the gutting of EPA, OSHA, FDA, the NLRB). Union protections are rapidly weakening in the face of a new employer offensive, which for the first time since the formation of the CIO has held union wage gains below those of non-union workers.[13] The line between the primary and the secondary workforce is dissolving. The sector once reserved for low-skill, marginal, unorganized employment—and particularly for women and minorities—is now setting the pattern for job standards throughout the economy.

We confront a labor market with the middle dropping out and with competition growing at every level. Contrary to the human capital theories so optimistically put forward by current education influentials, there will not be more room at the top to compensate for the losses in the middle. The promise of high technology is not a workforce filled with technicians and skilled operatives; as a distinct sector, high-tech production will account for only 5–7% of job growth by 1990. Job growth is expected to occur in the service sector—in trade, finance, and personal services. A profile of the fastest-growing occupations of the decade shows that they are overwhelmingly low-skill and/or low-pay positions.[14]

Top Growth Occupations of the 1980s

Occupation	Total Emp., 1981 (in 1,000s)*	Est. Increase, 1990 (in 1,000s)	% Female in 1981	Average Weekly Wage in 1981
All	72,491	16,800	39.5	$289
1. Secretaries	3,199	700	99.3	$230
2. Nurses' Aides	832	508	84.3	$172
3. Janitors	993	501	14.6	$219
4. Clerks (Sales)	1,032	479	60.3	$178
5. Cashiers	712	452	85.1	$227
6. Nurses	1,168	438	95.8	$332
7. Truckdrivers	1,560	415	2.1	$314
8. Fastfood	1,000	400	50.9	$171
9. Clerks (Office)	2,082	378	76.2	$201
10. Waiters	532	360	85.1	$150

*Full-time employees only.

In their enthusiasm for economic rationales, education policymakers have also widely ignored the displacement and deskilling effects of high technology on existing jobs. As Henry Levin and Russell Rumberger point out, the impact of new technology creates an initial increase in skill requirements, followed by a sharp and enduring decrease as mechanization proceeds. "Past applications of technology in the workplace, as well as the present evidence, suggest that future technologies will further simplify and routinize work tasks and reduce opportunities for worker individuality and judgment. Moreover, the displacement in jobs and the downgrading of skill requirements for most of the new positions will undermine employment generally, and especially the employment of skilled workers."[15]

The labor market of the future cannot be pictured as a bell-shaped curve, but rather as a bottom-heavy hourglass. The emerging top will include a small, elite strata of well-paid professional-technical employees, who themselves will face growing problems of skill devaluation and intense competition. The trend is already evident at the college level. Comparing jobs entered by college graduates from 1962 to 1969 with those entered from 1969 to 1978, the number of professional positions declined from 73.2% to 45.9%; the drop was taken up by sharp increases in clerical, sales, operative, service, and unemployed categories.[16]

On the bottom of the hourglass will be a shrinking number of blue-collar workers, faced with a continuous reduction of labor standards. The bottom will also include a growing segment of relatively skilled but low-paid employees in paraprofessional, technical, administrative, and service fields, a large proportion of them women. The bottom will include the traditional secondary workforce of low-skill, low-paid service jobs that are dead-end, unstable, and rapidly expanding. In addition, there will be a swelling pool of structurally unemployed workers, joining the vast reserve of irregular workers and hard-core unemployed.

Designating the Victims

What labor market trends tell us is that a long-standing paradox of schooling will become a more intense contradiction in coming years: education will mean more for a few and less for many. Access to rewarding jobs will require greater educational attainment and proficiency, but there will be fewer chances of success even with the fullest schooling. For the great majority, job destinies will not utilize intellectual skills beyond basic literacy, although years of schooling may still count in arbitrarily sorting out who gets hired and who gets rejected. These trends suggest a series of problems we have just begun to grasp. Poor and minority youth, who already receive substandard schooling and face 50% unemployment, are likely to be left entirely outside the job market. Working class youth, who have no particular advantage in their schooling, will not have compensating job or income opportunities as adults. And schools will be increasingly hard-pressed to motivate their students through career aspirations or goals.

Given the disjuncture between economic and educational rewards, the effort to link school reform to the market value of education threatens to abandon large segments of American youth. If one argues that schools should reflect the logic of a polarizing labor market, the necessary conclusion is that we must reinforce competitive schooling—raise elitist barriers, add new stratification mechanisms, reward only the most exceptional or advantaged. Few other options are left within a marketplace framework. When public education was less than universal and the job market more expansive, it was still possible to add new, selective layers on top while opening up the bottom. But today it is harder to exercise the traditional option of creating differential values for schooling by extending its upper levels. The institution is filling up at all levels, and, even at the highest rungs, students are not finding economic status commensurate with their schooling.

Since the market can no longer be served by extending competition, the elitists would serve it by intensifying competition. The result of strictly meritocratic reforms will not be a better future for the majority, but new convenience in designating the victims of both educational and economic deprivation. Today's get-tough policies work, in practice, as new ways to justify the enlargement of an underclass and the lowering of expectations for most others.

THE SCHOOL-ECONOMY CONNECTION: FINDING NEW IMPERATIVES

The economic imperatives that are cited to defend competitive standards are actually compelling reasons for rejecting such standards. If the marketplace offers so many students diminishing rewards for education—and demands more punitive schooling in the process—we need to look beyond the marketplace in defining the school mission. This does not mean that schools should ignore the occupational futures that await their students, but that schools should be more forcefully egalitarian in light of employment inequalities. Further, school change should be linked to changing the marketplace itself, working to reorder economic priorities so that skill and knowledge are socially useful for every young person. In reformulating the connection of schools to the economy, we see three levels of needed reform.

Democratizing Competition

The first challenge is to recognize that, within existing economic structures and polarities, there is a tremendous battle ahead simply to "democratize competition."[17] Even though job opportunities are limited, all children should have equal opportunities to succeed. Insistence on equity in access and in the quality of schooling will not transform the labor market, but equity can work to distribute labor market tyrannies more evenly. Although this represents only the minimum level of equal opportunity, we are far from fulfilling it. The focus today is on narrow forms of vocational training, with pressures for early tracking, test-driven and quantifiable curricula, and mastery of highly segmented and specific skills. School-to-work linkages, such as business partnerships and the federal JTPA program, are often only token efforts, frequently serving to cream the best students while neglecting the most needy.

To maximize their chances in a rapidly shifting and diversified job market, students need learning approaches that enhance their intellectual as well as vocational flexibility—a position firmly taken by the National Commission on Secondary Vocational Education, among others.[18] Students need schooling that emphasizes generic skills, reasoning capacity, and the social skills to interact with peers and teachers in tackling unfamiliar material. Schools also need to develop new approaches for economic literacy that go beyond instruction in filling out a job application or balancing a checkbook—students should have a realistic understanding of how the job market works and what barriers they will confront. Meaningful, paid work experience should accompany classroom training and be integrated with an academic program. Maximizing options also means challenging the rampant discrimination that prevails in vocational programs in the placement and instruction of female, minority, and low-income students. Along with affirmative action, there is an urgent need to address the counseling crisis in underfunded schools, particularly at the middle school level.

These are only some of the ingredients that could improve school-to-work linkages; the essential point is that the foundation for decent vocational preparation is a decent school, not just an extra program or a narrow skill. Deficient instruction, hostile school environments, attitudes of benign neglect based on low expectations are far more destructive than the absence of a computer science program, although computer science too should be demanded. Perhaps the basic priority is that we require schools to produce universal literacy—a feat nearly achieved by a number of very poor countries, far surpassing the United States, a very rich country that ranks 49th among 158 U.N. member nations in literacy.[19] Literacy is the minimal condition of labor market participation in tomorrow's economy, even in menial occupations, and it is the first order of failure in our schools.

Restructuring the Economy

Beyond adjusting the school to the realities of the economy, a second challenge is to recognize a larger agenda for adjusting the economy to meet the needs of youth. Addressing this question involves the pursuit of a genuine national full employment policy, which accepts that where the private sector does not provide sufficient jobs, based on its market needs, then the public sector must provide jobs based on social needs. Across the country, chronic needs exist both for job creation and for rebuilding our communities. Viable models exist, both here and abroad, for public service employment and job training programs applied to infrastructural repair, environmental protection, social and family services, cultural activities, even schooling.

One of the more promising proposals, rejected by the Reagan administration but still on the congressional agenda, is the creation of a national youth service corps, directed to conservation and community service and modeled on the Civilian Conservation Corps (CCC). States and some cities are also pursuing this concept, which integrates public service employment with vocational training and academic remediation. In addition, major reforms of labor policy, incomes policy, and industrial policy can substantially affect job futures for youth. The long list of needed reforms includes measures to reduce the standard work week, regulate the export of capital, protect civil and union rights, establish pay equity, finance community development ventures, and enforce fair labor standards. The Catholic bishops have stressed the importance of a viable family wage to both reduce job pressures and provide parents more time for family and community sustenance;[20] even a liveable minimum wage would be a step forward.

Our comprehensive goals should not only establish the right to a job but, in the process, reconceive job structures and definitions of socially productive work. While these structural interventions in the national labor market are not on Washington's agenda—indeed, they are hostilely received by the present administration—they speak to conditions that this society will have to face in the coming decades. Economic polarization is damaging the social fabric and democratic potential of America at a dangerously accelerating pace; our failure to recognize this now will only make the task of adjustment and reconstruction more difficult and painful in the future.

The task of generating a national commitment to full employment, or even to extensive youth employment through the public sector, involves a long-term and highly political process that is not familiar territory for school activists. Educators themselves tend to draw strict lines between institutional and social politics, while at the same time despairing over how little impact internal school change has in the face of corrosive economic and social trends. Yet the school constituency can be a significant element in making the case for new economic priorities and in building citizen coalitions to reverse the present politics of corporate trickledown. The new dynamism of state and urban politics, particularly the recent mobilization of minority electorates, represents an important opportunity to connect schooling needs to broader agendas for change and to initiate school-linked youth employment projects.

Schooling for Citizenship

A third challenge posed by economic decline and school devaluation is to define the mission of education in terms of its citizenship function, rather than its labor market function. The current emphasis on competitive achievement, punitive discipline, and the segregation of diverse student populations, all work to reproduce societal modes of discrimination and cultural elitism. Emphasis on quantitative tasks, standardized and test-driven curricula, narrow skills acquisition—along with a notable lack of interactive learning environments—discourages students from thinking critically about their society and the choices confronting them. The isolation of schools from their communities further undermines the sense of civic responsibility and solidarity that public education should but rarely does cultivate among students.

The citizenship role of schooling, broadly conceived, addresses new imperatives of community life far more compelling—and more readily influenced by schools— than the demands of the economy. This society has undergone tremendous social transformation in the post-war period, which schools can respond to in both how they teach and what they teach. We have seen a long-term decline in voting and political participation. We have witnessed the devastation of older industrial and rural centers, increased crime and family violence, rising indicators of substance abuse and personal distress. We have a more mobile population that is also more multi-racial and multi-national. We have a rising percentage of older people and a more distinct youth subculture.

Probably the most dramatic changes are occurring in the status of women and in child-raising patterns. In 1980, 54% of children under eighteen had working mothers. The number of female-headed households has risen sharply; in 1980, 23.4% of all children under eighteen—17.3% of white children, 57.8% of black children—were not living in two-parent households.[21] Schools are serving a majority of children who do not come from "traditional" homes. Functions that we previously relied on the family to serve—including childcare, recreation, educational enrichment, cultural initiation, community involvement—are increasingly shifting to other social institutions, particularly schools.

In addition, the burdens of poverty in this society have fallen increasingly on women and children. Nearly 40% of all poor people in America are children. One in five American children is poor, one in two black children is poor, two in five Hispanic children are poor. Of adults in poverty, two out of three are women; nearly 50% of all female-headed households are poor.[22] There is a direct correlation of poverty to undereducation—not because poor children cannot learn, but because poor children go to poor schools. Our schools rarely do well if the traditional prerequisites for academic learning are not already in place, including parent literacy, adequate nutrition and healthcare, high self-esteem, and other social endowments.

Demographic studies tell us these trends will accelerate and that the school population of the future will be markedly different from that which schools have been organized to serve in the past. There will be more children entering from poverty households and more poor children who do not get pre-school services, despite eligibility. There will be more children from single-parent households, more from families merged by remarriage, more "latchkey" children. There will be more children of teenage mothers, more children who were premature babies, more children whose parents were not married. And, if current practice holds, there will be more high school drop-outs and more college entrants who need both financial and academic assistance.[23]

Unfortunately, schoolpeople too often resent the added demands, blame under-parenting or social problems for school failure, and ultimately disclaim responsibility for making the school culture more supportive of the child. New demands on schools to meet social needs are not the enemy of school achievement; in fact, meeting these needs is a condition for effective instruction and a key to raising levels of achievement. The issue is not the demands that are placed on schools, but the resources that are provided to help schools meet these demands.

Education for citizenship means that schools should provide children with the social and intellectual skills to function well as members of families and communities, as political participants, as adult learners, as self-directed individuals. Education for citizenship means teaching children about the way the world works and arming them to influence how it works. Citizenship requires basic skills, but it requires other forms of learning as well: critical judgment, social awareness, connection to community, shared values. The prescription is not more civics classes for seniors, although we should certainly upgrade civics instruction and civic experience. The priority is developing educational values that recognize all student needs as legitimate and that prepare students for multiple roles as adults, regardless of their labor market destinies or economic status. The bottom line for democratic education is empowerment, not simply employment. Indeed, an attempt to reduce the disjuncture between schooling and job futures will require an empowered citizenry that is prepared to reorder our economic priorities. . . .

NOTES

1. Colin Greer, *The Great School Legend* (New York: Penguin, 1972), pp. 108–109.
2. Ibid., pp. 83–86, 93.
   See also Nathan Glazer and Daniel P. Moynihan, *Beyond the Melting Pot* (Cambridge, Mass.: MIT Press, 1964).
3. *A Children's Defense Budget*, report of the Children's Defense Fund (Washington, D.C.: CDF, 1984), p. 27 and chap. 8.
4. *Thirty Years After* Brown: *Three Cities That Are Making Desegregration Work*, report of the National Education Association (Washington, D.C.: NEA, May 1984).
5. Gary Orfield, *Working Paper: Desegregration of Black and Hispanic Students for 1968–80* (Washington, D.C.: Joint Center for Policy Studies, 1982).
6. Jennifer Hochschild, *Thirty Years After* Brown (Washington, D.C.: Joint Center for Policy Studies, 1985), p. 3.
7. Larry Farmer, program director of Mississippi Action for Community Education, presentation to the Educational Visions Seminar, New World Foundation, 31 May 1984.
8. Hochschild, *Thirty Years After* Brown, pp. 3, 5.
9. Regina Kyle, ed., *Kaleidescope: Emerging Patterns of Response and Action in ECIA Case Studies of Chapter 2 in Selected States*, report of the National Institute of Education by E. H. White & Co. (Washington, D.C.: U.S. Department of Education, July 1983), cited in *Education Week*, 5 December 1984, p. 1.
10. Thomas N. Bethell, "Economic Distress: Worse Than the Numbers Suggest," *Rural Coalition Report*, no. 10, December 1984, pp. 22–23.
11. *A Policy Blueprint for Community Service and Youth Employment*, report of the Roosevelt Centennial Youth Project (New York: Eleanor Roosevelt Institute, September 1984), pp. 3, 9.
    "The Youth Employment Situation," press release of the Roosevelt Centennial Youth Project, March 1984.

12. AFL-CIO Committee on the Evaluation of Work, cited in "Economy Gains but Changes," *New York Times*, 4 September 1983, p. A1.
13. "The Non-Union Edge," *New York Times*, 20 January 1985, p. D1.
14. Chart cited from Mike Davis, "The Political Economy of Late Imperial America," *New Left Review*, January 1984. His sources include data from U.S. Bureau of Labor Statistics figures cited in the following:

    Valerie Personick, "The Outlook for Industry Output and Employment through 1990," *Monthly Labor Review*, August 1981.

    A.F. Ehrbach, "The New Unemployment," *Fortune*, April 1981.

    See also Carol Boyd Leon, "Occupational Winners and Losers," *Monthly Labor Review*, June 1982.

    Robert Kuttner, "The Declining Middle," *Atlantic Monthly*, July 1983.

    Gene I. Maeroff, "The Real Job Boom Is Likely to Be Low Tech," *New York Times*, 4 September 1983, p. E16.

    Lester C. Thurow, "The Hidden Sting of the Trade Deficit," *New York Times*, 19 January 1986, p. F3.
15. Henry M. Levin and Russell W. Rumberger, *The Educational Implications of High Technology*, Project Report No. 83-A4, Institute for Research on Educational Finance and Governance (Palo Alto, Calif.: Stanford University, February 1983), pp. 9, 10–11.
16. Janet L. Norwood, "The Job Outlook for College Graduates thru 1990," *Occupational Outlook Quarterly*, Winter 1979, pp. 2–7.

    See also Maeroff, "The Real Job Boom."
17. "Democratizing competition" is a concept developed in David K. Cohen and Barbara Neufeld, "The Failure of High Schools and the Progress of Education," *Daedalus*, Summer 1981.
18. *The Unfinished Agenda*, report of the National Commission on Secondary Vocational Education (Washington, D.C.: NCSVE, December 1984).
19. Jonathan Kozol, *Illiterate America* (New York: Doubleday, 1985), p. 5.
20. "Bishops' Pastoral: Catholic Teaching and the U.S. Economy," *Origins*, 15 November 1984, pp. 358–359.
21. Andrew Hacker, ed., *U/S: A Statistical Portrait of the American People* (New York: Penguin, 1983), pp. 134, 90.
22. *Children's Defense Budget*, p. 21.

    See also *American Children in Poverty*, report of the Children's Defense Fund (Washington, D.C.: CDF, 1984).
23. Harold Hodgekinson, *All One System* (Washington, D.C.: Institute for Educational Leadership, 1985).

Tracking, Inequality, and the Rhetoric of Reform: Why Schools Don't Change

Jeannie Oakes

In these times of perceived scarcity, the question that most threatens American ideology surfaces at every turn: If there isn't enough to go around, who gets it? The current supply-side, trickle-down answer is clear: Those who have, shall get. In education the question has been forced by diminishing resources and the withdrawal of public support. The answer is confirmed in the recent reform reports and in policymakers' enthusiastic response to them. There is a cynical common thread that both the detractors and supporters of these reports share, and the metaphor of the swinging pendulum serves to illustrate it. Sometimes we're more conservative, sometimes more liberal; sometimes there's money and confidence, sometimes we feel poor and hopeless. Back and forth. Everyone senses that the change is illusory.

The intent of this paper is to respond to that pendulum phenomenon, for until it is understood clearly, a powerful force—as little "seen" as gravity—will continue to shape our schools. That force, present at the turn of the century, almost unchanged in the generous '60s, and with us today, is the differentiation of schooling experiences according to the belief that some children can more easily or more deservedly achieve excellence.

Current school reform proposals represent, for the most part, a stripping away of some of the contemporary guises of traditional schooling content and forms. This is differentiated schooling characterized by Anglo-conformity and meritocracy. Deemed "excellent" in the reform rhetoric, this mode of schooling has historically restricted both access to education and achievement of ethnic minority and poor

Jeannie Oakes, "Tracking, Inequality, and the Rhetoric of Reform: Why Schools Don't Change." *Journal of Education*, Volume 168, No. 1, Copyright 1986. Reprinted with permission of Editorial Board of the *Journal of Education*.

This paper is an extension of the analysis included in *Keeping Track: How Schools Structure Inequality* (Yale University Press, 1985). While the views expressed herein represent only those of the author, thanks are given to Martin Lipton and Gary Fenstermacher for helpful comments on this work.

children. Well-intentioned, progressive reformers have, at times, succeeded in mitigating the injustice inherent in these forms; even so, the current politics of social conservatism, far from inventing new inequities, appear to be largely capitalizing on endemic ones.

PREVAILING CONCEPTIONS OF EQUALITY AND SCHOOLING

Traditional schooling forms, so clearly symbolized by the practice of tracking, are deeply rooted in assumptions about student differences and the meritocratic nature of schooling. Political and economic trends generate changes in rhetoric without addressing these assumptions or affecting the essential nature of schools as social institutions. Straightforward intents to eliminate inequality have given way to various rationales for inequality. Both are charged with a tangle of myth, unexamined assumptions, good intentions, and accurate and inaccurate beliefs.

Rarely do either those who press for equality or those who see equality as a costly luxury articulate the relationship between equality and schooling that permeates American schools. The following is an attempt to make explicit the prevailing conceptions of equality and schooling.

1. Educational opportunity, not educational results, must be equal in school.
2. Equal educational opportunity means equal opportunity to develop quite fixed individual potential (intelligence and abilities) to its limit through individual effort in school, regardless of such irrelevant background characteristics as race, class, and gender.
3. Providing equal opportunities to develop individual potential has instrumental value to both individuals and society. For individuals, it provides fair access to the world of work by providing fair access to the technical knowledge, the skills, and the attitudes that make possible the production of goods and services. Work is the way to attain the material and nonmaterial resources of society (wealth, prestige, power). For society, equal educational opportunity means that individuals' talents are developed for the benefit of all. These are contributions that could be thwarted under patronage- or inheritance-based systems.
4. Equal educational opportunity does not guarantee equal social and economic benefits to all individuals, because the rewards for various occupations are not equal. Rather, it provides a fair competition for occupations and their accompanying unequal social and economic rewards. Thus, equal educational opportunity is the means for assuring equal economic and social opportunity.
5. Education provides students with the skills, attitudes, and technical knowledge required for participation in the workforce, but of course the requirements of different occupations vary greatly. They call for quite different levels of ability.
6. Equal educational opportunity does not require the same educational experiences for all individuals, but rather an equal opportunity to develop oneself for an appropriate future in the worklife of the community. This may,

and usually does, necessitate quite different educational experiences for individuals of varying abilities and future roles. Equal educational opportunity, then, requires the provision of different educational experiences and the proper match of these educations to individual ability and suitability for future work. In that way all are served equally well.

7. Publicly supported schooling is a neutral, fair, and meritocratic place to determine who is best suited for various kinds of technical knowledge and skill, to provide appropriate educational experiences toward those ends, and to certify individuals for work roles. Further, school provides immigrant and minority groups opportunities to learn mainstream attitudes, values, and behaviors that are required for successful participation in American social, political, and economic institutions. School, with the provision of equal educational opportunity, fairly stages the competition for adult positions in the social and economic hierarchy.

THE CONTENT OF EDUCATIONAL OPPORTUNITY

Equal educational opportunity, as expressed above, has shaped the structure of the contemporary school. This view has also led to the central struggle of contemporary schooling practice—the development of curriculum and instruction suited to the wide range of abilities and future needs of American children. Differentiated schooling is the structure for equalizing opportunity. But increasing evidence points to fundamental inequalities that result.

As a part of *A Study of Schooling*, data was collected about the curricular content, instructional processes, and classroom climates in nearly 300 secondary school English and mathematics classes. Over 200 of these classes were segregated by student ability or achievement levels.[1] Students had been assigned to these classes on the basis of teacher recommendations, test scores, or the advice of their counselors. Most of the students in upper-level classes were designated as academic-track students; most of the students in average or lower-track classes were in general or vocational programs. And, consistent with other studies of tracking, students in the upper tracks were disproportionately white; those in lower tracks were disproportionately minority. The data about these classes provided an unprecedented opportunity to look carefully at the principles of equal educational opportunity as they are played out in the everyday practice of schooling (Oakes, 1985).

There were considerable differences in the kinds of knowledge students in various tracks had access to. These differences did not represent equally valued alternative curricula. They were differences that could have important implications for the futures of the students involved. Students in high-track classes were exposed to "high status" content—literature, expository and thematic writing, library research, and mathematical ideas. Students in low-track classes were not expected to learn those topics and skills. They rarely, if ever, encountered them. They worked in workbooks and kits and practiced language mechanics and computation. The schools made decisions about the appropriateness of various topics and skills and, in doing so, limited sharply what some students would learn. The lower the track, the greater the limits.

Added to the unmistakable differences in the knowledge students had available to them were differences in their classroom learning opportunities. Both in the amount of time students were provided for learning and in the quality of instruction they received, there were significant differences among track levels. High-track students had more time to learn and more exposure to what seemed to be effective teaching than did other groups. These critical features of classrooms were not equally available to all students. Those students who were judged to learn most slowly and with greatest difficulty were provided the least time and the lowest quality of instruction.

Differences in the social milieus of the tracked classes were also found. In the high-track classes, teachers were perceived as more concerned and supportive; peers were often seen as nonthreatening allies. Students in low-track classes more often characterized their teachers as punitive and fellow students as unfriendly; their classes were more often seen as permeated with alienation, distance, and hostility.

What these students experienced in their classrooms shed considerable light on how equality of opportunity is manifested in classrooms. Despite meritocratic justifications and democratic intent, these data show an unequal distribution of learning opportunities in a direction that favors the already privileged. In the name of equal opportunity, track levels in schools, reflective of social and economic groupings in society, are provided with differential access to school opportunities that is likely to maintain or increase, rather than erase, the inequities in the larger social structure.

THE CONTEXT OF EDUCATIONAL OPPORTUNITY

To understand how schools arrived at this particular refinement of "separate-but-equal" one needs to look at the historical, political, and social context of differentiated students within schools. Shortly after the turn of the 20th century, as universal public secondary schooling was becoming a reality, the notions of equal opportunity and differentiated schooling converged in both the rhetoric and the organization of the urban high school. In 1908, the Boston school superintendent asserted, "Until very recently they [the schools] have offered equal opportunity for all to receive *one* kind of education, but what will make them democratic is to provide opportunity for all to receive such education as will fit them *equally well* for their particular life work" (Lazerson, 1974). Testing, tracking, and vocational education were the practices instituted to provide these equal opportunities. Both the rhetoric and the practices have changed little in this century.

Several related changes shaped the character of turn-of-the-century America: a switch from craftsman-based to industrial production, a population shift toward urban centers, a huge influx of poor, unskilled, and non-English-speaking immigrants, and the expansion of secondary schooling. Together they constituted a transformation of the economic, social, and political realities. All played a part in redefining the American conception of a democratic society. A central focus of this redefinition was establishing the prevailing 20th-century version of the relationship between equality and schooling. What resulted were the principles of equal educational opportunity outlined above.

The ideas undergirding these principles did not materialize from thin air. The air was thick with theories about the relationship of schooling to economic production and work, the value of a meritocracy, human evolution and the superiority of Anglo-Saxon cultures, and the unlimited potential of science and industry. A brief review of these ideas provides insight into the context of both turn-of-the-century and current definitions of educational equality.

School and Work

For the first time, students who would not become scholars, professionals, or gentle men were attending secondary schools. The traditional academic curriculum seemed a mismatch, especially for immigrants who were difficult to keep in school. Yet it seemed important and humane to postpone these children's entry into the grind of factory life. At the same time industrial employers needed immigrants socialized with the work habits and attitudes required to "fit in" as factory workers (proper deportment, punctuality, willingness to be supervised and managed) and, perhaps less important, technical skills. Native-born youth needed a changed conception of work as well. The autonomy and complexity of a craftsman-based workforce were of the past. Work in the factory required respect for the industrial, in part to make the monotony of factory work tolerable. These requirements of industry coincided with the curricular vacuum in schools. Preparation for work became a central mission of secondary schools (Edson, 1982).

Social Darwinism and Differentiated Education

The misapplication of the theories of Charles Darwin to human society—social Darwinism—provided a *scientific* basis for viewing immigrant and minority groups as of lesser social and moral development than others. Their lives of squalor could be accounted for biologically, just as the disproportionate economic and social power held by men of Anglo stock could be justified by their "fitness." This misapplied social Darwinism, too, explained the disproportionate school failure and "retardation" rates of immigrant children. They failed because they were incapable, biologically unfit for an academic curriculum. The provision of different school content for these children—namely, industrial training—seemed not only democratic, but humane. Tracking into vocational or academic programs clearly provided equal opportunities for students with such inherently different capabilities (Hall, 1905).

Americanization and Anglo-Conformity

Not surprisingly, given social Darwinism, the languages and habits of the southern and eastern European immigrants were threatening to native-born Americans. They were numerous, strikingly different, and poor. There emerged a great concern about preserving the dominant WASP culture, eliminating the immigrants' "depraved" life style, and making the cities safe. It seemed absolutely necessary to bring the foreign-born into the American cultural mainstream by teaching them the Protestant American values of hard work, frugality, modesty, cleanliness, truthfulness, and purity of thought and action. The program to do so, closely aligned with preparation for work, was termed Americanization and located in the public schools. The rhetoric was one of an American melting pot, but in reality only certain people were to be melted. Americanization was driven both by a belief in the goodness of Anglo ways and by fear of the immigrants. Along with industrialism, Americanization provided much of the content of educational opportunities that were provided the children of the poor (Cremin, 1964).

Scientific Management

The concept of industrial efficiency shaped the *form* schooling would take to provide different but equal educations. The country had fallen in love with the idea of the factory busily engaged in a neatly standardized and controlled process of mass production. In went raw materials and, through the application of scientifically determined "best" methods and tools, out came ready-made goods and machinery—all designed to improve the quality of American life. The essence of the factory was efficiency. Human energies were controlled, coordinated, and channeled into machine-like parts, with little waste of material or duplication of effort. The "Taylor System" of scientific management made possible a system of production based on top-down decision making, a rigid division of labor, elaborate rules and regulations, and an attitude of impersonality toward the individual (Nelson, 1980). Schoolmen welcomed and often spearheaded the incorporation of "scientific management" into schools. Compared with the factory, schools seemed to be inefficient and unsuccessful. In an era of specifiable and measurable outcomes, what better way to manage the diversity of children's abilities and provide different educational opportunities than through the infusion of division of labor, standardization, specialization, and a division of labor into the schools?

Meritocracy

Fundamental to American conceptions of democracy is the principle that, while material rewards need not be distributed equally among citizens, the contest for these rewards must be fair. The American view of a "fair" contest is that it be won by effort and ability rather than by inherited status and privilege. Because of the central role of schools in preparing for work, educational opportunities determined by merit were seen as the fair and neutral means of providing access to economic rewards. The development of intelligence testing lent a "scientific objectivity" to the assignment of students to different curricula. Predictions about the appropriate futures of students could be made on the basis of their scores and then the requisite training could be provided.[2] It was clear from the beginning that the different educational opportunities were not equally valued. After all, they led to quite different social and economic outcomes. That poor and immigrant children consistently demonstrated the least merit and were consistently placed in the least-valued programs was not troublesome given belief in the link between race, inherited social and economic status, and ability.

THE STRUGGLE FOR EQUALITY

Even with meritocratic selection, the consistent and obvious disproportionate placement of poor and minority students in inferior school programs required justification consistent with liberal and democratic intents. By mid-century biological explanations of group differences in capability gave way to environmental ones. Cultural deficits explained the gaps in achievement between minority and white student achievement. Poor and minority family life was disorganized, noncompetitive, and anti-intellectual; it provided little motivation for learning. The admission of environmental causes of inequities led, by the '60s, to efforts to use the regulatory power of government to "equalize" the competition by ameliorating these race and class barriers. Importantly, however, neither the neutrality of schools nor the concept of equal opportunity was questioned in these "compensatory" education efforts. School failure resided in the characteristics of the students, and it was these characteristics that must be altered. The influence of Darwinism had largely disappeared, but blaming the victim remained intact (Ryan, 1976). If disadvantaged children could begin school with a "head start," or be permitted to "catch up," equal results for children of various backgrounds would surely follow.

When equal results did not follow, political and social pressure led to the provision of more and more educational resources to poor and minority education. Generous funding was given to those programs that did not upset (a) the control of education, (b) the content or organization of schooling, (c) the pattern of distribution of educational resources, or (d) eventual social and economic payoff for differing educational credentials.

Some reform did question the *principles* of equality of opportunity. This questioning led to demands for educational interventions into previously protected areas. Affirmative action threatened "equal" competition for access; multicultural and bilingual education threatened the Anglo-conformity content and process of schooling (Banks, 1981; Cheng, Brizendine, & Oakes, 1979; Grant, 1977); and minority community control of schools, as in Ocean Hill-Brownsville, threatened elite power over education. Distributing educational resources on the basis of distributive justice threatened the concept of meritocracy (Bell, 1973). The push for reforms to enhance collective good, rather than individual gain (Cagan, 1978), threatened the very heart of society, i.e., individual competition for unequal economic benefits. And in fact those programs that called for significant restructuring to benefit poor and minority children were generally ignored, aborted, or only superficially implemented. What implementation did take place was accompanied by very little enthusiasm, great suspicion, and the closest of scrutiny (looking primarily for failures). For most people in decision-making positions, the only acceptable means of "equalizing" educational opportunities was to allocate additional resources to overcome deficits—to change individual students rather than to change the conduct of schooling or to examine its underlying assumptions.

What deserves our attention is not the evidence of a mid-century move toward greater equality. Far more striking is the evidence of the resilience of the ideology of opportunity and the intransigence of the essential structural properties of schooling.

Even in a period of abundant educational spending and generosity toward poor and minority children, differentiated schooling remained essentially unchanged; its justification with notions of individual and cultural differences and democratic opportunity remained virtually unchallenged.

THE SPECTRE OF SCARCITY

Seeing the mid-century push for better schooling for poor and minorities not as an *equalization* of education, but as an *extension* of educational opportunity permitted by a period of affluence and global supremacy, permits a clearer understanding of the retrenchment that quickly followed it. The 25 years following World War II were marked by unprecedented economic growth and material abundance. While this growth did not eliminate poverty, there was widespread optimism about prosperity trickling down to the poor. While inequalities and relative deprivation might still exist, in a period of abundance absolute deprivation could be alleviated.

The education enterprise experienced parallel surges in the amount of education and in the number of children served by the system of public schools. Demands for increased education were voiced by poor and ethnic minorities since schooling was seen as the means for commanding a greater share of the expanding wealth. The special needs and demands of poor and minority children in public schools were met by providing these children with additional educational resources, nearly always in the form of extra programs designed to ameliorate their background deficiencies and the difficulties they experienced in regular school programs. The add-on approach to enhancing educational opportunities and providing "equality" in schools was perfectly compatible with an expanding economy and abundant resources. In these times of seeming unlimited prosperity, society could provide Head Start, lunches, job training, and the like. Society could afford to be generous, even charitable, with the underprivileged. While these educational opportunities did begin to narrow the gap in educational attainment between the rich and the poor, they did not lead to any significant redistribution of economic, political, social, or educational power.

The 1970s, however, brought a set of social, political, and economic events that called this approach into serious question. For the first time, the prospects for unlimited economic growth and material abundance were called into question. The American economy reeled, first from the inflationary legacy of the Vietnam war and then from a dramatic rise in energy prices as Third World oil producers flexed their collective muscles. The second half of the decade of the '70s was plagued with inflation, recession, and unemployment.

Two quite different responses to the ecological and economic crises were voiced by scientists, politicians, and economists. One stressed the acceptance of the reality of shrinking world resources and encouraged the development of a cooperative human society in harmony with nature toward a no-growth end (see, e.g., Boulding, 1973; Commoner, 1977; Heilbroner, 1974; Schumacher, 1973). The second denied the doomsday prediction and condemned the limited vision of its spokespersons (see, e.g., Kahn, Brown, & Martel, 1976; Lipset, 1979; Macrae, 1972).

With the defeat of Jimmy Carter and the election of Ronald Reagan, the American public turned over political power to the champions of this second response. Government tinkering with the free play of the marketplace and excessive spending on social programs were blamed for inhibiting expansion, suppressing productivity, providing an easy life on the public dole, and leading to the current economic woes. "Social tinkering" had had a destructive effect on the healing and generating forces of economic growth, i.e. personal incentive, thrift, and hard work.[3] Economic recovery required a return to the values and approaches—hard work, free enterprise, and American ingenuity—that had earlier accompanied growth and prosperity. Government action must be limited to two goals: (a) eliminating controls and restrictions on the marketplace and (b) providing incentives to those with the talent, skills, and resources to spearhead the new technological advances. Gains to all would result from the "trickling down" of economic benefits. Needless to say, this approach has had ramifications for the schools.

TRICKLE-DOWN EXCELLENCE

Schools, as Seymour Sarason has so insightfully commented, serve as both scapegoats and sources of salvation (Sarason, 1983). That, of course, is the most salient message of current reforms. Although there have been hundreds of reports and state reform initiatives during the past two years, the tenor of reform is still best articulated in the 1983 round of commission reports. Their tone and substance have become recurrent themes in the educational pronouncements of politicians. Most states have followed their recommendations quite consistently in their efforts to upgrade their schools.

As the reports make plain, the current reform movement both blames schools for our current post-industrial economic woes and places on them the hope for recovery. We are all by now quite familiar with the warning in *A Nation at Risk* that "the educational foundations of our society are presently being eroded by a rising tide of mediocrity that threatens our very future as a Nation and as a people" (NCEE, 1983, p. 5). The reassertion of American dominance of a world of diminishing resources, voiced in terms of keeping and improving the "slim competitive edge we still retain in world markets," (p. 5) will result from re-establishing educational excellence in schools. "Knowledge, learning, information, and skilled intelligence are the new raw materials of international commerce and are today spreading throughout the world as vigorously as miracle drugs, synthetic fertilizers, and blue jeans did earlier" (p. 7). Given this conception of education itself as the medium of economic exchange it is not surprising that the report *Action for Excellence* claims, "Our future success as a nation—our national defense, our social stability and well-being and our national prosperity—will depend on our ability to improve education and training" (TFEEG, 1983, p. 14).

Equality issues are central to both the diagnoses of current educational troubles and the prescriptions for educational reform. The theme consistent in the diagnoses and prescriptions is that we have made a grave error in trying to be all things to all people. We have "squandered the gains in student achievement made in the wake of the Sputnik challenge" (NCEE, 1983, p. 5). After noting that efforts during the '60s and '70s to improve educational opportunities resulted in increased achievement for black students, *Action for Excellence* continues with an indictment of that era: "The fact remains, however, that overall performance in higher-order skills . . . declined in the seventies. . . . This suggests that we may be regressing from the standard of literacy which was considered adequate 15 years ago" (TFEEG, 1983, p. 24). The clear implication is that the price of extending educational opportunities was a decline in educational quality. Furthermore, providing resources to improve achievement exacted a social and economic price greater than the benefits received. *Making the Grade* is blatant in this regard: "Its [the federal government's] emphasis on promoting equality of opportunity in the public schools has meant a slighting of its commitment to educational quality" (TCF, 1983, p. 6).

The thrust of educational reform, then, is toward economic recovery through increased productivity and technological growth. Schools are to provide salvation from the crises of the '70s. The road to this salvation is clearly reflective of these crises and the lingering spectre of scarcity—even in the face of optimistic presidential promises for the future. It is clear that the central problem viewed by the makers of the reform reports is not an educational one. Educational issues have meaning only as they bear upon the issues of "real life": jobs, security, stability, defense, prosperity, and so on. And equality is given even less concern; it is tolerable as a goal only to the degree it is not perceived to stand in the way of these more important issues. And since the "real life" issues are so inextricably tied to perceptions of scarcity and abundance, education itself has meaning largely in the context of its contributions to the "good (economic) life"—Sarason's "salvation." Conversely, to the degree that prosperity, economic well-being, and so on are found wanting, all of education is suspect—Sarason's "scapegoat." If education is primarily a means to the goal of material well-being, it is not surprising that equality in education would receive little attention—no one has proven how to make equality pay. Still further, if equality is perceived as operating *against* life's real purposes (abundance) then it is all the easier to lay equality to rest with the claims that (a) we can't afford it, (b) it's bad for excellence, or (c) we solved the problem in the '60s.

It is in this context that current school reforms must be understood. Energy and resources for education are viewed as scarce. They must be expended judiciously and selectively with an eye toward maximizing economic returns. *Action for Excellence* seeks "more money *selectively invested* in efforts that promote quality" (TFEEG, 1983, p. 36). *Making the Grade* calls for public "report cards" assessing the effectiveness of funded programs (TCF, 1983, p. 18). Selective investment translates into extraordinary attention to preparing students for careers in scientific and technological fields and inattention to the worsening economic plight of the poor. This selectivity results in a reduced willingness to devote educational resources to poor and ethnic minority children. It is on those at the top that economic hopes, and therefore educational resources, are pinned.

It is in this regard that the College Board's report *Academic Preparation for College* (College Board, 1983) is of interest. The report focuses exclusively on the educational needs of the college-bound and is grounded in the view that improving college preparation is the first step toward educational reform. It is striking that a report so focused (and generated by an organization whose self-interest rests in the sale of SAT examinations) has assumed the status of a national report.[4] It symbolizes the current nearly exclusive attention on education for those students who can fulfill the hope for economic supremacy. In the current prevailing view, the provision of special opportunities or extra resources to those perceived as providing limited social and economic returns is a luxury permitted only in times of abundance. For these less promising students, financial stringency prohibits spending anything beyond what is required for preventing social disorganization (dropping out) and providing the minimum levels of competency required for low-level employment.

Still, those at the bottom are seen as benefiting educationally from this current emphasis. A more rigorously academic program at the top will create better programs for all students, it is claimed. Expanded course requirements and numbers of days and hours in school will benefit all—regardless of the differences that may exist inside their schools and classrooms. In this concentration of attention and resources on the best students there is clearly an expression of a "trickle-down" approach to educational excellence that parallels the prevailing mode of providing economic benefits. Emphasis on quality for those at the top will result in an enhanced quality of education for students throughout the system. This mood is made explicit by The College Board:

> Better preparation for the college-bound will spill over and improve the schooling of those who are not college-bound. . . . Just as the Advanced Placement Program has "rubbed off" on other teaching and learning in the schools, so better college preparation will strengthen the education of those who go directly from high school into the world of work or into the military. (Bailey, 1983, p. 25)

In all of this, little has really changed. The reform proposals are clearly shaped by the public response to scarcity. But the neglect of equality cannot be entirely explained as a response to the current economic crises. It must be viewed also in light of a neo-conservative reassertion of the turn-of-the-century values and beliefs considered earlier, beliefs that emerge virtually unaltered in the proposals for reform. The current crises have led to the stripping away of added-on programs that for a few years masked, but did not change, the fundamentally unequal structure of schooling.

Like the early 20th-century educational advocates, none of the current reformers state that equality should be sacrificed in the quest for excellence in schools. They even purport to uphold equality. But the view of equality presented—mostly by omission—is one firmly lodged in (a) a presumption of the neutrality of schools, (b) an Anglo-conformist perspective on educational excellence, and (c) faith in objective, quantifiable specifications of educational standards. From these proceeds a narrowly meritocratic allocation of educational opportunities and rewards. All of the above are simply variations on earlier themes—themes laid bare in times of crisis.

The Neutrality of Schools (Social Darwinism Revisited)

In their general indictment of schools, the authors of the reform reports do not attach particular importance to the fact that schools fail to serve all students equally well. Consequently, they do not consider as targets for reform the school content and processes that limit school achievement for poor and minority students. Schools are seen as essentially neutral, and the reforms are presented as color-blind and affluence-blind. The failure of disadvantaged children (especially if they have had the additional benefits of remediation, free lunches, or other "compensatory" help) becomes a matter of their own deficiencies—social, economic, educational, or linguistic—and not of the schools' inadequate response to them. Social and economic inequalities are not seen as affecting students' access to high educational expectations or excellent treatment in school. All children are seen as entrants in an equal, fair, and neutral competition.

Current reform efforts do not address the unequal quality of school facilities, programs, materials, counseling, expectations, and instruction. No interest is shown, for example, in the unequal distribution of competent teachers. Neither do they address school organizational changes likely to equalize access to high-quality educational contexts—desegregation, the elimination of tracking, and reconceptualizing vocational education programs, for example. Even as an issue is made emphatically of increasing the skills and knowledge of teachers, the assumption is that teachers simply need to get better at what they've always done. There is little or no mention of the need for teachers to be more knowledgeable about how poverty, racism, and limited expectations affect the educational treatment of poor and minority children. The omission of these concerns makes clear the prevailing conviction that schools, *as they are now*, are neutral places. While many faults are found with schools, unfairness is not one.

Special resources are seen as necessary to provide separate and different schooling for those children with deficits that prevent them from succeeding in the neutral process of schooling. The assumption that poor and minority children are *unable* to learn lurks close to the surface of these recommendations. It certainly lies behind the assertion in *A Nation at Risk* that disadvantaged children (along with other "special needs" children—gifted and learning disabled) constitute a "thin-Market area" in education. They are a group of students for whom *regular* instructional approaches are not suited. That these regular approaches themselves might be a source of disadvantage is unthinkable, given the assumption of school neutrality. And given this inattention to the race and class bias of schooling, *A Nation at Risk*'s final admonition to students becomes a sad and painful message to the poor and nonwhite:

> In the end it is *your* work that determines how much and how well you learn. When you work to your full capacity, you can hope to attain the knowledge and skills that will enable you to create your future and control your destiny. If you do not, you will have your future thrust upon you by others. Take hold of your life, apply your gifts and talents, work with dedication and self-discipline. Have high expectations for yourself and convert every challenge into an opportunity. (NCEE, 1983, pp. 35–36)

A Single Standard of Excellence (Return to Anglo-Conformity)

The elements proposed as the content and processes of excellent schooling are clearly reflective of Anglo-conformist values. Definitions of quality and standards are those that have historically served to discriminate against youngsters who are poor or members of ethnic minorities. There is nothing pluralistic or democratic about the educational content and processes that currently define "excellence." Perhaps *Making the Grade* is most straight-forward in this regard. In a major section entitled "The Primacy of English," the report recommends that bilingual programs be replaced with programs "to teach non-English-speaking children how to speak, read, and write English" and calls the failure of bilingual programs to assert the primacy of English "a grave error" (TCF, 1983, p. 12). There is no recognition of the unique contributions of different cultures or of the special problems that arise from a history of discrimination and racism. There is not even a recognition that cultural differences are legitimate and can contribute to a broad general education for all American students.

Provisions of compensatory education are not to be interpreted as provisions for pluralism or, in the words of *Making the Grade*, "abandoning a single standard of excellence. There cannot be a white standard or black standard or a Hispanic standard when measuring educational performance" (TCF, 1983, p. 22). This statement ignores the fact that there is a single standard posed in the reports, and that standard is undeniably white and middle-class.

Listen also to Secretary of Education William Bennett's response to a Latino teacher who had pleaded for a multicultural, multi-ethnic perspective in California schools. Bennett asserted, "I don't think it's the job of the public schools to introduce you to your grandparents" ("Bennett Says," 1985). Set next to Bennett's call for a reemphasis on the history and thought of Western Civilization in undergraduate collegiate eduction, the point becomes clear. Being introduced to your grandparents is an irrelevant educational matter—unless your grandparents represent the dominant cultural tradition. The current move in the Department of Eduction to dismantle bilingual education is a logical outgrowth of this perspective. Pluralism is seen as an intolerable shift from current dominance of Anglo values and interests.

At the same time, it is clear that what is valued for students with little academic promise is a quite different version of Anglo-conformity than that for the best students. The current system of differentiated curricula through tracking and ability grouping is clearly meant to be continued. The same subjects, the same "five new basics" of *A Nation at Risk*, are to be learned by everyone. But whereas the favored students will be helped to develop an *understanding* of science, mathematics, technology, and foreign language, a very different and "minimum-competency" education is envisioned for the rest who will be needed to fill low-status service jobs in a post-industrial economy. The emphasis for disadvantaged students is much as it has been, an emphasis on low-level basic literacy and computation skills (Oakes, 1985). There is no presumption that high-status knowledge is equally appropriate for all.

The Commodification of Educational Opportunity (Scientific Management Intensified)

In the current push for productivity, education is increasingly treated as a commodity, measurable by objective tests. Like the scientific managers early in the century, current reformers appear to consider notions such as learning, knowledge, and experience to be soft and airy words unless they can be translated into numbers. Quantification, as expressed in the reports, is used as a quality-control check against the educational "factory worker" who might otherwise certify as "safe" high-risk minorities and poor. This emphasis on quantitative measures, in fact, signals a lack of trust in the responsibility of educators and their professional judgment (see Sirotnik & Goodlad, 1985). A disturbing result is that quantitative determinations of quality have a disproportionately negative effect on poor and minority children (Gould, 1981; Wigdu, 1982). Witness the disproportionate placement of black males in classes for the educable mentally retarded based on standardized ability tests (Heller, Holtzman, & Messick, 1983).

A Narrowed Meritocracy ("Opportunity . . . as will fit them equally well for their particular life work")

As a marketable commodity, education is increasingly subject to the same individualistic, competitive, acquisitive norms as are material goods (Slaughter, 1985). These norms are all grounded in the presumption of inequality. And in a period of perceived scarcity, there is likely to be a shift in how the poor are provided for. In fact, the meager level of concern in the reports for those on the bottom of the schooling hierarchy clearly indicates "stinginess" in the distribution of educational goods. It is painfully clear that the least promising students are expected to do least well. Staying in school, passing an eighth-grade proficiency test, getting a job, not being a criminal, and staying off welfare become "success" indicators. No report advocates substantive reforms to keep larger number of poor and minority students in schools or improve the quality of what they experience there. The expectations for poor and minority students, in other words, are far lower than in the reform proposals of a more abundant time.

The conception of school as a meritocracy is clearly reflective of the belief that some students can learn and others cannot or will not. In current reforms, promotion, assignment to various programs, graduation, and the kind of diploma received are all to be governed by merit in terms of objective measures of student learning. The fact that retention and low-track placement do not lead to increased student learning is irrelevant (see Larabee, 1984). As part of a meritocratic system, retention and low-track placement serve primarily to deny advancement in the educational system of those *not worthy*. "Student progress should be measured through periodic tests of general achievement and specific skills; promotion from grade to grade should be based on mastery, not age" (TFEE, p. 11).

Separate educations based on meritocratic selection within schools (tracking) or at different schools are recommended in several of the reports for students who do well or poorly on tests. *A Nation at Risk* suggests "placement and grouping . . . should be guided by the academic progress of students" (NCEE, 1983, p. 30) and proposes "alternative classrooms, programs, and schools" for those students who don't conform to expected standards of behavior (p. 29). *Making the Grade* calls for federal stipends to allow those "unable to learn in public schools" to attend "small-scale academies." "Such an experiment . . . would free up the substantial resources now being spent on remediation with so little to show for it" (p. 20).

Little attention is paid to rethinking classroom instruction or school organization in such a way as to promote the achievement of poor children. The only concern raised about the race/class consequences of tracking or testing criteria as standards of excellence is in a footnote of *Making the Grade* (TCF, 1983, p. 20). No concern is evidenced regarding the "dead-end" educational experiences of segregated groups of poor students with curricula aimed at passing minimum competency exams (see Darling-Hammond & Wise, 1985, for a review of this literature). Providing different curricula for different students, as at the turn of the century, is seen as the appropriate way of meeting "individual needs." These are individual needs seen in terms of intellectual limits, not as means of enabling students to develop higher-order knowledge and skills. One commission member contributing to *Making the Grade* asserts, "I believe the mixing in the same class of students with vastly differing abilities in the name of equality has been a retrogressive step" (TCF, 1983, p. 21). Funding for children with special needs—poverty or handicaps—is to be used to support separate programs. No provisions for special access to the best educational programs—such as open admission to enriched programs, cultural criteria for placement in special programs for the gifted and talented, or affirmative action programs—are suggested.

The retreat to this narrowly meritocratic approach to the allocation of school opportunities and rewards is justified in part by the perceived successes of prior equality efforts. Both *A Nation at Risk* and *Action for Excellence* laud the gains in opportunity and achievement over the last 30 years. It is as if past wrongs have been redressed and it is now fair to return to the real purpose of education: excellence.

REFORM AND EQUALITY

Of course, all of the current reform proposals acknowledge educational equity as a national interest. *Educating Americans for the 21st Century*, the report of the National Science Board (NSB, 1983), has equity as a major theme. But little in the current discussion suggests an interest in reaching beyond turn-of-the-century conceptions of social Darwinism and meritocracy to equality in access to knowledge, skills, and educational experiences. Where the reports call for equality as well as excellence, they seem to lack conviction, and they provide no strategies toward this end. As with the emergence in the '80s of economic policies of a much earlier era, the school reforms exhibit a retrenchment into the values of an earlier time. Priorities are set according to prevailing economic interests—which value most highly the kind of human capital development likely to lead to the biggest payoff in the current economic crisis. At the same time, these priorities are also consistent with the interests of the professional elite that dominates educational institutions. It would be a mistake to doubt the sincerity of most educational reformers. It is clearly too crass to suggest that they are setting out deliberately to perpetuate privilege. If overt, villainous intent were the culprit, these problems would be more easily solved. It is harder to engage the well-intended in the critical scrutiny of prevailing assumptions than to oust rascals from positions of influence.

Given the educational "reforms" of the '60s and early '70s (which may have been of considerable benefit to many minority and poor individuals, but did little to change their relative educational or economic position), we may conclude that in times of prosperity a good bit of money may be spent in efforts to create illusions of the fairest possible meritocracy. To the extent that disadvantaged individuals can be helped without jeopardizing the overall structure or control of society, so much the better. (In fact, whatever their motivation, such programs can and do change lives; they deserve a hard fight to retain even if the ground in which they are sown is so infertile as to produce only marginal yields.) In times of scarcity, however, the costs of these "equalizing" programs are deemed intolerable. Recipients of special help are perceived as responsible for the decline of not only their own well-being, but the well-being of the socio-economic classes they supposedly aspire to join.

Only three years have passed since the nation's interest turned to educational reform, and it is too early for a full assessment. But reform has become national policy and the themes of the 1983 reports are sounded repeatedly in the statements of both the President and the Secretary of Education. Several states and hundreds of local school districts have rushed to implement reforms, and a number of scholars have assessed their likely effects. And, of course, many of the specific reforms were well underway at the time of the 1983 reports. In many respects the commissions only heralded and reiterated changes conceived in the economic crises and tax revolts of the 1970s.

Time adds conviction to the suspicion that the reforms will work largely to the advantage of those who are already well-off. Through differentiated schooling experiences, attention will be turned from the difficulties of those served less well by schools. Highly motivated, able students will be offered every opportunity to achieve in ways that will strengthen the US quest for technological, economic, and military supremacy. That the distribution of school achievement has racial and socio-economic dimensions is regrettable, but, as a consequence, there is little expectation that poor and minority children will contribute greatly to the national self-interest. While our humane and democratic ideology requires extending educational resources and opportunity to poor and minority children, the most pressing need at present is to cultivate those children with superior abilities, since they are seen as most likely to provide some relief from our national troubles.

All indications are that the current reform movement will produce success defined in its own terms: Children will spend more hours and days in school, more coursework will be taken in mathematics, science, and technology, and mean achievement test scores will probably rise. But beyond indicators of movement toward "excellence" (higher numbers) lies evidence of an ominous side of reform. We can already see a declining college attendance rate for minorities, increased underrepresentation of minorities in postgraduate and professional education, limited access of minority students to computers in schools and to instruction in programming, disproportionately large enrollment of minority students in low-track classes and high enrollment of whites in programs for the gifted, and disproportionately high failure rates on minimum competency tests for minority students.

The lack of evidence of advantages having "trickled-down" is not unique to education. While those at the top have declared the recovery to be in full swing, those at the bottom of the economic hierarchy experience a different reality. Today 20 million Americans—two thirds of whom are children—are estimated to be hungry, a dramatic shift from the "virtual elimination" of hunger in the 1970s (Physicians Task Force on Hunger, 1985). In current policies, social justice programs are seen as harmful to economic growth, just as equitable schooling policies are seen as destructive to educational excellence. For tangible benefits in either sphere, children who are poor and nonwhite must continue to wait.

NOTES

1. A Study of Schooling was a comprehensive inquiry into a national sample of schools. Results of the study are reported in Goodlad (1984).
2. As an aside, it should be noted that "scientifically" normed intelligence tests spearheaded the rationale for *all* testing even to the point of schoolwide testing and grade-level testing— even into the classroom. So, much of the "real work" of intelligence testing quickly passed down to schools and teachers, where poorer performance on tests, "scientific" or otherwise, justified the daily reinforcement of merit.
3. See Kuttner (1984) for a fascinating counter-argument to the negative influence of social justice programs on economic health.
4. It needs to be noted, however, that the College Board's Equality Project, from which the report came, pays far more attention to the provision of both opportunities and improved educational treatment for minority students than do most current proposals. See, for example, the report *Equality and Excellence: The Educational Status of Black Americans* (College Board, 1985).

REFERENCES

Bailey, A.Y. (1983). The educational equality project: Focus on results. *Kappan, 65* (September), 22–25.

Banks, J.R. (Ed.). (1981). *Education in the 80's: Multiethnic education.* Washington, DC: National Education Association.

Bell, D. (1973). *The coming of post-industry society.* New York: Basic Books.

Bennett says he is "consumer advocate." (1985). *Los Angeles Times*, March 3, p. 1.

Boulding, K. E. (1973). The shadow of a stationary state. *Daedalus*, 102, 93.

Cagan, E. (1978). Individualism, collectivism, and radical educational reform. *Harvard Educational Review, 48*, 227–266.

Cheng, C. W., Brizendine, E., & Oakes, J. (1979). What is an "equal chance" for minority children. *Journal of Negro Education, 48*, 267–287.

College Board. (1983). *Academic preparation for college: What students need to know and be able to do.* New York: College Board.

College Board. (1985). *Equality and excellence: The education status of black Americans.* New York: College Board.

Commoner, B. (1977). *The Poverty of Power.* New York: Bantam.

Cremin, L. A. (1964). *The Transformation of the school.* New York: Random House.

Darling-Hammond, L., & Wise, A. (1985). Beyond standardization: State standards and school improvement. *Elementary School Journal, 85*, 315–336.

Edson, C. H. (1982). Schooling for work and working at school: Perspectives on immigrant and working-class education in urban America, 1880–1920. In R. B. Everhart, (Ed.), *The public school monopoly.* Cambridge, MA: Ballinger.

Goodlad, J. I. (1984). *A place called school.* New York: McGraw-Hill.

Gould, S. J. (1981). *The mismeasure of man.* New York: W. W. Norton.

Grant, C. (Ed.) (1977). *Multicultural education: Commitments, issues, and applications.* Washington, DC: ASCD.

Hall, G. S. (1905). *Adolescence: Its psychology and its relations to physiology, anthropology, sociology, sex, crime, religion, and education.* New York: D. Appleton.

Heilbroner, R. L. (1974). *An inquiry into the human prospect.* New York: W. W. Norton.

Heller, K., Holtzman, W., & Messick, S. (Eds.) (1983). *Placing children in special education: Strategies for equity.* Washington, DC: National Academy Press.

Kahn, H., Brown, W., & Martel, L. (1976). *The next 200 years: A scenario for America and the world.* New York: Morrow.

Kuttner, R. (1984). *The economic illusion: False choices between prosperity and social justice.* Boston: Houghton-Mifflin.

Larabee, D. F. (1984). Setting the standard: Alternative policies for student promotion. *Harvard Educational Review, 54*, 67–87.

Lazerson, M. (1974). *Origins of the urban school.* Cambridge: Harvard University Press.

Lipset, S.M. (1978). Growth, affluence, and the limits of futurology. In *From abundance to scarcity: Implications for the American tradition.* Columbus: Ohio State University Press.

Macrae, N. (1972). The future of international business. *Economist, 22* (January), 5–7.

NCEE (National Commission on Excellence in Education). (1983). *A nation at risk: The imperative for educational reform.* Washington, DC: Government Printing Office.

NSB (National Science Board Commission on Precollege Education in Mathematics, Science, and Technology). (1983). *Educating Americans for the 21st century.* Washington, DC: National Science Foundation.

Nelson, D. (1980). *Fredrick W. Taylor and the rise of scientific management.* Madison: University of Wisconsin Press.

Oakes, J. (1985). *Keeping track: How schools structure inequality.* New Haven: Yale University Press.

Physicians Task Force on Hunger Report. (1985). Cambridge, MA: Harvard University Press.

Ryan, W. (1976). *Blaming the victim.* New York: Vintage Books.

Sarason, S. B. (1983). *Schooling in America: Scapegoat and salvation.* New York: The Free Press.

Schumacher, E. F. (1973). *Small is beautiful.* New York: Harper & Row.

Sirotnik, K. A., & Goodlad, J. I. (1985). The quest for reason amidst the rhetoric of reform: Improving instead of testing our schools. In W. J. Johnson (Ed.), *Education on trial: A midterm report.* San Francisco: Institute for Contemporary Studies.

Slaughter, S. (1985). *The pedagogy of profit: National commission reports on education.* Unpublished manuscript, State University of New York, Buffalo.

TCF (Twentieth Century Fund). (1983). *Making the grade: Report of the task force on federal elementary and secondary education policy.* New York: Twentieth Century Fund.

TFEEG (Task Force on Education and Economic Growth). (1983). *Action for excellence.* Washington, DC: Economic Commission of the States.

Wigder, S. (1982). *Ability-testing, uses and consequences.* Washington, DC: National Academy Press.

Reform versus Reality

Harold Hodgkinson

To begin, think of the following analogy. American education is like a house. This house was beautiful and well maintained, one of the nicest houses in the world. But over time, the owners allowed the house to deteriorate. First, a leak in the roof developed, allowing water to enter the attic, then to trickle down to the second floor, and then to the main floor. Floors buckled, plaster fell from the walls, electric systems rusted, windows began to fall out. The owners, returning after a long absence, hastily repaired the windows, the plaster, and the electric motors—but they neglected to fix the roof. The owners were surprised and angry when, after all their efforts, the house continued to deteriorate.

Basically, the publication of *A Nation at Risk* marked the return of the owners after a long absence to find education's house badly deteriorated. The first major sign of deterioration was declining scores on the Scholastic Aptitude Test (SAT), which Americans often hold to be *the* single barometer of educational quality. Since that time, a blizzard of education reform proposals has fallen, and states have raised the graduation standards for high schools, installed minimum standards for moving from one grade to the next, required new teachers to pass special examinations before being allowed to teach, instituted choice and magnet school programs, and so on.

But so far, there has been no change in high school graduation rates, in most test scores, or in other indicators of "quality." After nearly a decade, we have fixed the plaster in education's house, installed new windows, and repaired the electric motors. *But the roof still leaks.* Until we fix the roof, the house continues to deteriorate.

The leaky roof in our educational house is a metaphor for the spectacular changes that have occurred in the nature of the children who come to school. Until we pay attention to these changes, our tinkering with the rest of the house will

Harold Hodgkinson, "Reform versus Reality." *Phi Delta Kappa*, Volume 73, No. 1. Reprinted with permission of Harold Hodgkinson, Director, Center for Demographic Policy, Washington, D.C.

continue to produce no important results. The fact is that at least one-third of the nation's children are at risk of school failure even before they enter kindergarten. The schools did not cause these deficits, and neither did the youngsters. A few examples may suffice:

- Since 1987, one-fourth of all preschool children in the U.S. have been in poverty.

- Every year, about 350,000 children are born to mothers who were addicted to cocaine during pregnancy. Those who survive birth become children with strikingly short attention spans, poor coordination, and much worse. Of course, the schools will have to teach these children, and getting such children ready for kindergarten costs around $40,000 each—about the same as for children with fetal alcohol syndrome.

- Today, 15 million children are being reared by single mothers, whose family income averages about $11,400 in 1988 dollars (within $1,000 of the poverty line). The average family income for a married couple with children is slightly over $34,000 a year.

- Twenty percent of America's preschool children have not been vaccinated against polio.

- The "Norman Rockwell" family—a working father, a housewife mother, and two children of school age—constitutes only 6% of U.S. households today.

- One-fourth of pregnant mothers receive no physical care of any sort during the crucial first trimester of pregnancy. About 20% of handicapped children would not be impaired had their mothers had one physical exam during the first trimester, which could have detected potential problems.

- At least two million school-age children have no adult supervision at all after school. Two million more are being reared by *neither* parent.

- On any given night, between 50,000 and 200,000 children have no home. (In 1988, 40% of shelter users were families with children.)

- In 1987, child protection agencies received 2.2 million reports of child abuse or neglect—triple the number received in 1976.

This is the nature of education's leaky roof: about one-third of preschool children are destined for school failure because of poverty, neglect, sickness, handicapping conditions, and lack of adult protection and nurturance. There is no point in trying to teach hungry or sick children. From this we can deduce one of the most important points in our attempts to deal with education: *educators can't fix the roof all by themselves.* It will require the efforts of many people and organizations—health and social welfare agencies, parents, business and political leaders—to even begin to repair this leaky roof. There is no time to waste in fixing blame; we need to act to fix the roof. And unless we start, the house will continue to deteriorate, and all Americans will pay the price.

Indeed, the first of the national goals for education outlined by the President and the nation's governors states that, "by the year 2000, all children in America will start school ready to learn." Three of the objectives attached to this goal read as follows:

- All disadvantaged and disabled children will have access to high-quality and developmentally appropriate preschool programs that help prepare children for school.
- Every parent in America will be a child's first teacher and devote time each day to helping his or her preschool child to learn; parents will have access to the training and support they need.
- Children will receive the nutrition and health care needed to arrive at school with healthy minds and bodies, and the number of low-birthweight babies will be significantly reduced through enhanced prenatal health systems.

While these are noble statements about the need to fix the roof, they are not at all informative on how this should be done. (It has been estimated that meeting just the first objective would cost $30 billion to implement.) We need to know more about *why* the roof is leaking—why so many of our children are at risk of failure in school and in life.

The fact is that more than one-third of American children have the deck stacked against them long before they enter school. Although America's best students are on a par with the world's best, ours is undoubtedly the worst "bottom third" of any of the industrialized democracies. We need to take a brief look at the kinds of changes that have brought about this concentration of children at risk.

CHANGES IN THE FAMILY

During the 1980s the American family continued to undergo major changes in its structure (see Table 1). Every kind of "atypical" family increased in number during the decade, while the "typical" family—married couple with children—actually declined in number. Today, almost 50% of America's young people will spend some years before they reach age 18 being raised by a single parent. In 1988, 4.3 million

TABLE 1 U.S. Households, 1980–90

	1980	1990	% Change
All households	80,467,000	93,920,000	+16.7
Family households	59,190,000	66,652,000	+12.4
Married couples	48,990,000	52,837,000	+ 7.9
Married without children	24,210,000	28,315,000	+17.0
Married with children	24,780,000	24,522,000	− 1.0
Single female head	8,205,000	11,130,000	+35.6
Single male head	1,995,000	2,575,000	+29.1
People living alone	18,202,000	22,879,000	+25.7
Living with nonrelatives	3,075,000	4,500,000	+46.3

children were living with a mother who had never married (up 678% since 1970). Few have studied the consequences of being a child of an unmarried mother, but it's hard to think of this situation as an advantage. The 15 million children being raised by single mothers will have about one-third as much to spend on their needs as children being raised by two parents. (When both parents work, family income does not double; it *triples*.) For young children raised by a single mother, day care becomes a *vital educational issue,* as well as a matter of family survival. The 2.5 million fathers raising children by themselves have also discovered the vital nature of day care.

Some things show up clearly in these numbers. First, only about a quarter of America's households have a child in the public schools, a fact that will make school bond elections more difficult to pull off as time goes by. Second, 25 million people live by themselves or with nonrelatives, which explains why America's fertility rates are so low! Third, the feminization of poverty is not just a slogan: 23% of America's smallest children (birth to age 5) live in poverty, the highest rate of any industrialized nation. And many of them have a single parent, often a mother who works at a low-income service job. At present about six million workers in the U.S. earn the minimum wage, and more than five million others are within 50 cents of the minimum wage. Females over 25 with children to support—not teenage males saving for a car—account for the largest proportion of these low-wage workers. These women desperately need job skills to support their children, but they are not well represented in programs supported by the Job Training and Partnership Act or in other training programs.

We can begin to see how these areas interrelate when we think of a single mother with a low income who is raising a child. She must have a place to live; yet there are eight million qualified low-income households trying to play musical chairs with only four million low-income housing units. (Literally no one is building new low-income housing units in the U.S.) She will pay a higher percentage—in some cases more than 50%—of her income for housing than any other category of worker. It is highly unlikely that her living unit will have a quiet place for a child to study.

In addition, this woman must get to work, often on public transportation if she can't afford a car. If her child is a preschooler, she will have to get the child to day care before she gets herself to work, an arrangement that may involve four or more bus trips at the end of each day. (For women in this situation, daycare centers, housing, and jobs are not usually located close to one another.) If the child gets ill, the logistics get even more complex. A missed bus or a conked-out car can mean that the rent cannot be paid. Then the salary check may be changed for a welfare check, a switch that is painful not only to her and her child, but also to the taxpayer who must pay for the switch! (It would be much cheaper for us to prevent her from going into poverty than to pay for the very expensive consequences, including her child being in poverty and the loss of her self-esteem.)

If the President and the nation's governors are serious about the first objective associated with the first national goal, we must deal with this single parent and her child. For this woman and her child (let's call him Carlos), education services, health services. day-care services, transportation services, housing services, and employment services must all function together to prevent Carlos from having a diminished future. Carlos *is* education's leaky roof!

There is no way that the education system alone can be responsible for the economic difficulties of this woman and her son, although educators will have to teach the person who is at the end of the service chain: Carlos. In order for the national goals to be achieved, our leaders will have to think of a way for Carlos and his mother to have an improved base of services so that Carlos will not become a liability to the taxpayer and the nation. This may seem difficult, but Carlos' problems are much easier to solve than those of the 350,000 cocaine-addicted babies born every year. The national goals are silent about such children, although they are already showing up in the schools.

CHANGES IN ETHNIC DISTRIBUTION

One of the good things about the 1990 Census is that we already know many of the most important numbers. For example, the American population grew by 10% between 1980 and 1990, reaching a new total of 249.8 million, an addition of 23 million people. The fastest growing groups are the eldest members of our population: 57,000 Americans are at least 100 years old, according to the 1990 Census, up from 32,000 in 1980. Minority populations also grew rapidly.

Ninety percent of the 23-million-person increase occurred in the South and West, although some eastern states, such as New York and New Jersey, have started growing again. Only *three* states account for almost half of the nation's growth: Texas, Florida, and California increased their populations by a total of 11.7 million. We can link this growth to some political changes if we look at the increased votes in the House of Representatives by the year 2000.

It is very clear that the states with the most population growth (and the most new political clout) are states with a great deal of ethnic diversity. Table 2 shows the increases in population for various ethnic groups between 1980 and 1990.

While the white population increased by 15 million, the nonwhite population increased by 14 million. Even though whites grew by 8%, their share of the total U.S. population declined from 86% to 84%.

The numbers get even more interesting when we project changes in the youth population from 1990 to 2010 (see Figure 1). During those two decades, the nation

TABLE 2 Population Increases (in Millions) by Ethnic Group, 1980–90

	1980 Total	1990 Total	% Increase
White	194.7	210.3	8
Black	26.7	31.0	16
Asian, other	5.2	8.6	65
Hispanic	14.6	21.0	44

will gain in total population, but America's youth population will decline rapidly after 2000, because of the decline in women entering the childbearing years. However, as the total youth cohort moves from 64 million to 65 million, then down to 62 million, the nonwhite component of the nation's youth cohort will increase dramatically, from 30% in 1990 to 38% in 2010. Note also that the white youth population declines during *both* decades. In fact, in 2010, 12 states and the District of Columbia will contain 30 million of our 62 million young people, with the percentages of minority youths as follows: Washington, D.C., 93.2%; Hawaii, 79.5%; New Mexico, 76.5%; Texas, 56.9%; California, 56.9%; Florida, 53.4%; New York, 52.8%; Louisiana, 50.3%; Mississippi, 49.9%; New Jersey, 45.7%; Maryland, 42.7%; Illinois, 41.7%; South Carolina, 40.1%; U.S. total, 38.7%.

Many of these are large states, with a good deal of political and economic clout. But in all of them, a new question will arise: What do we call "minorities" when they constitute a majority? It behooves us all to make sure that *every* child in America has a good education and access to a good job. We cannot, as a nation, afford to throw *any* child away; we need them all to become successful adults if the economy, the community, the work force, the military—indeed, the nation—are to thrive. (And who else will generate the incomes that will pay for the Social Security benefits of the readers of this article?) Of the 20 million new workers who will be added to the American economy by 2000, only 18% of the net additions will be white males born in the U.S. The rest will be a combination of women, immigrants, or minorities.

By the 1980s the equity efforts of the 1960s had begun to pay off in terms of minority populations entering the middle class (defined by college education, suburban living options, and a whitecollar or professional job). About 40% of the black population can be called middle class in 1990; Hispanics are not far behind, and Asians are actually ahead. Different places in America have produced very different rates of black suburbanization, as the following list makes clear: Miami, 69%; Newark, 52.9%; Washington, D.C., 48.5%; Los Angeles, 46.5%; Atlanta, 46%; Oakland, 39.5%; St. Louis, 35.4%; Birmingham, 34.1%; Philadelphia, 27.7%; Cleveland, 27.2%; New Orleans, 24.6%; Baltimore, 23.5%; Memphis, 15.4%; Dallas, 15.3%; Detroit, 14.9%; Houston, 14%; and Chicago, 9%.

As jobs follow people to the suburbs, the ability of a city to allow either suburbanization or the development of middle-income homes and jobs within the city limits (the latter, known as "gentrification," has been a major failure in America) will have a large effect on the ability of the metropolitan area—city plus suburbs—to be economically healthy.

With money, jobs, houses, and (to some extent) brains and aspirations having moved to the suburbs, serious questions must be raised about our most serious problem: America's inner-city schools, where the highest percentage of "at-risk" students can be found; where classes are large (even though these children need the *most* individual attention); where health care, housing, transportation, personal security, and community stability are inadequate; where it is *very* hard to recruit and retain high-quality teachers and administrators; and where racial segregation still exists to an appalling degree, despite our best efforts. (It is pointless to desegregate schools if housing and jobs remain segregated.) The national education goals are conspicuous in their neglect of the special problems of inner-city schools in America.

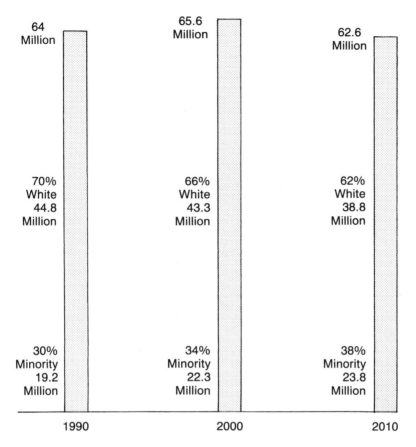

FIGURE 1   U.S. Youth (Birth–18) by Race, 1990–2010

SOURCE: Adapted from *American Demographics*, May 1989, p. 37.

It is particularly frustrating to realize that, if you equalize the environment in which a minority person lives (a home in the suburbs, parents who are college graduates and have managerial or professional jobs), you will tend to equalize his or her educational achievement as well. Indeed, for people of similar social and economic background, race *tends to go away as a predictor of educational achievement.* Figure 2 shows clearly that children of wealthy black families do *better* at math than do children of poor Asian families.

It is difficult to imagine a more exciting or optimistic conclusion. Nevertheless, millions of minority children and their parents are unable to enter the middle class, because they are locked into inner-city environments that offer no escape and scant possibility of improving conditions where they are. At the moment, there is no evidence of a truly permanent "underclass" in America, but give us two more generations of systematic neglect of inner-city youth, and there will be. By then, education's leaky roof will be beyond repair. Once again, schools cannot do the job in a social vacuum. Until job opportunities, health care, housing, transportation, and

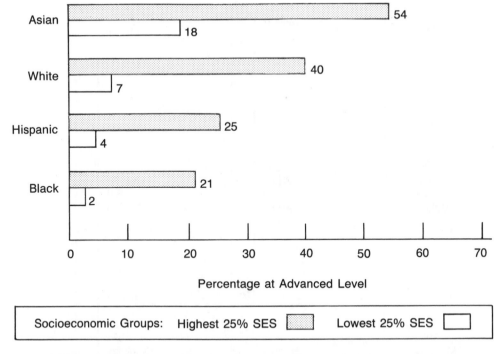

Percentage at Advanced Level

Socioeconomic Groups: Highest 25% SES   Lowest 25% SES

FIGURE 2 Percentage of Eighth-Graders in Low- and High-SES Groups Who Are Proficient in Advanced Mathematics, by Race

SOURCE: National Center for Education Statistics, *Profile of the American Eighth-Grader* (Washington, D.C.: U.S. Department of Education, 1990).

personal security improve in the inner cities, it is impossible to ask schools to get better. Trying to teach sick or hungry children is an exercise in futility.

INTERNATIONAL COMPARISONS

According to a study released by the Census Bureau in March 1990, American young people are at far greater risk for social, economic, and health problems than are children in the world's other developed nations. American children were the most vulnerable in most of the dimensions covered in the study particularly in the following areas:

- number of children affected by divorce,
- youth homicide rate,
- number (and percentage) of youngsters living in poverty,
- infant mortality rate, and
- teenage pregnancy rate.

From a different source, in 1988 America ranked 22nd in infant mortality, with a rate of 10 deaths per 1,000 live births. Young males in the U.S. are five times as likely to be murdered as are their counterparts in other nations. Twenty-three percent of America's youths live in poverty, and the younger the children, the higher the poverty rate.

As I mentioned above, 15 million children in this country are being reared by single parents, mostly as a result of divorce. Finally, though it might seem unlikely that any other nation could compete with our figure of 4.3 million children being reared by a mother who never married and 371,000 children being reared by a never-married father, the facts are otherwise. Although 23% of America's children are born out of wedlock today, the rate for Sweden is 48% and for Denmark, 40%. However, in Sweden and Denmark, infant mortality is low, and child hunger and poverty are virtually nonexistent.

Children can be at risk on a variety of factors, some of which reflect a social or educational problem: single-parent home (22% of eighth-graders), low-income family (21% of eighth-graders' families below the 1988 figure of $15,000), held back one or more grades (19% of eighth-graders), home alone three or more hours a day (14%), parent with a low level of education (11%), and limited English proficiency (2%).

Some children are at risk because of medical factors: fetal alcohol syndrome, no medical care in the first trimester of a mother's pregnancy, a drug-addicted mother, poor maternal nutrition during pregnancy, a mother who smoked during pregnancy, exposure to lead during pregnancy or in infancy, premature birth, low birthweight, having a "teenage mother," and being a victim of child abuse or neglect.

Some children are at risk because of a problem that develops in adolescence: teen pregnancy, criminal conviction, suicide attempts, and alcohol and/or drug abuse.

Indeed, may children are at risk on more than one of these factors.

Like the Reagan Administration before it, the Bush Administration has made a major point of saying that Americans overspend on education. "Throwing money at problems will not make them go away" became the recurrent litany of these Presidents and their advisors. However, the data they cite to show that Americans spend more than other industrialized nations on education include figures for *higher education,* on which we spend a prodigious amount. (The U.S. has 5% of the world's elementary and secondary students and 25% of the world's higher education students.)

On the other hand, if we compare the percent of its gross domestic product that America spends on K-12 education with similar expenditures in other nations, the results are spectacularly different (see Figure 3). Even with the difficulties of establishing "levels of effort" for different nations, it is clear that many nations invest a larger share of their wealth in their children's education than we do. In addition, the discrepancies in per-pupil expenditures *within* the U.S. are unmatched by any nation with a centralized education system. In many states in the U.S., the amount spent on *some* children is three or four times the amount spent on other children in the same state. Recent court decisions in Kentucky and Texas indicate that this is an area of future concern.

This range of effort and expenditure devoted to children and youths is most characteristic of our nation. In terms of infant mortality and care, one can go from some of the best infant care in the world to some of the worst merely by taking the short drive from Scarsdale to Harlem.

These are a few of the reasons for my earlier assertion that America's "bottom

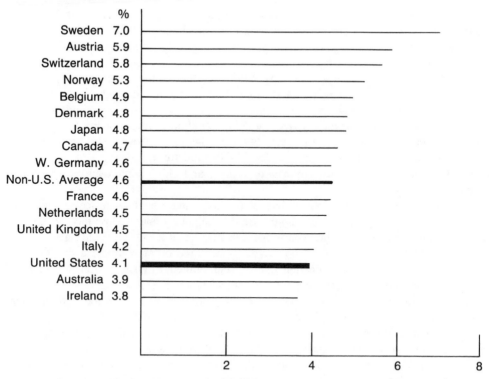

Spending on Grades K-12 as Percentage of Gross Domestic Product

FIGURE 3 International Comparison of Education Expenditures, 1985

SOURCE: M. Edith Rasell and Lawrence Mishel, *Shortchanging Education* (Washington, D.C.: Economic Policy Institute, 1990), p. 5.

third" of young people is more likely to fail than the "bottom third" of any nation with which we usually compare ourselves. If our goal is to ensure that every young person can graduate from high school with a high level of knowledge and skills, then we must concentrate a large measure of our fiscal and human resources on the children most likely to fail. At present, we concentrate our resources on those *least likely* to fail—children from relatively stable suburban families headed by parents who have high levels of education and income. The national education goals give us not a single clue as to how this reallocation of resources should be brought about. Just how do we fix the roof?

EDUCATION—THE BEST WEAPON AGAINST POVERTY AND CRIME

Think for a moment about two young families with children. In one of the families, one or both of the parents has a high school diploma. In the other family, neither parent does. Which family is more likely to live below the poverty line? A good

TABLE 3 High School Dropout Rates, 1987

State (Lowest)	%	State (Highest)	%
1. Minnesota	9.4	1. Florida	41.4
2. Wyoming	10.7	2. Louisiana	39.9
3. North Dakota	11.6	3. Michigan	37.6
4. Nebraska	13.3	4. Georgia	37.5
5. Montana	13.8	5. New York	37.1
6. Iowa	13.8	6. Arizona	35.6
7. Wisconsin	15.6	7. Mississippi	35.2
8. Ohio	17.2	8. Texas	34.9
9. Kansas	17.9	9. California	33.9
10. Utah	19.4	10. Alaska	33.3
11. Connecticut	19.5	11. South Carolina	33.1
12. South Dakota	20.3	12. Kentucky	32.6

SOURCE: *State Education Performance Chart* (Washington, D.C.: Office of Planning, Budget, and Evaluation, U.S. Department of Education, May 1989).

generalization is that increased levels of education will reduce the chances of living in poverty better than anything else. This is widely accepted.

But let's look at a different relationship. Let's look at the relationship between education and crime. Although it is not written about much, the relationship is quite strong. Today, more than 80% of America's one million prisoners are high school dropouts. Each prisoner cost taxpayers upwards of $20,000 a year. Moreover, the investment in prisoners is a bad one, in that 63% of released inmates are back in jail for serious crimes within three years. Taxpayers spend more by far on a prisoner than on *any other kind* of tax-supported individual. A college student is supported by about $3,300 of tax money—a very profitable investment indeed. Every dollar spent on a Head Start child will save taxpayers $7 in later services that the child will not need— a superb investment. Indeed, in Pennsylvania it is seven times more expensive for taxpayers to maintain someone in the *state pen* than it is to maintain someone at Penn State!

This correlation between being a high school dropout and becoming a prisoner is similar to the correlation between being a smoker and getting lung cancer. When you think about the public furor concerning the latter and the widespread ignorance concerning the former, you must wonder about America's youth policy. Table 3 shows the states with the highest and lowest high school dropout rates.[1] It is interesting to note that, with one exception, the states with the lowest dropout rates also have the lowest rates of prisoners per 100,000 people. With two exceptions, the states with the lowest graduation rates have the highest rates of prisoners per 100,000 people.

JAIL CONSTRUCTION VERSUS CRIME REDUCTION

America's prison population *doubled* in less than a decade, reaching 1.1 million prisoners in 1990. (The U.S. incarceration rate in 1991 was the highest in the world, ahead of the Soviet Union and South Africa. In fact, in 1988 a black male in the

U.S. was about five times as likely to be in prison as a black male in South Africa.) Given the increase in drug-related crime and the get-tough policies now in vogue, it is very likely that the number of inmates in U.S. prisons could reach two million before the decade is over. The cost of our prisons is increasing faster than that of *any other* social service, including education and health. Yet the return on the investment is extraordinarily low.

Many governors have discovered that, in order to show that they are "tough on crime," they can build a lot of jail cells and get reelected. Jails can also be built fairly quickly, which shows that the governor is a decisive leader. But there is one major problem with a campaign of building more jail cells: it doesn't reduce the crime rate. No sensible criminal is likely to stop committing crimes because more jail cells are available! (Criminals are not stupid.) There is, however, one thing that does reduce crime rates, and that is increased levels of education.

Let's return to our high school dropout family. With no high school diploma in the household, the best a family can usually manage is a minimum-wage job at $3.30 an hour. That adds up to about $9,000 a year for a full-time worker. Is that enough for our young family even to think about buying a house? Owning a car? Putting children through college? Clearly not. For young high school dropouts working minimum-wage jobs, there is little chance that the American Dream will become reality—unless, of course, they turn to crime. In 1989, four million Americans worked full-time but were still eligible for poverty benefits! Since Ben Franklin, America's deal with its citizens has been: if you work hard, you shouldn't be poor. Where is the reward for the work ethic for these four million people?

However, we know that as educational levels increase, so do earnings. And as earnings increase, the propensity for crime decreases. If you can make your way in the mainstream, a risky criminal "career" becomes less and less inviting. What we need to do is to work on America's crime rates, and the best policy for doing so is to make sure that *every* American child graduates from high school. Already, some school districts—e.g., Greeley, Colorado; and Springfield, Missouri—have developed strategic plans to achieve the goal of zero dropout by 1995. To do so is to achieve a reduction in crime also, but that result won't show up for many years. Unfortunately, political pressures force elected officials to look for quick-fix solutions like jail construction rather than long-term solutions like ensuring that every young person graduates from high school.

I hope that readers take away from this article two main points. First, for the reasons I specified above, America's children are truly an "endangered species." And second, educators alone cannot "fix" the problems of education, because dealing, with the root causes of poverty must involve health-care, housing, transportation, job-training, and social welfare bureaucracies.

We are left with two high-priority questions: What can educators do that they are not already doing to reduce the number of children "at risk" in America and to get them achieving well in school settings? And how can educators collaborate more closely with other service providers so that we all work together toward the urgent goal of providing services to the same client? These two questions must be answered by the nation before our schools will improve.

But we do *know* that it is possible to "fix education's leaky roof." With regard to the problems of children in America, President Bush has said, "We have more will than wallet." I think he has it backward. We have the resources to reduce the proportion of at-risk children to less than 5%. What we lack is the will to do it.

NOTE

1. While dropout rates are notoriously unreliable as absolute numbers, *comparing* rates obtained from the same source—numbers with a "commonly held bias"—is a valuable exercise. Something very different is happening in Minnesota, with its 9% dropout rate, than in Florida, with its 41% rate.

SOURCES OF DATA

Education and Human Services Consortium. *What It Takes: Structuring Interagency Partnerships to Connect Children and Families with Comprehensive Services.* Washington, D.C., 1991.

Hodgkinson, Harold. *All One System: Demographics of Education from Kindergarten Through Graduate School.* Washington, D.C.: Institute for Educational Leadership, 1985.

Hodgkinson, Harold. *The Same Client: Demographics of Education and Service Delivery Systems.* Washington, D.C.: Institute for Educational Leadership, September 1989.

House Select Committee on Children, Youth, and Families. *Children and Families.* Washington, D.C.: U.S. Government Printing Office, December 1988.

House Select Committee on Children, Youth, and Families. *U.S. Children and Their Families: Current Conditions and Recent Trends, 1989.* Washington, D.C.: U.S. Government Printing Office, 1989.

National Center for Education Statistics. *Profile of the American Eighth Grader.* Washington, D.C.: U.S. Department of Education, 1990.

National Health/Education Consortium. *Crossing the Boundaries Between Health and Education.* Washington, D.C., 1990.

Statistical Abstract of the United States, 1990. Washington, D.C.: U.S. Government Printing Office, 1989.

Waldrop, Judith, and Thomas Exter. "What the 1990 Census Will Show." *American Demographics*, January 1990.

Economics and Compassion

Matthew Fox

I do not write this chapter as an economist for I am not one. I am a citizen of the global village, however, and a theologian. Economists who are smug with the way their economics are currently operating will not want to hear about compassion from a theologian or anyone else. However, they should not forget that one of their heroes, Adam Smith, in an age that was not so overly specialized as ours, wrote a book on the *Theory of Moral Sentiments* and that he began his career as a moral philosopher. The morality he presumed for his economic system was, ironically, basically a religious one—this is one more reason for the datedness of Smith's economic theories, however, for religion as he knew it in his society is now dead. If we do not make every effort to relate compassion to economics, then compassion is only a hollow word and a pious sounding phrase. And economics becomes a highly developed form of violence.

The word "economics" comes from the words "to manage a house." Economics is about home-management—but clearly everything in economics will depend on what is meant at a given cultural or historical period by "home." Indeed, the passing of economic systems parallels the passing eras in which home was defined in a certain way. The first Christians responded to the new world-view that the joyous news of Christ gave to them by uniting in a communal life in which they shared all goods in common and in which the owners of lands and houses sold these and gave the proceeds to the apostles to distribute to the needy (Acts 2.44f; 4.32-35). This voluntary sharing with the poor later formed the basis of the monastic vow of poverty when monasticism was born as a response to a new definition given home by a new alliance between church and empire in the fourth century. Feudalism in the middle ages passed to capitalism when the lord-manor-serf system collapsed because people were leaving the land as home and moving to towns as home. Thus a more portable money system was needed for this kind of mobile revolution. The great revolutions of the sixteenth and seventeenth centuries in trade, in geographic discoveries and voyages, in the development of merchant capital, "forced a ceaseless expansion of the world market" (Marx) and brought about a new stage in economics. The new home for economics was big industry and with this stage feudalism finally gave way to capitalism. Economics underwent another giant break when the marketplace of local and in-house manufacturing was moved from family business and home-manufacturing to the factory—a movement of nineteenth century industrial expansion. The alienation or the feeling of *not being at home any longer* that the new economic system created gave birth to the Knights of Labor, the American Federation of Labor, Charles Dickens and Karl Marx as well as other critics of the economic order of their day. Labor Unions, socialisms, and communisms presented themselves as different alternatives to industrial capitalism.

Today we are involved in another economic break-up and with it a growing malaise of alienation, of not-feeling-at-home, of powerlessness and frustration the world over. This frustration is experienced in socialist *and* capitalist economics; it is experienced by employee and manager and the unemployed; by every-day citizens and by presidents of countries. People sense a chaos, a bottomless pit, over which they and their economic systems are suspended, for in fact *economics has not yet caught up with the new meaning of home in our time*. Economics is still running on Newtonian mechanistic "laws" such as Supply and Demand, with little questioning of what is supplied and for whom, and what is not being supplied and who is demanding, and how demands are channeled to manufacturers. Another "law" is that economic progress is synonymous with constant increase in Gross National Products. There is also a presumption, since Adam Smith's influential *Wealth of Nations*, that economics is primarily an issue of nationalist concern. In other words, that the proper 'home' for economics is the nation-state. People are beginning to question the frozen world of ordained economists who are unable to halt rampant inflation, to redirect resources to ensure the survival of the very poor, to guarantee employment for all fit workers, to stop the rich from getting richer and the poor from dying of starvation. People sense that our economic hierarchies are at least as much out of touch with reality as were churchmen of old who fought Galileo over his new discoveries. Fear grips people. Einstein sensed this when he said that "the production and distribution of commodities is entirely unorganized so that everybody must live in fear of being eliminated from the economic cycle." [Ein, p. 11]

What is the new name for "home" that economists have yet to adapt to? The poet has named it as follows: "The earth is your shoe/the sky is your hat."[2] The poet is more scientifically accurate than he had probably imagined, for the sky does in fact operate like a hat, shielding us from the millions of meteorites that fall against its outer limits each day and are thereby burned away. At the same time, this sky-canopy protects our oxygen supply from the ultraviolet light that would kill nucleic acids and protein. So, like any hat, the sky keeps unwelcome things off our heads and keeps welcome energies in.

"The earth is your shoe, the sky is your hat"—this is the lesson learned from the previous chapter: our home is indeed the universe and in a special way this unique planet earth. We are citizens no longer of any one tribe, kingdom, or nation, but of a planet. Our home is the world and our society is the universe—this is the lesson of interdependence that biology, physics and common awareness is driving home to us and that we dealt with in the previous chapter. People recognize the truth of this lesson more readily today, thanks to global communications and common global experiences of shared pain—whether war threats, unemployment, inflation, starvation, etc.—or of shared joy—including music, photos by orbiting astronauts, dancers, film-makers and other celebrators of life. We are no longer isolated entities—not in our domesticated houses—not in our isolated national identities. Nation-states, though they still strut about acting like they were, are not isolated entities any longer. What is becoming clearer and clearer to citizens the world over is that the earth is *our* shoe, the sky *our* hat and both are in jeopardy. Yet economists and their politicians, capitalist and socialist, have not yet caught up with the truth that increasing numbers of citizens are aware of.

The new name for home is "global village" but economics is only beginning to catch up with what the new realities of interdependency will mean. Economist Herman E. Daly of Louisiana State University is doing his part. He writes of the need for a new paradigm or model for economics:

> Continual growth in both capacity (stock) and income (flow) is a central part of the neoclassical growth paradigm. But in a finite world continual growth is impossible. Given finite stomachs, finite lifetimes, and the kind of man who does not live by bread alone, growth becomes undesirable long before it becomes impossible. But the tacit, and sometimes explicit assumption of the Keynesian-neoclassical growth mania synthesis is that aggregate wants are infinite and should be served by trying to make aggregate production infinite. . . . Even if we wish to be neutral or 'value-free' we cannot, because the paradigm by which people try to understand their society is itself one of the key determining features of the social system.[3]

. . . Even though our earth is round, our patriarchal economics remain ladder-like and with it the very name God and the name Justice and the name Compassion have been betrayed. For when you have a system that is ladder-like as in Figure A below, energies of all kinds including religious ones are ushered in to insure the survival of the ladder. We have seen how Jose Miranda demonstrated that this betrayal happened in Western religion with the very words "mercy" and "justice." Originally *saphat* meant Justice and the just God was the one on the side of the unjustly oppressed, the poor, the widow and the orphan. As the ladder grew in influence and power, however, the very name for God as justice was altered to God as Judge. Instead of standing with the poor, God became judge *over* the poor, aligned with the powerful at the top of the ladder. The poor could no longer call on God as a steadfast partner in justice-making but had to appeal to mercy, which became a buffer between the God of Judgment and the simple, non-privileged people. Thus appeals to mercy and to the God of mercy in fact accepted and encouraged the status quo. Mercy became a tender feeling but had nothing to do with changing structures or liberating people. Compassion then became synonymous with mercy and the word "justice" was exiled into introverted areas of religious concern about one's "righteousness" before God.

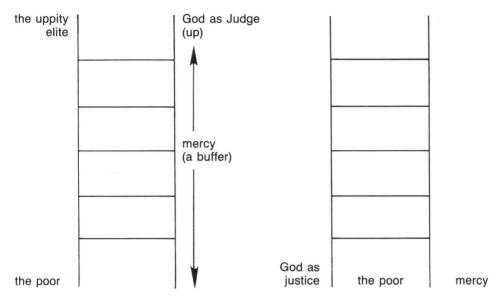

FIGURE A If God is Judge, mercy is buffer.   **FIGURE B** If God is Justice, mercy too is justice.

How far God-talk wandered from the Biblical tradition of God as Warrior on behalf of the oppressed, of God waging war for the slaves and the forgotten, of justice as what people need to crave instead of what a Final Judgment metes out to the powerless. "The true meaning of *saphat* is not 'to judge', but rather 'to do justice to the weak and oppressed.'"[32] Compassion becomes the carving of justice which is often an assertive kind of work, as in Psalm 143: "In his compassion he destroys my enemies." Those who remain close to the earth may be further from the judges who preside so handsomely from on high, but they live more closely to the justice which comes from below and which alone is a divine name. (See Figure B)

Amazing things happen at the top of the ladder where men and their manly corporations become buddies to one another. The rich, for example, receive more welfare that the poor do in such a ladder economy. According to Philip Stern, discriminatory and inequitable tax concessions give 2.2 billion dollars to 3,000 families whose incomes exceed a million dollars. According to Mr. Stern tax handouts to the wealthy amount to $77 billion annually—or twenty five times the amount we pay to support all the American poor who wander about at the bottom of the ladder.[33] This summer the House of Representatives has voted a tax deduction of $16.3 billion. Whom is it for? According to one critical analysis, it is "in all essentials, a handout to the very rich." Already capital gains deductions in the tax code amount to $11 billion annually and this bill adds another $1.9 billion. Two-thirds of the deductions in the new bill will go to taxpayers who make $200,000 or more per year or to 3/10 of one percent of U.S. taxpayers. The average income of the families who will receive this windfall is $400,000 per year. Each of these families will receive tax breaks of $30,000 from this bill. In contrast, the bill that was voted down would have provided tax relief to 98 per cent of the population of the country. Who lobbyied to get this tax relief for the wealthy? Mr. Charles Walker, one-time lobbying manager for the American banking industry who is head of the American Council on Capital Formation.[34] Justice Douglas was not talking idly when he said that in America we have socialism for the rich and "free enterprise" for the poor.[35]

The perpetuation of ladder economics perpetuates the lack of compassion that so characterizes our aggressive culture. It puts power in the hands of a few at the expense of the many who are, quite literally, at their "mercy." Popes have spoken out against such a system, encouraging instead a decentralized or Sarah-Circle approach to development. "At every level the largest possible number of people should have an active share in directing economic development."[36] Yet the irony of this statement is that the institutional Catholic Church, male dominated and patriarchal as it is, hierarchical and uppity as it often has been, remains part of the ladder structure we are criticizing. Which only goes to demonstrate how insidiously rooted the Jacob's-ladder syndrome is in the dominant institutions of the West. So insidious that their very spokesmen can condemn lack of participation in other spheres of living while not questioning their own.

Another dimension to sexism in economics is how the ladder-differentiation is split along sexual and racial lines. A.T. & T. is the largest private employer in the country. Among its one million employees, 80% of the females earn less that $7,000 annually, while 96% of its white males earn more. The Equal Opportunity Commission has called A.T. & T. "without a doubt the largest oppressor of woman workers in the U.S."[37] Racial discrimination also raises its head in these ladder models because 64% of Spanish-surnamed employees and 79% of black employees of A.T. & T. also earn less than $7,000 annually. Since this same company could afford to pay $3 billion in 1970 to its stock and bond holders who reside in the upper 1.6% of the economic ladder, it is clear that the workers at the ladder's bottom—especially women, blacks and hispanics—are subsidizing the continued good fortunes of that tiny elite at the ladder's top.[38]

It is not only salary differentiation that reveals sexism in our corporate economy but also the role that women are to play for that ladder. They are reduced from being makers of products—which their foremothers were who worked on farms or made cloth in their homes only a century ago—to being consumers of products. Thus, they are pictured as essentially passive to a system that is essentially active. As Anne Douglas points out in her study on women in the industrial nineteenth century, "women no longer marry to help their husbands get a living, but to help them spend their income."[39] Most of the advertising of products was directed at women for whom shopping now became a "feminine occupation." Reuther comments on this same sexual-economic formula: "Women became the chief buyers and the sexual image through which the appetites of consumption are to be stimulated to buy the products of consumer society. Women become a kind of self-alienated 'beautiful object' who sell consumer goods to themselves through the medium of their own sexual image. The home becomes the voracious mouth to be stimulated by every sensual image of consumer capitalism."[40] Here indeed is another definition of 'home' in our day—that of the "voracious mouth." Here lies much of the idolatry of Family (always with a capital F) that the consumer society and its giant institutions invest so heavily in, for the family becomes the basic cell; the first rung, of the ladder economy. Spiro Agnew declares that "the family is the cell of society." He should have added, "of consumer society." Greed, with its voracious mouth, is taught in that particular rung of the ladder these days or unless the family becomes critical and compassionate.

What happens to men who compete on the sexist ladder-climb upwards? A curious dimension to the all-male corporate existence is the role that gossip, backbiting and jealousy plays as one climbs up and up. As Larry Ross testifies: "Gossip and rumor are always prevalent in a corporation. There's absolutely no secrets." All that is holy is reduced to the overpowering appeal of the ladder itself. Corporate directors "really play God . . . They're interested in keeping a good face in the community—if it's profitable. You have the tremendous infighting of man against man for survival and clawing at the top." For at least one of his bosses, "there was nothing sacred in life except the business." Why did Mr. Ross leave the ladder? "I left that world because suddenly the power and the status were empty. I'd been there, and when I got there it was nothing. Suddenly you have a feeling of little boys playing at business." (534, 539) These little boys playing at business are unfortunately the little boys with the greatest influence over our priorities in education, medicine, international politics, legislation, industry, for they comprise the key-positions on boards of trustees of almost all of our institutions of research and "higher learning." More often than not, they are the ones to become advisors to presidents.

Another myth that is perpetuated as long as persons remain uncritical of the wors*hup* motif in the ladder economy is the myth that middle class living is what America wants for all its citizens and for all citizens of the world. Each American uses thirteen times more gasoline than the average citizen of Latin America. Who are we kidding? Who are we lying to when we imagine that we want Latin Americans to become like us? Should they succeed, we ourselves would no longer be able to sustain the life-styles we do, dependent as they are on the private automobile. It is a bold-face act of stupidity or a straight-out lie to preach middle class living as we know it in the United States to other countries. The earth's non-renewable resources such as gasoline will not tolerate such hypocrisies. When will the ladder give way to the circle? Reuther believes that "women's consciousness, the consciousness of all oppressed people, becomes redemptive when it reveals a cohumanity beneath the master/slave distortion as the authentic ground of our being, and fights its battle in a way that takes its stand upon and constantly reaffirms this ground." (B, 117) In other words, the new struggle away from the ladder and into circles will itself be the new way. A way of compassion which is dialectical and not dualistic. And this new way will never be able to occur within the structured society we now possess. For "the liberation of women as a caste is impossible within the present socio-economic system. Only in a new system, a restructuring of reality in all its basic interdependencies, especially in the relationship between work time, place and the domestic support system, can women emerge into the full range of human activities presently available to the dominant class and sexual caste." (111) There will be no birth without death. Most mothers know this. Many non-mothers who have spent themselves climbing ladders would just as soon forget it. But unless a seed falls into the ground and dies, nothing is born. No economics that is worthy of the name human economics, and no politics worthy of human ordering and organizing. Nothing is born. . . .

TOWARD AN ECONOMICS OF COMPASSION:
SEVEN PROPOSALS FOR DISCUSSION

We have established . . . that there will be no compassion without creativity and no creativity without imagination. Instead of our creative people being manipulated by our uneconomic economic system either to manufacture luxury goods that no one needs or to sell us ever-whiter detergents and teeth, softer bathroom tissue and longer-lasting deodorants, it would be healthier to use our creative powers to imagine and to implement an economic system that was truly compassionate. The time has plainly arrived to bring about economic alternatives that are more Sarah-circle in their dynamic and that will therefore make possible once again a way of life that is more eye-to-eye and less violently and compulsively ladder-like. One that reflects Einstein's universe of interdependencies instead of Newton's world of absolute isolation.

Economics is far too important and basic to the lives of all of us to be left to some kind of impersonal, quasi-divine and immutable Laws of Economics which were formulated in the nineteenth century under the exaggerated influence of mythologies derived from Darwinian Survival of the Fittest Laws. The ordained economic hierarchy who advise presidents represent an elite that has failed utterly in imagining basic solutions to the real economic realities of unemployment, violent employment, grotesque distribution, wealth, racism, sexism, inflation and competitive violence built into our economic system. I once listened to a live TV interview of one of these anointed ones who was President Nixon's main economic advisor. During the depths of the recession of '73–'74 he declared that: "Those who are suffering the most from the recession are the stock brokers." These economic priests should be served notice that hierarchies, whether sacred or secular, ought to either get off their high horses and down where the people live, work and play or they ought to step aside. They should recognize that as people learn that the word "hierarchy" means sacred and that transcendence is not up, they will no longer tolerate secular and mammon gods hiding at the top of ladders behind the skirts of religious mystical language that the believers of true religion no longer believe in.

Following is a basic guideline for discussion that I would propose for a compassionate economics containing seven points.

Local Control over Economics

I would like to see economics that encourages instead of discourages the small business owner or small farmer. Such an economics implies a non-elitist language and a thorough training in economics of interdependence instead of rugged independence. It also requires a removal of red tape, of giant bureaucratic intervention. A decision needs to be agreed upon about what amounts of merchandizing constitutes "small" businesses. One reason that small business continues to be a victim in the marketplace today is the propaganda that big business feeds about the "free enterprise system." It is imperative that small business people learn to disassociate themselves psychologically, mythically and economically from big business. The monopolies that the conglomerates create destroy the small business farmer, grocer or jeweler, and all the while the large groups propagandize about the need for non-interference of government agencies. In Kansas this past year I was told by family farmers who have worked the land there for generations that within ten years not a single family farmer would be left in that state. At present a quarter of a million family farmers leave their land yearly in America because they can no longer compete with the agri-businesses that are taking over the land of this country.[46] Non-interference for the small business person—Yes! For the large ones, No! Small businesses would do far better linking up with lobbyists of consumer agencies with whom they share so much in common than with lobbyists for large corporation interests. For what makes small business human, compassionate and a contribution to society is that in such a situation the buyer and seller look each other in the eye. It is a Sarah-Circle dynamic. There is a potential for knowledge and therefore for human understanding that is utterly lacking from the top of our skyscrapers.

Simplification of Income Tax Structure

The tax laws we now have are elitist—only accountants and lawyers can interpret them—and therefore those who can afford these specialists, especially the giant corporations, get the most mileage from them and, of course, from the legislative and judicial systems. How many small business people, for example can even afford the time or cost of court usage? Would it really be difficult, and would it not cut drastically the bureaucratic ballooning in IRS, to simplify the tax structure into a pattern that resembles the tithing of old? For example, a straight tax on income that might read as follows:

5% for those earning $10,000–$15,000

8% for those earning $15,000–$30,000

15% for those earning $30,000–$75,000

20% thereafter

With no deductions, no write-offs, etc., except for dependents. Those who earn less than $10,000 would simply not pay income tax.

Money that is earned by work should be untaxed or taxed minimally, while money that is earned by money ought to be greatly taxed. For anyone who has money to play with can afford to pay more taxes. People would be willing to pay income tax if they were convinced that, first, the tax were equitable and did not include constant welfare for the rich and the large corporations and, second, they saw results from their taxes in the form of decent housing, transportation, education, health and protection.

Institution of Land-tax

Outside of people, land is the most precious resource we know. All property presumes some kind of relationship to land, if only to store it. The relationship we all have to land is a sacred one, for no one of us created it ourselves and we will all return to it. And yet much land in America goes unused, abused, or becomes reduced to the status of one more object possessed. By taxing land more than we do and in a special way, we will be able to tax work and income derived from it considerably less. (Thus the reason for relatively light taxing in the previous section). A land-tax is meant to correct the monopoly of large corporations, of absentee landlords, and of State control. As such it would seem to be a useful device in a period when more and more observers were heard to remark that United States, home of multinational corporations and USSR, the granddaddy of State Control, seem to have more and more in common. A land-tax would tax all land but no improvements on the land and in this way would encourage initiative and jobs, rather than discourage them. It would run the land speculator and the absentee landlord out of town.

Henry George, an American pioneer in the land-tax movement, sees his movement as an alternative to Marxism and as a radical solution to an unjust economic system that rewards the speculator and puts millions out of work. In effect, he asks that everyone pay rent on whatever land he or she is occupying and that this rent be the only basic tax that a person pay. A land tax would encourage farmers who actually farm instead of those who speculate and, he feels, it would increase productivity, ingenuity and the creation of jobs. It would also lessen bureaucratic interference since basically it is simplifying the law code. Wealth would become "equally distributed. I do not mean that each individual would get the same amount of wealth. That would not be equal distribution, so long as different individuals have different powers and different desires. But I mean that wealth would be distributed in accordance with the degree in which the industry, skill, knowledge, or prudence of each contribute to the common stock . . . The non-producer would no longer roll in luxury while the producer got but the barest necessities of animal existence."[47] Just as we enslaved the one source of wealth, human beings, in the name of an economic institution for centuries but finally learned we could live without slavery, so we are still enslaving the second source of wealth, land. "The other source of wealth—the more passive one—is still held in bondage by a foolish economic system,"[48] and only when land is 'freed' from land speculators who sit on it or charge great rents for it without improving it will people themselves become free.

I do not know the full extent of the ramifications of George's economics though I do suspect that some basic income tax will still be required. But his starting points are impressively compassionate—which is more than can be said of the economic system we now grapple with. He says, for example: "Civilization is co-operation . . . What has destroyed every precious civilization has been the tendency to the unequal distributions of wealth and power." He believes that his system "will greatly benefit all those who live by wages, whether of hand or of head" and, because he is an American, he does not scare off Americans with talk of "nationalizing" the land or private property. For many Americans the latter carries with it a myth of self-independence. For all these reasons I believe that further investigation of a modified tax on land programs as George describes it might well be worth the efforts of our imaginative economists who are also compassionate. Several cities such as Pittsburgh and Baltimore already have adopted versions of George's land tax.

Emphasis on Distribution Rather than Production

Growthmania and myths of infinite possibilities of economic growth delude us all and distract us from the real purpose of economics which is to make a liveable home for our human family. Instead of idealistic mythical visions served up by so-called secular scientists whose world view is more mythical than that of most theologians even, we should begin economics with facts. The fact of economic life is that the poor are increasing in numbers and the poor are getting poorer while the few rich are getting richer. Anyone who visits a supermarket and observes the retired person on a fixed income having to turn down fresh vegetables and basic meats knows this fact of economic life. (I have observed, however, that very few of our very wealthy ever do their own shopping in supermarkets; and I wonder how many of our comfortable economists do either.) Harrington puts the starting point of economic facts of life this way: "We have in this country a *majority,* composed of the poor, the near-poor, more than half the workers and the lower middle class, which does not even have a 'moderate standard of living' as defined by the Government itself." (337, italics his)

What do we do about this situation? Economists sensitive to it call for a distribution revolution to replace our production compulsions and I agree. "Material growth as we have experienced it over the last century in *no* way has resulted in increased equality among the world's people. To the contrary, growth in its present form simply widens the gap between the rich and poor."[49] Boulding comments: "The essential measure of the success of the economy is not production and consumption at all, but the nature, extent, quality and complexity of the total capital stock, including in this the state of the human bodies and minds included in the system. . . . This idea that both production and consumption are bad things rather than good things is very strange to economists who have been obsessed with the income-flow concepts to the exclusion, almost, of capital-stock concepts." (p. 127) And Daly insists that "the important issue of the steady state will be distribution, not production." (19) The global home demands of all of us, economists included, a broader look at distribution of the basics for living. This necessarily means a cutting back on the luxuries that, as Keynes points out, while they may "satisfy the desire for superiority, may indeed be insatiable" in the desires they arouse and the production they require. John Stuart Mill also warned of an economics based on "consuming things which give little or no pleasure except as representative of wealth." (cited in Daly, 26) Who can say that an economics infused with the desire to distribute would not open up all new industries and job opportunities for many, many persons? The encouragement of those who create what Schumacher calls "good work" ought to be a priority in any humanly-oriented economics. This implies the encouragement of small businesses, of the uses to which land can be put, of the hiring of artists. Has anyone considered how many persons would derive not only employment but also delight and ecstasy by the hiring of mimes to walk our streets, clowns to invade our offices and factories and commuter trains, of musicians strolling through neighborhoods, of conductors organizing and leading neighborhood symphonies? In this kind of *good* work lies the end to unemployment, underemployment and even overemployment because a lot of overemployed are compulsive do-ers who have not learned to receive from the creative ones of society. The rewarding, for example, of inventions that truly save energy and that put people to work instead of eliminate persons from work, the rewarding of kinds of work that bring home-life and work-life closer together—all such rewards should be part of the fabric of a humanly based economy.

Skilling the Hard-Core Unemployed Where They Live

Around forty per cent of Harlem youth are unemployed and yet Harlem needs improved housing, shopping, safety, street-cleaning, parks, child-care centers, etc. All of these jobs—carpentry, policing, cleaning of streets, beautifying of parks and caring for children—can be done by local residents. And they are the ones who should do these jobs for from a commitment in group activity, community can happen. From a learning on the job, individuals committed to such neighborhood recovery work would also learn skills that can assist others in the neighborhood. An investment in materials and basic skilled leaders, who in fact do not have to be top dogs either in pay or expertise, would go a lot further than the money that otherwise will be lost in crime, prisons, drugs, or that ineffable loss of capital called the snuffing out of a potential citizen at an early age. Joe Selvaggio, director of Project for Pride in Living (PPL), has done exactly this in Minneapolis and St. Paul, proving the feasibility of it and demonstrating the community results of hope, pride and initiative that can follow from it.[50]

Making Economics Global

Economics must be world-oriented and world-aware and not merely nationalistic. Adam Smith's *Wealth of Nations* has been described as the first study in political economy "to constitute it for the first time as a separate science." It is, says J. Bullock, "the best all-around statement and defense of some of the fundamental principles of the science of economics."[51] This may have held true for the nineteenth century (though it may also help to explain the World Wars that have so characterized this century). But there is no future to our shrinking globe without a global economic perspective. We need to pass from a perspective on the Wealth of Nations to a perspective on the Wealth and Poverty of the Globe. With that perspective all else might change into a compassionate way of group-survival. Thus Barbara Ward and Rene Dubos can declare that "we have to place what is valuable in nationalism within the framework of a political world order that is morally and socially responsible as well as physically one."[52] Economics, like all sciences, must become truly interdependent.

Economics as an Ideal and Motivating Factor:
Towards an American Socialism

There is an intangible that is at stake in this 7-point Economic dream that can not be put in dollars and cents but is not thereby unimportant. In fact, it may be the single most important contribution of this or any other economic vision. It is the human factor of motivation, of idealism, of myth that arouses generosity and team-work and forgetting of one's own problems in working with others. *Time* magazine (and I deliberately cite *Time* because it is such a spokesperson for the 500 biggest American corporations that it admires so greatly and of which it is one) admits that Socialism is winning two battles around the world today. The battles are both very much related. One is the contribution that socialist societies make in what *Time* calls "quality of life" issues such as social services, education, medicine, employment. *Time* confesses that "state-provided social services are one promise that socialism has kept . . . The essential human services provided by Marxist-Leninist states often match and sometimes top those in Western democracies."[53] It would seem that this accomplishment, which even *Time* confesses to, is an important one from the point of view of compassion.

The second battle that *Time* confesses Socialism wins at is that of idealism. "In his ongoing debate with the socialist, the capitalist is at a disadvantage, unable to compete rhetorically with socialist idealism . . . Instead of a noble 'new man,' capitalism offers only the 'old man,' whose self-interest in profit—even though it may be condemned as greed—will ultimately benefit the commonwealth." (p. 36) This last assertion takes more faith to believe than does the Trinity itself! *Time* goes on: "The quintessential capitalist, whether or not he is religious, rejects the idea of man's perfectibility on earth." Here lies the moral and spiritual malaise of the West: our basic economic system, and here I cite not its critics like Karl Marx but its spokes-media, is pessimistic. Lacking in vision and hope and therefore in motivation. It is incapable of stirring us to cosmic vision or compassionate sharing or generosity. Therefore it has nothing intrinsic to it with which to capture the imagination of youth (who are not as easily fooled by the enticements of greed as their parents apparently are). It may accuse socialism of being "fundamentally utopian" which *Time* does but in doing so it reveals why socialism and not capitalism appeals to youth and other idealistic segments of the world: That socialism, for all its claims to being materialistic, is also compassionate. Yet capitalism's only effort at spirituality is in terms of sentimentalized, profit-oriented religion or in terms of philanthropy.

Given this lack of spiritual challenge in the capitalistic economic system as even *Time* itself confesses to, it is clear that the economics we now possess (or does it possess us?) is doomed. For it cannot rouse the hearts and minds and hands of people. Individual self-profit is *not* in the long run what economics is all about. It is about people, not profits. About the poor, not the wealthy. About conserving the goods of the earth that need to be conserved, not about the fast profiteering that destroys nonrenewable goods for other generations. Nor is competition as universal as capitalism would life us to believe. We need—the people need—an economics of interdependence. Yet how many of us have been invited to create or debate such an alternative economic svstem? Most of our 'education' in economics amounts either to, first, making money in the system we've got or, second, inciting us to worship the 'system' we have today by way of ideological propaganda and to hate the "other guy's" system. It is time for some creative alternatives.

Should the alternative be called Socialism? Sociologist Robert Bellah points out[54] that Americans resist that name born of a foreign philosophy developed in nineteenth-century Europe and associated as it is with philosophies of atheism from the same period. For many the term "socialism" has been tainted with too much expansionism, too much bureaucracy and too much dualistic fighting with capitalism to be very useful as a name for an alternative economics.[55] Yet, since an Economics of Interdependence and Compassion is what we seek and it is also what in theory socialism seeks, we should not isolate ourselves from what the socialist tradition can teach us. The time has come for our own adaptation of the socialist principle to our country's situation.

I have lived in American society and in its economic system for thirty-eight years. In those years I have observed the violence that that system perpetrates in very subtle ways—such as the building of greed by its mammoth advertising mania, its established unemployment and compulsive overemployment, its now-rampant inflation, its coddling of the over-wealthy (thirty senators in the US senate are millionaires), its ignoring of basic priorities such as health care, decent education, safety, housing, food, transportation and access to beauty for vast percentages of its citizens, its succumbing to an economy of luxury and trivia, its rendering of people into consumers and of festivities into orgies of buying and spending, its corruption of the media, its rendering citizens ignorant of their own economic system and bigoted toward alternative possibilities, its lack of idealism that can stir youth and old alike to work toward new and common visions, its pandering to decadence of the comfortable, its idolatry of rugged individualism that destroys a sense of the common good. I am now convinced that capitalism with its presuppositions is incompatible with compassion.

Therefore the time has come for a new kind of socialism—an American effort toward a truly democratic socialism. It would need to go beyond slogans and rhetoric and deal with complex issues of modern economics. It would reflect the uniqueness of our country and its peoples—its size and variety, for example, and will not merely borrow blindly from other efforts at socialism. Many of these efforts, as is well known in America, have failed at being both democratic and socialist—one thinks of Russia, of totalitarian regimes in Africa, etc. Yet there are many lessons to learn especially from European and middle European experiments with socialism. Socialists need to be patient people—after all, capitalism has evolved over eight centuries in the West and socialism has been with us for only one century. But this is precisely the point—recognizing the need for more creative expressions of socialism, expressions that truly utter Michael Harrington's goal of the "maximizing of human freedom and potential." It is time that Americans started to make the constructive contributions that they can make to a more compassionate economic system. But compassion will not be built in a day nor in our lifetime. The "quick fix" that McDonald's Corporation has taught Americans to believe in, the fast food fad, is not the way to set economics right.

The basic model for socialism is truly Sarah's-Circle, unlike capitalism's which is just as truly Jacob's-Ladder. Can America, which pioneered Sarah's Circle as a political ideal in the 18th century regain such courage and imagination to invent Sarah-Circle as an economic model for the 21st century? Here lies the most basic challenge that a spirituality of compassion hurls at us today.

SUMMARY

In this chapter we have considered the interdependence of economics to other levels of consciousness and compassion treated in this book: Namely, to psychology, sexuality, creativity, science and politics. We have called for an economic system that reflects the reality of the world we live in to replace that which only protects the privileges of the economic elite. I have presented a seven-fold path to consider in debating such an alternative economics. The key to the new economics will be Interdependence, the newly recognized "Law" of our world.

The basis of this Economics will be corporate and spiritual works of compassion. Do not tell us whether our economy is growing in Gross National Product yearly: rather, tell us whether our world-wide economics are accomplishing the following: housing for the homeless, feeding the hungry, educating the ignorant, caring for the sick, humanizing the prisons, creating good work for the unemployed, encouraging technology with a human face, celebrating with the forgotten, passing on nature's energies to other generations. This would be an economics of Interdependence. An economics as if the creation we lived in mattered.

The ultimate principle in any economics of compassion is that it is to the self-interest of all of us and it is to the private and greedy interests of none. Or, in Gandhi's words, there exists "enough for everyone's needs, but not for everyone's greed." Such an economics presumes that we have learned the difference between need and greed. Clearly we have a lengthy education ahead of us.

NOTES

2. Musician Anton Webern has set this folk song to music. Its title is "Armer Sunder, du." (Opus 17, Webern).
3. Herman E. Daly, "Introduction," in Herman E. Daly, ed., *Toward a Steady-State Economy* (San Francisco: W.H. Freeman & Co., 1973), p. 5.
32. Jose Miranda, *Marx and the Bible*, p. 113.
33. Philip Stern, *The Great Treasury Raid*, Cited in *A Teacher's Handbook on Christian Values and Economics* (St. Paul: Center for Economic Education, College of St. Thomas, Preliminary Review Edition, 1977), p. 13.
34. Alexander Cockburn & James Ridgeway, "How to Fix a Handout," *Village Voice*, August 21, 1978, pp. 15f.
35. William O. Douglas, *Points of Rebellion* (NY: Vintage Books, 1970), p. 68.
36. "Gaudium et Spes," (The Church in the Modern World), *Proceedings of the Second Vatican Council*, 1965, #672.
37. "A Unique Competence, A Study of Employment Opportunity in the Bell System," (Washington, D.C.: Equal Opportunity Commission, 1971), pp. 59, 238, 173; *Fortune* (NY: March, 1972), p. 17.
38. 1970 *Annual Report of A. T. & T.*
39. Anne Douglas, *The Feminization of American Culture* (NY: Knopf, 1977), p. 52.
40. In Eugene C. Bianchi, Rosemary Reuther, *From Machismo to Mutuality* (NY: Paulist, 1976), p. 51. Hereafter abbreviated B.
46. *Pocket Data Book, USA*, (U.S. Dept. of Commerce, 1971), p. 217.
47. James L. Busey, ed., *Progress and Poverty by Henry George* (NY: Robert Schalkenbach Foundation, 1968).
48. Frank McEachran, "Henry George and Karl Marx," Paper presented at the International Conference, London, Sept., 1936. (NY: Robert Schalkenback Foundation, n.d.), p. 6. Marx himself dismissed George as "capitalism's last ditch attempt to rear itself anew upon a firmer basis than its present one." (Letter from Karl Marx to a friend, June 20, 1881, reprinted in *The People,* June 5, 1892.)
49. Jorgen Randers and Donella Meadows, "The Carrying Capacity of our Global Environment: A Look at the Ethical Alternatives," in Daly, *ed. cit.*, p. 304.
50. See Pat Ryan Greene, "Advocate of Poor Honored: Winner Sold Shares in Self," *National Catholic Reporter*, May 26, 1978, p. 1.

51. C.J. Bullock, ed., "Introductory Note," to Adam Smith, *An Inquiry into the Nature and Causes of the Wealth of Nations* (NY: P.F. Collier & Sons, 1909), p. 3.
52. Barbara Ward and Rene Dubos, *Only One Earth: The Care and Maintenance of A Small Planet* (NY: Norton, 1972), p. 29.
53. "Socialism: Trials and Errors," *Time*, March 13, 1978. Time is itself the 217th largest corporation in America according to its brother publication, *Fortune*, May, 1977.
54. Robert Bellah, "The American Taboo on Socialism," in *The Broken Covenant* (NY: Seabury, 1975), chapter five.
55. Cf. Ivan Illich, "Total consumption of medicine is largely independent of cost or the kind of practice that is prevalent, i.e. private or socialized." In other words, industrialization and consumption are ideologies that threaten both right and left-wing economic systems. Ivan Illich, *Medical Nemesis* (NY: Pantheon, 1976), p. 73, note 119.

Marginality and Difference: The Fractured Community

Every migrant knows in his heart of hearts, that it is impossible to return. Even if he is physically able to return, he does not truly return, because he himself has been so deeply changed by his emigration. . . . Today, as soon as very early childhood is over, the home can never again be home, as it was in other epochs. This century, for all its wealth and with all its communication systems, is the century of banishment.[1]

John Berger's powerful words take us into the unifying theme of the third section of the book—a theme now of immense significance in the United States. For Berger and others, spiritual homelessness, or alienation, is the *defining* condition of humankind in the late twentieth century. Men and women feel estranged from their own labors and worlds, that is, unattached in any significant way to where they live; work; or as we see in this section, go to school. From this perspective, one sees a world deeply scarred by what has been called "the poison of separation." Our lives and our cultures are pervaded by fragmentation. Too little do we connect our creative selves to our labor, our private lives to the public world, or the traditionally masculine activities of production and agency to the typically feminine tasks of reproduction and nurturance. We find ourselves in a world that excludes, sometimes brutally, whole categories of people from any real participation in the collective making of the material or cultural conditions of their lives. Groups of people cast into the role of "surplus populations" find their lives, experiences, values, and ways of life demeaned and invalidated by those who are, or think they are, the central players in society. And as we will see later in this book, our world of separation places human beings on a path of fatal dissonance with the very context of our existence—the earth and our physical environment.

The phenomenon of alienation crosses national boundaries and the forms of political and social life. In the United States alienation and freedom are opposite sides of the same coin. Freedom in this country has always meant a "freedom from." It has meant bourgeois or liberal freedom, in which obligation, duty, and responsibility to the state or the community are minimal. Individuals are expected to become self-sufficient beings, unconstrained in their geographical and social mobility by the ties that bind them to others. *Individuality, autonomy,* and *independence* are the watchwords of the American ideology, the heart of the promise of American life. This promise has been enormously appealing to generations of immigrants from lands in which lives have been stunted or thwarted by repressive traditions, state coèrcion, or economic scarcity. Yet we have paid a heavy price for this type of freedom, founded as it is on separation. Our society denigrates common bonds and collective ties. However much we might wax nostalgic or sentimental about such social connections, the price for entry into the relative security of middle-class life is the dissolution of these ties. Success or achievement is attained primarily through the heartless, competitive, and egoistic drives demanded by the capitalist culture.

Success in America has meant abandonment of those communal ties that might limit the headlong rush for personal achievement. It has meant shredding the traditions of language, attitudes, beliefs, and values that stand in the way of conforming to the white, male, heterosexual, middle-class standards that constitute American "normalcy." For many, winning one's place in the American mainstream means submission to a brutal process of alienation. One must, in the first place, forfeit those ethnically, linguistically, and racially mediated cultures that are eschewed by the dominant culture. In other words, one must dissolve those historically constituted ties through which whole groups of human beings have learned to locate themselves in the world. doing so, one must not simply abandon social ties but also eliminate important aspects of one's identity. One must give up parts of oneself and struggle to become what has been called the "other." The price of some minimal degree of economic well-being or security is denial, shame, and inauthenticity.

This insistence on cultural homogenization has been accompanied historically by a process in which dominant groups rationalize their positions of privilege through myths about their superiority and the purported inferiority of those they oppress. Yet as our readings make clear, the process of homogenization is neither smooth nor conflict-free. Individually and collectively, human beings resist the Faustian bargain in which the price of economic survival is a denial of self or of one's community. In education, for example, students and parents have often fought to preserve social identities over which schools frequently ride roughshod. At times these struggles have borne fruit in the form of educational policies that recognize and attempt to assist racial, linguistic, ethnic, or other minorities in the preservation of their communal forms and cultures. Still, such instances do not characterize American education. More often what we witness is a system that falls far short of respecting human and cultural differences. Indeed, as the chapters (especially on gender and the education of handicapped people) show, we have not even begun to see how the prevailing logic of educational practice—even where it is intended to be ameliorative—confirms and reproduces the traditional structures of hierarchy, reward, and prejudice. More generally we have refused to confront the way in which such educational issues reflect questions of power—cultural, economic, and political. Exploring the enduring and pervasive forms of personal and collective alienation inside, as well as outside, the school means recognizing how institutions discount the voices of and exclude from meaningful participation many of its clients.

Jane Roland Martin begins with the saga of Richard Rodriguez and the human price that must sometimes be paid to achieve educational success—alienation from one's most intimate roots and the feelings and emotions that are nourished through them. In place of the self-congratulatory images of assimilation and acceptance of immigrants to America is the story of human lives lived at the edge of a strange, forbidding, and always foreign culture. Such alienation, Martin argues, is built into our very ideal of the educated person. Our ideal splits reason from emotion, mind from body, and thought from action. Rodriguez, Martin says, developed the capacity for "reasoned deliberation rather than spontaneous reaction, dispassionate inquiry rather than emotional response." Such attributes are a preparation for the public world—the place of productive processes. This world—a masculinized realm—excludes feeling, emotion, intimacy, and connection. Instead, Martin says, critical analysis, critical thinking, and self-sufficiency are valued. The education ideal, in other words, excludes the female-oriented, reproductive processes of society, which involve care, concern, connectedness, and nurturance—capacities that we need not just in the family but also increasingly to carry on society's economic, political, and social functions. The now imperiled fate of the earth, for example, demands an ethic of care resembling "the generative love of parents." Although not wishing to allocate values to men and women in stereotypical ways, the author argues that in order to conform to the ideal of an educated person, females are more likely to suffer an alienation from their own identity. For women this identity is more likely to emphasize emotional growth and intimate connections. And if they do become analytic, objective thinkers and autonomous agents, they are thought less feminine than they should be.

It is not enough merely to struggle for inclusion into the "mainstream" of educational achievement unless this struggle challenges the very basis of what currently constitutes the educational ideal. It must, in other words, question the tradition of Western thought that deems the functions, tasks, and traits associated with women less valuable than those associated with men. Martin concludes by outlining a vision of an educational realm expanded to include the reproductive processes of society and a corresponding redefinition of what it means to be educated.

In Signithia Fordham's piece on "racelessness," there is the same recognition of the terrible price that must be paid to enter the dominant cultural world. Access to the "American dream" requires a renunciation of one's allegiance to a native culture and community. Fordham demonstrates that the organizational structure of the school rewards racelessness in students. They must, in other words, learn to distance themselves from, even deny, their own communal identity and social roots. Schools communicate the message that black adolescents cannot be culturally different *and* achieve success as defined by the dominant society. Success in white American society requires learning to display little commitment to the African-American community. School and community stand in a dissonant relation, and students must juggle conflicting personae to deal with the resulting anxieties and conflicts. Ultimately, Fordham believes, black Americans must question whether they are willing to "sublimate" individual goals in favor of a commitment to the integrity of the existing cultural system and "the collective advancement of our people."

Carol D. Lee, Kofi Lomotey, and Mwalimu Shujaa examine this issue of what kind of education is now needed to allow African-Americans to thrive in a culture that has historically demeaned their character and denied their existence. What would it mean, the authors ask, to construct a genuinely African-centered pedagogy in the United States? Although providing a powerful statement of the need for such a pedagogy to reinforce "intra-ethnic solidarity and pride," the authors are also cognizant of living in a multiethnic society in which African-Americans must enter into coalitions with other groups with similar needs and interests. The authors leave no doubt that the goals of multicultural education must be political, in the sense that they are fundamentally concerned with reversing the structures of social, cultural, and economic racism and dispowerment.

The critical role of language in creating and reinforcing cultural inferiority and social exclusion through school is examined by Sonia Nieto. Paradoxically, she notes, there is still no common term for language discrimination (*linguicism* is suggested). Yet given the fact that by the year 2000 the number of children in the United States speaking a primary language other than English will be nearly 6 million, the issue is of enormous consequence. Nieto considers and explains the various meanings historically attributed to the idea of bilingual education. She insists that such education is always, at root, political because it concerns the class and ethnic group interests of traditionally dispowered groups. No less than racial integration, bilingual education is understood by language-minority groups as an important civil or human right—a means to empower their students, who are typically most disenfranchised.

The issue of educating individuals who are linguistically marginalized, as well as socially, politically, and economically excluded, is taken up by Eva Young and Mariwilda Padilla. The authors provide a description of "Mujeres Unidas en Acción," a nonprofit, community-based agency offering educational programs to low-income Latina women. The program is based on the belief that learning a language is more than learning grammatical rules. Rooted in Paulo Freire's conceptualization of oppression, education is viewed as a process in which language is communication; words are important, "not because of their grammatical characteristics, but because of the meanings and world vision they reflect." Education here is practiced as a liberating process in which, by learning to use language critically, it becomes possible to understand the conditions confronting economically and culturally oppressed women. The understanding such education provides makes it possible to engage in action that might challenge and change the social patterns of these women's lives and, more generally, the lives of Latina women in North American culture.

Finally, turning to another, frequently overlooked segment of society, Rebecca Blomgren describes the indignities suffered by those labeled as handicapped in our schools. The best intentions of special educators notwithstanding, those students are "helped" through a medical-scientific model of diagnosis, prescription, assessment, and remediation that views individuals as, "to a greater or lesser degree, impaired and thus in need of fixing." Within the framework of educational practice, Blomgren says, the unfixed, unproductive individual is blamed quickly for his or her lack of success. In the words of one student, she was an "interruption" in the schedule and class routine, an "interference" in the efficient operation of the educational process. The special-needs student is transformed rapidly into an object to be labeled and manipulated. This experience produces a profound alienation from oneself and from others—a doubt about one's own authenticity and a constant search for external validation. Paradoxically, of course, such programs are intended to promote a sense of integration and inclusion in the social mainstream.

Blomgren notes that neither the conventional model of educational reform nor the empowerment process associated with the critical pedagogy of Freire and others (which requires rational, critical, and expressive skills that many handicapped people lack) provides an adequate model of special education. Blomgren argues that in the light of the exclusion of the handicapped we need another starting point altogether—one in which help is not in any sense prescriptive but rather a matter of facing those who come before us in our classrooms as "valued and cherished human beings." The teaching-helping act, she says, is a call to participate in a partnership in such a way that we do not diminish our capacity to confirm or be confirmed. Our work, says Blomgren, must be conceived not as an act of fixing or shaping but of affirming the dignity and sanctity of human life.

All the writings in this section reflect an important shift in our view of cultures and human behaviors that do not conform to what has been considered "normal." In place of the widely held assumption that these "other" kinds of people are somewhat deficient or abnormal, we have begun to use a language of "difference" that seeks to treat all human beings with dignity and equal value. No human practices, values, or beliefs can set themselves up as *the* standards by which everyone should be judged and measured. Through the work of postmodern critics such as Michael Foucault, we have seen how claims about what is "normal" always cloak the power of one group or another to impose its views about the proper way to live, speak, think, feel, or value. It has become increasingly apparent how the discourse of normality masks the power to control others who are different because of race, nationality, religion, gender, sexual preference, language, class, physical appearance, mental or physical ability, and so on. From the perspective of "difference," a socially just world is impossible without a radically deepened appreciation and affirmation of cultural and human dignity.

NOTE

1. John Berger, *And Our Faces. My Heart, Brief on Photos* (New York: Pantheon, 1984), pp. 65–67.

Becoming Educated:
A Journey of Alienation
or Integration?

Jane Roland Martin

In his educational autobiography *Hunger of Memory*, Richard Rodriguez (1982) tells of growing up in Sacramento, California, the third of four children in a Spanish-speaking family. Upon entering first grade he could understand perhaps 50 English words. Within the year his teachers convinced his parents to speak only English at home and Rodriguez soon became fluent in the language. By the time he graduated from elementary school with citations galore and entered high school, he had read hundreds of books. He went on to attend Stanford University and, 20 years after his parents' decision to abandon their native tongue, he sat in the British Museum writing a PhD dissertation in English literature.

Rodriguez learned to speak English and went on to acquire a liberal education. History, literature, science, mathematics, philosophy: these he studied and made his own. Rodriguez's story is of the cultural assimilation of a Mexican-American, but it is more than this, for by no means do all assimilated Americans conform to our image of a well-educated person. Rodriguez does because, to use the terms the philosopher R. S. Peters (1966, 1972) employs in his analysis of the concept of the educated man, he did not simply acquire knowledge and skill. He acquired conceptual schemes to raise his knowledge beyond the level of a collection of disjointed facts and to enable him to understand the "reason why" of things. Moreover, the knowledge he acquired is not "inert": It characterizes the way he looks at the world and it involves the kind of commitment to the standards of evidence and canons of proof of the various disciplines that comes

Jane Roland Martin, "Becoming Educated." *Journal of Education*, Volume 167, No. 3, Copyright 1985. Reprinted with permission of the Editorial Board of the *Journal of Education*.

A version of this paper appears in Martin (1985, Ch. 7). The paper is based on my address to Division B at the annual meeting of the American Educational Research Association, April 26, 1984, New Orleans. An earlier version was presented under the title "Excellence and Curriculum: Alienation or Integration?" at the symposium on Excellence and the Curriculum in honor of Mauritz Johnson, November 5, 1983, Albany, New York.

from "getting on the inside of a form of thought and awareness" (Peters, 1961, p. 9).

Quite a success story, yet *Hunger of Memory* is notable primarily as a narrative of loss. In becoming an educated person Rodriguez loses his fluency in Spanish, but that is the least of it. As soon as English becomes the language of the Rodriguez family, the special feeling of closeness at home is diminished. Furthermore, as his days are increasingly devoted to understanding the meaning of words, it becomes difficult for Rodriguez to hear intimate family voices. When it is Spanish-speaking, his home is a noisy, playful, warm, emotionally charged environment; with the advent of English the atmosphere becomes quiet and restrained. There is no acrimony. The family remains loving. But the experience of "feeling individualized" by family members is now rare, and occasions for intimacy are infrequent.

Rodriguez tells a story of alienation: from his parents, for whom he soon has no names; from the Spanish language, in which he loses his childhood fluency; from his Mexican roots, in which he shows no interest; from his own feelings and emotions, which all but disappear as he learns to control them; from his body itself, as he discovers when he takes a construction job after his senior year in college.

John Dewey spent his life trying to combat the tendency of educators to divorce mind from body and reason from emotion. Rodriguez's educational autobiography documents these divorces, and another one Dewey deplored, that of self from other. Above all *Hunger of Memory* depicts a journey from intimacy to isolation. Close ties with family members are dissolved as public anonymity replaces private attention. Rodriguez becomes a spectator in his own home as noise gives way to silence and connection to distance. School, says Rodriguez, bade him trust "lonely" reason primarily. And there is enough time and "silence," he adds, "to think about ideas (big ideas)" (p. 47).

What is the significance of this narrative of loss? Not every American has Rodriguez's good fortune of being born into a loving home filled with the warm sounds of intimacy, yet the separation and distance he ultimately experienced are not unique to him. On the contrary, they represent the natural end point of the educational journey Rodriguez took.

Dewey repeatedly pointed out that the distinction educators draw between liberal and vocational education represents a separation of mind from body, head from hand, thought from action. Since we define an educated person as one who has had and has profited from a liberal education, these splits are built into our ideal of the educated person. Since most definitions of excellence in education derive from that ideal, these splits are built into them as well. A split between reason and emotion is built into our definitions of excellence too, for we take the aim of a liberal education to be the development not of mind as a whole, but of rational mind. We define this in terms of the acquisition of knowledge and understanding, construed narrowly (Martin, 1981b). It is not surprising that Rodriguez acquires habits of quiet reflection rather than noisy activity, reasoned deliberation rather than spontaneous reaction, dispassionate inquiry rather than emotional response, abstract analytic theorizing rather than concrete story-telling. These are integral to the ideal of the educated person that has come down to us from Plato.

Upon completion of his educational journey Rodriguez bears a remarkable resemblance to the guardians of the Just State that Plato constructs in the *Republic*. Those worthies are to acquire through their education a wide range of theoretical knowledge, highly developed powers of reasoning, and the qualities of objectivity and emotional distance. To be sure, not one of Plato's guardians will be the "disembodied mind" Rodriguez becomes, for Plato believed that a strong mind requires a strong body. But Plato designed for his guardians an education of heads, not hands. (Presumably the artisans of the Just State would serve as their hands.) Moreover, considering the passions to be unruly and untrustworthy, Plato held up for the guardians an ideal of self-discipline and self-government in which reason keeps feeling and emotion under tight control. As a consequence, although he wanted the guardians of the Just State to be so connected to one another that they would feel each other's pains and pleasures, the educational ideal he developed emphasizes "inner" harmony at the expense of "outward" connection. If his guardians do not begin their lives in intimacy, as Rodriguez did, their education, like his, is intended to confirm in them a sense of self in isolation from others.

Do the separations bequeathed to us by Plato matter? The great irony of the liberal education that comes down to us from Plato and still today as the mark of an educated person is that it is neither tolerant nor generous (Martin, 1981b). As Richard Rodriguez discovered, there is no place in it for education of the body, and since most action involves bodily movement, this means there is little room in it for education of action. Nor is there room for education of other-regarding feelings and emotions. The liberally educated person will be provided with knowledge about others, but will not be taught to care about their welfare or to act kindly toward them. That person will be given some understanding of society, but will not be taught to feel its injustices or even to be concerned over its fate. The liberally educated person will be an ivory tower person—one who can reason but has no desire to solve real problems in the real world—or else a technical person who likes to solve real problems but does not care about the solutions' consequences for real people and for the earth itself.

The case of Rodriguez illuminates several unhappy aspects of our Platonic heritage, while concealing another. No one who has seen Frederick Wiseman's film *High School* can forget the woman who reads to the assembled students a letter she has received from a pupil now in Vietnam. But for a few teachers who cared, she tells her audience, Bob Walters, a sub-average student academically, "might have been a nobody." Instead, while awaiting a plane that is to drop him behind the DMZ, he has written her to say that he has made the school the beneficiary of his life insurance policy. "I am a little jittery right now," she reads. She is not to worry about him, however, because "I am only a body doing a job." Measuring his worth as a human being by his provision for the sohool, she overlooks the fact that Bob Walters was not merely participating in a war of dubious morality but was taking pride in being an automaton.

High School was made in 1968, but Bob Walters's words were echoed many times over by 18- and 19-year-old Marine recruits in the days immediately following the Grenada invasion. Readers of *Hunger of Memory* will not be surprised. The underside of a liberal education devoted to the development of "disembodied minds" is a vocational education whose business is the production of "mindless bodies." In

Plato's Just State, where, because of their rational powers, the specially educated few will rule the many, a young man's image of himself as "only a body doing a job" is the desired one. That the educational theory and practice of a democracy derives from Plato's explicitly undemocratic philosophical vision is disturbing. We are not supposed to have two classes of people, those who think and those who do not. We are not supposed to have two kinds of people, those who rule and those who obey.

The Council for Basic Education has long recommended, and some people concerned with excellence in education now suggest, that a liberal education at least through high school be extended to all. For the sake of argument let us suppose that this program can be carried out without making more acute the inequities it is meant to erase. We would then presumably have a world in which no one thinks of him- or herself as simply a body doing a job. We would, however, have a world filled with unconnected, uncaring, emotionally impoverished people. Even if it were egalitarian, it would be a sorry place in which to live. Nor would the world be better if somehow we combined Rodriguez's liberal education with a vocational one. For assuming it to be peopled by individuals who joined head and hand, reason would still be divorced from feeling and emotion, and each individual cut off from others.

The world we live in is just such a place. It is a world of child abuse and family violence (Breines & Gordon, 1983), a world in which one out of every four women will be raped at some time in her life (Johnson, 1980; Lott, Reilly & Howard, 1982). Our world is on the brink of nuclear and/or ecological disaster. Efforts to overcome these problems, as well as the related ones of poverty and economic scarcity, flounder today under the direction of people who try hard to be rational, objective, autonomous agents but, like Plato's guardians, do not know how to sustain human relationships or respond directly to human needs. Indeed, they do not even see the value of trying to do so. Of course, it is a mistake to suppose that education alone can solve this world's problems. Yet if there is to be hope of the continuation of life on earth, let alone of a good life for all, as educators we must strive to do more than join mind and body, head and hand, thought and action.

REDEFINING EDUCATION

For Rodriguez, the English language is a metaphor. In the literal sense of the term he had to learn English to become an educated *American*, yet, in his narrative the learning of English represents the acquisition not so much of a new natural language as of new ways of thinking, acting, and being that he associates with the public world. Rodriguez makes it clear that the transition from Spanish to English represented for him the transition almost every child in our society makes from the "private world" of home to the "public world" of business, politics, and culture. He realizes that Spanish is not intrinsically a private language and English a public one, although his own experiences made it seem this way. He knows that the larger significance of his story lies in the fact that education inducts one into new activities and processes.

In my research on the place of women in educational thought (1982, 1985), I have invoked a distinction between the productive and the reproductive processes of society and have argued that both historians of educational thought and contemporary philosophers of education define the educational realm in relation to society's productive processes only. Briefly, the reproductive processes include not simply the biological reproduction of the species, but the rearing of children to maturity and the related activities of keeping house, managing a household, and serving the needs and purposes of family members. In turn, the productive processes include political, social, and cultural activities as well as economic ones. This distinction is related to the one Rodriguez repeatedly draws between public and private worlds, for in our society reproductive processes are for the most part carried on in the private world of the home and domesticity, and productive processes in the public world of politics and work. Rodriguez's autobiography reveals that the definition of education as preparation solely for carrying on the productive processes of society is not a figment of the academic imagination.

Needless to say, the liberal education Rodriguez received did not fit him to carry on all productive processes of society. Aiming at the development of rational mind, his liberal education prepared him to be a consumer and creator of ideas, not an auto mechanic or factory worker. A vocational education, had he received one, would have prepared him to work with his hands and use procedures designed by others. They are very different kinds of education, yet both are designed to fit students to carry on productive, not reproductive, societal processes.

Why do I stress the connection between the definition of education and the productive processes of society? *Hunger of Memory* contains a wonderful account of Rodriguez's grandmother telling him stories of her life. He is moved by the sounds she makes and by the message of intimacy her person transmits. The words themselves are not important to him, for he perceives the private world in which she moves—the world of childrearing and homemaking—to be one of feeling and emotion, intimacy and connection, and hence a realm of the nonrational. In contrast, he sees the public world—the world of productive processes for which his education fit him—as the realm of the rational. Feeling and emotion have no place in it, and neither do intimacy and connection. Instead, analysis, critical thinking, and self-sufficiency are the dominant values.

Rodriguez's assumption that feeling and emotion, intimacy and connection are naturally related to the home and society's reproductive processes and that these qualities are irrelevant to carrying on the productive processes is commonly accepted. But then, it is to be expected that their development is ignored by education in general and by liberal education in particular. Since education is supposed to equip people for carrying on productive societal processes, from a practical standpoint would it not be foolhardy for liberal or vocational studies to foster these traits?

Only in light of the fact that education turns its back on the reproductive processes of society and the private world of the home can Rodriguez's story of alienation be understood. His alienation from his body will reoccur so long as we equate being an educated person with having a liberal education. His journey of isolation and divorce from his emotions will be repeated so long as we define education exclusively in relation to the productive processes of society. But the assumption of inevitability underlying *Hunger of Memory* is mistaken. Education need not separate mind from body and thought from action, for it need not draw a sharp line between liberal and vocational education. More to the point, it need not separate reason from emotion and self from other. The reproductive processes *can* be brought into the educational realm thereby overriding the theoretical and practical grounds for ignoring feeling and emotion, intimacy and connection.

If we define education in relation to *both* kinds of societal processes and act upon our redefinition, future generations will not have to experience Rodriguez's pain. He never questions the fundamental dichotomies upon which his education rests. We must question them so that we can effect the reconciliation of reason and emotion, self and other, that Dewey sought. There are, moreover, two overwhelming reasons for favoring such a redefinition, both of which take us beyond Dewey.

All of us—male and female—participate in the reproductive processes of society. In the past, many have thought that education for carrying them on was not necessary: These processes were assumed to be the responsibility of women and it was supposed that by instinct a woman would automatically acquire the traits or qualities associated with them. The contemporary statistics on child abuse are enough by themselves to put to rest the doctrine of maternal instinct. Furthermore, both sexes have responsibility for making the reproductive processes of society work well. Family living and childrearing are not today, if they ever were, solely in the hands of women. Nor should they be. Thus, both sexes need to learn to carry on the reproductive processes of society just as in the 1980s both sexes need to learn to carry on the productive ones.

The reproductive processes are of central importance to society, yet it would be a terrible mistake to suppose that the traits and qualities traditionally associated with these processes have no relevance beyond them. Jonathan Schell (1982, p. 175) has said "The nuclear peril makes all of us, whether we happen to have children of our own or not, the parents of all future generations" and that the will we must have to save the human species is a form of love resembling "the generative love of parents." He is speaking of what Nancy Chodorow (1978) calls nurturing capacities and Carol Gilligan (1982) calls an "ethics of care." Schell is right. The fate of the earth depends on all of us possessing these qualities. Thus, although these qualities are associated in our minds with the reproductive processes of society, they have the broadest moral, social, and political significance. Care, concern, connectedness, nurturance are as important for carrying on society's economic, political, and social processes as its reproductive ones. If education is to help us acquire them, it must be redefined.

THE WORKINGS OF GENDER

It is no accident that in *Hunger of Memory* the person who embodies nurturing capacities and an ethics of care is a woman—Rodriguez's grandmother. The two kinds of societal processes are gender-related and so are the traits our culture associates with them. According to our cultural stereotypes, males are objective, analytical, rational, interested in ideas and things. They have no interpersonal orientation; they are not nurturant or supportive, empathetic or sensitive. Women, on the other hand, possess the traits men lack (Kaplan & Bean, 1976; Kaplan & Sedney, 1980).

Education is also gender-related. Our definition of its function makes it so. For if education is viewed as preparation for carrying on processes historically associated with males, it will inculcate traits the culture considers masculine. If the concept of education is tied by definition to the productive processes of society, our ideal of the educated person will coincide with the cultural stereotype of a male human being, and our definitions of excellence in education will embody "masculine" traits.

Of course, it is possible for members of one sex to acquire personal traits or qualities our cultural stereotypes attribute to the other. Thus females can and do acquire traits incorporated in our educational ideal. However, it must be understood that these traits are *genderized*; that is, they are appraised differentially when they are possessed by males and females (Beardsley, 1977; Martin, 1981a, 1985). For example, whereas a male will be admired for his rational powers, a woman who is analytical and critical will be derided or shunned or will be told that she thinks like a man. Even if this latter is intended as a compliment, since we take masculinity and femininity to lie at opposite ends of a single continuum, she will thereby be judged as lacking in femininity and, as a consequence, judged abnormal or unnatural. Elizabeth Janeway (1971, p. 96) has said, and I am afraid she is right, that "unnatural" and "abnormal" are the equivalent for our age of what "damned" meant to our ancestors.

Because his hands were soft Rodriguez worried that his education was making him effeminate.[1] Imagine his anxieties on that score if he had been educated in those supposedly feminine virtues of caring and concern and had been taught to sustain intimate relationships and value connection. To be sure, had his education fostered these qualities, Rodriguez would not have had to travel a road from intimacy to isolation. I do not mean to suggest that there would have been no alienation at all; his is a complex case involving class, ethnicity, and color. But an education in which reason was joined to feeling and emotion and self to other would have yielded a very different life story. Had his education fostered these qualities, however, Rodriguez would have experienced another kind of hardship.

The pain Rodriguez suffers is a consequence of the loss of intimacy and the stunting of emotional growth that are themselves consequences of education. Now it is possible that Rodriguez's experience is more representative of males than of females. But if it be the case that females tend to maintain emotional growth and intimate connections better than males do, one thing is certain: educated girls are penalized for what Rodriguez considers his *gains*. If they become analytic, objective thinkers and autonomous agents, they are judged less feminine than they should be. Thus, for them the essential myth of childhood is every bit as painful as it was for Rodriguez, for they are alienated from their own identity as females.

When education is defined so as to give the reproductive processes of society their due, and the virtues of nurturance and care associated with those processes are fostered in both males and females, educated men can expect to suffer for possessing traits genderized in favor of females as educated women now do for possessing traits genderized in favor of males. This is not to say that males will be placed in the double bind educated females find themselves in now, for males will acquire traits genderized in their own favor as well as ones genderized in favor of females, whereas the traits educated females must acquire today are *all* genderized in favor of males. On the other hand, since traits genderized in favor of females are considered lesser virtues, if virtues at all (Blum, 1980), and the societal processes with which they are associated are thought to be relatively unimportant, males will be placed in the position of having to acquire traits both they and their society consider inferior.

One of the most important findings of contemporary scholarship is that our culture embraces a hierarchy of values that places the productive processes of society and their associated traits above society's reproductive processes and the associated traits of care and nurturance. There is nothing new about this. We are the inheritors of a tradition of Western thought according to which the functions, tasks, and traits associated with females are deemed less valuable than those associated with males. In view of these findings, the difficulties facing those of us who would transform Rodriguez's educational journey from one of alienation to one of the integration of reason and emotion, of self and other, become apparent.

It is important to understand the magnitude of the changes to be wrought by an education that takes the integration of reason and emotion, self and other, seriously. Granted, when girls today embark on Rodriguez's journey they acquire traits gender-ized in favor of the "opposite" sex; but if on account of trait genderization they experience hardships Rodriguez did not, they can at least console themselves that their newly acquired traits, along with the societal processes to which the traits are at-tached, are considered valuable. Were we to attempt to change the nature of our educational ideal without also changing our value hierarchy, boys and men would have no such consolation. Without this consolation, however, we can be quite sure that the change we desire would not come to pass.

TOWARD AN INTEGRATED CURRICULUM

Just as the value structure I have been describing is reflected in our ideal of the educated person, so too it is reflected in the curriculum such a person is supposed to study. A large body of scholarship documents the extent to which the academic fields constituting the subjects of the liberal curriculum exclude women's lives, works, and experiences from their subject matter or else distort them by projecting the cultural stereotype of a female onto the evidence.[2] History, philosophy, politics; art and music; the social and behavioral sciences; even the biological and physical sciences give pride of place to male experience and achievements and to the societal processes thought to belong to men.

The research to which I refer reveals the place of women—or rather the absence thereof—in the theories, interpretations, and narratives constituting the disciplines of knowledge. Since the subject matter of the liberal curriculum is drawn from these disciplines, that curriculum gives pride of place to male experience and achievements and to the societal processes associated with men. In so doing, it is the bearer of bad news about women and the reproductive processes of society. Can it be doubted that when the works of women are excluded from the subject matter of the fields into which they are being initiated, students of both sexes will come to believe, or else will have their existing belief reinforced, that males are superior and females are inferior human beings? Can it be doubted that when in the course of this initiation the lives and experiences of women are scarcely mentioned, males and females will come to believe, or else believe more strongly than ever, that the ways in which women have lived and the things women have done throughout history have no value?

At campuses across the country projects are underway to incorporate the growing body of new scholarship on women into the liberal curriculum. Such efforts must be undertaken at all levels of schooling, not simply because women comprise one half the world's population, but because the exclusion of women from the subject matter of the "curriculum proper" constitutes a hidden curriculum in the validation of one gender, its associated tasks, traits, and functions, and the denigration of the other. Supporting our culture's genderized hierarchy of value even as it reflects it, this hidden curriculum must be raised to consciousness and counteracted (Martin, 1976). Introduction of the new scholarship on women into the liberal curriculum proper—and for that matter into the vocational curriculum too—makes this possible, on the one hand because it allows students to understand the workings of gender and, on the other, because it provides them with the opportunity to appreciate women's traditional tasks, traits, and functions.

In a curriculum encompassing the experience of one sex, not two, questions of gender are automatically eliminated. For the value hierarchy under discussion to be understood, as it must be if it is to be abolished, its genderized roots must be exposed. Furthermore, if intimacy and connection are to be valued as highly as independence and distance, and if emotion and feeling are to be viewed as positive rather than untrustworthy elements of personality, women must no longer be viewed as different and alien—as the Other, to use Simone de Beauvoir's expression (1961).

Thus, we need to incorporate the study of women into curricula so that females—their lives, experiences, works, and attributes—are devalued by neither sex. But simply incorporating the new scholarship on women in the curriculum does not address the alienation and loss Rodriguez describes so well. To overcome these we must seek not only a transformation of the content of curriculum proper, but an expansion of the educational realm to include the reproductive processes of society and a corresponding redefinition of what it means to become educated.

The expansion of the educational realm I propose does not entail an extension of a skill-oriented home economics education to males. Although it is important for both sexes to learn to cook and sew, I have in mind something different when I say that education must give the reproductive processes of society their due. The traits associated with women as wives and mothers—nurturance, care, compassion, connection, sensitivity to others, a willingness to put aside one's own projects, a desire to build and maintain relationships—need to be incorporated into our ideal. This does not mean that we should fill up the curriculum with courses in the three C's of caring, concern, and connection. Given a redefinition of education, Compassion 101a need no more be listed in a school's course offerings than Objectivity 101a is now. Just as the productive processes of society have given us the general curricular goals of rationality and individual autonomy, so too the reproductive processes yield general goals. And just as rationality and autonomy are posited as goals of particular subjects, e.g., science, as well as of the curriculum as a whole, so nurturance and connection can be understood as overarching educational goals and also as the goals of particular subjects.

But now a puzzling question arises. Given that the standard subjects of the curriculum derive from the productive processes of society, must we not insert cooking and sewing and perhaps childrearing into the curriculum if we want caring, concern, and connection to be educational objectives? Science, math, history, literature, auto mechanics, refrigeration, typing: these are the subjects of the curriculum now and these derive from productive processes. If for subjects deriving from productive processes we set educational goals whose source is the reproductive processes of society, do we not distort these subjects beyond recognition? But then, ought we not to opt instead for a divided curriculum with two sets of subjects? One set might be derived from the productive processes of society and foster traits associated with those, with the other set derived from the reproductive processes of society and fostering their associated traits. Is this the only way to do justice to both sets of traits?

If possible, a replication within the curriculum of the split between the productive and reproductive processes of society is to be avoided. So long as education insists on linking nurturing capacities and the three C's to subjects arising out of the reproductive processes, we will lose sight of their *general* moral, social, and political significance. Moreover, so long as rationality and autonomous judgment are considered to belong exclusively to the productive processes of society, the reproductive ones will continue to be devalued. Thus, unless it is essential to divide up curricular goal according to the classification of a subject as productive or reproductive, we ought not to do so. That it is not essential becomes clear once we give up our stereotypical pictures of the two kinds of societal process.

Readers of June Goodfield's *An Imagined World* (1981) will know that feeling and emotion, intimacy and connection can be an integral part of the processes of scientific discovery.[3] Goodfield recorded the day-to-day activities of Anna, a Portuguese scientist studying lymphocytes in a cancer laboratory in New York. Anna's relationship to her colleagues *and* to the cells she studied provides quite a contrast to the rationalistic, atomistic vision of scientists and scientific discovery most of us have. To be sure, some years ago James Watson (1969) made it clear that scientists are human. But Watson portrayed scientific discovery as a race between ambitious, aggressive, highly competitive contestants while Goodfield's Anna calls it "a kind of birth." Fear, urgency, intense joy; loneliness, intimacy, and a desire to share: these are some of the emotions that motivate and shape Anna's thought even as her reasoned analysis and her objective scrutiny of evidence engender passion. Moreover, she is bound closely to her colleagues in the lab by feeling, as well as by scientific need, and she empathizes with the lymphocytes she studies as well as with the sick people she hopes will one day benefit from her work.

If scientific activity can flourish in an atmosphere of cooperation and connection, and important scientific discoveries can take place when passionate feeling motivates and shapes thought, then surely it is not necessary for science education to be directed solely toward rationalistic, atomistic goals. And if nurturant capacities and the three C's of caring, concern, and connection can become goals of science teaching without that subject being betrayed or abandoned, surely they can become the goals of *any* subject.

By the same token, if rational thought and independent judgment are components of successful childrearing and family living, it is not necessary to design education in subjects deriving from the reproductive processes of society solely around "affective" goals. That they can and should be part and parcel of these activities was argued long ago, and very convincingly, by both Mary Wollstonecraft and Catharine Beecher (Martin, 1985) and is a basic tenet of the home economics profession today.

Thus, just as nurturance and concern can be goals of any subject, rationality and independent judgment can also be. The temptation to institute a sharp separation of goals within an expanded educational realm corresponding to a sharp separation of subjects must, then, be resisted so that the general significance of the very real virtues we associate with women and the reproductive processes of society is understood and these virtues themselves are fostered in everyone.

CONCLUSION

In becoming educated one does not have to travel Rodriguez's road from intimacy to isolation. His journey of alienation is a function of a definition of education, a particular ideal of the educated person, and a particular definition of excellence—all of which can be rejected. Becoming educated can be a journey of integration, not alienation. The detailed task of restructuring an ideal of the educated person to guide this new journey I leave for another occasion. The general problem to be solved is that of uniting thought and action, reason and emotion, self and other. This was the problem Dewey addressed, but his failure to understand the workings of gender made it impossible for him to solve it.

I leave the task of mapping the precise contours of a transformed curriculum for another occasion too. The general problem to be solved here is that of giving the reproductive processes of society—and the females who have traditionally been assigned responsibility for carrying them on—their due. Only then will feeling and emotion, intimacy and connection be perceived as valuable qualities so that a journey of integration is possible.

Loss, pain, isolation: It is a tragedy that these should be the results of becoming educated, the consequences of excellence. An alternative journey to Rodriguez's requires fundamental changes in both educational theory and practice. Since these changes will make it possible to diffuse throughout the population the nurturant capacities and the ethics of care that are absolutely essential to the survival of society itself, indeed, to the survival of life on earth, they should ultimately be welcomed even by those who would claim that the loss, pain, and isolation Rodriguez experienced in becoming educated did him no harm.

NOTES

1. Quite clearly, Rodriguez's class background is a factor in this judgment. Notice, however, that the form his fear takes relates to gender.
2. This scholarship cannot possibly be cited here. For reviews of the literature in the various academic disciplines see past issues of *Signs: Journal of Women in Culture and Society*.
3. See also Keller (1983).

REFERENCES

Beardsley, E. (1977). Traits and genderization. In M. Vetterling-Braggin, F. A. Elliston, & J. English (Eds.), *Feminism and philosophy* (pp. 117-123). Totowa, NJ Littlefield.

Blum, L. (1980). *Friendship, altruism, and morality.* London: Routledge & Kegan Paul.

Breines, W., & Gordon, L. (1983). The new scholarship on family violence. *Signs, 8*(3), 493–507.

de Beauvoir, S. (1961). *The second sex.* New York: Bantam.

Chodorow, N. (1978). *The reproduction of mothering.* Berkeley: University of California Press.

Galligan, C. (1982). *In a different voice.* Cambridge: Harvard University Press.

Goodfield, J. (1981). *An imagined world.* New York: Harper & Row.

Janeway, E. (1971). *Man's world, woman's place.* New York: Morrow.

Johnson, A. G. (1980). On the prevalence of rape in the United States. *Signs, 6* (1), 136–146.

Kaplan, A. G., & Bean, J. P. (Eds.). (1976). *Beyond sex-role stereotypes.* Boston: Little, Brown.

Kaplan, A. G., & Sedney, M. A. (1980). *Psychology and sex roles.* Boston: Little, Brown.

Keller, E. F. (1983). *A feeling for the organism.* San Francisco: W. H. Freeman.

Lott, B., Reilly, M. E. & Howard, D. R. (1982). Sexual assault and harassment: A campus community case study. *Signs, 8*(2), 296–319.

Martin, J. R. (1976). What should we do with a hidden curriculum when we find one? *Curriculum Inquiry, 6*(2), 135–151.

Martin, J. R. (1981a). The ideal of the educated person. *Educational Theory, 31*(2), 97–109.

Martin, J. R. (1981b). Needed: A new paradigm for liberal education. In J. F. Soltis (Ed.), *Philosophy and education* (pp. 37–59). Chicago: University of Chicago Press.

Martin, J. R. (1982). Excluding women from the educational realm. *Harvard Educational Review, 52*(2), 133–148.

Martin, J. R. (1985). *Reclaiming a conversation: The ideal of the educated woman.* New Haven: Yale University Press.

Peters, R. S. (1972). Education and the educated man. In R. F. Dearden, P. H. Hirst, & R. S. Peters (Eds.), *A critique of current eductional aims.* London: Routledge & Kegan Paul.

Peters, R. S. (1966). *Ethics and education.* London: Allen & Unwin.

Rodriguez, R. (1982). *Hunger of memory.* Boston: David R. Godine.

Schell, J. (1982). *The fate of the earth.* New York: Avon.

Watson, J. D. (1969). *The double helix.* New York: New American Library.

Racelessness as a Factor in Black Students' School Success: Pragmatic Strategy or Pyrrhic Victory?

Signithia Fordham

INTRODUCTION

In recent years, a major change appears to have occurred in the aspirations of Black Americans toward social mobility. Previous generations of Black Americans felt a great deal of pride and satisfaction when one member of the community "made it." For example, when Thurgood Marshall, Ralph Bunche, Lena Horne, and Jackie Robinson became "The First" Black Americans to break the color barrier in their chosen careers, most Black Americans saw their accomplishments as signs of the weakening of racial barriers and evidence that there would be less resistance to the efforts of other members of the group who wanted to pursue similar careers. These generations of Black Americans defined success for one Black person as success for all Black people.

Increasingly, however, today's Black Americans are rejecting the older generation's attitude toward social mobility: they do not view the accomplishments of individual members of the group as evidence of the advancement of the entire group; instead, they more often define Black achievement in terms of the collectivity (Dizard, 1970). Success now means that Blacks must succeed *as a people*, not just as individual Blacks. In other words, contemporary Black Americans are opting for a more inclusive view of success.

Black children who grow up in predominantly Black communities, then, are raised in the collective view of success, an ethos that is concerned with the Black community as a whole. But since an individualistic rather than a collective ethos is sanctioned in the school context, Black children enter school having to unlearn or, at least, to modify their own culturally sanctioned interactional and behavioral styles and adopt those styles rewarded in the school context if they wish to achieve academic success.[1]

At the heart of this paper is the struggle that Black adolescents face in having to "choose" between the individualistic ethos of the school—which generally reflects the ethos of the dominant society—and the collective ethos of their community. I will describe and analyze one strategy for achieving success that high school students (as well as adults) utilize: that is, the phenomenon of becoming raceless. Specifically, this paper examines the complex relationship between Black adolescents' racial identity and their school performance, and the role that the larger social structure plays in that relationship. I argue that, despite the growing acceptance of ethnicity and strong ethnic identification in the larger American society, school officials appear to disapprove of a strong ethnic identity among Black adolescents, and these contradictory messages produce conflict and ambivalence in the adolescents, both toward developing strong racial and ethnic identities and toward performing well in school. My assertions lead to this question: Is racelessness among Black adolescents a pragmatic strategy or Pyrrhic victory?

This paper is divided into five sections. The first section explains the concept of fictive kinship, the dominant cultural system that exists in Black communities, and its relation to the formation of an oppositional social identity (Fordham, 1981, 1982, 1985; Fordham & Ogbu, 1986). The second section of the paper introduces the phenomenon of racelessness and the efficacy of utilizing it as a strategy for vertical mobility. The third section of the paper describes the research setting. The fourth section presents and analyzes my research data, which suggest that Black students must develop a raceless persona in order to achieve academic success. The final section of the paper concludes with implications of racelessness and suggestions for minimizing the need for such a strategy for social mobility and academic excellence among Black adolescents.

The findings emerging from this research are not necessarily generalizable to all Black adolescents. The data were derived from a small segment of the larger group of "Black adolescents," and from a school located in a poor Black community. Thus, in order to formulate a general theory of Black adolescent school achievement, research must be conducted in a variety of settings, such as middle-class Black schools, predominantly White private schools, and parochial schools, and with Black adolescents who represent a cross section of cultural backgrounds and socioeconomic classes. The significance of this research is that it identifies a social phenomenon that must be examined if we are to fully understand the Black adolescent school experience in the United States.

FICTIVE KINSHIP AND OPPOSITIONAL SOCIAL IDENTITY

In studying the social identity and cultural frame of reference among Black Americans, I have found the anthropological concept "fictive kinship" useful (Fordham, 1982, 1983, 1985a). It refers to a kinship-like connection between and among persons in a society, not related by blood or marriage, who have maintained essential reciprocal social or economic relationships (Bloch, 1971; Brain, 1972; Folb, 1980; Fortes, 1969; Freed, 1973; Hale, 1982; Liebow, 1967; Norbeck & Befu, 1958; Pitt-Rivers, 1968, 1973; Stack, 1974; Staples, 1975, 1981). Among Black Americans the connection extends beyond the social and economic, and includes a political function as well. The term conveys the idea of "brotherhood" and "sisterhood" of *all* Black Americans; thus, a sense of peoplehood or collective social identity. This sense is evident in the various kinship terms that Black Americans use to refer to one another, such as "brother," "sister," and "blood" (Folb, 1980; Liebow, 1967; Sargent, 1985; Stack, 1974).

As used here, the term "fictive kinship" denotes a cultural symbol of collective identity among Black Americans, and is based on more than just skin color. The term also implies the particular mind-set, or world view, of those persons who are considered to be "Black," and is used to denote the moral judgment the group makes on its members (Brain, 1972). Essentially, the concept suggests that merely possessing African features or being of African descent does not automatically make one a Black person or a member in good standing of the group. One can be black in color, but choose not to seek membership in the fictive-kinship system. One can also be denied membership by the group because one's behavior, attitudes, and activities are perceived as being at variance with those thought to be appropriate and group-specific, which are culturally patterned and serve to delineate "us" from "them." An example is the tendency for Black Americans to emphasize *group loyalty* in situations involving conflict or competition with Whites.

Only Black Americans are involved in the evaluation of group members' eligibility for membership in the fictive-kinship system; thus, they control the criteria used to judge one's worthiness for membership. That is, the determination of the criteria for membership in the fictive-kinship system rests solely within the Black community. Furthermore, criteria for fictive kinship have a special significance for Black people, because they are regarded as the ideal by which members of the group are judged. This judgment is also the medium through which Black Americans distinguish "real" from "spurious" members of the community (Williams, 1981a, 1981b).

Additionally, as I view it, the fictive-kinship system described here has another important function. It symbolizes Black Americans' sense of peoplehood in opposition to White American social identity. In fact, the system was developed partly in response to two types of mistreatment from Whites: the economic and instrumental exploitation by Whites during and after slavery, and the historical and continuing tendency of White Americans to treat Black Americans as an undifferentiated mass of people, indiscriminately ascribing to them certain inherent strengths and weaknesses (Anderson, 1975; Bullock, 1970; Drake & Cayton, 1970; Myrdal, 1944; Spivey, 1978). Black Americans have generally responded to this mistreatment by inverting the negative stereotypes and assumptions of Whites into positive and functional attributes (Fordham, 1982; Holt, 1972; Ogbu, 1983). Thus, Black Americans may have transformed White people's assumptions of Black homogeneity into a collective identity system.

An example of collective treatment by White Americans is evident in one event that occurred following Nat Turner's "insurrection" in Southampton, Virginia, in 1831. Prior to Turner's insurrection, the general practice in Washington, DC, was to allow Black children to attend Sunday school with the White residents in the city. After that incident, Whites restricted the movement of Blacks into the predominantly White community and limited contact among Blacks themselves as well, regardless of their place of residence or personal involvement in the insurrection (Haley, 1976; Styron, 1966). Black children were forbidden to attend Sunday School with White children, although local Whites knew that the Black children had no part in the insurrection. What was well understood by Black people in Southampton, Virginia, in Washington, DC, and elsewhere in the country, was that the onus for Turner's behavior was extended to all Black Americans solely on the basis of their being Black. Numerous arbitrary mistreatments of this kind, coupled with a knowledge that they were denied true assimilation into the mainstream of American life, encouraged Black Americans to develop what DeVos (1967) calls "ethnic consolidation," a sense of peoplehood expressed in fictive-kinship feelings and language (Green, 1981).

Black children learn the meaning of fictive kinship from their parents and peers while they are growing up. It appears, moreover, that they learn it early enough, and well enough, so that they even tend to associate their life chances and "success" potential with those of their peers and other members of the community. The collective ethos of the fictive-kinship system is challenged by the individual ethos of the dominant culture when the children enter school, and when the children experience the competition between the two for their loyalty. For many Black adolescents, therefore, the mere act of attending school is evidence of either a conscious or semiconscious rejection of the indigenous Black American culture (Weis, 1985a, 1985b). Thus, in order to reinforce their belief that they are still legitimate members of the Black community, these students, wittingly and unwittingly, "create" (Weis, 1985b) an environment—for example, through the use of "Black English"—that reinforces the indigenous culture from which they are separated through the process of schooling. In recreating their indigenous culture in the school context, Weis (1985a, 1985b) argues, they inadvertently ensure their "failure" (see also MacLeod, 1987; Willis, 1981). Conversely, those students who minimize their connection to the indigenous culture and assimilate into the school culture improve their chances of succeeding in school. Unlike the students who seek to maintain their identification and affiliation with the indigenous culture, students who assimilate seek to maximize their success potential by minimizing their relationship to the Black community and to the stigma attached to "blackness." These students attempt to develop a raceless persona in order to succeed in school and in life. Racelessness, then, is the desired and eventual outcome of developing a raceless persona, and is either a conscious or unconscious effort on the part of such students to disaffiliate themselves from the fictive-kinship system described above.

RACELESSNESS AS A STRATEGY
FOR VERTICAL MOBILITY

I am a Black. . . . I suppose I still believe that there is a place in space or time where the pigmentation of my skin might be of only incidental relevance—where it could be possible to give a socially meaningful description of who I am and what I've done without using the word black at all. I have abandoned the belief that somewhere or someone will turn out to be here and now. So, for all practical purposes, I accept a belief that I have taken to calling "achromism" (from the Greek as meaning "not" and chroma, meaning "color"), which is that within the context of the society to which I belong by right—or misfortunate—of birth, nothing I shall accomplish or discover or earn or inherit or buy or sell or give away—nothing I shall ever do—*will outweigh the fact of my race in determining my destiny* [emphasis added]. (Bradley, 1982, pp. 58–59)

This self-description, quoted from David Bradley, the author of *The Chaneysville Incident*, asserts the critical importance of race, and places it as one of the most formidable obstacles in the lives of Black Americans. The practice of becoming raceless appears to have emerged as a strategy both to circumvent the stigma attached to being Black, and to achieve vertical mobility. In an effort to minimize the effects of race on their aspirations, some Black Americans have begun to take on attitudes, behaviors, and characteristics that may not generally be attributed to Black Americans. Out of their desire to secure jobs and positions that are above the employment ceiling typically placed on Blacks, they have adopted personae that indicate a lack of identification with, or a strong relationship to, the Black community in response to an implicit institutional mandate: Become "un-Black." The following examples from the world of corporate America illustrate this phenomenon.

In an article about the achievements of a Black disc jockey in Washington, DC, Gaines-Carter (1984) describes him in the following manner:

The voice is quiet thunder. Seductive. He stretches words, rolls them around in his mouth. Because his voice is neither black nor white and favors no geographical region, there has been some confusion about his racial identity. "I've had people look at me like I'm a ghost," says the 30-year-old disc jockey. "Some of them were expecting a white person. I hate for people to say I sound white. I don't. It's a matter of speaking properly, and anyone can do that." (Gaines-Carter, 1984, p. 6)

In a similar vein, Max Robinson, a Black reporter and one of three anchors on the ABC national news during the early 1980s, notes with bitter irony how his White superior's perception of him as a raceless person was influential in his achieving vertical mobility within that organization:

One of the problems I have is that we tend to separate everything, so at ABC Roone [Arledge; the director in charge of hiring news personnel] . . . mentioned on three occasions, he said, "I told you when I hired you, I didn't think you were black, or I didn't think of you as a black man." That's an incredible statement. I mean, I must be the funniest looking white man in this country. And the fact is, what he was trying to say, "I am going to give you credit. I admire you greatly, so therefore I will not think of you as black." (Transcript, The Oprah Winfrey Show, January 23, 1987, p. 4)

A third example of becoming "un-Black" can be found in the political arena. Here, particular Black candidates, in order to broaden their political base, often actively seek to minimize their allegiance to the Black community. This is evident in political elections in which the candidate is seeking election to a statewide or national office. MacPherson (1986) describes how Doug Wilder, a Black man who ran for the lieutenant-governor's seat in Virginia, won that election:

> In the state with the lowest percentage of blacks (17) of any southern state, he [Wilder] announced his candidacy in front of a picture of Harry Byrd and downplayed race until "people never perceived a Black candidate running." A statewide trek, backed up with television ads that included an archetypal white deputy sheriff endorsing Wilder, paid off. Wilder undid his tie and rolled up his sleeves in front of Confederate flags at country stores. Instant press, statewide and local, at every stop. (MacPherson, 1986, p. 4)

Although the examples above concern Black men adapting to the dominant ethos, Black women are also affected negatively by the phenomenon of racelessness. This is shown in a recent article discussing the success of Oprah Winfrey, television's latest talk-show host, who, the author claims, has very little emotional attachment to the Black community. Richman (1987) describes her as having suffered as a college student in a predominantly Black college in Tennessee because "she was uninterested in the compelling black issues of the day" (p. 56).

> They [the students at Tennessee State] all hated me—no, they resented me. I refused to conform to the militant thinking of the time. I hated, hated, hated college. Now I bristle when somebody comes up and says they went to Tennessee State with me. Everybody was angry for four years. It was an all-black college, and it was in to be angry. Whenever there was any conversation on race, I was on the other side, maybe because I never felt the kind of repression other black people are exposed to, I think I was called "nigger" once, when I was in fifth grade. (Richman, 1987, p. 56)

Perhaps no example more clearly typifies the tensions endemic to the racelessness issue in the work arena than the suicide of Leanita McClain, a journalist and the first Black American female to be elected to the Board of Directors of the *Chicago Tribune*. Having grown up in a predominantly Black community in Chicago, and subsequently having achieved enormous success in a White-dominated profession, McClain's sense of belonging and self-confidence were seriously undermined. To her White colleagues at the *Tribune*, McClain appeared raceless, indistinguishable from them.

Klose (1984) suggests that McClain was committed both to the development of a raceless persona and to racial integration as a social reality, and that she denied the existence of racism as an endemic feature of the social system in the United States. He cites as evidence a passage from a brief essay McClain wrote as a teenager:

> Why is there so much hate and contempt among people? I have never been blocked from anything because of my color, and I'm not ashamed of it either. My great-grandfather was Caucasian and so was my great-grandmother. . . . Why can't people just be people and live in peace and harmony? Maybe I'm in search of the perfect world. Or maybe I'm just me. That's it. I'm me. But to be me is to be nothing—to be nothing is to be me. And I love all people. Even pink polka-dotted ones with olive ears. (Klose, 1984, p. C2)

After having achieved the success she sought, McClain notes the personal transformation and the attendant anguish she feels:

> I am burdened daily with showing whites that blacks are people. I am, in the old vernacular, a credit to my race . . . my brother's keeper, and my sisters', though many of them have abandoned me because they think that I have abandoned them. . . . I assuage white guilt. I disprove black inadequacy and prove to my parents' generation that their patience was indeed a virtue. (McClain, cited in Klose, 1984, p. C3)

As she rose within the ranks of journalism, her commitment to the ideals espoused by the larger American society was constantly challenged, especially during and immediately after the election of Harold Washington, the first Black mayor of Chicago. Although McClain had previously denied the existence of racism, she slowly began to realize that it is a critical component of Black Americans' social reality that adversely affects all facets of their lives. This realization led to what she described as "hellish confusion" (McClain, 1983). Apparently, accepting this reality proved to be too burdensome for her.

Campbell (1982) further documents racelessness as a strategy used by Black Americans who choose, or who are chosen, to work in settings that historically have been off-limits to them. She notes the duality of their existence in such settings, and the resulting feelings of alienation and isolation.

> They consciously choose their speech, their walk, their mode of dress and car; they trim their hair lest a mountainous Afro set them apart. They know they have a high visibility, and they realize that their success depends not only on their *abilities* [emphasis added], but also on their white colleagues' feeling comfortable with them. (Campbell, 1982, p. 39)

Black Americans who gain entry into these predominantly White institutions are likely not only to experience enormous stress and feelings of isolation and ambivalence, but also to be viewed suspiciously by other Black people who are not themselves working in such institutions and who tend to view these members of the Black community as "un-Black" people.

> Many times, other blacks feel that these strange creatures with three-piece suits and briefcases have sold out. "A black manager can have a multi-million dollar deal on his mind," explains Dr. [Ronald] Brown of San Francisco. "But when he passes that black janitor, he knows that he'd better remember to speak; otherwise, he'll be labeled as 'acting white.' " (Campbell, 1982, p. 100)

Given the situation I have just presented, it is not surprising that many Black adolescents are keenly aware of the stigma associated with being successful in school, since school is seen as an agent of the dominant society. Based on the data gathered from my own research (which will be presented in the next section of the paper), I posit that *ambivalence* and *conflict* about academic effort appear to be at the center of Black students'—especially the high achievers'—responses to school and schooling.

Hence, they develop complex strategies that enable them to resolve, or, at least cope with, the ambivalence they experience. One such strategy is intended to minimize the influence and impact that the schooling process might have on their relationships to peers and to the community; the strategy follows what some researchers have termed the "anti-achievement ethic" (Granat, Hathaway, Saleton, & Sansing, 1986). Students who utilize this strategy, unfortunately, tend to fare poorly in school. The strategy that seems to be used frequently by adolescents who succeed in school is the phenomenon that I describe as developing a raceless persona.

Students who adopt a raceless persona do so with some risk of losing their feelings of belonging and of group membership:

> A black teenager in Price George's County [a suburban community outside Washington, DC] says many black kids "think if you succeed, you're betraying your color." Adds a friend: "The higher you get, the fewer blacks there are. You can succeed, but you feel like an outcast." (Granat et al., 1986, p. 166)

Recently, several articles in the press have illuminated the particularly painful consequences of being a successful student. In a headline story reported in *Newsweek*, Sylvester Monroe, a high-achieving prep school student, describes the attempts made by his school to separate and isolate him from his peers and indigenous community and to transform him from a group-centered Black person to a raceless "American."

> One of the greatest frustrations of my three years at St. George's [a predominantly White private school in New England] was that people were always trying to separate me from other black people in a manner strangely reminiscent of a time when slave owners divided blacks into "good Negroes" and "bad Negroes." Somehow, attending St. George's made me a good Negro, in their eyes, while those left in Robert Taylor [the housing project where he and his parents lived in Chicago] were bad Negroes or, at the very least, inferior ones. . . . Another St. George's teacher was surprised at my reaction when he implied that I should be grateful for the opportunity to attend St. George's, far away from a place like the Robert Taylors. How could I be, I snapped back, when my family, everyone that I cared most about were still there? But you're different, he continued. That's why you got out. . . . I'm not different, I insisted. I'm just lucky enough to have been in the right place at the right time. (Monroe, 1987, p. 57)

Monroe also talks about the alienation he experienced as a result of well-intended, yet implicitly racist, efforts on the part of school officials to integrate him into the school environment.

> Looking back on it, I was pleased to show what black boys were capable of. Yet, there was a faint disquiet. What bothered me was that some people found it easier to pretend I was something else. "We're colorblind here [at St. George's]," a well-meaning faculty member once told me. "We don't see *black* students or *white* students, we just see students." But black was what I was; I wasn't sure he saw me at all. . . .

The disquiet that Monroe describes is centered around the raceless persona he felt pressured to assume in order to be accepted at St. George's. Moreover, Monroe's description suggests that he had to become something other than an individual from the Black community. He had to become, instead, a "racial symbol," someone who embodies all the noble qualities necessary for a Black American to "make it" in the larger society (Trescott, 1977).

Morgan (1985) provides another example of how the school, as an institution that reproduces the dominant cultural values, pressures a 17-year-old student named Ellis to minimize his racial identity in order to achieve some measure of success. Ellis delineates the dual reality that confronts him in his predominantly White school in a suburban community outside Charlotte, North Carolina.

> Last year, the student council president, who was black, wanted to set aside a day to honor [Dr.] Martin Luther King. A lot of blacks said it was a good thing to do, but a lot of whites said it was a waste of time and was not fair. . . . I felt hurt that they [my White friends] would accept me as a black person but would not accept the idea of honoring a black person. . . . One of my white friends said, "I don't see you as a black friend, but as a friend." But I want them to look at me for what I am. *I am a black person* [emphasis added]. (Morgan, 1985, pp. 34–35; 90–92, 96–100)

The experiences of both Black males indicate the necessity of negotiating the duality, and the resulting ambiguities, of their existence.

In order to achieve academic success and, ultimately, vertical mobility, some Black students consciously choose risking membership in the fictive-kinship system to which, at one level, all persons socially defined as Black are "eternally bound." The following examples are illustrative cases:

> They [my friends and family] don't want [me] to change. They want me to be just like them. . . . I'm trying very hard to get away from black people. When I was in that all [Black] school, of course, my friends were all [Black]. But I don't have any more [Black] friends right now. I live in an all [Black] area, but I don't even talk to anybody who lives near me. I wanted to find out what white people were all about. So when I went to high school, I tried to make new friends and get away from the [Black] people as much as possible. . . . I've tried to maintain an image of myself in the school—getting away from those people. I work, and I buy my own clothes, and I study hard. In fact, I have all As in my classes and I'm in many of the white activities, like Speech—the only [Black person] in the whole group. . . ." (cited in Petroni & Hirsch, 1971, pp. 12, 20)

Similarly, Gray (1985) poignantly describes her largely unsuccessful efforts at disguising her racial identity, what she identifies as playing her "un-Black" role:

> During my pompous period, I dealt with my insecurities by wearing a veil of superiority. Except around my family and neighbors, I played the role—the un-Black. . . . To whites, I tried to appear perfect—I earned good grades and spoke impeccable English, was well-mannered and well-groomed. Poor whites, however, made me nervous. They seldom concealed their contempt for blacks, especially "uppity" ones like me. . . . To blacks, I was all of the above and extremely stuck up. I pretended not to see them on the street, spoke to them only when spoken to

and cringed in the presence of blacks being loud in front of whites. The more integrated my Catholic grammar school became, the more uncomfortable I was there. I had heard white parents on TV, grumbling about blacks ruining their schools; I didn't want anyone to think that I, too, might bring down Sacred Heart Academy. So I behaved, hoping that no one would associate me with "them" [other Black Americans]. (Gray, 1985, pp. E1, E5)

The common theme in all of the examples presented here is the conflict and ambivalence experienced by Black Americans in both school and work settings, and the persistent questioning of how they are accepted by both Black and White people. Not surprisingly, the conflict and ambivalence appear to be more pronounced and debilitating among those Black Americans who achieve the greatest degree of success as defined by the dominant society, and relative to the success of peers in their indigeous communities.

THE RESEARCH SETTING: THE CAPITAL HIGH COMMUNITY

Capital High[2] is a public school located in a predominantly poor Black neighborhood of Washington, DC. As is typical of such urban neighborhoods, the main thoroughfare near the school, Hunter Avenue, is lined with fast food chain restaurants like McDonald's and Kentucky Fried Chicken, various Catholic and Protestant churches, and a variety of corner stores. On the side streets there are detached single-family homes, similiar to those on The Avenue, but with small, well-cared-for front yards. During the spring, many of these yards are adorned with begonias, petunias, tulips, and other blooming plants, strongly contrasting with the brick and cement of the major thoroughfares in the neighborhood.

The Physical Structure

The school itself is located on a large plot of land in the middle of the block on a major thoroughfare. One section of the building was completed during the early 1960s; the other was completed during the academic year 1970–71. The lapse in time between construction of the two sections is clearly evident in the amenities featured in the two structures. For example, in the new section there is both a basement and sub-basement level; this is not the case in the original structure. The new section is completely air-conditioned, while the older section of the building is not.

The school's cafeteria, auditorium, and gymnasium are all located in the original section of the school. Since the addition of the new section allowed the enrollment to double, the gymnasium, cafeteria, and auditorium are no longer large enough to accommodate the student population.

Nowhere is this problem of space more apparent than in the auditorium. The lack of adequate space means that there is never an assembly of the entire student body at one time. Moreover, this structural limitation appears to have justified the administration's decision to limit assembly attendance primarily to students who are taking courses in the Advanced Placement program at the school. In addition to the lack of adequate space, there is also limited accessibility to the building for students who are physically disabled.

In spite of the relative newness of the physical plant, during the period of my research, it was not in the best condition. Some areas of the building, such as the cafeteria, were in critical need of repair. When it rained, there was always a possibility of seeing trash barrels sitting in the middle of the cafeteria floor to prevent the rain from soaking the floor and flooding the hallways. Yet in spite of the state of disrepair, the building was spotless. The fastidiousness of Mr. McGriff, the current principal, was apparent everywhere; he believed that cleanliness and the ability to decipher educational symbols were inextricably commingled. Consequently, he constantly picked up paper and other debris in the halls and on the streets adjacent to the school. Moreover, he regularly admonished the students to keep the building clean by following his example, and constantly urged teachers and other school personnel to remind the students of the importance of keeping the building clean.

Because of the layout of the building, herculean efforts were necessary to maintain departmental and organizational integrity at the school. Although it was not always easy to discern why certain departments and programs were placed where they were in the building, it was apparent that enormous effort was made to keep them in proximity according to academic discipline. The exceptions to this were made to insure that students with handicapping conditions, particularly those in wheelchairs, had access to certain basic courses. So, for example, even though most courses in the mathematics department were taught on the second floor of the building, three were taught on the first floor.

The Students

According to official statistics of the District of Columbia Public Schools, Capital had a total enrollment of 1,886 students (at the start of the 1982–83 school year), with Blacks constituting 99 percent of the student body. During the regular fall registration, 490 students enrolled; there were 130 discharges by the third week of November. There were 476 graduates in the class of 1982, representing 75 percent of the twelfth graders. Most of the students come from one-parent homes, many of them live in public or low-income housing, and approximately one-fourth of the student body is eligible for the reduced-cost lunch program.[3]

The School Personnel

There was a total of 172 school personnel at Capital. Of this total, 130 were teachers, including four special education teachers, one transition teacher (who helped students bridge the gap between junior and senior high), and two math and reading skills teachers. Most of the teachers were tenured, and most had between six and ten years of classroom teaching experience. The administrative staff consisted of a principal, four assistant principals, five counselors, and two librarians (although the school was without a certified librarian until after the spring break of 1983). The support staff was made up of ten cafeteria workers, five clerical aides, two community aides, twelve custodians (including the engineering staff), and one school nurse.

The racial composition of the personnel reflected that of the student body: It was predominantly Black. The English department had the largest number of White teachers, but most departments, including Special Education, had at least one White member. Interestingly, the White teachers taught the more advanced or "difficult" courses, such as Chemistry, Physics, Government, and the Advanced Placement classes. They were also the ones who served as sponsors for academically oriented activities such as the club "It's Academic" and the Chess Club.

The Curriculum

Capital High offered students a wide range of courses and programs of study. The academic programs included Advanced Placement courses and basic and advanced computer courses; woodshop, printing, auto mechanics, and stage and television productions were offered in the non-academic curriculum. In other words, the "shopping mall" concept of schooling (Powell, Farrar, & Cohen, 1985) was part and parcel of the educational landscape at Capital High.

The school had a four-tier curricular structure that consisted of two special programs (Advanced Placement and Humanities), the regular curriculum in which most of the students were placed, and a program for students in need of special education. Where there were areas of overlap in the regular curriculum and the two special programs, students were grouped according to performance on standardized examinations, and were either permitted or required to take the appropriate courses for their skill levels.

In the school's regular curriculum, the norm appeared to be for students to take *only* the courses that were required for graduation. The counselors, however, urged the students to take courses in subjects the students generally believed to be difficult, such as math, science, and foreign languages, and to remain in them even though they might experience some difficulty. The students, however, did not generally follow the suggestions of their counselors; instead, they dropped the so-called difficult courses once they had been given a "Letter of Understanding" apprising them of what courses they had to take in order to meet graduation requirements. In the rare instance in which a senior student did not reject the suggestion of his/her counselor, and remained in the difficult course, the student resorted to behaviors that made him or her "appear to but not to": (1) he or she continued in the course, but rarely attended class, thus virtually assuring failure; or (2) he or she took the body to class but left the mind somewhere outside the classroom.

Students who are assigned courses or who sign up for more courses than they need for graduation are generally thought of as "strange" or "crazy." However, those few students are usually able to convince their peers that they are unable to get out of the class or classes by attributing their deviation from the norm to the intractability of their counselors. "Man, Mr. Collins would not let me drop this class."

Unlike students in the regular curriculum, students in the special academic programs, although few in number (the larger of the two programs included just over 400 of the nearly 2,000 students enrolled in the school), were exposed to a curriculum whose minimal requirements far exceeded those of the regular curriculum. They were required to complete a math course and a science course at each grade level and to take two years of a foreign language.[4] Moreover, class assignments included an additional time period (so that these students took seven courses instead of the six taken by those in the regular curriculum), and a flexible curriculum that enabled students to spend longer periods of time in some classes.

The students in the two academic programs were provided special academic and support services intended to enhance their school experience and to improve their chances for academic success. These students were assigned teachers who had the most prestigious credentials and who were regarded as the most skilled in their particular subject areas. They were advised by a special counselor whose primary responsibility was to help them achieve their goals. She provided students with the specific information they needed in order to make the appropriate educational and career choices and organized specialized courses in test-taking and other auxiliary skills to help them perform as well as mainstream White students on standardized measures of academic success. Furthermore, these students were even transported to and from school, and were not allowed to be employed after school during the academic year because, it was argued, work interferred with their homework and extracurricular academically oriented activities.

How the Study Was Conducted

I gained entry to Capital High as an ethnographer at the start of the fall semester of 1982, and the data were collected over a two-year period. During the first year, formal and informal interviews were conducted with students, teachers, counselors, and parents. Observations of students were made both inside and outside of the classrooms. Out-of-class observations took place at school and at other places such as churches, work sites, recreation centers, and sports events. The second year of the study was devoted to the administration of a 55-page, 201-item questionnaire to 600 students from all the grades, and findings were compared to those obtained in the first year.

The sample for the first year of the study was selected from a pool of students referred by both teachers and counselors. The teachers and counselors were asked to identify eleventh-grade high achievers and underachievers who they thought would be willing to participate in this intensive and time-consuming study, and whose parents would approve of their participation. I verified the claims of the teachers and counselors by analyzing the cumulative folder of each student. Thirty-three students participated in the study; twenty-one of them were identified as underachievers; twelve of them were identified as high achievers, and constituted the primary sample. In this paper, data on six of the high-achieving students—three males and three females—will be presented and analyzed.

RACELESSNESS AT CAPITAL HIGH

Racelessness and school success appear to be linked at Capital High. This is evident in many aspects of the lives of the students and in their responses to questions regarding Black life and culture. Also, racelessness appears to be more prevalent among the high-achieving students, although the verbal responses of both high- and underachieving students indicate a tendency to disaffiliate themselves from other Black Americans. Essentially, the high-achieving students' responses indicate a strong belief in the dominant ideology of the American social system: equality of opportunity for all, regardless of race, color, creed, or national origin; and merit as the critical factor in social mobility. Some examples from my research are illustrative.

The Female High-Achieving Students

The most salient characteristic shared by the female members of the research sample is their unequivocal commitment to the values and beliefs of the dominant social system. Unlike the male students, whose "duality of socialization" is clearly evident in both their behaviors and responses, the female students appear to be much less victimized by the fact that they are required to live in two worlds concurrently. Indeed, they appear to be more unanimously committed to the ideology and values of the larger society than they are to the norms and values of the existing fictive-kinship system. The following three examples are illustrative of how the female students' commitment to racelessness as a strategy for vertical mobility structures their behavior and performance in the school context.

Rita

Rita is one of the highest achieving female students in the sample group. She is a 16-year-old student who takes most of the courses available to eleventh graders from the Advanced Placement program at Capital. She is also the student with the highest score on the verbal component of the PSAT this academic year (1982–83). The best adjectives to describe Rita are: intelligent, creative, hostile, sarcastic, assertive, garrulous, comedic, and manipulative. It is also appropriate to describe her as kind, caring, complex, clever, confused, and troubled. She often challenges the values and rules of the school with conviction, vacillating between demanding total adherence to these ideals on the part of her teachers and other school administrators, and discounting and disparaging these same values and rules herself in ways that display a blatant disregard for and arrogance toward their sanctity and value.

These characteristics appear to make Rita a very unfeeling and thoughtless person. Yet this is not an accurate picture. Admittedly, she is confused and angry, and she does not know how to focus her anger; however, she is also a very sensitive person whose "hellish confusion" (McClain, 1983) is the result of her efforts to cope with the disparaged economic and social conditions of Black Americans. Her confusion is so intense and so rampant that she told me on more than one occasion that she is often flabbergasted when people ask her if she views herself as a White person:

> *Some—a lot of times I have people ask me that—"Do you think you are a white person?"! But I don't know, maybe it's me. Maybe I don't carry myself like a Black person. I don't know. But I'm Black. And I can't go painting myself white or some other color, it's something that I have to live with. So it's the way it is, and it's not like having herpes or something—it's not bad. It's—I think it's just the same as being white, as far as I'm concerned—everybody's equal. (Formal Interview, May 4, 1983)*

However, despite her verbal claims that she does not view being Black in America as a negative factor, her constant disparagement of those activities and events generally associated with Black Americans negates her claims, suggesting, instead, a preference for those activities her family and some of her friends view as "White activities." She insists that her mother and sisters view her as an antisocial person because she does not like to do the things they like to do, such as going to shows at Constitution Hall and the Capital Center and attending cabarets and other places frequented by Black Washingtonians.

> They [my family] go to all the shows, go out to the Capital Center and all that crap, and listen to all that trash—as far as I'm concerned. But I don't really like going out [there], you know, but if I ask them to go see the Washington Philharmonics with me, they won't go. "Is that opera?" [they want to know]. . . . And they don't go to the museums with me either, 'cause they don't think, they'd go crazy, they'd rather go to the movies to see Eddie Murphy in "48 Hours" than to go see "To Fly" at the Air and Space Museum, and so. . . . (Formal Interview, January 12, 1983)

Rita's desire to dissociate herself from the Black community is even more evident in her response to a question about the kind of music she listens to and the kind of albums she buys:

> Black music is meaningless to me. . . . The lyrics. I mean, they, "Oh, it got a nice beat, so it must be good," you know, but that's not always, you know, like that. And so . . . on, well . . . you know . . . it's just meaningless, you know. You listen to the lyrics sometime, and Black artists, you know, just into meaningless music. And I think I listen to Stevie Wonder because, you know, all of his records usually have, you know, some sort of meaning, like his "Hotter Than July" album, you know, like—what is it?—"Happy Birthday," "Hotter Than July" . . . it's meaningful. But Vanity 6, "Nasty Girls," I mean, what's that, really? It's not—it's just trash . . . as far as I'm concerned. . . . So I start[ed] listening to WPGC [a contemporary non-Black music format] . . . instead of OK-100 (a station which plays music sung primarily by Black artists]. (Formal Interview, January 12, 1983)

There are other, even stronger, indicators of Rita's desire to dissociate herself from the fictive-kinship system prevalent in the Black community. This is particularly apparent in her response to a question about her identification with Black people:

> I identify with Blacks and whites alike—I don't—see, that's one thing I don't go for: I don't like when people ask me do I identify with Black people or do I identify with white people? I identify with people. People are people, Black or white, Spanish, red, white or blue, we're all the same. (Formal Interview, May 4, 1983)

However, the tone of her voice when she responded to the above question conveyed to me much more than her idealistic response ever could. She was clearly offended by my question and felt personally attacked by my inquiry. I apologized, but felt compelled to try and understand the latent feelings this young woman has about her identity as a Black American. Apparently, she subordinates her identity as a Black American to her identity as an American, hoping that a raceless persona will mitigate the harsh treatment and severe limitations in the opportunity structure that are likely to confront her as a Black American.

Despite Rita's assertions that she does not feel any pressure to separate from Black Americans, her response to the large amount of literature she has begun to receive from various colleges since her PSAT scores were posted is clearly indicative of her ambivalence and confusion about racial identity. She has been forced to acknowledge that distinctions between people based on race are quite rampant, and that they are even found in the "halls of ivy." Rita's racelessness was directed at the core of the ideology of the American social system that maintains that differences of race, religion, and national origin are not important. However, her belief in this ideology was constantly tested when she was forced to acknowledge—or others around her constantly reminded her—that such distinctions not only exist but are critically important in the dominant American society. The literature she received from colleges, indicating that special consideration is given to Black and other "minority" students, was a case in point.

> *I mean—okay, this college sent me a Third World—I mean, they said, "We have a Third World Club"—place for Blacks! I mean, the audacity! To even think that I would go to a college that has a club for Blacks! I was. . . . Okay, Middlebury—I went to the college—but they sent me this little pamphlet that said, "Minorities at Middlebury"—like, "Do they exist?" or something like that. . . . I mean, it's like— "well, we put them aside in some other place," or something—I don't care. I say, well, I mean, I* suppose *minorities go there—I mean, I guess at least a few of them—there* were *only twenty-five there, out of the whole school. But, nevertheless, I* know *they're there by you sending me this pamphlet. I don't appreciate it! (Formal Interview, May 4, 1983)*

Rita is convinced that if only people—Black and White—would seriously begin to discount race as a factor in their interactions with each other, discrimination and other invidious distinctions would disappear. She does not view racism in America as an institutionalized phenomenon. It is in connection with this belief system that she has built the raceless persona she presents in the school and nonschool context. Her commitment to the ideology of the dominant social system is what structures her academic effort and performance in the school context, motivating her to strive for academic excellence.

Katrina

Katrina presents another example of racelessness as a factor in the academic achievement of high-achieving females. She had the highest grade-point average of any student in the research sample and she graduated as the valedictorian of the Class of '84. Her best performance was in math and math-related subjects as computer science; her weakest performance was in the humanities and social sciences. Her performance on the math component of the PSAT was at the 95th percentile. Only one other student scored higher than she, and only one other student had a score that was comparable to hers. Her overall score on the PSAT was higher than that of most of her class- and schoolmates.

Katrina admits that she has had to put brakes on her academic performance in the school context in order to minimize the stress she experiences. In most instances she is much better at handling the subject matter than her peers are, but, like many of the other high achievers, she tries not to be conspicuous.

> *Junior high, I didn't have much [of a] problem. I mean, I didn't have—there were always a lot of people in the classroom who did the work, so I wasn't like, the only one who did this assignment. So—I mean, I might do better at it, but I wasn't the only one. And so a lot of times, I'd let other kids answer—I mean, not let them, but. . . . All right, I let them answer questions [laughter], and I'd hold back. So I never really got into any arguments, you know, about school and my grades or anything. (Formal Interview, February 8, 1983)*

The important point to keep in mind is that, although she was extremely fearful of what might happen to her if she acted in ways which were not sanctioned by her peer group, she was, and still is, unwilling to give up on her desire to do well in school. Hence, she chose to "go underground," to become a visible yet invisible person. By using this technique, she did not draw attention to herself, thereby minimizing the possibility of appearing to be different from those around her. Katrina constantly worries, even today, about appearing to be over-confident. An example from one interview session with her supports this observation. The "It's Academic" club is perhaps the most "intellectual" extracurricular activity at the school. In order to participate on the three-person team, students must compete by answering correctly a "test" the school sponsor has prepared for the participants. The students obtaining the three highest scores are identified and are then eligible to participate on the team representing the school on television. Katrina was unable to avoid taking the test because of her relationship with the club's sponsor, who was her physics teacher. However, she established certain preconditions for participation in the qualifying activity: she would take the test, but even if she earned a score that would make her eligible for participating on the school's team, she was not to be selected to participate on television. Having abstained the consent of the club's sponsor and her counselor to these preconditions, she took the qualifying test. As a result of her score on the qualifying exam (she scored higher than all the other participants), she was obviously one of the three students eligible to participate on the school's team. However, since she had made it quite clear to the club's advisor and all other interested parties that she was not to be chosen as one of the team's members, she was made an alternate. She found this arrangement quite satisfying for several reasons: (1) it allowed her to display her knowledge to her teachers and some of her supportive friends, thereby validating her academic capabilities; (2) at the same time, she was able to retain her invisibility as a high achiever, a much-desired status on her part; and (3) she satisfied, at least in part, her teacher's request that she compete for one of the most highly sought academic honors at the school (Formal Interview, March 7, 1983). Katrina was pleased with herself because she had proved herself capable of out-performing most of her peers at the school—even those students who were twelfth-graders. At the same time, she was able to remain anonymous and invisible in the school context. Her invisibility had made it so much easier to pursue her goal of academic excellence.

In comparison with Rita, Katrina's personality seems dull. Nevertheless, she, too, is insightful and fun to be with. She also has the kind of personality that makes it easy for those who interact with her to do so comfortably. Like Rita, she is able to perform well on school measures of success, both in the classroom context and on standardized measures. Also like Rita, Katrina is not sure that Black Americans have a viable cultural system. Her uncertainty stems from her lack of attention to the issue rather than some strongly held view on the matter. When I insisted that she describe for me what she thinks of when she thinks of Black culture, she sighed and finally responded by saying: "Music. Dance." Like Rita, Katrina does not like contemporary Black music and avoids those radio stations that are most often identified with the Black community. She views the music played on those stations as being too "rowdy"; she also does not like the regular TV serials, preferring old movies, especially the ones with such stars as Doris Day, Fred Astaire, and Ginger Rogers. The fact that both she and Rita tend to eschew Black music is an important aspect of their raceless personae, given the symbolic significance of indigenous music in the Black community.[5]

Like many of the other student members of the research sample, Katrina believes in the democratic ideals of the nation, and wants Black and White Americans to live peaceably and contentedly together. In fact, she opposes any effort on the part of Black Americans to separate themselves from the majority culture. Her belief in the fairness and openness of the opportunity structure is primarily responsible for her commitment to school norms and academic achievement.

Katrina's responses to the questions about Black life and culture, and her explanation for the massive poverty in the Black community, suggest that she is not the least bit certain about the answers she offers. What is more important, her responses indicate that she has not given much thought to the nature and configuration of the social organization of the Black community. She has not given much thought to these questions, in part because they are rarely discussed in the school context as part of the core curriculum. This has had a negative effect on her perception of her racial group membership and her sense of herself as an individual. Moreover, the lack of a strong attachment to the Black community in her home environment and a limited focus on the value of that membership in the school context have led her to embrace a raceless persona so as to minimize the harm that is likely to result from an acknowledgment that she is Black.

Katrina also admits that she has no real preference for how she should be identified, racially or ethnically. The fact that she has no preference suggests a desire to appear raceless, or non-Black. Like Rita, she believes that hard work on the part of Black Americans is the key to the elimination of economic and social differences between Black and White Americans, and, as noted above, she holds Black Americans primarily responsible for their present lower-class status because, in her mind, Black Americans are basically lazy. Her acceptance of the widely held stereotypical image of Black Americans motivates her to try to be an exception to the rule. She does not want other people to view her in the same way; in other words, as a lazy person. This persistent negative perception of Black Americans motivated her to develop the kind of raceless persona which is so much a part of the person she is today. Because she has defined success as going "to college, and graduate in the highest percentile . . . a nice steady job [which] pays well . . . travel . . . and friends," she constantly seeks to disassociate herself from the negative stereotypes which are so much a part of the daily social reality of Black Americans.

Katrina has been able to maintain a high level of proficiency on school measures of success while at the same time muting the hostility of her peers and classmates who might otherwise use boundary-maintaining mechanisms to limit her efforts at social mobility. She has done this by developing a persona which makes her appear virtually raceless in the school context. Among her schoolmates and peers, Katrina's raceless persona is characterized by her inconspicuousness and seeming invisibility; to her teachers and other representatives of the dominant society, her racelessness is evident in her strong commitment to the values and norms condoned in the school context and the larger society, as well as her disavowal of those features of the Black community which are rejected by the school and the larger social system (for example, speaking non-standard English, commitment to group advancement rather than individual mobility, and so on). Racelessness as a strategy for social mobility is also evident in her willingness to put forth the effort necessary to excel in those arenas and aspects of the school curriculum which have traditionally been defined as the purview of White Americans.

Maggie

Maggie is the third example of how high-achieving females work to develop a raceless persona. She is a 17-year-old student with a high GPA who scheduled her core courses from the regular curriculum. Choosing regular courses instead of Advanced Placement courses is not a particularly unproductive strategy for Maggie, since her mother and maternal family members provide her with a strong support system for academic achievement. Her mother, who forms the base of this support system, is uncompromising in her insistence on behavior befitting a "young lady" and the appropriate grades at this level of schooling. In fact, the support system is so strong that it tends to have many unintended consequences, at least from Maggie's perspective.

Maggie does not consider herself to have a lot of friends, either at school or in her immediate neighborhood. Indeed, she insists that she has virtually no contact with the people who live near her; that all her friends are either fellow students or, in a more limited number, people she knows from church. She claims to know no one from her neighborhood, despite the fact that she has lived with her parents in the same single-family townhouse for more than ten years. She insists that her knowledge of the people in the neighborhood is so severely limited because her parents, particularly her mother, are afraid that she will start using drugs and engage in other undesirable behaviors if she becomes too familiar with the neighborhood residents. They, therefore, demand that she avoid such relationships. This avoidance of the people who are constantly around her has taught her to view herself as being different from those people, despite the fact that racially they are the same: they too are Black Americans.

Perhaps the most contradictory component of Maggie's life—both in and outside the school context—is reflected in her efforts to come to grips with being Black in a country where being Black is devalued. This reality has led to the development of identity problems for her; problems which are exacerbated by her lighter skin color. She admits that her fairer skin color is not as problematic today as it was when she was in elementary and junior high school, where she was frequently referred to as "yellow." This description of her was so pervasive when she was in elementary school that she came to see herself as being raceless, neither Black nor White. When asked to choose one of the various labels used to identify Black Americans ("Black," "Negro," "Colored," "Afro-American," and so forth), she responded in the following manner:

> *I wouldn't consider myself as none of them. When I was small, people used to say I was yellow, right?, so I thought—I really thought I was yellow. I didn't think I was Black. I thought I was a Mongoloid. So all these—all this time I've been—well, not recently—I thought I was yellow until I got into—maybe around the sixth, seventh grade. Then my mother told me I wasn't yellow, 'cause on the papers when we used to fill out, I used to put "Yellow" on it, you know, for "Black, White or Other"? . . . I would put "Other" or put "Yellow" on it, 'cause people used to call me "yellow." And my mother told me that I was Black.*
>
> *. . . I kind of felt different. I felt like a different person. I said, "All this time I thought I was yellow. And now I'm Black. . . ."* (Formal Interview, February 25, 1983)

The residual effect of this misidentification is still a part of Maggie's identity structure, aiding and abetting her conscious and unconscious desire to be an "exception to the rule." Part of the reason for her reluctance to be identified as a Black American stems from the fact that, perhaps unwittingly, she accepts many of the popular negative stereotypes regarding the behavior and lifestyles of Black Americans, magnifying her desire to disso-ciate herself from the larger Black community. As with most of the other female high achievers, her family reinforces her perception of being different. In the school context, this perception is supported by her teachers and other school officials, who constantly reassure her that her willingness to work at achieving school success is evidence of her lack of affiliation with her peers and other Black Americans. The juxtaposition of her desire to disaffiliate from her eternal and unbreakable bond and her obligation to the Black community (Taylor, 1973) exacerbates her uncertainty and confusion regarding racial loyalty.

In summary, racelessness among the female students described in this analysis is a strategy for social mobility both in and out of the school context. These young women tend to internalize the values, beliefs, and ideals taught and learned in school, making them a part of their behavior pattern in their family and community environments. In this way, racelessness becomes a definite part of their lives, creating enormous stress and anxiety. Moreover, this raceless response to the duality of their existence puts social distance between them and their less successful peers, enabling them to pursue goals and objectives that, under the scrutiny and careful eyes of their peers, might be severely criticized. Also, as this analysis shows, the female high-achievers vacillate between inconspicuousness among their less successful peers and carefully constructed racelessness in the presence of their teachers and other representatives of the dominant society. The raceless personae they present appear to be mandated by the school—the price they pay if they desire to achieve vertical mobility. These students appear to understand that the school and their teachers expect them to distance themselves from the "Black" aspects of their home, peers, and immediate community in ways that suggest an individualistic orientation toward success and social mobility.

The Male High-Achieving Students

A common theme in the responses—verbal and behavioral—of the male high-achieving students is their commitment to the ideology of the American social system, and the sense of conflict and uncertainty about their dual relationship with the larger dominant society and the indigenous fictive-kinship system of the Black community. This uncertainty and the resultant conflict force them to question their identity repeatedly, leading to a response pattern that highlights their relationship to the dominant society while at the same time maintaining their relationship to the Black community and the existing fictive-kinship system. Hence, the male high achievers differ from their female counterparts in that they appear to be much more victimized in the school context by the "double consciousness" attendant on the dual socialization pattern that appears to be an endemic feature of the childrearing practices prevailing in the Black community. In other words, presenting a raceless persona appears to be much more difficult for the male students in the sample group. Nevertheless, as in the female high achievers, racelessness appears to be a quality which enhances the academic potential of the male students in the research sample. Some examples from my research are instructive of how the development of a raceless persona enables them to succeed in the school context. Kent is a case in point.

Kent

Kent is one of the most unusual students at Capital High in that he appears to be unaffected by his peers' perception or acceptance of him. He appears to be both adult- and goal-oriented. He was the male valedictorian of his junior high school graduating class. He makes good grades and never cuts class.

> I haven't missed a day of school ever since I was in seventh grade. And it's just come to me now, if I miss a day—I don't want to miss a day. Sometime my mother say, "Stay home. You deserve to stay home, relax and everything." I say, "I can't do that, I gotta go to school." And I want to stay home, but it's hard for me now that I've become adjusted to that and everything. And it's like when I'm going to bed at night sometime—I used to go to bed something like nine o'clock. Now I don't go to

bed till about two, two-thirty, or three o'clock [A.M.]. . . . 'Cause I'm used to staying up studying and everything and thinking about my plans for tomorrow, and it just became a habit. I just kept on doing it and kept on doing it. (Formal Interview, February 23, 1983)

Kent loves track and could probably earn a track scholarship were he to participate in that sport at Capital; however, he recently resigned from the track team because he concluded that it interfered with his ability to complete his math homework when he went home after practice.

I wasn't doing that well in math at first, but because I wanted to run track, and I was practicing and everything . . . when you taking Algebra II, Trig, you cannot be tired going home. You cannot be tired and study at the same time, 'cause if you do, you won't comprehend that algebra and stuff. So now, this third advisory and everything, I got hundreds on all my math tests, 'cause I quit track, for one thing, and I told myself I'm gonna get my work, my work come first and everything. . . . (Formal Interview, February 23, 1983)

Kent's teachers generally consider him to be hardworking and serious young man. He is often asked to introduce guests or make oratorical presentations at school assemblies. As a tenth grader, he won First Place in the citywide and regional Science Fair competitions, and was a finalist at the national level. He also took first honors in the citywide History Fair for a project he undertook on the relationship between the Japanese and American automobile industries. He attends the Upward Bound program at Georgetown University on Saturdays on his own initiative. No one demands that he attend this program, nor does he get extra credit for doing so. It is an activity he enjoys, and it reinforces his desire to "be somebody." His commitment to the value of schooling is unquestioned. He is convinced that if an individual does well in school, he will succeed in the larger society.

Kent's explanations for the poverty conditions experienced by Black Americans, like those of most of the high-achieving males participating in this study, are ambivalent and contradictory. He attributes the widespread poverty to inadequate schooling caused by Black Americans' general resistance to investing great effort in education. He identifies effort as an important factor in an individual's achieving his or her goal.

Interestingly, however, Kent camouflages his scholastic efforts and the importance placed on education as a vehicle for success by developing a comedic persona. This transformation minimizes negative or hostile reactions from his peers. From his description of his behavior and interactions in the school situation, one can perceive his strong commitment to the "achievement ideology" (MacLeod, 1987). Evidence from his interview and my observations shows that he uses humor as a strategy to diffuse the emergence of a raceless persona in the classroom when interacting with the teacher as well as in bantering with his classmates during class time.

. . . I start saying some of my jokes . . . and make the class laugh and get things moving or something. Like, if [the teacher] might . . . say he was talking to us about some kind of bonds, chemical bonds and he spelled this word wrong on the board. So he look[ed] at it and he said, "I can't spell today," and I say, "Yes, you can, Doc—it's t-o-d-a-y. My little brother can spell that." And he wasn't talking about that. He was talking about his word on the board be messed up. And everybody thought that was so funny. I do—sometimes I do things like that. (Formal Interview, February 23, 1983)

Although Kent has decided to put the values, beliefs, and ideology of the larger society over those of the indigenous fictive-kinship system when these values collide, he has been able to minimize his peers' perception of his emerging raceless persona. Many of them see him as somewhat "strange," but a nice fellow, nonetheless. Not surprisingly, he is constantly juggling his various personae in order to minimize the risks associated with the pursuit of school success. Hence, Kent feels the conflict between the two cultural systems competing for his loyalty. His efforts to dissociate himself from the fictive-kinship system and the Black community have negative consequences for him.

Wendell

Wendell is another example of a Black male who develops a persona to achieve academic excellence and acceptance in the dominant society. Wendell prides himself on his achievement of excellent grades in school while preserving the appearance of commitment to the Black community. He has maintained the balance because, until this point in his schooling, he rarely had to study to receive good grades.

> . . . I think that I catch on quick. . . . That's how I got academic—not smart, you know. I don't consider myself smart. . . . When people think smart, like, they know everything. I think people who are academic know some things, but, you know, to a certain point. That's how I think. (Formal Interview, March 23, 1983)

Wendell indicates the extent of his ambivalence about the relationship between academic excellence and his identity as a Black American male student, pointing specifically to the conflict he experienced around the issue of being separated from his friends and those with whom he identifies.

> I would have been in [the Advanced Placement courses], but they kept pressing me. . . . They [school officials] kept on—like, almost begging me to be in the [AP courses]. . . . I wouldn't do it 'cause they kept . . . pressing. They kept on. They almost was trying to make me get in [the AP courses]. I would have got in, too. Like when I was doing my grades, they looked, and my grades checked. "Oh, he goin' be in [the AP courses]." I said, "No, I'm not." They said. "Put him down for [the AP courses]," they was telling me I was going to be [in those courses]. I was in junior high. And they was telling me. All through the summer they kept calling me, "You want to be in [the AP courses]?" "No, that's all right." So that's why I didn't get in [the AP courses]. And they—some things they don't let you do [if you take the AP courses], either. You know, like sports-wise and stuff. I don't like that. They almost run your life. (Formal Interview, March 23, 1983)

Apparently this conflict stems from Wendell's desire to be identified in a way that allows him to be acceptable to both school officials and to his friends.

Prior to attending Capital High School, Wendell envisioned a career as a chemist in a major corporation; his excellent grades in junior high school earned him the title of valedictorian of his ninth-grade class. Belatedly, he now realizes that his decision to forego his assignment to the AP courses at the school has undermined his attempts to convince his teachers that he is not dumb. In high school, unlike the way he felt before, he is confused and uncertain about whether to pursue academic excellence. In junior high school, Wendell was able to achieve school success without much effort and without being differentiated by the school officials from his less successful peers and friends. At the high school level, where the distinctions between successful and not-so-successful students are sharper, it is more difficult for him to bridge these two groups.

His decision not to attend the National Honor Society induction ceremony at his school illustrates Wendell's ambivalence about his academic role. When asked why he chose not to participate in the ceremony honoring his achievements during his first year (tenth grade) and the first semester of his second year at the school, he simply shrugged his shoulders, indicating that he did not have an acceptable response. A later response to a question about the meaning of the term "brainiac" provides insight into his behavior. He admitted that most of the students at the school seek to avoid being so labeled even though they might earn grades that, given the definition of the term, warrant such a label. Wendell stated that he himself is in such an undesirable position. I asked him to tell me why most students do not want to be identified as brainiacs.

> *Because they think people won't like them, if they smart. Like, my French teacher was saying that—well, my—she said—she was saying that I'm good and everything, right?—in class, around her, want everybody to act like me. And I tried to say, "No! Don't say that!",* you know, 'cause I know people get mad at me and stuff. So—it seem like sometime you want to have your friends. . . . [When brainiac is considered *a negative term, it is intended to say,]* like, when you're—like, you're [out]cast, since you're smart. Outcast. . . . [T]hey say, "Since he smart, you know, he think he too smart. You know, we don't want to deal with him." Like that. (Formal Interview, March 29, 1983)

Wendell admits that he does not want to be identified as being different from his peers, but the pressure of trying to live up to the expectations associated with being "smart" while at the same time trying to minimize the social distance between him and his peers is overwhelming.

From the discussion above we see that Wendell's earlier belief in the efficacy of school and the attendant commitment to racelessness are undergoing a precipitous change. Prior to the second semester of this, his eleventh-grade year, he has consistently earned above-average grades in school. The present change in his perception of the value of school and schooling can be linked to his changing perception of what it means to be a young Black American male and of the importance of school credentials for the adult roles he believes are available to males who share his ethnic and racial background. Wendell's emerging disillusionment is so severe that it points up the critical need for future research to address the question: "Are Black male adolescents who become racially conscious in the high school context likely to respond in a negative way to school-sanctioned norms?" There is limited evidence to support a positive answer to this question, but the sample represented in this study is too small to offer unequivocal proof (Reeves, 1972).

Wendell began to pursue academic excellence in response to the persistence of stereo-typical myths that suggest that Black Americans, as a social group, are "ignorant." As the son of an unmarried woman whose major means of supporting her children is through public assistance (AFDC), Wendell, throughout his school experience, has fought to minimize the stereotypes frequently attributed to such families: lazy, unproductive, under-achieving in the school context, and so forth. The primary strategy available to him is to minimize his identity as a Black person, because—as he is quick to point out—the best way Black people can enhance their potential for success is to remember: "Don't be looked upon as Black" (Formal Interview, May 20, 1983, p. 98). In Wendell's mind, doing well in school is a good way to make a political statement about himself and his family and similarly economically disadvantaged families. Hence he is driven to do well in school. Insofar as the children of welfare recipients are subjected to a more pronounced stigma than Black children whose parents are not on welfare, he felt compelled to disavow his resemblance to those with whom he was racially and economically identifiable.

Because Wendell has recently begun to see his future as being intimately linked to his racial group affiliation, his academic effort has diminished considerably. He no longer seeks to distinguish himself from his peers in the one way in which he had sought distinction prior to senior high school: getting high grades without much effort. He has come to this stage of his development primarily because his perception of the opportunity structure is governed less by the official ideology of the dominant social system than it is by the informal rules and regulations that operate in the present fictive-kinship system. He has come to believe that a raceless persona is not all he had thought it to be. Hence, the only distinction he made between himself and his peers—obtaining good grades in school—is no longer a worthwhile option for him, especially since he must now put forth effort in order to receive grades comparable to those he received in elementary and junior high school.

Martin

Martin is another example of how male high achievers seek to distinguish themselves from their peers by the development of a repertoire of skills and behaviors that are generally attributed to non-Black students. Although Martin maintains that he is in many ways different from his peers at Capital, primarily because he earns good grades in school and "care[s] about what people think of [him]," he also notes with unintended anguish his efforts to cloak a raceless persona. Because he earns good grades in school, he is constantly mindful of being labeled "brainiac" or "pervert."

> *A pervert is like a brainiac . . . a pervert won't have his mind on girls or [on] nothing but his schooling, that's it! He'll come to school, do this work, won't say nothing to nobody, and leave. . . . That's all I know he'll do (Formal Interview, March 23, 1983)*

Martin believes it is important for a male high-achieving student at Capital High to be protective of his image and to cloak it in other activities to minimize the harm that is likely to follow from being known as a brainiac. Moreover, he says that there are persistent rumors that some of the male students who take all or a large number of the Advanced Placement courses at the school are gays, or "perverts."

> *INTERVIEWER: Are there many "perverts" or squares or brainiacs at this school?*
> *MARTIN: In [the Advanced Placement courses], yes. . . . [For example,] I know one guy, he call boys "Egberts"—'cause a guy named Egbert he knew one time was very smart. I call them—some of them—well, I hate to say it about some of them, but some of them be acting like gays. (Formal Interview, March 23, 1983)*

To minimize the possibility of being known as a brainiac and thereby bringing their manhood into question, high-achieving male students who are doing well in school often resort to "lunching"—behaviors suggestive of clowns or comedians or some other unconventional personalities.

Martin's perception of Black Americans is full of conflicts and contradictions. For example, he identifies discrimination and prejudice as being widely practiced by White Americans, thus limiting Black Americans' ability to improve their economic, political, and social conditions. At the same time, he believes they (Black people) "don't care."

Like I said, they [Black Americans] don't care. That's what I say. They don't care. . . . I mean, they'll stand on the corner, smoke marijuana, and all that. I don't know why . . . they won't get [themselves] together, but I think they just don't care. (Formal Interview, March 23, 1983)

Martin sees himself as being different from most other Black Americans in that he "care[s] what people think of [him]. [He] always tr[ies] to [make] a good impression on people. [He] always care[s] . . ." (Formal Interview, March 23, 1983). His view of himself as being different from the masses of Black people is a factor to a limited extent in his commitment to school achievement. His commitment to "impression management," as well as to dispelling persistent negative stereotypes associated with Black Americans, motivates him to work at the development of a raceless persona.

SUMMARY AND IMPLICATIONS

In this paper I have tried to capture the endemic tensions and conflicts experienced by Black high-achieving students as they seek to define their dual relationship to the indigenous Black American cultural system and the individualistic, impersonal cultural system of the dominant society. Because the individualistic ethos predominates in the school context, high achievers often make choices that either put social distance between them and their peers or undermine group solidarity. They do not appear to believe—nor does their experience support—the idea that they can truly be bicultural and actualize what Edwards (1987) describes as their "crossover dreams"—the widely touted dreams of wealth, fame, and fortune. Instead, their experiences, both in and out of school, support the value of appearing raceless to their teachers and other adults in the school context.

Indeed, various indicators at Capital High suggest that a raceless persona is valued in school. The structure of the curriculum that separates the "winners" from the "losers" is the primary example. Although not perceived by either the parents or the students as having the malevolent intentions overwhelmingly attributed to most tracking systems, the Advanced Placement courses form a subtle track that fosters a distinctive individualistic ideology within those students selected to enroll in them. Furthermore, the school implicitly weakens the collective ethos in the Capital High community—an extension of the collective ethos of the fictive-kinship system prevailing in the Black community—by enticing students who display signs of having only a marginal relationship to the collectivity into participating in the special programs. Separating students in this manner isolates them from the masses in ways comparable to the experiences reported earlier in this paper (Campbell, 1982; Gray, 1985; McClain, 1983; Monroe, 1987; Petroni & Hirsch, 1971). In short, the high achievers described in this paper have learned the value of appearing to be raceless—a clear example of internalizing oppression—in their efforts to "make it."

Because the high-achieving students believe firmly in the "American dream," they willingly, and in some instances not so willingly, seek to distance themselves from the fictive-kinship system in the Black community. The organizational structure of the school rewards racelessness in students and thus reinforces the notion that it is quality necessary for success in the larger society. As a result, the students are also led to believe in the view of racism and discrimination as the practices of individuals rather than as part and parcel of institutionally sanctioned social policies.

What high-achieving students often forfeit in their development toward becoming raceless, however, is strong allegiance to the Black community and connection to the fictive-kinship system. This trade-off becomes problematic because many of their less successful peers do not share the value of becoming raceless. Consequently, many of the successful students find themselves juggling their school and community personae in order to minimize the conflicts and anxieties generated by the need to interact with the various competing constituencies represented in the school context.

My analysis also demonstrates that racelessness among the Black adolescents at Capital High may be influenced by gender, with the female high-achieving students appearing to be more willing to be closely identified with the values and beliefs of the dominant social system than their male counterparts. When compared with the female students, the high-achieving males appear to be less committed to the cultural system of the larger society and far more confused and ambivalent about the value of forsaking their indigenous beliefs and values. Hence, the high-achieving male students mask their raceless personae to a far greater degree than their female counterparts in the school context. In spite of these differences, both male and female students do believe that school and schooling are the primary means of achieving vertical mobility for Black Americans in the existing social system.

The resistance of high-achieving students to identifying too strongly with the Black community parallels that of Black adults in the workforce who have achieved some measure of success above the existing job ceiling. In other words, successful students, like their successful adult counterparts, seek to minimize the discomfort experienced by members of the dominant society who evaluate them as they enter institutions that are governed by dominant group norms and standards. If they are not successful in minimizing their ethnic group membership—that is, appearing raceless—their chances of achieving vertical mobility are seriously diminished, despite clear evidence of academic excellence on standardized measures of success.

The critical question this paper addresses, therefore, is whether the development of raceless personae by the high-achieving students at Capital High in order to achieve academic excellence is a pragmatic strategy or a Pyrrhic victory. The answer to this question is complex. At the individual level, the high-achieving student's attainment of his or her self-defined goals appears to be enhanced by the development of a raceless persona. At the level of the individual, then, racelessness appears to be a pragmatic strategy.

This is true, in part, because at Capital High, and perhaps in other schools, the message conveyed to Black adolescents is that they cannot be culturally different and, at the same time, achieve success as defined by the dominant society. This is an important observation because, unlike many other ethnically distinctive markers, Blackness is a barrier that limits and inhibits vertical mobility in the larger American society. As Aplin-Brownlee (1984, p. D5) notes, it is difficult for White Americans, when interacting with Black Americans, to "get past the look of blackness to actually hear what's being said."

Yet, given the Black community's penchant for the collectivity, what kind of support from peers can be expected by Black adolescents whose behaviors and values in the school context appear to be at odds with the indigenous social organization of

Black people? At Capital High School there is not much support for students who adopt the individualistic ethos, because succeeding in school is invariably associated with movement away from the community and is seen as a sign of having been co-opted by the dominant society. Hence, even those high achievers who camouflage their efforts at academic excellence are viewed with suspicion, and are tested constantly by their less successful peers to determine whether their appearance of being "drylongso" (Gwaltney, 1980) is in fact who they are. This surveillance helps the group to maintain established cultural boundaries, ensuring the survival of the group as well as its cultural integrity (Staiano, 1980). Unfortunately, this constant surveillance of the behaviors of members of the school community—both high- and under-achieving—drains the energy of students which might be devoted to the pursuit of academic excellence and other creative endeavors. Thus, while the development of a raceless persona is a prerequisite for success in the Advanced Placement curriculum of the school, it is equally the case that the development of such a persona is marked by conflict and ambivalence.

In my analysis, the larger questions are directed to the Black community. It is imperative that Black Americans, particularly parents, ask themselves the following questions to determine what they can give up in order for their children to achieve academic success: (1) Are we willing to have our children defined as successful even though they display very little commitment to the Black community? (2) Or are we more committed to the integrity of the existing cultural system in the Black community and, therefore, willing to sublimate our individual goals for the collective advancement of our people? Another equally compelling question must be directed to school officials: Are you willing to modify existing school curricula to incorporate a more group-centered ethos, thereby enabling Black students to "seek self-realization through personal effort in service to the group" (LeVine & White, 1986, p. 103). The answer to each of these questions has important, and drastically different, implications for Black adolescents' school performance and the continued integrity of the existing fictive-kinship system in the Black community.

As my analysis suggests, within the school structure, Black adolescents consciously and unconsciously sense that they have to give up aspects of their identities and of their indigenous cultural system in order to achieve success as defined in dominant-group terms; their resulting social selves are embodied in the notion of racelessness. Hence, for many of them the cost of school success is too high; it implies that cultural integrity must be sacrificed in order to "make it." For many Black adolescents, that option is unacceptable. For the high achievers identified in this paper, achieving school success is not marked only by conflict and ambivalence, as noted earlier, but with the need to camouflage efforts directed at behaviors that the group identifies as "acting White." Moreover, Black Americans' changed perceptions of what it means to be successful in America will dictate to some degree how Black adolescents respond to the system of schooling in this country. The ethos that values the collectivity over individual mobility has an important impact on the academic efforts and perceptions of Black adolescents.

Given the continued domination of the individualistic ethos in public schooling in the United States, if the Black community continues to sanction group rather than individual mobility, Black adolescents' academic achievement is likely to remain unchanged. But if Black Americans as a people are willing to have their children evince behaviors and attitudes that suggest a lack of connectedness to the larger Black community, then racelessness is a pragmatic strategy that more Black Americans should embrace, and not a Pyrrhic victory. The issue of pragmatic strategy or Pyrrhic victory can and should be determined only by Black Americans. Although further research is clearly indicated, it is imperative that Black Americans define explicitly their relationship to the larger society, and hence their expectations for their children in the school context.

NOTES

1. I hypothesize that this response is prevalent not only among Americans of African descent but also among most subordinated populations in the United States. The desire to succeed— as defined by the dominating population—causes subordinated peoples to seek social distance from the group with which they are ethnically or racially identified. However, efforts at dissociation or disidentification are often characterized by conflict and ambiguity about both the individual's value and identity. Because it is virtually impossible to eliminate all traces of the markers associated with one's indigenous cultural system, efforts at dissociation are often only marginally successful.
2. The name of the school and names of individuals used in this paper are fictitious.
3. As stated previously, the community is beset by poverty and other effects of structural inequality. Thus, many—though not all—of the students from the community who attend Capital High are poor. High school students in the District of Columbia School System are allowed to attend the schools of their choice; therefore, many parents from other communities throughout the District encourage their children to attend Capital because of the wide range of courses offered there. Hence, although the student body is best characterized as poor, it includes working-class and middle-class students.
4. It should be noted that this list of requirements changed during the second year of the study, but they were in place during the base year of the research and had been for several years.
5. The findings emerging from this study regarding Black music and other forms of indigenous entertainment in the Black community indicate that they are critical symbols of group unity and solidarity. Consequently, students who do not identify with these aspects of Black American culture are perhaps unwittingly avoiding an important symbol of membership in the fictive-kinship system and shared behavioral patterns.

REFERENCES

Anderson, J. D. (1975). Education as a vehicle for the manipulation of Black workers. In W. Feinberg and H. Rosemont, Jr. (Eds.), *Work, technology, and education: Dissenting essay in the intellectual foundations of American education*. Chicago: University of Illinois Press.

Aplin-Brownlee. V. (1984, July 8). July 4 reminds me . . . : Black and Whites still talk to each other through masks. *The Washington Post*, p. C4.

Bloch, M. (1971). The moral and tactical meaning of kinship terms. *Man, 6*, 79–87.

Bradley, D. (1982, May). Black and American, 1982. *Esquire*, pp. 58–64, 69.

Brain, J. J. (1972). Kinship terms. *Man, 7*, 137–138.

Bullock, H. A. (1970). *A history of Negro education in the South: From 1619 to the present* (2nd ed.). New York: Praeger.

Campbell, B. M. (1982, January 17). Black executives and corporate stress. *The New York Times Magazine*, pp. 1–42.

DeVos, G. A. (1967). *Japan's invisible race: Caste in culture and personality.* Berkeley: University of California Press.

Dizard, J. (1970). Black identity, social class, and Black power. *Psychiatry, 33*, 195–202.

Drake, S. C., & Cayton, H. R. (1970). *Black metropolis; A study of Negro life in a northern city* (Vols. 1 and 2). New York: Harcourt Brace Jovanovich.

Edwards, A. (1987). Crossover dreams: For Blacks, the cost of corporate success too often is bicultural stress. *Essence, 17*, pp. 53–68.

Folb, E. (1980). *Runnin' down some lines: The language and culture of Black teenagers.* Cambridge: Harvard University Press.

Fordham, S. (1981, October 24). *Differentiated schooling in internally colonized social systems: A cultural ecological perspective.* Paper presented at the 24th Annual Meeting of the African Studies Association, Bloomington, IN.

Fordham, S. (1982, December 3–7). *Cultural inversion and Black children's school performance.* Paper presented at the 81st Annual Meeting, American Anthropological Association, Washington, DC.

Fordham, S. (1983, November 17–20). *Afro-Caribbean and native Black American school performance.* Paper presented at the 82nd Annual Meeting, American Anthropological Association, Chicago.

Fordham, S. (1985). *Black student school success as related to fictive kinship: An ethnographic study in the Washington, DC. Public School System* (Final report). Washington, DC. National Institute of Education.

Fordham, S., & Ogbu, J. (1986). Black students' school success: "Coping with the burden of 'acting White'." *The Urban Review, 18*, 176–206.

Fortes, M. (1969). *Kinship and the social order: The legacy of Lewis Henry Morgan.* Chicago: Aldine.

Freed, S. A. (1973). Fictive kinship in a northern Indian village. *Ethnology, 2*, 86–103.

Gaines-Carter, P. (1984, June 17). Quiet thunder: On a roll with Donnie Simpson. *The Washington Post Magazine*, pp. 6–7.

Granat, D., Hathaway, P., Saleton, W., & Sansing, J. (1986). Blacks and Whites in Washington: How separate? How equal? A special report. *The Washingtonian, 22*, pp. 152–182.

Gray, J. (1985, March 17). A Black American princess: New game, new rules. *The Washington Post*, pp. E1, E5.

Green, V. M. (1981). Blacks in the United States: The creation of an enduring people? In G. P. Castile & G. Kushner (Eds.), *Persistent peoples: Cultural enclaves in perspective.* Tucson: University of Arizona Press.

Gwaltney, J. L. (1980). *Drylongso: A self-portrait of Black America.* New York: Random House.

Hale, J. (1982). *Black children: Their roots, culture and learning styles.* Provo, UT: Brigham Young University Press.

Haley, A. (1976). *Roots: The saga of an American family.* Garden City, NY: Doubleday.

Holt, G. S. (1972). "Inversion" in Black communication. In T. Kochman (Ed.), *Rappin' and stylin' out.* Urbana: University of Illinois Press.

Klose, K. (1984, August 5). A tormented Black rising star dead by her own hand. Leanita McClain: A pioneer at the racial frontier who lost her way. *The Washington Post*, pp. C1, C2.

LeVine, R., & White, M. (1986). *Human conditions: The cultural basis of educational development.* New York: Routledge & Kegan Paul.

Liebow, F., (1967). *Tally's corner: A study of Negro street-corner men.* Boston: Little, Brown.

MacLeod, J. (1987). *Ain't no makin' it: Leveled aspirations in a low-income neighborhood.* Boulder, CO: Westview Press.

MacPherson, M. (1986, February 2). Doug Wilder. *The Washington Post*, pp. G1–G2.

McClain, L. (1983, July 24). How Chicago taught me to hate Whites. *The Washington Post*, pp. C1, C4.

Monroe, S. (1987, March 23). Brothers: A vivid portrait of Black men in America. *Newsweek*, pp. 55–86.

Morgan, T. (1985). The world ahead: Black parents prepare their children for pride and prejudice. *The New York Times Magazine*, pp. 34–35, 90–92, 96–100.

Myrdal, G. (1944). *An American dilemma: The Negro problem and modern democracy.* New York: Harper.

Norbeck, F., & Befu, H. (1958). Informal fictive kinship in Japan. *American Anthropologist*, *60*, 102–117.

Ogbu, J. (1983, October 21–22). *Crossing cultural boundaries: A comparative perspective on minority education.* Paper presented at a Symposium on "Race, Class, Socialization and the Life Cycle," in Honor of Allison Davis. University of Chicago, Chicago, IL.

The Oprah Winfrey Show. (1987, January 23). Prejudice against Black men. Transcript.

Petroni, F. A., & Hirsch, F. A. (1971). *Two, four, six, eight, when you gonna integrate?* New York: Behavioral Publications.

Pitt-Rivers, J. (1968). Pseudo-kinship. In D. L. Sills (Ed.), *The international encyclopedia of social scenes.* New York: Macmillan.

Pitt-Rivers, J. (1973). The kith and kin. In J. Goody (Ed.). *The character of kinship.* New York: Cambridge University Press.

Powell, A., Ferrar, F., & Cohen, D. (1985). *The shopping mall high school: Winners and losers in the educational marketplace.* Boston: Houghton Mifflin.

Reaves, D. (1972). *Notes of a processed brothers.* New York: Pantheon Books.

Richman, A. (1987). Oprah Winfrey. The best talker on TV (and a movie star to boot). *People Weekly, 27*(2), 48–50, 55–56, 58.

Robinson, M. (1987, January 23). Prejudice. Transcript, The Oprah Winfrey Show.

Sargent, E. (1985, February 10). Freeing myself: Discoveries that unshackle the mind. *The Washington Post*, pp. D1, D4.

Spivey, D. A. (1978). *Schooling for the new slavery: Black industrial education, 1868–1915.* Westport, CT: Greenwood Press.

Stack, C. (1974). *All our kin: Strategies for survival in a Black community.* New York: Harper & Row.

Staiano, K. V. (1980). Ethnicity as process: The creation of an Afro-American identity. *Ethnicity, 7*(1), 27–33.

Staples, R. (1975). To be young, Black and oppressed. *The Black Scholar, 6*, 2–9.

Staples, R. (1981). The Black American family. In C. H. Mindel & R. W. Habenstein (Eds.). *Ethnic families in America: Patterns and variations.* New York: Elsevier.

Styron, W. (1966). *The confessions of Nat Turner.* New York: Random House.

Taylor, S. A. (1973). Some funny things happen on the way up. *Contact, 5*(1), 12–17.

Trescott, J. (1977, April 1). Anchorman-reporter Ed Bradley: Like it or not, a symbol. *The Washington Post*, pp. B1, B3.

Weis, L. (1985a). *Between two worlds: Black students in an urban community college.* New York: Routledge & Kegan Paul.

Weis, L. (1985b). Without dependence on welfare for life: Black women in the community college. *Urban Review, 17*(4). 233–255.

Williams, M. D. (1981a). *On the street where I lived.* New York: Holt, Rinehart & Winston.

Williams, M. D. (1981b). Observations in Pittsburgh ghetto schools. *Anthropology and Education Quarterly, 12*(3), 211–220.

Willis, P. (1977). *Learning to labor: How working-class kids get working-class jobs.* Lexington, MA: D. C. Heath.

How Shall We Sing Our Sacred Song in a Strange Land? The Dilemma of Double Consciousness and the Complexities of an African-Centered Pedagogy

Carol D. Lee, Kofi Lomotey, and Mwalimu Shujaa

What manner of education will provide African-Americans the voice to sing the sacred liturgy of their own culture? What manner of education will mold the African personality to thrive in a culture that has historically demeaned its character, denied its existence, and coordinated its destruction? How shall we sing our sacred song in a strange land? This is the fundamental contradiction that stands before African-centered pedagogy in the United States.

The conceptual foundations of Western education reveal assumptions about humanity that offer no recognition of the differences among human beings. For example, in 1657 John Amos Comenius wrote, "The education that I propose includes all that is proper for a man and it is one in which all men who are born into this world should share . . . [to be] educated fully to full humanity." In *Treatise on Pedagogies*, Immanuel Kant, according to John Dewey, "defines education as the process by which man becomes man" (Dewey, 1916, p. 95). This same theme is reiterated today in the cultural literacy movement as articulated by E. D. Hirsch (1987) and the Paideia movement as articulated by Mortimer Adler (1982). The fundamental flaw in these conceptions of education is their narrow interpretation of what it means to be fully human—to be man, woman, and child. Is it desirable or even possible to produce such definitions in a way that ignores time, space, gender, and culture?

Conceptions of humanness are not universal, but culturally and historically specified, although there are generalizations that apply across cultures. However, the extent

Carol Lee, Kofi Lomotey, and Mwalimu Shujaa, "How Shall We Sing Our Sacred Song in a Strange Land?" *Journal of Education*, Volume 172 No. 2, Copyright 1990. Reprinted with permission of the Editorial Board of the *Journal of Education*.

The research reported in this essay was supported by a grant from the Spencer Foundation. The opinions expressed in this essay do not necessarily reflect the position or the endorsement of the Spencer Foundation.

to which such generalizations regarding human cognition are useful for effective teaching has been called into question by recent studies in cross-cultural psychology (Cole, 1985; Ginsburg et al., 1981; Kulah, 1973; Laboratory of Human Cognition, 1986; Lave, 1977; Petitto, 1982; Petitto & Ginsburg, 1982; Reed & Lave, 1981; Saxe, 1982; Scribner & Cole, 1981; Stigler & Baranes, 1989).

In this paper we address why African-American people need an African-centered pedagogy, the problems inherent in its conception, what an African-centered pedagogy should do, and finally, why and how the independent school movement in the United States is in a unique position to implement such a pedagogy.

THE NEED FOR AN AFRICAN-CENTERED PEDAGOGY

African-American people need an African-centered pedagogy because racism and worldwide Eurocentric hegemonic attitudes and practices are still the order of the day. The existing pedagogy in public education remains European-centered. Despite the upward mobility of many middle- and upper-middle-class African-Americans, the majority of African-Americans remain in poverty and do not achieve educational parity in American schools (Lomotey, 1990). The status of the majority of African-Americans relative to whites has not changed significantly throughout the history of the United States. In this regard, Haki Madhubuti (1990) summarizes key points from a report by the National Research Council (Jaynes & Williams, 1989):

1. Black poverty rates have been two to three times higher than those of whites at all times.

2. Residential separation of Blacks and Whites has remained practically unchanged since the 1960's.

3. "Segregation and differential treatment of Blacks continue to be widespread in the elementary and secondary schools," the committee reported. . . . [Rates of Black college attendance] remain significantly lower than those of the 1970's.

4. Blacks [account for] 13% . . . of the U.S. population . . . [but] still make up only about 1% of all elected officials.

5. "Blacks are disproportionately victims of crime," the committee found. [The prison population is approximately 50% Black.]

6. There are wide gaps in the mortality and morbidity of Blacks compared to Whites at all ages except for individuals 85 and older.

7. The majority of Black children under the age of 18 live in families that include their mothers but not their fathers, while one in every five White children lives with just his or her mother. These figures are particularly significant considering the fact that female-headed families were 50% of all Black families with children in 1985, but they received only 25% of total Black family income. (pp. vii–viii)

It is neither popular nor comforting to look at these figures. Moreover it is insufficient to attribute culpability totally to racism and white supremacy. The response of the African-American community to these conditions has been incomplete and short sighted (Cruse, 1967, 1987; Karenga, 1982; Madhubuti, 1990; Woodson, 1933). Nevertheless, enslavement and the African holocaust interrupted and depoliticized the cultural memory as well as disrupted historical continuity for Africans in the Diaspora.[1] Slavery and colonialism had similar effects on development within the African continent (Akbar, 1984; Bennett, 1964; Madhubuti, 1984; Rodney, 1972; Williams, 1974). The picture presented here for African-Americans is representative of the condition of Africans worldwide. Generally speaking, anywhere in the world where Africans and whites are living together, Africans are threatened by white supremacy—a universal framework that all people, African, European, or Asian, must struggle to overcome.

Currently, most theories of learning and development produced by Western educational research tend to reproduce and reinforce Eurocentric paradigms. Conclusions are drawn from observations of white, middle-class samples and postulated as universal norms for development and learning (Apple, 1979; Banks, 1988; Miller-Jones, 1988; Ogbu, 1988; *Saving the African-American Child,* 1984; Slaughter & McWorter, 1985; Stigler & Baranes, 1989). An African-centered pedagogy is needed to support a line of resistance to these conditions; it is needed to produce an education that contributes to achieving pride, equity, power, wealth, and cultural continuity for Africans in America and elsewhere.

In addition, an African-centered pedagogy is necessary in order to foster an ethical character development grounded in social practice within the African community. The African cultural character is neither monolithic nor static. However, even in its historical and geographic formations—whether Yoruba or Zulu, African-Brazilian or African-American—there is an ontological foundation that remains constant (Asante, 1988; Diop, 1978; Karenga, 1990; Mbiti, 1970; Nobles, 1980; Sofola, 1973; Stuckey, 1987; Warfield-Coppock, 1990). That constant is well represented in the ancient Egyptian concept of *Maat,* which, according to Dr. Maulana Karenga (1990), includes the following propositions:

1. the divine image of humans;
2. the perfectability of humans;
3. the teachability of humans;
4. the free will of humans; and
5. the essentiality of moral social practice in human development. (p. 26)

Cultivation of this historical model of ethical character is required not only for resistance to political and cultural oppression, but also to sustain independent development. Dr. Maulana Karenga (1990) reinforces this perspective when he says,

> The key crisis and challenge in African life [is] . . . one of culture, the challenge to rescue and reconstruct the best of ancient African culture and use it as a paradigm for a renewed modern African culture and community. . . . Only in this way . . . [can] they speak their own special truth to the world and make their own unique contribution to the forward flow of human history. (p. xi)

This historical paradigm can be supported by pedagogical practices that cultivate the following characteristics in students (New Concept Development Center Parent Handbook, 1977):

1. think critically and question everything;
2. understand history;
3. set good examples and accept just criticism;
4. practice a life-style which recognizes the importance of African and African-American heritage and traditions, and is geared to the values which will facilitate the present and future development of African people;
5. learn to be critical of self first and recognize that African values are only as just and correct as those who practice them. (pp. 1–2)

PROBLEMS CONFRONTING AN AFRICAN-CENTERED PEDAGOGY

In the context of a multi-ethnic, democratic society, attention to African-centered pedagogy amidst calls for multicultural education arouses serious tensions (Hancock, 1990). We who seek to articulate such a theory of learning and teaching must address many delicate questions. Among them is to discuss how this theory is both similar to and dissimilar from other progressive pedagogical frameworks, such as Freire's liberation pedagogy (1970). Because we live in a multi-ethnic society, we must also address how an African-centered pedagogy reinforces intra-ethnic solidarity and pride without promoting inter-ethnic antagonisms. An African-centered pedagogy must include a conceptualization of American society as a culturally diverse entity within which ethnic solidarity is required in order to negotiate, acquire, and maintain power. An African-centered pedagogy should promote intra-ethnic solidarity among African-Americans while at the same time providing strategies for coalitions with other groups with similar needs and interests. American society is not a melting pot, but rather a mosaic of diversity. We must honestly address the question of what the implementation of an African-centered pedagogy means for a classroom in which many ethnic groups are represented as well as for a public school whose population is entirely African-American.

In addition to the complexities within the United States, there are also complex international considerations. Issues related to the formulation of an African-centered pedagogy are relevant to Africans worldwide. However, the functions and cultural specificity of such a pedagogy will be qualitatively different in such diverse countries as the United States, Brazil, Australia, Nigeria, and Azania (South Africa). For example, there are sociopolitical and historical contexts which are important in accounting for the level of educational achievement of Caribbean Blacks in the United States as compared with their lack of educational achievement in Britain. A similar comparison may be made of the differences in educational achievement between Koreans in Japan and Koreans in the United States (Cortes, 1986; Ogbu & Matute-Bianchi, 1986).

Considering these complexities, how does an African-centered pedagogy fit into the framework of American public education? We believe that public education can achieve the following ends:

1. Foster the development of adequate skills in literacy, numeracy, the humanities, and technologies that are necessary to negotiate economic self-sufficiency in the society;

2. Instill citizenship skills based on a realistic and thorough understanding of the political system, and support such citizenship skills by promoting questioning and critical thinking skills and teaching democratic values (Gutman, 1987; McNeil, 1988);

3. Provide historical overviews of the nation, the continent, and the world which accurately represent the contributions of all ethnic groups to the storehouse of human knowledge.

Accomplishing these goals represents a major challenge to public education. However, their attainment, although necessary, is not adequate for the achievement of ethnic pride, self-sufficiency, equity, wealth, and power for Africans in America. For Africans in America to achieve these goals will require a collective (although not monolithic) cultural and political worldview. Public education currently does not impart such a worldview to African-Americans. The political perspective that guides public education will depend on who controls the schools in a given community. It is hard to believe that public education in a democratic and ethnically diverse country such as the United States has the responsibility to liberate any particular group of people. It is precisely these limitations of public education, as presently constructed, which argue for the articulation, research, and implementation of an African-centered pedagogy.

African-Americans are not the only group focusing on the articulation of pedagogical principles specific to their cultural group. Such pedagogical principles have been articulated for native Hawaiian children (Gallimore et al., 1982; Tharp, 1982; Tharp et al., 1984), for Navajo children (Jordan et al., 1985; White & Tharp, 1988), for Pueblo Indian children (John-Steiner & Osterreich, 1975; Winterton, 1977), for Athabascan Alaskan children (Barnhardt, 1982; Scollon, 1981), and for Hispanic students (Moll, 1990). This focus is critical given the current limitations of western research. Rogoff and Morelli (1989) note:

> Cross-cultural research provides a breadth that has been more difficult to achieve when researchers have looked at cultural variation in our own nation and have tended to assume that the majority's practices are normal and the minority's practices involve deficits. (p. 341)

The February 1989 issue of *American Psychologist* addresses the issue of culture and American education from diverse perspectives. Dalton Miller-Jones (1988) has noted the positive effects for all children that research into issues of African-American cultural styles and their relationship to education has had over the past 30 years. In a similar fashion, we expect that research and implementation of African-centered pedagogical principles will broaden our knowledge of human learning by broadening the base of cases that instantiate our premises.

AFRICAN-CENTERED PEDAGOGY: A RELEVANT PRAXIS

The following goals are common attributes of all conceptions of pedagogy. However, the specific pedagogical practices that reflect these attributes require cultural specificity. An effective African-centered pedagogy:

1. legitimizes African stores of knowledge;
2. positively exploits and scaffolds productive community and cultural practices;
3. extends and builds upon the indigenous language;
4. reinforces community ties and idealizes service to one's family, community, nation, race, and world;
5. promotes positive social relationships;
6. imparts a worldview that idealizes a positive, self-sufficient future for one's people without denying the self-worth and right to self-determination of others;
7. supports cultural continuity while promoting critical consciousness.

The challenge to researchers and practitioners who undertake the development of an African-centered pedagogy which encompasses these attributes is to enact them in ways that are culturally accurate, politically viable, developmentally appropriate and subject matter sensitive. *This task requires an integration of research and practice as well as an environment that does not consciously inhibit culturally sensitive development and practice.*

In the arena of educational research, there are many fundamental questions regarding human development that are needed to support an African-centered pedagogy. In urban, poor, single-parent African-American households, what is the nature of play and what are the cognitive foundations and socialization strategies that undergird that play? What story schema do African-American children display during oral story telling in naturalistic environments and what are the implications of those schema or story grammars for story comprehension in early literacy and for writing instruction in creative writing, exposition, and argument in later grades?[2] What are the experiences that promoted African-American writers' creation of what Henry Louis Gates (1988) calls the "speakerly text"? How can educators use African-American English speakers' understanding of and production of metaphoric and ironic talk in the form of signifying, sounding, etc. to promote children's comprehension of metaphor and irony in literature?[3] How can educators use African-American English speakers' signifying and sounding to enhance student writing?[4] What informal experiences in play and work do poor African-American children in urban and rural environments have with spatial relationships, quantities, logical operations, classification schemes, money, weight, and volume? What characteristics of these informal mathematical experiences share sufficient attributes of formal school-based mathematics so as to provide productive scaffolding for school learning? What effect can the incorporation of African contributions to mathematics, science, and technology into school-based curricula have on student motivation? How does the African and African-American tradition of socializing children through the indirect talk of proverbs and storytelling affect cognitive processing? How are the inferences from such indirect talk constructed and what are the implications of such construction for teaching African-American children (or other children) who are socialized in this way? These questions are the tip of the iceberg of the potential foci for research that will support the articulation and elaboration of an African-centered pedagogy. Research in some of these areas has begun, but clearly more research will need to follow. This theoretical research must be coupled with strategic curricular implementation in environments that can maximize the effectiveness of instruction. Independent Black schools have served and continue to serve as models for the implementation of an African-centered pedagogy.

IMPLEMENTATION OF AFRICAN-CENTERED PEDAGOGY: THE IBI

The implementation of African-centered pedagogical principles continues within Black independent schools and within other educating institutions outside the public sector, including churches, social and fraternal collectives, and community organizations (Ratteray & Shujaa, 1988). Moreover, historically African-American colleges as well as national school systems in independent African nation states provide fertile ground for research, reflection, implementation, revision, and proselytizing.

African-centered pedagogy is not a new phenomenon in the education of African-American youth. The African-American free schools during Reconstruction (Anderson, 1988; Bennett, 1964; Harding, 1981) and the Freedom Schools of the civil rights movement (Howe, 1965) represent two historical poles of this continuum. The Black independent schools since 1970 have provided the most contemporary stage for the practice of African-centered pedagogy. However, in order to articulate a more cohesive educational philosophy sensitive to both current and future conditions, researchers and practitioners must collaborate in lab school settings. These lab school settings must have the philosophical and material resources as well as the historical practices to provide adequate support for the collaborative activities. Black independent schools and African-centered educational researchers make an ideal alliance for implementation. Conclusions and practices drawn from such an alliance offer relevant and tested sources of curriculum content and pedagogical principles for the African-American component of multicultural curricula in public schools. Consider the shortcomings of the African-American component of the Portland school system's multicultural models and the political turmoil surrounding the report "Curriculum of Inclusion" issued by the Task Force on Minorities: Equity and Excellence from the New York State Board of Education (Hancock, 1990).[6] It is naive to believe that significant comprehensive development of African-centered curriculum based on an African-centered pedagogy will occur under such conditions.

The implementations of an African-centered pedagogy demands teachers who advocate and are well grounded in the following principles:

1. The social ethics of African culture as exemplified in the social philosophy of *Maat* (Karenga, 1990);
2. The history of the African continent and Diaspora;
3. The need for political and community organizing within the African-American community;
4. The positive pedagogical implications of the indigenous language, African-American English (Delain, Pearson, & Anderson, 1985; Gee, 1989; Heath, 1989);
5. Child development principles that are relevant to the positive and productive growth of African-American children (Hale, 1982; Warfield-Coppock, 1990; Wilson, 1978);
6. African contributions in science, mathematics, literature, the arts, and societal organization;
7. Teaching techniques that are socially interactive, holistic, and positively affective (Hale, 1982; Warfield-Coppock, 1990; Willis, 1989);

8. The need for continuous personal study;

9. The African principle that "Children are the reward of life";

10. The African principle of reciprocity (Armah, 1979; Mbiti, 1970; Nobles, 1980); that is, a teacher sees his or her own future symbiotically linked to the development of students.

These attributes are extremely demanding, but are fundamental to the liberating aims of this pedagogy.

One important environment for the articulation and implementation of African-centered pedagogical principles has been the independent Black school as embodied through the Council of Independent Black Institutions (CIBI). Since the early 1970s, hundreds of community-based schools across the country have developed and implemented a challenging curriculum which incorporates African and African-American history and culture. Students in these community-based institutions demonstrate a high level of mastery of academic skills as evaluated by standardized achievement tests (Ratteray, 1986, 1989). The brief overview that follows describes some of the kinds of curricular activities that are common in CIBI schools and that reflect some of the goals we have identified as crucial to an African-centered pedagogy. Space will not allow presentation of a fuller range of activities. The following activities do not engage all the aims identified for this pedagogy. However they do legitimize African stores of knowledge, idealize community service, and impart a worldview in which Africans master technology and support cultural continuity while promoting critical consciousness.

Many of the following activities were conducted in preparation for the annual National Science EXPO sponsored by CIBI since 1977. These particular units were done by students in grades one through five. We mention the grade level of the students because the work was challenging for such young students. The challenge was undertaken, however, because in the spirit of such educators as Septima Clark and Mary McLeod Bethune, African-American educators in these institutions take for granted that all children are capable of learning and that the role of teacher is an extension of the role of parent. This means that whatever time, energy, and strategies are required to achieve success for these children will be used. Such an attitude is required by an African-centered pedagogy because this conception of teaching means that the teacher sees his or her own personal future in the lives of these children, a point poignantly made by Sarah Lawrence Lightfoote in a 1989 television interview with Bill Moyers. These activities in science and technology are highlighted also because much of the current emphasis on African-centered curriculum focuses primarily on the arts and secondarily on the humanities, but rarely on the sciences. When activities that may be construed as science-related are put forward, they are generally nothing more than storytelling—biographies of great African men and women.

Exemplary units include one on the principles of aeronautics, one on architecture, and one on computer science. In the unit on aeronautics, students built a model wind tunnel and tested the effects of the position of the tail, rudder, and ailerons on the direction of an airplane in simulated flight. This set of activities was preceded by units on air pressure and air lift as exemplified by Bernoulli's principle. In conjunction with this unit, students researched and wrote about the role of Africans in

American aviation, including the story of the famous Tuskegee Airmen. They also developed scenarios speculating on the source of the wooden glider in the Cairo Museum, presumed to be preliminary evidence of early attempts at flight by the ancient Egyptians (Van Sertima, 1983).

In the unit on architecture, students tested the strength of certain shapes in construction, particularly the truss in bridge and building construction. They then identified the triangle as the building block of the truss and traced the Egyptians' understanding of this function through the construction of the ancient pyramids.[7] For the actual science EXPO, students built model buildings and bridges out of straw and popsicle sticks. An African-American architect came in not only to evaluate the projects, but also to talk with the students about how he used his skills and his architectural firm to promote development in the Black community.

In the computer science unit, several student volunteers in the computer science program at a local public high school came in to work after school with a group of elementary students on simple programming. The elementary students accumulated information from studies in Black history and developed a Black history quiz. With the assistance of the high school volunteers, the students then translated the quiz into a simple computer program. Other students worked on the base two binary system and developed an elementary circuit board illustrating how the computer counts and operates using binary based on/off switches. At the science EXPO, an African-American businessman who not only builds computers but also owns a computer company came in to talk with the children about computers and to show them the inner workings of a computer. For the children, the computer specialist represented a living model of what they could become as well as an example of an adult who gives his skills back to the community from which he came.

Other projects have included a hands-on demonstration of the Yoruba counting system. This activity was important in legitimizing a new source of knowledge for the students and also expanded their examples of how people count. In conjunction with units on Kemetic (Egyptian) history, students have demonstrated the Egyptians' use of fractions in the marketplace and their use of simple machines in the building of the obelisk of Queen Hatshepsut. Several students from a CIBI school, while visiting the Washington Monument observed that the monument was an obelisk. They noted that it differed from the Egyptian model in that Hatshepsut's obelisk was carved out of solid granite, while the Washington Monument appeared from the naked eye to be built from blocks.

The independent Black school affirms the strengths that economically disadvantaged African-American children, in particular, bring to schools. This unswerving belief, coupled with the kind of curricular activities described, promote a qualitative development that is beyond simple literacy and beyond skills for getting a job to work for someone else. Instead, these kinds of activities reflect African-centered pedagogical principles aimed at empowering students to create and to reflect on their creations and the impact such creations can have on their communities and families. Such activities inspire both a vision of the past and a future in which Africans exert self-determination in the space over which they walk.

An African-centered pedagogy must direct African-American children and African-American people out of the "peculiar sensation" observed by W.E.B. DuBois

(1903), of "this double-consciousness, this sense of always looking at one's self through the eyes of others." Rather, African-centered pedagogy must take up the mantle of the griots as Ghanaian novelist Ayi Kwei Armah reveals in the prophetic novel *Two Thousand Seasons* (1979). African-centered pedagogy must help students to see beyond "the howling cacophony" that may engulf them. Its activities must link them to "those gone, ourselves here [and] those coming." African-centered pedagogy can help students to "listen far toward origins," and can offer them some tools with which they can figure out their "way." Their voices and self-analysis must be strengthened in order to "make this knowledge [of themselves] inevitable [and] impossible to lose."

There is a lesson to learn from scholar/practitioners as diverse as George Washington Carver, W.E.B. DuBois, Ida B. Wells, Cheikh Anta Diop, Mary McLeod Bethune, and Carter G. Woodson. They have demonstrated that with a strong cultural sense of self, with a commitment to and connection with our people, we may emerge out of lowly circumstances, take in the knowledge of the world, and give special gifts to all of humanity.

NOTES

1. During the African holocaust of enslavement, despite attempts to dismantle the language, religion, social practices, and family structures which constituted and gave meaning to African identity, many African cultural forms withstood the attack (Bastide, 1971; Herskovitz, 1955; King, 1976; Nobles, 1974). Those cultural forms are most evident in the Africanisms which undergird African-American English (Dillard, 1972; Smith, 1972a, 1972b; Smitherman, 1977; Turner, 1949; Vass, 1979), in expressions of African-American spirituality (Mbiti, 1970; Stuckey, 1987) as well as in music and dance (Jones, 1963; Pasteur & Toldson, 1982; Southern, 1971).

2. We acknowledge the important contributions to this question made by Heath (1983), Michaels (1981, 1986), and Gee (1989). We also applaud Shirley Brice Heath's (1988) admonition that "Relatively few Black anthropologists or linguists have chosen to focus their research on language and culture patterns of Black Americans" (p. 32). Several significant projects in naturalistic environments by African-American researchers include Mitchell-Kernan (1971), Potts (1989), and Stockman & Vaughn-Cooke (1982, 1989) as well as ongoing research by Mahiri (1990). It has become more commonly accepted in ethnographic research that indigenous participant-observers may have insights into the discourse that others do not (Heath, 1988; Saville-Troike, 1989). The investigations of stories of personal experience within diverse communities by Miller, Potts, and Fung (1989) reflect sensitivity to the potentially privileged role indigenous researchers of a speech community may have in ethnographic research.

3. Taylor & Ortony (1980) and DeLain, Pearson, & Anderson (1985) have established a relationship between expertise in African-American English, sounding (a form of signifying), and comprehension of figurative language in metaphor and simile. However, these studies do not use naturalistic texts and so the question of any transferability of this relationship to literary understanding remains open. Carol Lee (1990) addresses the issue of transfer and the conditions of instruction which might promote transfer.

4. Arnetha Ball (1990) has initiated an excellent study which identifies structural patterns of discourse that emerge in writing samples from African-American high school students. How

to exploit these structural patterns in enhancing student writing, however, remains an open question.

5. The unit plans developed by the Portland Board of Education do not meet the quality expected as a result of the superb baseline essays developed by Afro-centric scholars to provide a historical and philosophical framework for the African-American component of the Portland multicultural curriculum (Asa Hilliard, personal communication).

6. Critics of this report cited by Hancock (1990) assume that history is apolitical and that education is not an ideological as well as an intellectual enterprise. These critics cite Asian-American students and the fact that Japanese students learn to master Western culture as evidence that the Eurocentrism in American textbooks does not hinder the scholastic achievement of these populations. This argument skirts the issue of the limitations of Eurocentric bias in American textbooks and curricula. More importantly, it does not address the strong cultural foundations and ethnic solidarity, as well as ethnic complexities, which inspire the academic performance of many groups of Asian-American and Japanese students (Slaughter et al., 1990).

7. This curriculum reinforces the fact that classical Egyptian or Kemetic civilization was created primarily by Black people. For further references see Carruthers and Karenga (1986), Diop (1974, 1977, 1978a, 1978b, 1981), Houston (1985), Jackson (1970), James (1970), and Williams (1974). Kemetic civilization is highlighted because, according to Dr. Cheikh Anta Diop, "ancient Egypt was the key classical African civilization given its abundance of documents, its level of achievement in various areas of culture and human knowledge and its resultant significance to other African cultures as well as to world culture" (Karenga, 1990, p. xii).

REFERENCES

Adler, M. (1982). *The Paideia proposal: An educational manifesto.* New York: Macmillan.

Akbar, N. (1984). *Chains and images of psychological slavery.* Jersey City, NJ: New Mind Productions.

Anderson, J. (1988). *The education of Blacks in the South, 1860–1935.* Chapel Hill: University of North Carolina Press.

Apple, M. (1979). *Ideology and curriculum.* London: Routledge & Kegan Paul.

Armah, A. K. (1979). *Two thousand seasons.* Chicago: Third World Press.

Asante, M. K. (1988). *Afrocentricity.* Trenton, NJ: Africa World Press.

Ball, A. (1990). *A study of the oral and written descriptive patterns of Black adolescents in vernacular and academic discourse communities.* Paper presented at the annual meeting of the American Research Association.

Banks, J. (1988). Ethnicity, class, cognitive and motivational styles: Research and teaching implications. *Journal of Negro Education, 57*(4), 452–466.

Barnhardt, C. (1982). Tuning-in: Athabaskan teachers and Athabaskan students. In R. Barnhardt (Ed.), *Cross-cultural issues in Alaskan education* (Vol. 2). Fairbanks: University of Alaska, Center for Cross-Cultural Studies. (ERIC Document Reproduction Service No. ED 232 814).

Bastide, R. (1979). *African civilization in the new world.* London: C. Hurst.

Bennett, J. (1964). *Before the Mayflower: A history of the Negro in America 1619–1964.* Chicago: Johnson Publishing Company.

Carruthers, J., & Karenga, M. (Eds.). (1986). *Kemet and the African world view: Selected papers of the proceedings of the first and second conferences of the Association for the Study of Classical African Civilization.* Los Angeles: University of Sankore Press.

Cole, M. (1985). The zone of proximal development: Where culture and cognition create each other. In J. Wertsch (Ed.), *Culture, communication and cognition* (pp. 146–161). New York: Cambridge University Press.

Comenius, J. A. (1967). *The great didactic of John Amos Comenius* (M. W. Keatinge, Trans. & Ed.). New York: Russell & Russell.

Cortes, C. (1986). The education of language minority students: A contextual interaction model. In California State Department of Education, *Beyond language: Social and cultural factors in schooling, language minority children* (pp. 73–142). Los Angeles: Evaluation Dissemination and Assessment Center, California State University.

Cruse, H. (1967). *The crisis of the Negro intellectual*. New York: William Morrow.

Cruse, H. (1987). *Plural but equal: A critical study of Blacks and minorities and America's plural society*. New York: William Morrow.

Delain, M. T., Pearson, P. D., & Anderson, R. C. (1985). Reading comprehension and creativity in Black language use: You stand to gain by playing the sounding game. *American Educational Research Journal, 22*(2), 155–173.

Dewey, J. (1916). *Democracy and education*. New York: Macmillan.

Dillard, J. L. (1972). *Black English*. New York: Random House.

Diop, C. A. (1974). *The African origin of civilization: Myth or reality* (Mercer Cook, Trans.). New York: Lawrence Hill & Company.

Diop, C. A. (1977). *Parente genetique de l'Egyptien pharaonique et des langues Negro-Africaines*. Dakar, Senegal: Les Nouvelles Editions Africaines.

Diop, C. A. (1978a). *The cultural unity of Black Africa*. Chicago: Third World Press.

Diop, C. A. (1978b). The peopling of the ancient Egyptians and the deciphering of Meroitic script. *Proceedings of the symposium held in Cairo from 28 January to 3 February, 1974*. Paris: UNESCO.

Diop, C. A. (1981). The origins of the ancient Egyptians. In P. Mokhtar (Ed.), *The general history of Africa: Ancient civilizations of Africa* (Vol. 2, pp. 27–57). Berkeley: University of California Press.

DuBois, W. E. B. (1903). *The souls of Black folk*. Chicago: A. C. McClurg.

Freire, P. (1970). *Pedagogy of the oppressed*. New York: Seabury Press.

Gallimore, R., Tharp, R. G., Sloat, K., Klein, T., & Troy, M. E. (1982). *Analysis of reading achievement test results for the Kamehameha early education project: 1972–1979* (Tech. Rep. No. 102). Honolulu: Kamehameha Schools/Bishop Estate.

Gates, H. L. (1988). *The signifying monkey: A theory of Afro-American literary criticism*. New York: Oxford University Press.

Gee, J. (1989). The narrativization of experience in the oral style. *Journal of Education, 171*(1), 75–96.

Ginsburg, H., Posner, J. K., & Russel, R. L. The development of mental addition as a function of schooling and culture. *Journal of Cross-Cultural Psychology, 12*, 163–178.

Gutman, A. (1987). *Democratic education*. Princeton: Princeton University Press.

Hale, J. E. (1982). *Black children: Their roots, culture and learning styles*. Provo, UT: Brigham Young University Press.

Hancock, L. (1990, April 24). Whose America is this anyway? *Village Voice*, pp. 37–39.

Harding, V. (1981). *There is a river: The Black struggle for freedom in America*. New York: Harcourt Brace Jovanovitch.

Heath, S. B. (1983). *Ways with words: Language, life and work in communities and classrooms*. Cambridge: Cambridge University Press.

Heath, S. B. (1988). Language socialization. In D. Slaughter (Ed.), *Black children and poverty: A developmental perspective* (pp. 29–42). San Francisco: Jossey-Bass.

Heath, S. B. (1989). Oral and literate traditions among Black Americans living in poverty. *American Psychologist, 44*(2), 367–373.

Herskovitz, M. (1955). *Cultural anthropology*. New York: Alfred A. Knopf.

Hirsch, E. D. (1987). *Cultural literacy: What every American needs to know*. Boston: Houghton Mifflin.

Houston, D. D. (1985). *Wonderful Ethiopians of the ancient Cushite empire*. Baltimore: Black Classic Press.

Howe, F. (1965). Mississippi's freedom schools: The politics of education. *Harvard Educational Review, 35*(2), 144–160.

Jackson, J. (1970). *Introduction to African civilizations*. New York: University Books.

James, G. (1954). *Stolen legacy*. San Francisco: Julian Richardson Associates.

Jaynes, G. D., & Williams, R. M. (Eds.). (1989). *A common destiny: Blacks and American society*. Washington, DC: National Academy Press.

John-Steiner, V. P., & Osterreich, H. (1975). *Learning styles among Pueblo children: Final report to National Institute of Education*. Albuquerque: College of Education, University of New Mexico.

Jones, L. (1963). *Blues people: Negro music in white America*. New York: William Morrow.

Jordan, C., Tharp, R. G., & Vogt, L. (1985). *Compatibility of classroom and culture: General principles with Navajo and Hawaiian instances* (Working Paper No. 18). Honolulu: Kamehameha Schools/Bishop Estate.

Karenga, M. (1982). *Introduction to Black studies*. Los Angeles: Kawaida Publications.

Karenga, M. (Translation and Commentary). (1990). *The book of coming forth by day: The ethics of the declarations of innocence*. Los Angeles: University of Sankore Press.

King, J. R. (1976). African survivals in the Black community: Key factors in stability. *Journal of Afro-American Issues, 4*(2), 153–167.

Kulah, A. A. (1973). *The organization and learning of proverbs among the Kpelle of Liberia*. Unpublished doctoral dissertation, University of California, Irvine.

Laboratory of Human Cognition. (1986). Contributions of cross-cultural research to educational practice. *American Psychologist, 41*(10), 1049–1058.

Lave, J. (1977). Cognitive consequences of traditional apprenticeship training in west Africa. *Anthropology and Education Quarterly, 7*, 177–180.

Lee, C. (1990). *Signifying in the zone of proximal development*. Unpublished paper, University of Chicago.

Lomotey, K. (1990). Introduction. In K. Lomotey (Ed.), *Going to school: the African-American experience* (pp. 1–9). Albany, NY: SUNY Press.

Madhubuti, H. (1984). *Earthquakes and Sunrise Missions*. Chicago: Third World Press.

Madhubuti, H. (1990). *Black men: Single, dangerous and obsolete*. Chicago: Third World Press.

Mahiri, J. (1990). *Language use and literary features of pre-adolescent African-American males in a neighborhood based organization*. University of Illinois at Chicago.

Mbiti, J. (1970). *African religion and philosophy*. New York: Anchor Books.

McNeil, L. (1988). *Contradictions of control: School structure and school knowledge*. New York: Routledge & Kegan Paul.

Michaels, S. (1981). Sharing time: Children's narrative styles and differential access to literacy. *Language in Society, 10*, 423–442.

Michaels, S. (1986). Narrative presentations: An oral preparation for literacy with first graders. In J. Cook-Gumperz (Ed.), *The social construction of literacy* (pp. 94–116). Cambridge: Cambridge University Press.

Miller, P., Potts, R., & Fung, H. (1989). *Minority perspectives on narrative development*. Paper presented at the annual meeting of the American Educational Research Association.

Miller-Jones, D. (1988). The study of African-American children's development: Contributions to reformulating developmental paradigms. In D. Slaughter (Ed.), *Black children and poverty: A developmental perspective* (pp. 75–92). San Francisco: Jossey-Bass.

Mitchell-Kernan, C. (1971). *Language behavior in a Black urban community*. Monographs of the Language Behavior Laboratory, University of California, Berkeley, No. 2 (February 1971).

Moll, L. (1990). *Literacy research in community and classrooms: A socio-cultural approach*. Paper presented at the conference on Multi-disciplinary Perspectives on Research Methodology in Language Arts, National Conference on Research in English, Chicago.

New Concept Development Center parent handbook. (1977). Chicago: Institute of Positive Education.

Nobles, W. (1974). African roots and American fruit: The Black family. *Journal of Social and Behavioral Sciences, 20*(2), 52–64.

Nobles, W. (1980). African philosophy: Foundations for Black psychology. In R. Jones (Ed.), *Black Psychology* (pp. 23–36). New York: Harper and Row.

Ogbu, J. (1988). Cultural diversity and human development. In D. Slaughter (Ed.), *Black children and poverty: A developmental perspective* (pp. 11–28). San Francisco: Jossey-Bass.

Ogbu, J., & Matute-Bianchi, M. E. (1986). Understanding sociocultural factors: Knowledge, identity, and school adjustment. In California State Department of Education, *Beyond language: Social and cultural factors in schooling, language minority children* (pp. 73–142). Los Angeles: Evaluation Dissemination and Assessment Center, California State University.

Pasteur, A., & Toldson, I. (1982). *Roots of soul: The psychology of Black expressiveness*. Garden City, NY: Anchor Press/Doubleday.

Petitto, A. (1982). Practical arithmetic and transfer: A study among west African tribesmen. *Journal of Cross-Cultural Psychology, 13*, 15–28.

Petitto, A., & Ginsburg, H. (1982). Mental arithmetic in Africa and America: Strategies, principles, and explanations. *Internal Journal of Psychology, 17*, 81–102.

Potts, R. (1989). *West Side stories: Children's conversational narratives in a Black community*. Paper presented at the biennial meeting of the Society for Research Child Development.

Ratteray, J. D. (1986). *Access to quality: Private schools in Chicago's inner city* (Heartland Policy Study, No. 9). Chicago: Heartland Institute.

Ratteray, J. D. (1989). *What's in a norm: How African-Americans score on achievement tests*. Washington, DC: Institute for Independent Education.

Ratteray, J. D. & Shujaa, M. (1988). Defining a tradition: Parental choice in independent neighborhood schools. In D. Slaughter & D. J. Johnson (Eds.), *Visible now: Blacks in private schools* (pp. 184–198). Westport, CT: Greenwood Press.

Reed, H. J., & Lave, J. (1981). Arithmetic as a tool for investigating relations between culture and cognition. *Language, culture and cognition. Anthropological perspectives*. New York: Macmillan.

Rodney, W. (1972). *How Europe underdeveloped Africa*. Washington, DC: Howard University Press.

Rogoff, B., & Morelli, G. (1989). Culture and American children: Section introduction. *American Psychologist, 44*(2), 341–342.

Saville-Troike, M. (1989). *The ethnography of communication: An introduction*. New York: Basil Blackwell.

Saving the African-American child. (1984). A report of the National Alliance of Black School Educators, Inc., Task Force on Black Academic and Cultural Excellence. Washington, DC.

Saxe, G. B. (1982). Culture and the development of numerical cognition: Studies among the Oksapmin of Papua, New Guinea. In C. Brainerd (Ed.), *Children's logical and mathematical cognition* (pp. 157–176). New York: Springer-Verlag.

Scribner, S., & Cole, M. (1981). *The psychology of literacy*. Cambridge: Harvard University Press.

Slaughter, D., & McWorter, G. (1985). Social origins and early features of the scientific study of Black American families and children. In M. Spencer, G. Brookins, & W. Allen (Eds.),

Beginnings: The social and affective development of Black children (pp. 5–18). Hillsdale, NJ: Lawrence Erlbaum Associates.

Slaughter, D., Nakagawa, K., Takanishi, R., & Johnson, D. (1990). Toward cultural/ecological perspectives on schooling and achievement in African and Asian-American children. *Child Development, 61*(2), 363–383.

Smith, A. (1972a). Markings of an African concept of rhetoric. In A. Smith (Ed.), *Language, communication and rhetoric in Black America.* New York: Harper and Row.

Smith, A. (1972b). Socio-historical perspectives of Black oratory. In A. Smith (Ed.), *Language, communication and rhetoric in Black America.* New York: Harper and Row.

Smitherman, G. (1977). *Talkin' and testifyin': The language of Black America.* Boston: Houghton Mifflin.

Sofola, J. A. (1973). *African culture and the African personality.* Ibadan, Nigeria: African Resources.

Southern, E. (1971). *The music of Black Americans: A history.* New York: W. W. Norton.

Stigler, J., & Baranes, R. (1989). Culture and mathematical learning. *Review of Research in Education, 15,* 253–306.

Stockman, I., & Vaughn-Cooke, A. F. (1982). Reexamination of the research on the language of Black children: The need for a new framework. *Journal of Education, 164,* 157–172.

Stockman, I., & Vaughn-Cooke, A. F. (1989). Addressing new questions about Black children's language. In R. W. Fasold & D. Schiffrin, *Language change and variation.* Philadelphia: John Benjamin.

Stuckey, S. (1987). *Slave culture.* New York: Oxford University Press.

Taylor, M., & Ortony, A. (1980). Rhetorical devices in Black English: Some psycholinguistic and educational observations. *Quarterly Newsletter of the Laboratory of Human Cognition, 2*(2), 21–26.

Tharp, R. (1982). The effective instruction of comprehension: Results and descriptions of the Kamehameha early education program. *Reading Research Quarterly, 17*(4), 503–527.

Tharp, R. G., Jordan, C., Speidel, G., Au, K. H., Klein, T. W., Sloat, K. C. M., Calkins, R. P., & Gallimore, R. (1984). Product and process in applied developmental research: Education and the children of a minority. In M. E. Lamb, A. L. Brown, & B. Rogoff (Eds.), *Advances in developmental psychology* (Vol. 3, pp. 91–144). Hillsdale, NJ: Lawrence Erlbaum Associates.

Turner, L. (1949). *Africanisms in the Gullah dialect.* Chicago: University of Chicago Press.

Van Sertima, I. (Ed.) (1983). *Blacks in science.* New Brunswick, NJ: Transaction Books.

Vass, W. K. (1979). *The Bantu speaking heritage of the United States.* Los Angeles: Center for Afro-American Studies, University of California.

Warfield-Coppock, N. (1990). *Afrocentric theory and applications, Volume one: Adolescent rites of passage.* Washington, DC: Baobab Associates.

White, S., & Tharp, R. G. (1988, April). *Questioning and wait-time: A cross-cultural analysis.* Paper presented at the annual meeting of the American Educational Research Association, New Orleans.

Williams, C. (1974). *The destruction of Black civilization.* Chicago: Third World Press.

Willis, M. G. (1989). Learning styles of African-American children: A review of the literature and interventions. *Journal of Black Psychology 16*(1), 47–65.

Wilson, A. (1978). *The developmental psychology of the Black child.* New York: Africana Research Publications.

Winterton, W. A. (1977). *The effect of extended wait-time on selected verbal response characteristics of some Pueblo Indian children.* Unpublished doctoral dissertation, University of New Mexico, 1976. Dissertation Abstracts International, 38, 620-A. (University Microfilms No. 77-16, 130).

Woodson, C. G. (1933). *Miseducation of the Negro.* Washington, DC: Associated Publishers.

Linguistic Diversity
in Multicultural Classrooms

Sonia Nieto

OVERVIEW

Language is inextricably linked to culture. It is a primary means by which people express their cultural values and the lens through which they view the world. Yet it is often overlooked when referring to cultural differences. The language that children bring to school inevitably affects how and what they learn. Because of the close link between language and culture, it is important to understand that it is an essential component of multicultural education. Nevertheless, some of the most comprehensive approaches to multicultural education, while including race, class, and gender concerns, have failed to include language issues in their conceptual framework.[1]

Part of the reason for the exclusion of language issues is related to the lack of relevant terms in general use. Terms that describe discrimination based on race, gender, and class, among others, are part of our general vocabulary. *Racism, sexism, ethnocentrism, anti-Semitism, classism,* and so on are widely understood by the general public. Until recently, no such term existed for language discrimination, although this does not mean that language discrimination as such did not exist. Skutnabb-Kangas, by coining the term *linguicism* to refer to discrimination based specifically on language, has helped to place it under the same general umbrella as the other terms.[2]

The purpose of this chapter is to investigate the impact of linguistic differences on student achievement. Specifically, we will explore bilingual education as a way to approach language differences in a positive and empowering manner. Before doing so, we will discuss some of the ways in which language differences have been viewed in classrooms.

The stripping away of students' native language and culture is often done for what teachers and schools believe are good reasons. One study of the repression of Spanish in Texas, for instance, found that schools often make a direct link between the students' English assimilation and their economic and social mobility. Thus, students who speak a language other than English are frequently viewed as "handicapped." It was found that Spanish was repressed in school in what teachers believed were the best interests of students. Teachers felt that continuing to speak Spanish was a way of persisting in being "foreign" and in effect refusing to be "American." Although 90 percent of the students were U.S. citizens, their status as "outsiders" was maintained, at least in the eyes of teachers, if they persisted in speaking Spanish.[3] The influence this devaluation of native language in the school may have cannot be dismissed.

LINGUISTIC DIVERSITY AND IMPACT ON LEARNING

In spite of the enormous impact that language has on children's schooling, it is important to emphasize that lack of English skills *alone* cannot explain the poor academic achievement of students. It is tempting to fall back on this explanation and thus count on simple solutions like English "sink or swim" programs to solve the problem. Cuban students, for example, have been found to have the *highest* educational level of all Latinos, yet they are the most likely to speak Spanish at home.[4] They are also more likely to come from middle-class backgrounds than any other Latino children. One study focusing on the relationship between Spanish-language background and achievement among first-, second-, and third-generation Mexican American high school students concluded that contrary to the conventional wisdom, Spanish is *not* an impediment to student achievement. Another large-scale study of Latino high school sophomores and seniors found that those who were highly proficient in Spanish actually performed *better* on achievement tests and had higher educational aspirations than those who were not. In spite of such findings, the fact that students speak Spanish is treated by many teachers as a social problem.[5] There is also evidence that teachers interact more negatively with students who do not speak English than with those who do.[6] If this is the case, the language dominance of students is not really the issue; rather, *the way in which teachers and schools view their language may be even more crucial to student achievement.*

Speaking a language other than English is not in and of itself a handicap. On the contrary, it can be a great asset to learning, as will be documented later. How language and language use are perceived by the schools and whether modifications in the curriculum are made as a result are important factors to keep in mind. The fact that English speakers rarely have the opportunity to enter bilingual education programs reinforces the inferior status of these programs. Bilingualism, at least in the case of dominated groups, is generally viewed as a burden, although it is seen as an asset among middle-class and wealthy students. It is not unusual to find in the same high school the seemingly incongruous situation of an entire group of students having their native language wiped out while another group of students struggles to learn a foreign language. Issues of social class may have an even greater effect than language on academic performance.

EXPLORING LINGUISTIC DIVERSITY
THROUGH BILINGUAL EDUCATION

Because bilingual education has been a consistent and controversial educational concern in the United States since the 1960s, it will be examined as one of the fundamental ways in which language differences are handled in the schools. This is not meant to downplay the importance of other language differences. *Black English,* the vernacular spoken by a great many African American children, increasingly being called *African American Language,* is one such language difference. It affects the educational experiences of a large number of students because they must cope with the burden of the negative stigma attached to the language they speak at the same time they learn a different variant of the language when they enter school.[7] Nor is the discussion of bilingual education meant to diminish the difficult and traumatic experiences that students from *low incidence populations* have in our schools. This term refers to students who speak a particular language for which there may not be sufficient speakers to entitle them legally to a bilingual program. Such is often the case with Asian, Southeast Asian, and some European languages. In this situation, the most common programmatic practice is some kind of ESL approach.

We will focus on bilingual education because it represents an intriguing case study of the policies and practices that have evolved over the years to deal with language differences in our schools. In addition, bilingual education needs to be understood as a fundamental part of multicultural education. The purpose of this section is to review the need for bilingual education, its history and program models, and its connection with multicultural education.

BILINGUAL EDUCATION: THE NEED GROWS

The number of students who are classified as having *limited English proficiency* in the United States is growing dramatically. This term refers to students whose lack of facility in the English language may have negative consequences for their academic achievement in monolingual English classrooms. One report estimates that there are currently between 1.2 million and 1.7 million such students.[8] Even more dramatic is the expectation that by the year 2020, the number of children speaking a primary language other than English will be almost 6 million.[9] Asian children are supplanting those from Spanish-speaking countries as the leading group entering the country, doubling the number of Asian children already in the United States.[10] These changes are part of a larger immigrant trend in the United States, which in the last two decades has been among the largest in our history. The reasons for this new trend are varied, from a rise in the number of refugees from countries where the United States has been involved in aggression (as in Central America and Southeast Asia) to a loosening of immigration restrictions for some parts of the world. Legal immigration alone between 1980 and 1990 will probably have equaled that of 1900 to 1910. The largest numbers of new immigrants are now from Asia and Latin America, a marked departure from previous times, when they were overwhelmingly from Europe.[11]

All of these changes in the demographics of the United States have profound implications for education. Yet most students who need and could benefit from bilingual programs are not currently receiving them Only about 15 percent of students needing special language services are in federally funded bilingual programs; only about one-third are receiving *any* language assistance at all. In addition, the percentage of students in bilingual programs has actually declined in some places since 1980, precisely when they are most needed.[12] The reasons for this decline are varied, from the fact that many states do not have bilingual education statutes to poor enforcement of those state and federal mandates that do exist. Finding qualified personnel has been another major problem, and the fact that fewer bilingual people are entering the teaching profession makes the problem even more serious.

DEFINITIONS AND PROGRAM MODELS

Bilingual education is generally defined as an educational program that involves the use of two languages of instruction at some point in a student's school career. This definition is broad enough to include the many program variations that are classified as bilingual education. For example, a child who speaks a language other than English, say Vietnamese, may receive instruction in content areas in Vietnamese while at the same time learning English as a second language. The culture associated with the primary language of instruction is generally part of the curriculum, as is that of the second language. The approach is sometimes called *bilingual/bicultural education* and is based on the premise that the language and culture children bring to school are assets that must be used in their education. Thus there is an emphasis on students' native culture, including their history and traditions, within the curriculum. The bicultural aspect of bilingual education is unfortunately neglected or downplayed in some programs. For example, the materials used in some programs, that is, textbooks, curricula, and so on, are simple translations into other languages of the English-language materials used in monolingual classrooms. This practice helps to defeat the purpose of bilingual/bicultural education, which is to use students' prior knowledge for new learning.

There are numerous interpretations of bilingual education in the schools, ranging all the way from ESL to developmental bilingual education. Some of these will be briefly described, although it should be pointed out that there is not always agreement on what these program options are.[13]

Although *English as a second language (ESL)* is sometimes viewed as a kind of bilingual education, it is not generally considered to be bilingual education in and of itself because the child's native language is not used in instruction. Sometimes ESL classrooms have aides who speak the children's language and help in translating or explaining concepts, but this alone does not make them bilingual classrooms. The ESL approach, if not part of a bilingual program, simply focuses on teaching language skills in English so that children can learn their content in English. While they are learning English, these students may be languishing in their other subject areas because they do not understand the language of instruction. Education, for them, usually consists only of learning English until they can function in the regular English-language environment.

It must be emphasized that a primary objective of bilingual education is to have students become proficient and literate in the English language. As such, ESL is an integral and necessary component of all bilingual programs. That is, ESL goes hand in hand with native-language instruction in content areas. Rather than seeing these as separate areas of the curriculum, successful bilingual programs use students' talents, including their knowledge and literacy in another language, to help them learn new skills. In this way, student learning is reinforced in two languages.[14]

Probably the most common model of bilingual education in the United States is the *transitional bilingual education* approach. In this approach, students receive their content area instruction in their native language while learning English as a second language. As soon as they are thought to be ready to benefit from the monolingual English-language curriculum, they are "exited" out of the program. The rationale behind this model is that native-language services should serve only as a transition to English. Therefore, there is a limit on the time a student may be in a bilingual program, usually three years. This limit was established in 1971 by Massachusetts, the first state to mandate bilingual education, and has served as a model for subsequent states. The number of states that mandate bilingual education has fluctuated over the years, depending on the political climate in different states at different times.[15] The primary objective of a transitional program is to teach students English as quickly as possible so that they can continue their education in a monolingual English classroom.

Another approach is called *maintenance bilingual education,* a more comprehensive and long-term model. As in the transitional approach, students receive content area instruction in their native language while learning English as a second language. The difference is that there is generally no limit set on the time students can be in the program. The reasoning here is that a child's native language is worth maintaining because it is an asset in its own right and therefore an appropriate channel for continued learning. That children literate in their native language will be more successful students than those whose language is ignored, denied, or replaced has been documented repeatedly.[16] This approach builds on their literacy and extends it to a second language as well. The objective is for the children to become fluent in both languages by using them both for instruction. Students may, in theory, remain in a maintenance bilingual program throughout their education. The longer they remain in the program, the more functionally bilingual they become and, therefore, the more balanced is the curriculum to which they are exposed. That is, they can potentially receive equal amounts of instruction in English and in their native language.

In recent years, the term *developmental bilingual education* has been substituted for the more politically charged term *maintenance,* as the latter has become associated in the minds of some opponents of bilingual education with separatism. Some opponents have raised the specter of terrorism and even civil war as possible results of bilingual education. This has been the case generally with right-wing groups or other organizations waging the battle for "English only."[17]

The positive effects of maintenance bilingual education have been highlighted by Warren in an ethnographic study of one such program. He found that although the curriculum in the program was what he called "culturally Anglo," it was nevertheless highly successful because it had an important mediating role in the students' achievement. Although the school's curriculum was not totally Mexican American or Latino, the continuing importance of bilingual competency for the students was assumed by all staff. For example, students could express their needs in the language that was most meaningful to them at every grade level. In this way, the maintenance model affirmed the equal worth of the ethnicity and language of the students.[18]

Two-way bilingual education is a program model for integrating students whose native language is English with those for whom English is a second language. The purpose of this approach is to develop bilingualism in both. Therefore, all students learn content in their native language while they learn the other language as a second language. Let us take the example of a Spanish-English bilingual program. English-speaking children would learn Spanish as a second language, and those who speak Spanish as their native language would learn English (ESL). They would each learn content in their stronger language, but they would be integrated for some academic work. The more fluent students become in their second language, the more time they are integrated for instruction. This approach also lends itself quite well to cooperative learning and peer tutoring since all the students have important skills to share with one another. There is generally no time limit to this approach, although some two-way programs are part of existing transitional programs and therefore have the same entrance and exit criteria, at least for the students who do not speak English.

Finally, *immersion bilingual education* represents quite a different approach to learning a second language. In these programs, students are generally immersed in their second language for a year or two before their native language is introduced as a medium of instruction. By their fifth or sixth year of schooling, they may be receiving equal amounts of instruction in their two languages, or they may continue to receive the lion's share in their second language. Immersion has been found to be quite effective with middle-class students whose language is the dominant language of the society. Thus, in Canada, English-speaking students have been quite successful learning in French.[19] Unfortunately, the success of this kind of program has been used by opponents of bilingual education as the basis for suggesting *submersion bilingual education* for linguistic minority students in the United States. It has been suggested that linguistic minority students be placed in a totally English-language environment in order for them to learn English as quickly as possible and thus benefit from their schooling. The fallacy of this kind of thinking will be reviewed later as we investigate the results of research in bilingual education. To understand the context for this kind of thinking, however, it is important to explore first the history of bilingual education in the United States.

THE HISTORY AND POLITICS OF BILINGUAL EDUCATION

Bilingual education is not new. It is as old as the United States and can probably be traced as well to the many Indian Nations before the arrival of the Europeans. Castellanos has said that the history of bilingual education is also the history of the United States; he is probably not far from the mark.[20] That is, the cycle of policies and practices related to languages and language use in society in general and schools in particular reflects the many ways in which the United States has attempted to resolve the issue of language diversity. These have ranged all the way from "sink or swim" policies (i.e., immersing language minority students in English-only classrooms to fend on their own), through the imposition of English as the sole medium of instruction, to allowing and even encouraging German-English bilingual schools in the last century. By 1900, for example, it was estimated that over 200,000 children were being taught in German in public elementary schools, with smaller numbers being taught in Polish, Italian, Norwegian, Spanish, French, Czech, Dutch, and other languages.[21]

Where bilingual education is concerned, everyone from parents to presidents has gotten into the fray. Theodore Roosevelt, very much a spokesperson for the restrictive language policies at the beginning of the century, which were a response to the huge influx of primarily East European immigrants to the United States, stated; "We have room for but one language here, and that is the English language; for we intend to see that the crucible turns our people out as Americans, of American nationality, and not as dwellers in a polyglot boardinghouse; and we have room for but one sole loyalty, and that is loyalty to the American people."[22] Roosevelt's views were widely shared by many people who felt threatened by the new wave of immigrants. The language policies of the time, particularly those restricting instruction in a language other than English, reflect these concerns.

The issue of language use and patriotic loyalty have often been bound together, especially in the teaching of German after World War I.[23] It remains true today, particularly with regard to Spanish. The fact that bilingual education has as one of its fundamental goals the learning of English is often overlooked. Note, for example, the words of a more recent president. Ronald Reagan, responding to a reporter's question about support for bilingual education, stated, "It is absolutely wrong and against American concept to have a bilingual education program that is now openly, admittedly dedicated to preserving their native language and never getting them adequate in English so they can go out into the job market."[24] The "English-only" movement of the past decade is a reflection of this feeling.[25]

The zigzag of support and rejection of languages other than English demonstrates the schizophrenia with which language diversity has been viewed in the United States. The latest cycle of support for bilingual education, albeit at times lukewarm, began with the passage of the Elementary and Secondary Education Act of 1968. Even in times of support, bilingual education has always been controversial and the target of much antagonism. Why this should be so is no mystery. First, the use of languages other than English has generally been perceived in our society as a threat to national unity. This view has at times resulted in counterproductive policies that inhibit the learning of foreign languages as well as the understanding of other peoples. That our society continues to be ignorant of other languages and cultures is self-evident; that it is now jeopardized by this monolingualism and monoculturalism in a world becoming increasingly interdependent is becoming more and more apparent. Second, bilingual education has been perceived as a threat because it questions the very basis of much of our educational system. The fact that it has been successful at all thus becomes problematic. That is, successful bilingual programs have demonstrated that students *can* learn in their native language while *also* learning English *and* achieving academically. This achievement contradicts the conservative agenda of the 1980s, which called for a return to a largely European American curriculum and pedagogy. Successful bilingual education threatens to explode the myth of the "basics" if the basics means only valuing a Eurocentric curriculum and the English language.

This brings us to one of the most salient aspects of bilingual education. Bilingual education is now, has always been, and will no doubt continue to be a fundamentally *political* issue. It is concerned with the relative power or lack of power of various groups in our society. This assertion is not at all meant to detract from the sound pedagogical basis of bilingual education or from its primarily positive results. However, in spite of these results, bilingual education continues to be controversial. By representing the class and ethnic group interests of traditionally disempowered groups, bilingual education has been characterized by great controversy and debate. The issue is not whether or not it works but the real possibility that it might. Bilingual education is a political issue because both its proponents and opponents have long recognized its potential for empowering these traditionally powerless groups. The closer such programs come to using students' language and culture in a liberating way, the more they are criticized. For example, maintenance programs tend to be much more controversial than transitional programs; ESL programs, with no bilingual assistance, are viewed as less problematic than either. Understanding the political nature of bilingual education, and of multicultural education in general, is essential if we are to develop effective programs geared toward meeting the needs of all our students. Both the political nature of bilingual education and its research results have to be kept in mind.

RESULTS OF BILINGUAL EDUCATION: WHAT WORKS AND WHY?

Bilingual education has been characterized by major achievements in providing equal educational opportunity to students whose native language is not English. Nevertheless, opponents to bilingual education in the United States have attempted to use the success of immersion programs in Canada as a rationale for such programs in this country. However, the issues are quite different. First, most bilingual programs in the United States serve children of economically oppressed communities. Second, the native language of the majority of these students is what is called a *marked* language, that is, a language not highly valued by the society at large. This situation is in stark contrast to the use of standard English in a primarily English-speaking country. Finally, an immersion program in this country would not mean placing limited English-proficient students in all-English classrooms. On the contrary, such a program would place native English-speaking students in another language setting until the second or third year of their schooling. Even the researchers associated with Canada's immersion program have cautioned against using it as a model with language minority students in the United States.[26] The immersion model, if applied to language minority students, would properly be called *submersion*.

There is a dizzying array of program alternatives in bilingual education, each claiming to be more successful than the others. In general, most research has found that bilingual programs, either transitional or maintenance in approach, are effective not only in teaching students content area knowledge in their native language but also in teaching them English. This has proven time and again to be the case in research analyses and specific program reviews.[27] Even more important, however, bilingual programs may have secondary effects such as motivating students to remain in school rather than dropping out, making school more meaningful, and in general making the school experience more enjoyable.[28] According to Hakuta, the most significant effect of bilingual education may not be that it promotes bilingualism, which he claims it does not, but rather that it "gives some measure of official public status to the political struggle of language minorities, primarily Hispanics."[29] Official public status may have a positive effect on the achievement of students.

A related phenomenon may be that bilingual education reinforces important relationships among students and their family members, allowing them to engage in more communication than would be the case if they were instructed solely in English and lost their native language. In a prize-winning essay on the importance of bilingual education, a seventh-grade Navajo student wrote, "The ability to communicate in two languages is an advantage because I can talk and understand my elders." He explains, "Being bilingual is also important for maintaining the native tongue. Without this, our language will die out. This cannot happen because it is the basis of our culture."[30] A nationwide survey of over 1,000 families for whom English is a second language echoes these findings. Researchers found evidence of serious disruptions of family relations when young children learn English in school and lose their native language. Attempts to get three- and four-year-old preschoolers into programs in which they are taught English before kindergarten are linguistically and culturally unsound and may have negative consequences on language, social, and intellectual development.[31]

The fact is that bilingual education is generally more effective than other programs such as ESL alone, not only in learning content through the native language but also in learning English. This apparently contradictory finding can be understood if one considers that students in bilingual programs are given continued education in content areas *along with* structured instruction in English. In addition, they are building on a previous literacy. This becomes what Lambert has called an *additive* rather than a *subtractive* form of bilingual education.[32] This may not be the case in other programs, even in ESL programs, which may concentrate on English grammar, phonics, and other language features out of context with the way in which the real, day-to-day language is used.

Even in programs in which English is not used, results often show dramatic gains in students' achievement. This achievement helps prepare them for the academic demands of school, no matter what language is used. Campos and Keatinge, for example, found that Hispanic children enrolled in a Spanish-only preschool program developed more skills that would prepare them for school than comparable children in a bilingual preschool program whose main objective was to develop English proficiency.[33]

The claim that immersion programs are appropriate for language minority students has not been borne out. Although a small number of studies find that immersion is effective in teaching English skills, a large-scale comparative evaluation of immersion and bilingual education programs by Ramirez concluded that students in bilingual programs do as well or better than those in immersion programs, even in their English-language performance.[34] Ironically, the more native-language instruction students received, the more likely they were to be reclassified as proficient in English. Even if the primary purpose of instruction is to learn English (a debatable position), immersion programs do not seem to work as well. In contrast, the positive effects of bilingual education, from lowering dropout rates to literacy development, have been found time and again.[35]

The Ramirez study, as well as others, provides yet another rationale for late-exit models of bilingual education, that is, programs in which students remain until they have developed adequate proficiency for high-level academic work. By continuing to use students' native language in substantive ways, late-exit programs encourage them to maintain close relationships with family members, particularly linguistic interactions, thus helping students' in their schoolwork and emotional needs at the same time. In addition, late-exit models tend to encourage parental involvement to a greater degree than early-exit models because parents feel more comfortable in settings where their native language is used.

BILINGUAL EDUCATION AND EQUAL EDUCATIONAL OPPORTUNITY

There is an important relationship between bilingual education and equity. Bilingual education has frequently been addressed as simply an issue of language, but it goes much deeper than this. Bilingual education is a civil rights issue because it is the only guarantee that children who do not speak English will be provided education in a language they understand. Without it, millions of children may be doomed to educational underachievement and limited occupational choices in the future.

The U.S. Supreme Court has recognized the relationship of language and equal educational opportunity. In 1969, plaintiffs representing 1,800 Chinese-speaking students sued the San Francisco Unified School District for failing to provide students who did not speak English with an equal chance to learn. They lost their case but in 1974 had taken it all the way to the Supreme Court. In the landmark *Lau* v. *Nichols* case, the Court ruled unanimously that the civil rights of students who did not understand the language of instruction were indeed being violated. Based on Title VI of the Civil Rights Act, the Court stated, in part,

> There is no equality of treatment merely by providing students with the same facilities, textbooks, teachers, and curriculum; for students who do not understand English are effectively foreclosed from any meaningful education. Basic skills are at the very core of what these public schools teach. Imposition of a requirement that, before a child can effectively participate in the educational program he must already have acquired those basic skills is to make a mockery of public education.[36]

Although the decision did not impose any particular remedy, its results were immediate and extensive. By 1975, the Office for Civil Rights and the Department of Health, Education, and Welfare issued a document called "The *Lau* Remedies," which has served as the basis for determining whether or not school systems through-out the country are in compliance with the findings of *Lau*. In effect, the document provides guidance in identifying, assessing the language abilities, and providing appropriate programs for students with a limited proficiency in English. Bilingual programs are the common remedy of most school systems.

The Equal Educational Opportunities Act (EEOA) of 1974 has also been instrumental in protecting the language rights of students for whom English is not a native language. This law interprets the failure of any educational agency to "take appropriate action to overcome language barriers that impede equal participation by its students in its instructional programs" as a denial of equal educational opportunity.[37] A number of federal cases have resulted in a strong interpretation of this statute. In both *Lau* and the EEOA, bilingual education has emerged as a key strategy to counteract the language discrimination faced by many students in our schools.

Linguicism, or discrimination based on language use, has been fairly widespread.[38] Entire communities have been denied the use of their native language, not only for instruction or in schools but also in social communication of all kinds. Throughout our history, the language rights of substantial numbers of people have been denied, from prohibiting enslaved Africans from speaking their languages to the imposition of recent "English only" laws in a growing number of states.[39] Landry has charged that the government, in favoring one language over all others, is in effect violating the language rights of everybody whose primary language is not English. Through its massive support for only one language, particularly in schools, he maintains that the government is failing to protect other language rights. He says that at least Native American languages, Spanish, and French can be considered native to the United States and are therefore entitled to special consideration in light of the Helsinki agreement, in which national minority rights are protected. He makes this claim because in the case of these particular languages, territory was incorporated into the United States without the consent of the people involved.[40]

Even if one does not go so far as Landry in defense of language rights, it can be said that bilingual education services represent one important guarantee of a fundamental right. As such, a bilingual education is an equitable education for over a million students in our schools. Just as racial integration has been considered an important civil right for those who were segregated and doomed to an inferior education, bilingual education is understood by language minority communities as an equally important civil right. Thus bilingual education is an essential, although often overlooked, part of multicultural education. Skutnabb-Kangas has proposed what she calls "The Declaration of Children's Linguistic Human Rights," a proposal that puts linguistic rights on the same level as other human rights and includes the right to identify positively with one's mother tongue, to learn it, and to choose when to use it.[41] For language majority children, these rights are self-evident, but not for those who speak a language with a negative stigma. Because language and culture are so intertwined, and because both bilingual and multicultural approaches attempt to involve and empower students, particularly the most disenfranchised, it is essential that their natural links be understood.

PROBLEMS AND ISSUES

Although bilingual education represents an important advance over monolingual education, there are a number of problems with proposing it as the only alternative. One is that it is often perceived as a panacea for all the educational problems of language minority students. Yet even with a bilingual education, many children are likely to face educational failure, which is true of multicultural education in general as well. No approach or program can cure all the problems, educational and otherwise, facing our young people if it does not also address the fundamental issues of discrimination and stratification in schools and society. Only a comprehensively conceptualized approach can hope to achieve success for most students. Simply substituting one language for another, or books in Spanish with Dick and Jane in brownface, will not guarantee success for language minority students. Expecting too much of even good programs is counterproductive because in the absence of quick results, the children are again blamed for their failure.

Cummins's work on student empowerment through bilingual programs is based on this important premise. In fact, he claims that the crucial element in reversing students' school failure is not the language of instruction but rather the extent to which teachers and schools attempt to reverse the institutionalized racism of society as a whole. Although this statement is not meant to downplay the great benefits of native language instruction, unless bilingual education becomes "anti-racist education," according to Cummins, "it may serve only to provide a veneer of change that in reality perpetuates discriminatory educational structures."[42]

One of the implications for teachers is to consider how modifications can be made in their instruction and curriculum to help students achieve. Effective pedagogy is not simply teaching subject areas in another language but rather finding ways to use the language, culture, and experiences of students in their education. Therefore, the traditional environments, strategies, and policies of many bilingual programs—in which straight rows of desks, ditto sheets, and silence are viewed as signs of "real learning," whereas questioning, talking, and other signs of active participation are viewed as either disrespectful or culturally inappropriate—need to be challenged. Montero-Sieburth's ethnography of a bilingual teacher faces this challenge squarely.[43] The bilingual teacher with whom she worked turned her classes into "problem-posing forums," where the issues that the students faced on a daily basis became the curriculum.

A further problem has to do with the definition of success of most bilingual programs. Bilingual programs, particularly those with a transitional focus, are meant to "self-destruct" within a limited time. Success in these programs is measured by the rapidity with which they mainstream students. That being the case, their very existence is based on a "compensatory education" philosophy and departs very little from the "deficit" theories reviewed in Chapter 3. Students who enter school knowing little or no English are regarded as needing compensation. Their knowledge of another language is not considered an asset but at best a crutch to use until they master the "real" language of schooling. This is at best a patronizing and at worst a racist position.

Given this perspective, it is little wonder that many parents do not want their children in bilingual programs or that these programs are often isolated and ghettoized in the schools. This message is not lost on students either. In an ethnographic study of four bilingual students, Nancy Commins found that some children are reluctant to speak Spanish because it is perceived to be the language of the "dumb kids."[44] Thus, children may unconsciously jeopardize their own language development by dropping Spanish, a language that benefits their academic achievement by allowing them to use higher-level cognitive skills than with their English, which they do not speak as well. Commins concludes, "Both the overt hostility expressed by some towards Spanish and the implicit message sent by the supremacy of English in the environment reinforced the students' perceptions, internalized over many years, that the use of Spanish in school was unacceptable. . . ."[45]

There are other problems with this self-destruct aspect of bilingual education. For example, these programs are in perpetual limbo because the number of students of limited English proficiency may vary from year to year. The program, perceived as unstable, may be granted low priority in the school. This practice places an unnecessary burden on bilingual teachers, who are in a precarious situation because it is their job to "exit" students out of their program. These teachers, sometimes from the same linguistic and cultural background of the students they teach, bring an important element of diversity into the school. But because they are often isolated and marginalized in the schools, they tend to have little interaction with other staff.

In spite of the "quick exit" philosophy of most bilingual programs, much of the research has documented that students generally need a minimum of five to seven years to develop the level of English proficiency needed to succeed academically in school.[46] With most programs permitting students to remain a maximum of only three to four years, only partially positive results can be expected. The research evidence is in direct contrast to program implementation, although many programs are successful nevertheless.

Equally troublesome for some school districts is that they have numerous language groups in their student population. That is, they may have small numbers of students representing a great many languages. Providing a bilingual program for each of these small groups would not only be impractical but also impossible. Research by Trueba has suggested that even when bilingual education is not possible, instruction can still be tailored to children's "cultural knowledge and experiences," for example, placing students in learning environments that promote success, identifying their learning strengths and modifying instructional strategies to match, and developing a group of teachers who become colleagues and effective supporters of innovative approaches.[47] Such options may become necessary in dealing with low-incidence groups.

Another problematic feature of bilingual education concerns its need to separate students. Bilingual education has been characterized by some as tracking because students are separated from their peers for instruction. Although the reasons for this separation are legitimate and based on sound research and pedagogy, tracking as a practice flies in the face of equal educational opportunity. These issues need to be sorted out carefully. Landry has suggested that whereas discrimination in race, class, gender, and disability tends to be resolved by *integration,* the opposite is true for bilingual education. That is, bilingual education demands the opportunity to *separate* students, at least for part of their education.[48] This makes it a particularly thorny issue in a democratic society. Add the research evidence suggesting that students should remain in bilingual classrooms until they develop sufficient academic competency in English, and we would be left with some students in segregated settings for the major part of their schooling.

Although this dilemma seems particularly disturbing in a multicultural philosophy, there are ways in which the needs of limited English-proficient and mainstream students can be served at the same time. Within every bilingual program, there are opportunities for integrating students for nonacademic work. Students in the bilingual program can take art, physical education, and other nonacademic classes with their English-speaking peers. In addition, bilingual programs can be integrated into the school rather than separated in a wing of the building, so that teachers from both bilingual and nonbilingual classrooms are encouraged to collaborate on projects.

Two-way bilingual programs provide another opportunity for integration. Few programs have attempted to incorporate both language majority and language minority students in one setting, although the results have generally been quite positive when they have been documented. Collier, for example, in a preliminary follow-up study of one two-way program, found that both the English-speaking and Spanish-speaking students, now in early adulthood, had benefited substantially from their involvement in such a program.[49] They were all still bilingual, years after leaving the program. Even their worldviews and career choices were being influenced directly by their positive experiences in a cross-cultural and bilingual setting. For example, many of the English-speaking graduates of the program were very involved in Spanish-speaking communities in the United States. A great many of the former students had become advocates of multilingual and multicultural education. In addition, most were in college, in spite of the fact that at least the Latinos in the program were from primarily poor and working-class backgrounds and therefore greatly exceeded the average educational expectations for their group. Finally, that English-speaking students had to undergo the difficult process of learning a second language tended to make them more sensitive to the situation of their Spanish-speaking peers and to cultural differences in general.

Other approaches to resolving the integration/segregation dilemma of bilingual education have been explored,[50] for example, setting aside times for joint instruction and setting up bilingual options in desegregation plans and magnet schools. The fact remains, however, that much remains to be done in this regard. Although the programmatic imperatives of separating students for literacy development must be respected, ways to make bilingual education a central concern for all schools have to be found.

SUMMARY

There are numerous ways in which linguistic differences may affect students' learning. Language differences per se are not necessarily barriers to learning, but the history of linguicism in our society has resulted in making them so. Language policies and practices in the United States have ranged from a grudging acceptance of language diversity to outright hostility. We have seen the positive impact that recognizing and affirming students' languages can have on their learning. We have also pointed out some of the issues and concerns that arise when students are separated for instruction, as is often the case with bilingual education.

Bilingual education is certainly not the only approach for dealing with linguistically diverse students. The claim that it can completely reverse the history of failure of linguistic minority students is both unrealistic and naive. Nevertheless, bilingual education still represents the best and most effective program for most students for whom English is a second language. The fact that it alone cannot change the achievement of students is an indication of the complexity of factors that affect learning. Following the case studies, Part II will explore a more comprehensive explanation of school success and failure by taking into account some of these factors.

NOTES

1. An excellent example of a comprehensive and progressive approach to understanding multicultural education can be found in Christine E. Sleeter and Carl A. Grant, "A Raltionale for Integrating Race, Gender, and Social Class," in *Class, Race, and Gender in American Education*, ed. Lois Weis (New York: State University of New York Press, 1988). Even here, however, language differences are not included as a separate category. Gollnick and Chin, however, have included linguistic diversity as a separate issue in their conceptualization of multicultural education; see Donna M. Gollnick and Philip C. Chin, *Multicultural Education in a Pluralistic Society*, 3rd ed. (New York: Maxwell Macmillan International Publishing, 1990).
2. By *linguicism* she means "*ideologies and structures which are used to legitimate, effectuate and reproduce an unequal division of power and resources (both material and non-material) between groups which are defined on the basis of language. . . .*" See Tove Skutnabb-Kangas, "Multilingualism and the Education of Minority Children," in *Minority Education: From Shame to Struggle*, ed. Tove Skutnabb-Kangas and Jim Cummins (Clevedon, Eng.: Multilingual Matters, 1988), p. 13.
3. Aída Hurtado and Raúl Rodriguez, "Language as a Social Problem: The Repression of Spanish in South Texas," *Journal of Multilingual and Multicultural Development*, 10, 5 (1989), 401–419.
4. Ray Valdivieso and Cary Davis, *U.S. Hispanics: Challenging Issues for the 1990s* (Washington, DC: Population Trends and Public Policy, December 1988).
5. See the studies by Raymond Buriel and Desdemona Cardoza, "Sociocultural Correlates of Achievement Among Three Generations of Mexican American High School Seniors," *American Educational Research Journal*, 25, 2 (1988), 177–192; Francois Nielson and Roberto M. Fernandez, *Hispanic Students in American High Schools: Background Characteristics and Achievement* (Washington, DC: National Opinion Research Center, National Center for Education Statistics, 1981).
6. U.S. General Accounting Office, *Bilingual Education: A New Look at the Research Evidence* (Washington, DC: U.S. Government Printing Office, March 1987)
7. See Selase W. Williams, "Classroom Use of African American Language: Educational Tool or Social Weapon?" in *Empowerment Through Multicultural Education*, Christine E. Sleeter, ed. (Albany, NY: State University of New York Press, 1991).
8. Laurence Steinberg, Patricia Lin Blinde, and Kenyon S. Chan, "Dropping Out Among

Language Minority Youth," *Review of Educational Research,* 54, 1 (Spring 1984), 113–132.

9. Gary Natriello, Edward L. McDill, and Aaron M. Pallas, *Schooling Disadvantaged Children: Racing Against Catastrophe* (New York: Teachers College Press, 1990).

10. Dorothy Waggoner, "Foreign-Born Children in the U.S. in the Eighties," *NABE Journal,* Fall 1987, pp. 23–49.

11. Cited in John B. Kellogg, "Forces of Change," *Phi Delta Kappan,* November 1988, pp. 199–204.

12. See Sonia Nieto, "Excellence and Equity: The Case for Bilingual Education," *Bulletin of the Council on Interracial Books for Children,* 17, 3 and 4 (1986); *Barriers to Excellence: Our Children at Risk* (Boston: National Coalition of Advocates for Students, 1985); *Federal Education Funding: The Cost of Excellence* (Washington, DC: National Education Association, 1990); *Hispanic Education: A Statistical Portrait* (Washington, DC: National Council of La Raza, 1990).

13. For an excellent description and analysis of the many program models and their implications, see Carlos J. Ovando and Virginia P. Collier, *Bilingual and ESL Classrooms: Teaching in Multicultural Contexts* (New York: McGraw-Hill, 1985).

14. For examples of how children's literacy in their native language is used as the basis for further learning, see Jim Cummins, "The Role of Primary Language Development in Promoting Educational Success for Language Minority Students," in Office of Bilingual Bicultural Education, *Schooling and Language Minority Students: A Theoretical Framework* (Sacramento: Evaluation, Dissemination, and Assessment Center, California State University, 1981); see also Carole Edelsky, "Bilingual Children's Writing: Fact and Fiction," in *Richness in Writing: Empowering ESL Students,* ed. Donna M. Johnson and Duane H. Roen (White Plains, NY: Longman, 1989).

15. The National Clearinghouse for Bilingual Education, Washington, DC, has current data on bilingual programs throughout the country.

16. See Shirley Brice Heath, "Questioning at Home and at School: A Comparative Study," in *Doing the Ethnography of Schooling: Educational Anthropology in Action,* ed. George Spindler (New York: Holt, Rinehart & Winston, 1982); Francois Nielsen and Roberto M. Fernández, *Hispanic Students in American High Schools: Background Characteristics and Achievement* (Washington, DC: National Opinion Research Center, National Center for Education Statistics, 1981); Virginia P. Collier, "How Long? A Synthesis of Research on Academic Achievement in a Second Language," *TESOL Quarterly,* 23, 3 (September 1989), 509–531; Ruben G. Rumbaut and Kenji Ima, *The Adaptation of Southeast Asian Refugee Youth: A Comparative Study,* Final Report. (San Diego: Office of Refugee Resettlement, September 1987).

17. *On Creating a Hispanic America: A Nation Within a Nation?* (Washington DC: Council on Inter-American Security, 1986).

18. Richard L. Warren, "Schooling, Biculturalism, and Ethnic Identity: A Case Study," in *Doing the Ethnography of Schooling: Educational Anthropology in Action,* ed. George Spindler (New York: Holt, Rinehart & Winston, 1982).

19. See, for example, Jim Cummins, "Linguistic Interdependence and the Educational Development of Bilingual Children," *Review of Educational Research,* 49 (Spring 1979), 222–251; Merrill Swain, "Bilingual Education for the English-Speaking Canadian," in *Georgetown University Round Table on Languages and Linguistics 1978: International Dimensions of Bilingual Education,* ed. J. Alatis (Washington, DC: Georgetown University Press, 1978).

20. Diego Castellanos, *The Best of Two Worlds* (Trenton: New Jersey State Department of Education, 1983).

21. Ibid.; see also Gary S. Keller and Karen S. van Hooft, "A Chronology of Bilingualism and Bilingual Education in the United States," in *Bilingual Education for Hispanic Students in the United States,* ed. Joshua Fishman and Gary Keller (New York: Teachers College Press, 1982); Charles Leslie Glenn, Jr., *The Myth of the Common School* (Amherst: University of Massachusetts Press, 1988); David Tyack, *The One Best System: A History of American Urban Education* (Cambridge, MA: Harvard University Press, 1974).

22. As cited by Stephan F. Brumberg, *Going to America, Going to School: The Jewish Immigrant Public School Encounter in Turn-of-the-Century New York City* (New York: Praeger, 1986), p. 7.

23. For a review of some of these policies, see Kenji Hakuta, *Mirror of Language: The Debate on Bilingualism* (New York: Basic Books, 1985).

24. *New York Times,* March 3, 1981.

25. For a review of the "English only" movement, see *English Plus: Issues in Bilingual Education,*" a special issue of *The Annals of the American Academy of Political and Social Science,* ed. Courtney B Cazden and Catherine F. Snow, 508 (March 1990); Harvey A. Daniels, *Not Only English: Affirming America's Multilingual Heritage* (Urbana, IL: National Council of Teachers of English, 1990).

26. See, for example, W. E. Lambert, "The Two Faces of Bilingual Education," *Focus,* No. 3 (Rosslyn, VA: National Clearinghouse for Bilingual Education, 1980); "An Overview of Issues in Immersion Education," in *Studies on Immersion Education: A Collection for U.S. Educators* (Sacramento: California State Department of Education, 1984); G. R. Tucker, "Implications for U.S. Bilingual Education: Evidence from Canadian Research," *Focus,* No. 2 (Rosslyn VA: National Clearinghouse for Bilingual Education, 1980).

27. See, for example, Kenji Hakuta, *Bilingualism and Bilingual Education: A Research Perspective,* No. 1 (Washington, DC: National Clearinghouse for Bilingual Education, Spring 1990). A. C. Willig, "A Meta-Analysis of Selected Studies on the Effectiveness of Bilingual Education," *Review of Educational Research,* 55 (1985), 269–317; James Crawford, *Bilingual Education: History, Politics, Theory, and Practice* (Trenton, NJ: Crane Publishing, 1988); Cummins, "Role of Primary Language."

28. See Christina Bratt Paulston, *Bilingual Education: Theories and Issues* (Rowley, MA: Newbury House, 1980); *Locked In/Locked Out: Tracking and Placement Practices in Boston Public Schools* (Boston: Massachusetts Advocacy Center, March 1990).

29. Hakuta, *Mirror of Language.*

30. Aaron Jones, "Why Being Bilingual Is Important to Me and My Family," award-winning essay reported in *NABE News,* February 1, 1991, p. 13

31. This research was reported in "The NABE No-Cost Study on Families," *NABE News,* February 1, 1991, p. 7.

32. For research on additive and subtractive bilingualism, see W. E. Lambert, "Culture and Language as Factors in Learning and Education," in *Education of Immigrant Students,* ed. A. Wolfgang (Toronto: OISE, 1975); Collier, "How Long?"

33. J. Campos and R. Keatinge, "The Carpinteria Language Minority Student Experience: From Theory, to Practice, to Success," in *Minority Education: From Shame to Struggle,* ed. Tove Skutnabb-Kangas and Jim Cummins (Clevedon, Eng.: Multilingual Matters, 1988).

34. For a study on the effectiveness of immersion, see "Adequate Motivation and Bilingual Education," *Southwest Journal of Linguistics,* 9, 2 (1990). The results of the large-scale study were first reported by Jim Crawford, "Immersion Method Is Faring Poorly in Bilingual Study," *Education Week,* 5 (April 23, 1986), pp. 1, 10; and later by Julie A. Miller, "Native-Language Instruction Found to Aid LEP's," *NABE News,* 14, 3 (December 1, 1990). Although its results were withheld from the general public for a long time, the report was finally officially released in March 1991; see J. David Ramirez, *Final Report:*

Longitudinal Study of Structured English Immersion Strategy, Early-Exit and Late-Exit Transitional Bilingual Education Programs for Language Minority Children (Washington, DC: Office of Bilingual Education, 1991). This massive study of 4,000 students of limited English proficiency was proposed and funded by the Reagan administration, which was openly hostile to bilingual education.

35. The Massachusetts Advocacy Center, for instance, has found that bilingual education in Boston appears to act as a "buffer" against dropping out. See *Locked In/Locked Out.*
36. *Lau* v. *Nichols,* 414 U.S. 563 (1974).
37. Equal Educational Opportunities Act of 1974, 20 U.S.C. 1703 (f).
38. See Meyer Weinberg, *A Chance to Learn: A History of Race and Education in the U.S.* (Cambridge: Cambridge University Press, 1977); Cummins, "Linguistic Interdependence"; Hurtado and Rodriguez, "Language as a Social Problem"; Deirdre E Jordan, "Rights and Claims of Indigenous People," in *Minority Education: From Shame to Struggle,* ed. Tove Skutnabb-Kangas and Jim Cummins (Clevedon, Eng.: Multilingual Matters, 1988); Hakuta, *Mirror of Language.*
39. According to U.S. English, a national organization founded in 1983 "to preserve our national unity by protecting our common language—English" (from their promotional brochure), there are currently 17 states with official English-only laws. See "U.S. English—A Common Language Benefits Our Nation and All Its People" (Washington, DC: U.S. English, n.d.).
40. Walter J. Landry, "Future *Lau* Regulations: Conflict Between Language Rights and Racial Nondiscrimination," in *Theory, Technology, and Public Policy on Bilingual Education,* ed. Raymond V. Padilla (Rosslyn, VA: National Clearinghouse for Bilingual Education, 1983).
41. Skutnabb-Kangas, "Multilingualism and the Education of Minority Children."
42. Cummins, *Empowering Minority Students,* p. 51.
43. Martha Montero-Sieburth, *"Echar Pa'lante,* Moving Onward: The Dilemmas and Strategies of a Bilingual Teacher," *Anthropology and Education Quarterly,* 18, 3 (September 1987), 180–189.
44. Nancy L. Commins, "Language and Affect: Bilingual Students at Home and at School," *Language Arts,* 66, 1 (January 1989), 29–43.
45. Ibid., p. 38.
46. Cummins, "The Role of Primary Language Development in Promoting Educational Success"; see also the research synthesis by Collier, "How Long?" for an excellent review of pertinent studies.
47. Henry T. Trueba, "Instructional Effectiveness: English-Only for Speakers of Other Languages? *Education and Urban Society,* 20, 4 (August 1988), 341–362.
48. Landry, "Future *Lau* Regulations."
49. Virginia P. Collier, "Academic Achievement, Attitudes, and Occupations Among Graduates of Two-Way Bilingual Classes," paper presented at the annual meeting of the American Educational Research Association, San Francisco, March 1989.
50. Tony Baez, "Desegregation and Bilingual Education: Legal and Pedagogical Imperatives," *Bulletin of the Council on Interracial Books for Children,"* 17, 3 and 4 (1986).

Mujeres Unidas en Acción:
A Popular Education Process

Eva Young and Mariwilda Padilla

Mujeres Unidas en Acción (Women United in Action) is a nonprofit community-based agency offering educational programs to low-income Latina women living in Dorchester, Massachusetts. All of the women attending Mujeres's programs are outside the United States's social, political, and economic mainstream, because we live in poverty.[1] In addition, we contend that institutionalized racism and other forms of oppression, such as sexism, classism, and discrimination, can be understood as other causes that keep Latina women outside the mainstream.[2] We believe that our lack of education is rooted in a system that perpetuates exclusion and provides no options for people who are not privileged. Therefore, at Mujeres we are working for change by creating opportunities and developing educational programs that generate our advancement as women, and particularly as women of color.

Mujeres is based upon the right and the control we believe each woman should have over her own education. Its processes guarantee and institutionalize active participation in the agency's administrative, academic, and social development. We like to think of Mujeres Unidas en Acción as a "social incubator" through which Latina women have the opportunity and access to develop their skills in community organization, development, and leadership. We believe that a safe environment in which all people are committed to sharing skills and supporting each other will enable women to advance.

This article provides an overview of our agency, as well as an in-depth description of one of its educational components, the Spanish program. Specifically, we focus on the agency's origins, its current structure, and its educational activities. The discussion of administrative and educational philosophies illustrates how they are put into practice. We also give examples of the agency's participatory approach—the active participation of Mujeres members in all educational and administrative decision-making processes—and its educational objectives—creating a critical vision of society and developing literacy skills in the native language to reinforce the process of second-language acquisition.

A HOLISTIC VIEW OF MUJERES

Mujeres Unidas en Acción began in 1979 as a pilot project under the auspices of a nonprofit community agency called WeCan. The agency's principal mission was to develop programs to rehabilitate vacant lots and abandoned buildings, advocate for low-income housing, and organize the residents of twenty-two blocks around Codman Square in Dorchester, Massachusetts.[3]

During the winter of 1979, while teaching residents how to set up insulation material, a WeCan volunteer discovered that a great number of Latinas did not know how to speak English. The volunteer noticed major differences between native English speakers and the Spanish-speaking women who had lived in the United States for years. These women clearly seemed left behind. The majority, from Puerto Rico, were also low-income, unmarried mothers with little or no education in their native language. Faced with this great need for education, We-Can volunteers organized a program to teach English as a second language (ESL) in a local church basement. The purpose of the ESL program, called Mujeres Latinas de Dorchester (Latina Women of Dorchester), was to include the Latinas in WeCan community activities.[4]

Through the use of a participatory approach,[5] various community affairs activities were developed. Originally, there were two volunteer teachers and one childcare worker offering services. The Latina women's enthusiastic response to the English program was unexpected, and in less than a year the number of women attending classes grew from eight to twenty. Initially, teachers were using the same beginning English curriculum for students with widely different skills. Students who were illiterate received extra help. Also, once a week the agency offered remedial courses in reading, conversational English, and writing. During initial stages the agency's growth accelerated in a variety of ways. As the number of women attending classes increased, the number and range of classes were no longer sufficient to meet diverse student needs, and so the agency reached beyond its original goal, expanding from only providing ESL classes to providing a wide range of support services.

We believe that Mujeres's accelerated growth is due to our unique and innovative approach to supporting and helping low-income Latinas in their struggle to become active members of society. The agency's fiscal conduit, WeCan, disappeared in 1981 due to federal government budget cuts. In 1982, when the center was able to incorporate itself as a nonprofit agency to serve the community of low-income Latinas, the name was changed to Mujeres Unidas en Acción, Inc. At Mujeres, all services are free. Funds come from the City of Boston, private foundations, corporations, and community fund-raising activities.

The mission of Mujeres Unidas is to provide opportunities for low-income women to participate in and take control of their education and use it as a liberating tool. This is evident in each and every component of Mujeres Unidas's programs. Today Mujeres Unidas offers services to over one hundred women and thirty-five children aged one to five. At present, we are unable to accommodate all of the women who are interested in our services. All services, including emotional counseling and academic and technical education, are participant-based. We offer four levels of ESL: beginner; intermediate; advanced intermediate; and advanced English. This last course is offered in collaboration with Bunker Hill Community College and allows students to earn four college-level credits of ESL. In addition, Mujeres Unidas offers a preparatory course for the Graduate Equivalency Diploma (GED), and a literacy course, both of which are taught in Spanish. These educational programs have become the pillar of our participatory process.

Recently, we began to offer job and educational counseling, sponsored by the Gateway Cities Program.[6] Since the agency's formation, students have initiated support groups in accordance with their needs. In this way, they share experiences and help each other. Support groups include individual and group emotional counseling, and an alcoholism and substance-abuse support group. In 1987, a meditation group was initiated because a student, Nora Zuñiga, expressed a need to have a space for meditation. In her own words: "humans need food not only for the body but also for the soul." After a year, these students decided to merge with the alcoholism and substance-abuse group. This group, called *compañeras* (sisterhood), meets once a week and is open to all women from the community. It was formed by a recovering alcoholic who studied at Mujeres, and is the first of its kind in Massachusetts for Latinas.

In January 1989, as part of a pilot project in collaboration with Boston's Department of Public Health (DPH), one of the agency's counselors began to develop a support group for battered women. Created by Latinas for low-income Latina women, it will be unique in Massachusetts. The idea for organizing this support group came from a student who had attended a workshop at Mujeres in the fall of 1988, given by Dr. Elba Crespo from the Prevention of Family Violence Unit for DPH. Other women also expressed concern about dealing with domestic violence or not wanting to confront it.

Two other types of programs, forums and minicourses, further illustrate how the participatory approach is put into practice. Since its beginning, Mujeres Unidas has sponsored a community issues forum every Friday; ideas come from student suggestions. After these ideas are developed into topics, students select them in a meeting early in the semester. Guest speakers are subsequently invited to address them.

In response to many students who wanted to learn more practical skills, Mujeres Unidas started a series of minicourses this past winter. Tina Cueva, the outreach worker and a graduate of Mujeres Unidas's program, affirms that "when we learn something practical, it gives us a sense of achievement. After we finish this first step, we look at the next one with greater ease." Practical minicourses are offered in areas such as typing, citizenship, and driving. Nine students have already passed the written part of the driving exam and are preparing to take the practical exam. During the spring semester four students studied to take the citizenship exam. Two women took the test and passed, and one has been sworn in as a U.S. citizen. The other two continue to study, and plan to take the test soon. Six other students are enrolled in the typing courses.

A childcare program supports Mujeres's students through their years at the center. Under the supervision of two teachers, both former graduates of our ESL program, children gather from Monday to Friday in an environment where learning experiences are shared, while their mothers are attending classes. This is the first time that many of the children have been separated from their mothers and are not under the care of other family members. Although this can be a difficult experience for them, we have found that as time passes, especially because their mothers are close by, the experience becomes a positive one. After a while, children willingly let go of their mothers' hands to walk into their own childcare room. It has also been positive because any time there is a childcare activity, attendance is great. Of thirty-five children enrolled in childcare, twenty-five children and their mothers participate in practically all of the activities organized for special days. Since one of the teachers is from the Cape Verde Islands, the children learn Cape Verdean Creole in addition to Spanish and English. We think that first-hand experience with different languages is valuable for the children's development of vocabulary and for their appreciation of language diversity.

The participatory approach is also practiced in the agency's administrative structure. Mujeres has chosen to function as a collective since its origin. It is composed of the ten Mujeres Unidas staff workers. In addition, student representatives are elected to this body at the beginning of each semester. The student representatives serve as liaisons between students and the collective. They are responsible for raising issues that are relevant to the students. Through their participation in bimonthly collective meetings, they are an integral part of the decisionmaking process. The meetings are open to all students and volunteers; everyone's opinions and ideas are welcomed and discussed.

The collective's major responsibilities are: 1) to develop programs based on the needs expressed by the student population; 2) to make recommendations about expanding the program; 3) to develop long- and short-term plans; and 4) to discuss topics related to the Latina community, particularly those affecting low-income Latinas.

Volunteers, although welcome, usually do not attend collective meetings, because the majority serve on a part-time basis or conduct home visits on weekends. The volunteers are primarily Anglo, middle-class, educated women who want to learn more about the Latina community, develop their teaching skills, and support efforts for the advancement of other women. The responsibility of the volunteers is to support students who are unable to register because of a lack of space, or who need special attention or additional instruction. Specifically, they meet with students one-on-one or in small groups, providing citizenship classes and tutorials in participants' homes and at the agency in subjects such as math, English, and understanding cultural differences. There is also a volunteer representative on the staff, who is responsible for bringing volunteers' ideas to the collective meeting discussions.

In the collective we see and treat each other as equals, despite our cultural, class, social, and educational differences. Of course, in the group's dynamics, differences are periodically observed, depending upon the topic being discussed. Nevertheless, these differences are seen as necessary and positive for the development of equal community participation. During our collective meetings we respect and take into consideration the different levels and types of knowledge each has on a given issue. As Tina Cueva, the outreach worker, says, "the fact that we don't have a boss inspires each one of us to develop ideas, and to be innovative, instead of just waiting for someone to tell us what to do."

It would be impossible to talk about social transformation—particularly in the case of the Latina, who has historically been raised to be a mother, daughter, sister, or wife—without including radical changes in the power structure to validate her own voice.[7] One structure which may oppress many women is the hierarchically organized family. In many low-income families, the male figure, when present, is the one who represents authority, giving orders and making the decisions. Some of our students, for example, have been forbidden by their husbands, partners, or lovers to continue their education (since learning English is considered to be enough), or to participate in other activities sponsored by the agency. Other students need to fulfill certain obligations, such as food preparation and ensuring that the home is cleaned, before they can participate in any activity outside the home. In many such households the mother is the sole provider for the emotional needs and social upbringing of the children. This situation is oppressive because these women are kept from pursuing other options, such as furthering their education or pursuing other interests.

Radical changes are needed both inside and outside of the woman. Internally, women need to identify their own feelings of oppression and gain the strength to confront them. Externally, stereotypical roles need to be confronted; the roots of gender roles need to be discussed openly and addressed in a way that gives equal responsibility to men and women. Women need freedom to work and study, to change the traditional roles of mother, daughter, sister, and emotional supporter. We believe that for these roles to be changed, society must reinvest resources in our educational processes and our social structures. Socialization based on gender roles needs to be questioned, critically analyzed, and changed. For example, a more equitable sharing of responsibility for childrearing would require, among other things, reassessing job priorities and schedules, creating childcare centers, and achieving parity in salaries for males and females.

It would be absurd to maintain a hierarchical system in an organization such as Mujeres Unidas, because that would perpetuate the present social oppression women face. The decision for Mujeres to be a collective grew out of an urgent need to provide women, particularly low-income women, with the space to express their opinions freely. The participatory approach allows Mujeres to function in an environment where the importance of the collective process minimizes the risk of one person taking on all of the power.

The dynamics of development for the dispossessed must include practical and immediate action to validate our voices—to appreciate, understand, and learn from what each woman experiences, thinks, and speaks. At Mujeres Unidas, workers and students learn the value of their own words. They learn to be assertive in what they are trying to express. One example of this is the review process for Mujeres's Personnel Manual, which began in June 1987, when we realized that the manual needed revision. Policies for maternity leave, temporary workers, and other issues of current concern to staff were not included in the old manual. In June of 1988, Mujeres Unidas, with technical assistance from the Boston Women's Fund, began revising the personnel manual. A typical revision process, in which the agency's director reviews the manual, makes necessary changes, and then sends a memorandum to workers and the Board of Directors[8] for approval, was not used because this approach worked against the participatorial principles of the agency. Instead, we created a committee composed of members of the collective and students. The process of developing the personnel manual took about six months. Each article, amendment, and phrase was read and reread until all of the workers and students present at the meetings understood, analyzed, criticized, and expanded the content, so that it was based on their own experiences. The collective's members and students joined efforts to produce something in common. The different skills of each of the participants converged to create a new personnel manual. We consider this a concrete example of education functioning as a liberating tool. While we recognize that the extenuating efforts, time commitments, and slow pace of the process can be cumbersome and sometimes overburdening, we feel that the results are worthwhile. At present the personnel manual is at the Board of Directors for their approval.

The Board of Directors of Mujeres Unidas is an essential component of the agency's structure. It has several different functions. The first is to be its legal representative, in accordance with regulations governing nonprofit organizations. At the same time, our Board maintains a system of checks and balances. The Board of Directors is composed of 40 percent professional women and 60 percent low-income Latinas. This duality in composition means that Board members necessarily have the responsibility of educating themselves. The professional women learn from the community women's experiences, struggles, and survival. Simultaneously, the women from the community learn from the professional women the skills needed to become active members, not only of the Board of Directors, but of other decisionmaking structures as well. For example, when the position of secretary of the Board was vacant, Nelly, a newly arrived immigrant from Puerto Rico who had become involved with Mujeres's Board, was nominated by her peers to fill it. Nelly brings to the Board firsthand knowledge of single parenting and experience with the challenges faced by an immigrant learning a new language. In turn, the Board can help Nelly develop the skills to become a good secretary. Before committing herself, Nelly asked to see a job description and other information necessary for performing her job well. She stated, "I need to know really well what my responsibilities are." This is one way Board members exchange ideas, resources, and skills.

Board members also participate in Mujeres Unidas's working committees. These were created to organize the daily work needed to operate a community-based agency; they also involve students, staff, and Board members in collaboration for learning diverse skills. There are three working committees: Evaluation, Planning, and Personnel; Fund-Raising and Special Events; and the Development, Maintenance, and Dissemination of the Board of Directors' Information.

The formation of these committees represents another part of our liberating process, providing an additional forum for our students to develop their creative ideas, critical thinking, and leadership skills, and become active in the structure and functioning of the agency. Working committees comprise at least two members and meet approximately every three months, depending on the particular situation. The committees have organized a variety of activities, including selling food at lunchtime for fund-raising; publishing a booklet on AIDS and safe sex for mothers; and the Community Unity Festival, a day of celebration and solidarity in Roxbury and Dorchester for communities of color.

We believe that the success of Mujeres Unidas is demonstrated by the lar e number of women who come to register for our programs. At the end of the most recent Spring cycle, eighty-four students had already registered for the current Fall-Winter cycle. We get at least two or three phone calls a week asking for information about our courses. For our five-week Summer cycle, in which we offer two classes instead of our usual four, we could only register twenty-four students; an additional twenty-nine students were placed on a waiting list due to a lack of available space. Furthermore, we can see success in the number of Mujeres graduates who are now either working or in college or technical schools. After our incorporation in 1982, we began graduating students in the fiscal year of 1983–1984. Since 1983, sixty-five out of ninety-five students have graduated from the Advanced ESL class, and twenty-eight out of a group of thirty-five have obtained their GED. One student from the ESL program has obtained a B.A. in Economics from the University of Massachusetts, Boston. She is currently a member of the Board of Directors. Another student finished Mujeres's ESL program in 1986 and obtained certification in Word Processing at the Humphrey Occupational Center of the Boston Public Schools. She also finished Advanced English at Bunker Hill Community College and is currently enrolled in the School of Management at the University of Massachusetts, Boston. Most of our students would never have thought it possible to continue their education at a local university; Mujeres has opened the door to the future for many of them.

One of the reasons for our success has been our ability to recognize, identify, and overcome the barriers faced by Latinas in their struggle for self-development. These barriers are often deeply rooted in Latino culture. The Latina immigrant not only confronts the difficulties of a competitive, individualistic society in the United States, which oppresses her in a variety of ways; she also brings her own internalized marks of oppression. The roles of the obedient woman and mother, as well as other cultural stereotypes, are handicaps to the liberation process. Specifically, many women who come to Mujeres want only to learn English; they do not want to deal with other issues and problems at home. Their participation in class discussions allows them to realize that the problems each of them may face at home or in their lives are not theirs alone. For example, many women experienced problems with health-care providers. They learn that problems often have the same roots—lack of education, lack of job opportunities, racism, discrimination—and that the solutions can only be found collectively. The role of the obedient woman, who follows orders and does not think critically, interferes with the search for self. In fact, many come to Mujeres precisely because they want to change and improve their status as women in order to be better role models for their children.

One of the educational components at Mujeres, the Spanish program, has attempted to sensitively explore these barriers. In this program the women have begun to identify problems, thus obtaining control over their education and, ultimately, over their lives.

AN IN-DEPTH LOOK AT THE SPANISH PROGRAM

In one Spanish class we were working with photographs of Latino working families doing different household chores. The family structure varied in each; some showed mothers and children, others had both the parents and children. The *compañeras* wrote about the contents of the photographs. Each person read her work aloud. Later, we commented on what we had written, and compared the families in the pictures to our own families. Maria, Carmen, and Brunilda, all single mothers—like the women in some of the photographs—responded to the question: "Does this family look like yours?" by agreeing that these families were very similar to their own. Juanita, also a single mother, holding a picture of a mother, father, and their children, said, "Yes, this family looks like mine, but in my family the only thing that is missing is the father of my children, but I'm that too."

There are so many Latina women like Juanita, who have the responsibility of raising a family alone. It is difficult to raise healthy human beings capable of leading productive lives—teaching them good values, giving them proper support, being a good role model for their socialization, financially maintaining the home—while playing the role of both mother and father. Eighty percent of the women who participate in Mujeres's Spanish Educational Program are single mothers.[9] While some of these women have been in the United States for as short a time as two or three months and others have been here for as long as twenty-five years, the majority have lived in the States for a total of ten years. The women in this program mainly come from Puerto Rico and Dominican Republic, although we have had students from Guatemala, El Salvador, and the Cape Verde Islands. Their level of education varies. Some have never been to school, others have completed three to four years of elementary schooling; still others have completed some years of high school. But none have studied beyond high school. All of them receive public assistance. This description clearly demonstrates this group's lack of economic resources. The reasons that these women give for wanting to strive for a good education and claim their right to a better life include insufficient economic resources, lack of a support system, low level of formal education, and the necessity to be a good mother. Matilde, a forty-one-year-old Puerto Rican woman, expressed her feelings this way: "I left school because I had to help my family. But I have to start depending on myself, finish high school in order to get a good job and take stock in my self-worth without constantly waiting for help from Welfare."

The Spanish Program is based on the following four premises: 1) education is a universal right; 2) it is necessary to strengthen the native language in order to facilitate the acquisition of a second language; 3) there is a lack of educational resources for low-income families in Latin American countries; and 4) there are few educational opportunities in the United States for low-income Latinas. At Mujeres, education is a right, and not a privilege. With this in mind, the collective started an educational program in Spanish. In this way Mujeres Unidas is contributing to the quality of Latina women's lives.

In order to bridge the gap between these women's lack of education and their adaptation to a new culture and language, Mujeres provides literacy courses in their native language, Spanish. We believe that in order to promote learning a foreign language, it is necessary to master basic reading and writing skills in one's own language (Cummins, 1981). If such skills are not developed, it is difficult to learn another language beyond the acquisition of some listening comprehension and oral communication skills. Furthermore, to approach a complete education, one should at least learn to read and write in one's native language. The need to develop literacy skills in the native language was evident in the women's verbal testimonies of their lives, and the oral dialogues done in ESL classes.

Program participants range in age from twenty to fifty-eight, with an average age of thirty-four. Almost all are heads of household. Primarily because of social conditions in their countries, most of these women—as mentioned earlier—suffer from a lack of formal schooling. Their economic and social development corresponds to that found in some Third World countries, where the possibility of an education is rare, if not nonexistent.[10] Our own personal experiences as Latina women from lower- and lower-middle-class backgrounds have shown us that the educational resources available in our countries are highly limited for the poor. In the Dominican Republic, for example, 33 percent of the population is illiterate, and 40 percent of the labor force is unemployed (Hilsum, 1983). Although Hilsum does not indicate specifically what percentage of women are illiterate, these data suggest that access to social resources such as education and employment is scarce for the poor, including poor women. Indeed, one of the reasons, Hilsum offers for these high percentages is the poverty of the country: "A lot of people cannot go to school because they must work from a very young age to help their families attain the basic needs of food, housing, and clothing."[11]

Think for a moment of what life is like for a single woman, with two or more children, who emigrates from her native country to raise her family in the United States. Latin American countries are exploited countries, where a lack of resources for poor people and—in many cases—war combine to force people to emigrate to find better living conditions, a stable income, and adequate health services for their children. Women participating in the Spanish Program often give these as their reasons for coming to the United States. The historical realities of poverty, migration, and war in Latin America serve as evidence in the testimonies of these women. For example, the migration of Puerto Ricans fleeing poverty throughout the 1920s, 1940s, and 1950s has been well documented (see López, 1980; Maldonado-Denis, 1970; Nieves-Falcón, 1971; Rodríguez, 1989). Currently, the migration of Dominicans to cities in Massachusetts is primarily a result of the poverty and lack of educational opportunities in their country. The presence of war in Central America has caused women to emigrate into the United States (see Mental Health Committee, 1989; Organización Panamericana de la Salud, 1988). In addition, the women have described some of the personal conditions that motivated them to look for new horizons in the United States. Many of these women emigrated in order to flee from personal problems and psychological and physical abuse by their husbands or partners.

Seven current participants in the Spanish Literacy course were forced to leave school when they were younger. In the patriarchal societies of their Latin American countries, especially in low socioeconomic groups, learning to add, subtract, read, and write is still believed to be sufficient education. Once they are educated at that level, young women must stay home to help support the rest of the family. Carmen, a forty-eight-year-old Puerto Rican woman and a pre-GED student, states, "My father took me out of school as soon as I learned to read and write a little. According to him that was all I needed to learn since I had to help my mother with the housework and take care of my little brothers and sisters." Society has forced women to take on the responsibilities of home and family; this is true not only in Latin American countries, but even in those, like Puerto Rico, that are more industrialized. Carmen's testimony reflects current realities: even though women may be part of the labor force, society still imposes on them the additional role of housewife. This is what is known as *doble carga* (double work). Women must work outside the home to support their families in addition to doing all the housework. Society limits the educational opportunities of women, and does not recognize the value of their roles. Thus, we can say that women's lack of education is closely tied to social factors.

Marcia Rivera-Quintero, a Puerto Rican feminist, writes that

> The home constituted the center of activity for women given that the biological reproductive functions developed there. The duties that peasant women carried out, set the basis for generalization and hegemony of the conceptualization of housework as women's work. The production and biological reproduction of the human species were closely linked processes and the former was subordinated to the patriarchal family. (1980, p. 13)

Even though Quintero's study examined the lives of women at the beginning of this century, it remains relevant today, chiefly because industrialization in Puerto Rico is situated in the capital and coastal towns—the areas of highest economic value. Therefore, the benefits of industrialization—such as job opportunities, modernization, and more education—did not, and in many cases still have not, reached rural areas of the island, particularly the center.

For many of our students the home environment has provided the only means of socialization. Since they do not have jobs, they do not have the opportunity to leave the house regularly. If they have children, they do not have money for childcare or for public transportation. At Mujeres, we face this reality daily. Because of these limitations and the scarce resources available, the need for these women to be educated is vital. We believe that if women are educated, they increase their opportunities to find decent jobs, which will improve their financial situation and better their living conditions. At Mujeres, women have the chance and the space to socialize by exchanging concerns, ideas, and realities with other women and, therefore, to discover new things that can improve their lives.

Finally, we would like to point out that the scarcity of educational opportunities for many of these women in the United States makes our Spanish Program indispensable. In 1980 women made up 52 percent of the Latino population in Massachusetts, and women single heads of household made up 19.4 percent of the Latino population in the United States.[12] We want to note that many low-income Latinas who are single heads of household are not counted in the population census because they are undocumented in this country. The crucial need for education becomes even more striking when we add that only 43 percent of Latinas in the nation have completed high school.[13] The testimonies of women at Mujeres link the high dropout rate to language barriers and the quality of the education they received in the United States.[14]

The Spanish Program has two components: the Literacy Program (pre-GED) and the course for preparation for the GED exam. Mujeres Unidas's literacy program has been named pre-GED because it prepares students to develop basic skills in reading, writing, and arithmetic. Mastery of these skills is required for the GED. Nearly 90 percent of the women enter directly into the GED course because they already have these skills. Ideally, when women finish the pre-GED course they will move on into the GED program. In fact in the summer of 1989 we had our first student, Georgina Cruz, move from the pre-GED to the GED course.

Our experience with the program has shown us that learning to read and write is a slow process for adult women, many of whom have not had previous experience in an educational program. Thus, we have built into the program the time and space for the women to adapt to and feel at ease in a new environment, an environment with different responsibilities from those of their households. The program's final objectives are to prepare women to obtain their high school diplomas and pursue higher education. We encourage them to work on their English reading and writing skills so that fluency in both Spanish and English is developed and strengthened.

The Spanish program began in September, 1987, and so far, twenty women have obtained their high school diplomas. Currently, 28 women are enrolled in the Spanish courses: 11 Dominicans, 15 Puerto Ricans, 1 Guatemalan, and 1 Cape Verdean. Included in this total are two former GED students who are now paid tutors for the Spanish program and are currently students in the ESL program. By allowing graduates of the program to stay on as tutors, we feel we are encouraging the women's participation in their own educational process.

Students actively participate in the development of curriculum based on their learning needs. The curriculum is open to the integration of topics and themes the students deem necessary. For example, if a student feels the need to have information about an issue, she will express this need to the group, which then decides how to address this in the discussion. Some of the topics suggested include: domestic violence, rape, machismo, racism, child psychology, welfare benefits, adolescent problems, menopause, drugs, AIDS, and historical facts about their respective countries. In practice, it is a very informal process, based on the principle that education should go beyond what is dictated in books.

We believe that effective education is one which generates meaningful change—for example, changing the roles imposed by society on women. Specific examples of social roles imposed by society are the tripartite role of women in society (mother, wife, and housewife) and stereotypes of women's behavior, such as submissiveness and obedience. We realize that women are oppressed as a consequence of the imposition of such roles. The existence of these beliefs in patriarchal societies of Third World countries, as well as in societies of industrialized countries such as the United States, makes us affirm the need for social change which will allow us, as women, to transform our roles. We understand that education is one of the means by which we can achieve meaningful change in women's history and the history of society. Based on this, the Spanish program utilizes a methodology that springs from the pedagogical philosophy of Brazilian educator Paulo Freire. The program is based on four beliefs: that we must develop a process to understand oppression; that learning language is more than learning grammatical rules; that reading the word is reading the world; and that education is action.

First, we understand that in order to achieve social changes there must be a liberating process that allows us to recognize our condition as oppressed women (Freire, 1971). To engage in such a process we need to have a clear understanding of our native language (Cummins, 1981). We confront the question: How can we begin to liberate ourselves in a language that we do not understand?

Second, using Freire's conceptualization of oppression, we believe that understanding a language goes beyond familiarity with grammatical forms of that language. That is to say, grammatical rules are only one part of any language system; such rules are subject to a communicative context. Language is communication. Through it we can express what and how we feel and think, and we facilitate social interrelationships among people. In this view, words are seen as important, not because of their grammatical characteristics, but because of the meanings and world visions they reflect. Therefore, words are not detached from reality, but rather, the reality is signified by the words.

When we learn to use our language critically we gain a deeper understanding of our reality. Thus, we not only educate ourselves with respect to the text we study, but also with respect to its context. For instance, if we are discussing the word *educación* (education), not only do we learn to write it, but also to understand its significance in terms of the influence it can have on our own lives. The text is a word, *educación,* with its grammatical form, spelling, and any identifying accent rules. The context is understanding what education means for us. Education could be a way of understanding and reacting to the social and political environment, or of identifying and understanding oppressive structures and obtaining control over ourselves and our lives.

To put this methodology into practice we use popular theater techniques as learning tools. These techniques are adapted from the work of the French director, Auguste Boalt, who incorporates Freire's pedagogical theory into theater as a means of social education. Good results can be achieved working with Latino people through theater, because culturally we are very expressive, frequently using body language to communicate. There is no teacher in the theater forum, although students can volunteer to serve as facilitators for a specific session. There is also no philosophy of instruction per se, other than the desire to look for solutions to certain problems.

Theater forum is one of our most successful resources, a vehicle for presenting alternative solutions to enacted situations. First, a theme is suggested and a drama created to present it. The drama is performed, utilizing both language and physical expression. An anti-model, or a response to a negative or unacceptable aspect of the situation being performed, is then chosen by the participants. Those watching the action interrupt it when they feel that there is a disagreement between their own interpretation of the event and what is being presented. In order to present their alternative they must in turn become actresses, replacing the person whose message they disagree with. Through verbal and physical expression they present their alternative solutions. At the end there is an open discussion with all the participants to stimulate a critical view of the theme presented.

An activity during Mujeres's AIDS education month will serve to illustrate this process. The Spanish and ESL classes met for a theater forum session. After completing a values-clarification exercise in which myths and realities about AIDS were discussed, the students developed a theater piece on a situation involving AIDS. One situation concerned a mother who found that her son was gay and at a very high risk of getting or being exposed to the disease. Two women played the roles of the mother and the son. The woman playing the mother was told by the facilitator to be the antimodel—a mother who cannot accept the homosexuality of her son. The situation was presented in a conversation between the mother and the son that developed into an argument. The son wanted to be accepted as a homosexual, and as a homosexual at risk of getting AIDS. The mother blamed him for all that was happening in their lives. At some point during the situation one of the students in the audience watching stopped the action and took on the role of the mother herself. In her performance, she tried to be more open to her son's problems and to look for professional help, thus suggesting an alternative.

At the beginning of each semester we carry out an exercise of theater forum, using the meaning of education in the lives of the participants as a theme. This is how we try to recognize the importance and influence that education might have on us. Another session of theater forum serves to illustrate this point. This time the situation was about a woman sent to Mujeres to study by a local Welfare office. The woman was very reluctant to do it, because education had no meaning to her at that time; she was content with watching soap operas on television—the antimodel. Different students stopped the action to provide alternatives to the antimodel by talking about what education meant to them. Some of their ideas, as they presented them in the theater forum, were that education was a way to improve the qualities of their lives by providing them and their children with more opportunities for development and growth, enabling them to face the world as active participants.

The impact that this nontraditional teaching approach has had is amazing; according to these students, expanding their reality in new and refreshing ways has led them to become more involved in their own educational process. Expanding their reality is very important for the women who attend our program, given the limited socialization to which they have been subjected. One participant states:

> Mujeres Unidas and its Spanish program have opened up doors for my future. Not only do I learn specific subject matters, but I also have learned a lot about the realities of the world around me and how to face the world better. I've grown tremendously as a human being.—*Genoveva, Puerto Rican mother of two*

Third, we believe that reading a word is reading reality. When women understand the meaning of a word and the impact that meaning may have in their lives, they understand a reality which in one way or another is linked to the role they are playing in society. Thus, conditions are created to stimulate critical thinking of the historical moment in which we are living. This is how we begin to become conscious of the reality we live in as Latinas in this country.

We need to understand that we are cultural beings and that we respond to the cultural patterns we have internalized. When women have a clear understanding of these patterns, they reassert their own culture; who they are, and the goals they wish to achieve for their own growth, become clearer. This process makes it easier to question the assumptions of other cultures as well. North American culture has standards very different from those of Latino cultures. Our experience as Latina women tells us that if we understand where we come from we will know better where we are going.

The final objective of liberation pedagogy is action. Once we know who we are and where we come from, we can better confront North American culture and change patterns of women's oppression in this country. When knowledge leads to action, social change is achieved, because "one makes one's presence known." An example of taking action comes from Carmen Torres, a student of the GED class who participated as Mujeres's spokeswoman in a rally for the Gateways City Program in March of 1989. She spoke to the members of the Gateways Advisory Council about the problems that low-income Latina women face in getting an education in this country. She stated: "We do not have money to afford daycare services so we can go to school. We really need programs like this [Gateways] to have the chance to contribute in a better way to the future." Clearly, she is articulating her concerns and the concerns of other women in similar situations. She brought an issue to a governing body to let them know that issues facing Latina women need to be addressed. We feel that women's experiences in class discussions, participation in theater forums, and other activities at Mujeres that allow women to speak, serve as a practice arena for speaking their voice in society in general.

Implementation of this methodology presents us with certain disadvantages. In many cases, for example, fear of the challenge that comes along with knowledge of an oppressive reality is hard to overcome. The learning process is often slow because it requires full participation of the students in their educational process. Despite these difficulties, we reaffirm the effectiveness of this method, reflected in student work and achievement. At the present time, all the *compañeras* in the GED class who have taken the exam have passed it with very high scores.

The learning process has been one in which mutual support between student and teacher is essential to success. The communication and solidarity developed by women in the class, at the root of the participatory process, helped overcome fears one by one, such as fear of the challenge, fear of coming to school after being an adult, fear of the unknown, fear of power, fear of failure, fear of not being able to learn to read and write, fear of speaking another language, and fear of being rejected.

Also, it is important to mention that the students' attendance and retention has been astounding; the women who were able to get here stayed here. Of the few who have left most keep in constant contact with Mujeres Unidas, and the ones who do not keep in touch often return. One student states:

> I was a student at Mujeres from 1984–86. I finished the level 4 ESL class and I had to move on. What I learned at Mujeres was the most important learning I have done in my life. After leaving Mujeres I went to Puerto Rico for two years. . . . I believe now that I lost a lot of time there. On returning to the United States I was feeling very frustrated and when I asked for my treasured school I found out that they were offering GED preparation and I immediately signed up. Now I feel so much happier with the hope that I am reaching my fulfillment.—*Carmen Fortis, mother of three*

We cannot overlook the impact of the Spanish program at an individual level, where women are raising their consciousness as oppressed people and are realizing the importance of education in their native language. The impact can also be seen at the community level, with the creation of new leaders. One example of this is Mujeres's support group, *compañeras*. As mentioned earlier, this group was formed thanks to the initiative of a student who is at present a recovering alcoholic. She has an incredible will to move forward in her life, as the formation of the support group reflects. She has just received her high school equivalency degree after taking the GED course at Mujeres. The program's impact is also manifested at a societal level in the form of student action, for example, in uniting to demand rights at a local or national rally. Another example of students taking action occurred during "AIDS Month," when, after presenting a video on AIDS, one student from the GED class and another student from the pre-GED class suggested showing the video to their husbands and partners in order to educate the men on AIDS prevention. We see these kinds of actions as contributing to the transformation of society and the creation of history.

One way of measuring success is to document what the students accomplish once they have graduated. One of the program's students published two of her poems in the book, *Need I Say More,* published by the Adult Literacy Resource Institute in Boston (Spring, 1988). Another student received an award from the Boston Public Schools for her work in the struggle to maintain bilingual programs in certain high schools. Both carried out their work in their native language, Spanish.

In one way or another, in spite of economic, societal, political, and familial barriers, all the women involved in the development of Mujeres Unidas are committed to social change. When you acknowledge the tremendous necessity for changing the present power structures which perpetuate racism, the patriarchal system, sexism, and homophobia, and you acknowledge the economic and political oppression of certain parts of society, you begin to understand the depth of the commitment the women have made toward taking action in order to achieve social change. We believe that in order to take action, it is necessary to continue discovering our truth, our language, and our word. With these discoveries we can then challenge the existing forces of oppression and institutionalize change. At Mujeres Unidas, change has been institutionalized through painstaking educational activities and an innovative administration; here everyone learns from each other.

NOTES

1. Recent research literature shows that, in general, Puerto Ricans in the United States suffer from lack of economic resources. Rodríguez (1989) cites studies which indicate that "the economic situation of Puerto Ricans in the United States has worsened with time" (p. 36). She writes:

   > Tienda and Jensen (1986), in their analysis of the 5% decennial census data (1960–80), found Puerto Ricans in the states to be the only group to experience a drop in real family income between 1970 and 1980 and to show a steadily increasing concentration in the lowest income quartile (other groups compared were Blacks, Mexicans, other Hispanics, and Native Americans). . . . Bean and Tienda (1988) also found Puerto Ricans to have declining economic well-being, as measured by falling labor force participation, high unemployment, poverty, and declines in real family income. (p. 47)

   In addition, women in particular fall consistently into the low economic end of the scale. Rodríguez (1989) mentions a study done by Darity and Myers (1987) which found that Puerto Rican female-headed households were among the poorest families. A study done by the Hispanic Office for Planning and Evaluation (HOPE) and the Massachusetts Institute of Technology (MIT) in 1987 states that

> Half of all Hispanic families with children under 18 supported by single mothers. This family structure has important implications for the prevalence of poverty among families as well as for the strategies to promote full employment for Hispanics. When families are supported by a sole earner, especially women, they are much more likely to be poor. For single-parent families to survive above the poverty level, it becomes even more crucial for the breadwinner to gain access to higher wage jobs. (Borges, Vázquez-Fuentes, & Kluver, 1987, p. 36).

This study also states that "in Massachusetts, current Assistance for Families with Dependent Children benefits (usually the only option for unemployed single mothers) are approximately 30 percent below the poverty level" (p. 13). As the statewide Massachusetts Commission for Hispanic Affairs stated in 1986, "The availablity of services sought by single-parent households, such as daycare, after-school programs or counseling is crucial to the well-being of Hispanic families" (p. 33). According to a survey commissioned by the Boston Redevelopment Authority (BRA) in 1985, females made up 63 percent of all Hispanics. The 1980 census shows that 52 percent of Hispanics in Boston had no high school diploma. These figures suggest that there is a disproportionate number of women who have been kept outside the mainstream.

2. There is some literature that has dealt with the racial experience of Puerto Ricans in the United States. For example, Rodríguez (1989) states:

> As Puerto Ricans entered into "the American dilemma" (Myrdal, 1944) two facts about the racial order were quite clear. One was that the context in which Puerto Ricans stepped offered only two paths—one to the White World and one to the not-White world. Choice of path was dependent on racial classification according to U.S. standards. Use of these standards divided the group, negated the cultural existence of Puerto Ricans, and ignored their expectations that they be treated, irrespective of race, as a culturally intact group. The other quite obvious fact about the race order was that those Americans who were White were socioeconomically better off. (p. 56)

3. The state census of 1985 showed the following percentages for Hispanics in the following areas in and around Dorchester: North Dorchester, 13 percent Hispanics of a population of 26,005; South Dorchester, 7 percent of a total population of 16,373; Roxbury, 13 percent of a total population of 58,475; and Mattapan, 6 percent of a total population of 40,395.

4. To this date there are very few written documents that trace the specific growth of the agency. Currently, Mujeres is dedicated to documenting the early growth and development of the agency through oral histories.

5. Our participatory approach means that women are given the opportunity and are encouraged to express their opinions and ideas at all levels of the agency. For example, classroom curriculum is developed around students' needs as articulated by them. For women who have never before been asked to express an opinion, doing so and being respected for it makes them active participants and is empowering. Providing learning experiences that promote critical thinking skills allows women to make decisions about their own lives and take a more active and assertive role in them.

6. The Gateway Cities Program is a local aid initiative, created in fiscal year 1987 by a legislative State order. Gateway Cities funds have helped municipalities and local commu-

nity groups provide services in such areas as immigration assistance, housing, economic development, interpreter and translation services, specialized education, and municipal access programs. As of fiscal year 1989, however, the Gateway Cities Program funds were not renewed due to budget cuts.

7. Social transformation in this context refers to a transformed society in which people can see themselves in control of their lives, having the access, the options, and the opportunities to develop skills and as being able to control their destinies. And one in which people can see themselves as members of a collective process in which diversity in race, culture, language, gender, and sexual orientation is respected and tolerated.

8. The Board of Directors is formed by former Assistance for Families with Dependent Children (AFDC) recipients, current AFDC recipients who are students at Mujeres, graduates of Mujeres, and professional Latina women.

9. By "single mothers" we mean women heads of household with children raising a family by themselves without the presence of a paternal figure.

10. Philip Berryman (1987) states: "Today Latin America is in its worst economic crisis since the 1930s. Servicing the foreign debt ($360 billion) consumes 40 percent of the continent's exports. In some countries, such as Peru, living standards have fallen back to the levels of twenty years ago. Latin America produces less food per capita than it did forty years ago. . . ." (p. 183). He bases his data on the work of Morris David Morris (1979). Information on the economic conditions in Latin America can also be found in: *North American Congress on Latin America (NACLA), 22*(4) (July–August, 1988); *Mujeres Adelante, 9* (October–December, 1986).

11. Hilsum (1983) explains that in the Dominican Republic, government credit, irrigation, and desalination schemes are directed almost exclusively into export crops. For example, research undertaken by Women of the South in 1980 showed that 90 percent of the cattle from the region was eaten elsewhere, as was 80 percent of the fish, 92 percent of the bananas, and 80 percent of the grapefruit and kidney beans. She states: "As the men tramp the region looking for work, the women often are left to support and bring up the children. When women manage to find work, it is usually as small traders, domestic servants, or farm laborers. They fight a never-ending battle against poor housing, lack of sanitation, ill health and malnutrition" (p. 116).

12. Data from the 1980 population census, projections for 1985.

13. Data from the 1980 population census.

14. The quality of education received by minority groups in the United States has been questioned in recent literature (see, for example, Rodríguez, 1989).

REFERENCES

Berryman P. (1987). *Liberation theology: The essential facts about the revolutionary movement in Latin America and beyond*. Oak Park, IL: Meyer Stone.

Borges, R., Vázquez-Fuentes, R., & Kluver, J. (1987). *Background paper for developing a job: A strategy for Hispanics in Boston*. Unpublished manuscript, Hispanic Office for Planning and Evaluation and the Massachusetts Institute of Technology.

Cummins, J. (1981). The role of primary language development in promoting education success for language minority students. In *Schooling and language of minority students: A theoretical framework*. Sacramento: California State Department of Education, Office of Bilingual and Bicultural Education.

Freire, P. (1971). *Pedagogy of the oppressed*. New York: Seabury Press.

Hilsum, L. (1983). Nutrition, education, and social change: A women's movement in the

Dominican Republic. In D. Morley, J. Rhode, & G. Williams (Eds.), *Practicing health for all*. Cambridge: Oxford University Press.

López, A. (1980). *The Puerto Ricans: Their history, culture, and society*. Cambridge: Schenkman.

Maldonado-Denis, M. (1970). *The emigration dialectic: Puerto Rico and the U.S.A.* New York: International Publisher.

Massachusetts Commission for Hispanic Affairs. (1986). *Hispanics in Massachusetts: A demographic analysis*. Unpublished manuscript.

Mental Health Committee. (1989). *Threatened lives: Undocumented Central American refugees*. Report distributed by members of the Mental Health Committee of the Boston Committee for Health Rights in Central America (BCHRICA), Chestnut Hill, MA.

Nieves-Falcón, L. (1971). *Diagnóstico de Puerto Rico* [Diagnosis of Puerto Rico]. Río Piedras, Puerto Rico: Editorial Edil.

Organización Panamericana de la Salud. (1988). *Mortalidad materna en America Latina* [Maternal mortality in Latin America]. Washington, DC: Pan American Sanitary Bureau.

Rivera-Quintero, M. (1980). Incorporación de las mujeres al mercado del trabajo en el desarollo del capitalismo [The inclusion of women into the labor force in the development of capitalism]. In E. Acosta-Belén (Ed.), *La mujer en la sociedad Puertorriqueña*. Río Piedras: Ediciones Hurracàn.

Rodríguez, C. (1989). *Puerto Ricans born in the U.S.A.* Winchester, MA: Unwin Hyman.

Special Education and the Quest for Human Dignity

Rebecca Blomgren

Within the context of education, we occasionally ponder the purpose of our actions and the direction in which those actions and resulting choices turn us. As special educators, many of these reflections and methodological choices revolve around issues of help, remediation and compensation. How do we envision our help and what are the realities within which we practice these concerns? How do we regard those who come before us in their various stages and states of disability? What do we do to them and with them in the name of help? What are the discrepancies between our desire to help and the voices with which we have chosen to express this assistance? Where does this leave us educationally? personally? and collectively? What does this say about our humanity or inhumanity?

This chapter, while situated within the arena of special education, will attempt to delve into the dilemmas we all face when we attempt to understand the purpose of school, the meaning of help and the hope we hold for education. As we strive to couple our democratic ideals of equality, freedom and inclusion with productivity, competition and education within the process of education, the tensions of this structure begin to emerge. The tensions become increasingly painful and horrifying as they are filtered through the lives, realities and experiences of the handicapped. Special education offers an intense focusing point in which the tensions, dilemmas, and paradoxes are illuminated and magnified.

In reflecting upon the issues that press upon special educators, the message of Martin Buber offers an opportunity to seriously consider how we prepare ourselves to encounter the challenges that teaching presents.

> He [the modern educator] enters the school room for the first time, he sees them crouching at the desks, indiscriminately flung together, the misshapen and the well-proportioned, animal faces, empty faces and noble faces in indiscriminate confusion,

like the presence of the created universe; the glance of the educator accepts and receives them all. (Buber, 1965, p. 94)

Buber's image addresses the dignity of the noble acts of teaching and further sparks the vision that many of us, as educators, initially held.

It is my impression, as an educator, that most of us enter into the varying fields of educational practice with some degree of concern for and awareness of an underlying impulse for care and a compassion for humanity. Those of us in special education, at least initially, seem to be very sensitive to and aware of this helping impulse. However, ironically, special educators frequently find themselves knowingly and obliviously performing the most inhumane deeds, ranging from obvious acts of violence as manifest in severe behavior modification programs that are justified by assertive discipline plans to the more subtle abuses of person as witnessed in the detrimental effects of assessment and labeling that are the prerequisites for special education placement and intervention.

The discrepancy between our initial concern for helping and the reality of our practices in the classroom surfaces as we ponder over just how we meet those who appear before us. How do we respond to the "animal faces," the "misshapen," the "noble faces" and the "empty ones"? Our current and for the most part unexamined response becomes one of efficiently and thoroughly categorizing, tracking and controlling those who come before us year after year. Our educational efforts center upon being absolutely certain that we can label and identify the "animal faces" and the "empty ones" so that we may direct and divert those students into more appropriate programs, where we deceive ourselves, our students and their parents into believing that this special education process will enable these "animal faces" to fulfill their potential and be the most they can be.

We seek to identify and repair these "misshapen ones" and we respond to them with an understanding gained from the medical, scientific models of help. Our desire to help is expressed in terms of diagnosis, prescription, assessment and remediation. The implication of such medical language results in our viewing these individuals as being, to a greater or lesser degree, impaired and thus in need of fixing. As educators, it becomes our responsibility to perform our teaching tasks in the roles of diagnosticians and technicians. It is our job to meet those who come before us prepared to prescribe a task analysis, an Individual Education Program (IEP) and behavioral objectives that will enable these students to acquire techniques and skills that will fix them or at least help them compensate for their problems. As teachers, we attempt to prescribe an education program that will guide them to conformity so they can be as "normal" as possible. As Kliebard suggests, in his critique of Tyler's transmission models of education, "our teaching responsibility becomes one of turning out as useful and as finished a product as possible" (Gress & Purpel, 1978, p. 266).

Helping as diagnosis, teaching as prescription and learning as remediation and production turns very quickly into an educational dilemma in which the unfixed, unproductive, non-useful individual is blamed for his or her lack of success. We rapidly degenerate into blaming the victim for his or her learning disability, educable mental retardation or emotional handicap. When our best prescriptive attempts to to remediate an individual fail, we begin to accuse the individual for his or her inability to become a useful product. With the hope that success resides in some elusive technique or method, we quicken our pace as we search for a better task analysis or a more comprehensive behavior contract. All the while, we continue to blame ourselves and our students for the failure. We delude ourselves into thinking that this is being done in the best interest of the student and in the name of help.

Only upon a deeper look or an examination of our taken-for-granted assumptions regarding help and teaching can we begin to penetrate the destructive cycle of blaming the victim. Whose interest is being served as we meet one another for the purpose of categorizing and prescribing? How might we reconstruct our perception of help? Who is being uplifted by our diagnostic procedures in education? As Camus so poignantly writes, "The evil that is in the world always comes of ignorance, and good intentions may do as much harm as malevolence, if they lack understanding" (Camus, 1972, p. 124). As educators responding to an impulse to help through an unexamined practice which encompasses prescription, remediation, assessment and competitive productivity, we might, as Camus suggests, be ushering in evil through our unexamined good intentions.

In considering resistance as an analytical construct, Giroux provides a vehicle for revealing and examining the painful paradoxes that surface as the tensions between special education, help and productivity are seriously examined. Resistance critique enables us to question our good intentions and to articulate our concerns regarding interest by looking at those who resist conformity and standardization, regardless of the obvious reasons as indicated by the various labels we have placed upon them. The learning disabled, the mentally retarded and the emotionally disturbed who are unable to produce and compete efficiently and who consequently do not fit into our existing educational picture are those who resist the propulsion of our transmission-productivity paradigm. They are the ones who slow down the general productivity in the classroom by seeking explanations for assignments, by requiring additional assistance in order to complete a project or by interrupting the class routine because they are unable to keep pace with the others. They are often cast out, dismissed or viewed as problems by today's educators. These are the students who present us with non-deliberate and frequently unintended pictures of resistance. Although unintended, their resistance serves as a focusing point for analytical critique.

Giroux points out, however, "not all oppositional behavior has 'radical significance,' nor is all oppositional behavior rooted in a reaction to authority and domination" (Giroux, 1983, p. 103). Further, he points out that all behaviors do not automatically "speak for themselves; to call them resistance is to turn the concept into a term that has no analytical preciseness" (p. 109).

However, when resistance, as an analytical tool, is reframed and placed into the dimension of criticism, we are able to examine our "good intentions." Oppositional behaviors and school failures are moved into the political arena in which the questions of interest surface. Functional explanations and understandings based upon educational psychology that tend to contribute to the phenomenon of blaming the victim no longer provide the educational solutions. Rather than being viewed as the result of individual psychology and learned helplessness, oppositional behavior is regarded as having to do with moral and political indignation. Resistance, when understood from this perspective, contains "an expressed hope, an element of transcendence, for radical transformation" (Giroux, 1983, p. 108).

When resistance critique is used to examine our good educational intentions, the actual voices of those who have not fit into the production, transmission models of traditional educational practice begin to be heard. Resistance critique offers a personal and powerful tool for examining our good intentions and for revealing the political dimensions of culture and knowledge. It calls into focus the actual, lived experiences of those who have been denied access or who have felt anguished by the production, transmission pulse of most educational practice. It is through these voices that we may begin to glimpse an insight into the truly alienating conditions of our human existence as manifest through the unexamined, taken-for-granted and good intended practices in education that we call "help" and "teaching."

The voices of Dee and Kay articulate two such stories of resistance that begin to point to the depth of alienation created by our unexamined educational good intentions. Their stories provide us with an opportunity to give voice to the experience of many who have been traditionally dismissed and unheard. Even so, it is difficult to hear the extent of their hegemony, to attend to the depths of their despair and to admit the degree to that they have been prevented from engaging in the process of inquiry. However, Dee and Kay only touch upon the beginnings of voicing the anguish that must be the experience of the excluded handicapped. The vast majority of severely and profoundly handicapped persons in our society remain inarticulate, without language, non-communicative and voiceless. They are placed in the precarious care of those who must speak for them! What about those stories that we may never hear? What can these people reveal to us regarding our good intentions? What are our responsibilities in light of such reflection?

As I began these interviews I did so with a concern for human affirmation, feeling that labeling and special education, although well intended, perpetuated more harm than good. Initially, I felt that I would hear these young women express evidence of poor self-concepts and reveal injured self-esteem; however, their pain was much deeper and their anguish was directed toward the frustration and despair of having been denied their human dignity. These women revealed stories that spoke directly to the issues of exclusion and marginality and of the struggle to be recognized as being human!

Dee

Dee, a 21-year-old interior design student had been labeled as having a learning disability and was placed in a special program when she was in the third grade. She remained in special education programs through the eighth grade. As she reflects upon her special education experience in a resource room, she focuses upon the extensive evaluation and continual assessment that seemed to dominate her school life. Most of these evaluations were not explained, leaving her with a sense of alienation. She recalls feeling extremely frustrated with a third-grade standardized test: "I remember barely being able to read everything that was on there, because most of it was too hard. . . . I felt stupid and frustrated." She goes on to describe a hearing test she was administered in the third grade:

> At one point . . . they even tested me for hearing because they thought I couldn't hear. . . . You had to put those ear, headphones on. I was so nervous all I could do was hear my heart beat. So, they told my parents I couldn't hear.

At the conclusion of this interview, I asked Dee if there was anything else she would like to mention and she stated further her feelings with regard to testing:

> *I feel like an IQ's more the experiences you have instead of all of your book learning. I think people are intelligent in different areas and you can't be perfect in everything. I guess the tests are for society's perfect persons. I don't know. . . . I just don't think the whole testing thing is fair. I mean that's something that's sort of circumstantial. I mean, everything that's been going on in your life, whether you're stressed or not, has a great deal to do with how you do, how well you do, and how you feel that day.*

Although she has experienced the injustice of testing and has a sense of the discomfort it caused, she does not question the validity of the function of testing and has internalized the value for the necessity of tests designed to determine whether or not one has learned the important facts considered to be knowledge. Throughout the interview, she blames herself for her lack of success and her academic problems. She says, "If I was older and had more experience, I'm sure I could apply it, but I didn't." She goes on to say, "I was just slower and didn't put forth the effort that I really should have, in study."

She is unclear as to whether or not the resource center was helpful in providing her with assistance in remediating her reading and spelling problems, but she did feel that it offered her a pleasant escape from the regular classroom. "I felt relieved because the resource teacher was so much nicer and I really liked doing that, getting away from my [classroom] teacher." She goes on to say, however, with regard to the effectiveness of the resource center, "I don't know, I feel if I had had a private tutor early on, I would have been OK." Although she had had tutors from fourth through ninth grades, after school and during the summer, Dee felt that maybe she would not have had as many difficulties in school if tutoring had begun at an earlier point. The significance lies in the fact that Dee perceived herself as not being OK and that the cure required assistance from an external authority.

Dee goes on to describe herself: "I wasn't as smart as the average student. . . . I think I was as smart as the other students, I was just slower and I didn't put forth the effort that I really should have, in study, I mean, I did my homework." She is ambiguous about her own ability and once again partially sees her difficulties as being her own fault. She blames herself for her problems and for her inability to solve them. Dee was unsure about the actual label that she had been given in elementary school but remembered it as having been associated with being slow. "I was labeled, I've forgotten, they had two different labels. One meant you were just a little bit slow and the other one meant you were a little bit retarded . . . and I was the one that was a little bit slow."

In describing the actual resource center experience she commented, "I'd go down [the hall] and we'd have to have hall passes and all that stuff. I've had hall passes all my life!" The labeling process brought with it tickets of admission and identification. The "hall pass" indicated that permission was required for entrance and if denied permission, one might face the existential dilemma of remaining in the hall, therefore not being allowed to participate and at the same time wondering why. Essentially, she was being placed into a position, with the hall pass, which potentially denied her admission to the conditions that enable one to construct meaning within the competitive framework existing in our schools. Those who carry hall passes are designated as marginal; they may or may not be granted permission to compete.

Feelings of being different permeate Dee's experiences and relationships. She felt most intensely alienated from the teachers for whom she perceived herself as being a structural problem in terms of causing an interruption.

I think they [teachers] were hostile because they wanted everyone to do this, this and this, [to] be very structured. I messed up the structure because I was slower and went to the resource room, more from being slower.

She perceived herself as an interruption to the routine because she needed to have things explained and therefore she caused a problem for the efficient functioning of the classroom.

Dee felt also that the expectations of the teachers were lowered as a result of her being placed in the resource center.

I remember Mrs. B [a sixth-grade teacher] not letting me be on my level of math because I did go to the resource room. . . . She was telling me that I needed to do this and finally I convinced her to let me be in there, it was a little bit above average, and I did fine. . . . Her expectation was a lot lower; it was back to the math I did in second grade, just addition and subtraction of single digits.

Generally her memories of teachers were unpleasant, remembering teachers as being impatient and herself as being an interruption.

With regard to feelings about herself, she recalls that throughout elementary school and junior high school she felt she was slower than other students and that she needed more time. She felt different and stressed. She says she is still insecure about spelling and reading aloud. She also expressed insecurity with regard to encountering new situations and leaving familiar settings. She recalls the time of high school graduation as being an especially frightening period:

When I graduated from high school, I didn't know what I would do because I felt so stupid. I had a very good GPA and I still have one, but I didn't think I could go to college because I wasn't smart enough to do the work.

Self-doubt and a feeling of inadequacy continue to be a part of her living experience. She comments that during her studies in interior design she still experiences moments of uncertainty:

I'm very cautious to look up words, sometimes every single word, especially when I'm stressed. [Sometimes I'll] have somebody proofread my work before I hand it in. . . . I think I could do it in the real world, [but] before I would hand anything to a client, I would not have it written in my scribbly writing. I think that would be uncalled for.

In referring to the insights gathered from Giroux, Freire and other critical theorists, my interpretations of Dee's view of school is one that is shaped by a consideration of alienation and resistance.

It seems that Dee's view of school, as shaped by her experiences, revolves around the idea that school is a place of much testing and that this testing transformed her into an object to be labeled and manipulated. She felt victimized by the whims of teachers who decided how she was to be grouped, what she was taught and where she was to go. She also victimized herself by feeling that the problems were her fault and that if she tried harder, put forth more effort, had had tutoring earlier, she would have been "OK." She viewed herself as being a bureaucratic problem. She was an interruption to the schedule and class routine, and she interfered with the efficiency of the educational process. She has had "hall passes all her life"; she is different, alienated and removed. She requires a "pass" in order to gain entrance into the educational game. She lives her life with the fear that the admission may be denied at any point along the way, that she may be designated to remain in the hall and that if that happens it would somehow be her own fault.

Kay

The second young woman, Kay, a 17-year-old high school junior, had also been labeled as having a learning disability and had been placed in a special education resource program while in the first grade and was dismissed from special programs upon completion of fifth grade. Kay's school activities include various school clubs, honor society, track team and theatre. She has a part-time job and engages in an assortment of physical activities ranging from biking to weight lifting.

Kay's school memories are also filled with recollections of extensive and unexplained testing, leaving her feeling like a specimen.

> *I can't remember anyone ever talking to me about the tests. They probably talked to my parents, but I don't know. . . . I sort of felt like a specimen. I just felt like a guinea pig when it came to those books. You know you look at the books or something and you say what is it. And then, not knowing whether it is right or wrong and nobody tells you. . . . I feel like they are deciding. When it comes to the things that I have to do every day, I do feel like everyone is deciding if, you know, what kind of person I am or if. . . . I'm smart. . . . I've been tested so much. I remember those big books. You look at them all the time. The teachers won't tell you if you've done them right or wrong. You're just sitting there all the time.*

Tests are a tremendous source of anxiety for Kay and evoke waves of feelings of self-doubt. She recalls the competency testing in high school as causing her a great deal of fear. She was afraid because she didn't know what to expect, and she wondered whether or not she should hire a tutor in order to do as well as the other students who would be taking the competency test. She also didn't know how to fill out the information section on the test: "I have those little decisions, should I say that I'm this special person or should I go on and act normal?" She was uncertain as to whether or not she should check the learning disabilities box. In retrospect she describes the test as having been as "easy as pie" and she is aggravated with herself for having been so nervous about it. But she says,

> *So, it scares me when I don't know my results on tests and that goes back to learning disabilities. Because when I had LD, I didn't know the results. It's not like it is today, you know your results, PSAT, SAT, and competency. Then I didn't know how I was doing at all.*

With regard to resource class experiences, Kay doesn't remember exactly how she got into it, but does remember it as "not being that bad." Basically, she just feels that she has been through "a lot of schooling."

> *They put me in a resource room and then I started improving. I don't know exactly how I got in there. I might have been tested. . . . I just remember being in there and that I had to go. No one told me why I had to go. I don't remember. I don't remember when I think back to school. I've been through so much school. When I*

think back, I remember going to the classroom and having different special classes and I feel I've had a lot of schooling.

She recalls that being in a resource program did make her feel different and insecure.

I remember being in class and working and I remember one day sitting in there and it was time for me to go to the resource room and everyone asking, "Where are you going?" I felt weird because no one else had to go, except a few other people. I didn't want to go; I wanted to stay in that class. I felt dumb that I had to go to special class. I didn't want anyone to know, or to miss out on something in class and have to catch up.

In retrospect Kay considers the resource experience as having been a positive event in her life. She says, "Then it was bad, but now it's good." This is because the resource program provided her with a condition that she wanted to get away from. When she got out of the resource program, she considered it as having been the accomplishment of a goal that has given her confidence that she might not otherwise have had.

See, I was in there but that gave me, I mean, everyone has a goal in their life, and you see, I've already accomplished one goal. You see, a lot of people haven't done that yet and they're 17, and that was a big goal. And so, like if anyone ever asked me, "What goal have you ever accomplished?" You know, just wondering. They [might] say, "Oh, well. . . . I tried out for and made the theatre." I'd say, "I made the theatre, too, and made the track team, too, and I did everything you did, and I also did one more thing that you didn't do. . . . I got out of the resource room!"

Getting out of the resource room was an achievement and a source of confidence for Kay. She says, "It was an achievement. . . . It was a big responsibility on a little mind, that's exactly what it was. But I'm glad I'm not in it now. Even though I've got my mind now, I'm glad I'm not in there." Part of Kay's "getting her mind" seems to be in being able to fully participate in the educational game. She seems to have fully accepted the necessity for and consequences of the hierarchical competitive structure of school. Although the evaluations inherent in competition are a source of fear and anxiety for her, she tenaciously hangs on to the unquestionable necessity for and legitimacy of competition. She has earned the right to play the game and to act "normal."

Kay was very clear about her label as that of being learning disabled and recalls,

It was a great excuse. . . . I could say, "Well, I have a learning disability, leave me alone! I'll pick it up in a minute. You might pick it up, but I'll pick it up, maybe longer." I was relieved. I was still scared that I wasn't going to do my best, but not as scared.

She views the label as providing her with a sense of relief. Before she had been labeled learning disabled, she couldn't understand what was happening to her or why she couldn't learn in the prescribed way. "I just remember that I couldn't do anything and that I just felt dumb." The learning disability label provided Kay with a reason for her difficulties and a sense that something could be done about them. However, even though it gave her hope, it also carried with it the fear that if she didn't try hard enough, she couldn't be successful. So, in some removed way, it was still somehow her fault but not completely; she was still scared but not as scared.

Interestingly enough, although Kay considers getting out of the resource room as being one of her major life accomplishments, her actual removal from the resource room seems to have been a vague, mysterious process. She recalls, "I was getting tired of it; I didn't want to go anymore. I didn't want to be different. I was ready to get out and I got out." She remembers forgetting to attend her resource classes and the teacher deciding that she probably didn't need to come anymore. She doesn't remember any specific tests or conferences. She just remembers being told that she didn't need resource anymore. She honestly recalls that she forgot about it and then she was told she didn't have to go. So, her achievement was accomplished through an act of passive resistance of which she is not actually conscious.

Basically, Kay regarded her peers as being smarter than she and was fearful that they would think she was dumb. She describes herself as having been friendly with other students, while at the same time feeling removed from them and different. She felt that they thought she was different, but she was even more fearful that others would get the labels confused and think even worse of her.

I was afraid people would get confused. I don't think slow learner is as bad as mentally retarded. If they thought I was mentally retarded, I'd probably freak. I wonder what thought they'd think . . . that I was weird, I strange, or different? I think they thought I was different, not strange or weird.

Kay felt alienated from her regular classroom teachers, describing them as "impatient, old bats. I felt like some teachers were angry with me because it would take [them] longer to explain it to me." Consequently, Kay also felt that she caused a disruption of the daily school and class routine. She felt removed from the flow of the class because she was slower and needed explanations.

Kay's learning disability was considered to be a "family thing" in the sense that the other family members helped Kay. Her mother and sister also participated in local community activities that were aimed at working with the handicapped. Kay recalls that when she went to summer school her mother and sister went with her. She described her mother as being "another tutor who drilled stuff into my head." Generally she felt good about her family involvement and support. The only major conflict that Kay had with her family was concerned with Kay's attending a summer school tutorial program the summer following her dismissal from the resource program. Kay had always resented attending this program and was extremely upset with the idea of having to continue in that program after having been removed from the resource room. Kay sensitively realized that her mother was anxious about whether or not she could succeed without the additional assistance, but Kay recalls, "I was scared, scared enough for both of us."

Feelings of being different and of being fearful permeate Kay's memories regarding herself at the time of placement in a resource room. However, she now perceives herself as being confident, more determined and responsible as a result of her past experiences. She is not concerned with whether others know that she was in a resource program because she feels that most would not believe that she had actually been in the program. She says, "It's fine with me. It makes me feel good that they can't believe I was in there." Kay feels that she has her learning disability "under control" and is determined to keep it from resurfacing. She regards herself as being an example to other learning disabled individuals. "I think I'm an example, not an exception. I don't know anyone like me, but I know there are other people about like me." In a sense, she objectifies herself and places herself on display for others to note. She has committed herself to the rigors of competition and at this moment she is winning. However, I feel that in some ways this activity is displayed for the purpose of proving that she is "normal" or OK. Without being conscious of it, I feel that Kay senses that she is in a period of remission and that there is always an underlying fear that she might experience a relapse that would cause her disability to surface. I view her frantic achievement-oriented actions as being an attempt to construct a "buffer" in order to ward off the potential reoccurrence of the disease.

In general Kay's view of school is that of being a place that is to be approached with suspicion—a place where there is a lot of testing and where people are deciding about you and keeping the results hidden. School is a place where one is examined impersonally and made to feel like a specimen. She felt objectified by the testing process and alienated from herself and others as a result of that process. Decisions were being made about her in which she had no participation or awareness. She was labeled and officially recognized as being different. She sensed that she was somehow to blame for her problems and felt that if she tried hard enough to "act normal" that she would be OK. School is a place where Kay has learned well the lesson of winners and losers. She has absorbed that lesson into her very soul. She views her determined acts as being the safeguards that will hopefully enable her to remain on the winning side. She senses, but does not give voice to, the possibility that this game of "acting normal" could collapse and she would once again find herself disabled.

The evolving worldview of these two women, as having been shaped by their school experiences as a result of having been labeled and placed in special educational programs, seems to be one that is interpenetrated with themes of alienation and resistance. Their alienation from self and others is manifest in the fear and suspicion they experience in various concrete and abstract situations. Their fears are concretely recognized in testing situations and classroom settings in which the circumstances for success or failure are more or less clearly established. Voiced fears of general failure, time limitations and testing seem to be consciously recognized, but their expressions are not the consciously recognized voices of resistance!

The more subtle forms of alienation seem to be more abstractly formulated in feelings of anxiety. There is a vague sense of discomfort that seems to haunt both of these young women as they move through their lives wondering where, when, or if their existing reality is going to collapse, leaving their disabilities exposed. They walk on the border-line, "acting normal" but always carrying their "hall passes." They are extremely vulnerable to the possibility of being "found out" and consequently being denied access to commonly agreed upon conditions of competition in which meaning is constructed in our schools and our greater society. They live with an unvoiced anxiety that accompanies them in the form of doubt.

They are alienated from themselves in the sense that they doubt their authenticity and are constantly seeking validation from external sources. The ever present nagging doubt has damaged their sense of self-worth; their dignity has been diminished by doubt. They are alienated from others as a result of not being able to name themselves; they are officially recognized as being different. In Tillich's (1952) sense of the "courage to be," they have been denied the dignity which would have allowed them to construct the meaning that would have enabled them to "be as oneself." In so doing, they are denied the possibility of constructing meaning as "being as oneself" in community. They are robbed of dignity and ultimately alienated form self and others. They have been objectified and denied the opportunity of reciprocally engaging in relationships in which there is the possibility of dynamic interchange between subjects.

The theme of resistance, manifest as an attempt to hold on to one's dignity and to affirm oneself as a human being with the right to name oneself, is apparent in the few but persistent acts of not accepting the prescribed labels and placements. Although not so apparent to themselves or others, both women resisted attempts by authorities to completely determine their fate. Passively forgetting to attend the resource program, not fully recognizing the label that had been prescribed and actively confronting teachers about academic groupings are examples of acts of resistance. In spite of these few acts, it seems that a worldview dominated by a sense of alienation prevails. The anguish of this alienation is made more painful as one recognizes that neither Kay nor Dee is able to name her condition.

Their worldview is one in which the hegemony, transmission-productivity, educational paradigm is reflected. Dee and Kay have been perceived by others and themselves as being on the margin and, in wishing and hoping to be admitted, have not questioned seriously the existing flaws in the dominant structure as reflected in the educational system. They have not examined the value of the conditions that enable one to construct meaning or that allow one to be received into the school hierarchy. They have internalized the ethic of competition and abide by the rules of evaluation which determine one's worth. The diagnostic-prescriptive educational view has contributed to their further oppression as they perceive their own problems and difficulties within a psychological framework. They are unable to place themselves within the social context by constructing a history that is sociologically framed. They are the victims of the productivity-transmission rationality, and they have internalized the consciousness of their oppressors. Dee and Kay are alienated in their isolation. Their acts of resistance have been precarious efforts to become a part of the dignity-denying, oppressive structure that further intensifies their anxiety and insecurity.

These stories reach far beyond our typical educational concerns regarding positive self-esteem to much more serious and wrenching problems of marginality, exclusion and alienation. The voices of Dee and Kay call into our consciousness the responsibility we have as educators for responding to and embracing those who come before us, the animal faces, the empty faces and the noble ones alike. Their stories cause us to confront the inconsistencies in our educational practices in which we purposefully seek to exclude and avoid the misshapen and empty ones. The voices of these two women point out that our good intentions and our focus upon productivity and competition are handicapping evils that we can no longer afford to avoid. Camus cautions us regarding the consequences of such a lack of scrutiny:

> On the whole, men are more good than bad; that however isn't the real point; but they are more or less ignorant, and it is this that we call vice or virtue; the most incorrigible vice being that of ignorance that fancies it knows everything and therefore claims for itself the right to kill. The soul of the murderer is blind; and there can be no true goodness nor true love without the utmost clear-sightedness. (Camus, 1972, p. 124)

We must examine our taken-for-granted practice of meeting those who come before us. Our good intention as expressed in our educational desire to help has degenerated into the practice of sorting, labeling and tracking special education students so that we can provide them with what we refer to, from an unexamined position, as being the most appropriate and specialized instruction. This must be revealed as the dignity-denying and alienating process it is. In assuming that we know everything, we have claimed the right to kill, we dismiss the already disenfranchised and we blame them for their disempowerment. We must look more closely at our medical model of help and reappraise our notion of successful education as it is currently understood in terms of utility, productivity and competition. Evaluation and competition, the prized elements of today's educational practice, need to be exposed for the roles they play in establishing and maintaining the educational hierarchy, a hierarchy that systematically excludes and dismisses vast numbers of our students and prevents them from obtaining the promised "keys to the kingdom" as they participate in the educational obstacle course.

As we listen to the voices of the handicapped expressing their moral outrage at being labeled and excluded, the taken-for-granted assumptions that this process is the "lesser of evils" or in the "best interest" of those being identified begins to turn on itself. The unexamined acceptance of competition and productivity also begins to surface as we listen to the outrage of those who have been denied access to success as a result of an inability to compete and/or produce. In hearing the stories of Dee and Kay, we take a second look at our good intentions and the ways in which we respond to those who come before us. Currently, who you are and how far you go on the educational hierarchy depends upon how much you can produce and what you can do. In special education, no matter how much we talk about enabling one to aspire to his/her full potential, the current framework for success, specifically competition and productivity, ultimately requires that some of us will be more highly prized and valued in this system than others. Some of us have more worth and greater potential as competitors and producers than others and therefore will be the recipients of the educational rewards and benefits at the cost of those who have been excluded.

The voices of the labeled, when contemplated critically and when examined with clear-sightedness, affirm the insights of Maria Montessori as she discusses the rewards and punishments of educational competition and productivity:

> . . . in school there is only one prize for all those of good will who enter the race, a fact that generates pride, envy and rivalries instead of that thrill coming from effort, humility and love which all can experience. In this way we create conflict not simply between school and social progress but also between the school and religion. One day a child will ask himself if the prizes won at school were not rather obstacles on the way to eternal life, or if the punishments with which he was humiliated when he was in no position to defend himself did not make him one of those "hungering" and thirsting after justice. . . . (Montessori, 1976, pp. 13 and 14)

The stories of our handicapped, the misshapen, the empty faces and the animal faces, poignantly reveal the injustice that is manifest in our current educational practice grounded in competition and production, which serve exclusive ends.

The critical consciousness of emancipatory praxis, which has given us the "clear-sightedness" to examine our "good intentions," has also provided us with the tools to begin to rethink the educational values of productivity and competition. Thus the anguish of the handicapped is felt as we recognize that the vehicles of educational success are denied them. The handicapped personify the greater failings of the transmission, productivity ethic in educational practice. Regardless of how well we sort, track and label, many of our handicapped will remain unable to participate in the educational game. As educators, many of us avoid a deeper examination of the failing of the handicapped because it highlights the more profound alienation of our general educational practices. Namely, the handicapped point out the inadequacy of remediation and the futility of help when help and remediation are placed within a context of evaluation, competition and utility.

To become clear-sighted so that we as educators do not sustain a fundamentally evil practice seems to be the message illuminated by the anguish, hegemony and confusion of Dee and Kay. The process of becoming clear-sighted appropriately addresses the educational needs of many of our labeled students who are disproportionately represented in our underclasses by racial and ethnic minorities and are frequently the victims of poverty.

The educational response would be one of engaging in dialogue for the purpose of facilitating the conversation out of which students could acquire more language with which to begin to name themselves and their experiences. Finding one's voice and naming oneself as oppressed and outraged rather than slow, strange, weird or different offers the opportunity to criticize the existing educational hierarchy and to move beyond the defeating cycle of blaming the victim for failure. As Freire points out,

> Only when the people of a dependent society break out of the culture of silence and win their right to speak—only, that is when radical structural changes transform the dependent society—can such a society as a whole cease to be silent toward the director society. (Freire 1985, p. 73)

This is a liberating pedagogy based upon finding one's voice while engaging in critical dialogue about one's actions and experiences and which can result in sustained critical reflection, examined practice and empowerment.

It seems that fostering a critical consciousness is truly a noble educational ideal and one toward which the acts of teaching ought to be directed. After all, it is Dewey who writes, "We are free to the degree in which we act knowing what we are about" (Dewey 1929, p. 250). Further, Dewey reminds us,

> Genuine freedom, in short is intellectual; it rests in the trained power of thought, in ability to "turn things over" to look at matters deliberately, to judge the amount and kind of evidence requisite for decision is at hand, and if not, to tell where and how to seek such evidence. (Dewey, 1934, p. 67)

For many teachers and students alike, educational aims grounded in dialogue and critical consciousness offer the hope of freedom and empowerment.

However, just as many handicapped individuals are alienated by their inability to produce and compete, so too are they excluded by the empowerment process that requires rational, critical, logical and expressive skills that many handicapped people lack. Consequently, they may remain in the precarious care of the emancipated who may or may not view them affectionately. The vulnerable population of the handicapped, who lack the intellectual and emotional capacities necessary to participate in the empowering relationship and emancipating dialogue, remain excluded and voiceless.

As John Merrick, the Elephant Man, screams, "I am a human being!" and as the mentally retarded adolescent boy coloring a Thanksgiving picture asks, "Am I a people?" while the aide taunts him by saying, "Turkey, color yourself! Turkey!", one becomes painfully aware that the anguish expressed here comes from a much more fundamental exclusion. It is an exclusion that has resulted not in a damaged self-concept or a lowered self-esteem but in the denial of one's human dignity. The outrage and pain expressed by the handicapped as they come up against the competitive, productive sorting practice of our educational structure are a response to their objectification and a resistance to their being denied the relationship within which they can be affirmed.

In reexamining our good intentions in light of the exclusion of the handicapped that takes place not only as a result of the production-transmission-competition values of traditional educational practice but also occurs within the empowering thrust of critical pedagogy, one begins to rethink the purpose of teaching and the composition of help. If the fundamental starting point, as the Elephant Man suggests, is the recognition of our humanity, then the character of help changes radically. The task of facing those who come before us is one of recognizing and beholding them as valued and cherished human beings. Help becomes not an act of fixing, imposing or shaping but instead one of love, commitment and responsibility. This is not to be trivialized or sentimentalized but to be gravely contemplated.

We are humbled and sobered by the words of Abraham Heschel as he addresses a class of graduating nursing students. Although he recognizes the nobility of all "helping" professions and affirms those who choose to do such work, he seriously reminds us of the sacredness and weight of genuine help when he says, "We must never forget that when we truly wish to help our fellow human beings we must remove our shoes, for the ground we walk upon, when we seek to help, is sacred ground."

Help is not prescriptive; we do not know nor can we determine how someone else should be; however, within a partnership we might foster the care and compassion with which to affirm each other's dignity. The teaching-helping act is a calling to participate in the partnership in such a way that we do not diminish our capacity to confirm or be confirmed. The educational mission and calling require action that passionately propels us to engage in the mystery. Such engagement leaves us with awe and wonder, enabling us to become aware of the mystery but never resulting in our comprehension of it. Heschel writes,

> Awe is an intuition for the dignity of all things, a realization that things not only are what they are but also stand, however remotely, for something supreme. Awe is a sense for the transcendence, for the reference everywhere to mystery beyond all things . . . what we cannot comprehend by analysis, we become aware of in awe. (Heschel, 1965, pp. 88–89)

"With an intuition for the dignity of all things," we must face those who come before us, recognizing the wonder and the mystery. The alienation of Dee and Kay, the anguish of the Elephant Man and the confusion of the young man inquiring into his humanity direct us to the fundamental ground upon which the acts of teaching rest. The voices and the faces of the handicapped require us to center ourselves as educators within the caring acts of love that illuminate the questions that deal with who we are and what we are about. We must be prepared to meet and receive those who come before us, the empty, the misshapen and the noble, not to make them less misshapen or more noble but so that we may each gain a deeper understanding of what it means to be here or at least to be able to wonder why.

This wondering process and its significance are poetically and simply illustrated by Albert in Alice Walker's *The Color Purple*. As Albert grapples with the dilemma of why we suffer, why we are men or women he concludes that "it don't mean nothing if you don't ask why you here, period." He goes on to say,

> I think us here to wonder, myself. To wonder. To ast. And that in wondering bout the big things and asting bout the big things, you learn about the little ones, almost by accident. But you never know nothing more about the big things than you start out with. The more I wonder, he say, the more I love. (Walker, 1982, p. 247)

In our more reflective moments, the examination of the exclusion of the handi- capped enables us to seriously contemplate educational theories, policies and prac- tices. The recognition of the marginality and the hegemony of these individuals as they deny who they are as they strive for inclusion enables us to wonder. Their existence and their resistance help us to focus upon the big questions, finding the pieces that address the smaller ones in the process. The handicapped challenge us and remind us that we are here to wonder why! Their presence requires us to ponder the tensions and the paradoxes.

So where are we? If educational aims and ideals should be generated from a platform of love and affirmation of human dignity rather than from the existing positivistic, technical, productive, competitive frameworks, then is there not a cry for a different way of conceptualizing and conversing about our educational theory and practice? If we take seriously the voices of Dee and Kay, then do we not have a responsibility for attempting to construct a liberating and empowering pedagogy? Further, if the screams of the Elephant Man and the confusion of the mentally retarded adolescent have any significance, then what is it educationally that we can no longer afford to leave to chance?

We must take clear-sighted action and be willing to accept the responsibility for the risk we take as we turn toward a different discourse and as we turn away from the technical language that frames our existing view of educational practice. As Philip Jackson points out, if we do not examine the serious problems of our current educa- tional practice with an intent to do more than just remediate the symptom, then we may, through our good intentions, be repairing a structure that is moving in the wrong direction:

> After all, it is easier to put oil on squeaky wheels than to ask about where the vehicle is headed in the first place and to ponder the necessity of a change in direction. The danger of course, is that by so doing we may create a smoothly running machine that is moving in the wrong direction or not at all. (Noll, 1987, p. 111)

In light of the dilemmas illuminated while reflecting upon issues of inclusion, affirmation, love and help within the context of special education, it seems apparent that the current technical language, although facilitating a superficially smoothly functioning practice, ultimately highlights a vacuum. Technically framed educational discourse does not have the words for contemplating relationship, compassion or confirmation. It points to an empty, lifeless void, one in which we are inarticulate and illiterate when it comes to dignity-talk, which Donald Vandenberg refers to as "talk of the heart." "It may be that dignity-talk is less intelligible to the intellect than to the heart" (Vandenberg, 1983, p. 31). We can no longer ignore the evil that is being perpetuated by our unexamined good intentions. We must at the risk of appearing "sentimental, fuzzy and pious, thereby repelling many of our readers, (Macdonald & Purpel, 1987, p. 186), turn to the religious language that allows us to begin to voice love, relationship and justice.

It becomes apparent that whatever action we take, it entails moral responsibility. We are as responsible for our unexamined good intentions as we are for our clear-sighted ones. We, as educators, must have the courage to move from a naive, unexamined position of neutral, technical, objective, lifeless practice to intellectually and compassionately responsible action framed by spiritual discourse. Such discourse enables us to examine our good intentions and to change our direction.

REFERENCES

Buber, M. (1965). *Between man and man*. New York: Macmillan Publishing Company.

Camus, A. (1972). *The plague*. New York: Vintage Books.

Dewey, J. (1929). *The quest for certainty: A study of the relation of knowledge and action*. New York: Minton, Balch and Company.

Dewey, J. (1934). *A common faith*. New Haven: Yale University Press.

Freire, P. (1985). *Politics of education*. New York: The Continuum Publishing Company.

Giroux, H. A. (1983). *Theory and resistance in education: A pedagogy for the opposition*. South Hadley, MA: Bergin and Garvey Publishers, Inc.

Gress, J., & Purpel, D. E. (1978). *Curriculum: An introduction to the field*. Berkeley, CA: McCutchan Publishing Corporation.

Heschel, A. J. (1965). *Who is man?* Stanford, CA: Stanford University Press.

Macdonald, J. B., & Purpel, D. E. (1987). *Curriculum and planning visions and metaphors. Journal of Curriculum and Supervision*, 2(2), 178–192.

Montessori, M. (1976). *The discovery of the child*. New York: Ballantine Books.

Noll, J. W. (1987). *Taking sides: Clashing views on controversial educational issues*. Guilford, CT: The Dushkin Publishing Group, Inc.

Tillich, P. (1952). *The courage to be*. New Haven: Yale University Press.

Vandenberg, D. (1983). *Human rights in education*. New York: Philosophical Library, Inc.

Walker, A. (1982). *The color purple*. New York: Washington Square Press.

Curriculum and Teaching: Dangers and Dreams

This book has so far mostly dealt with broad social, cultural, and educational issues and policies that emerge from social theories, economic models, intellectual paradigms, and historical forces. In this section we extend the theme of the connections between social-cultural forces and educational issues to the classroom, to the issues of curriculum and teaching. We are concerned here with the theories and orientations that inform the most basic of all pedagogical questions: What should we teach? Since these questions cannot be separated from instructional considerations, we also include materials on vital questions concerning the role of teachers in the struggle for significant educational reform.

The field of curriculum studies reflects the major cultural and educational trends of the times. The 1960s and early 1970s were times of major curriculum innovation, although it would be misleading to characterize the era as a radical one for curriculum. In fact, a great deal of the change was directed at revitalizing the traditional school disciplines, particularly science and mathematics, with some significant concern for foreign languages. It was the aftermath of the American reaction to Sputnik, the first space satellite, interpreted as a sign of Soviet educational superiority. Interestingly, much of this curriculum movement was directed at encouraging student creativity and deep understanding, as represented in the popularity of such terms as *problem solving* and *problem posing, discovery,* and *structure* (a marked contrast to the current emphasis on *mastery* and *mini-*

mum competencies). This curriculum movement was greatly aided by significant funding from the federal government and from foundations. In addition, many major universities were deeply involved in these efforts, as prominent academics helped develop curriculum materials. Some of these materials gained wide national distribution and acceptance, in part because they were of a very high academic quality. These packages were often given alphabetic signatures—for example, SMSG (School Mathematics Study Group), PSSC (Physical Science Study Committee), and BSCS (Biological Sciences Curriculum Study)—and often included sophisticated content (e.g., "the new math"), pedagogy (e.g., a stress on experiential and inductive learning), and teaching materials such as films.

At about the same time, there was renewed interest in elementary education, some of it directed at such organizational and structural aspects as team teaching and nongraded instruction. However, there was also considerable interest in imaginative curriculum "packages" designed for younger children, particularly in science, mathematics, and foreign languages. The most famous innovation in elementary education, however, was an orientation that came to be known as "open education." Never a coherent and definable theory, this orientation nonetheless did have a number of identifying themes, for example, concern for individual rates and modes of learning, experiential learning, stress on learning rather than instruction, concern for student responsibility, fluid structure, and so on.

These interesting and imaginative projects were to become victims of the general cultural and educational backlash of the 1970s and 1980s. However creative these curriculum reforms of the 1950s and 1960s may have been, they never seriously challenged the basic structural dimensions of educational ideology, although they did raise questions about some well-established practices within the existing structure. However, even if we accept these reforms as provocative and challenging, their impact on the schools was very slight. Indeed, their failure to have a major effect on the schools led many curriculum theorists to the bleak land of disenchantment. The development of the curriculum packages of the 1950s and 1960s had been to some extent the realization of the theorist's fantasy—to bring together bright, knowledgeable, and creative people; a large budget; and a commitment to modern pedagogic insights. The disenchantment emerged from the realization that even with the availability of wonderful curriculum materials, the schools maintained their steady course of conformity and competition. What many educators came to recognize was that what schools teach and what students learn goes beyond what is contained in course syllabi and lesson plans. The focus of curriculum research shifted from issues of content and technique to the school's structure, ideology, intent, and values—to what is called the "hidden curriculum."

The reality of the way in which curriculum and teaching are shaped by social forces can be seen vividly in the enormous popularity of the back-to-basics movement of the 1970s and 1980s. This movement, with its renewed emphasis on mastery, achievement, and discipline and with its concern for knowledge retention, cultural transmission, and teacher control, mirrors society's backlash to the cultural stirrings of the 1960s—the antiwar movement, the struggle for civil rights, and the pressures for participatory democracy. Those who saw these activities as destabilizing and threatening included schools on the list of contributing offenders. The mildly interesting educational innovations were seen as promoting permissiveness, if not license; insufficient structure, if not chaos; laxity, if not sloth.

Simultaneous with the cultural backlash came the severe recession of the 1970s, and with it the end of the consciousness of continuous and boundless economic growth. A new cycle of fear, protectiveness, and resentment culminated in a climate of renewed narcissism, greed, and hyperindividuality. The metaphors of the 1970s shifted from growth to "steady state," from making peace and love simply to "making it." The language of educational reform shifted correspondingly from such terms as *discovery, structure, self-paced*, and *creativity* to *accountability, competence tests, mastery*, and *excellence*. In a more hostile and economically competitive world, what was needed, according to our leaders, was a leaner, tougher, more skilled work force not enervated by the seductions of freedom and choice. Life is tough and real, they say in so many words, and there are serious competitors out there willing and eager to work harder, to endure more, and to compete more ruthlessly. These people are succeeding because America has grown soft and flabby, the consequences of a permissive and lazy educational system. Educators thought much less about Deweyan democracy and much more about social Darwinism; they shifted their interests from Bruner's notions of structures of learning to Skinner's ideas about maximizing learning.

For curriculum theorists this was an era with only two games in town. One involved the dreary, reactionary, and anti-intellectual efforts to improve the technology of instruction—or more precisely, to find ways in which students could do well on tests. The other challenge was the much more intellectually rewarding and productive one of critically analyzing the social and cultural context and meaning of curriculum. A great deal of this work has been enormously helpful, insightful, and liberating (as reflected in many of the selections in this collection), but until recently curriculum critics tended to maintain an analytic posture and to slight the continuously important task of affirming an educational program congruent with a cultural and social vision. One of the exciting portents of hope is the relatively recent emergence of a third body of work, that is, a spate of bold, creative, and affirmative curriculum theorizing (some included in this section).

There clearly has been a creative burst of energy directed at fundamental changes in how curriculum should be conceptualized and developed. However, there is an important anomaly associated with these efforts: Even as we ritualistically support and venerate teaching, we continue to marginalize teachers. Largely absent from major educational policy-making and theorizing to this date is concern for what one would think is an absolutely critical dimension of educational policy—the role of the teacher. What do we make of this failure to include teachers (both as contributors and as concerns) in the creation of new educational theory? This puzzling omission of teachers' perspectives and presence in major decision making is pervasive. Time after time, the major reports, commission findings, legislation, and so on are written and directed by groups with only nominal teacher representation. Why would this be so?

In truth, society is ambivalent about teachers (and education). Society demands a great deal from teachers but allocates to them very few resources. We demand high-quality teachers but tend to encourage our ablest students to seek other, more lucrative and prestigious professions. We put our children in teachers' care but tend to demean educators. We demand professional expertise but deny them professional autonomy. We are not sure whether teaching really ought to be a profession, whether education is too important to be left to the educators.

And what of teachers themselves? In spite of powerful organizations such as the National Education Association and the American Federation of Teachers, teachers generally have failed to develop a strong professional voice, one powerful enough to have an impact on broad educational policy. In many locales, teachers' organizations have been allowed (often grudgingly) to participate in decisions regarding salary and working conditions. In addition, national organizations can exercise considerable lobbying clout in many legislative arenas. Despite these gains, however, teachers tend to be neither proactive in determining public policy nor a force in shaping educational theory, although there are a number of encouraging signs of change. In many communities teachers are organizing themselves on a grass-roots basis to produce teaching materials, develop networks, produce newsletters, and so on. In addition there is a small but growing movement to allow teachers more autonomy in schools.

The readings in this section are designed to give some insight into the reasons for the general situation and to suggest how teachers can acquire power. In the first selection Michael Apple uses the lens of social class and gender to clarify the plight of teachers. He describes how a systematic program of tighter and tighter control has increasingly "de-skilled" and "proletarianized" the teaching profession. He believes that the intense concern for more efficiency and control has led to more emphasis on testing and competence-based instruction and that the emphasis on predetermined objectives has increased teachers' managerial work. This development in turn has undermined the efforts of teachers to focus on curriculum development and on adopting personally appropriate teaching styles. The addition of long-standing gender discrimination has resulted in a teaching force that is increasingly powerless, divided, and demoralized.

Henry A. Giroux examines the implications of an increasingly de-skilled teaching profession for an education directed at personal empowerment and social justice. He criticizes the strongly technical and instrumental orientation toward teacher education as well as the tendency to separate teachers from policy-making. Giroux's position is that teachers should (and can) be involved in critical political reflection and thereby actually participate in "making the pedagogical more political and the political more pedagogical." In this view, teachers should not be passive technicians implementing policies but "transformative intellectuals" participating in the struggle for a more just society.

David E. Purpel compares teachers to a conscripted army because they are asked to perform nobly and heroically but are undertrained, overworked, underpaid, and underutilized. He writes of the huge gulf between the enormity of real social problems and the trivial nature of proposed educational reforms. More particularly, he offers specific suggestions on how teachers can be actively involved in raising the appallingly low quality of public discourse on education.

The selections that stress issues of curriculum and instruction (as opposed to the teachers' role) are varied in their approach but share a common view: The conventional curriculum is at best maladaptive and at worst a contributor to our social and cultural crises. H. Svi Shapiro links his curriculum analysis to the work of one of the foremost cultural critics of our time, Christopher Lasch. Lasch has written eloquently and powerfully about an increasingly narcissistic culture in which people focus on their own minimal needs for survival in a highly personalistic and hedonistic manner. Shapiro sees a connection between a curriculum that focuses on so-called basic skills, which he calls "individual-adaptive," and a trend that Lasch notes permeates our present culture—defensive competition, that is, working to avoid pain rather than trying positively to achieve pleasure. Shapiro sees current curriculum as a model not for seeking meaning, but rather for providing a way for students to develop only the minimum skills needed to cope individually with a difficult environment. In contrast to this negative mode of individual survival, Shapiro suggests a positive, community-oriented curriculum that would stress the achievement of critical social understanding, which can enhance personal empowerment in the service of social reform.

Even though educational critics from the left have written for years about the ideological nature of the curriculum, this point, ironically enough, came into public consciousness mostly through the efforts of the "new right." It was Ronald Reagan after all (echoing the analysis of the hidden curriculum) who proclaimed on innumerable occasions that the schools could not be value-neutral. The issues had shifted from *whether* schools should be ideological to *which* ideology should be reflected. This shift has had the salutary effect of moving (at least in some places) the discourse of curriculum away from technical instructional concerns to those of basic cultural and social significance. The change is reflected in a critique of two highly influential books by two highly influential educational theorists. Stanley Aronowitz and Henry A. Giroux present serious social as well as educational criticism of *The Closing of the American Mind* by Allan Bloom and *What Every American Needs to Know* by E. D. Hirsch, Jr.

Aronowitz and Giroux see these books as heavily and determinedly ideological, as polemics for an America founded on a common cultural tradition. In their critique, they warn that these books reflect an elitist and anti-democratic orientation with hints of racism and sexism. They claim that the cry for higher cultural and academic standards is an aspect of a political orientation that sees chaos where others see freedom and moral laxity where others see cultural relativity. Aronowitz and Giroux accuse Hirsch and Bloom of ignoring the critical question of how power is distributed, and thereby promoting a culture of elitism, privilege, and exclusivity. It is their view that by focusing on the traditional canon, Bloom and Hirsch opt not to enhance the richness and diversity of the culture, and thereby implicitly reject the vision of an informed, critically literate population prepared to transform rather than merely perpetuate the status quo.

Maxine Greene is a philosopher who has focused on the dangers of a taken-for-granted reality, one in which people, rich and poor, advantaged and disadvantaged, accept their lives as inevitable and permanent. She has energetically and passionately championed the study of the humanities and the arts as powerful educational agents for challenging this sense of futility and unawareness. In this selection Greene focuses on education for freedom and choice, which she urges us to see as involving "relatedness, communication, and disclosure." Curriculum for her needs to be grounded in the kind of critical and creative thinking that allows us both to be aware of existing multiple perspectives and to be open to new realities and dimensions. Her educational ideas allow for traditional as well as emerging areas of study—for example, history *and* popular music; classical literature *and* contemporary novels by women and blacks—as long as they reveal, awaken, and intensify our awareness and our possibilities. Schools in Greene's vision can become forceful and creative institutions of continuous re-searching and risk taking rather than purveyors of safety and conventional wisdom.

The last selection, "Education in a Prophetic Voice," is a chapter from David E. Purpel's book *The Moral and Spiritual Crisis in Education*. Purpel sees the problems of education as primarily moral and spiritual and urges educators and the public to respond imaginatively to the enormous issues of our era. He speaks directly to a new curriculum paradigm, one that provides a moral framework and cultural vision to ground a new set of curriculum goals. This curriculum framework seeks to address in moral and educational terms the horrors of global hunger, worldwide suffering, nuclear nightmare, and ecological catastrophes.

The critiques that emerge from the articles in this section of the book suggest several important issues for educators. The selections all indicate that considerations of school reform must be seen in systematic terms. Issues of curriculum, educational policy, social priorities, and cultural goals are intertwined and hence must be addressed as a whole, not compartmentally. Moreover, these chapters reveal a deep dissatisfaction with the quality of the current so-called educational reform movement, which seems for the most part to focus (at best) on short-term amelioration rather than on long-term transformation. Higher pay for teachers will not improve the quality of teaching if they are forced to submit to a narrowly conceived and control-oriented evaluation. A policy of rigid planning and frequent testing is antithetical to the development of a fundamental shift in the curriculum.

The selections reflect significant changes in scholarly approaches to the study of curriculum and the analysis of the teacher's role. There is clearly a rejection of Tylerian thinking, with its emphases on clearly stated goals, resonant techniques, and close testing and measurement. In its place is a concern about the "hidden curriculum," a concept that reflects a much broader sense of the social, political, and cultural implications of the curriculum. Moreover, this concern reflects a change in the tremendous reliance educators have placed on the social sciences. In these selections, we see perspectives other than those of psychology and sociology. We see instead aesthetic, philosophical, and moral viewpoints used to provide insight and understanding.

We also see a new orientation toward teaching, one that moves away from the concept of the teacher as an applied psychologist, a master craftsperson, and an expert in the skills of diagnosing students' needs and prescribing appropriate pedagogical responses. Instead we see the concept of the teacher as an intellectual involved in educational ideology, social leadership, and cultural transformation. Most important, these selections contain not only critiques but also alternative perspectives of considerable imagination and boldness. They bring excitement and hope to the project of recreating life in the classroom and the possibility of transforming schools into educational rather than socializing institutions.

Controlling the Work of Teachers

Michael Apple

PROLETARIANIZATION: CLASS AND GENDER

An examination of changes in class composition over the past two decades points out something quite dramatically. The process of proletarianization has had a large and consistent effect. There has been a systematic tendency for those positions with relatively little control over their labor process to expand during this time period. At the same time, there was a decline in positions with high levels of autonomy.[1]

This should not surprise us. In fact, it would be unusual if this did not occur, especially now. In a time of general stagnation and of crises in accumulation and legitimation, we should expect that there will also be attempts to further rationalize managerial structures and increase the pressure to proletarianize the labor process. This pressure is not inconsequential to educators, both in regard to the kinds of positions students will find available (or not available) after completing (or not completing) schooling, and also in regard to the very conditions of working within education itself. The labor of what might be called 'semi-autonomous employees' will certainly feel the impact of this. Given the fiscal crisis of the state, this impact will be felt more directly among state employees such as teachers as well. One should expect to see a rapid growth of plans and pressures for the rationalization of administration and labor within the state itself.[2] This is one of the times when one's expectations will not be disappointed.

In earlier work, I argued that teachers have been involved in a long but now steadily increasing restructuring of their jobs. I claimed that they were more and more faced with the prospect of being deskilled because of the encroachment of technical control procedures into the curriculum in schools. The integration together of manage-

From *Teachers and Texts* by Michael Apple. Reprinted with permission of Routledge.

ment systems, reductive behaviorally based curricula, pre-specified teaching 'competencies' and procedures and student responses, and pre and post testing, was leading to a loss of control and a separation of conception from execution. In sum, the labor process of teaching was becoming susceptible to processes similar to those that led to the proletarianization of many other blue-, pink-, and white-collar jobs. I suggested that this restructuring of teaching had important implications given the contradictory class location of teachers.[3]

When I say that teachers have a contradictory class location, I am *not* implying that they are by definition within the middle classes, or that they are in an ambiguous position somehow 'between' classes. Instead, along with Wright, I am saying that it is wise to think of them as located simultaneously in two classes. They thus share the interests of both the petty bourgeoisie and the working class.[4] Hence, when there is a fiscal crisis in which many teachers are faced with worsening working conditions, layoffs, and even months without being paid—as has been the case in a number of urban areas in the United States—and when their labor is restructured so that they lose control, it is possible that these contradictory interests will move closer to those of other workers and people of color who have historically been faced with the use of similar procedures by capital and the state.[5]

Yet, teachers are not only classed actors. They are gendered actors as well—something that is too often neglected by investigators. This is a significant omission. A striking conclusion is evident from the analyses of proletarianization. In every occupational category, *women* are more apt to be proletarianized than men. This could be because of sexist practices of recruitment and promotion, the general tendency to care less about the conditions under which women labor, the way capital has historically colonized patriarchal relations, the historical relation between teaching and domesticity, and so on. Whatever the reason, it is clear that a given position may be more or less proletarianized depending on its relationship to the sexual division of labor.[6]

In the United States, it is estimated that over 90 percent of women's (paid) work falls into four basic categories: (1) employment in 'peripheral' manufacturing industries and retail trades, and considerably now in the expanding but low-paid service sector of the economy; (2) clerical work; (3) health and education; and (4) domestic service. Most women in, say, the United States and the United Kingdom are concentrated in either the lowest-paid positions in these areas or at the bottom of the middle-pay grades when there has been some mobility.[7] One commentator puts it both bluntly and honestly: 'The evidence of discrimination against women in the labour market is considerable and reading it is a wearing experience.'[8]

This pattern is, of course, largely reproduced within education. Even given the years of struggle by progressive women and men, the figures—most of which will be quite familiar to many of you—are depressing. While the overwhelming majority of school teachers are women (a figure that becomes even higher in the primary and elementary schools), many more men are heads or principals of primary and elementary schools, despite the proportion of women teachers.[9] As the vertical segregation of the workforce increased, this proportion actually increased in inequality. In the United States in 1928, women accounted for 55 percent of the elementary school principalships. Today, with nearly 90 percent of the teaching force in elementary schools being women, they account for only 20 percent of principals.[10] This pattern has strong historical roots—roots that cannot be separated from the larger structures of class and patriarchy outside the school.

In this chapter, I shall want to claim that unless we see the connections between these two dynamics—class and gender—we cannot understand the history of and current attempts at rationalizing education or the roots and effects of proletarianization on teaching itself. Not all teaching can be unpacked by examining it as a labor process or as a class phenomenon, though as I have tried to demonstrate in some of my previous work much of it is made clearer when we integrate it into theories of and changes in class position and the labor process. Neither can all of teaching be understood as totally related to patriarchy, though why it is structured the way it is is due in very large part to the history of male dominance and gender struggles,[11] a history I shall discuss in considerably more detail in the next chapter. The two dynamics of class and gender (with race, of course) are not reducible to each other, but intertwine, work off, and codetermine the terrain on which each operates. It is at the intersection of these two dynamics that one can begin to unravel some of the reasons why procedures for rationalizing the work of teachers have evolved. As we shall see, the ultimate effects of these procedures, with the loss of control that accompanies them, can bear in important ways on how we think about the 'reform' of teaching and curriculum and the state's role in it.

ACADEMIC KNOWLEDGE AND CURRICULAR CONTROL

So far I have made a number of general claims about the relationship between proletarianization and patriarchy in the constitution of teaching. I want to go on to suggest ways we can begin to see this relationship in operation. Some sense of the state's role in sponsoring changes in curricular and teaching practice in the recent past is essential here.

The fact that schools have tended to be largely organized around male leadership and female teachers is simply that—a social fact—unless one realizes that this means that educational authority relations have been formally patriarchal. As in the home and the office, male dominance is there; but teachers—like wives, mothers, clerical workers, and other women engaged in paid and unpaid labor—have carved out spheres of power and control in their long struggle to gain some autonomy. This autonomy only becomes a problem for capital and the state when what education is for needs revision.

To take one example outside of education: in offices clerical work is in the process of being radically transformed with the introduction of word-processing technologies, video display terminals, and so on. Traditional forms of control—ones usually based on the dominance of the male boss—are being altered. Technical control, where one's work is deskilled and intensified by the 'impersonal' machinery in the office, has made significant inroads. While certainly not eliminating patriarchal domination, it has in fact provided a major shift in the terrain on which it operates. Capital has found more efficient modes of control than overt patriarchal authority.[12]

Similar changes have occurred in schools. In a time when the needs of industry for technical knowledge and technically trained personnel intersect with the growth in power of the new petty bourgeoisie (those people in technical and middle management positions) and the reassertion of academic dominance in the curriculum, pressures for curricular reform can become quite intense. Patience over traditional forms of control will lessen.

Patriarchal relations of power, therefore, organized around the male principal's relations to a largely female teaching staff, will not necessarily be progressive for capital or the state. While they once served certain educational and ideological ends, they are less efficient than what has been required recently. Gender relations must be partly subverted to create a more efficient institution. Techniques of control drawn from industry will tend to replace older styles which depended more on a sexual division of power and labor within the school itself.

Perhaps an example will document the long and continuing history of these altered relationships. In the United States, for instance, during the late 1950s and the 1960s, there was rather strong pressure from academics, capital, and the state to reinstitute academic disciplinary knowledge as the most 'legitimate' content for schools. In the areas of mathematics and science especially, it was feared that 'real' knowledge was not being taught. A good deal of effort was given to producing curricular programs that were systematic, based on rigorous academic foundations, and, in the elementary school material in particular, were teacher-proof. Everything a teacher was to deal with was provided and prespecified. The cost of the development of such programs was socialized by the state (i.e., subsidized by tax dollars). The chance of their being adopted by local school districts was heightened by the National Defense Education Act, which reimbursed school districts for a large portion of the purchase cost. That is, if a school system purchased new material of this type and the technology which supported it, the relative cost was minimal. The bulk of the expense was repaid by the state. Hence, it would have seemed irrational not to buy the material—irrational in two ways: (1) the chance of getting new curricula at low cost is clearly a rational management decision within industrial logic, and (2) given its imprimatur of science and efficiency, the material itself seemed rational.

All of this is no doubt familiar to anyone who lived through the early years of this movement, and who sees the later, somewhat less powerful, effects it had in, say, England and elsewhere. Yet this is not only the history of increasing state sponsorship of and state intervention in teaching and curriculum development and adoption. *It is the history of the state, in concert with capital and a largely male academic body of consultants and developers, intervening at the level of practice into the work of a largely female workforce.* That is, ideologies of gender, of sex-appropriate knowledge, need to be seen as having possibly played a significant part here. The loss of control and rationalization of one's work forms part of a state/class/gender 'couplet' that works its way out in the following ways. Mathematics and science teaching are seen as abysmal. 'We' need rapid change in our economic responsiveness and in 'our' emerging ideological and economic struggle with the Soviet Union.[13] Teachers (who just happen to be almost all women at the elementary level) aren't sophisticated enough. Former ways of curricular and teaching control are neither powerful nor efficient enough for this situation. Provide both teacher-proof materials and financial incentives to make certain that these sets of curricula actually reach the classroom.

One must integrate an analysis of the state, changes in the labor process of state employees, and the politics of patriarchy to comprehend the dynamics of this history of curriculum. It is not a random fact that one of the most massive attempts at rationalizing curricula and teaching had as its target a group of teachers who were largely women. I believe that one cannot separate out the fact of a sexual division of labor and the vision of who has what kinds of competence from the state's attempts to revamp and make more 'productive' its educational apparatus. In so doing, by seeing these structurally generated relationships, we can begin to open up a door to understanding part of the reasons behind what happened to these curriculum materials when they were in fact introduced.

As numerous studies have shown, when the material was introduced into many schools, it was not unusual for the 'new' math and 'new' science to be taught in much the same manner as the old math and old science. It was altered so that it fitted into both the existing regularities of the institution and the prior practices that had proven successful in teaching.[14] It is probably wise to see this as not only the result of a slow-to-change bureaucracy or a group of consistently conservative administrators and teachers. Rather, I think it may be just as helpful to think of this more structurally in labor process and gender terms. The supposed immobility of the institution, its lack of significant change in the face of the initial onslaught of such material, is at least partly tied to the resistances of a female workforce against external incursions into the practices they had evolved over years of labor. It is in fact more than a little similar to the history of ways in which other women employees in the state and industry have reacted to past attempts at altering traditional modes of control of their own labor.[15]

A NOTE ON THE STATE

The points I have just made about the resistances of the people who actually work in the institutions, about women teachers confronted by external control, may seem straightforward. However, these basic arguments have very important implications not only about how we think about the history of curriculum reform and control, but more importantly about how many educators and political theorists have pictured the larger issue of the state's role in supporting capital. In the historical example I gave, state intervention on the side of capital and for 'defense' is in opposition to other positions within the state itself. The day-to-day interests of one occupational position (teachers) contradict the larger interests of the state in efficient production.[16] Because of instances such as this, it is probably inappropriate to see the state as a homogeneous entity, standing above day-to-day conflicts.

Since schools *are* state apparatuses, we should expect them to be under intense pressure to act in certain ways, especially in times of both fiscal and ideological crises. Even so, this does not mean that people employed in them are passive followers of policies laid down from above. As Roger Dale has noted:

Teachers are not merely 'state functionaries' but do have some degree of autonomy, and [this] autonomy will not necessarily be used to further the proclaimed ends of the state apparatus. Rather than those who work there fitting themselves to the requirements of the institutions, there are a number of very important ways in which the institution has to take account of the interests of the employees and fit itself to them. It is here, for instance, that we may begin to look for the sources of the alleged inertia of educational systems and schools, that is to say what appears as inertia is not some immutable characteristic of bureaucracies but is due to various groups within them having more immediate interests than the pursuit of the organization's goals.[17]

Thus, the 'mere' fact that the state wishes to find 'more efficient' ways to organize teaching does not guarantee that this will be acted upon by teachers who have a long history of work practices and self-organization once the doors to their rooms are closed. As we shall see in a moment, however, the fact that it is primarily women employees who have faced these forms of rationalization has meant that the actual outcomes of these attempts to retain control of one's pedagogic work can lead to rather contradictory ideological results.

LEGITIMATING INTERVENTION

While these initial attempts at rationalizing teaching and curricula did not always produce the results that were anticipated by their academic, industrial, and governmental proponents, they did other things that were, and are, of considerable import. The situation is actually quite similar to the effects of the use of Tayloristic management strategies in industry. As a management technology for deskilling workers and separating conception from execution, Taylorism was less than fully successful. It often generated slowdowns and strikes, exacerbated tensions, and created new forms of overt and covert resistance. Yet, its ultimate effect was to legitimate a particular ideology of management and control both to the public and to employers and workers.[18] Even though it did not succeed as a set of techniques, it ushered in and finally brought acceptance of a larger body of ideological practices to deskill pink-, white-, and blue-collar workers and to rationalize and intensify their labor.

This too was one of the lasting consequences of these earlier curriculum 'reform' movements. While they also did not completely transform the practice of teaching, while patriarchal relations of authority which paradoxically 'gave' teachers some measure of freedom were not totally replaced by more efficient forms of organizing and controlling their day-to-day activity, they legitimated both new forms of control and greater state intervention using industrial and technical models and brought about a new generation of more sophisticated attempts at overcoming teacher 'resistance.' Thus, this new generation of techniques that are being instituted in so many states in the United States and elsewhere currently—from systematic integration of testing, behavioral goals and curriculum, competency-based instruction and prepackaged curricula, to management by objectives, and so forth—has not sprung out of nowhere, but, like the history of Taylorism, has grown out of the failures, partial successes, and resistances that accompanied the earlier approaches to control. As I have claimed, this is not only the history of the control of state employees to bring about efficient teaching, but a rearticulation of the dynamics of patriarchy and class in one site, the school.

INTENSIFICATION AND TEACHING

In the first half of this chapter, we paid particular attention to the historical dynamics operating in the schools. I would like now to focus on more current outgrowths of this earlier history of rationalization and control.

The earlier attempts by state bureaucrats, industry, and others to gain greater control of day-to-day classroom operation and its 'output' did not die. They have had more than a decade to grow, experiment, and become more sophisticated. While gender will be less visible in the current strategies (in much the same way that the growth of management strategies in industry slowly covered the real basis of power in factories and offices), as we shall see it will be present in important ways once we go beneath the surface to look at changes in the labor process of teaching, how some teachers respond to current strategies, and how they interpret their own work.

Since in previous work I have focused on a number of elements through which curricula and teaching are controlled—on the aspects of deskilling and reskilling of labor, and on the separation of conception from execution in teachers' work—here I shall want to concentrate more on something which accompanies these historically evolving processes: what I shall call *intensification*. First, let me discuss this process rather generally.

Intensification 'represents one of the most tangible ways in which the work privileges of educational workers are eroded.' It has many symptoms, from the trivial to the more complex—ranging from being allowed no time at all even to go to the bathroom, have a cup of coffee or relax, to having a total absence of time to keep up with one's field. We can see intensification most visibly in mental labor in the chronic sense of work overload that has escalated over time.[19]

This has had a number of notable effects outside of education. In the newspaper industry, for example, because of financial pressures and the increased need for efficiency in operation, reporters have had their story quotas raised substantially. The possibility of doing non-routine investigative reporting, hence, is lessened considerably. This has had the effects of increasing their dependence 'on prescheduled, preformulated events' in which they rely more and more on bureaucratic rules and surface accounts of news provided by official spokespersons.[20]

Intensification also acts to destroy the sociability of non-manual workers. Leisure and self-direction tend to be lost. Community tends to be redefined around the needs of the labor process. And, since both time and interaction are at a premium, the risk of isolation grows.[21]

Intensification by itself 'does not necessarily reduce the range of skills applied or possessed by educated workers.' It may, in fact, cause them to 'cut corners' by eliminating what seems to be inconsequential to the task at hand. This has occurred with doctors, for instance; many examinations now concentrate only on what seems critical. The chronic work overload has also caused some non-manual workers to learn or relearn skills. The financial crisis has led to shortages of personnel in a number of areas. Thus, a more diverse array of jobs must be done that used to be covered by other people—people who simply do not exist within the institution any more.[22]

While this leads to a broader range of skills having to be learned or relearned, it can lead to something mentioned earlier—the loss of time to keep up with one's field. That is, what might be called 'skill diversification' has a contradiction built into it. It is also part of a dynamic of intellectual deskilling[23] in which mental workers are cut off from their own fields and again must rely even more heavily on ideas and processes provided by 'experts.'

While these effects are important, one of the most significant impacts of intensification may be in reducing the *quality*, not the quantity, of service provided to people. While, traditionally, 'human service professionals' have equated doing good work with the interests of their clients or students, intensification tends to contradict the traditional interest in work well done, in both a quality product and process.[24]

As I shall document, a number of these aspects of intensification are increasingly found in teaching, especially in those schools which are dominated by behaviorally prespecified curricula, repeated testing, and strict and reductive accountability systems. (The fact that these kinds of curricula, tests, and systems are now more and more being mandated should make us even more cautious.) To make this clear, I want to draw on some data from recent research on the effects of these procedures on the structure of teachers' work.

I have argued here and elsewhere that there has been a rapid growth in curricular 'systems' in the United States—one that is now spreading to other countries.[25] These curricula have goals, strategies, tests, textbooks, worksheets, appropriate student response, etc., integrated together. In schools where this is taken seriously,[26] what impact has this been having? We have evidence from a number of ethnographic studies of the labor process of teaching to be able to begin to point to what is going on. For example, in one school where the curriculum was heavily based on a sequential list of behaviorally defined competencies and objectives, multiple worksheets on skills which the students were to complete, with pre-tests to measure 'readiness' and 'skill level' and post-tests to measure 'achievement' that were given often and regularly, the intensification of teacher work is quite visible.

In this school, such curricular practice required that teachers spend a large portion of their time evaluating student 'mastery' of each of the various objectives and recording the results of these multiple evaluations for later discussions with parents or decisions on whether or not the student could 'go on' to another set of skill-based worksheets. The recording and evaluation made it imperative that a significant amount of time be spent on administrative arrangements for giving tests, and then grading them, organizing lessons (which were quite often standardized or pre-packaged), and so on. One also found teachers busy with these tasks before and after school and, very often, during their lunch hour. Teachers began to come in at 7:15 in the morning and leave at 4:30 in the afternoon. Two hours' more work at home each night was not unusual, as well.[27]

Just as I noted in my general discussion of the effects of intensification, here too getting done became the norm. There is so much to do that simply accomplishing what is specified requires nearly all of one's efforts. 'The challenge of the work day (or week) was to accomplish the required number of objectives.' As one teacher put it, 'I just want to get this done. I don't have time to be creative or imaginative.'[28] We should not blame the teacher here. In mathematics, for example, teachers typically had to spend nearly half of the allotted time correcting and recording the worksheets the students completed each day.[29] The situation seemed to continually push the workload of these teachers up. Thus, even though they tended to complain at times about the long hours, the intensification, the time spent on technical tasks such as grading and record-keeping, the amount of time spent doing these things grew inexorably.[30]

Few of the teachers were passive in the face of this, and I shall return to this point shortly. Even though the elements of curricular control were effective in structuring major aspects of their practice, teachers often responded in a variety of ways. They subtly changed the pre-specified objectives because they couldn't see their relevance. They tried to resist the intensification as well: first by trying to find some space during the day for doing slower-paced activities; and second by actually calling a halt temporarily to the frequent pre- and post-tests, worksheets and the like and merely having 'relaxed discussions with students on topics of their own choosing.'[31]

This, of course, is quite contradictory. While these examples document the active role of teachers in attempting to win back some time, to resist the loss of control of their own work, and to slow down the pace at which students and they were to proceed, the way this is done is not necessarily very powerful. In these instances, time was fought for simply to relax, if only for a few minutes. The process of control, the increasing technicization and intensification of the teaching act, the proletarianization of their work—all of this was an absent presence. It was misrecognized as a symbol of their increased *professionalism*.

PROFESSION AND GENDER

We cannot understand why teachers interpreted what was happening to them as the professionalization of their jobs unless we see how the ideology of professionalism works as part of both a class and gender dynamic in education. For example, while reliance on 'experts' to create curricular and teaching goals and procedures grew in this kind of situation, a wider range of technical skills had to be mastered by these teachers. Becoming adept at grading all those tests and worksheets quickly, deciding on which specific skill group to put a student in, learning how to 'efficiently manage' the many different groups based on the tests, and more, all became important skills. As responsibility for designing one's own curricula and one's own teaching decreased, responsibility over technical and management concerns came to the fore.

Professionalism and increased responsibility tend to go hand in hand here. The situation is more than a little paradoxical. There is so much responsibility placed on teachers for technical decisions that they actually work harder. They feel that since they constantly make decisions based on the outcomes of these multiple pre- and post-tests, the longer hours are evidence of their enlarged professional status. Perhaps a quote will be helpful here.

> One reason the work is harder is we have a lot of responsibility in decision-making. There's no reason not to work hard, because you want to be darn sure that those decisions you made are something that might be helpful . . . So you work hard to be successful at these decisions so you look like a good decision maker.[32]

It is here that the concept of professionalism seemed to have one of its major impacts. Since the teachers thought of themselves as being more professional to the extent that they employed technical criteria and tests, they also basically accepted the longer hours and the intensification of their work that accompanied the program. To do a 'good job,' you needed to be as 'rational' as possible.[33]

We should not scoff at these perceptions on the part of the teachers. First, the very notion of professionalization has been important not only to teachers in general but to women in particular. It has provided a contradictory yet powerful barrier against interference by the state; and just as critically, in the struggle over male dominance, it has been part of a complex attempt to win equal treatment, pay, and control over the day-to-day work of a largely female labor force.[34]

Second, while we need to remember that professionalism as a social goal grew at the same time and was justified by the 'project and practice of the market professions during the liberal phase of capitalism,'[35] the strategy of professionalism has historically been used to set up 'effective defenses against proletarianization.'[36] Given what I said earlier about the strong relationship between the sexual division of labor and proletarianization, it would be not only ahistorical but perhaps even a bit sexist as well wholly to blame teachers for employing a professional strategy.

Hence, the emphasis on increasing professionalism by learning new management skills and so on today and its partial acceptance by elementary school teachers can best be understood not only as an attempt by state bureaucrats to deskill and reskill teachers, but as part of a much larger historical dynamic in which gender politics have played a significant role.

Yet the acceptance of certain aspects of intensification is not only due to the history of how professionalism has worked in class and gender struggles. It is heightened by a number of internal factors as well. For example, in the school to which I referred earlier, while a number of teachers believed that the rigorous specification of objectives and teaching procedures actually helped free them to become more creative, it was clear that subtle pressures existed to meet the priorities established by the specified objectives. Even though in some subject areas they had a choice of how they were to meet the objectives, the objectives themselves usually remained unchallenged. The perceived interests of parents and their establishment of routines helped assure this. Here is one teacher's assessment of how this occurs.

> Occasionally you're looking at the end of the book at what the unit is going to be, these are the goals that you have to obtain, that the children are going to be tested on. That may affect your teaching in some way in that you may by-pass other learning experiences simply to obtain the goal. These goals are going home to parents. It's a terrible thing to do but parents like to see 90's and 100's rather than 60's on skills.[37]

In discussing the use of the skills program, another teacher points out the other element besides parents that was mentioned: 'It's got a manual and you follow the manual and the kids know the directions and it gets to be routine.'[38]

Coupled with perceived parental pressure and the sheer power of routine is something else: the employment practices surrounding teaching. In many schools, one of the main criteria for the hiring of teachers is their agreement with the overall curricular, pedagogic, and evaluative framework which organizes the day-to-day practice. Such was the case in this study. Beyond this, however, even though some investigators have found that people who tend to react negatively to these pre-packaged, standardized, and systematized curricular forms often leave teaching,[39] given the depressed market for new teachers in many areas that have severe fiscal problems and the conscious decision by some school districts to hire fewer teachers and increase class size, fewer jobs are available right now. The option of leaving or even protesting seems romantic, though current teacher shortages may change this.

GENDERED RESISTANCE

At this point in my argument it would be wise to return to a claim I made earlier. Teachers have not stood by and accepted all this. In fact, our perception that they have been and are passive in the face of these pressures may reflect our own tacit beliefs in the relative passivity of women workers. This would be an unfortunate characterization. Historically, for example, as I shall demonstrate in the following chapter, in England and the United States the picture of women teachers as non-militant and middle-class in orientation is not wholly accurate. There have been periods of exceptional militancy and clear political commitment.[40] However, militancy and political commitment are but one set of ways in which control is contested. It is also fought for on the job itself in subtle and even 'unconscious' (one might say 'cultural') ways—ways which will be contradictory, as we shall now see. Once again, gender will become of prime importance.

In my own interviews with teachers it has become clear that many of them feel rather uncomfortable with their role as 'managers.' Many others are less than happy with the emphasis on programs which they often feel 'lock us into a rigid system.' Here the resistance to rationalization and the loss of historically important forms of self-control of one's labor was very contradictory outcomes, partly as a result of sexual divisions in society. Thus, a teacher using a curricular program in reading and language arts that is very highly structured and test-based states:

> While it's really important for the children to learn these skills, right now it's more important for them to learn to feel good about themselves. That's my role, getting them to feel good. That's more important than tests right now.

Another primary grade teacher, confronted by a rationalized curriculum program where students move from classroom to classroom for 'skill groups,' put it this way:

Kids are too young to travel between classrooms all the time. They need someone there that they can always go to, who's close to them. Anyway, subjects are less important than their feelings.

In these quotes, discomfort with the administrative design is certainly evident. There is a clear sense that something is being lost. Yet the discomfort with the process is coded around the traditional distinctions that organize the sexual division of labor both within the family and in the larger society. The *woman's* sphere is that of providing emotional security, caring for feelings, and so on.

Do not misconstrue my points here. Teachers should care for the feelings and emotional security of their students. However, while these teachers rightly fight on a cultural level against what they perceive to be the ill-effects of their loss of control and both the division and the intensification of their labor, they do so at the expense of reinstituting categories that partly reproduce other divisions that have historically grown out of patriarchal relations.[41]

This raises a significant point: much of the recent literature on the role of the school in the reproduction of class, sex, and race domination has directed our attention to the existence of resistances. This realization was not inconsequential and was certainly needed to enable us to go further than the overly deterministic models of explanation that had been employed to unpack what schools do. However, at the same time, this literature has run the risk of romanticizing such resistances. The fact that they exist does not guarantee that they will necessarily be progressive at each and every moment. Only by uncovering the contradictions within and between the dynamics of the labor process *and* gender can we begin to see what effects such resistances may actually have.[42]

LABOR, GENDER, AND TEACHING

I have paid particular attention here to the effects of the restructuring of teachers' work in the school. I have claimed that we simply cannot understand what is happening to teaching and curriculum without placing it in a framework which integrates class (and its accompanying process of proletarianization) and gender together. The impact of deskilling and intensification occurs on a terrain and in an institution that is populated primarily by women teachers and male administrators—a fact that needs to be recognized as being historically articulated with both the social and sexual divisions of labor, knowledge, and power in our society.

Yet, since elementary school teachers are primarily women, we must also look beyond the school to get a fuller comprehension of the impact of these changes and the responses of teachers to them. We need to remember something in this regard: women teachers often work in *two* sites—the school and then the home. Given the modification of patriarchal relations and the intensification of labor in teaching, what impact might this have outside the school? If so much time is spent on technical tasks at school and at home, is it possible that less time may be available for domestic labor in the home? Other people in the family may have to take up the slack, thereby partly challenging the sexual division of household labor. On the other hand, the intensification of teachers' work, and the work overload that may result from it, may have exactly the opposite effect. It may increase the exploitation of unpaid work in the home by merely adding more to do without initially altering conditions in the family. In either case, such conditions will lead to changes, tensions, and conflicts outside of the sphere where women engage in paid work.[43] It is worth thinking very carefully about the effects that working in one site will have on the other. The fact that this dual exploitation exists is quite consequential in another way. It opens up possible new avenues for political intervention by socialist feminists, I believe. By showing the relationship between the home and the job and the intensification growing in both, this may provide for a way of demonstrating the ties between both of these sphere and between class and gender.

Thinking about such issues has actually provided the organizing framework for my analysis. The key to my investigation in this chapter has been reflecting about changes in *how* work is organized over time and, just as significantly, *who* is doing the work. A clearer sense of both of these—how and who—can enable us to see similarities and differences between the world of work in our factories and offices and that of semi-autonomous state employees such as teachers.

What does this mean? Historically the major struggles labor engaged in at the beginning of the use of systematic management concerned resistance to speed-ups.[44] That is, the intensification of production, the pressure to produce more work in a given period, led to all kinds of interesting responses. Craft workers, for example, often simply refused to do more. Pressure was put on co-workers who went too fast (or too slow). Breaks were extended. Tools and machines suddenly developed 'problems.'

Teachers—given their contradictory class location, their relationship to the history of patriarchal control and the sexual division of labor, and the actual conditions of their work—will find it difficult to respond in the same way. They are usually isolated during their work, and perhaps more so now given the intensification of their labor. Further, machinery and tools in the usual sense of these terms are not visible.[45] And just as importantly, the perception of oneself as professional means that the pressures of intensification and the loss of control will be coded and dealt with in ways that are specific to that workplace and its own history. The ultimate effects will be very contradictory.

In essence, therefore, I am arguing that—while similar labor processes may be working through institutions within industry and the state which have a major impact on women's paid work—these processes will be responded to differently by different classes and class segments. The ideology of professional discretion will lead to a partial acceptance of, say, intensification by teachers on one level, and will generate a different kind of resistance—one specific to the actual work circumstances in which they have historically found themselves. The fact that these changes in the labor process of teaching occur on a terrain that has been a site of patriarchal relations plays a major part here.

My arguments here are not to be construed as some form of 'deficit theory.' Women have won and will continue to win important victories, as I will demonstrate in the following chapter. Their action on a cultural level, though not overtly politicized, will not always lead to the results I have shown here. Rather, my points concern the inherently *contradictory* nature of teachers' responses. These responses are victories and losses at one and the same time. The important question is how the elements of good sense embodied in these teachers' lived culture can be reorganized in specifically feminist ways—ways that maintain the utter importance of caring and human relationships without at the same time reproducing other elements on that patriarchal terrain.

I do not want to suggest that once you have realized the place of teaching in the sexual division of labor, you have thoroughly understood deskilling and reskilling, intensification and loss of control, or the countervailing pressures of professionalism and proletarianization in teachers' work. Obviously, this is a very complex issue in which the internal histories of bureaucracies, the larger role of the state in a time of economic and ideological crisis,[46] and the local political economy and power relations of each school play a part. What I do want to argue quite strongly, however, is the utter import of gendered labor as a constitutive aspect of the way management and the state have approached teaching and curricular control. Gendered labor is the absent presence behind all of our work. . . .

NOTES

1. Erik Olin Wright and Joachim Singelmann, 'The Proletarianization of Work in American Capitalism,' University of Wisconsin-Madison Institute for Research on Poverty, Discussion Paper No. 647–81, 1981, p. 38.
2. *Ibid.*, p. 43. See also Michael W. Apple, 'State, Bureaucracy and Curriculum Control,' *Curriculum Inquiry* 11 (Winter 1981), 379–88. For a discussion that rejects part of the argument about proletarianization, see Michael Kelly, *White Collar Proletariat* (Boston and London: Routledge & Kegan Paul, 1980).
3. Deskilling, technical control and proletarianization are both technical and political concepts. They signify a complex historical process in which the control of labor has altered— one in which the skills employees have developed over many years on the job are broken down into atomistic units, redefined, and then appropriated by management to enhance both efficiency and control of the labor process. In the process, workers' control over timing, over defining appropriate ways to do a task, and over criteria that establish acceptable performance are all slowly taken on as the prerogatives of management personnel who are usually divorced from the actual place in which the work is carried out. Deskilling, then, often leads to the atrophy of valuable skills that workers possessed, since there is no longer any 'need' for them in the redefined labor process. The loss of control or proletarianization of a job is hence part of a larger dynamic in the separation of conception from execution and the continuing attempts by management in the state and industry to rationalize as many aspects of one's labor as possible. I have discussed this in considerably more detail in Michael W. Apple, *Education and Power* (Boston and London: Routledge & Kegan Paul, 1982). See also Richard Edwards, *Contested Terrain* (New York: Basic Books, 1979), and Michael Burawoy, *Manufacturing Consent* (Chicago: University of Chicago Press, 1979).
4. Erik Olin Wright, 'Class and Occupation,' *Theory and Society* 9 (No. 2, 1980), 182–3.
5. Apple, *Education and Power*.
6. Wright, 'Class and Occupation,' 188. Clearly race plays an important part here too. See Michael Reich, *Racial Inequality* (Princeton: Princeton University Press, 1981), and Mario

Barrera, *Race and Class in the Southwest: A Theory of Racial Inequality* (Notre Dame: Notre Dame University Press, 1979).

7. Janet Holland, 'Women's Occupational Choice: The Impact of Sexual Divisions in Society,' Stockholm Institute of Education, Department of Educational Research, Reports on Education and Psychology, 1980, p. 7.

8. *Ibid.*, p. 27.

9. *Ibid.*, p. 45.

10. Gail Kelly and Ann Nihlen, 'Schooling and the Reproduction of Patriarchy,' in Michael W. Apple (ed.), *Cultural and Economic Reproduction in Education: Essays on Class, Ideology and the State* (Boston and London: Routledge & Kegan Paul, 1982), pp. 167–8. One cannot fully understand the history of the relationship between women and teaching without tracing out the complex connections among the family, domesticity, child care, and the policies of and employment within the state. See especially, Miriam David, *The State, the Family and Education* (Boston and London: Routledge & Kegan Paul, 1980).

11. For an interesting history of the relationship among class, gender and teaching, see June Purvis, 'Women and Teaching in the Nineteenth Century,' in Roger Dale, Geoff Esland, Ross Fergusson, and Madeleine MacDonald (eds.), *Education and the State, Vol. 2: Politics, Patriarchy and Practice* (Barcombe, Sussex: Falmer Press, 1981), pp. 359–75. I am wary of using a concept such as patriarchy, since its very status is problematic. As Rowbotham notes, 'Patriarchy suggests a fatalistic submission which allows no space for the complexities of women's defiance' (quoted in Tricia Davis, 'Stand by Your Men? Feminism and Socialism in the Eighties,') in George Bridges and Rosalind Brunt (eds.), *Silver Linings: Some Strategies for the Eighties* (London: Lawrence & Wishart, 1981), p. 14. A history of women's day-to-day struggles falsifies any such theory of 'fatalistic submission.'

12. Jane Barker and Hazel Downing, 'Word Processing and the Transformation of the Patriarchal Relations of Control in the Office,' in Dale, Esland, Fergusson and MacDonald (eds.), *Education and the State, Vol. 2*, pp. 229–56. See also the discussion of deskilling in Edwards, *Contested Terrain*.

13. For an analysis of how such language has been employed by the state, see Michael W. Apple, 'Common Curriculum and State Control,' *Discourse* 2 (No. 4, 1982), 1–10, and James Donald, 'Green Paper: Noise of a Crisis,' *Screen Education* 30 (Spring 1979), 13–49.

14. See, for example, Seymour Sarason, *The Culture of the School and the Problem of Change* (Boston: Allyn & Bacon, 1971).

15. Apple, *Education and Power*, and Susan Porter Benson, 'The Clerking Sisterhood: Rationalization and the Work Culture of Sales Women in American Department Stores,' *Radical America* 12 (March/April 1978), 41–55.

16. Roger Dale's discussion of contradictions between elements within the state is very interesting in this regard. See Roger Dale, 'The State and Education: Some Theoretical Approaches,' in *The State and Politics of Education* (Milton Keynes: The Open University Press, E353, Block 1, Part 2, Units 3–4, 1981), and Roger Dale, 'Education and the Capitalist State: Contributions and Contradictions,' in Apple (ed.), *Cultural and Economic Reproduction in Education*, pp. 127–61.

17. Dale, 'The State and Education,' p. 13.

18. I have examined this in greater detail in Apple, *Education and Power*. See as well Edwards, *Contested Terrain*, and Daniel Clawson, *Bureaucracy and the Labor Process* (New York: Monthly Review Press, 1980).

19. Magali Larson, 'Proletarianization and Educated Labor,' *Theory and Society* 9 (No. 2, 1980), 166.

20. *Ibid.*, 167.

21. *Ibid.* Larson points out that these problems related to intensification are often central grievances even among doctors.

22. *Ibid.*, 168.

23. *Ibid.*, 169.

24. *Ibid.*, 167.

25. Apple, *Education and Power.* See also Carol Buswell, 'Pedagogic Change and Social Change,' *British Journal of Sociology of Education* 1 (No. 3, 1980), 293–306.

26. The question of just how seriously schools take this, the variability of their response, is not unimportant. As Popkewitz, Tabachnick and Wehlage demonstrate in their interesting ethnographic study of school reform, not all schools use materials of this sort alike. See Thomas Popkewitz, B. Robert Tabachnick, and Gary Wehlage, *The Myth of Educational Reform* (Madison: University of Wisconsin Press, 1982).

27. This section of my analysis is based largely on research carried out by Andrew Gitlin. See Andrew Gitlin, 'Understanding the Work of Teachers,' unpublished Ph.D. dissertation, University of Wisconsin, Madison, 1980.

28. *Ibid.*, 208.

29. *Ibid.*

30. *Ibid.*, 197.

31. *Ibid.*, 237.

32. *Ibid.*, 125.

33. *Ibid.*, 197.

34. This is similar to the use of liberal discourse by popular classes to struggle for person rights against established property rights over the past one hundred years. See Herbert Gintis, 'Communication and Politics,' *Socialist Review* 10 (March/June 1980), 189–232. The process is partly paradoxical, however. Attempts to professionalize do give women a weapon against some aspects of patriarchal relations; yet, there is a clear connection between being counted as a profession and being populated largely by men. In fact, one of the things that are very visible historically is the relationship between the sexual division of labor and professionalization. There has been a decided tendency for full professional status to be granted only when an activity is 'dominated by men—in both management and the ranks.' Jeff Hearn, 'Notes on Patriarchy: Professionalism and the Semi-Professions,' *Sociology* 16 (May 1982), 195.

35. Magali Larson, 'Monopolies of Competence and Bourgeois Ideology,' in Dale, Esland, Fergusson, and MacDonald (eds.), *Education and the State, Vol. 2*, p. 332.

36. Larson, 'Proletarianization and Educated Labor,' p. 152. Historically, class as well as gender dynamics have been quite important here, and recent research documents this clearly. As Barry Bergen has shown in his recent study of the growth of the relationship between class and gender in the professionalization of elementary school teaching in England, a large portion of elementary school teachers were both women and of the working class. As he puts it:

> Teaching, except at the university level, was not highly regarded by the middle class to begin with, and teaching in the elementary schools was the lowest rung on the teaching ladder. The middle class did not view elementary teaching as a means of upward mobility. But the elementary school teachers seemed to view themselves as having risen above the working class, if not having reached the middle class. . . . Clearly, the varied attempts of elementary teachers to professionalize constitute an attempt to raise their class position from an interstitial one between the working class and middle class to the solidly middle class position of a profession.

See Barry H. Bergen, 'Only a Schoolmaster: Gender, Class, and the Effort to Professionalize Elementary Teaching in England, 1870–1910,' *History of Education Quarterly* 22 (Spring 1982), 10.

37. Gitlin, 'Understanding the Work of Teachers,' p. 128.
38. *Ibid.*
39. Martin Lawn and Jenny Ozga, 'Teachers: Professionalism, Class and Proletarianization,' unpublished paper, The Open University, Milton Keynes, 1981, p. 15 in mimeo.
40. Jenny Ozga, 'The Politics of the Teaching Profession,' in *The Politics of Schools and Teaching* (Milton Keynes: The Open University Press, E353, Block 6, Units 14–15, 1981), p. 24.
41. We need to be very careful here, of course. Certainly, not all teachers will respond in this way. That some will not points to the partial and important fracturing of dominant gender and class ideologies in ways that signal significant alterations in the consciousness of teachers. Whether these alterations are always progressive is an interesting question. Also, as Connell has shown, such 'feminine' approaches are often important counterbalances to masculinist forms of authority in schools. See R. W. Connell, *Teachers' Work* (Boston and London: George Allen & Unwin, 1985).
42. See Henry Giroux, 'Theories of Reproduction and Resistance in the New Sociology of Education: A Critical Analysis,' *Harvard Educational Review* 53 (August 1983), 257–93, even though he is not specifically interested in gender relations.
43. While I have focused here on the possible impacts in the school and the home on women teachers, a similar analysis needs to be done on men. We need to ask how masculinist ideologies work through male teachers and administrators. Furthermore, what changes, conflicts, and tensions will evolve, say, in the patriarchal authority structures of the home given the intensification of men's labor? I would like to thank Sandra Acker for raising this critically important point. For an analysis of changes in women's labor in the home, see Susan Strasser, *Never Done: A History of American Housework* (New York: Pantheon, 1982).
44. Clawson, *Bureaucracy and the Labor Process*, pp. 152–3.
45. In addition, Connell makes the interesting point that since teachers' work has no identifiable object that it 'produces,' it can be intensified nearly indefinitely. See Connell, *Teachers' Work*, p. 86.
46. Apple, *Education and Power*, and Manuel Castells, *The Economic Crisis and American Society* (Princeton: Princeton University Press, 1980).

Teachers as Transformative Intellectuals

Henry A. Giroux

Unlike many past educational reform movements, the present call for educational change presents *both* a threat and a challenge to public school teachers that appears unprecedented in our nation's history. The threat comes in the form of a series of educational reforms that display little confidence in the ability of public school teachers to provide intellectual and moral leadership for our nation's youth. For instance, many of the recommendations that have emerged in the current debate either ignore the role teachers play in preparing learners to be active and critical citizens or they suggest reforms that ignore the intelligence, judgment and experience that teachers might offer in such a debate. Where teachers do enter the debate, they are the object of educational reforms that reduce them to the status of high-level technicians carrying out dictates and objectives decided by experts far removed from the everyday realities of classroom life.[1] The message appears to be that teachers do not count when it comes to critically examining the nature and process of educational reform.

The political and ideological climate does not look favorable for teachers at the moment. But it does offer them the challenge to join in a public debate with their critics as well as the opportunity to engage in a much-needed self-critique regarding the nature and purpose of teacher preparation, in-service teacher programs and the dominant forms of classroom teaching. Similarly, the debate provides teachers with the opportunity to organize collectively to improve the conditions under which they work and to demonstrate to the public the central role that teachers must play in any viable attempt to reform the public schools.

In order for teachers and others to engage in such a debate, it is necessary that a theoretical perspective be developed that redefines the nature of the educational crisis while simultaneously providing the basis for an alternative view of teacher training and work. In short, recognizing that the current crisis in education largely has to do

Reprinted by permission from National Council for the Social Studies *Social Education*.

with the developing trend towards the disempowerment of teachers at all levels of education is a necessary theoretical precondition for teachers to organize effectively and establish a collective voice in the current debate. Moreover, such a recognition will have to come to grips not only with a growing loss of power among teachers around the basic conditions of their work, but also with a changing public perception of their role as reflective practitioners.

I want to make a small theoretical contribution to this debate and the challenge it calls forth by examining two major problems that need to be addressed in the interest of improving the quality of "teacher work," which includes all the clerical tasks and extra assignments as well as classroom instruction. First, I think it is imperative to examine the ideological and material forces that have contributed to what I want to call the proletarianization of teacher work; that is, the tendency to reduce teachers to the status of specialized technicians within the school bureaucracy, whose function then becomes one of managing and implementing curricular programs rather than developing or critically appropriating curricula to fit specific pedagogical concerns. Second, there is a need to defend schools as institutions essential to maintaining and developing a critical democracy and also to defending teachers as transformative intellectuals who combine scholarly reflection and practice in the service of educating students to be thoughtful, active citizens. In the remainder of this essay, I will develop these points and conclude by examining their implications for providing an alternative view of teacher work.

DEVALUING AND DESKILLING TEACHER WORK

One of the major threats facing prospective and existing teachers within the public schools is the increasing development of instrumental ideologies that emphasize a technocratic approach to both teacher preparation and classroom pedagogy. At the core of the current emphasis on instrumental and pragmatic factors in school life are a number of important pedagogical assumptions. These include: a call for the separation of conception from execution; the standardization of school knowledge in the interest of managing and controlling it; and the devaluation of critical, intellectual work on the part of teachers and students for the primacy of practical considerations.[2]

This type of instrumental rationality finds one of its strongest expressions historically in the training of prospective teachers. That teacher training programs in the United States have long been dominated by a behavioristic orientation and emphasis on mastering subject areas and methods of teaching is well documented.[3] The implications of this approach, made clear by Zeichner, are worth repeating:

> Underlying this orientation to teacher education is a metaphor of "production," a view of teaching as an "applied science" and a view of the teacher as primarily an "executor" of the laws and principles of effective teaching. Prospective teachers may or may not proceed through the curriculum at their own pace and may participate in varied or standardized learning activities, but that which they are to master is limited in scope (e.g., to a body of professional content knowledge and teaching skills) and is fully determined in advance by others often on the basis of research on teacher effectiveness. The prospective teacher is viewed primarily as a passive

recipient of this professional knowledge and plays little part in determining the substance and direction of his or her preparation program.[4]

The problems with this approach are evident in John Dewey's argument that teacher training programs that emphasize only technical expertise do a disservice both to the nature of teaching and to their students.[5] Instead of learning to reflect upon the principles that structure classroom life and practice, prospective teachers are taught methodologies that appear to deny the very need for critical thinking. The point is that teacher education programs often lose sight of the need to educate students to examine the underlying nature of school problems. Further, these programs need to substitute for the language of management and efficiency a critical analysis of the less obvious conditions that structure the ideological and material practices of schooling.

Instead of learning to raise questions about the principles underlying different classroom methods, research techniques and theories of education, students are often preoccupied with learning the "how to," with "what works," or with mastering the best way to teach a *given* body of knowledge. For example, the mandatory field-practice seminars often consist of students sharing with each other the techniques they have used in managing and controlling classroom discipline, organizing a day's activities, and learning how to work within specific time tables. Examining one such program, Jesse Goodman raises some important questions about the incapacitating silences it embodies. He writes:

> There was no questioning of feelings, assumptions, or definitions in this discussion. For example, the "need" for external rewards and punishments to "make kids learn" was taken for granted; the educational and ethical implications were not addressed. There was no display of concern for stimulating or nurturing a child's intrinsic desire to learn. Definitions of *good kids* as "quiet kids," *workbook work* as "reading," *on-task time* as "learning," and *getting through the material on time* as "the goal of teaching"—all went unchallenged. Feelings of pressure and possible guilt about not keeping to time schedules also went unexplored. The real concern in this discussion was that everyone "shared."[6]

Technocratic and instrumental rationalities are also at work within the teaching field itself, and they play an increasing role in reducing teacher autonomy with respect to the development and planning of curricula and the judging and implementation of classroom instruction. This is most evident in the proliferation of what has been called "teacher-proof" curriculum packages.[7] The underlying rationale in many of these packages reserves for teachers the role of simply carrying out predetermined content and instructional procedures. The method and aim of such packages is to legitimate what I call management pedagogies. That is, knowledge is broken down into discrete parts, standardized for easier management and consumption, and measured through predefined forms of assessment. Curricula approaches of this sort are management pedagogies because the central questions regarding learning are reduced to the problem of management, i. e., "how to allocate resources (teachers, students and materials) to produce the maximum number of certified . . . students within a designated time."[8] The underlying theoretical assumption that guides this type of pedagogy is that the behavior of teachers needs to be controlled and made consistent and predictable across different schools and student populations.

What is clear in this approach is that it organizes school life around curricular, instructional, and evaluation experts who do the thinking while teachers are reduced to doing the implementing. The effect is not only to deskill teachers, to remove them from the processes of deliberation and reflection, but also to routinize the nature of learning and classroom pedagogy. Needless to say, the principles underlying management pedagogies are at odds with the premise that teachers should be actively involved in producing curricula materials suited to the cultural and social contexts in which they teach. More specifically, the narrowing of curricula choices to a back-to-basics format and the introduction of lock-step, time-on-task pedagogies operate from the theoretically erroneous assumption that *all* students can learn from the same materials, classroom instructional techniques and modes of evaluation. The notion that students come from different histories and embody different experiences, linguistic practices, cultures, and talents is strategically ignored within the logic and accountability of management pedagogy theory.

TEACHERS AS TRANSFORMATIVE INTELLECTUALS

In what follows, I want to argue that one way to rethink and restructure the nature of teacher work is to view teachers as transformative intellectuals. The category of intellectual is helpful in a number of ways. First, it provides a theoretical basis for examining teacher work as a form of intellectual labor, as opposed to defining it in purely instrumental or technical terms. Second, it clarifies the kinds of ideological and practical conditions necessary for teachers to function as intellectuals. Third, it helps to make clear the role teachers play in producing and legitimating various political, economic and social interests through the pedagogies they endorse and utilize.

By viewing teachers as intellectuals, we can illuminate the important idea that all human activity involves some form of thinking. No activity, regardless of how routinized it might become, can be abstracted from the functioning of the mind in some capacity. This is a crucial issue, because by arguing that the use of the mind is a general part of all human activity we dignify the human capacity for integrating thinking and practice, and in doing so highlight the core of what it means to view teachers as reflective practitioners. Within this discourse, teachers can be seen not merely as "performers professionally equipped to realize effectively any goals that may be set for them. Rather [they should] be viewed as free men and women with a special dedication to the values of the intellect and the enhancement of the critical powers of the young."[9]

Viewing teachers as intellectuals also provides a strong theoretical critique of technocratic and instrumental ideologies underlying an educational theory that separates the conceptualization, planning and design of curricula from the processes of implementation and execution. It is important to stress that teachers must take active responsibility for raising serious questions about what they teach, how they are to teach, and what the larger goals are for which they are striving. This means that they must take a responsible role in shaping the purposes and conditions of schooling. Such a task is impossible within a division of labor in which teachers have little influence over the ideological and economic conditions of their work. This point has a normative and political dimension that seems especially relevant for teachers. If we believe that the role of teaching cannot be reduced to merely training in the practical skills, but involves, instead, the education of a class of intellectuals vital to the development of a free society, then the category of intellectual becomes a way of linking the purpose of teacher education, public schooling and inservice training to the very principles necessary for developing a democratic order and society.

I have argued that by viewing teachers as intellectuals we can begin to rethink and reform the traditions and conditions that have prevented teachers from assuming their full potential as active, reflective scholars and practitioners. I believe that it is important not only to view teachers as intellectuals, but also to contextualize in political and normative terms the concrete social functions that teachers perform. In this way, we can be more specific about the different relations that teachers have both to their work and to the dominant society.

A starting point for interrogating the social function of teachers as intellectuals is to view schools as economic, cultural and social sites that are inextricably tied to the issues of power and control. This means that schools do more than pass on in an objective fashion a common set of values and knowledge. On the contrary, schools are places that represent forms of knowledge, language practices, social relations and values that are particular selections and exclusions from the wider culture. As such, schools serve to introduce and legitimate *particular* forms of social life. Rather than being objective institutions removed from the dynamics of politics and power, schools actually are contested spheres that embody and express a struggle over what forms of authority, types of knowledge, forms of moral regulation and versions of the past and future should be legitimated and transmitted to students. The struggle is most visible in the demands, for example, of right-wing religious groups currently trying to institute school prayer, remove certain books from school libraries, and include certain forms of religious teachings in the science curricula. Of course, different demands are made by feminists, ecologists, minorities, and other interest groups who believe that the schools should teach women's studies, courses on the environment, or black history. In short, schools are not neutral sites, and teachers cannot assume the posture of being neutral either.

In the broadest sense, teachers as intellectuals have to be seen in terms of the ideological and political interests that structure the nature of the discourse, classroom social relations, and values that they legitimate in their teaching. With this perspective in mind, I want to conclude that teachers should become transformative intellectuals if they are to educate students to be active, critical citizens.

Central to the category of transformative intellectual is the necessity of making the pedagogical more political and the political more pedagogical. Making the pedagogical more political means inserting schooling directly into the political sphere by arguing that schooling represents both a struggle to define meaning and a struggle over power relations. Within this perspective, critical reflection and action become part of a fundamental social project to help students develop a deep and abiding faith in the struggle to overcome economic, political and social injustices, and to further humanize themselves as part of this struggle. In this case, knowledge and power are inextricably linked to the presupposition that to choose life, to recognize the necessity of improving its democratic and qualitative character for all people, is to understand the preconditions necessary to struggle for it.

Making the political more pedagogical means utilizing forms of pedagogy that embody political interests that are emancipatory in nature; that is, using forms of pedagogy that treat students as critical agents; make knowledge problematic; utilize critical and affirming dialogue; and make the case for struggling for a qualitatively better world for all people. In part, this suggests that transformative intellectuals take seriously the need to give students an active voice in their learning experiences. It also means developing a critical vernacular that is attentive to problems experienced at the level of everyday life, particularly as they are related to pedagogical experiences connected to classroom practice. As such, the pedagogical starting point for such intellectuals is not the isolated student but individuals and groups in their various cultural, class, racial, historical and gender settings, along with the particularity of their diverse problems, hopes, and dreams.

Transformative intellectuals need to develop a discourse that unites the language of critique with the language of possibility, so that social educators recognize that they can make changes. In doing so, they must speak out against economic, political and social injustices both within and outside of schools. At the same time, they must work to create the conditions that give students the opportunity to become citizens who have the knowledge and courage to struggle in order to make despair unconvincing and hope practical. As difficult as this task may seem to social educators, it is a struggle worth waging. To do otherwise is to deny social educators the opportunity to assume the role of transformative intellectuals.

NOTES

1. For a more detailed critique of the reforms, see Stanley Aronowitz and Henry A. Giroux, *Education Under Siege* (Massachusetts: Bergin & Garvey, 1985); see also the incisive comments on the impositional nature of the various reports in Charles A. Tesconi, Jr., "Additive Reforms and the Retreat from Purpose," *Educational Studies* 15 (Spring 1984): 1–11; Terrence E. Deal, "Searching for the Wizard: The Quest for Excellence in Education," *Issues in Education* 2 (Summer 1984): 56–57; Svi Shapiro, "Choosing Our Educational Legacy: Disempowerment or Emancipation?" *Issues in Education* 2 (Summer 1984): 11–22.
2. For an exceptional commentary on the need to educate teachers to be intellectuals, see John Dewey, "The Relation of Theory to Practice," in John Dewey, *The Middle Works, 1899– 1924.* JoAnn Boydston, ed. (Carbondale, Ill.: Southern Illinois University Press, 1977), [first published 1904]. See also Israel Scheffler, "University Scholarship and the Education of Teachers," *Teachers College Record* 70 (1968): 1–12; Giroux, *Ideology, Culture and the Process of Schooling.* (Philadelphia: Temple University Press, 1981).
3. See, for instance, Herbert Kliebard, "The Question of Teacher Education," in D. McCarty, ed., *New Perspectives on Teacher Education* (San Francisco: Jossey-Bass, 1973).
4. Kenneth M. Zeichner, "Alternative Paradigms on Teacher Education," *Journal of Teacher Education* 34 (May–June 1983): 4.
5. Dewey, "Relation of Theory to Practice."
6. Jesse Goodman, "Reflection on Teacher Education: A Case Study and Theoretical Analysis," *Interchange* 15 (1984): 15.
7. Michael Apple, *Education and Power.* (Boston: Routledge & Keagan Paul, 1982).
8. Patrick Shannon, "Mastery Learning in Reading and the Control of Teachers," *Language Arts* 61 (Sept. 1984): 488.
9. Scheffler, "University Scholarship," p. 11.

Educational Discourse and Global Crisis: What's a Teacher to Do?

David E. Purpel

This chapter focuses on the remarkable and dangerous chasm between mainstream educational discourse and the urgent social, political, and moral crises of our time. Public debate on education tends to focus on issues such as academic achievement, test scores, computer literacy, study skills, and merit pay while most professional academic educators busy themselves with developing more sophisticated evaluation instruments and more effective instructional techniques, and teachers and administrators strive to respond to public pressures. Clearly a similar gap between crisis and response can be seen in other social institutions such as politics and the media; for example, the current presidential campaign in the United States is eerie in how far removed it is from dealing with the immediate specters of human misery, ecological calamity, and nuclear war. However, the reality that professional educators exemplify a high degree of denial, complacency, and passivity in the face of enormous crises ought to be a matter of serious concern for those who have faith that knowledge, creativity, insight, and understanding (i.e., education) are key to overcoming our current perils. The basic themes of this chapter involve an affirmation of the importance of education without succumbing to the fiction that education (meaning here basically public schools) can by itself be the only or even the prevailing force for fundamental social and cultural change. Schools do indeed have *a* role to play in this realm—to what particular degree is in some ways irrelevant since each of us has a responsibility to work diligently for a better world within our own sector. Another theme of this chapter is that there is danger in both bashing and romanticizing teachers—indeed we will not do them or ourselves honor by denying them and us our humanity. The dilemmas and frustrations that teachers face reflect as well as affect the tangles and complexities of our times—there is no reason to believe that schoolteachers have been any less or any more wise, heroic, or imaginative than any other group of educators such as academics, researchers, and administrators. The difficulty, of course, is that what is required for survival from us is a great deal more wisdom, courage, and imagination than we have seen. Is it reasonable to ask even more of teachers, a group clearly overworked, underpaid, and undervalued—a profession with strong traditions of passivity, gentleness, and modesty, a group that is so overshadowed by administrators, school board members, political leaders, and academics? A great deal is asked of teachers but not much is given to them.

I believe that the plight of teachers can be at least to some extent compared to the frustrations and dilemmas of an army at war. I use this metaphor not in terms of violent and destructive images but rather as it illuminates the role, functions, and conflicts in how a public task of great importance is defined, organized, and performed. In this image, I see an army that is recruited in a burst of energetic affirmation and idealism—for example, to defend honor, to restore democracy, and to fight evil. There is great public support for this effort as articulated and crystallized by its leaders, and although everyone is asked to make some contribution and sacrifice to the war effort, the burden will inevitably fall most heavily on the shoulders of a relative few. Those few will be strenuously trained, but surprisingly briefly, their pay low, their quality of life difficult, but all is made endurable by the majesty of their cause. Indeed, many people volunteer to serve and yearn for the opportunity to fight for Principle, God, and Country. It is a very familiar image, one represented many times in novels, songs, films, newsreels, and family stories. Some of these stories have a triumphant quality; some speak to despair. All reflect the best and worst of us—courage, heroism, sacrifice, idealism, and solidarity, on the one hand, and cowardice, cynicism, pain, destruction, and cruelty, on the other. For purposes of this chapter, however, I will focus only on a narrow part of this broad metaphor, that of the response of the rank-and-file soldier, the person in the trenches, the "dog-soldier," that is, the counterpart to the classroom teacher.

The sagas and narratives of this aspect to the story often speak to starkly unromantic dimensions of being a soldier—of boredom, loneliness, fright; of feeling isolated, manipulated, and powerless. By the time soldiers confront their actual day-to-day tasks, the initial emotional energy will probably have faded, the powerful reasons for fighting are likely to have become blurred and perhaps even questionable, and there is a growing suspicion that their pain and suffering is unappreciated and that their contributions will be forgotten or unaffirmed. Some will believe that there are those back home who actually profit from the continuation of a war that seems increasingly endless and futile, and that others who presumably are their colleagues (e.g., officers, chaplains, and support personnel) have a much more comfortable tour of duty. Soldiers differ and quarrel among themselves—complaining can be seen as whining, criticism of the war as lack of patriotism and cowardice—whereas others accept their lot fatalistically if not heroically. However depressed, lonely, and terrifying the task might be, one cannot but be struck by the reality that virtually everyone returns to the task despite the risks, frustration, and powerlessness. Since this is a very large army, responses to these tasks vary—some perform heroically (only some of whom are recognized); some desert, are wounded, or suffer psychological wounds; but probably most do their routine task remote from the action and even more remote from the larger, strategic concerns.

Like any metaphor, this one surely has limits and can distort as well as illuminate but there are a few parallels that I would like to stress. Society tends to have a similar and ambivalent attitude toward teachers, on the one hand extolling them in a rhetoric of virtue and dedication but simultaneously affording them relatively low status and resources. Teachers tend to be seen as agents of policies determined by their professional leaders and elected officials and only vaguely understood by the public. Teachers largely see themselves as powerless, misunderstood, and undervalued, and educational theorists are apt to criticize them for lack of depth if not for incompetence. There is at least one extremely significant difference between soldiers and teachers and that is that although the military ethic strongly affirms discipline, loyalty, and obedience, the ethic of educators does not. Military personnel are expected to follow lawful orders, to attend strictly to the prerogatives of a very well-defined hierarchy, and to see regimentation and uniformity as necessary dimensions of their tasks. Educators, in contrast, emerge from a tradition that stresses criticism, reflection, and dissent. Indeed, the entire theoretical framework for education rests on the assumption of the free pursuit of truth. Obviously, there is enormous variation in practice, and no doubt there is space within the military for dissent and criticism, but I would guess that the opportunity is limited to certain spheres. I wish to speak, however, more directly to this matter as it relates to teachers.

Once again, teachers find themselves in an ambiguous and paradoxical situation when it comes to the issue of their professional autonomy. Teachers are in effect asked to be both loyal and autonomous, team players and stars—they are told they will be rewarded for contributing to school goals but are rarely given a serious opportunity to determine them. Schools tend to be hierarchical, but school leaders are likely to invoke the rhetoric of family and community. Theorists and administrators are apt to speak to the critical importance of teachers but do little to change their political status. However, most central to the focus of this chapter is not so much the powerlessness of teachers but their voicelessness—that is, unlike infantrymen whose voicelessness is to some extent sanctioned, teachers have a very weak public voice even though the official rhetoric speaks otherwise. Indeed it can easily be said that teachers have an ethical imperative to go far beyond their conventional passivity.

Let me try to be a little clearer about teacher power and teacher voice. There are realms where teachers exercise considerable influence and times when a teacher's voice is clear and energetic. National and state teachers' organizations have considerable political clout in supporting candidates and legislation, and in a great many communities they engage in serious collective bargaining largely on issues of salaries and work conditions. In individual situations of practice, particular teachers provide highly valued expertise on instructional matters and often offer very helpful personal support to troubled students. However limited these situations are, they do indicate the potential for extending teachers' influence and autonomy. At the same time they indicate the limited range in which teachers have chosen to exercise their responsibilities.

Teachers, parallel with other educators, tend to use a technical instructional discourse within the profession and with their clients and with the public. Teachers as teachers can and do talk about such matters as students' developmental readiness, appropriate instructional strategies, curriculum scope and sequence, and valid testing techniques. Teachers as public employees tend to speak with their administrators about ameliorating the problems of the existing system—for example, raising wages, reducing class size, and adding services. This discourse is for the most part not directed at social transformation but at fine-tuning the existing structures. What teachers tend not to do is to engage in serious moral and political discourse; that is, to the extent that they are reflective and articulate, their criticism tends to be of a technical and instrumental nature. Like soldiers at war, no doubt many teachers sense that there are fundamental difficulties involved in their frustration, issues of a strategic rather than a tactical nature. Like the foot soldier, teachers sense a loss of their early energy, which emerged out of a shining vision that is now blurry if not stained. Teachers, like a forgotten army, often feel helpless and inarticulate in trying to give voice to these feelings.

I wish now to return to the beginning of this chapter and to the point I made about the enormous gap between current social crises and educational discourse, and later I will try to link this problem with the issue of teacher voice. When I speak of these crises I refer to those that seriously threaten both our highest and minimum hopes. Our highest aspirations have to do with creating a world of justice, love, peace, community, joy, and beauty for all. Our minimum hope is plain and simple survival. Both possibilities have become highly problematic. This is certainly not the first time in history when we are disappointed in our efforts to create a better world, but it is the first time in the modern era that we have reason to fear for any kind of world at all. The threats are not remote, and indeed they are so familiar and frightening that their mention often engenders resistance and denial. Statistics and warnings abound, the media speak daily and vividly about the perils, and even politicians have been known to make reference to them (although to do so can put them at political risk). Here are some examples:

1. More than one billion people are chronically undernourished. Deaths related to hunger and starvation average 50,000 a day.
2. Two billion people . . . do not have safe water to drink.
3. The twentieth-century has already had 207 wars and an estimated 78 million lives lost . . . more than five times as many deaths in the past century.[1]

These issues are incredibly complex and of enormous magnitude, involving a myriad of dimensions and perspectives. As a citizen and as an educator I have come to see their presence both as indicators of failure in our fundamental structures and as evidence of moral confusion. Clearly, responding to these issues requires a great deal of new knowledge and intellectual acuity; but we have also come to see that intellectual abilities have not been sufficient in preventing our crises. Indeed, we have seen genius applied to the creation of the very crises that threaten us.

We must confront certain realities—that a wealthy society like ours that allows so many infants to die unnecessarily has serious flaws; that a culture that produces both a Holocaust and the concept of unconditional love is at war with itself; and that an ethic that celebrates a freedom to create both a Garden of Eden and a hole in the atmosphere represents lunacy. We must also confront two other realities—that overcoming these threats will require transformation, not reform, and paradoxically that we seem very reluctant to own up to the severity of these crises. I say paradoxically because I believe that there is an emerging consensus that we do indeed face calamity even though, of course, there is a wide diversity of interpretations on the source and nature of the calamity and what our response should be. I am convinced that a vital element in confronting all of these realities is to address them in moral discourse. By that, I do not limit myself to moral analysis, as critical and vital as that process is, but I also strongly believe that our task must include forging a moral vision—one that can inform and energize our political will and educational strategy.

Teachers, as other educators, must confront some of the painful and anguishing dimensions of current educational practice. They, as the rest of us, are caught up in a system in which individual achievement, competition, success, and aggressiveness are essential and central elements. It is a system in which education becomes an instrument in legitimizing and defining hierarchy; in which schools are a site where people are sorted, graded, classified, and labeled, hence giving credence to the tacit social value that dignity is to be earned. Teachers are asked to prepare students differently— some are to be given the encouragement and skills to be leaders, whereas others are taught to endure their indignities quietly and proudly. It is a system that helps sustain and legitimize a society reveling in consumerism, jingoism, hedonism, greed, and hierarchy.

We also must confront the problematics and limitations of the various reforms and critiques that range from criticisms of teachers' working conditions and wages to basic curriculum reform. Many of the suggestions offered (e.g., more stringent testing for students and teachers) are clearly presented as efforts to solidify rather than alter the basic structures of the educational systems. However, there are a number of serious critiques that not only provide for sharper insight into the system's fundamental problematics but also offer sweeping and exciting suggestions for change. I will very briefly note three general types of these more progressive critiques—those that urge for a much more thorough emphasis on critical dialogue, those that urge that democratic processes permeate the curriculum including classroom and school life, and those that urge us to work for a more enlightened consciousness.

I believe these represent serious, important, and valuable critiques, ones that merit inclusion in any dialogue concerned with the transformation of education. In our enthusiasm for these issues, however, we must not be blinded by their own problematic relationship to the nature of our current crises. We have come to know the anguish of realizing that highly intelligent, sensitive, and creative people (many with a serious spiritual or religious sensibility) are capable of being involved in brutality and oppression. We are aware that it is possible to value both democracy *and* materialism; critical thinking *and* aggression; spiritual peace *and* hierarchy. The ecological crisis needs more than deeper understanding of its dimensions and etiology; the alternative to competition and alienation will not emerge totally from intellectual insight, nor only from conducting the dialogue democratically. A New Age will not emerge only from meditation and peak experiences, nor will any Utopia be built on a foundation that does not seek to integrate body, mind, and spirit.

What I believe is lacking in these alternative approaches and what I believe can better inform them is the development of a moral vision that can provide direction and energy. I further believe that there are within our traditions ample resources in the way of images, metaphors, myths, and visions that are available for this task. Indeed, I believe that it is possible to achieve a great deal of consensus on the broad contours of that vision and yet still allow a great deal of space for diversity, dissent, and creativity. I believe with other critics that there is a crisis in community, that we are increasingly fragmented and isolated, but I disagree that a greater sense of community can be enhanced solely by the possession of common knowledge. Instead, I believe that we can, as we have done momentarily and from time to time, forge a greater share of community through a common moral vision. Such a vision would almost certainly build on such commitments as a concern for social justice, dignity, love, joy, and fulfillment for all. We have extremely rich traditions that give voice to our impulse to care, to be connected with others and with nature, and to live a life of meaning.

However, the reconstruction of a moral vision is surely not without numerous difficulties and dangers. It is also a task that needs to involve all elements of our society, but our focus here is on teachers and their role in this task. In one sense, the difficulties that teachers might have with this orientation very likely parallel those that other large groups would face. Surely, teachers, as the rest of us, would have to wrestle with the ambiguities, paradoxes, and contradictions of our current vision, blurry as it might be. Clearly there would be significant differences among teachers on the definition and validity of the existing visions as well as likely uncertainty and conflict within individual teachers. All this can be seen as conflicts and ambiguities reflective of the larger culture. My position, however, is that teachers have a very special role and opportunity in the process of wrestling with these issues.

Teachers, like the soldiers I spoke of before, are intimately involved with the dialectic between aspirations and reality and with the high price that is paid when they are in sharp conflict. Teachers can in the heat of day-to-day battle become deeply involved in technique and trivia, thereby losing sight of the higher vision. It is even possible that the classroom as well as the trenches are places where good, decent people find themselves working at cross purposes with their own aspirations. Teachers, like soldiers, perhaps are often not even sure of what the vision is; whether it is a good idea to have one; whether it is their place to challenge the existing vision, never mind the possibility of trying to replace it.

It is my position, nonetheless, that teachers must be involved in this endeavor and that those who prepare and lead teachers must also be involved. Teachers have at least three very significant forums in which to exercise this responsibility—in their teaching, in their relationships with parents, and in their interaction with other teachers and professionals. I will speak briefly to each one of these arenas, but I need to stress that what I have in mind is dialogue, not didactics. My hope is not that teachers will assume the role of moral visionaries and leaders but will become involved in the difficult, complex, and profoundly important process of engaging in moral discourse. It is a process that asks us to share our questions, doubts, and insights with the goal of reaching important degrees of consensus on the shape of a moral vision.

Teachers have an extraordinary opportunity in the classroom, obviously, to teach, to raise important issues, to provide appropriate language and background, and to engage students in serious inquiry. However limited and truncated the prescribed written curriculum (which is in many places becoming increasingly so), the teacher has ample opportunities at the very least to raise the fundamental challenges that face us—for example, it is inconceivable to me that ecological issues could not be appropriately and authentically related to virtually any course of study. Surely, it is possible to voice the dangers of nuclear war and mass starvation within an intellectual and academic framework. Even if some teachers in some situations find this to be overly difficult, there is always the agenda of school and classroom life. In these interactions issues of dignity, affirmation, power, and community are always present and always in need of dialogue and the possibility of modification. This is only to repeat the obvious, that the schools represent a microcosm of society and have to face the task of building community while at the same time have the further opportunity to engage in the issues of larger worlds. It is in schools that people are taught (not the first or last place or time) to deal with competition, individual success, hierarchy, and instrumentalism, and it is teachers who have the day-to-day responsibility to monitor these processes. It is surely possible (and to me vital) that teachers surround their responsibilities with a profound concern for their implications for the serious social and cultural crises of our time. Surely, teachers can reflect by themselves and surely they can raise the question of whether and to what degree the stuff of school life contributes to the problems or to their solutions. Surely, such questions will produce different reactions, and no doubt there will be complexity, contradiction, and ambiguity. What is central here is not for teachers to provide answers and certainty but to engage their students in the most important issues that face us—the very real possibilities of ecological calamity; nuclear war; mass starvation; and immense, unnecessary human misery.

When teachers talk to other teachers and professionals they have a further opportunity to develop this discourse. Beyond the important curricular issues just mentioned, teachers are in a position to at least infuse this discourse in the discussion of such school policies as grading, attendance, requirements, dress code, and testing. Many, if not most, teachers have little direct power or influence on such matters, but they almost always have at least token opportunity to express their views. Certainly, teachers do talk informally to one another on professional issues, and in many cases teachers routinely work collegially (e.g., in departments and co-teaching situations). Most schools have faculty meetings (even though in many cases they may be pro forma and strictly controlled), which provide at the least an opportunity for teachers to raise questions in the manner described above. The point, again, is to urge a widening of professional discourse to include, to a significant extent, consideration of major current crises, particularly as they relate to our responsibility to participate in a reconstruction of our moral vision.

Perhaps most important, teachers have an opportunity to work closely with parents and to some extent with a larger public. In the dialectic between schools and society it is clearly the society that dominates the shape of educational discourse and policy. Schools more often than not react to public pressures and demands and are clearly under the political and financial control of society. As we have noted, public discourse on education tends to be conducted within a narrow range of technical concerns (e.g., teachers' salaries and graduation requirements) or within a framework of social instrumentalism (e.g., job training, college admissions, and foreign policy concerns). Often there are intense local issues that generate wider and deeper dialogue, but in general the public dialogue on education is appallingly naive and uncritical. There is precious little public debate on the basic assumptions and structural dimensions of our educational system.

There is little opportunity for the public to examine the relationships between some of our culture's highest aspirations (justice, love, dignity, and community) and educational policies and practices. Ironically enough, there *is* public dialogue that extends to the notion that profound social and cultural changes might be required to overcome the major crises of our times. There are, for example, public voices that urge us to develop a global consciousness or at least a bio-regional rather than a national one; there are suggestions that we respond to national security issues by studying peace rather than war; there are ideas about economics, decentralization, alternative technologies, and new concepts at work. I say ironically because there is very little (I could say no) parallel, strong public voice that speaks to fundamental changes in the educational system. This may very well be an index of the public's confusion and ambivalence about the necessity for major change. These radical proposals require giving up what constitute important dimensions of the existing vision: success, the acquisition of material wealth, a sense of personal well-being, personal autonomy, national pride, and individual achievement. To move the various proposals for fundamental cultural and social changes to the educational sphere is to move from theory to practice, from fantasy to reality. Just as people from both the right and the left are apt to seek out conservative bankers and lawyers in their personal lives, it may be that the schools are too risky a site to deal with truly fundamental change. The schools thus offer a site of continuity, stability, and buffering—a predictable place where newer cultural values can be filtered and modified to limit their potency.

Teachers have a wonderful opportunity here to engage with the lay public in a more direct encounter with the problematics of our existing educational vision. For one thing, like those soldiers fighting in the mud and jungles, teachers need not and should not have to shoulder the full burden of their awesome responsibilities. It is for teachers and educators not only to remind the public of the ambiguity and contradictions of its expectations and of the public's refusal to match the quality of resource allocation to the magnitude of these expectations but also to urge and require them to work together in a common struggle. In a word, we cannot afford to continue a policy of letting the public off the hook, a policy that keeps the profession as the scapegoat.

Let me illustrate the possibilities of this forum with the issue of grading, surely a perplexing and central one in educational practice. Teachers certainly spend a great deal of time discussing policies for grading as well as actually determining them for their students. There are many informal discussions among parents, teachers, counselors, and administrators about the validity, significance, and interpretation of grades of individual students. It is also well known that many parent meetings focus on grades and grading policy. There has also been a great deal of modest experimentation, particularly on the nature of report cards, although most of these changes are at a surface level, for example, moving from letter grades to phrases like "needs improvement." What is rarely heard, particularly at public forums, is a more searching examination of the deeper significance of grading, not only its implications for educational theory but also its moral and social significance. Many if not most teachers are seriously conflicted about grading, certainly to the point of worrying about its impact on students' motivation, initiative and self-esteem. Many teachers see it as counterproductive to an education that focuses on openness, creativity, autonomy, trust, and safety. In addition, many if not most teachers are troubled by technical issues of their testing and grading policies, particularly as they impinge on their commitment to both fairness and compassion.

Beyond these questions are deeper, more troubling issues of how grading is related to hierarchy, competitiveness, success, and perhaps to divisiveness, alienation, and egocentricity. Teachers are asked continuously to rank their students, thereby sometimes subtly but more often quite directly creating a setting where most students put enormous energy into and experience high anxiety about seeking approval. A few are honored and quite a few humiliated in the process, one in which teachers and students alike are debased by becoming parties to a system of allocating various degrees of dignity and self-worth. The unnecessary difficulty that teachers face is that even though many confront these problematics, complexities, and dangers, they typically face them alone. The public has not been seriously forced to grapple with these issues, which at their most significant are not in their nature professional but moral and political. Teachers in their silence and passivity have allowed the issues to be defined at best as professional and at worst as technical. Although, for example, there is some dialogue on standardized testing, the discourse is mostly on issues of cultural sensitivity, validity, and degree of predictability. What is virtually absent from public discourse is dialogue on the basic elements of our society that necessitate grading—class, hierarchy, competitiveness, and individualism.

Teachers have an opportunity to share the burdens of dealing with grading, and beyond that they have a responsibility to engage the public in a broader and deeper awareness. The teaching profession has excellent and ongoing opportunities to raise the dilemmas and problematics of grading and has the experience and sophistication to help in framing and posing deeper, more profound, and more illuminating questions. Teachers can exercise this responsibility in the classroom, in their discussions with other teachers, in their conferences with parents, and in various public forums. Teachers' organizations have a wider opportunity to raise these issues and indeed have an ethical responsibility to infuse discussions of grading policies with serious consideration of their moral and political significance. Grading is in its least important dimensions a professional matter in which expertise is required; in its most significant aspect it involves moral and social policy and hence is a matter for public dialogue and debate.

The sad and ironic reality, however, is that such a role for teachers goes clearly against the grain of public expectations and of professional self-definition. Teachers typically are not expected by the public or by their leaders to engage in serious moral discourse nor to confess their deep ambivalence toward school policies. The public tends to regard teachers as civil servants—valuable and decent civil servants to be sure—who are expected to channel their technical expertise toward social policies largely determined by nonprofessionals. The poignancy and arrogance of this position is that the public does not typically have access to the powerfully valuable insight of the very adults who have the most intimate involvement with the day-to-day impact of school policies. Thus, teachers, as soldiers, are both valued and ignored, relied upon and distrusted, and both serve as easy targets for blame when there is confusion in the ranks.

A morally critical consciousness for teachers also flies in the face of the form and substance of how teachers are trained, before and after the fact. Teacher training first of all must deal with students who typically have neither well-developed critical skills nor effective teaching skills. Undergraduate students in teacher education are asked to squeeze a great deal of new information and insights about teaching and education into an already stressful and bewildering bachelor's program. These students tend to be quite anxious about their ability to teach and their long-range job prospects in addition to dealing with all the other pressures of undergraduate life. Added to this is the likelihood that such students tend to be more passive and docile than students entering other professions. We would seem to have a group of particularly vulnerable and naive prospective teachers. Such a group would hardly seem likely candidates for engaging the public and the profession in a controversial, volatile, and anguishing moral discourse.

The possibilities for such a transformation are, however, appreciably diminished by preparation programs that barely address such matters. Instead, teacher training tends to be oriented around technical concerns, with a strong emphasis on social and behavioral science discourse. Many if not most programs stress the application of psychological theories and the importance of classroom effectiveness. To the degree that students encounter social and philosophical issues, my guess would be that the strong emphasis is on the understanding and analysis of particular conceptual or historical processes. In my experience, it is very rare for teacher trainees to be encouraged to develop and project a moral critique of educational policy and practices. Much of this may have to do with students' readiness—for example, their lack of background and their strong concern for classroom survival—but these issues are less relevant in the case of graduate programs in education, where I believe the emphasis changes only slightly.

If we have people going into the profession who are passive and who focus on mastering classroom teaching skills and who are trained and led mostly by people who are mostly concerned with analysis and scholarly research, then it is no wonder that teachers remain silent and voiceless on issues of greatest magnitude. Those in the academics who have been silent and shy about these issues must confront the political implications of their reluctance. To those who insist on the paramountcy of rigorous research and academic distance, I urge and plead with you to consider the seriousness of our current crises—indeed I urge us all to listen to the ticking of the clock, for I share with others the deep conviction that we are in a race with time for the survival of the planet and human existence. If there were ever a time for us to decide when the "long run" has arrived, this is probably it—for in the long run we have come to recognize that only basic transformation will save us from the calamities of environmental pollution, human misery, nuclear disaster, and armed conflict. The task is surely formidable but urgent—this is hardly the time to say only "more research is needed." Nor is it of course the time for zealotry and arrogant self-righteousness. Rather it is, as it always has been, a time for serious reflection, outrage, and action.

NOTE

1. Ruth Leger Sivard, *World Military and Social Expenditures* (Washington, DC: 1988) 1985 World Priorities.

Curriculum Alternatives in a Survivalist Culture: Basic Skills and the "Minimal Self"

H. Svi Shapiro

INTRODUCTION: FROM CRITICAL THEORY TO POLITICAL AGENDA

Perhaps the most disappointing aspect of what has been, in other ways, the immensely successful project of elaborating a critical social theory of education, is the failure to develop this into a meaningful and catalytic political agenda. There are, of course, a number of possible reasons for this. One of these, perhaps, is the frequently determinist leanings of so much of the educational analysis carried on within this framework. This point has recently been made by Henry Giroux[1] in his attempt to retreive a more dialectical recognition of the importance of actor and action in social 'reality' to balance the frequent emphasis on the social subject's apparent passive accommodation to structure and institutions. This argument addresses the importance of conscious human interventions in the construction of the social world, not simply incorporation in an unchanging reality. There is also the often 'totalistic' frame of analysis which attempts to so integrate education into the social matrix that change in any one area of society is inconceivable outside of change in all areas of the society.[2] This makes for interesting theory, but is useless as a guide to political action within, and around, specific institutions or domains of social practice. There is little that can be done by those desiring social change in the places within which we work, live or are educated, short of waiting for a radical transformation of the entire system. Of course we may also have to admit to the difficulties that stem from 'translating' the often difficult linguistic and conceptual frameworks of critical social inquiry into the everyday world of political mobilization. There are surely other reasons in addition. In any event it is clear that the task of formulating, on the basis of our critical educational theory, an agenda for a politics of educational change has hardly begun.

It does seem to me that the attempt to construct such an agenda would have to take very seriously the way in which educational concerns mediate the larger social world. Indeed, educational issues must be seen as part of a wider set of concerns and demands that attempt, in some way, to address the problems of this world. Such demands, concerns and assertions constitute the oppositional moments of ideology and culture. They will, more than likely, find a variety of ways in which to express themselves within the context of our social practices (in the workplace, in political life, in the neighborhood, on the street as well as around schooling). At times it is also possible that such moments of opposition cohere into a structure or pattern of dissent, opposition, or revolt. In other words, there comes into being a social movement which has self-conscious political, cultural or economic goals. Of course, it must be recognized that the relationship between these forms of opposition and the reality of social existence is a highly mediated one. Its connections may be enormously convoluted, or its proffered solutions to problems massively displaced. The attempt to deal with reality in all of its hardships, suffering, and deprivation, may well take place through forms that do little but compound or exacerbate the original oppression, providing little but 'otherworldly' solace, or false comfort.

Both in this paper and elsewhere I have attempted to make the point that movements for educational reform are best understood when located within broader movements for political, cultural or economic change.[3] From this perspective educational demands can, and do, become a powerful way of focusing the concerns, demands and needs of this larger movement. They become a way of giving concrete political expression to moments of opposition and resistance in the wider culture. Of course, from this viewpoint too, changes in educational policy have complex social origins. They must be seen as far more than the simple impositions of dominant elites or ruling groups. They incorporate those oppositional moments of ideology that well-up from the bottom or the middle of the social structure. Ideological hegemony involves a complex transformation of these oppositional moments so that they can become part of the dominant ideology and no longer pose a significant challenge or threat to the real forms of domination and control in the society. When this transformation is impossible outright suppression, exclusion or censorship is likely to be attempted.

What, then, is crucial here is the notion that political agendas for educational change must be constructed out of the fabric of social experience. It must, if it is to be successful, mediate the struggles, the travail, the anxieties, and concerns that accompany this experience, and provide a focus for dissent and opposition as well as affirmation and assertion. And, of course, as with all political agendas, its capacity for wide appeal cannot be separated from its ability to capture the popular imagination.

THE BASIC SKILLS MOVEMENT
AND MIDDLE CLASS REACTION

In this paper I have returned to a previously explored theme, that of the 'basic skills movement'. My concern here, as in previous papers, has been the way in which the educational movement cannot be fully understood outside of its connections to the experience and ideological expression of specific social groups.[4] I have, however, felt compelled to extend my analysis under the influence of the recent work by Christopher Lasch, *The Minimal Self.*[5] While this work does not deal with education in any direct sense, I believe its principal theme—the psychic impact of a culture preoccupied with questions of survival—has enormous relevance to a critical understanding of the contemporary politics of education. Lasch's study, I believe, offers crucial insight into the social ground out of which conservative educational discourse has flourished. It helps provide important clues about the connections between the dominant educational agenda in the '80s and the larger political agenda of which this is a part. Such analysis is, however, important not only as a study in the interpretation of human experience, ideology, and educational politics. It also offers potential openings into the formulation of a viable and effective progressive educational agenda—one that is rooted in the social reality of everyday life and that addresses the collective and individual suffering produced here. This time, in contradiction to the movement concerned with 'basics' and 'minimum competencies', a pedagogy is suggested that offers not an illusionary response to the travail of the human situation, but one that prepares us to collectively intervene and change it. However, whatever the immanent value or logic of this latter pedagogy, it is certain that only through its capacity to clearly articulate current concerns, and deal with the issues that all too painfully confront the mass of people in this society, will it stand a chance of constituting a political agenda around which people can be enthusiastically mobilized.

In an earlier study of the 'basic skills' movement I argued that it had to be understood, first and foremost, as a reaction to social and educational changes that occurred in the 1960s. Of course, rooting the demand to 'return to basics' in the turbulence of that time was not an especially original idea. Indeed, abolishing that era's curricular and institutional reforms was the explicit goal of many 'basics' advocates. Their charge that the period's liberal reforms had undermined standards, replaced serious academic concerns with frivolities and frills, inflated grades, reduced the ability to read, write and achieve simple numeracy, and made school into an extension of the hedonistic culture concerned mainly with entertaining and gratifying students, has filled the print and electronic media for over a decade. Decrying the era's educational reforms and charging them with being responsible for the nation's scholastic mediocrity have become more than familiar complaints. And, of course, eliciting the truth of these claims, and the counter-claims of liberals, has occupied more than one professional research career. Though, it must be added, judging by the way in which the center of educational discourse and practices have moved to the right, it is the conservative critics who must be declared the victors.

My concern, however, has not been to adjudicate on the effectiveness of conservative and liberal education reforms. I am concerned, instead, with making sense of the larger social and political implications of this struggle. The passionate, at times vitriolic, arguments over the appropriate forms of curriculum and instruction in the nation's public schools, was about much more than education and disagreements over educational practice. Much more has been and continues to be at stake. The question of returning the schools to 'basics' is related to some much larger and more fundamental set of concerns. It was precisely this belief that earlier led me to suggest a number of underlying tensions that provided the impetus to this educational struggle over the past decade and more. These tensions are social, ideological, and economic in nature. Without grasping the way in which the curriculum battles frequently were surrogates for the broader social ideological and economic conflicts, it was impossible to understand what has really been at stake in educational politics in recent years. Thus, I have argued that the emergence of the 'basics' movement is connected to the larger belief that the curriculum and other school reforms emerging from the equalitarianism of this period undermined the relationship of school to the social division of labor and the reproduction of the distinctions between middle class and working class life. The expansion and diversification of curriculum during this period, for example, reduced the ordered, hierarchical character of school knowledge.[6] In this sense the curriculum reforms initiated during the 1960's undermined the epistemological basis for social ranking and hierarchy that are integral to the process of schooling. More directly the incorporation of experiences and knowledge more closely related to the lives of students (particularly those most often excluded from, or unsuccessful in, the educational process) eroded the traditional separation of school experiences from everyday life. It is precisely this distinction that has been shown to sustain the notion of 'becoming educated' with all of its elitist and hierarchical implications. To become 'educated', in this sense, refers to the selective process in which a particular segment of the population has transmitted to them especially valued aspects of the culture; i.e. highly regarded and honored elements of the society's intellectual and literary heritage. The transmission of this 'cultural capital' is a process that requires that schools provide experiences marked by their very separateness from the life of students (from some more than others), and whose availability or accessibility can thus be regulated and controlled by the school and by the state. As Michael Young has shown, the character of school knowledge or experience has traditionally underpinned this separation—its compartmentalization, abstraction, concern with literariness, and symbolic manipulation, as well as the emphasis on the impersonal, the past or the distant, and the spurning of the language or the culturally particularistic traits of the student (particularly of lower class students and those of a minority culture).[7]

Given the fundamental social distinctions that are transmitted and reinforced by the ability to cope with or succeed at the academic curriculum, it is no wonder that the movement for curriculum change centered around notions like 'relevance' was met with such hostility. It was perceived by some in the middle class as a challenge to the selective process that underpins the social division of labor—the very basis of middle class status. By allowing the inclusion of a significantly extended range of curriculum experiences (many of which were more directly related to the lives of poor or minority students) meant that the particular character of the 'cultural capital' which is both the source and product of middle class advantage was threatened. A larger and less exclusive set of symbols, meaning, knowledge and values could be utilized as 'cultural capital'. In short, with a drastic increase in the accessibility to or availability of the 'cultural capital' required for educational success, the middle class felt itself threatened by a devaluation of its most precious resources—the ability to transmit the cultural advantages of the division of labor to its offspring.

The curriculum changes initiated in the 1960's[8] posed an important threat to the stable reproduction of class advantage. Those sections of the middle class who most clearly felt this threat could do no more than insist on a return to some standard through which their cultural advantage would be restored and maintained. With the utilitarian erosion of any notion of being educated connected to general intellectual, moral or aesthetic development, such a return was the bare-bones concept of 'basics'—a simplified inventory of capabilities that marked one as able or not to perform mental work and hence be fit for white collar or professional training.

The competitive social impulses that I have described above as being associated with the reassertion of 'traditional' curricular goals for schools must be conjoined to the crisis of a growing scarcity of employment opportunities commensurate with long years of schooling. The promise of such work—high interest, autonomy, creativity, and responsibility,—is in sharp contradiction to the routinized, closely monitored, and fragmented experiences increasingly found in white collar and professional occupations.[9] The dissatisfaction engendered by such changes is clearly evidenced in the rapid spread of white-collar unionization, and the industrial-style militancy of many professional groups (public school teachers being, perhaps, the clearest example).

Alongside changes in the notion of 'intellectual' work has been the effect of what is seen as the overproduction of educated workers.[10] The apparent surplus of potential workers with degrees and diplomas has led to the general devaluation of educational credentials. The tendency has been exacerbated by the fiscal crisis of the state which has ensured a dramatic restriction in the employment of those involved in agencies of the state—human service workers, and employees of regulatory agencies. The general reduction of opportunities for work of a professional nature is blamed less on economic policies that fail to promote full employment and the generation of work situations commensurate with lengthy educational preparation and professional training, and more on the problems of schooling. 'Open-door' policies of schools, 'social promotion', 'grade inflation,' and the erosion of educational standards are seen as being at the root of the job problem in their tendency to reduce the selectivity of the educational process thus overproducing educated workers. In other words, the eroding position of white-collar or professional workers in many fields is viewed as a problem that reflects less the absence of adequate employment opportunities than a consequence of schooling that has become too easy.

Within this context of the 'proletarianization' of white-collar and professional work, and the perception of a surplus among educated workers, it is clear why policies that have as their consequence greater selectivity among students might be pursued. Such policies, in reducing the supply of educated workers would, it is felt, likely restore the hitherto valued and prestigious position of such workers. More simply, it would increase the pay-off—both monetary and in the quality of the work itself—for those most diligent or successful in the classroom. The result of such a perspective, is, of course, the demand for great restrictiveness in schooling through an intensified process of evaluating students—whether through standardized tests, competency exams, or other selective measures. Such measures are likely to benefit the middle class in their competition with students from working class homes. All of this, as we have seen, occurs in a framework which asserts the need to restore the traditional basis of school evaluation—a need to 'return' to the ordered epistemological universe of the 3R's or a related curricular outlook.

The basic skills movement, then, represents at one level, an attempt to restore the eroding relationship between schooling and the reproduction of the class structure—at least insofar as it affects groups in the lower and middle levels of the social structure.

This relationship has become an increasingly tenuous one—schooling as an investment in intergenerational mobility is viewed, increasingly, as a dubious venture. It is, indeed, paradoxical that a movement which is, in itself, in many ways the living indictment of educational developments in bourgeois society should purport to be its savior. The pursuit of 'basic skills' is the very embodiment of a pedagogy that is entirely instrumental. Its claims to human enlightenment are couched in terms of basic human survival. Its real paradox is that while it attempts to assert those distinctions characteristic of class-divided societies—between 'culture' and 'civilization', 'mental' and 'manual' labor, the very notion of 'basic skills' is an admission of the disintegration of these distinctions. Thus, while schools are moved in the direction of ever-more specialized, fragmented, and utilitarian concerns, they are also expected to affirm those generalized cultural attributes that legitimate the superior status of those employed in the areas of conceptualization, planning and administration, and the subordination of those relegated to manual labor. And yet it is precisely the erosion of any notion of culture that is embodied in the present focus on basic skills and minimum competencies. Education has replaced any concern with the general apprehension of the meaning and values of society and the development of faculties concerned with critical inquiry, with a concern for the acquisition of those instrumentalities necessary only to attain and maintain one's place in the labor market.

The 'Minimal Self': The Culture of Survival

It is now my belief that the analysis of the basic skills movement that I have summarized above[11] is too restrictive. For one thing it does not begin to enter into the social psychological domain in order to find the psychic roots of this educational movement. Beyond the class dynamics and conflicts elaborated above are social and cultural changes whose impact has been on the very fabric of psychic adjustment and equilibrium in this society. Changes in educational concerns, ideas and practices in the last decade must be seen as emanating from the life experiences of far broader categories of people than I have hitherto suggested. While certainly mediated via class, race, gender and other social groups in distinct ways, conservative educational discourse mirrors a cultural crisis of far larger proportions than could be concluded from what I have so far presented. Christopher Lasch's 1984 study, *The Minimal Self*, provides an important opening into this much broader crisis—one whose effects on education can be drawn from the author's description of the general social psychological character of these 'troubled times'. Thus the basic skills phenomenon can be understood at least partly, as rooted in what Lasch calls 'The Survival Mentality.' Such a mentality, he argues, is the product of "people who have lost confidence in the future. Faced with an escalating arms race, rising crime and terrorism, environmental deterioration, and long-term economic decline, they have retreated from commitments that presuppose a secure and orderly world. Self-concern, so characteristic of our time, has become a search for psychic survival."[12] In an uneasy age, he continues, the problem of survival overshadows loftier concerns. It has entered so deeply into popular culture and political debate that every issue, however fleeting or unimportant, presents itself as a matter of survival. A list of recent books on survivors and survivalists, says Lasch, would include books on ecology and nuclear war, books on the Holocaust, books on technology and automation, and a flood of 'future studies' not to mention an outpouring of science fiction that takes a coming apocalypse as its major premise. Such a list would also include the huge psychiatric literature on 'coping' and the equally enormous sociological literature on victims and 'victimology'. It would include books setting forth 'survival strategies' for oppressed minorities, 'survival in the executive jungle', and 'survival in marriage'. The grim rhetoric of survivalism, says Lasch, invades the rhetoric of everyday life—even in the most trivial forms of expression. He notes that the left-wing magazine *Mother Jones* advertises itself as a 'survival guide' to the 'political Dark Ages' brought about by the election of Ronald Reagan; a Los Angeles radio station commends itself as 'your survival station of the eighties'; Samsonite, a manufacturer of luggage, advertises its latest briefcase as the 'Survivor'; a basketball coach praises one of his players for his capacity to learn from his mistakes and to 'survive them'; at Yale a 'Student Rescue Committee' urges parents to send their sons and daughters a 'survival kit' ('nourishing snack food in a humorously packed box') to help them weather final exams; Erma Bombeck introduces her latest collection of columns as a book 'of surviving'; and an antifeminist tirade, publishing with the usual media fanfare, announces itself as 'A Survival Guide for the Bedeviled Male.'

The concern with survival, notes Lasch, is connected with the widely-shared perception of the way in which all of us are victims or potential victims. The growing belief that we are all victimized in one way or another, by events beyond our control owes much of its power, he says, not just to the general feeling that we live in a dangerous world dominated by large organizations, but to the memory of specific events in twentieth century history that have victimized people on a mass scale. Lasch notes that in the preface to the revised edition of William Ryan's well-known book *Blaming the Victim*, Ryan apologizes for devoting the first edition largely to the plight of black people and the poor. He has come to see that almost everyone is vulnerable to disaster; to catastrophic illness; to the deliberate manipulation of inflation and unemployment; to grossly unfair taxes; to pollution, unsafe working conditions, and the 'greed of the great oil companies'. Returning to a theme of his earlier book, *The Culture of Narcissism*,[13] Lasch believes that competition, as a central value in our culture, now centers not so much on the desire to excel as on the struggle to avoid a crushing defeat. A willingness to risk everything in the pursuit of victory gives way to a cautious hoarding of the resources necessary to sustain life over the long haul. The heroic rebel, warrior, or robber baron, earlier prototypes of successful competition, yield their place in the modern imagination to the wily veteran determined not so much to outstrip his opponents as to outlast them. Survivalism, says Lasch, leads to a devaluation of heroism. The purpose of success, he continues, has been reconceived as a daily struggle for survival. Americans now see money not as a measure of success but as a means of survival. Books addressed to executives, bearing such titles as *Survival in the Executive Jungle*, recommend a 'strategy for survival' based on watchfulness, suspicion and distrust.

The results of the survivalist mentality, says Lasch, are seen in a variety of ways: for example, by concentrating our attention on the small immediate obstacles that confront us each day. Recent success manuals, he says, stress the importance of narrow, clearly defined objectives and the danger of dwelling in the past or looking too far into the future. The implications of such thinking for education and curriculum design are, as we will see, apparent. Lasch writes:

> Success manuals are not alone in urging people to lower their sights and to confine their attention to the immediate moment. The human potential movement, the medical and psychiatric literature on coping, the growing literature on death and dying all recommend the same strategy for dealing with the 'predictable crises of everyday life . . .' (The Survivor) keeps his eyes fixed on the road just in front of him. He shores up fragments against his ruin. His life consists of isolated acts and events. It has no story, no pattern, no structure as an unfolded narrative . . . Both time and space have shrunk to the immediate present, the immediate environment. . . .[14]

There is also in the survivalist mentality, says Lasch, an implicit but extreme form of individualism—cut your ties, simplify your needs, get back to basics. There is a need for a kind of self-sufficiency. It is self-sufficiency, he continues, which is premised on the idea that the fundamental crises of late 20th century society have no collective or political solutions. The survivalist, Lasch asserts, has lowered his sights from history to everyday immediacy. The heavy price that is paid for this is the radical restriction of perspective that precludes moral judgments and intelligent political activity. All of this "allows him to remain human—no small accomplishment in these times. But it prevents him from exercising any influence over the course of public events."[15] Lasch adds that the result is also a personal life that is sadly attenuated: "Long term commitments and emotional attachments carry certain obligations under the best of circumstances: in an unstable, unpredictable world . . . people find it increasingly difficult to accept."[16] In order to achieve this emotional disengagement survivors are urged to learn the trick of observing themselves as if the events of their lives were happening to someone else:

> One reason people no longer see themselves as the subject of a narrative is that they no longer see themselves as subjects at all but rather as the victims of circumstance: and this feeling of being acted on by uncontrollable external forces prompts another mode of moral armament, a withdrawal from the beleaguered self into the person of a detached, bemused, ironic observer.[17]

Basic Skills and the 'Minimal Self'

It is clear, I believe, that there are strong connections between Lasch's survivalist mentality/culture and some of the assertions found in conservative educational discourse—especially centered around the demand for a 'return to basics' in matters of curriculum. Such discourse can be understood as a response to, and an expression of, survivalism. It must, however, be understood that such a response to the contemporary crisis (or crises) of survival is but one choice among several possibilities. That is to say, the way in which we respond—educationally or otherwise—to the crisis, is one selection from a number of different possible ways in which we might react. Each selection, of course, contains within it values, prejudices, and assumptions about human and societal possibilities; what we can do to deal with, or overcome, the difficult and precarious social reality in which we find ourselves living. In other words, as a way of dealing with our precarious and threatening situation, the 'basics' approach to curriculum is an ideological statement about the nature of the wider crisis, and how we must act towards it; it contains, implicitly, meanings and values that structure the nature and possibilities of human action. For want of a better term I shall refer to the ideological principle structuring the 'basics' curriculum and pedagogy as *individual-adaptive*. In contrast to this I think it is possible to identify as a response to the crisis of survival an alternative educational approach—one structured around an ideological principle that I have called *social-interventionist*. The latter suggests a radically different set of possibilities for dealing with the social crisis. In the prevailing notions of 'basics' and 'minimal competencies' (i.e. those structured around the individual-adaptive principle) there is the implicit demand for the development of self-sufficiency and self-reliance. As we have seen, it is just such characteristics that are at the core of the survivalist personality. Curriculum experiences in which such concerns are paramount are ones that promise to each individual the fundamental knowledge or skills that make possible one's survival—in the labor market and as consumers. Such a notion of education, which is seen as the medium for the acquisition of certain fundamental and minimum competencies to ensure an individual a minimum degree of agency in the pursuit of one's livelihood, forms a powerful focus for the mobilization of educational opinion. Its power is associated with the way in which schooling is directly connected to the possibilities for individual self-sufficiency and self-reliance; not merely for those at the higher levels of educational achievement, but for all those who are successful at some officially sanctioned test of intellectual ability. To be 'minimally competent' implies some basic ability to effectively negotiate one's way in the world. It suggests that the appropriately schooled graduate is the proprietor of capacities that might insulate him or her from the hazardous nature of market values in our society. Of course, education defined in this way becomes the quintessential expression of the survivalist mentality. It is a belief that connects schooling with the acquisition of those skills or knowledge that might, in some way, protect individuals from the insecurity and predatory nature of our social and economic environment. As with other aspects of survivalist discourse, basic skills oriented schooling offers a curriculum with little or no attention to questions of personal meaning. There is little concern with the transmission of a cultural literacy that might provide the kind of narrative threads that allow one to apprehend one's place in the totality of social life. To the contrary, such forms of schooling with its curriculum that is a discontinuous and unconnected inventory of skills, information and behaviors, is remote from an education that might foster the intellectual capacity to connect history with the present or to link individual experience with that of the collectivity. In this sense, and in other ways we have referred to, it is profoundly individualistic—an approach in which our collective problems and difficulties must be faced by the solitary individual who, with the help of schooling, has learned to 'cope' with the world alone. The basic skills minimum competencies perspective is, as Lasch described, a manifestation of that larger orientation to the world in which life consists of isolated acts and events; in which there is no pattern, structure or unfolding narrative. Time and space have shrunk to the immediate present and the immediate environment. The 'basics' approach to curriculum has little interest in making sense of the world, in connecting experience with meaning, and meanings in one part of our world to those in another. To the contrary, 'basics' oriented curriculum offers disconnected skills and unrelated facts. The knowledge conveyed through such schooling is characterized by its fragmented nature, and experienced as isolated bits of information. Both within and between curriculum areas and subjects there is little in the way of structure or pattern with which to connect meanings and knowledge. Of course, none of this should be too much of a surprise. The 'basics' imbued curriculum is connected not with matters of awareness, insight, or imagination, but with supplying a set of skills and knowledge needed to simply (if not easily) 'get by' in the world. Its utilitarian emphasis is on the ability to cope with, or adapt to, what appears to exist in the immediate present, and in the immediate vicinity. In its fragmented and high circumscribed concerns it mirrors the survivalist mentality. Of course, notions of 'coping with' or 'adapting to' what exists (or appears to exist) implies a process of dealing with the world in which structures and institutions are reified. It is the atomized individual that must adapt to a reality that is substantially unchangeable and unchallengeable. Instead, curricular concerns are oriented around what Lasch calls "the predictable crises of everyday life"—a process that avoids any significant intellectual or moral engagement with the dangerous and catastrophic problems that confront humanity. In this sense the basic skills orientation represents, in the same manner as the mentality of survivalism, an intensification of a self-sufficient individualism. In that vein a pragmatic and utilitarian individualism is more meaningful than any attempt to comprehend critically the shared culture. Instead this curriculum attempts to facilitate the individual's adaptation to the shoals and currents of a turbulent reality.

Of course, as I have argued elsewhere, there is an important element of mystification in all of this. Such thinking connects high levels of unemployment among young people with inadequate training in literacy and numeracy. From this perspective improved acquisition of these capabilities would appear to augur improved capacity to determine one's own economic future. It is, as we know, exactly this aspect of our ideology which results in the notion of 'blaming the victim'; the individual as the sole proprietor of his own person or capacities,[18] becomes the lone determinant of one's economic success or failure. Indeed, the concept of 'minimum competencies' implies the acquisition of some basic capacity to survive or cope with contemporary society. Whether this assumes higher levels of literacy as the route to great job opportunities or advancement, the ability to balance a check-book as the means to remain solvent in an inflationary economy, or greater consumer awareness as the vehicle for dealing with corporate deception or exploitation, the emphasis is personalistic. The assumption is of an individual's accommodation to, or acceptance of, social reality. The development of individual capacities through the acquisition of appropriate knowledge or skills at school becomes, in short, the vehicle for human survival in contemporary American society. The perspective of 'basic skills' and 'minimum competencies' asserts, ultimately, an individualistic world-view in which personal effort and ability, not structural change, becomes the means to deal with the present harsh reality. It is my belief that the frequent association of 'basics' and 'competencies' with the concept of survival ('survival skills') points to the petit-bourgeous ideological underpinnings of recent educational policies. It is, certainly, emblematic of such ideology. From this perspective the individual enters a Hobbesian world of unmitigated agency, a world in which, through the appropriate education, one may be prepared to cope with a deteriorating struggle for survival.

Of course, the emphasis on individual adaptation to reality, while foreclosing possibilities of social change and reconstruction, does not rule out a nostalgic desire to return to more salutary times. Those observers who have described a reactionary aspect to the 'basic' mentality are surely correct. There is, certainly, an implicit wish among some social groups for schools to prepare youngsters for jobs and roles such as they grew up among; the desire to perpetuate a world it understood, a world limited to a particular era and culture.[19] There is here what appears as a paradoxical blend in which, while the present is reified, there is a wish to return to the past. Perhaps this can be explained if the present reality—or at least those parts of it which are viewed as desirable—is seen as organically linked to the past, while the undesirable aspects of the present appear as disconnected from the core features of American life, as these have developed historically. The result is the conservative inability to see the moral and spiritual crisis of American society as rooted in its fundamental historic structures, especially those related to capitalistic institutions. The disintegrative effect on traditional values of a consumption-oriented system, and the pervasive commodification of human activity, with all its dire effects on moral and spiritual life, is not easily attributed to these core institutional influences. To do so undercuts the conservative romanticization of what this society is all about. The moral rot must be seen as an unnatural interruption, an abberation from what is the fundamental nature of the society. Returning to basics is thus connected to a larger concern which is the desire to return to what is taken to be the good, sound, wholesome roots of the nation. In both its restructured pedagogic sense, as well as in the larger cultural sense, such a perspective avoids engagement with the structural and social determinant of the present crisis of human survival.

THE SOCIAL-INTERVENTIONIST CURRICULUM: TOWARDS AN ALTERNATIVE PEDAGOGY

As a response to the crisis of survival the return to basics represents an ideology that is the prevailing, though not the only possible, approach. Against the 'individual-adaptive' ideological principle underpinning basics pedagogy one can identify an alternative pedagogy organized around what I have referred to as a 'social-interventionist' world-view. While both approaches have as their central concern issues of survival, they differ sharply in matters of theory and practice. In describing the social-interventionist approach to curriculum we can see more clearly the taken-for-granted assumptions that structure the dominant form of educational discourse. In dealing with the issue of survival, in education or elsewhere, we assume, through this discourse, not only the causes of the crisis but means through which to address it.

In the first place, *adapting* to the difficult and threatening circumstances of present day social reality is contrasted with an approach which emphasizes the possibilities of intervening in what exists and *changing* reality. In this sense the concern with 'adapting to' or 'coping with' the situation is contrasted with a notion of empowerment. While the first approach reifies the world, the second emphasizes the possibilities of challenging and transforming what presently exists. The first approaches the world as a fundamentally immutable phenomenon in which individuals must be helped to make the best accommodation possible; the second asserts the historically and socially-conditioned nature of the present reality. In emphasizing the need to make society adaptive to human concerns and needs (rather than vice-versa), the curriculum must be one that emphasizes the knowledge and skills that might ensure a more responsive culture. Central to this is education for purposes of citizenship and the capacity of democratic participation. Citizenship here embraces a concern for those public spheres of activity that impinge on our lives as individuals and as members of a collectivity; as students, as workers, as consumers, as neighborhood residents, and as voters. The concern with such spheres of public activity ensures that citizenship education is rooted in the issues, concerns and struggles of the everyday world, not in the rarified abstractions typically found in school-book discussion of democracy and governance. In addition, apprehension of the reality of democratic participation, and of popular governance of institutions—in the workplace, in the market, and in our communities—implies a collective rather than individual mode of intervention into the conditions of our lives. Intervention into the conditions of our everyday lives can only mean, for the mass of people, a collective, rather than personal form of empowerment. Instead of the emphasis on individual self-reliance and self-sufficiency, there is the notion of an interdependent community in which individual capabilities and skills are pooled in order to exert a shared control of our social world. Instead of individual adaption to a world out of control, there is, instead, the attempt to confront, in an agentic manner, the circumstances that are responsible for our hazardous and dangerous disordered social situation.

While knowledge for democratic practice in the everyday world implies a training of sorts—a transmission of information, skills and knowledge—what is suggested here is far more than a utilitarian, fragmented, behavioristic, and technically dominated curriculum associated with the 'basics' in the individual-adaptive mode. At the core of the social-interventionist approach to curricular knowledge is the notion of cultural literacy.[20] Its central concern is not the accumulation of discrete skills or the segmented topics of subject-oriented schooling, but broad apprehension of the social/cultural formation which structures our everyday world. In this sense the curriculum is concerned with the connection of human practices among and between the moral/cultural, the political, the economic, the religious, the artistic and literary, and elsewhere. It must also emphasize, in the study of these spheres, the need for critical insight—awareness that penetrates the ideology of surface description in which our world is named in particular and distorting ways. Of course, a cultural literacy that attempts to provide critical awareness of the social/cultural information cannot be a continuation of the remote abstraction of the liberal arts tradition.[21] It must, instead, be deeply rooted in the experience of individuals daily struggling with the crises of survival—material, moral, spiritual and psychological. This requires that education provide a means through which the anxiety, confusion, disintegration, degradation and suffering of everyday life can be confronted and understood in terms of rootedness in the common circumstances of our lives. The curriculum, in other words, must link the individual's experience to the shared experience, and this, in turn, must be situated in the dynamics and the structures of the social world. In this education integrates self-reflection and self-awareness into the process of social analysis so that, for example, (and as suggested by Z. Bauman)[22] by exposing the intimate links between the limits of individual gratification and freedom of action on the one hand and societal networks of power and wealth (normally invisible to the unaided individual eye), the private experience of individual suffering and frustration may be understood in terms of the social dynamics of a class society.

As a pedagogy concerned with addressing the crisis of survival, awareness of its structural roots and its shared effects in our lived experience must be joined to a pedagogy of vision for transforming our present circumstances. Social-interventionist pedagogy is concerned both with what is and with what might be. The critical spirit underpinning such an education is not one of sheer negativity but is one of a coin whose reverse face is concerned with reconstructive possibilities. While the first face is analytical and relentlessly probing, the latter face is creative, imaginative and also hopeful. The classroom must open a public space in which to imaginatively recreate our everyday world. Of course this imaginative recreation seeks to transform the dangerous and threatening disorder of the present reality with arrangements that facilitate secure, loving, just and empowered lives. Naturally a pedagogy that places imaginative recreation of human life at its centre, whose epistemology is centred in understanding our lived experience, implies a fundamental reordering of what we traditionally assume about being teachers and students. This is not the place to elaborate of what we traditionally assume about being teachers and students. This is not the place to elaborate its qualities and characteristics. Its emphasis on the classroom as a place of dialogue, on the student and teacher as co-inquirers, the centrality of the interpretation of experience and the pursuit of meaning, and the relationship between the practical and the theoretical, have been well elaborated in a tradition that stretches from Dewey to Freire.

EDUCATIONAL CHANGE AND THE RULES
OF RADICAL POLITICAL DISCOURSE

I began this paper with the assertion that effective educational agendas (i.e. ones that have popular mobilizing power) do not do so as the result of a magical process. Their success is grounded in the agenda's ability to effectively give expression to widely shared experiences. An educational agenda of this sort is able to offer, at a discursive level, a resonant representation of this experience. Of course, this is more than mere representation: it interprets and mediates the structural conditions of our existence. It creates, in Althusser's formulation, our imaginary relationship to the world. We have seen here, for example, the relationship between the crises that permeate our world at every turn, and the explicit and implicit claims of a basics oriented curriculum. One that promises to facilitate individuals' negotiation of these crises so as to achieve, in the precarious conditions that we face, a level of self-sufficiency that might enable us to survive. However illusory these promises, (no amount of basic skills training, for example, would enable black youth in America's ghettos to avoid the 40% or so unemployment rate found there). Their powerful hold on the educational imagination is rooted in the ability to articulate real human concerns in a form expressive of the dominant rationality.

Radical educational agendas—such as the one described briefly here—must take seriously such limitations. They must be rooted in widely shared human concerns and experience. And, befitting the world of political mobilization not theoretical discourse, they must have the capacity for popular appeal and a resonant vision of what should, and could, conceivably be. At the same time radical agendas must contain a logic that, even if quite different from the dominant rationality, must correspond with practices and traditions that form a significant, if subordinate, part of the culture and ideological landscape. Too many radical prescriptions for education (and perhaps in other domains too) ignore these rules. They ignore the need to root alternative educational ideas and practices in the ground of widely felt human concerns. I have, here, suggested that the pervasive crises of survival, so incisively described by Christopher Lasch, offers a resonant starting point not only for conservative educational nostrums, but for radical interventions in schooling. In this case educational prescriptions offer not an adaption to the precarious and disordered nightmare of our present reality but a discourse concerned with human empowerment and social transformation; not a preparation for coping single-handedly with our dangerous and threatening world, but skills and knowledge to facilitate our collective capacity for intervening and reconstructing this world. It must be said that however appealing this vision might be, the social-interventionist logic which is its mainspring, reflects in America, a subordinate cultural and ideological viewpoint. Unlike the individual-adaptive rationality at the heart of the basics movement, it is only weakly represented in the offical discourse of American society. While we have attempted to root our educational agenda in the broadly felt concerns and anxieties of people, this in no way guarantees the possibility of addressing such concerns through an alternate logic than that which is prevalent. The latter, of course, is more than a clever deception planted, or imposed, in the minds of individuals. Far from this, such logic is constitutive of our commonsense; it is inseparable from important aspects of subjectivity itself—from the basic assumptions, meanings and values which are used to organize and cohere our sense of self, and our relationship to society and to nature. At the same time, however, the alternate logic—the social-interventionist principles underlying our radial pedagogy—is not an entirely abstract configuration without ties to culture and our way of life. The democratic and collective pedagogy advocated as a means to address the crisis of survival can certainly draw on traditions—however eroded or weakened—found in American society. Notions of self and collective empowerment, whether through social movements, labor unions, or neighborhood activism are not without cultural resonance in American life, as are traditions that speak to the democratic capacity to shape or reshape our social lives. We must be honest, however, in acknowledging that the most important opening to acceptance of an alternate logic in education (or elsewhere) is the disintegrative effects of the crisis itself—a crisis (or crises) that, as we have seen in Lasch's description embraces larger and larger segments of the population. The inability of conservative interventions, whether around matters of basic skills or prayer in school amendments, or elsewhere, to seriously address underlying causes will widen the openings to serious alternatives that do. At these moments it is possible to pry consciousness loose from the prevailing rationality. As 'acceptable' levels of unemployment rise, promises of creative and responsible work go unmet, awareness of sexual and other forms of subordination widens, personal life becomes as insecure and as fractious as public life, and fear of nuclear annihilation threatens all of our futures so there is the possibility to move beyond what is consciously assumed and accepted. It may be possible to encourage those alternative or oppositional moments of culture that form, in Gramsci's words, our 'commonsense' world. In the quest for educational change we must be cognizant of the social conditions that both enable, as well as limit, what is possible. At the same time we need to remember that it is not conditions, or structures, but human beings, who must, in the final analysis, grasp the possibilities of each situation and struggle to transform them. The theoretical discourse of radical analysis has done well at describing the structured circumstances of education; it has much more to do in developing a political discourse that can effectively contribute to transforming them.

NOTES

1. Henry Giroux, *Theory and Resistance in Education* (Mass: Bergin and Garvey, 1983).
2. For an important discussion of the concept of 'totality' in Marxist thought see Martin Jay, *Marxism and Totality* (Berkeley: University of California, 1984).
3. See, for example, H. Svi Shapiro, 'Education and Ideology: a Sociological Study of Educational Thought in the American Radical Movement, 1900–25,' in *Philosophy and Social Criticism*, Vol. 6, No. 4 (1979).
4. See, H. Svi Shapiro, 'Class, Ideology, and the Basic Skills Movement: A Study in the Sociology of Education Reform,' in *Interchange*, Vol. 14, No. 2 (1983).
5. Christopher Lasch, *The Minimal Self* (New York: W. W. Norton, 1984).
6. The surge of equalitarianism in this period was fed by the civil, economic and social struggles of minorities and women, and by the anti-hierarchical and anti-bureaucratic concerns of the student movement. The cultural (and related, educational) revolt that resulted from the equalitarianism had, at its heart, a number of common pressures. These included the attempt to reduce the separation between (or merge) what constitutes 'culture' as opposed to real life; the attempt to assimilate politics and culture; the concern to eclipse the separateness of personal and cultural experience; and the attempt to reduce or eliminate the traditional hierarchies that restrict who may participate in the 'making' of culture, what counts as comprising culture, and who is able to appreciate it. Daniel Bell, in his discussion of the effects of this radical temper on the arts noted that there was "stylistically . . . an attempt to eclipse 'distance'—psychic distance, social distance, and aesthetic distance— and insist on the absolute presentness, the simultaneity and immediacy, of experience." In all, he said, "there was a 'democratization' of culture in which nothing could be considered high or low . . . and a world of sensibility which was accessible to all."

    The result of this movement for greater equality in American Society, sought by minorities, women, the poor, students and others, generated tendencies then, leading towards a radical redefinition or reinterpretation of the meaning of culture. There was a movement towards reducing the hierarchically ordered separation between these practices, meanings, symbols, knowledge, etc., that were associated with the notion of 'culture' from those relegated to what members of the Frankfort School of Social Research have called 'civilization'. Included in the latter were the practices, meanings, etc., associated with the 'daily round of existence'—work, community, family, etc. Culture, meanwhile, retaining its connotation of 'high culture'—the select heritage of intellectual, artistic, literary and aesthetic products claimed to represent more noble concerns. From this perspective culture could no longer be seen as restricted to only certain human activities or endeavors, or found in only a very select number of locations. Instead, culture was to be viewed as existing wherever man makes the world the object of his knowledge, submitting it to a process of transformation, altering reality. It becomes synonymous with the *entire* range of human practice and social experience. The street, factory, neighborhood, etc., are no less a part of the cultural matrix than the more traditional sites of cultural transmission—schools, museums, etc. Nor is culture quite so connected to the abstract, the symbolic, or things past—it is less the accumulation of a select tradition than the ongoing product of the total human experience. It is preeminently concerned with the life presently lived, and the language, concerns, meanings, values and activities of those living.

The result of all this was precisely a legitimation of educational reforms that led to an extended and broadened version of what constitutes educational experience or 'counts' as educational knowledge. Media 'literacy' no less than the 'classics'; Black culture no less than U.S. History, ecological awareness no less than algebra or trigonometry, could be viewed as valid components of school curriculum. Nor, indeed, did school constitute the only, or even the best, site for education—that could be had in many other areas in which man engaged in his world. Indeed, the school was seen as suffering from its cloistered, unrelatedness to the real world outside.

7. Michael F. D. Young, 'An approach to the Study of Curricula as Socially Organized Knowledge,' in Michael F. D. Young (Ed.), *Knowledge and Control* (London: Collier-MacMillan, 1971).

8. The general effects of the educational reform movement, as is widely recognized, was the proliferation of courses in schools which included most notably, studies in the history and culture of disadvantaged minorities, in environmental and ecological concerns, contemporary politics, the mass media, current events and social issues, a widening of literary instruction into contemporary themes, a concern with 'relevance' in history and social studies, and the exploration of personal experience—sexual activity and relationships, drugs, family life, moral and value concerns, etc. In addition to the widely heralded proliferation and diversification of curriculum was the emergence (though to a more limited scale) of curricula that focused upon—and offered direct experience of—the local or surrounding community (the 'school-without-walls' being perhaps, the best noted example of this focus). In that most visible or notorious symbol of the reforms of this period— the 'alternative' school—many of these tendencies merged, a concern with contemporary social issues, a pedagogy that often included direct, out-of-the-classroom experience and an exploration of the students' particular cultural experience and personal identify.

Taken as a whole, such reform can be seen as an affirmation (or more accurately, a reaffirmation) of a powerful and enduring educational theme in which schooling is identified with the apprehension of the collective or common culture. While the curricular, institutional, and pedagogic elements mentioned above cannot be said to form a clearly articulated presentation of such a view, the concern is, I believe, still a central one. It is evidenced in changes in the curriculum so that its focus shifts toward an exploration of contemporary social experience (encapsulated in the often trivializing notion of 'relevance'), and institutional changes that move school toward embodying or reflecting the social and cultural context in which it is located through integration, mainstreaming, etc.). The underlying assertion is that the 'culture' of school needs to comprise many, if not all, of those values, beliefs, meanings, and experiences which are found within the wider society, and that the purpose of school is connected to the process of transmitting, facilitating access to, and widespread apprehension of this culture. The powerful assertion of this view, beginning in the 1960's, engendered, inevitably, important curricular and institutional demands—demands which have, despite the more recent changes, continued to reverberate within education. In curriculum, the focus on issues of sexual, ethnic, racial and social 'relevance' embodied these demands with its concerns for life in the present, not in the past; and as it is experienced by those who are a part of the society—not just a select group. At the institutional level, the public school, in order to more truly reflect the common culture moved to become more representative of the entire social order—black and white, rich and poor, 'normal' or handicapped, etc.

9. For a moving picture of the contradictions between the promise and reality of white-collar work see Richard Sennett and Jonathan Cobb, *The Hidden Injuries of Class* (New York: Knopf, 1972).

10. For an important discussion of the relationship between employment opportunities and education see Henry M. Levin and Russell W. Rumberger, *The Educational Implication of High Technology* (Stanford: Institute for Research on Educational Finance and Governance, 1983).

11. This account is an abbreviated version of that presented in my paper, 'Class, Ideology and the Basic Skills Movement: A Study in the Sociology of Educational Reform,' in *Interchange*, Vol. 14, No. 2 (1983).

12. Lasch, *The Minimal Self*.

13. Christopher Lasch, *The Culture of Narcissism* (New York: Warner Books, 1979).

14. Lasch, *The Minimal Self*, pp. 95–96.

15. Ibid., pp. 93–94.

16. Ibid., p. 96.

17. Ibid., p. 96.

18. C. B. Macpherson, *The Political Theory of Possessive Individualism* (Oxford: Clarendon Press, 1962).

19. James Moffett, 'Hidden Impediments to Improving English Teaching,' in *Phi Delta Kappan*, vol. 67, No. 1 (Sept. 1985).

20. The term 'cultural literacy' is probably best associated with the work of the Brazilian educator Paulo Freire. See, for example Paulo Freire, *Cultural Action for Freedom* (Harvard Education Review Monograph). See, also, C. A. Bowers, *Cultural Literacy for Freedom* (Eugene, Oregon: Elan, 1974).

21. For an excellent recent discussion of the dissonance between liberal arts education and social reality see Christopher Lasch, 'Excellence in Education: Old Refrain or New Departure?' in *Issues in Education*, Vol. 3, No. 1 (Summer 1985). See also Stanley Aronowitz and Henry Giroux, *Education Under Siege* (S. Hadley, Mass: Bergin and Garvey, 1985).

22. Zygmunt Bauman, *Towards a Critical Sociology* (London: Routledge and Kegan Paul, 1976).

Schooling, Culture, and Literacy in the Age of Broken Dreams: A Review of Bloom and Hirsch

Stanley Aronowitz and Henry A. Giroux

Since the second term of the Reagan administration, the debate on education has taken a new turn. Now, as before, the tone is principally set by the Right, but its position has been radically altered. The importance of linking educational reform to the needs of big business has continued to influence the debate, while the demands for schools to provide the skills necessary for domestic production and expanding capital abroad have slowly given way to an overriding emphasis on schools as sites of cultural production. The emphasis on cultural production can be seen in current attempts to address the issue of cultural literacy, in the development of national curriculum boards, and in reform initiatives bent on providing students with the language, knowledge, and values necessary to preserve the essential traditions of Western civilization.[1] The Right's position on cultural production in the schools arose from a consensus that the problems faced by the United States can no longer be reduced to those of educating students in the skills they will need to occupy jobs in more advanced and middle-range occupational levels in such areas as computer programming, financial analysis, and electronic machine repair.[2] Instead, the emphasis must be switched to the current cultural crisis, which can be traced to the broader ideological tenets of the progressive education movement that dominated the curriculum after World War II. These include the pernicious doctrine of cultural relativism, according to which canonical texts of the Western intellectual tradition may not be held superior to others; the notion that student experience should qualify as a viable form of knowledge; and the idea that ethnic, racial, gender, and other relations play a significant role in accounting for the development and influence of mainstream intellectual culture. On this account, the 1960s proved disastrous to the preservation of the inherited virtues of Western culture. Relativism systematically downgraded the value of key literary and philosophical traditions, giving equal weight to the dominant

Aronowitz, Stanley and Giroux, Henry A., "Schooling, Culture, and Literacy in the Age of Broken Dreams: A Review of Bloom and Hirsch," *Harvard Educational Review*, 58:2, pp. 172–194. Copyright © 1988 by the President and Fellows of Harvard College. All rights reserved. Reprinted with permission.

knowledge of the "Great Books" and to an emergent potpourri of "degraded" cultural attitudes. Allegedly, the last twenty years have witnessed the virtual loss of those revered traditions that constitute the core of the Western heritage. The unfortunate legacy that has emerged during the recent past has resulted in a generation of cultural illiterates. In this view, not only is the American economy at risk, but civilization itself.

Allan Bloom and E. D. Hirsch represent different versions of the latest and most popular conservative thrust for educational reform. Each, in his own way, represents a frontal attack aimed at providing a programmatic language with which to defend schools as cultural sites; that is, as institutions responsible for reproducing the knowledge and values necessary to advance the historical virtues of Western culture. Hirsch presents his view of cultural restoration through a concept of literacy that focuses on the basic structures of language, and applies this version of cultural literacy to the broader consideration of the needs of the business community, as well as to the maintenance of American institutions. His view of literacy represents an attack on educational theories which validate student experience as a key component of educational formation and curriculum development. For Hirsch, the new service economy requires employees who can write a memo, read within a specific cultural context, and communicate through a national language composed of the key words of Western culture. Within the same spirit, Bloom offers a much wider critique of education. Advancing a position that claims schools have contributed to the instrumentalization of knowledge and that the population has fallen victim to a widespread relativism and rampant anti-intellectualism, Bloom proposes a series of educational reforms that privileges a fixed idea of Western culture organized around a core curriculum based on the old Great Books. Bloom writes:

> Of course, the only serious solution [for reform in higher education] is almost universally rejected: the good old Great Books approach, in which a liberal education means reading certain generally recognized classical texts, just reading them, letting them dictate what the questions are and the method of approaching them—not forcing them into categories we make up, not treating them as historical products, but trying to read them as their authors wished them to be read. . . . But one thing is certain: wherever the Great Books make up a central part of the curriculum, the students are excited and satisfied, feel they are doing something that is independent and fulfilling, getting something from the university they cannot get elsewhere. The very fact of this special experience, which leads nowhere beyond itself, provides them with a new alternative and a respect for study itself. (p. 344)

This propensity for making sweeping claims without even a shred of evidence raises serious questions about the nature of Bloom's position as well as the quality of his own scholarship. Moreover, Bloom's position is hardly novel. It has been with us since the Enlightenment and has long been invoked as an argument for the reproduction of elites. It is a position that advocates a social system in which a select cadre of intellectuals, economically privileged groups, and their professional servants are the only individuals deemed fit to possess the culture's sacred canon of knowledge, which assures their supremacy.

Both of these books represent the logic of a new cultural offensive, one of the most elaborate conservative educational manifestos to appear in decades. Similarly, both books have broad implications for educational reform and for the wider crisis in democracy. We intend to analyze the ideological and pedagogical content of these books in the context of the current debates, beginning with an analysis of Bloom's *The Closing of the American Mind*.

Bloom's critique of American education does not address the indifference of schools to the realities of the international marketplace, as in the old technicist discourse which reduces schooling to job training. Instead, Bloom attacks modernity, especially what he considers the rampant relativism that marks the last one hundred years of Western history. Like José Ortega y Gasset, his illustrious predecessor, Bloom seeks to restore the dominance of Platonism—that is, the belief in the trans-historical permanence of forms of truth—to education. Where President Reagan's Secretary of Education, William Bennett, and the older elitists reiterated the call for "excellence," but never succeeded in articulating its substance, Bloom presents his proposals in more concrete terms.

Bloom's attack on liberal educational practice and the philosophy that underlies it is a sobering reminder that political and social analyses, which have identified them-selves with modernity as a critique of advanced industrial societies, constitute power-ful weapons in the hands of both the Right and the Left. Here we have all the elements of an elitist sensibility: abhorrence of mass culture, a rejection of experience as the arbiter of taste and pedagogy, and a sweeping attack on what is called "cultural relativism," especially on those who want to place popular culture, ethnic and racially based cultures, and cultures grounded in sexual communities (either feminist or gay and lesbian) on a par with classical Western traditions. For conservatives, each of these elements represents a form of anti-intellectualism that threatens the moral au-thority of the state. Consequently, much more than economic survival is at stake: at issue is the survival of Western civilization as it represents itself through 2,500 years of philosophy, historiography, and literature.

Bloom's sweeping agenda intends to eliminate culture as a serious object of knowledge. According to Bloom, the culturalist perspective is what Plato meant by the allegory of the cave. Thus, we are prevented from seeing the sunlight by culture, which is the enemy of what Bloom calls "openness." Although vaguely apologetic on the subject, Bloom ends up arguing that Western tradition is superior to non-Western cultures precisely because its referent is not "cultural" but the universal and context-free love of wisdom; for the underlying ethic of Western civilization, according to Bloom, is its capacity to transcend the immediate circumstances of daily life in order to reach the good life. Lower cultures are inevitably tied to "local knowledge"—to family and community values and beliefs, which are overwhelmingly context-specific. As it so happened in the course of history, the Greeks managed to teach some thinkers—Bloom being one—the way to universal truth.

For Bloom, the teachings of Plato and Socrates provide the critical referents with which to excoriate contemporary culture. Bloom systematically devaluates the music, sexuality, and pride of youth, and traces what he envisions as the gross excesses of the 1960s (the real object of his attack) to the pernicious influence of German philosophy from Nietzsche to Heidegger as refracted through the mindless relativism of modernizers. Feminism is equated with "libertinism," or making sex easy; "affirmative action now institutionalizes the worst aspects of separatism"; and rock music "has the beat of sexual intercourse" and cannot qualify, according to Bloom's Socratic standard, as a genuinely harmonic reconciliation of the soul with the passions of the body. Instead, rhythm and melody are viewed as a form of barbarism when they take on the explicit sexual coloration of modern rock 'n' roll music. For Bloom, popular culture, especially rock 'n' roll, represents a new form of barbarism whose horror he conjures up in the image of a thirteen-year-old boy watching MTV while listening to a Walkman radio.

> He enjoys the liberties hard won over centuries by the alliance of philosophic genius and political heroism, consecrated by the blood of martyrs; he is provided with comfort and leisure by the most productive economy ever known to mankind [*sic*]; science has penetrated the secrets of nature in order to provide him with the marvelous, lifelike electronic sound and image reproduction he is enjoying. And in what does progress culminate? A pubescent child whose body throbs with orgasmic rhythms; whose feelings are made articulate in hymns to the joys of onanism or the killing of parents; whose ambition is to win fame and wealth in imitating the drag-queen who makes the music. In short, life is made into a nonstop, commercially prepackaged mastubational fantasy. (p. 75)

Bloom's sentiments, in this case, have been shaped by what he perceives as indications of a serious moral and intellectual decline among American youth: a challenge to authority formed by the student movements of the 1960s and the leveling ideology of democratic reform characteristic of radical intellectuals.[3]

These judgments merely provide a prologue to a much more forceful and unsparing attack on nihilism, which, according to Bloom and his political and intellectual peerage, consistently devalues scholarship, or, in its more universal aspect, the life of the mind. Nihilism in Bloom's philosophy is a code word for the glorification of action and power and represents the real threat to contemporary civilization. Nihilism has a number of historical roots: the modernism of the good life that stresses pluralism and diversity; the vacillations of democracy that permit the ignorant a degree of freedom which, in four undergraduate years, students are not prepared to use; a fragmentation born out of the uncertainties of a moral order that cannot present to the young either a unified world view or goals to overcome the greed of modern life; and, in a more politically charged context, the decade of the 1960s, which was marked by a flagrant disrespect for authority, especially the authority of the intellect. Here we have more than the usual tepid porridge of conservative discourse. Bloom invokes images of "chaos and decay" in the moral fabric of our society. However, the sources of decay are rarely seen to be economic and political. Indeed, there is not a whisper of criticism of capitalism. In fact, capitalism appears only as a sidelight in Bloom's rather indirect discussion of Marxism.

This brief description does not exhaust the breadth of Bloom's hyperbolic tirade. Our concern is, of course, focused on Bloom's vision of the crucial role schools can perform in correcting the current state of academic and public national culture he so roundly despises. Naturally, Bloom does not expect all schools to participate in reversing our country's spiritual malaise. The task falls to the literally twenty or thirty first-rate colleges and universities that are blessed with the best students but are regrettably frittering away their mission to restore to the West the mantle of greatness.

Commanding his minions to revise radically the curriculum, to purge it of allusions to student experience (which, in any case, is mired in ignorance), Bloom seeks to rid the classroom of cultural relativism and of all those areas of study that do not venerate the traditions of the past. Bloom's call for curriculum reform is clear: End the sham of the sexual, racial, and cultural revolution that animated the generation who confronted the White men at the Pentagon and at other institutions of economic, political, and cultural power twenty years ago. Reinstate Latin as the lingua franca of learning and transmit Western civilization through the one hundred greatest books that embody its system of values.

Of course, the state universities and colleges are now populated by the casualties of contemporary culture: large numbers of children of divorced parents, who are portrayed by Bloom as unfortunate—even tragic—products of current conditions; Blacks and other minorities whose university experience is "different from that of other students" because of their history of "disadvantage," and whose dedication is, except in rare instances, not to learning but to practical advantage; and dispirited faculty members whose dreams of living in a community of scholars have been destroyed by the "interruptions" of modern social problems. For Bloom, these conditions disqualify the state universities and colleges as appropriate sites for professors and students to experience the awe and wonder of confronting the "Great Minds" of the ages.

It would be too easy to dismiss this frankly aristocratic vision of education as simply an effort to establish a new status quo conforming to Clark Kerr's model—a three-tier postsecondary education system in which theoretical knowledge is confined to the Ivy League institutions and major state universities—principally the University of California and some of the Big Ten—and private institutions such as Chicago, Duke, and Emory. But this would not do justice to the political intention in the neoconservatives' attack on higher education, or comprehend the danger and novelty of their argument.

For, unlike Irving Kristol's rantings against the 1960s' New Left (who were trying to create an "adversary culture" in opposition to the supremely democratic and capitalist society that had become America), Bloom joins Hilton Kramer and the professors of the Cold War intelligentsia of the 1950s in advocating a return to the age of the medieval Schoolmen, or at least to the high European culture of the nineteenth century. Rather than praising democracy, he yearns for the return of a more rigidly stratified civilization in which the crowd is contained within the land of the marketplace and its pleasures are confined to the rituals of the carnival. What he wants to exclude are the majority of the population from the precincts of reason. At the same time, he would drive the vox populi from the genuine academy where the Absolute Spirit should find a home, but does not, because of the confusion that reigns amidst the dangerous and flabby influence of the discourse of social commitment, politics, and equality. Bloom identifies the impulse to egalitarianism as the chief culprit in the decay of higher learning as well as the worst impasse of democracy. But university administrators bear equal responsibility for pandering to these base motives. Instead of feeling bound by tradition to transmit the higher learning which, after all, is the repository of what is valuable in schooling, they gave away the store. Universities lost their way in the scandal that is culture.

Pluralists and democrats might dismiss these elitist ruminations without grasping the valid elements of the complaint. For there can be no doubt that the reception which Bloom's book has enjoyed signifies that he has tapped the elitists' collective nerve. Intellectuals are uneasy about their role as teachers because their own experiences, interests, and values seem profoundly at odds with the several generations they have taught since the 1960s. But even more searing is their growing feeling of irrelevance, not only with respect to the process of education, but also with respect to their role within public life.

In Bloom's exegesis, the past must play a crucial role in formulation of the future. Intellectuals are to join in a classical evocation of a mythically integrated civilization that becomes the vantage point from which to criticize the current situation. In all of its versions, the integrated past is marked by the existence of a community of the spirit; it is a time when at least a minority was able to search for the Good and the True, unhampered by temporal considerations such as making a living. For the idyllic past is always constructed in the images of leisure, or to be more fair, in an environment where society provides a sufficient social surplus to support a priest class, or their secular equivalents. In contrast, the contemporary construction of the intellectual is on the model of technical rather than pure reason. The intellectual transmits algorithms rather than ideas, and orients students to careers rather than criticizes the social structure.

Bloom's attack on higher education conveniently excludes the degree to which the existing arrangements of social and economic power have contributed to the shaping of the intellectual life that he so stridently laments. What Bloom fails to mention in his attack on the servants of higher education is that the disappearance of political intellectuals corresponds to the passing of politics from "public" life. Educational institutions, once charged with the task of providing a little learning to ruling elites and providing them with a mandarin class, have assumed a crucial place in the economic and cultural order. Their task is no longer to preserve civilization as it has been defined by the Greek and Roman aristocracies; these institutions are now filled with knowledge-producers, who, in advanced capitalist societies, have become part of the process of material and social reproduction. The idea of the intellectual as adversary of the dominant culture is utterly foreign to current arrangements (for example, the president of Barnard College, a former corporate lawyer, appears on television commenting as an insider on the stock market crash and barely refers to her role as educator except to observe that students are calling home nervously asking their parents, "How are we doing?").

In his last chapter Bloom alludes to business civilization and describes negatively the way economics has overwhelmed the social sciences in "serious" universities (taking the place once held by sociology in the days when students desired to "help" people rather than looking out for themselves). Sounding like the Frankfurt school of critical theory, he even manages to criticize the belief, common among natural scientists, that their disciplines yield the only "real" knowledge. Characteristically, Bloom appeals to the elite schools to introduce philosophy as a key component of liberal education in order to counter the threat to higher education being posed by the rigid empiricisms of economics and natural science.

The tension between tradition and innovation plagues all who are seriously concerned with education. But Bloom refuses to go beyond scapegoating and ask how classical texts have failed to address the generations that came into postsecondary education after World War II: why Latin and Greek were no longer deemed essential for even the elite university curricula; why students, administrators, and the overwhelming majority of faculty came to view universities as degree mills, at worst, or, at best, places where the enterprising student could be expected to receive a good reading list. These questions cannot be addressed, much less answered, by invective.

The conservative appeal to the past takes on the character of an ideological flag against the future. It is not that the relativists, of both left and liberal persuasion, want to destroy the spirit and form of Western cultural heritage. Rather, they seek to reveal how such a heritage has often been employed as a weapon against those who would democratize institutions, who would change relations of power. Every achievement of civilization—the pyramids, great works of Greek philosophy and science, the wonderful representations of the human body and the soul that emerged during the Renaissance—has been built on the backs of slaves, on a faraway peasantry; in short, on a material foundation that undermines the notion of an uncomplicated marriage between high culture and humanism. Ignoring this fact, as Walter Benjamin reminds us, helps to sustain the culture and civilization in general.[4] For this reason, the rebellion against privilege is frequently accompanied by an attack against the intellectuals. What oppressed people understand better than most is that intellectuals are typically servants of the mighty; they often provide the legitimacy for deeds of state, private violence, and exploitation. This, of course, is the meaning of the argument that every achievement of high culture is preceded by the blood of those who make it possible.

When Bloom calls for reviving Latin as a requirement for educated youth, he opposes one of the crucial reforms of the eighteenth- and nineteenth-century democratic revolutions: establishing the vernacular as the language not only of commerce and manufacture but also of public life, literature, and philosophy. His fealty to classical texts excludes the pre-Socratics and Aristotle and focuses instead on Socrates and his disciple Plato precisely because of their attempt to separate truth from knowledge. Truth in Plato's *Symposium* requires no external object for its justification but refers instead to itself, particularly the purity of form. Knowledge is always one-sided, referring to an external object. It constitutes a representation of things and not, in Plato's terms, the things themselves. This distinction was challenged during the Enlightenment. Increasingly, truth and knowledge have the same external referent; subjectivity is removed from the realm of science and occupies, as ethics, psychology, and philosophy, a quasi-religious margin.

The virtue of Bloom's tirade, despite its reactionary content, is to remind us of what has been lost in the drive for rationalization, for the supremacy of science over philosophy, history over eternal essences. That is, the twentieth-century obsession of both defining and celebrating history as an evolutionary mode of ideological and material progress, produced through the marriage of science and technology, has resulted in a refusal to give primacy to the important and problematic relationship between truth, power, and knowledge. From the point of view of a conservative for whom the past is all that is worth preserving, the consequence of Enlightenment ideology finds its apogee in the brutality of the cultural revolutions of 1789 and 1968, but, of course, he forgets to mention the response of traditional Schoolmen to Galileo's discoveries. The intellect, in this case, defends itself by threatening to obliterate its adversaries.

In effect, the historical legacy of technicization has been to turn universities into training institutions, which creates few spaces for intellectuals. Within the ranks of the democratic professoriate, a debate often rages between those who spurn the elitism that emanates from the new conservative attack on affirmative action, open admissions, and student-centered learning and others who would try to extract some self-serving half-truths from Bloom's critique of contemporary postsecondary education (for example, open admissions is detrimental to quality education, affirmative action is unfairly discriminatory, and so forth).

What must be accepted in Bloom's discourse is that anti-intellectualism in American education is rampant, influencing even those whose intentions are actually opposed to closing the doors to genuine learning. We know that the environment in most universities is inimical to broadly based, philosophically informed scholarship and dialogue concerning burning questions of politics and culture. In a few places, liberal and radical intellectuals are building micro-institutions (centers, institutes, programs) within the universities as outposts that attempt to resist the larger trends toward instrumentalized curricula. These programs wisely accept that they are engaged in an intellectual as well as a political project; but, for the most part, their influence is confined to the already initiated.

On the front lines, some teachers, buffeted and bewildered, continue to maintain a fresh creative and critical approach to their tasks. In doing so, they receive little or no sustenance from the intellectuals. The challenge, in our view, is to combine the intellectual work of cultural reclamation with the work of pedagogy. This would entail a deliberate effort to avoid the tendency toward exclusivity on the part of intellectuals; to refuse the temptation to reproduce the "community of scholars" that is the heart of Bloom's program, even if the scholars are democratic intellectuals. The intellectuals who boldly announce that the search for truth and the good life is not the exclusive property of the Right and, in fact, is largely opposed to the conservative sensibility, would be required to engage with students—to start, not from the new great texts, much less the old great texts, but from the texts of the vernacular experience; from popular culture, not only in its written forms but in its visual artifacts as well. As Bertolt Brecht quipped, "Let's start not from the good old things but from the bad new things."

This need not imply leaving aside consideration of the tradition. But the task of reworking it might be explicitly combined with current concerns. For if tradition is to become part of a popular canon, it would have to justify itself either by its claim to pertinence or as a sociological and historical trace of the culture against which the present contends. In this connection, it is instructive to follow the fate of scientific texts. Except for historians, practicing physicists and their students rarely, if ever, read the works of Newton, Galileo, Kepler, and Copernicus. Similarly, Darwin is left to the scholars. Surely, one would not want to construct a curriculum in which this rich past was left to gather cobwebs. Science has no need for a literary canon, because it has long since abandoned the search for truth, and is intent on discovery. In other words, science is interested only in knowledge that can be derived from mathematics and experiment. Consequently, with few exceptions, it discourages the focus on meaning that still dominates the humanities. Like the social sciences, the natural sciences are content with explanation, and have forgotten that any object of knowledge is grasped not only quantitatively or by perception, but also historically.

The relationship between literary tradition and history is the most important one. For, unless we are to take the position made popular by Henry Ford that "history is bunk," we are obliged to take a historical perspective on the present and the future. That is to say, what we know is conditioned by historical precedents, and our natural and social world is constituted rather than merely given. For this reason, both knowledge and the truth of subjects themselves presuppose the elements of their formation. The danger lies in a position of sheer determination of the present by the past, in which case nothing really ever happens; events are reworkings of their antecedents. Instead, we propose that both disruption and continuity are characteristic of the nature of things. Disruption is a name for the proposition that things are constituted by interactions; in the first place, by intersubjective relations, but also by relations between what humans produce in the present and the past that appear as a part of the natural order. To critique the reification of the social as an unproblematic category does not dissolve everything into intersubjective relations including our own "nature," since our relation to what is taken as nature is part of human formation. This double relation has a history which is, to a great extent, embodied in literature and philosophy and in folk narratives that are incorporated into popular cultural forms.

While it is possible to make a strong case that reading classic texts is necessary even today because they continue to speak to our condition, we must take into account the massive shift that has occurred in the terms of the discourse; vernacular speech and popular language are now deeply embedded in the collective imagination. Thus, any effort to displace this language must be perceived as an imposition from on high, an effort by professional intellectuals to destroy or ignore what has happened in the last two hundred years. We do not want to argue that none of the privileged texts of Western culture should be incorporated into the curriculum. Nor are we defending anti-intellectualism, even as we explain some of its democratic impulses. But the responsibility of intellectuals for the current state of affairs must be acknowledged before the tension between tradition and modernity or post-modernity can be ameliorated. When intellectuals, whose alliance with the established order is their last best hope to save their status, make proclamations about educational reform, they must remain suspect. For what Bloom means by reform is nothing less than an effort to make explicit what women, minorities, and working-class students have always known: the precincts of higher learning are not for them, and the educational system is meant to train a new mandarin class. Their fate is tied to technical knowledge. This is Bloom's program. In part, this becomes clear not only in Bloom's complaint that "Harvard, Yale, and Princeton are not what they used to be—the last resorts of aristocratic sentiment within the democracy" (p. 89), but also in his attack on ethnicity and subordinate cultures. According to Bloom,

When one hears men and women proclaiming that they must preserve their *culture*, one cannot help wondering whether this artificial notion can really take the place of the God and country for which they once would have been willing to die. The "new ethnicity" or "roots" is just another manifestation of the concern with particularity, evidence not only of the real problems of community in modern mass societies but also of the superficiality of the response to it, as well as the lack of awareness of the fundamental conflict between liberal society and culture. . . . The "ethnic" differences we see in the United States are but decaying reminiscences of old differences that caused our ancestors to kill one another. (pp. 192–193)

In commenting on the "sample" of students Bloom uses to construct his view of university life, Martha Nussbaum provides an illuminating insight into Bloom's treatment of students who do not inhabit the world of elite universities, particularly subordinate groups who make up the Black, ethnic, and White working class.

[Bloom's students who] are materially well off and academically successful enough to go to a small number of elite universities and to pursue their studies there without the distraction of holding a job are equated with those having "the greatest talents" and the "more complex" natures. They are said to be the people who are "most likely to take advantage of a liberal education," and to be the ones who "most need education." It would seem that the disadvantaged, as Bloom imagines them, also have comparatively smaller talents, simpler natures, and fewer needs. But Bloom never argues that they do. He simply has no interest in the students whom he does not regard as the elite—an elite defined, he makes plain, by wealth and good fortune as much as by qualities of the mind that have deeper value.[5]

For Bloom, philosophy after Hegel abandons the search for truth, becoming the servant of technical knowledge and thereby losing its claim to wisdom. But whereas Bloom wants to reconstruct the category of truth through an unproblematic, quasi-essentialist and elitist reading of history, we believe that recovering a notion of truth grounded in a critical reading of history that validates and reclaims democratic public life is fundamental to the project of educational reform. Consciousness must take itself as its object, recognize that the process of forging an identity should be tied not to representations of what *should be* the goals to which students should aspire, but to what students themselves want, what they think and feel, and—most important—what they already know. The assumption that students are a tabula rasa upon which the teacher, armed with the wisdom of ages, places an imprint, is the basis of the widespread distrust of education among today's students. The elite professoriate is recruited from that tiny minority of every generation for whom the life of the mind represents the pinnacle of life. Such ideals are by no means shared by the preponderance of professors, much less by their students.

We are arguing for the parity of canonical text and popular text as forms of historical knowledge. In fact, what counts as high cultural text often originates as popular novels (the work of Dickens, Dostoevsky, and Rabelais are just a few examples). Their narratives were inevitably drawn from the everyday lives of their readers as well as those who had not (yet) gained their own voice, either in the public sphere or in literature. The novelist, argues Mikhail Bakhtin, creates a narration worthy of canonization when a multiplicity of voices, analogous to a polyphonic musical work, are placed in dialogic relation to one another.[6] Among these, one can discover the popular, if by that term we mean those excluded from literate culture, a basic feature of the early bourgeois epoch. In this example we read literature as a social semiotic, as a string of signifiers that illuminate our past, that reveal our selves, that provide us with a heritage for our own times. But the rediscovery of the popular is not the only treasure that can be scrounged from the established canon. We may discover in Gustave Flaubert's *Madame Bovary,* in Mark Twain's *Huckleberry Finn,* and in Theodore Dreiser's *Chronicles of American Plunder*—descriptions of the human sacrifices that were made for the sake of progress at the turn of the century—the modern tragedies and comic narratives of which the dark side of middle-class and native American culture is made, a revelation that is rarely unearthed by reading traditional narrative history or philosophy. In short, we may take literature as social knowledge, but the knowledge is not of an object, it is a part of the truth about ourselves.

We are sure that Bloom would find this program objectionable because it preserves what should be destroyed—historicity—placing our lives in relation to our times, seeing history as less than the unfolding of the Absolute Spirit, but instead, as the deconstruction of the myths of "civilization." The democratic use of literary canons must always remain critical. Above all, the canon must justify itself as representing the elements of our own heritage. In the final instance, it is to be appropriated rather than revered—and, with this appropriation, transformed. The canon is to be pressed, then, in the service of definite ends—freeing us from its yoke, which, even if unread, is acknowledged as the unquestioned embodiment of Truth.

At first glance, Hirsch's *Cultural Literacy* has little in common with Bloom's work. Bloom directs his attack against a number of institutions, social practices, and ideologies which challenge the dominant assumptions of contemporary social life. As we have mentioned, his targets include cultural relativism, higher education, popular culture, Nietzsche, the Left, feminism, rock music, and the social movements of the 1960s. Hirsch's focus is narrower; he argues for a view of cultural literacy that serves both as a critique of many existing theories of education and a referent for a reconstructed vision of American public schooling. Whereas Bloom attacks the notion of culture as a referent for self- and social formation, Hirsch attempts to enlist the language of culture and the culture of literacy as a basis for rethinking the American past and reconstructing the discourse of public life. But the differences that characterize these two positions are minor compared to the ideological and political project that they have in common.[7] In the most general sense, Hirsch and Bloom represent different versions of the same ideology, one which is deeply committed to cleansing democracy of its critical and emancipatory possibilities.

At the same time, Hirsch and Bloom share a common concern for rewriting the past from the perspective of the privileged and the powerful. In this view, history becomes a vehicle for endorsing a form of cultural authority that legitimates an unproblematic relationship between knowledge and truth. Both disdain the democratic implications of pluralism, and each argues for a form of cultural uniformity in which difference is consigned to the margins of both history and everyday life. From this perspective, culture, along with the authority it sanctions, is not a terrain of struggle: it is merely an artifact, a warehouse of goods, posited either as a canon of knowledge or a canon of information that has simply to be transmitted as a means for promoting social order and control. Learning, for both Hirsch and Bloom, has little to do with dialogue and struggle over the meanings and practices of a historical tradition. On the contrary, learning is defined primarily through a pedagogy of transmission, and knowledge is reduced to a culture of great books or related catalogues of shared information. As we indicated earlier, their positions are both part of the most recent frontal attack by the aristocratic traditionalists to restore knowledge as a particular form of social authority, pedagogy, and discipline in the classroom in order to replace democratic educational authority. Each of their positions espouses a view of culture removed from the trappings of power, conflict, and struggle, and in doing so, each attempts to legitimate a view of learning and literacy that not only marginalizes the voices, languages, and cultures of subordinate groups but also degrades teaching and learning to the practice of implementation and mastery. Both of these discourses are profoundly anti-utopian and correspond with a more general vision of domination and control as it has been developed during the Reagan era. Specifically, Bloom and Hirsch represent the most popular expression of the resurgent attempt on the part of right-wing intellectuals and ruling groups to undermine the basis of democratic public life as we have known it over the last two decades. In what follows, we analyze in greater detail some of these assumptions through an analysis of the major themes presented in Hirsch's version of the conservative educational credo.

Hirsch has entered the debate on the nature and purpose of public schooling by way of a discourse that has gained public attention within the last six years. In the manner of conservatives such as William Bennett, Diane Ravitch, Chester Finn, and Nathan Glazer, Hirsch begins with the assumption that a state of crisis exists in the United States which reflects not only the demise of public schooling but also the weakening of a wider civic and public culture. Schools in this view are frontline institutions that have reneged on their public responsibility to educate students into the dominant traditions of Western culture.

Appropriating the radical educational position that schools are agencies of social and cultural reproduction, conservatives such as Hirsch defend this position rather than criticize it, and make it a measure for defining both the quality of school life and the society at large. Implicit in this position is the notion that schools represent a preparation for and legitimation of particular forms of social life; they are cultural institutions that name experience and in doing so presuppose a vision of the future. It is in these terms that Hirsch's book becomes important. For Hirsch insists that schools be analyzed as sites of learning in which knowledge, not merely skills, constitutes the most important consideration, if public schooling is to fulfill its imperative as a transmitter of civic and public culture. To Hirsch's credit, he enters the debate regarding public schooling by arguing for a particular relation between culture and power on the one hand and literacy and learning on the other. In doing so, he not only provides an important corrective to the view that the curriculum in general and learning in particular should be organized around the developmental organization of learning skills; he also argues for a definition of literacy that embraces a particular relationship between knowledge and power. Knowledge, in this case, is the basis not only for learning but also for entering the social and economic possibilities that exist in the wider society. These issues have been analyzed critically by a number of educational theorists, but Hirsch has developed them from the perspective of a con- servative discourse that challenges the critical perspective while refusing to openly engage its arguments. Hirsch has decided to ignore completely the critical tradition, thus limiting the possibility for making visible and problematic the ideological inter- ests that structure his own arguments.

In what follows, we want to provide and extend some important theoretical insights offered by the critical educational tradition as a key referent for challenging some of Hirsch's major assumptions. To pursue this analysis we will examine Hirsch's view of the crisis in education, his reading of history and tradition, his construction of the relationship between culture, language, and power and its contribution to a view of literacy, and finally, the book's implications for teachers and classroom pedagogy.

Reiterating the arguments of Bennett, Ravitch, and Finn, Hirsch identifies the crisis in education through the general level of cultural ignorance exhibited in recent years by American students. In this view, students lack the knowledge necessary to "thrive in the modern world" (p. xiii). Relying heavily on the declining test scores of college-bound students, particularly those of the Scholastic Aptitude Test (SAT) and the National Assessment of Educational Progress, as well as on anecdotal evidence, Hirsch argues that there is indeed a literacy crisis in the United States. For Hirsch, the SAT is essentially a "test of advanced vocabulary," and as such is a "fairly sensitive instrument for measuring levels of literacy" (p. 4). In these assertions, the relationship between ignorance and learning, between knowledge and ideology, first becomes evident in Hirsch's book. At issue is a definition of literacy that is organized within categories that favor knowledge as a shared body of information, and a definition of learning as the appropriation of this information. For Hirsch, the defining character of this knowledge is that it represents the unifying facts, values, and writings of Western culture. In this instance, the relationship between knowledge and power is legitimated through claims to a body of information that resides beyond the sphere of historical conflict and the shifting terrain of ideological struggle. Authority and meaning come together within a view of history that appears unproblematic and unchangeable in its determining influence on the present and the future. What you see is what you get.

More important, Hirsch's view of history is the narrative of the winners. It is the discourse of the elites in history that constitutes the fund of cultural knowledge that defines literacy. Assured by his son, who taught high school Latin, Hirsch recognizes that students do in fact know something. Ignorance, for Hirsch, is not merely the absence of information. At stake is *what* the students know. Literacy and illiteracy are defined by the information students possess regarding the canon of knowledge that constitutes, for Hirsch, the national culture. Hirsch characterizes the crisis in literacy by the lack of familiarity students have with Western culture's canon bequeathed by history as a series of facts—dates of battles, authors of books, figures from Greek mythology, and the names of past presidents of the United States. In effect, the crisis of literacy is defined primarily as an epistemological and political problem. In the first instance, students cannot read and write adequately unless they have the relevant background information, a particular body of shared information that expresses a privileged cultural currency with a high exchange value in the public sphere. In the second instance, students who lack the requisite historical and contemporary information that constitutes the canon of Western tradition will not be able to function adequately in society. In Hirsch's terms, the new illiteracy is embodied in those expanding ranks of students who are unable either to contextualize information or to communicate with each other within the parameters of a wider national culture.

Hirsch does more than rely on the logic of verification and personal anecdote to signal the new illiteracy. He also attempts to analyze the causes for its emergence in the last half of the twentieth century. Hirsch begins by arguing that schools are solely responsible for the current cultural blight that plagues contemporary youth. If students lack the requisite historical and literary knowledge, it is because both schools of education and the public schools have been excessively influenced by the theoretical legacies of the early progressive movement of the 1920s. Influenced by the theories of John Dewey and the liberal ideas embodied in the 1918 Cardinal Principles of Education, public schooling is alleged to have historically shifted its concern from a knowledge-based curriculum to one that has emphasized the practical application of knowledge. The result has been, according to Hirsch, the predominance in public schools of a curriculum dominated by a concern with developmental psychology, student experience, and the mastery of skills. Within this line of reasoning, progressive educational theory and practice have undermined the intellectual content of the curriculum and further contributed to forms of public schooling marked by an increasing loss of authority, cultural relativism, lack of discipline, poor academic performance, and a refusal to train students adequately to meet the demands of the changing industrial order.

Hirsch is not content merely with criticizing the public schools. He is also intent on developing a programmatic discourse for constructing curriculum reform. Hirsch's message is relatively simple. He believes that since literacy is in a decline caused by an overemphasis on process at the expense of content, schools should begin to subordinate the teaching of skills to what he calls common background knowledge. For Hirsch, this common background knowledge consists of information from mainstream culture represented in standard English. Its content is drawn from what Hirsch calls the common culture, which in his terms is marked by a history and contemporary usefulness that raises it above issues of power, class, and discrimination. In Hirsch's terms, this is "everybody's culture," and the only real issue, as he sees it, is that we outline its contents and begin to teach it in schools. For Hirsch, the national language, which is at the center of his notion of literacy, is rooted in a civic religion that forms the core of stability in the culture itself. "Culture" in these terms is used in the descriptive rather than anthropological and political sense; it is the medium of conservation and transmission. Its meaning is fixed in the past, and its essence is that it provides the public with a common referent for communication and exchange. It is the foundation upon which public life interacts with the past, sustains the present, and locates itself in the future. Psycholinguistic research and an unchallenged relationship among industrialization, nationalism, and historical progress provide the major referents mobilized in the name of cultural literacy. The logic underlying Hirsch's argument is that cultural literacy is the precondition for industrial growth, and that with industrial growth comes the standardization of language, culture, and learning. The equation is somewhat baffling in its simplicity, and Hirsch actually devotes whole chapters to developing this particular version of historical determinism. The outcome of his Hegelian rendering of history and literacy is a view of Western culture that is both egalitarian and homogeneous.[8] Hirsch dismisses the notion that culture has any determinate relation to the practices of power and politics or is largely defined as a part of an ongoing struggle to name history, experience, knowledge and the meaning of everyday life in one's own terms. Culture for Hirsch is a network of information shrouded in innocence and goodwill. This is in part reflected in his reading of the relationship between culture and what he describes as nation building:

Nation builders use a patchwork of scholarly folk materials, old songs, obscure dances, and historical legends all apparently quaint and local, but in reality selected and reinterpreted by intellectuals to create a culture upon which the life of the nation can rest. (p. 83)

There is a totalitarian unity in Hirsch's view of culture that is at odds with the concept of democratic pluralism and political difference. In fact, where difference is introduced by Hirsch, as in reference to multiculturalism or bilingualism, it appears to vacillate between the category of a disrupting discourse and of a threat to the vitality and strength of the Western cultural tradition. Hirsch's defense of a unified version of Western tradition ideologically marks his definition of cultural literacy as more than a simplistic call for a common language and canon of shared information. Hirsch's argument that to be culturally literate is "to possess the basic information needed to thrive in the modern world," or enable us to master the standard literate language so that we can become "masters of communication, thereby enabling us to give and receive complex information orally and in writing over time" (p. 3), is not merely a prescription for a particular form of literacy and schooling. It is part of a hegemonic discourse that is symptomatic of the crisis in history currently facing this nation, and a threat to democracy itself.

We will analyze some of the major arguments made by Hirsch in defense of his notion of cultural literacy. In doing so we will not restrict our analysis to the defining ideas that Hirsch develops, but will also analyze the significant gaps in Hirsch's view of history, literacy, culture, and schooling. We hope to show that Hirsch's argument is more than a popular and politically innocent treatise on educational reform, but rather serves at best as a veiled apology for a highly dogmatic and reactionary view of literacy and schooling. At worst, Hirsch's model of cultural literacy threatens the very democracy he claims to be preserving.

For Hirsch, the starting point for the crisis in literacy and education is the decline of student achievement as measured by the SAT and similar tests. Hirsch and other conservatives presume that the test scores accurately measure academic proficiency, and that the progress of educational reform can be accurately inferred from an upturn in SAT scores. In recent times this wisdom has been highly disputed. Not only is the validity of the SAT and other national measurement schemes being questioned despite their alleged objectivity, but it is also being strongly argued that the reliance on test scores as a measure of school success contains in itself an ideology that is highly detrimental to improving the quality of school life and providing the basis for critical learning.[9]

We believe that Hirsch's reliance on such scores to analyze the nature of the problems public schools currently face in this country is theoretically impoverished and politically visionless. This position ignores the wider complex of social and political forces that deeply influence the way schools are structured to benefit some students at the expense of others. For instance, this position is silent regarding the ways that tracking, the hidden curriculum, the denial of student experience as a valid basis for knowledge, and school practices predicated on class, sexist, and racial interests discriminate against students. Nothing in Hirsch's position speaks to the 50 to 80 percent dropout rate of high school students in inner-city schools, or to the fact that in major urban cities like Chicago, schools with over a 50-percent Black and Hispanic enrollment manage to retain only 39 percent of the entering freshmen by their senior year.[10] These figures highlight a number of problems that cannot be accounted for or even understood through analysis of so-called aptitude tests. Hirsch's reliance on test scores also ignores the effect that the technical rationality of this position has had on the deskilling of teachers within the last few years. State-mandated efforts to raise test scores, especially in the areas of reading and writing, have been part of a much broader educational reform movement tied to instrumental-izing teaching and learning around a variety of accountability schemes. As Linda Darling-Hammond reports, the results have had very little to do with genuine reform and a great deal to do with teacher disempowerment and despair.

> Viewing teachers as semiskilled, low-paid workers in the mass production of educa-tion, policymakers have sought to change education, to improve it, by "teacher-proofing" it. Over the past decade we have seen a proliferation of elaborate accountability schemes that go by acronyms like MBO (management by objectives) PBBS (performance-based budgeting systems), CBE (competency-based education) . . . and MCT (minimum competency testing). . . . we learned from teachers that in response to policies that prescribe teaching practices and outcomes, they spend less time on untested subjects. . . . they use less writing in the classrooms in order to gear assignments to the format of standardized tests; they resort to lectures rather than classroom discussion in order to cover the prescribed behavioral objectives without getting "off the track"; they are precluded from using teaching materials that are not on prescribed textbook lists, even when they think these materials are essential to meet the needs of some of their students; and they feel constrained from following up on expressed student interests that lie outside the bounds of mandated curricula. . . . And 45 percent of the teachers in this study told us that the single thing that would make them leave teaching was the increased prescriptiveness of teaching content and methods—in short, the continuing deprofessionalization of teaching.[11]

Hirsch appears unaware that the politics of verification and empiricism that he supports frame his own agenda for reform in a way that is at odds with an ethical and substantive vision of what schools might be with respect to their potential for empow-ering both students and teachers as active and critical citizens. Hirsch's reliance on narrow models of psycholinguistic research forces him to use absolute categories; that is, categories which appear to transcend historical, cultural, and political contingen-cies. By ignoring a wide range of sociological, cultural, and historical research on schooling, Hirsch wrongly names the nature of the crisis he attempts to address. He completely ignores those theories of schooling that in recent years have illustrated how schools function as agencies of social and cultural reproduction.[12] He completely ignores existing critical research that points to how working-class and minority chil-dren are discriminated against through various approaches to reading;[13] he exhibits no theoretical awareness of how schools frequently silence or discriminate against stu-dents;[14] and he completely ignores the research that points out ways in which the state and other social, economic, and political interests bear down on and shape the daily practices of school organization and classroom life.[15] Consequently, Hirsch's analysis and prescriptions are both simplistic and incorrect. The crisis in education is not about the background information that young people allegedly lack, or the inability of students to communicate in order to adapt more readily to the dictates of the dominant culture. Rather, it is a crisis framed in the intersections of citizenship, historical consciousness, and inequality, one which speaks to a breakdown at the heart of democratic public life.

The limitations of Hirsch's view of the crisis are evident not only in the research which he selects to define the problem, but also in the factors he points to as causes of the crisis in literacy and schooling. Among the chief historical villains in Hirsch's script are the progressive principles embodied in the work of John Dewey. Hirsch holds Dewey responsible for promoting a formalism in which the issues of experience and process become a substitute for focussing on school knowledge in the school curriculum. Hirsch argues that Dewey is the major theoretical architect of a content-neutral curriculum (as if such a thing ever existed). Dewey's crime in this view is that he has influenced later generations of educators to take critical thinking seriously as opposed to learning the virtues of having students accumulate information for the purpose of shoring up the status quo.

Hirsch misinterprets Dewey's work. Even the most casual reading of Dewey's *The Child and the Curriculum* and *The School and Society* reveals a blatant refusal to accept any division between content and process or between knowledge and thinking. Rather than support this bifurcation, Dewey argued that information without the benefit of self-reflection and context generally resulted in methods of teaching in which knowledge was cut off from its organic connection to the student's experiences and the wider society. Dewey was not against facts, as Hirsch argues; he was against the mere collection of facts both uninformed by a working hypothesis and unenlight-ened by critical reflection. He was against the categorization of knowledge into sterile and so-called finished forms. We are certainly not suggesting that Hirsch's misreading of Dewey represents an act of intellectual dishonesty; more probably, since Dewey's views are so much at odds with Hirsch's theory of learning and schooling, it was easier for him to misread Dewey than to engage his ideas directly on specific issues. For example, Hirsch's claim that memorization is a noble method of learning, his refusal to situate schooling in broader historical, social, and political contexts, and his belief that public culture is historically defined though the progressive accumulation of information, represent major ideas that Dewey spent a lifetime refuting as education-ally unsound and politically reactionary. But Hirsch refuses to argue with Dewey on these issues; instead, he cavalierly attributes to Dewey a series of one-dimensional ideas that Dewey never advocated. This is not merely a distortion of Dewey's work; it also represents a view of history and causality that is, as we explain below, deeply flawed. Moreover, Hirsch reproduces in this view of educational history and practice a slightly different view of Bloom's profoundly anti-democratic tirade.

Underlying Hirsch's view of the major causes of the problem influencing Ameri-can education is a notion of history that is reductionist and theoretically flawed. It is reductionist because it assumes that ideas are the determining factor in shaping history, somehow unfolding in linear fashion from one generation to the next. There is no sense of how these ideas are worked out and mediated through the ideological and material conditions of their times, or of how history is shaped through the changing patterns of communication, technology, language conflicts, struggles between different social groups, and the shifting parameters of state power. Hirsch's history lacks any concrete political and social referents, its causal relations are construed through a string of ideas, and it is presented without the benefit of substantive argument or historical context. While ideas are important in shaping history, they cannot be considered so powerful as to alter history beyond the density of its material and social contexts. Ideas are not so powerful that they exist, as Hirsch believes, in a realm of autonomy and independence from human activity.[16]

Hirsch practices historical inquiry not as a form of social memory but as a form of repression. It is history stripped of the discourse of power, injustice, and conflict. For instance, the struggle over curriculum in the United States emerged in the first half of the twentieth century amidst an intense war of ideological positions, each attempting to stamp its public philosophy and view of learning on the curriculum of the public schools. As Herbert Kliebard points out, curriculum represented a terrain of struggle among different groups over questions regarding the purpose of schooling, how children learn, whose knowledge was to be legitimated, and what social relations would prevail.[17] The contending groups included social efficiency advocates whose priorities were based on the interests of corporate ideology, humanists who were advocates of the revered traditions of Western cultural heritage, developmentalists who wanted to reform the curriculum around the scientific study of child development and, finally, social meliorists who wanted to shape the curriculum in the interests of social reform. Kliebard not only provides a complex and dense history of the struggle for control of the curriculum in the public schools, he also argues that the most important force in shaping curriculum in the United States came not from the progressives but from the social efficiency movement. Given the history of public schooling since the rise of the Cold War and the launching of Sputnik, there can be little doubt that the efficiency and accountability models for curriculum have carried the day.

History for Hirsch is not a terrain of struggle;[18] it is a museum of information that merely legitimates a particular view of history as a set of sacred goods designed to be received rather than interrogated by students. We have stressed Hirsch's view of history, because it influences every category he relies upon to develop his major arguments. We began our criticism of his work by arguing that his discourse of crisis and cultural restoration missed the point. We want to return to this issue and argue that the real crisis in American schooling can be better understood through an analysis of the rise of scientism and technocratic rationality as a major ideological force in the 1920s; the increasing impingement of state policy on the shaping of school curricula; the anti-communism of the 1950s; the increasing influence of industrial psychology in defining the purpose of schooling; the rise of individualism and consumerism through the growth of the culture industry in which the logic of standardization, repetition, and rationalization define and shape the culture of consumption; the gendered nature of teaching as manifested in the educational labor force and in the construction of school administration and curriculum; the racism, sexism, and class discrimination that have been reinforced through increasing forms of tracking and testing; and the failure of teachers to gain an adequate level of control over the conditions of their labor. While this is not the place to discuss these issues, they need to be included in any analysis of the problems that public schools are now facing. Moreover, these issues point to a much broader crisis in the schools and the wider society than Hirsch is willing to recognize.[19] It is a crisis that has given rise to cynicism about the promise of democracy, to a vast and unequal distribution of ideological and material resources both in the schools and in the wider society, and to the repression of those aspects of our history that carry the voices and social memories of groups who have been marginalized in the struggle for democratic life.

Central to Hirsch's concept of literacy is an understanding of the relationship between culture and literacy that also warrants close theoretical scrutiny. For Hirsch, culture, which is the central structuring category in his approach to literacy and learning, appears as a mythic category that exists beyond the realm of politics and struggle. It is systematically reduced to a canon of information that constitutes not only a fund of background knowledge but also a vehicle for social and economic mobility. Hirsch writes:

> Literate culture has become the common currency for social and economic exchange in our democracy, and the only available ticket to full citizenship. Getting one's membership card is not tied to class or race. Membership is automatic if one learns that background information and the linguistic conventions that are needed to read, write, and speak effectively. (p. 22)

There is a false egalitarianism defining Hirsch's view of culture, one which suggests that while it is possible to distinguish between mainstream and what he calls ethnic culture, the concept of culture itself has nothing to do with struggle and power. Culture is seen as the totality of the language practices of a given nation, and merely "presents" itself for all to participate in its language and conventions. Hirsch refuses to acknowledge how deeply the struggle for moral and social regulation inscribes itself in the language of culture. He makes no attempt to interrogate culture as the shared and lived principles of life, characteristic of different groups and classes as these emerge within unequal relations of power and struggle. Not unlike Bloom's position, Hirsch's view of culture expresses a single, durable history and vision, one which is at odds with the notion of difference, and maintains an ominous ideological silence—an ideological amnesia of sorts—regarding the validity and importance of the experiences of women, Blacks, and other groups excluded from the narrative of mainstream history and culture. Thus there emerges no sense of culture as a field of struggle or domain of competing interests in which dominant and subordinate groups live out and make sense of their given circumstances and conditions of life. This is an essentialist reading of culture. It deeply underestimates the most central feature of cultural relations in the twentieth century. That is, by failing to acknowledge the multilayered relations between culture and power, Hirsch ignores how the ideological and structural weight of different cultural practices operates as a form of cultural politics. In this case, he not only ignores how domination works in the cultural sphere, he also refuses to acknowledge the dialectic of cultural struggle between different groups over competing orders of meaning, experience, and history.

The failing of Hirsch's view of culture is most evident in his analysis of public schools. He provides little, if any, understanding of the forms of struggle that take place in schools over different forms of knowledge and social relations. This is best exemplified in the research on culture and schooling that has emerged within the last twenty years both in the United States and abroad. Theorists such as Pierre Bourdieu, Basil Bernstein, Paulo Freire, Michael Apple, and others have investigated the relationship between power and culture, arguing that the culture transmitted by the school is related to the various cultures that make up the wider society, in that it confirms and sustains the culture of dominant groups while marginalizing and silencing the cultures of subordinate groups of students.[20] This is evident in the way in which different forms of linguistic and cultural competency, whether they are manifested in a specific way of talking, dressing, acting, thinking, or presenting oneself, are accorded a privileged status in schools. For example, Ray Rist, Jean Anyon, and Hugh Mehan have demonstrated that White middle-class linguistic forms, modes of style, and values represent honored forms of cultural capital and are accorded a greater exchange rate in the circuits of power that define and legitimate the meaning of success in public schools.[21] Students who represent cultural forms that rely on restricted linguistic codes, working-class or oppositional modes of dress (long hair, earrings, bizarre patterns of clothing), who downplay the ethos of individualism (and who may actually share their work and time), who espouse a form of solidarity, or who reject forms of academic knowledge that embody versions of history, social science, and success that are at odds with their own cultural experiences and values, find themselves at a decided academic, social, and ideological disadvantage in most schools.

A more critical understanding of the relationship between culture and schooling would start with a definition of culture as a set of activities by which different groups produce collective memories, knowledge, social relations, and values within historically constituted relations of power. Culture is about the production and legitimation of particular ways of life, and schools often transmit a culture that is specific to class, gender, and race. By depoliticizing the issue of culture, Hirsch is unable to develop a view either of literacy or pedagogy which acknowledges the complex workings of power as they are both produced and mediated through the cultural processes that structure school life. Thus, Hirsch ends up with a view of literacy cleansed of its own complicity in furthering cultural practices and ideologies that reproduce the worst dimensions of schooling.

Given Hirsch's view of culture, it is not surprising that he espouses a clothesline-of-information approach to literacy that ignores its function as a technology of social control, as a feature of cultural organization that reproduces rather than critically engages the dominant social order. When the power of literacy is framed around a unifying logic consistent with the imperatives of the dominant culture, the voices of those groups outside of the dominant tradition are often silenced because their voices and experiences are not recognized as legitimate. Hirsch's view of literacy decontextualizes learners both from the culture and mode of literacy that give their voices meaning and from that which is legitimated as knowledge in the name of the dominant version of literacy. Literacy for Hirsch is treated as a universal discourse and process that exists outside "the social and political relations, ideological practices, and symbolic meaning structures in which it is embedded."[22] Not only is the notion of multiple literacies (the concept of cultural difference) ignored in this formulation, but those who are considered "illiterate" bear the burden of forms of moral and social regulation that often deny their histories, voices, and sufferings. To argue for a recognition of the dialectical quality of literacy, that is, its power either to limit or enhance human capacities as well as the multiple forms of expression it takes, is a deeply political issue. It means recognizing that there are different voices, languages, histories, and ways of viewing and experiencing the world, and that the recognition and affirmation of these differences is a necessary and important precondition for extending the possibilities of democratic life. June Jordan has captured the importance of this issue in her comments regarding the problems in a democratic state:

> If we lived in a democratic state our language would have to hurtle, fly, curse, and sing, in all the common American names, all the undeniable and representative and participating voices of everybody here. We would not tolerate the language of the powerful and, thereby lose all respect for words, per se. We would make our language conform to the truth of our many selves and we would make our language lead us into the equality of power that a democratic state must represent.[23]

To acknowledge different forms of literacy is not to suggest that they should all be given equal weight. On the contrary, it is to argue that their differences are to be weighed against the capacity they have for enabling people to locate themselves in their own histories while simultaneously establishing the conditions for them to function as part of a wider democratic culture. This represents a form of literacy that is not merely epistemological but also deeply political and eminently pedagogical. It is political because literacy represents a set of practices that can provide the conditions through which people can be empowered or disempowered. It is pedagogical because literacy always involves social relations in which learning takes place; power legitimates a particular view of the world, and privilege, a specific rendering of knowledge.[24]

This view of culture, knowledge, and literacy is far removed from the language and ideology of Hirsch and Bloom. The refusal to be literate in their terms means that one has refused to appropriate either the canon of the Great Books or the canon of information that characterizes the tradition of Western culture. In this view, refusal is not resistance or criticism; it is judged as ignorance or failure. This view of culture and literacy is also implicated in the theories of pedagogy put forth by Bloom and Hirsch. Both subscribe to a pedagogy that is profoundly reactionary and can be summed up in the terms "transmission" and "imposition." Both authors refuse to analyze how pedagogy, as a deliberate and critical attempt to influence the ways in which knowledge and identities are produced within and among particular sets of social relations, might address the reconstruction of social imagination in the service of human freedom. The categories of meaning that students bring to the classroom and that provide them with a basis for producing and interpreting knowledge are simply denied by Bloom and Hirsch as viable categories of learning. Pedagogy, for both Bloom and Hirsch, is an afterthought. It is something one does to implement a preconstituted body of knowledge. The notion that pedagogy represents a method or technique for transmitting information, as well as an essential dynamic in the production and exchange of knowledge, necessitates that educators attend to the categories of meaning that students bring to the classroom as well as to the fundamental question of why they should want to learn anything in the first place. This is an especially important consideration for those students in the public schools who know that the truth of their lives and experiences is omitted from the curriculum. A pedagogy that takes their lives seriously would have to begin with a question that June Jordan has suggested such students constantly pose to teachers through their absences and overt forms of school resistance: "If you don't know and don't care about who I am then why should I give a damn about what you say you do know about?"[25] To legitimate or address a question of this sort would constitute for Bloom and Hirsch not merely bad teaching, but a dangerous social practice.

Read against the recent legacy of a critical educational tradition, the perspectives advanced by both Bloom and Hirsch reflect those of the critic who fears the indeterminacy of the future and who, in an attempt to escape the messy web of everyday life, purges the past of its contradictions, its paradoxes, and ultimately, of its injustices. Hirsch and Bloom sidestep the disquieting, disrupting, interrupting problems of sexism, racism, class exploitation, and other social issues that bear down so heavily on the present. This is the discourse of pedagogues afraid of the future, strangled by the past, and refusing to address the complexity, terror, and possibilities of the present. Most important, it is a public philosophy informed by a crippling ethnocentrism[26] and a contempt for the language and social relations fundamental to the ideals of a democratic society. It is, in the end, a desperate move by thinkers who would rather cling to a tradition forged by myth than work toward a collective future built on democratic possibilities. This is the philosophy and pedagogy of hegemonic intellectuals cloaked in the mantle of academic enlightenment and literacy.

NOTES

1. For an example of this position, see William Bennett, " 'To Reclaim a Legacy': Text of Report on Humanities in Higher Education," *Chronicle of Higher Education,* November 28, 1984, pp. 16–21; Diane Ravitch and Chester Finn, Jr., *What Do Our 17-Year-Olds Know?* (New York: Harper & Row, 1988); for an excellent critique of this position, see Robert Scholes, "Aiming a Canon at the Curriculum," *Salmagundi, 72* (Fall 1986), 101–117.

2. This issue is taken up in Martin Carnoy and Henry M. Levin, *Schooling and Work in the Democratic State* (Stanford: Stanford University Press, 1985).

3. Given Bloom's tirade on popular culture and rock 'n roll, it is both somewhat surprising and ironic that when a reporter asked him if he had anticipated the popular success of *The Closing of the American Mind,* he responded with "Sometimes I can't believe it. . . . It's like being declared Cary Grant, or *a rock star. All this energy passing through you*" (my emphasis). Maybe Bloom has missed the contradiction here, but it appears that his new-found energy undermines both his own critique of the affective value of popular culture, and his own need to interrogate the underlying dichotomy he constructs between pleasure and learning. He may be surprised to find that the terrain of pleasure may be more complex and contradictory than he first imagined. See Henry A. Giroux and Roger I. Simon, "Popular Culture and Critical Pedagogy," *Culture Studies* (forthcoming). Bloom's comment is taken from James Atlas, "Chicago's Grumpy Guru: Best-Selling Professor Allan Bloom and the Chicago Intellectuals," *The New York Times Magazine,* January 3, 1988, p. 25.

4. See Walter Benjamin, "Theses on the Philosophy of History," in *Illuminations,* ed. Hannah Arendt (New York: Schocken Books, 1963), pp. 253–264.

5. In Martha Nussbaum, "Undemocratic Vistas," *The New York Review of Books,* November 5, 1987, p. 22.

6. Mikhail Bakhtin, *The Dialogic Imagination,* ed. Michael Holquist, trans. Caryl Emerson and Michael Holquist (Austin: The University of Texas Press, 1981).

7. Robert Scholes provides an illuminating commentary on the conservative agenda underlying the differences and commonalities that characterize the Bloom and Hirsch books.

> Hirsch wants to save us through information. He thinks that knowing about things is more important than knowing things. Bloom, on the other hand, thinks that the only thing that can save us is a return to really knowing and experiencing the great books, especially the great works of political and social philosophy that follow in the train of Plato's *Republic*. Hirsch concerns himself with what every American student should know, whereas Bloom is concerned only about a tiny elite. Together, they set the conservative agenda for American education. Hirsch will make sure that everyone knows what the classics are and respects them, while Bloom will see to it that an elite can be defined by actually knowing these classics. In this way, the masses will be sufficiently educated to respect the superior knowledge of their betters, who have studied in a few major universities. Both Hirsch and Bloom emphasize certain kinds of traditional learning, but it is important to recognize that the attitude they take toward this learning is very different. For Bloom nothing less than a prolonged, serious engagement with the great books themselves can save the souls of our students. For Hirsch, just knowing the names of the great books and authors will suffice. Both Hirsh and Bloom share, however, a nostalgia for a not very close examined past in which things were better. (Robert Scholes, "Three Views of Education: Nostalgia, History, and Voodoo," *College English, 50* [1988], 323–324.)

8. The simplicity, ignorance, and political interests that often inform this particular view of Western culture are brilliantly analyzed and deconstructed in James Clifford, *The Predicament of Culture: Twentieth-Century Ethnography, Literature, and Art* (Cambridge: Harvard University Press, 1988).
9. For a criticism of this form of testing, see Allan Nairn and Associates, *The Reign of ETS: The Corporation that Makes Up Minds* (Washington, DC: Ralph Nader, 1980); David Owen, *None of the Above: Behind the Myth of Scholastic Aptitude* (Boston: Houghton Mifflin, 1985); Peter Schrag, "What the Test Scores Really Mean," *The Nation*, October 4, 1986, pp. 311–314; Peter Schrag, "Who Wants Good Teachers?" *The Nation*, October 11, 1986, pp. 342–345.
10. For both a statistical and theoretical analysis of these problems, see National Coalition of Advocates for Students, *Barriers to Excellence: Our Children at Risk* (Boston: Author, 1985).
11. Linda Darling-Hammond, "Valuing Teachers: The Making of a Profession," *Teachers College Record, 87* (1985), 210.
12. For a review of this literature, see Henry A. Giroux, *Theory and Resistance in Education* (South Hadley, MA: Bergin & Garvey, 1985).
13. See for example, Pat Shannon, "The Use of Commercial Reading Materials in American Elementary Schools," *Reading Research Quarterly, 19* (1983), 68–85; Patrick Shannon, "Reading Instruction and Social Class," *Language Arts, 63* (1985), 604–611; Kenneth S. Goodman, "Basal Readers: A Call for Action," *Language Arts, 63* (1986), 358–363.
14. See, for example, Michelle Fine, "Silencing in Public Schools," *Language Arts, 64* (1987), 157–174; Henry A. Giroux, *Schooling and the Struggle for Public Life* (Minneapolis: University of Minnesota Press, 1988).
15. Martin Carnoy and Henry M. Levin, *Schooling and Work in the Democratic State* (Stanford: Stanford University Press, 1985); Ira Katznelson and Margaret Weir, *Schooling for All: Class, Race, and the Decline of the Democratic Ideal* (New York: Basic Books, 1985); Stanley Aronowitz and Henry A. Giroux, *Education under Siege: The Conservative, Liberal & Radical Debate over Schooling* (South Hadley, MA: Bergin & Garvey, 1985).

16. Hirsch's view of history represents what Harvey J. Graff calls a radically idealist conception of historical causation, in which one speaks "in historical claims without studying or interpreting any range of historical evidence or [presumes] the universality and power of ideas without inquiring into them and their actual or alternative historical contexts or consequences." Harvey J. Graff, "A Review of: *The Closing of the American Mind:* How Higher Education Has Failed Democracy and Impoverished the Souls of Today's Students," *Society* (November/December, 1987), 101.

17. Herbert M. Kliebard, *The Struggle for the American Curriculum 1893–1958* (New York: Routledge & Kegan Paul, 1986).

18. Hirsch's view of history is strikingly similar to that expressed by William J. Bennett in his "To Reclaim a Legacy." In this view, as Harvey J. Kaye has pointed out, history is not conveyed as a "sense of the conflicts between social and political groups over ideas, values, and social relations. Nor does it posit the necessity of examining the distance between 'ideal' and 'experience' in Western Civilization and world history." In Harvey J. Kaye, "The Use and Abuse of the Past: The New Right and the Crisis of History," *Socialist Register 1987,* ed. Ralph Miliband, Leo Panitch, and John Saville (London: The Merlin Press, 1987), p. 354.

19. Hirsch argues for a notion of cultural literacy that suffers both from a misplaced faith in its social and economic possibilities and a refusal to take seriously how a pedagogy might be constructed that is consistent with the aims of this particular form of literacy. In the first instance, Hirsch argues that literacy is an essential precondition for eliminating just about every social and economic evil that plagues contemporary industrial societies. In this view, literacy becomes an independent variable that operates as part of a simple cause and effect relationship to produce particular outcomes. The issue here is not simply that Hirsch claims more for literacy than it can actually do as an ideological and social practice; more important, Hirsch presents an argument for literacy that both ignores and mystifies the role that wider cultural, historical, and social forces play in defining both the different forms of literacy and in supporting particular political and economic inequities. Hirsch's view of literacy is one that is silent about the wider problems and inequities that plague American society, problems that are rooted in configurations of power and structural relations that call into question not simply the dominant forms of literacy but the political, economic and social fabric of the society itself. This issue is discussed in Harvey Graff, *The Literacy Myth: Literacy and Social Structure in the Nineteenth-Century City* (New York: Academic Press, 1979); see also Colin Lankshear with Moira Lawler, *Literacy, Schooling and Revolution* (New York: Falmer Press, 1987). But Hirsch does more than mystify the nature and effects of literacy, he also completely ignores the issue of what makes students want to learn, to be interested, or to listen to pedagogues such as himself. As we point out in the latter section of this essay, pedagogy for Hirsch is an unproblematic and uncritical construct, a technique to be employed after one has decided on the content to be taught. Given the wide gap between what Hirsch expects from his view of literacy and the simplistic and reactionary view of pedagogy he employs, it is not surprising that he ends up with what Scholes has called "voodoo education." (See Scholes, "Three Views of Education," p. 327.)

20. This literature is extensively reviewed in Giroux, *Theory and Resistance in Education.*

21. Ray Rist, "On Understanding the Process of Schooling: The Contribution of Labeling Theory," in *Power and Ideology,* ed. J. Karabel and A. H. Halsey (New York: Oxford University Press, 1977); Jean Anyon, "Social Class and the Hidden Curriculum of Work," in *Curriculm and Instruction,* ed. Henry A. Giroux, Anthony Penna, and William Pinar (Berkeley: McCutchan Publishing, 1981); Hugh Mehan, *Learning Lessons* (Cambridge: Harvard University Press, 1979).

22. Kathleen Rockhill, "Gender, Language and the Politics of Literacy," *British Journal of Sociology of Education, 8* (1987), p. 158.

23. June Jordan, *On Call: Political Essays* (Boston: South End Press, 1987), p. 30.

24. The notion of literacy as a form of cultural politics that embodies a particular pedagogical practice is most evident in the works of Paulo Freire. See, for example, Paulo Freire, *Pedogogy of the Oppressed*, trans. Myra Bergman Ramos (New York: Seabury Press, 1968); Paulo Freire and Donaldo Macedo, *Literacy: Reading the Word and the World* (South Hadley, MA: Bergin & Garvey, 1987).

25. Jordan, *On Call*, p. 29.

26. Martha Nussbaum's comment on the narrowness of Bloom's reading of the fruits of Western civilization is worth repeating. She writes:

> His special love for these books [the old Great Books of the ancient philosophers] has certainly prevented him from attending to works of literature and philosophy that lie outside the tradition they began. For he makes the remarkable claim that "only in the Western nations, i.e., those influenced by Greek philosophy, is there some willingness to doubt the identification of the good with one's own way." This statement shows a startling ignorance of the critical and rationalist tradition in classical Indian thought, of the arguments of classical Chinese thinkers, and beyond this, of countless examples of philosophical and nonphilosophical self-criticism from many parts of the world. (Nussbaum, "Undemocratic Vistas," p. 22)

Education, Art, and Mastery:
Toward the Spheres of Freedom

Maxine Greene

Our exploration began in an awareness of a taken-for-grantedness and a void where present-day thinking is concerned, of a lassitude and a lack of care. The void exists with regard to the question of freedom, the givenness of which is taken for granted. We have, in the course of this inquiry, distinguished freedom from liberty for the purpose of highlighting the tension and the drama of personal choosing in an intersubjective field—choosing among others in a conditioned world. Liberty may be conceived of in social or political terms: Embodied in laws or contracts or formulations of human rights, it carves out a domain where free choices can be made. For Isaiah Berlin, the sense of freedom entails "the absence of obstacles to possible choices and activities—absence of obstructions on roads along which a man can decide to walk" (1970, p. xxxix). We recognize, as he did, that among the obstructions to be removed (and preferably through social action) are those raised by poverty, sickness, even ignorance. We recognize as well that the removal of obstacles to "possible choices and activities" may, in many cases, lead to domination by the few and the closing off of opportunities for the many. We know too that, even given conditions of liberty, many people do not act on their freedom; they do not risk becoming different; they accede; often, they submit.

The problems for education, therefore, are manifold. Certain ones cluster around the presumed connection between freedom and autonomy; certain ones have to do with the relation between freedom and community, most significantly moral community. Autonomy, many believe, is a prime characteristic of the educated person. To be autonomous is to be self-directed and responsible; it is to be capable of acting in accord with internalized norms and principles; it is to be insightful enough to know and understand one's impulses, one's motives, and the influences of one's past. There are those who ascribe to the autonomous person a free rational will, capable of making rational sense of an extended objective world. Values like independence, self-sufficiency, and authenticity are associated with autonomy, because the truly autonomous person is not supposed to be susceptible to outside manipulations and compulsions. Indeed, he/she can, by maintaining a calm and rational stance, transcend compulsions and complexes that might otherwise interfere with judgment and clarity.

As is well known, the attainment of autonomy characterizes the highest state in the developmental patterns devised by Jean Piaget (1977) and, later, by Lawrence Kohlberg (1971). Piaget saw autonomy as emergent from experience of mutual reciprocity and regard. A life plan, he wrote, is "an affirmation of autonomy"; and "a life plan is above all a scale of values which puts some ideals above others and subordinates the middle-range values to goals thought of as permanent" (p. 443). For Kohlberg, whose primary interest was in moral development, people who reach a high-enough cognitive stage of development become autonomous enough to guide their choices by universalizable principles of justice and benevolence. "That welfare and justice," he said, "are guiding principles of legislation as well as of individual moral action points to the fact that a principle is always a maxim or a rule for making rules or laws as well as a maxim of individual situational conduct" (p. 60). If the presumption is that autonomy is associated with "higher order" thinking and with the ability to conceptualize abstractions like human rights and justice, and if indeed such principles become maxims of individual conduct, many conclude that autonomous persons can be considered free persons. To abide by internalized principles, after all, is to acknowledge the rule of "ought" or "should." R. M. Hare has written that it is because we *can* act in this way or that, that we ask whether we ought to do this or that (1965, p. 51ff.). Granting the various usages of words like "ought" and "should," we can still understand why persons who are capable of principled action and who are responsive to ideals they have incarnated for themselves are considered self-determining and therefore free.

The implications for education have had to do with cognition—with logical thinking, the resolution of moral dilemmas, the mastery of interpersonal rules. For R. S. Peters, this kind of education involves the nurture of a "rational passion" associated with commitment to the worthwhile. Peters wrote: "Respect for truth is intimately connected with fairness, and respect for persons, which together with freedom, are fundamental principles which underlie our moral life and which are personalized in the form of the rational passions" (1970, p. 55). The problem with this highly cognitive focus in the classroom has in part to do with what it excludes. Also, it has to do with whether or not reasoning is enough when it comes to acting in a resistant world, or opening fields of possibilities among which people may choose to choose. There have been many reports on classroom discussions of issues ostensibly of moment to the students: cheating, betraying confidences, nonviolent resistance, sexual relations, discrimination. Not only has there been little evidence that the participants take such issues personally; there has been little sign of any transfer to situations in the "real world," even when there were opportunities (say, in a peace demonstration) to act on what were affirmed as guiding principles. We will touch, before long, on the importance of imagination and the exploration of alternative possibilities. It seems clear, as Oliver and

Bane have said, that young people "need the opportunity to project themselves in rich hypothetical worlds created by their own imagination or those of dramatic artists. More important, they need the opportunity to test out new forms of social order—and only then to reason about their moral implications" (1971, p. 270).

Most of the writers to whom we have referred in these paragraphs are, of course, interested primarily in moral commitments, not freedom *per se*. It does appear, as has been said, that there is a presupposition linking autonomy to personal freedom, autonomy in the sense of rational and principled self-government. For many, a movement out of heteronomous existence, with all its conditioning and shaping factors, cannot but be a movement in the direction of a kind of rule-governed self-sufficiency and independence. And this (at least where qualified students are concerned) is viewed by numbers of educators as the most desirable end of pedagogy, to be achieved by liberal education and commitment to the worthwhile.

Such inquiries into women's moral development as Carol Gilligan's *In a Different Voice* (1981) and into women's distinctive modes of reflection as *Women's Ways of Knowing* by Mary Field Belenky and her colleagues (1986) have, at the very least, made problematic the focal emphasis on separateness and responsiveness to purely formal principle. Gilligan has pointed time and time again to the neglect of the patterns of women's development, whose "elusive mystery . . . lies in its recognition of the continuing importance of attachment in the human life cycle. Woman's place in man's life cycle is to protect this recognition while the developmental litany intones the celebration of separation, autonomy, individuation, and natural rights" (p. 23). Belenky's work emphasizes the relational thinking and the integration of voices that characterize women's life stories. Where freedom is concerned (and it is rarely mentioned in contemporary women's literature), it is taken to signify either liberation from domination or the provision of spaces where choices can be made. There is a general acknowledgment that the opening of such spaces depends on support and connectedness. "Connected teaching," for example, involves what Nel Noddings describes as "care" (1984, pp. 15–16). Rather than posing dilemmas to students or presenting models of expertise, the caring teacher tries to look through students' eyes, to struggle *with* them as subjects in search of their own projects, their own ways of making sense of the world. Reflectiveness, even logical thinking remain important; but the *point* of cognitive development is not to gain an increasingly complete grasp of abstract principles. It is to interpret from as many vantage points as possible lived experience, the ways there are of being in the world.

This recent attentiveness to mutuality and to responsiveness to others' wants and concerns cannot but recall the contextual thinking of Dewey, Merleau-Ponty, Hannah Arendt, Michel Foucault, and others. Dewey wrote of the habit of viewing sociality as a trait of an individual "isolated by nature, quite as much as, say, a tendency to combine with others in order to get protection against something threatening one's own private self" (1938/1963, p. 22). He believed it essential to consider the problem of freedom within the context of culture, surely within a context of multiple transactions and relationships. Part of the difficulty for him and those who followed him had to do with the positing of a "free will" associated with a mysterious interiority, even as it had to do with a decontextualization that denied the influences of associated life.

Hannah Arendt found some of the century's worst contradictions in the distinction made between "inner" freedom and the kind of outward "unfreedom" or causality described by Immanuel Kant and his successors. The search for a freedom within, she said, denied notions of *praxis* and the public space. For her, as we have seen, freedom was identified with a space that provided room for human action and interaction. She believed that freedom was the major reason persons came together in political orders: it is, she wrote, "the *raison d'être* of politics" and the opposite of "inner freedom," which she called "the inward space into which we may escape from external coercion and *feel* free." (1961, pp. 141–146).

The relationships and responsibilities stressed by women inquirers are not to be identified entirely with the cultural matrix of such importance to Dewey; nor is either emphasis precisely the same as Arendt's concern with the public space. Nonetheless, all these strains of thought are significant responses to present calls, in philosophy and the human sciences, for some reconstitution of core values, some rebuilding of community today. Attention is being repeatedly called to the crucial good of "friendship" in the Aristotelian qualitative-moral sense (see *Nicomachean Ethics*, Bk. VIII)—the relation between those who desire the good of friends for their friends' sake, no matter how different that "good" may be from what a companion chooses and pursues. In some degree, this is a way of acknowledging and respecting another's freedom to choose among possibilities, as it involves a desire to foster that choosing, because the other is a friend. There is talk of "solidarity" as well, as in the case of Richard Rorty talking about human beings giving sense to their lives by placing them in a larger context. There are two ways of doing this, he says: "by telling the story of their contribution to a community" or "by describing themselves as standing in immediate relation to a nonhuman reality." He calls the first story an example of the desire for solidarity, the second an example of the desire for objectivity. "Insofar as a person is seeking solidarity, he or she does not ask about the relation between the practices of the chosen community and something outside that community" (1985, p. 3). Rorty associates the notion of solidarity with pragmatism, especially when the suggestion is made that the only foundation for the sense of community is "shared hope and the trust created by such sharing." This removes not only objectivism but absoluteness; it returns us to the ideas of relatedness, communication, and disclosure, which provide the context in which (according to the viewpoint of this book) freedom must be pursued.

It is because of people's embeddedness in memory and history, because of their incipient sense of community, that freedom in education cannot be conceived either as an autonomous achievement or as merely one of the principles underlying our moral life, personalized (as R. S. Peters said) "in the form of rational passions." It is because of the apparent normality, the givenness of young people's everyday lives, that intentional actions ought to be undertaken to bring things within the scope of students' attention, to make situations more palpable and visible. Only when they are visible and "at hand" are they likely to cry out for interpretation. And only when individuals are empowered to interpret the situations they live together do they become able to mediate between the object-world and their own consciousness, to locate themselves so that freedom can appear.

Aware of how living persons are enmeshed, engaged with what surrounds them, Merleau-Ponty wrote:

> It is because we are through and through compounded of relationships with the world that for us the only way to become aware of the fact is to suspend the resultant activity . . . to put it out of play. Not because we reject the certainties of common sense and a natural attitude to things—they are, on the contrary, the consistent theme of philosophy—but because, being the presupposed basis of any thought, they are taken for granted and go unnoticed, and because in order to arouse them and bring them into view we have to suspend for a moment our recognition of them. (1962/1967, p. xiii)

He was not talking about withdrawing into some interior domain. Nor was he calling for a deflection of attention from ordinary life. Rather, he was exploring the possibilities of seeing what was ordinarily obscured by the familiar, so much part of the accustomed and the everyday that it escaped notice entirely. We might think about the clocks that play such important parts in schoolrooms, or school bells, or loudspeakers blaring at the beginning and end of the day; about calling individual children "third graders" or "lower track"; about threats to summon the remote principal; even about the Pledge of Allegiance, and about the flags drooping in the public rooms. Why *should* these phenomena be presupposed as a "basis" for thought and self-identification? We might think of the way the chalkboard is placed, of the peculiar distancing of the teacher at the front desk, of books firmly shut before the reading is done. The point is to find a means of making all this an object of thought, of critical attention. And we may be reminded again of Foucault's remark that "thought is freedom in relation to what one does." Part of the effort might be to defamiliarize things, to make them strange. How would a Martian view what was there, a "boat person" newly arrived? What would happen if the hands were removed from the clock? (No one, for instance, who has read William Faulkner's *The Sound and the Fury* is likely to forget the strangeness of what happens when Quentin pulls the hands off his watch on the day of his suicide. "Hearing it, that is," thinks Quentin, "I don't suppose anybody ever deliberately listens to a watch or a clock. You don't have to, You can be oblivious to the sound for a long while, then in a second of ticking it can create in the mind unbroken the long diminishing parade of time you didn't hear" [1946, p. 96]. Later, he remembers that "Father said clocks slay time. He said time is dead as long as it is being clicked off by little wheels; only when the clock stops does time come to life" [p. 104]. Reading that, one cannot but find the clock-field, the clock-world, expanding. And the possibilities of thinking multiply.) What of paper? Why is there so much paper? So many files? (George Konrad's novel about a Hungarian social worker, called *The Caseworker*, also makes a reader see—and ask, and question. "I question, explain, prove, disprove, comfort, threaten, grant, deny, demand, approve. . . . The order I defend is brutal though fragile, it is unpleasant and austere; its ideas are impoverished and its style is lacking in grace. . . . I repudiate the high priests of individual salvation and the sob sisters of altruism, who exchange commonplace partial responsibility for the aesthetic transports of cosmohistorical guilt or the gratuitous slogans of universal love. I refuse to emulate these Sunday-school clowns and prefer—I know my limitations—to be the sceptical bureaucrat that I am. My highest aspiration is that a medium-rank, utterly insignificant civil servant should, as far as possible, live with his eyes open" [1974, p. 168]. Again, familiar bureaucratic orders in one's own world thrust themselves into visibility. Seeing more, feeling more, one reaches out for more to do.)

Walker Percy's narrator in *The Moviegoer* says it in another way. He is trying to relieve his own boredom, a boredom verging on despair; and the idea of a search suddenly occurs to him.

> What is the nature of the search? you ask.
> Really, it is very simple, at least for a fellow like me; so simple that it is easily overlooked.
> The search is what anyone would undertake if he were not sunk in the everydayness of his own life. This morning, for example, I felt as if I had come to myself on a strange island. And what does such a castaway do? Why, he pokes around the neighborhood and he doesn't miss a trick.
> To become aware of the possibility of the search is to be onto something. Not to be onto something is to be in despair. (1979, p. 13)

To undertake a search is, of course, to take an initiative, to refuse stasis and the flatness of ordinary life. Since the narrator says he was "sunk in everydayness," his search is clearly for another perspective, one that will disclose what he has never seen. Even to realize that he can be "onto something" is to begin perceiving lacks in his own life. The question as to what the "neighborhood" holds and implies remains open. He may be moved to "poke around" because others have taken heed of him, because he has appeared in the open for almost the first time. If this is so, he may acquire the space that will free him from his environment of everydayness. The experience may be one denoting a willingness "to learn again to see the world"—and to restore "a power to signify, a birth of meaning, or a wild meaning, an expression of experience by experience" (Merleau-Ponty, 1962/1967, p. 60). I am suggesting that there may be an integral relationship between reaching out to learn to learn and the "search" that involves a pursuit of freedom. Without being "onto something," young people feel little pressure, little challenge. There are no mountains they particularly want to climb, so there are few obstacles with which they feel they need to engage. They may take no heed of neighborhood shapes and events once they have become used to them—even the figures of homelessness, the wanderers who are mentally ill, the garbage-strewn lots, the burned-out buildings. It may be that no one communicates the importance of thinking about them or suggests the need to play with hypothetical alternatives. There may be no sense of identification with people sitting on the benches, with children hanging around the street corners after dark. There may be no ability to take it seriously, to take it personally. Visible or invisible, the world may not be problematized; no one aches to break through a horizon, aches in the presence of the question itself. So there are no tensions, no desires to reach beyond.

There is an analogy here for the passivity and the disinterest that prevent discoveries in classrooms, that discourage inquiries, that make even reading seem irrelevant. It is not simply a matter of motivation or interest. In this context, we can call it a question having to do with freedom or, perhaps, the absence of freedom in our schools. By that I do not necessarily mean the ordinary limits and constraints, or even the rules established to ensure order. I mean, in part, the apparent absence of concern for the ways in which young people feel conditioned, determined, even *fated* by prevailing circumstances. Members of minority groups, we are repeatedly informed, do not see the uses of commitment to schooling and studying. No matter how they yearn for success in society, they are convinced of inimical forces all around them, barricades that cannot be overcome. Poor children and others often experience the weight of what is called "cultural reproduction," although they cannot name it or resist it. By that is meant not only the reproduction of ways of knowing, believing, and valuing, but the maintenance of social patterings and stratifications as well. The young people may not chafe under the inequities being kept alive through schools, as inequities often are; they are likely to treat them as wholly "normal," as predictable as natural laws. The same might be said about advantaged children who grow up with a sense of entitlement and privilege, but still feel they have no choice.

The challenge is to engage as many young people as possible in the thought that is freedom—the mode of thought that moved Sarah Grimké, Elizabeth Cady Stanton, Septima Clark, Leonard Covello, the Reverend King, and so many others into action. Submergence and the inability to name what lies around interfere with questioning and learning. Dewey had something much like this in mind when he emphasized the dangers of "recurrence, complete uniformity," "the routine and mechanical" (1934, p. 272). What he sometimes called the "anaesthetic" in experience is what numbs people and prevents them from reaching out, from launching inquiries. For Dewey, experience becomes fully conscious only when meanings derived from earlier experience enter in through the exercise of the imaginative capacity, since imagination "is the only gateway through which these meanings can find their way into a present interaction; or rather . . . the conscious adjustment of the new and the old is imagination" (p. 272). The word, the concept "conscious" must be emphasized. Experience, for Dewey, becomes "human and conscious" only when what is "given here and now is extended by meanings and values drawn from what is absent in fact and present only imaginatively." Conscious thinking always involves a risk, a "venture into the unknown"; and it occurs against a background of funded or sedimented meanings that must themselves be tapped and articulated, so that the mind can continue dealing consciously and solicitously with lived situations, those situations (as Dewey put it) "in which we find ourselves" (p. 263).

Education for freedom must clearly focus on the range of human intelligences, the multiple languages and symbol systems available for ordering experience and making sense of the lived world. Dewey was bitterly opposed to the anti-intellectual tendencies in the culture and frequently gave voice to what he called "a plea for casting off that intellectual timidity which hampers the wings of imagination, a plea for speculative audacity, for more faith in ideas, sloughing off a cowardly reliance upon those partial ideas to which we are wont to give the name facts" (1931, p. 12). He spoke often as well about the kinds of inquiry that deliberately challenge desires for certainty, for fixity. He would undoubtedly have agreed with John Passmore's more recent call for "critico-creative thinking," the kind that is consciously norm-governed but at once willing to challenge rules that become irrelevant or stultifying. No principle, Passmore wrote, no person or text or work of art should be kept beyond the reach of rational criticism. There should nonetheless be a continuing initiation into the great traditions in which we are all, whether we are aware of it or not, embedded. Passmore went on:

> Critical thinking as it is exhibited in the great traditions conjoins imagination and criticism in a single form of thinking; in literature, science, history, philosophy or technology, the free flow of the imagination is controlled by criticism and criticisms are transformed into a new way of looking at things. Not that either the free exercise of the imagination or the raising of objections is in itself to be despised; the first can be suggestive of new ideas, the second can show the need for them. But certainly education tries to develop the two in combination. The educator is interested in encouraging critical discussion as distinct from the mere raising of objections; and discussion is an exercise of the imagination. (1975, p. 33)

A concern for the critical and the imaginative, for the opening of new ways of "looking at things," is wholly at odds with the technicist and behaviorist emphases we still find in American schools. It represents a challenge, not yet met, to the hollow formulations, the mystifications so characteristic of our time. We have taken note of the forms of evangelism and fundamentalism, the confused uneasiness with modernism that so often finds expression in anti-intellectualism or an arid focus on "Great Books." Given the dangers of small-mindedness and privatism, however, I do not think it sufficient to develop even the most variegated, most critical, most imaginative, most "liberal" approach to the education of the young. If we are seriously interested in education for freedom as well as for the opening of cognitive perspectives, it is also important to find a way of developing a *praxis* of educational consequence that opens the spaces necessary for the remaking of a democratic community. For this to happen, there must of course be a new commitment to intelligence, a new fidelity in communication, a new regard for imagination. It would mean fresh and sometimes startling winds blowing through the classrooms of the nation. It would mean the granting of audibility to numerous voices seldom heard before and, at once, an involvement with all sorts of young people being provoked to make their own the multilinguality needed for structuring of contemporary experience and thematizing lived worlds. The languages required include many of the traditional modes of sense-making: the academic disciplines, the fields of study. But none of them must ever be thought of as complete or all-encompassing, developed as they have been to respond to particular kinds of questions posed at particular moments in time. Turned, as lenses or perspectives, on the shared world of actualities, they cannot but continue resonating and reforming in the light of new undercurrents, new questions, new uncertainties.

Let us say young high school students are studying history. Clearly, they require some understanding of the rules of evidence where the historical record is concerned. They need to distinguish among sources, to single out among multiple determinants those forces that can be identified as causal, to find the places where chance cuts across necessity, to recognize when calculations are appropriate and when they are not. All this takes reflective comprehension of the norms governing the discipline of history. But this does not end or exhaust such study. There is a consciousness now, as there was not in time past, of the significance of doing history "from the ground up," of penetrating the so-called "cultures of silence" in order to discover what ordinary farmers and storekeepers and elementary schoolteachers and street children and Asian newcomers think and have thought about an event like the Holocaust or the Vietnam War or the bombing of Hiroshima or the repression in South Africa that continues to affect them directly or indirectly even as it recedes into the visualizable past. They need to be empowered to reflect on and talk about what happened in its varying connections with other events in the present as well as the past. And they may be brought to find out that a range of informed viewpoints may be just as important when it comes to understanding the Civil War, or the industrial revolution, or the slave trade, or the Children's Crusade. Clearly, if the voices of participants or near-participants (front-line soldiers, factory workers, slaves, crusaders) could be heard, whole dimensions of new understanding (and perplexity and uncertainty) would be disclosed. The same is true with respect to demographic studies, studies based on census rolls or tax collections, studies that include diaries and newspaper stories and old photographs. Turning the tools and techniques of history to resources of this kind often means opening up new spaces for study, metaphorical spaces sometimes, places for "speculative audacity." Such efforts may provide experiences of freedom in the study of history, because they unleash imagination in unexpected ways. They draw the mind to what lies beyond the accustomed boundaries and often to what is not yet. They do so as persons become more and more aware of the unanswered questions, the unexplored corners, the nameless faces behind the forgotten windows. These are the obstacles to be transcended if understanding is to be gained. And it is in the transcending, as we have seen, that freedom is often achieved.

The same can be said for the other disciplines and fields of study in the social and natural sciences; and, even among the exact sciences, a heightened curiosity may accompany the growth of feelings of connection between human hands and minds and the objects of study, whether they are rocks or stars or memory cores. Again, it is a matter of questioning and sense-making from a grounded vantage point, an interpretive vantage point, in a way that eventually sheds some light on the commonsense world, in a way that is always perspectival and therefore forever incomplete. The most potent metaphor for this can be found at the end of Melville's chapter called "Cetology" in the novel *Moby Dick*. The chapter deals with the essentially futile effort to provide a "systematized exhibition of the whale in his broad genera," or to classify the constituents of a chaos. And finally:

> It was stated at the outset, that this system would not be here, and at once, perfected. You cannot but plainly see that I have kept my word. But now I leave my cetological System standing thus unfinished, even as the great Cathedral of Cologne was left, with the crane still standing upon the top of the uncompleted tower. For small erections may be finished by their first architects; grand ones, true ones, ever leave the copestone to posterity. God keep me from ever completing anything. This whole book is but a draught—nay, but the draught of a draught. Oh, Time, Strength, Cash, and patience! (1851/1981, p. 148)

To recognize the role of perspective and vantage point, to recognize at the same time that there are always multiple perspectives and multiple vantage points, is to recognize that no accounting, disciplinary or otherwise, can ever be finished or complete. There is always more. There is always possibility. And this is where the space opens for the pursuit of freedom. Much the same can be said about experiences with art objects—not only literary texts, but music, painting, dance. They have the capacity, when authentically attended to, to enable persons to hear and to see what they would not ordinarily hear and see, to offer visions of consonance and dissonance that are unfamiliar and indeed abnormal, to disclose the incomplete profiles of the world. As importantly, in this context, they have the capacity to defamiliarize experience: to begin with the overly familiar and transfigure it into something different enough to make those who are awakened hear and see.

Generalizations with regard to what forms possess such potential for different people are tempting, but they must be set aside. Jazz and the blues have long had a transformative, often liberating effect on many populations, for example. We have only to read the musical history of our country, recall the stories of our great black musicians, heed such novels as *Invisible Man* (constructed, its author said, according to the patterns of the blues), take note of the importance of jazz in European art forms throughout the century, see how the Jazz Section of the Czech dissident movement has become the live center of dissent. The ways in which the blues have given rise to rock music and what are called "raps" testify as well to a power, not merely to embody and express the suffering of oppressed and constricted lives, but to name them somehow, to identify the gaps between what is and what is longed for, what (if the sphere of freedom is ever developed) will some day come to be.

Recent discoveries of women's novels, like discoveries of black literature, have certainly affected the vision of those reared in the traditions of so-called "great" literature, as they have the constricted visions of those still confined by outmoded ideas of gender. The growing ability to look at even classical works through new critical lenses has enabled numerous readers, of both genders, to apprehend previously unknown renderings of their lived worlds. Not only have many begun coming to literature with the intent of *achieving* it as meaningful through realization by means of perspectival readings. Many have begun engaging in what Mikhail Bakhtin called "dialogism," viewing literary texts as spaces where multiple voices and multiple discourses intersect and interact (1981, pp. 259–422). Even to confront what Bakhtin calls "heteroglossia" in a novel is to enlarge one's experience with multiplicity of perspectives and, at once, with the spheres that can open in the midst of pluralities.

With *Invisible Man* in mind, we might recall the point that invisibility represents a condition in the mind of the one who encounters the black person and draw implications for the ways we have looked at other strangers, and even for the ways we have looked at those posited as "other" or as enemies. We can find ourselves reading so-called canonical works like *Jane Eyre* and become astonished by a newly grasped interpretation of the "madwoman" imprisoned upstairs in Mr. Rochester's house. Shocked into a new kind of awareness, we find ourselves pushing back the boundaries again, hearing new voices, exploring new discourses, unearthing new possibilities. We can ponder such works as Tillie Olsen's "I Stand There Ironing" or "Tell Me a Riddle" and uncover dimensions of oppression, dream, and possibility never suspected before. We can look again at Gabriel García Márquez's *One Hundred*

Years of Solitude and find ourselves opening windows in our experience to startling renderings of time, death, and history that subvert more of our certainties. It is not only, however, in the domains of the hitherto "silent" cultures that transformations of our experience can take place. There is a sense in which the history of any art form carries with it a history of occasions for new visions, new modes of defamiliarization, at least in cases where artists thrust away the auras, and broke in some way with the past.

It has been clear in music, pushing back the horizons of silence for at least a century, opening new frequencies for ears willing to risk new sounds. It has been true of dance, as pioneers of movement and visual metaphor uncover new possibilities in the human body and therefore for embodied consciousnesses in the world. In painting, it has been dramatically the case. An example can be found in the work of the painter John Constable, who abandoned old paradigms of studio painting and studio light and began sketching his subjects in the open air. Breaking through "horizons of expectation," as the critic Ernst Gombrich writes (1965, p. 34), Constable enabled spectators to perceive green in the landscape, rather than rendering it in the traditional manner in gradations of brown. He defamiliarized the visible world, in effect, making accessible shadings and nuances never suspected before. We can say similar things about numerous visual artists, if we are enabled, say, to see them against their forerunners; moving through the "museums without walls," listening to those Merleau-Ponty called the "voices of silence," we can discover ourselves variously on an always-changing place on earth. Giotto, della Francesca, Botticelli, Michelangelo, Raphael, Poussin: The names sound, the doors open to vista after vista. Exemplary for moderns may be Claude Monet making visible the modelling effects of light on objects once seen as solidly and objectively *there*. Some can recall the multiple studies of haystacks in his garden at different seasons of the year or of Rouen Cathedral at different times of day. Recalling, we are reminded again how visions of fixity can be transformed, how time itself can take on new meanings for the perceiver, for the one choosing to journey through works of visual art. And we can (we ought to) recall Pablo Picasso's abrupt expansion of Western observers' conceptions of humanity and space with his "Demoiselles d'Avignon" and its African and Iberian visages, or his imaging of unendurable pain in the "Guernica."

Of course, such visions are unknown in most of our classrooms; and relatively few people are informed enough or even courageous enough actually to "see." And it must be acknowledged that, for all their emancipatory potential, the arts cannot be counted on to liberate, to ensure an education for freedom. Nonetheless, for those authentically concerned about the "birth of meaning," about breaking through the surfaces, about teaching others to "read" their own worlds, art forms must be conceived of as ever-present possibility. They ought not to be treated as decorative, as frivolous. They ought to be, if transformative teaching is our concern, a central part of curriculum, wherever it is devised. How can it be irrelevant, for example, to include such images as those of William Blake, with contraries and paradoxes that make it forever impossible to place the "lamb" and the "tiger" in distinctive universes, to separate the "marriage from the "hearse"? How can it be of only extracurricular interest to turn to Emily Dickinson, for instance, and find normal views of experience disrupted and transformed? She wrote:

I stepped from plank to plank
So slow and cautiously;
The stars about my head I felt,
About my feet the sea.
I knew not but the next
Would be my final inch,—
This gave me that precarious gait
Some call experience.

(1890/1959, p. 166)

The spaces widen in the poem—from plank to plank under an open sky. She identifies experience itself with a "precarious gait"; and the risk involved is emphasized. Reading such a work, we cannot but find our own world somehow defamiliarized. Defamiliarized, it discloses aspects of experience ordinarily never seen. Critical awareness may be somehow enhanced, as new possibilities open for reflection. Poetry does not offer us empirical or documentary truth, but it enables us to "know" in unique ways. So many poems come to mind, among them W. H. Auden's "Surgical Ward," which may emerge from memory because of the AIDS epidemic, or because of a concern about distancing and lack of care. He wrote of the remoteness of those who "are and suffer; that is all they do" and of the isolation of the sufferers compared with those who believe "in the common world of the uninjured and cannot imagine isolation—" (1970, pp. 44–45). Any one of a hundred others might have come to mind: the choice is arbitrary. A writer, like the writer of this book, can only hope to activate the memories of *her* readers, to awaken, to strike sparks.

The same is true, even more true, when it comes to novels and plays: The occasions for revelation and disclosure are beyond counting. In my train of thought (and readers will locate themselves in their own), I find Antigone, committed to her sense of what is moral and dying for her cause; King Lear, with all artifice and "superfluity" abandoned on the heath in the raging storm. I somehow see Lucifer falling in *Paradise Lost* and continually falling, reappearing at the end of James Joyce's *A Portrait of the Artist as a Young Man* when Stephen Dedalus says, "I will not serve." And then, remembering Joyce, I hear that resounding "Yes" at the end of Molly Bloom's soliloquy in *Ulysses*. In the background, softly, stubbornly, there is Bartleby's "I prefer not to" in the Melville story; there is the dying Ivan Ilyitch in the Tolstoy story, speaking of himself as "little Vanya" to the peasant holding his legs; there is the shadow of the little girl who hung herself in Dostoevsky's *The Possessed*. There are the soldiers described in Malraux's *Man's Fate,* young soldiers about to be executed on the Lithuanian front and forced to take off their trousers in the snow. They begin to sneeze, "and those sneezes were so intensely human in that dawn of execution, that the machine-gunners, instead of firing, waited—waited for life to become less indiscreet" (1936, p. 76). Indiscreet—and I see the house beaten by the storms and the dilapidations of time in the "Time Passes" section of Virginia Woolf's *To the Lighthouse*; Willa Cather's Paul (in "Paul's Case") and the winter roses and a boy's death on the railroad tracks. There are the spare, lace-curtained bedrooms and the slave women in red in Margaret Atwood's *The Handmaid's Tale*; and, in another future, there is the stark transcendence of the rocket in *Gravity's Rainbow* by Thomas

Pynchon. There is Mark Helprin's white horse in the snow-bound city in *Winter's Tale,* the "air-borne toxic event" in Don DeLillo's *White Noise.*

Any reader might go on to recall how, as Herbert Marcuse has put it, "art is committed to that perception of the world which alienates individuals from their functional existence and performance in society" (1978, p. 9). An education for freedom must move beyond function, beyond the subordination of persons to external ends. It must move beyond mere performance to action, which entails the taking of initiatives. This is not meant to imply that aesthetic engagements, because they take place in domains of freedom, separate or alienate learners so fully from the tasks of the world that they become incapacitated for belonging or for membership or for work itself. Marcuse also spoke of an aesthetic transformation as a "vehicle of recognition," drawing the perceiver away from "the mystifying power of the given" (1978, p. 72). He was pointing to an emancipatory possibility of relevance for an education in and for freedom. Encounters with the arts alone will not realize it; but the arts will help open the situations that require interpretation, will help disrupt the walls that obscure the spaces, the spheres of freedom to which educators might some day attend.

With situations opening, students may become empowered to engage in some sort of *praxis,* engaged enough to name the obstacles in the way of their shared becoming. They may at first be identified with the school itself, with the neighborhood, with the family, with fellow-beings in the endangered world. They may be identified with prejudices, rigidities, suppressed violence: All these can petrify or impinge on the sphere of freedom. As Foucault would have it, persons may be made into subjects, docile bodies to be "subjected, used, transformed, and improved" (1977, p. 136). It is not merely the structures of class, race, and gender relations that embody such power and make it felt in classrooms. Much the same can happen through the differential distribution of knowledge, through a breaking of what is distributed into discrete particles, through an unwarranted classification of a "chaos."

Having attended to women's lives and the lives of many strangers, we are aware of the relation between the subjugation of voices and the silencing of memories. All these have often been due to the insidious workings of power or the maintenance of what has been called "hegemony" (Entwhistle, 1979, pp. 12–14). Hegemony, as explained by the Italian philosopher Antonio Gramsci, means direction by moral and intellectual persuasion, not by physical coercion. That is what makes it a matter of such concern for those interested in education for freedom. The persuasion is often so quiet, so seductive, so disguised that it renders young people acquiescent to power without their realizing it. The persuasion becomes most effective when the method used obscures what is happening in the learners' minds. Strangely, the acquiescence, the acceptance, may find expression through dropping out or other modes of alienation, as much as through a bland compliance to what is taken to be the given. This may be because the message or the direction emphasizes an opportunity system or a stratification system offering a limited range of possibilities, apparently attentive to but a few modes of being. This becomes most drastically clear in the case of youngsters whose IQs, according to current testing practices, are low. Ours is not a society that ponders fulfilling options for people with low IQs. Lacking an awareness of alternatives, lacking a vision of realizable possibilities, the young (left unaware of the messages they are given) have no hope of achieving freedom.

In the classroom opened to possibility and at once concerned with inquiry, critiques must be developed that uncover what masquerade as neutral frameworks, or what Rorty calls "a set of rules which will tell us how rational agreement can be reached on what would settle the issue on every point where statements seem to conflict" (1979, p. 315). Teachers, like their students, have to learn to love the questions, as they come to realize that there can be no final agreements or answers, no final commensurability. And we have been talking about stories that open perspectives on communities grounded in trust, flowering by means of dialogue, kept alive in open spaces where freedom can find a place.

Looking back, we can discern individuals in their we-relations with others, inserting themselves in the world by means of projects, embarking on new beginnings in spaces they open themselves. We can recall them—Thomas Jefferson, the Grimké sisters, Susan B. Anthony, Jane Addams, Frederick Douglass, W.E.B. DuBois, Martin Luther King, John Dewey, Carol Gilligan, Nel Noddings, Mary Daly—opening public spaces where freedom is the mainspring, where people create themselves by acting in concert. For Hannah Arendt, "power corresponds to the human ability . . . to act in concert. Power is never the property of an individual; it belongs to a group and remains in existence only so long as the group keeps together" (1972, p. 143). Power may be thought of, then, as "empowerment," a condition of possibility for human and political life and, yes, for education as well. But spaces have to be opened in the schools and around the schools; the windows have to let in the fresh air. The poet Mark Strand writes:

It is all in the mind, you say, and has
nothing to do with happiness. The coming of cold,
The coming of heat, the mind has all the time in the world.
You take my arm and say something will happen,
something unusual for which we were always prepared,
like the sun arriving after a day in Asia,
like the moon departing after a night with us.

(1984, p. 126)

And Adrienne Rich, calling a poem "Integrity" and beginning, "A wild patience has taken me this far" (1981, p. 8). There is a need for a wild patience. And, when freedom is the question, it is always a time to begin.

REFERENCES

Arendt, H. 1961. *Between Past and Present*. New York: The Viking Press.
Aristotle. *Nichomachean Ethics*. Book VIII. Trans. W.D. Ross. In *Introduction to Aristotle*, ed. R. McKeon. New York: The Modern Library, 1972.
Auden, W.H. 1970. *Selected Poetry of W.H. Auden*. New York: Vintage Books.
Bakhtin, M.M. 1981. *The Dialogic Imagination*. Austin: University of Texas Press.
Belenky, M.F., et al. 1986. *Women's Ways of Knowing*. Basic Books.
Berlin, I. 1970. *Four Essays on Liberty*. New York: Oxford University Press.
Dewey, J. 1934. *Art as Experience*. New York: Minton, Balch & Co.

Dewey, J. 1938. *Experience as Education*. New York: Collier Books, 1963.

Dickinson, E. 1890. *Selected Poems and Letters of Emily Dickinson*, ed. R.N. Linscott. Garden City, NY: Doubleday/Anchor Books, 1959.

Faulkner, W. 1946. *The Sound and the Fury*. New York: Modern Library.

Foucault, M. 1977. *Languages, Counter-Memory, Practice*, ed. D.F. Bouchard. Ithaca: Cornell University Press.

Gilligan, C. 1982. *In a Different Voice*. Cambridge: Harvard Univeristy Press.

Gombrich, E. 1965. *Art and Illusion*. New York: Pantheon Press.

Hare, R.M. 1965. *Freedom and Reason*. New York: Oxford University Press.

Kohlberg, L. 1971. "Stages of Moral Development as a Basis for Moral Education." In *Moral Education: Interdisciplinary Approaches*, eds. C.M. Beck, B.S. Crittenden, & E.V. Sullivan. New York: Newman Press.

Konrad, G. 1974. *The Caseworker*. New York: Harcourt Brace Jovanovich.

Marcuse, H. 1978. *The Aesthetic Dimension*. Boston: Beacon Press.

Melville, H. 1851. *Moby Dick*. Berkeley: University of California Press, 1981.

Merleau-Ponty, M. 1962. *Phenomenology of Perception*. New York: Humanities Press, 1967.

Noddings, N. 1984. *Caring: A Feminine Approach to Ethics and Moral Education*. Berkeley: University of California Press.

Oliver, D.W. & Bane, M.J. 1971. "Moral Education: Is Reasoning Enough?" In *Moral Education: Interdisciplinary Approaches*, eds. C.M. Beck, B.S. Crittenden, & E.V. Sullivan. New York: Newman Press.

Passmore, J. 1975. "On Teaching to be Critical." In *Education and Reason,* eds. R.F. Dearden, P.H. Hirst, & R.S. Peters, pp. 415-433. London: Routledge & Kegan Paul.

Percy, W. 1979. *The Moviegoer*. New York: Alfred A. Knopf.

Peters, R.S. 1970. "Concrete Principles and the Rational Passions." In *Moral Education*, eds. N.F. Sizer & T.R. Sizer. Cambridge: Harvard University Press.

Piaget J. 1977. *The Essential Piaget*, eds. H.E. Gruber & J.J. Voneche. New York: Basic Books.

Rich, A. 1981. *A Wild Patience Has Taken Me This Far*. New York: W.W. Norton.

Rorty, R. 1985. "Solidarity Or Objectivity?" In *Post-Analytic Philosophy*, eds. J. Rachman & C. West. New York: Columbia University Press.

Strand, M. 1939. "So You Say." In *Selected Poems*. New York: Viking Press.

Education in a Prophetic Voice

David E. Purpel

> *The two dominant attitudes of prophetic faith are gratitude and contrition: Gratitude for creation and contrition before judgment; or in other words, confidence that life is good in spite of its evil and that it is evil in spite of good. In such faith both sentimentality and despair are avoided.*
> *Reinhold Niebuhr,* An Interpretation of Christian Ethics

A basic theme of this book is the intimate interconnection between culture and education, and in this chapter we will focus more sharply on the implications of the proceeding moral and religious analysis for educational practice. The remainder of the book is an attempt to lay out the meaning of our interpretation for the profession, for curriculum and instruction, and for broad educational policy. In this chapter we will deal primarily with issues concerning the profession itself, with particular focus on the possibilities inherent in the profession for significant cultural and educational leadership. Our basic position is that the profession must confront its possibilities, as well as its structural limitations, and that its redemption can emerge from a frank and courageous recognition of its responsibilities and capabilities. Therefore, we begin our specific analysis of educational practice with a consideration of the single most vital professional element, the profession itself.

THE EDUCATION PROFESSION

When we talk of an educational program we cannot limit ourselves to discussion of materials, techniques, course of study, etc., for as we well know one's educational experiences are shaped by a host of other phenomena. We have already spoken at length on how cultural, social, and moral views permeate the schools and classrooms in powerful ways, but the hidden curriculum includes not only the values and attitudes but the quality of school life, its atmosphere and tone, and the nature of human relationships. The quality of school life is, in turn, significantly influenced by the nature and background of the staff, the conditions under which they work, their values, and their professional beliefs. Clearly, what students learn is strongly related to the school's constitutive structural elements and the sum total of human experiences in that school. Although it is a cliché to say that teachers and administrators are part of the "curriculum," it is cliché because it is said so frequently and not because we pay a great deal of attention to its significance. We need, therefore, to address more sharply the nature of the profession itself, as a major constitutive and structural element of educational experience.

We are, alas, a very weak profession, captured in part by our difficulty in admitting to our condition. I believe, however, that we are not weak by chance and that our weaknesses reflect the culture's basic ambivalence about the power and value of education as discussed in chapter one. What is maddening is that although we have been constituted to be weak, we are nonetheless brutally criticized by the culture for the consequences of our weakness. We are criticized for not being intellectually strong, yet the culture tends to channel its best and brightest students to other professions, such as law, medicine, and the sciences. We are berated for our sloppy theorizing and numbing jargon, yet scholars in older, well-established fields tend to ignore the serious study of education or insist on substituting their naivete about educational matters for informed dialogue. Teachers are asked to perform at very high-level tasks of profound importance and yet are given resources that are absurd and insulting. Moreover, because school budgets tend to be prominent and distinguishable, they are often subjected to minute and haggling examination, which puts the educational community in the posture of beggars who ought to be content with their customary dole.

We have also been unable to stem the forces that seriously work to make our profession reluctant to take initiative and assume leadership, and this is because in part our resources and destinies are largely controlled by people who want to keep down the budget, the complaints, the demands, and the quality of thinking. There are, of course, exceptions, such as the case of teacher organizations and unions pressing very aggressively for somewhat better working conditions and pay. However, it is often the case that in these situations, even when the professional groups ask for quite modest changes, there is at best cool community support and often community hostility. We are also a docile and passive profession for another basic and more troubling reason, one that we are reluctant to discuss publicly. I believe that we must confront our own inadequacies as a profession; we must deal with the reality that our members include a great many who are not very gifted intellectually, many who are timid or narrow about exercising leadership, and many who see teaching as a job requiring fairly modest technical skills and lots of hard work. Yes, there are lots of incompetents in other professions, and yes, the culture does do a lot to keep brighter, abler, more energetic people out of our profession. It is also true that the well-known defensiveness of the profession is partly a function of the cruelty and ignorance that permeates much of the public criticism of the schools.

However, we do not do ourselves or the culture any favor by refusing to acknowledge serious deficiencies in the basic structure of the system (which includes our competence) and the culture's very significant responsibility for those deficiencies (including ours). We are more feeble than we need be because we have allowed, if not encouraged, the culture to set the terms and boundaries of the debate and discussion of educational issues. Educators are typically put in a reactive posture and usually find themselves co-opted to work within a parameter of policies that many educators find fundamentally false. In this way educators become technical staff engaged to administer and execute policies set by those who are likely to have serious reservations about providing serious education for all. This has worked to let the profession off the hook of exercising its own responsibility to participate in, and enrich the process of, providing broad cultural leadership. The profession finds itself in a vicious circle—it is looked upon with disdain or perhaps indifference because it lacks the intellectual clout of genuine authority, and yet those in power see a confident, authoritative, and persuasive profession as a serious threat to existing arrangements. Our profession is further weakened by our own brand of specialization, divisiveness, and fragmentation. There are walls among and between teachers and administrators, among and between schools and universities. There is a myriad of worlds within worlds (gifted and talented; elementary; such organizational rubrics as science, middle school), a wide range of educational ideologies ranging from those that are "child-centered" to those totally loyal to institutional concerns. As professionals, we are divided and conquered.

Stanley Aronowitz and Henry Giroux (1985) have provided a concise and powerful analysis of the growing erosion of teacher autonomy and what they call the "proletarianization of teacher work." It is their position that there are steady pressures to reduce the significance of the teachers by increasing administrative controls, using such techniques as competency testing, the development of "teacher-proof" materials, and by emphasizing an increasingly technical and instrumental orientation toward instruction.

> Teachers are not simply being proletarianized; the changing nature of their roles and functions signifies the disappearance of a form of intellectual labor central to the nature of critical pedagogy itself. Moreover, the tendency to reduce teachers to either high-level clerks implementing the orders of others within the school bureaucracy or to specialized technicians is part of a much larger problem within western societies, a problem marked by the increasing division of intellectual and social labor and the increasing trend toward the oppressive management and administration of everyday life. (1985:24)

In their brilliant essay on intellectualism and teaching, Aronowitz and Giroux distinguish among various forms of intellectual activities and maintain a firm view that the requirements of serious and sensitive teaching include the capacity for serious intellectual inquiry. Their commitment, however, is clearly to a kind of teacher they label as a "transformative intellectual," a concept that seems ideally fitted to the teacher as prophet.

> Central to the category of transformative intellectuals is the task of making the pedagogical more political and the political more pedagogical. In the first instance, this means inserting education directly into the political sphere by arguing that schooling represents both a struggle for meaning and a struggle over power relations. Thus schooling becomes a central terrain where power and politics operate out of a dialectical relationship between individuals and groups, who function within specific historical conditions and structural constraints as well as within cultural forms and ideologies that are the basis for contradictions and struggles. Within this view of schooling, critical reflections and action become part of a fundamental social project to help students develop a deep and abiding faith in the struggle to overcome injustice and to change themselves. (1985:36)

It does not seem to be in the interest of those currently in power to encourage and empower the education profession to seek that intellectual and moral authority. On the other hand, there are educators who believe strongly that it is very much in the interest of those who struggle for a culture of love, joy, and justice to demand that our profession develop such a vision. These educators also believe that members of our profession have a basic right to pursue their calling (vocation) with integrity and pride and to seek to fulfill their responsibilities to participate in the struggle to achieve those conditions. All educators must come to define their autonomy in relationship to these broader struggles rather than as a minor component of an existing bureaucratic apparatus. Individual members of the profession have the opportunity and indeed the imperative to search for their own meaning within the context of their work as calling rather than as job. Therefore, they need not see their professional interests as necessarily coinciding with those of school boards, college admission offices, personnel offices, state departments of education, nor even those of school administrators. Professional autonomy in this sense is not to be confused with the self-serving, self-protective ethic of so-called professionalism, which translates into a consciousness of being quiet, polite, and deferential (e.g., "we mustn't wash our dirty linen in public" and "don't make waves"). It is nothing short of tragic that the concept of professionalism has become so distorted that it can connote narrow protectionism rather than dedication to high principles. We should as a profession profess our high ideals rather than being fearful to confess our shortcomings.

We must accept the responsibilities of being the kind of a profession which involves independence and autonomy, and in order to merit that independence and autonomy we must be competent; we must have a sound basis for our authority, and we must have a set of principles and ideas that can inform our professional ethic. As long as we see ourselves as employees or staff or technicians, we will not be a profession that leads but a camp that follows the parade. But we need more than power to lead; we need moral, intellectual, and professional authority that influences rather than imposes. As a profession we need to develop our own overarching professional mythos—a shared set of images and ideals that can guide and inform all our various specializations and concentrations. We suggest that the prophetic tradition provides direction for such a mythos.

EDUCATION AND PROPHECY

Both the culture and individual educators need a profession with a critical capacity and the courage and expertise to provide insights into cultural problems and suggest reasonable responses to them. There are many people and institutions charged with the responsibility of noting and detecting our achievements and shortcomings and of suggesting ways of dealing with them. We urge that the education profession be one of those institutions which accepts that responsibility. In this way, educators would be working within the prophetic tradition that seeks to remind us of our highest aspirations, of our failures to meet them, and of the consequences of our responses to these situations. In order to act in this tradition, educators need to be well-equipped with intellectual powers, expertise, psychological strength, moral courage, strong convictions, and inner strength that derive from a sense of responding seriously to profoundly important issues. Again, it is not in the interest of the existing power structure to stress the extraordinary power and importance of teaching, but it is to our common interest that we all be mindful of the magnificence and nobility of those who seriously teach.

The educator as prophet does more than re-mind, re-answer, and re-invigorate—the prophet-educator conducts re-search and joins students in continually developing skills and knowledge that enhance the possibility of justice, community, and joy. His concern is with the search for meaning through the process of criticism, imagination, and creativity. Such a role (as Socrates found out) is in fact seriously threatening to those fearful of displacing the status quo. Most importantly, the educator as prophet seeks to orient the educational process toward a vision of ultimate meaning. The prophetic model, hence, does not allow the individual educator to go in individual or happenstance direction, for the great prophets like Socrates, Moses, Jesus, Gandhi, and King have performed their critical and creative functions within a broad but particular conception of the meaning and significance of human creation and destiny. Educators who accept the concept of their profession as having a prophetic function must then affirm a set of sacred and moral principles—a mythos, a set of metaphysical or religious assumptions—or commit themselves to that which has ultimate meaning to them. As human beings we need to consciously participate in the process of both forming and being informed by these principles, and as educators we need to help our students to learn how to participate in that process. We have indicated what at least some of these principles might be, and note that educators not only have a responsibility to be reflective, thoughtful, and critical about these principles but also have a responsibility to reflect on their own basic assumptions, however implicit, tacit, or preconscious they may be. A profession without a mythic dimension that provides a vision of ideals and goals is not capable of providing serious cultural leadership and instead serves as a tool that is manipulated by those who have such a vision in place.

Educators are culturally well positioned to have a sense of how the culture is responding to its highest ideals and, consequently, ought to be able to respond to its opportunities for providing social criticism. Traditionally, however, the profession has not seen itself as an institution with such responsibilities and has tended to acquiesce to the dominant culture's self-definition of what the major problems and needs are. The profession needs to establish as its central concerns those policies that correspond to the culture's highest ideals and not those that distort them or deceive us. Although it is reasonable to make some link between cultural success and failure with educational success and failure, it is crucial that the profession be free to focus on what actually constitutes success and failure. For example, schools are criticized, perhaps appropriately, when S.A.T. scores go down, but perhaps they should also be criticized when there is a war or when charitable donations drop. Educators must point out serious social and moral problems of our culture as part of their responsibility to be self-critical and as a way of setting a professional agenda for action. When brilliant economists and other social scientists say they can't control the economy, they are, at least partly, saying something about the inadequacy of their knowledge, of the limitations of their research, of their lack of imagination (i.e., of their education). Such problems should not logically lead us to intensify the very schooling that produced these difficulties but rather to seriously reconsider some of its basic assumptions.

As educators we must confront ourselves and the public with the harsh reality of the basic ignorance and intellectual failures of those who by conventional standards have had the very best education. The fact that the best and the brightest have done very well in some areas and very poorly in others should not fill us with defensiveness or shame but with humility and determination.

Our failures surely speak at least partly to the limits of our knowledge, or perhaps to the political constraints on inquiry, as well as to the failure of the educational system to provide enough opportunities for greater insight and imagination. Educators must reflect on how they have contributed to major structural failures like persistent unemployment and poverty rather than focus on their inability to lower the dropout rate or keep schooling costs down. Educators must confront our moral failure by seriously considering the relationship between the realities of hunger, poverty, and misery and the nature of existing educational programs. The culture that produces and allows any such oppression or degradation fails, and all its institutions must share in the responsibility for that failure. The profession must begin with the perspective of hunger, war, poverty, or starvation as its starting point, rather than from the perspective of problems of textbook selection, teacher certification requirements, or discipline policies. If there is no serious connection between education and hunger, injustice, alienation, poverty, and war, then we are wasting our time, deluding each other, and breaking faith. I believe, however, that there are strong connections and it is these connections which give educators purpose and enable us to see ourselves as having prophetic responsibilities.

In order for educators to accept and meet their responsibilities as social critics and leaders, they obviously will need to have sufficient resources. One of the most telling indications of the weakness and timidity of our profession is its acceptance of the basic framework of the conditions under which teachers in elementary and secondary schools are expected to work. Even though there is a consensus that teachers are grossly overworked and underpaid, efforts directed at change are almost always ameliorative rather than transformative in character. In fact, it takes enormous efforts simply to maintain workload and pay standards at their currently absurd levels lest they become worse, as they have in many communities. As has been said, we see in this situation evidence of the dominant culture's fear of a strong educational program and its respect for the potential impact of schools populated by stimulating and imaginative teachers who have been given sufficient resources and a reasonable work load. We must also, however, closely examine the reality that the profession has not made a serious concerted effort to convince the American public that its allocations to the schools are not merely inadequate but shocking, insane, and destructive. There is, for example, the extraordinary variance in salaries and working conditions between those who teach in grades K-12 and those who teach at the university level, private and public. Salaries in universities are two or three times what they are in the lower grades, opportunities for advancement and development are infinitely greater, and the differences in teacher load are astounding (i.e., typically twelve hours vs. thirty hours). Moreover, the differences in autonomy, respect, and status are such that it is extremely difficult to consider teachers in both institutions as being in the same profession. The profession itself has contributed to the glib and irrational belief that these differences are "natural" and perhaps even desirable. Do we really want to take the position that teaching at the elementary or high school is less important or less taxing than university teaching? Are we prepared to defend a position that says that those who do not teach at the university do not need or want to do scholarly research? More to the point, why has the profession failed to address seriously not only this particular lunacy but broader question of what a proper, high-quality environment for serious teaching and learning would really entail?

One explanation is that, sadly enough, many members of the profession have come to accept the existing framework as reasonable, perhaps needing adjustment from time to time, and have failed to reflect seriously on its inadequacies. A related explanation speaks more clearly to the basic fear in our profession, a fear which produces our prodigious docility and passivity. What one hears regularly from many professionals in response to the pitiful working conditions for teachers is the belief that "we" should not seriously rock the boat lest "they" react in anger and retribution. This is the employer-employee, master-slave mentality in which we are reminded of our place and our powerlessness, urged to count our blessings, and warned about the consequences of protest. We are a profession which has, to a very large degree, internalized the oppressors' consciousness.

Let us contrast this posture of appeasement and passivity with that of the biblical prophets. Of course we cannot in any way return to those times, but we can hope that their example will help illuminate our present condition. First of all, there was, according to some scholars, a recognized role and function for prophets in ancient Israel. Prophecy as the process of reminding, criticizing, and warning was considered to be a necessary role in that society; and while prophets were not always given official status, they were accepted and valued as legitimate, if sometimes difficult or troublesome, members of the quasi-formal leadership. They were often consulted by the priests and kings and sometimes, nevertheless, imprisoned for their views and their agitations. However, there seems to be strong evidence that the *prophetic function* was considered necessary even though the acceptance of individual prophets varied enormously. Buber describes their functions not as magical but as functional:

> The Israelite prophet utters his words, directing them into an actual and definite situation. Hardly ever does he foretell a plainly certain future. YHVH does not deliver into his hand a completed book of fate with all future events written in it,

calling upon him to open it in the presence of his hearers. It was something of this kind the "false prophets" pretended, as when they stood up against Michaiah (v. 11ff) and prophesied to the king, "Go up and prosper!" Their main "falsity" lay not in the fact that they prophesy salvation, but that what they prophesy is not dependent on question and alternative. This attitude is closer to the divination of the heathen than to true Israelite prophecy. The true prophet does not announce an immutable decree. He speaks into the power of decision lying in the moment, and in such a way that his message of disaster just touches this power. (1960:103)

The power structure no doubt paid attention to the prophets for a variety of reasons. First, like anyone else, they were particularly interested in a prophet's capacity to foretell the future, even though prophets were definitely not in the same category as sorcerers and magicians. The prophetic capacity of predicting the future is more akin to the aspirations of contemporary social science or punditry—that is, it emerges from a keen understanding of how underlying forces are affecting events. Second, prophets probably both reflected and influenced community attitudes and, hence, their views had important political meaning. Third, and not necessarily least of all, prophets claimed to have privileged communication with God, or at the very least to have special sensitivity to know God's will. The power structure for whatever combination of reasons, would certainly want to connect their decisions and policies to what were accepted as sacred imperatives. The priests on the other hand were too closely identified with the power structure and were probably more interested in dealing with issues of ritual and observance than with political issues. The culture apparently felt it was well served by the existence of a group whose independence, special sensitivities, and intense concerns would serve the function of actually preserving the culture by pointing out the necessity of appropriate change. Prophets were neither wholly inside nor wholly outside the system but clearly committed to the system's long-range well-being, and, therefore, their criticisms and cries of outrage could not be dismissed (although they sometimes were) as work of cranks or subversives. This is certainly not to make a historical claim that prophecy was without its serious problems and resistances in ancient Israel, but only to point to a model of a culture's attempt to institutionalize a way of maintaining its commitments to its conceptions of the sacred through continuous criticism and affirmation.

Buber, in talking of the role of prophets in ancient Israel, speaks of the reluctance of that nation to have "kings" in the modern sense. Israel held onto the idea that the spirit of God should serve as sufficient governance, but eventually the Israelites came reluctantly to accept first "judges" and later "kings." Buber believes that the inevitable tensions created by monarchy contributed to the importance of prophecy.

The dynastic continuity implies a continuity of responsibility to fulfill the divine commission. . . . The fundamental and practical opposition of the kings to this constitutional obligation resulted in the mission of the prophets. . . . Against the tendency of the kings (frequently supported it seems by the priests with their sole concern for the autonomy of the social domain) to sublimate the commission into a divine right without any obligation, a divine right granting the kings to stand in accordance with ancient customs, as sons of the deity invested with full powers (cf. Ps. 2,7)—against this tendency the prophets set up the theopolitical realism which does not admit any "religious" subtlety. Over and against YHVH's vicegerent on the royal throne, acting unrighteously and therefore unlawful, but powerful, there stands the bearer of YHVH's word, without any power, but certain of his mission, reproving and claiming, reproving and claiming in vain. (1960:152–53)

Clearly our culture is inevitably very different from that tiny society that struggled and flourished four thousand years ago. However, as cultures surely differ, they also have a great number of challenges in common—particularly those involved with the struggles for survival and fulfillment. Our culture does not formally recognize the prophetic function, although many individuals and institutions seek to perform it, and we are certainly not suggesting any formal institutionalization of it by creating something like the Department of Prophecy. Ideally, all our institutions and every individual could incorporate those dimensions within their work, and indeed, the nourishment of those impulses should be considered as a prime goal of the educational process. In order to encourage "prophecy," educators themselves need to be "prophets" and speak in the prophetic voice that celebrates joy, love, justice, and abundance and cries out in anguish in the presence of oppression and misery. Educators share this prophetic responsibility with others in the culture, but they have special and critical roles in applying the prophetic perspective to professional issues, concerns, and standards. The educator as prophet needs to be particularly concerned about the degree to which the culture and the profession are keeping their sacred commitments. Prophetic educators must facilitate the dialogue on what these sacred commitments are, how they are to be interpreted in the light of particular situations, and what constitutes appropriate responses to them. In this way we can respond to this challenge from Walter Brueggemann: "The educational task of the community is to nurture some to prophetic speech. But for many others, it is to nurture an awareness that we must permit and welcome and evoke that prophetic tongue among us. Otherwise we will be diminished into the prose world of the king and, finally, without hope. Where there is no tongue for new truth, we are consigned to the coldness of the old truth" (1982:54).

Prophetic educators focus not only on the culture and the profession but on their more specialized practice. Educators have parallel responsibilities to be guided in their practice by their vision of the ultimate/sacred/holy and their responsibilities to be critical of shortcomings as well as to be responsive to them. Such educators must regard themselves and their students as holy and sacred, not as tools and mechanisms, hence as ends not means; they must be committed to the development of institutions of learning in which all those involved (teachers, administrators, staff, students) are full citizens, each of whom has the inherent right of personal and social fulfillment, each of whom has inherent and full dignity, and each of whom has the inherent right to grow, learn, and create as much as he/she possibly can. Thus, schools can be transformed from warehouses and training sites into centers of inquiry and growth where participants share their different abilities and talents in the pursuit of the common goal of creating a culture of deepest meaning. Such a conception of the profession will, I believe, serve the culture and educators well, for although it certainly puts the profession into a service role, it does not put it in the service of pursuing the profane, but rather the sacred. Paradoxically, such a role limits the profession, yet liberates it from servility and collaboration in unworthy tasks to a role of participating in the creation of freedom and justice.

Educators as prophets must therefore be mindful that their specialization plays a crucial moral and social role; they must be mindful of the professional and personal requirements necessary to meet these responsibilities. They must act simultaneously as citizens, professionals, technicians, and leaders. If educators are indeed to be prophets, it is obviously critical that they be aware of a vision that informs and guides their practice. It is to the delineation of this vision that we must now turn.

CREDO AND HISTORY: THE DIALECTIC OF EDUCATIONAL GROUND

We are at the point of articulating our basic orientation toward educational practice, one grounded in the dialectical relationship between a commitment to a broad vision of what is sacred and an understanding of the significance of this particular moment in history. As prophet educator in the tradition of Moses and Jesus, we must be in touch with our highest aspirations; as educator-prophets in the tradition of Socrates, Marx, and Freud, we must be aware of the problems involved in our understanding of this vision, and as educator-prophets in the tradition of Martin Luther King and Paulo Freire, we must be alert to its significance in the light of contemporary events. Education is a dynamic, ever-changing process that must be able to respond to the shifts and twists of this dialectic process, and hence I believe it both appropriate and imperative to attempt a basic statement on an educational framework that ought to guide our work for the next generation.

The historical grounds for this statement have already been discussed in prior sections of this book, but it is perhaps useful to summarize them in the form of several propositions:

1. We live in a moment of utmost precariousness, a time unlike other times, when particular cultures, nations, and groups are at risk, but when the entire civilization and planet confront the possibility of extinction.
2. We live in a time of massive injustice, ranging in severity from serious and devastating to unimaginably horrible. We confront staggering conditions of starvation, unemployment, poverty, misery, exploitation, and oppression.
3. We live in a time of estrangement and apartheid, ranging from moral and spiritual alienation, narcissism and personalism, to the legitimized structures of racial, economic, and social separation. Paul Tillich helps us to understand the relationship between this alienation and our concern for the sacred, an alienation he calls estrangement.

Estrangement as sin has a threefold character. It is the wilful turning away from the divine ground of our being (unbelief), combined with the elevation of our own selves to the center of all things, thus usurping the place of God (*hubris*). It expresses itself also in "concupiscence"—the lustful striving not only for sexual conquest, but for knowledge and power as well—in other words "the unlimited desire to draw the whole of reality into one's self." (Quoted in Porteous 1966: 113–14)

4. We live in a time of particularly dangerous self-deception and arrogance derived from our reluctance to accept the extent of our ignorance. Peter Berger has written on how organized religion (and by extension the schools) can contribute to moral numbness. In *The Precarious Vision* he has this to say:

To reject the comforts and security of religious submission is to have the courage to admit the precariousness of existence and to face the silence of the universe. This certainly does not mean that one must resign oneself to meaninglessness or that one must give up the quest for meaning. It does mean the surrender of illusionary meanings and false reassurances. This also involves a relentless intellectual honesty which abhors bad faith and seeks always to be conscious to the fullest possible clarity. Such intellectual honesty forces the admission that there are many questions, even vital questions, of which we are ignorant. (1961:151)

5. We live in a time of increasing despair, a time when more and more people perceive themselves as victims and as powerless even in the face of the realization that "powerlessness corrupts and absolute powerlessness corrupts absolutely." More and more we have edged into a paranoic state where the "system," however irrational and unwise, becomes ever stronger, more remote, and less responsive. José Miranda characterizes this view and its effect on, or commitment to, social justice and community:

The system forces the man to surrender himself, with all his existential weight, to assuming his economic future and to regarding the problems of others as completely foreign to himself. It forces him to surrender himself to the spirit of calculation, to the ideology which says that a man's value depends on his cleverness in situating himself within the system. And he must do this because of the system itself, independently of indoctrination by propaganda or education or ideology; he must do this necessarily, to be someone, to be able to survive, in order not to be crushed by the social machinery. (1974:8–9)

6. We also live in a time of hope that emerges from increased consciousness and sensitivity, as well as from the achievements and potentials of our creative, artistic, scientific, and intellectual genius. We are experiencing enormously exciting and profound changes in our knowledge, theories, and paradigms in our arts, sciences, crafts. and professions. We continue to demonstrate our creative capacities to recreate the world with the increasing demands for justice, joy, and meaning for all as we widen the realm of possibility.

Given these possibilities as educators and citizens we *must* regard this moment as a time of utmost crisis and, therefore, must respond to these priorities with all our energy and imagination. We cannot disregard the horrors of misery, starvation, poverty for millions of people, nor the possibility of nuclear destruction of billions of people. Not to act or not to respond fully are acts of enormous consequence. As educator-prophets we can be guided by Heschel's precept that "it is an act of evil to accept the state of evil as either inevitable or final. Others may be satisfied with improvement, the prophets insist upon redemption" (1962: 181). Nor can we disregard the immense human capacity and interest in continuing the struggle for a world of love and joy. We must confront our enormous capacities for both good *and* evil: what we have broken we surely can fix, what we have yet to create we can surely construct.

AN EDUCATIONAL CREDO: A STATEMENT OF GOALS

As educators we have the specific responsibility of forging a broad educational belief system ever mindful of the problems of any such effort as well as the problems involved in not making such an attempt. The following represent an effort, therefore, to sketch out broad educational goals which reflect our cultural mythos and which, together with the just completed historical perspective, can help generate the somewhat more specific educational objectives described in the next chapter. The credo represents very basic values and assumptions that are in a sense "non-negotiable," even though we are simultaneously convinced of their "truth" and nervous about their problems. In recognition of the twin dangers of being either dogmatic or uncommitted, we affirm that the goals of current educational practices ought to include:

1. *The examination and contemplation of the awe, wonder, and mystery of the universe.* As educators we have the responsibility to examine the world and universe we live in and to share our reactions authentically and rationally and have a concomitant responsibility to be aware of and share with our students the process of observation and examination used by different scholars and observers. When we do so, we *always* find at least one common result—namely, enormously different observations, reactions, and explanations across and within time and place. Not only is there an immensely different assortment of cosmic explanations, but there is diversity even within very narrow fields of explanation. We find not only differences of opinion but also agreement that every field is extraordinarily complicated.

We can and should confront this reality as a reflection of our comparative youth as a species in a universe which numbers its birthdays in the billions of years. Thus, we are appropriately humble as any novice would be, maintaining however the confidence that over time we have come to know more and more, and perhaps at an accelerating rate. However paradoxically, our knowledge explosion has also led to a deeper sense of the mystery of the most fundamental process of origin and destiny. The areas of the unknown may have been narrowed, but their mystery has been heightened. When we look at the incredible biological process within the human body, or the physical process that forms mountains and continents, or when we contemplate the immensity of space, we are struck with the sheer wonder of it all—we are left (almost) speechless, in awe. Whatever cosmic explanations we use, it is inevitably and inherently breathtaking and incredible in scope. It is just as mind-blowing to posit a God who created the universe as it is to posit a universe created without a God. This awe and wonder need not and should not be sentimentalized, nor should it be a matter of indifference. It is intellectually honest to recognize the mystery and to examine ways in which to reduce the needlessly mysterious—that is, to do the research and the teaching designed to reduce ignorance. It is intellectually necessary to be honest not only about what we do know but about what we do not know. This is not humility for the sake of religious ritual, but necessary for the pursuit of truth, knowledge, and meaning.

Educators perforce provide a basic context for their program of studies, and as part of this context we need to establish the reality of the immense mystery that is the surround of our existence of awesome complexity. This context is critical in that it locates us not only as an interested observer of the mystery but as an aspect of the mystery as well. Thus, we have to establish from the beginning our ontological dimension (i.e., that we are a people engaged in a process of defining our being). Moreover, this context helps to establish that such a process is an ongoing one, fraught with uncertainty and, hence, one that requires serious knowledge, reflection, and research. Furthermore, it is a context that posits that such a process will require that we be ever mindful of the profundity of the task and the modest nature of our progress. In this way we also catch a glimmer of our responsibilities—we are required to respond to our condition, for if humans are to survive they must respond.

2. *The cultivation and nourishment of the processes of meaning making.* With the experience of awe and mystery comes the recognition that though we as a species are required to take initiative for survival purposes (e.g., we have to build shelter and search for food), we are also a people intent on creating systems of thought that explain our past and guide our present and future. When educators examine these various thought systems, they confront the same kind of diversity and complexity of cosmic explanations. In a parallel way, educators must also deal with the context of meaning within which educational activities are to be presented. The educational goal is not so much to teach a particular meaning system but rather to teach for the process of responding to that challenge. Educators must remind themselves and their students that any civilization or any culture is a human construction, and it is a human responsibility to create and re-create culture; thus, it is intellectually unsound to encourage the notion that cultural institutions, values, and beliefs are given. We are to a very significant degree, though certainly not entirely responsible for the creation of our lives—we create our culture and our culture creates us. We live in dialectical relationship with the mystery, with nature, and with the culture. Therefore, in recognition of our important though limited role in the vast drama of existence, it is incumbent that we respond to our creative responsibilities.

Educators must help us all to see the nature of this creative process by sharpening our creative capacities and by exposing us to a variety of cultural creations. We need to create not only a culture that enables us to live but one that needs to know that such a possibility exists and that there are others who have responded to that opportunity. The educational process is based on a very basic notion that the world makes sense and that we are involved in both determining and creating that sense. From almost the very beginning of their lives, people try to understand and control their world, and educational institutions must elaborate and nourish these impulses. This is not say that educators should in any way encourage solipsism and self-indulgence. Rather they should stress the collectively human basis of our culture, regarding subjectivity and imagination not so much as channeled into self-expression but as necessary to the impulse to create a life of moral significance.

3. *The cultivation and nourishment of the concept of the oneness of nature and humanity, with the concurrent responsibility to strive for harmony, peace, and justice.*

Here we very definitely enter a realm of affirmation—that is, the acceptance of basic cosmological and moral principles. In this statement we accept as an assumptive belief that there is an ultimate sense in which we are essentially connected with each other, with nature, and with the universe. We posit, therefore, that our goals should include the development of a consciousness in which peace, harmony, and justice are integral. We assume that in a universe of harmony and meaning each individual human is inherently of worth and that the dignity of all elements of the universe is significantly interrelated. Harmony, therefore, by definition demands justice and peace—dignity is indivisible. As public educators we have special responsibilities to remind ourselves of this truth and to find ways in which to make this truth real. Since we have already assumed that we have a responsibility to help create a world of meaning, we can set in motion this process by affirming these very basic metaphysical assumptions—namely, that we add to our educational context the notion that we are directed toward the struggle for harmony among the cosmic elements. We are happy to reaffirm and, as educators, to act upon these universal truths—that *all* people are created with equal worth and dignity and that it is our responsibility to sustain and nourish that initial position through our lifetimes. We would urge educators to provide the intellectual and emotional resources needed to take on the struggle that is involved in maintaining this commitment.

We must also be mindful of our place in the universe and our relationship to nature, particularly in our responsibilities to preserve and enrich our environment. We must confront without hyperbole how we as species have threatened not only certain social institutions but the very existence of the planet as a living organism. Our struggle is to participate in the cosmic impulse for an ecology of natural, human, and universal joy, love and justice, or, as we sometimes call it, harmony. Indeed, we see major and exciting possibilities emerging in this area in the emergence of the extraordinary consciousness-raising efforts represented in both the women's and ecological movements. Both of these broad movements have at their center a fundamental concern for intimacy and harmony, based on the recognition of our interdependence and our vision of wholeness.

By accepting these principles, we as educators need to model and instruct in ways so that we can actually participate in this struggle. We need not only to be encouraged and supported in our impulse to love, to do justice, and to be one with our humanity and nature, but we also need to learn that we must work continuously, creatively, and intensely to act on these impulses. Educators must become aware of and share the techniques of the theory *and* practice of meaning making, and the making of a world. Educators must, however, also be candid about the complexities, paradoxes, and contradictions of human existence. We can celebrate harmony as a goal, but we must also recognize the enormous difficulties and serious resistance to the struggle for universal justice and peace.

As educators we must honestly and candidly share our knowledge of the plurality of modes of consciousness and of cultural variation. We must also note that our traditions, including educational ones, put stress on sharp divisions, as seen in the dualisms of mind and body, the individual and the group, and in the nurture vs. nature controversy. Given the mystery we have discussed, and by the same token given our assumption about the ultimate universal harmony, we can sustain our faith in the face of these dualisms by affirming the concept of the dialectic. We cannot avoid the danger of dualistic thinking by denying the power of one of the dyads (e.g., by denying that our lives have a significant degree of determinism to them, or that the body has a reality of its own).

4. *The cultivation, nourishment, and development of a cultural mythos that builds on a faith in the human capacity to participate in the creation of a world of justice, compassion, caring, love, and joy.* Educators here again are in a posture of affirmation, not only of these moral principles but of their "sacred" quality. As public educators in an American context, we cannot and should not paint ourselves into an ideological corner by identifying ourselves totally with one of a number of sects, denominations, or movements with a religious or quasi-religious orientation. As educators we can and should confront ourselves and our students with the serious and important questions and issues that are inherent in these matters and offer us insight and tools of analysis to increase our understanding. However, as I have tried to demonstrate, teaching for understanding is not enough, for we must also teach for meaning.

Educators can and should include in their broad context of practice the broad areas of moral consensus that we have discussed in the previous chapter. Educators can and should also offer to their students the opportunity and responsibility to wrestle with the moral and religious dilemmas and paradoxes that permeate our culture. We can as educators offer and act on our wisdom that we are well advised to accept a sacred/profane distinction of some kind, leaving open of course the question of whether such a conception represents revelation or sociology. We can as educators and humans also in very good faith insist that we accept and act on the moral principles of love, justice, compassion, and joy for all. As educators we must also stress the enormous difficulties inherent in the ways in which these terms are defined, experienced, and implemented.

5. *The cultivation, nourishment, and development of the ideals of community, compassion, and interdependence within the traditions of democratic principles.* As educators we should not in the least be embarrassed by embracing and nourishing our democratic heritage, which is a political response to the moral requirements of equality and individual dignity as well as the social realties of interdependence. Democratic theory is a pragmatic response to a culture's desire to deal with the everyday requirements of living within the moral contexts of two profound but potentially contradictory values: equality and freedom. Democracy both affirms a moral position and offers concrete procedures and principles to allow us to work on the challenges of this contradiction. We as a people have faith that we can at least approach a society where every person can do as they like provided that it does not, paradoxically, interfere with what others may want to do. Our heritage calls for individual autonomy *and* concern for others; it speaks to individual freedom *and* social justice, to independence *and* compassion.

As educators and humans we should celebrate this tradition, and as educators we should be mindful of the problems, difficulties, and complexities that arise and will continue as a consequence of this moral orientation. There is surely no contradiction in affirming the broad principles and intentions of democracy and in being mindful of their problems. It is in fact the very spirit of democracy that allows, indeed encourages, continuous critical reflection and free inquiry by free people. Let us, however, not interpret this to mean a community without boundaries; flexible and supportive as we may be, the cultural/sacred mythos we have been sketching does not allow for oppression, injustice, and inequality. We must also be ever mindful of considering the meaning of democratic institution in the particular context of the social and political realities of specific historical moments. Indeed, democratic procedures must be examined in the light of their impact on moral and spiritual aspirations, even in the faith that they are of one piece.

6. *The cultivation, nourishment, and development of attitudes of outrage and responsibility in the face of injustice and oppression.* As educators we must in our celebration of democracy also be mindful of the extraordinary importance of individual participation in the life of the community. Democracy demands a great deal from each person and rests on the faith that an informed public will be alert to its failures and responsive to the need to overcome those failures. If we are to take the major and broad elements of our mythos seriously, then we will see that oppression, injustice, and indignity are collective concerns, even though they may be focused on individuals or groups. Educators must also recognize that passion is an inevitable part of human experience and that it needs to be seen in its constructive as well as its destructive sense. We will not do our cause of justice and love any service by being merely civil in the face of oppression (i.e., being polite and decorous are totally inappropriate in the context of misery). At the same time, we must recognize that passion by itself is no guarantee of the presence of deep moral principles.

Outrage at oppression is, however, an intelligent and rational response to a situation where our highest values are being violated. We must be wary when we pass off certain violations as minor or modest—as in an acceptable level of unemployment or casualties. Oppression and misery are horrid and unacceptable for one person, and when that horror extends to large numbers of people, the horror becomes more horrible. However, we cannot use the logic of reversing this process in such a way that horror for a few became less horrible than horror for many for otherwise we will become tolerant of some horror. As Heschel says,

> Modern thought tends to extenuate personal responsibility. Understanding the complexity of human nature, the interrelationship of individual and society, of consciousness and subconsciousness, we find it difficult to isolate the deed from those circumstances in which it was done. But new insights may obscure essential vision, and man's conscience grow scales: excuses, pretense, self-pity. Guilt may disappear: no crime is absolute, no sin devoid of apology. Within the limits of the human mind, relativity is true and merciful. Yet the mind's scope embraces but a fragment of society, a few instants of history; it thinks of what has happened, it is unable to imagine what might have happened. . . . Above all, the prophets remind us of the moral state of a people: Few are guilty, but all are responsible. If we admit that the individual is in some measure conditioned or affected by the spirit of society, an individual's crime discloses society's corruption. In a community not indifferent to suffering, uncompromisingly impatient with cruelty and falsehood, continually concerned for God and every man, crime would be infrequent rather than common. (1962:14, 16)

THE ISSUE OF INDOCTRINATION

We have to this point been discussing educational goals that are mostly those involving assumptions, beliefs, and values. The values and attitudes represented in these goals are derived from the dimensions of broad cultural consensus that might serve as a statement of our sense of the sacred, of our mythos, and of our platform of beliefs. We offer no apologies for being explicit about the place of values and beliefs in education, since we operate under the assumption that education cannot and should not be "value-free." Indeed, concern for fairness and openness represents values, and educators need to affirm them. Another way of expressing these values is to raise a concern about indoctrination, manipulation, and the imposition of teacher values upon students.

As educators we must recognize and confront this dilemma and be mindful of the difficulties and risks involved in teaching. There is no way of avoiding this risk, but attempts to avoid it are bound to distract and deceive us and, hence, will likely exacerbate the problem. Educators can be more authentic by sharing the problem with each other, the public, and their students. We also should be mindful that there are both gray areas and black-and-white ones in this realm. We can easily point to conditions which we can call manipulative and oppressive—situations in which coercion is used as a teaching technique (either crudely, as in punishment and grading, or more subtly, as in the denial of affection), or situations in which undue pressures are used (such as ridicule and ostracism).

The single most effective way to reduce the inherent political advantage of teachers is to reduce as much as possible, and as soon as possible, crucial politically significant gaps between teacher and student. These gaps include differences in the amount and nature of knowledge; modes of analysis; critical and creative capacities; poise, confidence, personal strength, and stability. Educators must maintain their legitimate authority but give away all their coercive power as soon as possible, and in this way they, as well as students, can be free to *study* the problems rather than to use them as part of a struggle for power and domination. Ironically enough, teachers are also oppressed by the presence of the fear of indoctrination and manipulation, since many sensitive and caring teachers bend over backwards to avoid even the appearance of taking advantage of their political position. A casualty of this process can be students losing out on the fully passionate consciousness of a teacher's commitments. Teachers and students need to be free of the fears of dominating and of being dominated in order to facilitate free common inquiry. For this reason alone, the primitive practice of "grading" students should be abolished. Grading degrades and dehumanizes in its inherent process of creating hierarchies. It is also anti-intellectual in its irrational and arbitrary character, and it is a serious barrier to the true educational process of inquiry, sharing, and dialogue.

The more specific educational goals to be discussed in the next chapter can be seen as not only vital to the overall purpose of education, as indicated, but also as part of the way we can help students and teachers avoid the possibilities of indoctrination and manipulation. They can be seen as intellectual equalizers, capacities that are enabling and empowering and that help us to be liberated from the oppressions of ignorance, incompetence, and powerlessness, and at the same time free us to make our moral commitments a reality.

REFERENCES

Aronowitz, Stanley, and Henry A. Giroux. 1985. *Education Under Siege: The Conservative, Liberal, and Radical Debate Over Schooling*. South Hadley, MA: Bergin and Garvey.

Berger, Peter L. 1961. *The Precarious Vision: A Sociologist Looks at Social Fictions and Christian Faith*. Garden City, NY: Doubleday.

Brueggemann, Walter. 1982. *The Creative Word: Canon as a Model for Bibical Education*. Philadelphia: Fortress Press.

Buber, Martin. 1960. *The Prophetic Faith*. New York: Harper & Row.

Heschel, Abraham Joshua. 1962. *The Prophets*, 2 Vols. New York: Harper & Row.

Miranda, José P. 1974. *Marx and the Bible: A Critique of the Philosophy of Oppression*. Trans. John Eagleson. Maryknoll, NY: Orbis Books.

Porteous, Alvin G. 1966. *Prophetic Voices in Contemporary Theology: The Theological Renaissance and the Renewal of the Church*. Nashville: Abingdon Press.

Toward the Twenty-first Century: Global Catastrophe or Social Transformation?

This anthology contains the work of a great many highly diverse authors writing from a plurality of perspectives. The book as a whole, however, has a smaller number of significant themes.

1. The interpenetration of clusters of social, cultural, economic, and political forces and clusters of educational issues; the importance of confronting the seriousness of the problems; and the importance both to understanding their origin and to overcoming them.
2. The crucial importance of developing fresh, imaginative, and daring ideas—formulations and concepts that can provide intellectual and moral exits from our current stagnation.
3. The importance of forging a cultural vision energized by deep moral commitment that can drive the engine of cultural and educational transformation.

In this last section, these three themes coalesce in articles that reflect both criticism and hope, despair and possibility. Although it is our strong belief that we live in a time of extraordinary peril and crisis, we reaffirm our faith in the importance and power of education to help us avert and transcend these dangers. Our basic criticism of our profession is that educators have either failed to recognize the seriousness of our difficulties or decided that education cannot possibly overcome them. Perhaps they lack faith in human potential for the extraordinary creativity and imagination required. For as the authors in this section demonstrate, this is *not* the time for conventional thinking or common sense but for break-throughs, "breakouts," and creativity. We have come to learn in the very hardest way possible, however, that rational thinking alone cannot lead us to a more loving and caring world, for we have seen the fruits of human intellectual genius used for destructive and evil purposes. What our culture yearns for is a moral vision, a set of deeply felt commitments, and a communal sense of profound purpose that can give meaning to our work as well as to the work of those who precede and follow us. The dangerous myth of objective and neutral education is dead, if not buried, and we must replace it with a renewed commitment to the struggle for a more just and loving community, which perforce requires perplexing moral choices. This is a task for all institutions, not just schools; for all people, not just educators. How-ever, we as educators have special duties in addressing the responsibilities, oppor-tunities, and possibilities that face us in our work, duties that include but do not end at honest and penetrating criticism.

These are times, then, not only of enormous crises but also of great possibili-ties. Although much of the highly creative reconceptualizing of our cultural, so-cial, and educational process is not available to the larger public, there is an abundance of such work and every indication that there will be even more. This section contains a very small sample of these works in the belief that they offer more hope and possibility *because* they do not blink at the seriousness of the problems nor at the possibility of resolution. In different ways the writings point to or embrace aspects of what has been called a "postmodern" worldview. Although defining in precise terms what it means to talk of the postmodern is not easy, we can suggest some of its dimensions. They involve a rejection of the pretensions of scientific or rationalistic methods of "truth gathering" and an assertion of the way in which all knowledge is inevitably historically situated and discursively con-structed. Postmodernism also refuses to imagine human liberation in terms that tie it to ever more powerful modes of dominating nature as well as hierarchical and instrumental relations among people. And it conceives of freedom in ways that value and validate the profusion of differences—cultural, sexual, and racial—that constitute human identity. Such freedom recognizes the sensual and creative char-acter of full human existence.

It is not unusual for educational theorists to grapple with the future and to suggest the necessity to adapt to a radically new world. Typically, these analysts deal with major technological and scientific changes—computers, artificial intelli-gence, cloning, medical breakthroughs, and so on. However, these selections put far more emphasis on the importance of human consciousness. Furthermore, what stamps these selections as unique is that they urge us to reformulate our ways of being in the world through serious reflection on moral and spiritual considerations. In this way, we avoid the dangers of extreme relativism inherent in postmodern thinking.

All of the selections affirm the necessity and possibility of fundamental structural change in the culture and in our consciousness. Central to these analyses is the significance of creativity and subjectivity, which has emerged from a profound critique of positivism and science. Although a view of reality as socially constructed clearly undermines a sense of certainty, it need not, as the writers here demonstrate, paralyze us. These authors provide powerful illustrations of the human capacity to reconnect and recreate our images of ourselves and our possibilities. We need not accept a world in which poverty and competition are inevitable nor define ourselves as "naturally" greedy and aggressive. We have the creative capacity to reframe who we are and where we can go. Our lives reflect our humanly constructed narratives of who God is, what it means to be human, and what constitutes knowledge. This view of truth and knowledge has immense educational significance since it speaks to a curriculum that focuses on the reality of uncertainty and celebrates the imaginative possibilities. This is a far cry from our present curricular emphasis on mastery, certainty, and knowledge transmission. A culture of reliance on metaphors, images, subjectivity, and imagination is a culture that will require and produce very different forms of education.

These selections also emphasize the importance of spiritual language. We have come to see the aridity and dangers of a life limited to personal success and self-indulgence. The yearning for renewed and reenergized images that unite us yield exciting responses, particularly from feminist theologians. These theologians have shown how traditional religious images have fostered domination and hierarchy, and they are developing religious languages that evoke our impulse for deeper community and a greater sense of inclusiveness and interdependence. The images of such interdependence extend beyond the psychological and social spheres to the cosmic, involving our connection to the planet and the universe. A greater sense of wholeness and interconnectness replaces conventional images of dualism and autonomy. These new images both illuminate our present darkness and provide us with hope. These articles point to an education that aims to change our consciousness from rigidity to creativity and from gloomy paralysis to joyous energy, an education aimed not at division and hierarchy but at wholeness and justice.

Fritjof Capra's article is taken from his book *The Turning Point*. Capra, a physicist, describes a new paradigm of truth emerging from Eastern philosophy and the new physics. He sees us in a difficult period of transition involving fundamental changes in our attitudes toward patriarchy, fossil fuels, and scientific thinking. He suggests that a fundamental restructuring of our thinking—for example, moving away from dualistic thinking and including intuitive and creative thinking in our education—can lead us to a more balanced life.

Herbert Marcuse, a very influential figure of the 1960s, writes from a neo-Marxist perspective and as a social theorist. In this selection he speaks to the possibility of creating a new consciousness, one that rejects aggression, competition, and performance and instead celebrates joy, play, and community. He urges an education that "involves the mind *and* the body, reason *and* imagination, the intellectual *and* the instinctual needs. . . ."

C. A. Bowers, a curriculum theorist, writes movingly about an educator's response to the real possibilities of ecological catastrophe. In a unique blending of educational theory, ecological perspective, and Native American consciousness, Bowers offers a sober and powerful analysis of both peril and possibility.

In the final selection, Sallie McFague writes from the perspective of feminist Christian theology. She also sees us on the verge of a new era, poised on the brink of troubling and exciting possibilities precipitated by major changes of perspective—"a holistic vision of reality" (similar to that described by Capra), "the nuclear nightmare," and "the consciousness of the constructive character of all activities." It is this last perspective that leads her to describe the human origins of conceptions of God and to offer a new set of theological metaphors arising out of a feminist critique of traditional Christianity. McFague talks of the centrality and dangers of the language of patriarchy and suggests that feminine metaphors of caring and nurturance should inform the theology and worldview that our times require.

The task reflected in these selections is the transformation of our society and culture—surely an ambitious, if not pretentious, undertaking. However, if our world is to survive, transformation is required. As educators we are well placed to participate in this sacred endeavor. We have the opportunity to increase awareness and participate in the development of new educational discourses. We are also in a position to ward off the paralyzing effects of despair and helplessness with the hope and energy in the very soul of education. This last section of the book, therefore, provides vivid examples of the enormous and seemingly infinite potential for human genius. We hope and pray that there will be further bursts of positive energy and that they come before it is too late.

The Turning of the Tide

Fritjof Capra

. . . To understand our multifaceted cultural crisis we need to adopt an extremely broad view and see our situation in the context of human cultural evolution. We have to shift our perspective from the end of the twentieth century to a time span encompassing thousands of years; from the notion of static social structures to the perception of dynamic patterns of change. Seen from this perspective, crisis appears as an aspect of transformation. The Chinese, who have always had a thoroughly dynamic world view and a keen sense of history, seem to have been well aware of this profound connection between crisis and change. The term they use for "crisis"—*wei-ji*—is composed of the characters for "danger" and "opportunity."

Western sociologists have confirmed this ancient intuition. Studies of periods of cultural transformation in various societies have shown that these transformations are typically preceded by a variety of social indicators, many of them identical to the symptoms of our current crisis. They include a sense of alienation and an increase in mental illness, violent crime, and social disruption, as well as an increased interest in religious cultism—all of which have been observed in our society during the past decade. In times of historic cultural change these indicators have tended to appear one to three decades before the central transformation, rising in frequency and intensity as the transformation is approaching, and falling again after it has occurred.[10]

Cultural transformations of this kind are essential steps in the development of civilizations. The forces underlying this development are complex, and historians are far from having a comprehensive theory of cultural dynamics, but it seems that all civilizations go through similar cyclical processes of genesis, growth, breakdown, and disintegration. The following graph shows this striking pattern for the major civilizations around the Mediterranean.[11]

Among the foremost if more conjectural studies of these patterns in the rise and fall of civilizations is Arnold Toynbee's *A Study of History*.[12] According to Toynbee, the genesis of a civilization consists of a transition from a static condition to dynamic activity. This transition may occur spontaneously, through the influence of some civilization that is already in existence or through the disintegration of one or more civilizations of an older generation. Toynbee sees the basic pattern in the genesis of civilizations as a pattern of interaction which he calls "challenge-and-response." A challenge from the natural or social environment provokes a creative response in a society, or a social group, which induces that society to enter the process of civilization.

The civilization continues to grow when its successful response to the initial challenge generates cultural momentum that carries the society beyond a state of equilibrium into an overbalance that presents itself as a fresh challenge. In this way the initial pattern of challenge-and-response is repeated in successive phases of growth, each successful response producing a disequilibrium that requires new creative adjustments.

The recurrent rhythm in cultural growth seems to be related to processes of fluctuation that have been observed throughout the ages and were always regarded as part of the fundamental dynamics of the universe. Ancient Chinese philosophers believed that all manifestations of reality are generated by the dynamic interplay between two polar forces which they called the yin and the yang. Heraclitus, in ancient Greece, compared the world order to an ever living fire, "kindling in measures and going out in measures." Empedocles attributed the changes in the universe

Rise-and-fall patterns of the major civilizations around the Mediterranean.

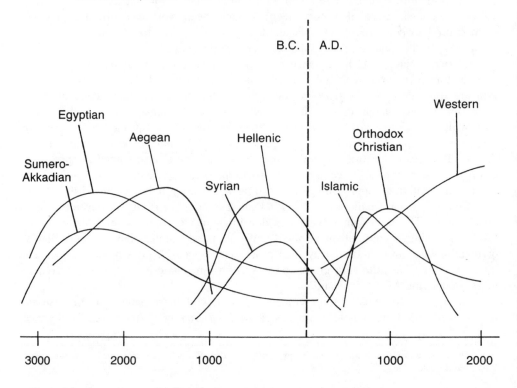

to the ebb and flow of two complementary forces, which he called "love" and "hate."

The idea of a fundamental universal rhythm has also been expressed by numerous philosophers of modern times.[13] Saint-Simon saw the histories of civilizations as a series of alternating "organic" and "critical" periods; Herbert Spencer viewed the universe as moving through a series of "integrations" and "differentiations"; and Hegel saw human history as a spiral development from one form of unity through a phase of disunity, and on to reintegration on a higher plane. Indeed, the notion of fluctuating patterns seems always to be extremely useful for the study of cultural evolution.

After civilizations have reached a peak of vitality, they tend to lose their cultural steam and decline. An essential element in this cultural breakdown, according to Toynbee, is a loss of flexibility. When social structures and behavior patterns have become so rigid that the society can no longer adapt to changing situations, it will be unable to carry on the creative process of cultural evolution. It will break down and, eventually, disintegrate. Whereas growing civilizations display endless variety and versatility, those in the process of disintegration show uniformity and lack of inventiveness. The loss of flexibility in a disintegrating society is accompanied by a general loss of harmony among its elements, which inevitably leads to the outbreak of social discord and disruption.

However, during the painful process of disintegration the society's creativity—its ability to respond to challenges—is not completely lost. Although the cultural mainstream has become petrified by clinging to fixed ideas and rigid patterns of behavior, creative minorities will appear on the scene and carry on the process of challenge-and-response. The dominant social institutions will refuse to hand over their leading roles to these new cultural forces, but they will inevitably go on to decline and disintegrate, and the creative minorities may be able to transform some of the old elements into a new configuration. The process of cultural evolution will then continue, but in new circumstances and with new protagonists.

The cultural patterns Toynbee described seem to fit our current situation very well. Looking at the nature of our challenges—not at the various symptoms of crisis but at the underlying changes in our natural and social environments—we can recognize the confluence of several transitions.[14] Some of them are connected with natural resources, others with cultural values and ideas; some are parts of periodic fluctuations, others occur within patterns of rise-and-fall. Each of these processes has a distinct time span, or periodicity, but all of them involve periods of transitions that happen to coincide at the present moment. Among these transitions are three that will shake the very foundations of our lives and will deeply affect our social, economic, and political system.

The first and perhaps most profound transition is due to the slow and reluctant but inevitable decline of patriarchy.[15] The time span associated with patriarchy is at least three thousand years, a period so long that we cannot say whether we are dealing with a cyclical process because the information we have about prepatriarchal eras is far too tenuous. What we do know is that for the past three thousand years Western civilization and its precursors, as well as most other cultures, have been based on philosophical, social, and political systems "in which men—by force, direct pressure, or through ritual, tradition, law and language, customs, etiquette, education, and the division of labor—determine what part women shall or shall not play, and in which the female is everywhere subsumed under the male."[16]

The power of patriarchy has been extremely difficult to understand because it is all-pervasive. It has influenced our most basic ideas about human nature and about our relation to the universe—"man's" nature and "his" relation to the universe, in patriarchal language. It is the one system which, until recently, had never in recorded history been openly challenged, and whose doctrines were so universally accepted that they seemed to be laws of nature; indeed, they were usually presented as such. Today, however, the disintegration of patriarchy is in sight. The feminist movement is one of the strongest cultural currents of our time and will have a profound effect on our further evolution.

The second transition that will have a profound impact on our lives is forced upon us by the decline of the fossil-fuel age. Fossil fuels[17]—coal, oil, and natural gas—have been the principal sources of energy for the modern industrial era, and as we run out of them this era will come to an end. From the broad historical perspective of cultural evolution, the fossil-fuel age and the industrial era are but a brief episode, a thin peak around the year 2000 on our graph. Fossil fuels will be exhausted by the year 2300, but the economic and political effects of this decline are already being felt. This decade will be marked by the transition from the fossil-fuel age to a solar age, powered by renewable energy from the sun; a shift that will involve radical changes in our economic and political systems.

The third transition is again connected with cultural values. It involves what is now often called a "paradigm[18] shift"—a profound change in the thoughts, perceptions, and values that form a particular vision of reality.[19] The paradigm that is now shifting has dominated our culture for several hundred years, during which it has shaped our modern Western society and has significantly influenced the rest of the world. This paradigm comprises a number of ideas and values that differ sharply from those of the Middle Ages; values that have been associated with various streams of Western culture, among them the Scientific Revolution, the Enlightenment, and the Industrial Revolution. They include the belief in the scientific method as the only valid approach to knowledge; the view of the universe as a mechanical system composed of elementary material building blocks; the view of life in society as a competitive struggle for existence; and the belief in unlimited material progress to be achieved through economic and technological growth. During the past decades all these ideas and values have been found severely limited and in need of radical revision.

From our broad perspective of cultural evolution, the current paradigm shift is part of a larger process, a strikingly regular fluctuation of value systems that can be traced throughout Western civilization and most other cultures. These fluctuating changes of values and their effects on all aspects of society, at least in the West, have been mapped out by the sociologist Pitirim Sorokin in a monumental four-volume work written between 1937 and 1941.[20] Sorokin's grand scheme for the synthesis of Western history is based on the cyclical waxing and waning of three basic value systems that underlie all manifestations of a culture.

Sorokin calls these three value systems the sensate, the ideational, and the

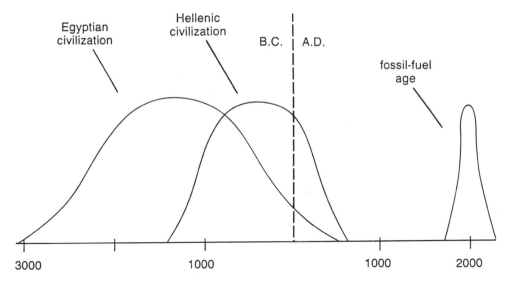

Fossil-fuel age in the context of cultural evolution.

idealistic. The sensate value system holds that matter alone is the ultimate reality, and that spiritual phenomena are but a manifestation of matter. It professes that all ethical values are relative and that sensory perception is the only source of knowledge and truth. The ideational value system is profoundly different. It holds that true reality lies beyond the material world, in the spiritual realm, and that knowledge can be obtained through inner experience. It subscribes to absolute ethical values and super-human standards of justice, truth, and beauty. Western representations of the ideational concept of spiritual reality include Platonic ideas, the soul, and Judeo-Christian im-ages of God, but Sorokin points out that similar ideas are expressed in the East, in different form, in Hindu, Buddhist, and Taoist cultures.

Sorokin contends that the cyclical rhythms of interplay between sensate and ideational expressions of human culture also produce an intermediate, synthesizing stage—the idealistic—which represents their harmonious blending. According to ide-alistic beliefs, true reality has both sensory and supersensory aspects which coexist within an all-embracing unity. Idealistic cultural periods thus tend to attain the highest and noblest expressions of both ideational and sensate styles, producing balance, integration, and esthetic fulfillment in art, philosophy, science, and technology. Exam-ples of such idealistic periods are the Greek flowering of the fifth and fourth centu-ries, B.C., and the European Renaissance.

These three basic patterns of human cultural expression have, according to Soro-kin, produced identifiable cycles in Western civilization, which he has plotted on dozens of charts for belief systems, wars and internal conflicts, scientific and techno-logical development, and law and various other social institutions. He has also charted fluctuations of styles in architecture, painting, sculpture, and literature. In Sorokin's model the current paradigm shift and the decline of the Industrial Age are another period of maturation and decline of sensate culture. The rise of our current sensate era was preceded by the ascendancy of ideational culture during the rise of Christianity and the Middle Ages, and by the subsequent flowering of an idealistic stage during the European Renaissance. It was the slow decline of these ideational and idealistic epochs in the fifteenth and sixteenth centuries that gave way to the rise of a new sensate period in the seventeenth, eighteenth, and nineteenth centuries, an era marked by the value system of the Enlightenment, the scientific views of Descartes and Newton, and the technology of the Industrial Revolution. In the twentieth century these sensate values and ideas are on the decline again, and thus in 1937, with great foresight, Sorokin predicted as the twilight of sensate culture the paradigm shift and social upheavals we are witnessing today.[21]

Sorokin's analysis suggests very forcefully that the crisis we are facing today is no ordinary crisis but one of the great transition phases that have occurred in previous cycles of human history. These profound cultural transformations do not take place very often. According to Lewis Mumford, there may have been fewer than half a dozen in the entire history of Western civilization, among them the rise of civilization with the invention of agriculture at the beginning of the neolithic period, the rise of Christianity at the fall of the Roman Empire, and the transition from the Middle Ages to the Scientific Age.[22]

The transformation we are experiencing now may well be more dramatic than any of the preceding ones, because the rate of change in our age is faster than ever before, because the changes are more extensive, involving the entire globe, and because several major transitions are coinciding. The rhythmic recurrences and patterns of rise and decline that seem to dominate human cultural evolution have somehow conspired to reach their points of reversal at the same time. The decline of patriarchy, the end of the fossil-fuel age, and the paradigm shift occurring in the twilight of the sensate culture are all contributing to the same global process. The current crisis, therefore, is not just a crisis of individuals, governments, or social institutions; it is a transition of planetary dimensions. As individuals, as a society, as a civilization, and as a planetary ecosystem, we are reaching the turning point.

Cultural transformations of this magnitude and depth cannot be prevented. They should not be opposed but, on the contrary, should be welcomed as the only escape from agony, collapse, or mummification. What we need, to prepare ourselves for the great transition we are about to enter, is a deep reexamination of the main premises and values of our culture, a rejection of those conceptual models that have outlived their usefulness, and a new recognition of some of the values discarded in previous periods of our cultural history. Such a thorough change in the mentality of Western culture must naturally be accompanied by a profound modification of most social relationships and forms of social organization—by changes that will go far beyond the superficial measures of economic and political readjustment being considered by today's political leaders.

During this phase of revaluation and cultural rebirth it will be important to minimize the hardship, discord, and disruption that are inevitably involved in periods of great social change, and to make the transition as painless as possible. It will therefore be crucial to go beyond attacking particular social groups or institutions, and to show how their attitudes and behavior reflect a value system that underlies our whole culture and that has now become outdated. It will be necessary to recognize and widely communicate the fact that our current social changes are manifestations of a much broader, and inevitable, cultural transformation. Only then will we be able to approach the kind of harmonious, peaceful cultural transition described in one of humanity's oldest books of wisdom, the Chinese *I Ching*, or Book of Changes: "The movement is natural, arising spontaneously. For this reason the transformation of the old becomes easy. The old is discarded and the new is introduced. Both measures accord with the time; therefore no harm results."[23]

The model of cultural dynamics that will be used in our discussion of the current social transformation is based in part on Toynbee's ideas about the rise and fall of civilizations; on the age-old notion of a fundamental universal rhythm resulting in fluctuating cultural patterns; on Sorokin's analysis of the fluctuation of value systems; and on the ideal of harmonious cultural transitions portrayed in the *I Ching*.

The major alternative to this model, which is related to it but different in several aspects, is the Marxist view of history known as dialectic or historical materialism. According to Marx, the roots of social evolution lie not in a change of ideas or values but in economic and technological developments. The dynamics of change is that of a "dialectic" interplay of opposites arising from contradictions that are intrinsic to all things. Marx took this idea from the philosophy of Hegel and adapted it to his analysis of social change, asserting that all changes in society arise from the development of its internal contradictions. He saw the contradictory principles of social organization as being embodied in society's classes, and class struggle as a consequence of their dialectic interaction.

The Marxist view of cultural dynamics, being based on the Hegelian notion of recurrent rhythmic change, is not unlike the models of Toynbee, Sorokin, and the *I Ching* in that respect.[24] However, it differs significantly from those models in its emphasis on conflict and struggle. Class struggle was the driving force of history for Marx, who held that all important historical progress was born in conflict, struggle, and violent revolution. Human suffering and sacrifice was a necessary price that had to be paid for social change.

The emphasis on struggle in Marx's theory of historical evolution paralleled Darwin's emphasis on struggle in biological evolution. In fact Marx's favorite image of himself is said to have been that of "the Darwin of sociology." The idea of life as an ongoing struggle for existence, which both Darwin and Marx owed to the economist Thomas Malthus, was vigorously promoted in the nineteenth century by the Social Darwinists, who influenced, if not Marx, certainly many of his followers.[25] I believe their view of social evolution overemphasizes the role of struggle and conflict, overlooking the fact that all struggle in nature takes place within a wider context of cooperation. Although conflict and struggle have brought about important social progress in our past and will often be an essential part of the dynamics of change, this does not mean that they are the source of this dynamics. Therefore, following the philosophy of the *I Ching* rather than the Marxist view, I believe that conflict should be minimized in times of social transition.

In our discussion of cultural values and attitudes throughout this book we will make extensive use of a framework that is developed in great detail in the *I Ching*, and that lies at the very basis of Chinese thought. Like Sorokin's framework, it is based on the idea of continuous cyclical fluctuation, but it involves the much broader notion of two archetypal poles—yin and yang—underlying the fundamental rhythm of the universe.

The Chinese philosophers saw reality, whose ultimate essence they called Tao, as a process of continual flow and change. In their view all phenomena we observe participate in this cosmic process and are thus intrinsically dynamic. The principal characteristic of the Tao is the cyclical nature of its ceaseless motion; all developments in nature—those in the physical world as well as those in the psychological and social realms—show cyclical patterns. The Chinese gave this idea of cyclical patterns a definite structure by introducing the polar opposites yin and yang, the two poles that set the limits for the cycles of change: "The yang having reached its climax retreats in favor of the yin; the yin having reached its climax retreats in favor of the yang."[26]

In the Chinese view, all manifestations of the Tao are generated by the dynamic interplay of these two archetypal poles, which are associated with many images of opposites taken from nature and from social life. It is important, and very difficult for us Westerners, to understand that these opposites do not belong to different categories but are extreme poles of a single whole. Nothing is only yin or only yang. All natural phenomena are manifestations of a continuous oscillation between the two poles, all transitions taking place gradually and in unbroken progression. The natural order is one of dynamic balance between yin and yang.

The terms yin and yang have recently become quite popular in the West, but they are rarely used in our culture in the Chinese sense. Most Western usage reflects cultural preconceptions that severely distort the original meanings. One of the best interpretations is given by Manfred Porkert in his comprehensive study of Chinese medicine.[27] According to Porkert, yin corresponds to all that is contractive, responsive, and conservative, whereas yang implies all that is expansive, aggressive, and demanding. Further associations include, among many others:

YIN	YANG
EARTH	HEAVEN
MOON	SUN
NIGHT	DAY
WINTER	SUMMER
MOISTURE	DRYNESS
COOLNESS	WARMTH
INTERIOR	SURFACE

In Chinese culture yin and yang have never been associated with moral values. What is good is not yin or yang but the dynamic balance between the two; what is bad or harmful is imbalance.

From the earliest times of Chinese culture, yin was associated with the feminine and yang with the masculine. This ancient association is extremely difficult to assess today because of its reinterpretation and distortion in subsequent patriarchal eras. In human biology masculine and feminine characteristics are not neatly separated but occur, in varying proportions, in both sexes.[28] Similarly, the Chinese ancients believed that all people, whether men or women, go through yin and yang phases. The personality of each man and each woman is not a static entity but a dynamic phenomenon resulting from the interplay between feminine and masculine elements. This view of human nature is in sharp contrast to that of our patriarchal culture, which has established a rigid order in which all men are supposed to be masculine and all women feminine, and has distorted the meaning of those terms by giving men the leading roles and most of society's privileges.

In view of this patriarchal bias, the frequent association of yin with passivity and yang with activity is particularly dangerous. In our culture women have traditionally been portrayed as passive and receptive, men as active and creative. This imagery goes back to Aristotle's theory of sexuality and has been used throughout the centuries as a "scientific" rationale for keeping women in a subordinate role, subservient to men.[29] The association of yin with passivity and yang with activity seems to be yet another expression of patriarchal stereotypes, a modern Western interpretation that is very unlikely to reflect the original meaning of the Chinese terms.

One of the most important insights of ancient Chinese culture was the recognition that activity—"the constant flow of transformation and change," as Chuang Tzu called it[30]—is an essential aspect of the universe. Change, in this view, does not occur as a consequence of some force but is a natural tendency, innate in all things and situations. The universe is engaged in ceaseless motion and activity, in a continual cosmic process that the Chinese called Tao—the Way. The notion of absolute rest, or inactivity, was almost entirely absent from Chinese philosophy. According to Hellmut Wilhelm, one of the leading Western interpreters of the *I Ching*, "The state of absolute immobility is such an abstraction that the Chinese . . . could not conceive it."[31]

The term *wu wei* is frequently used in Taoist philosophy and means literally "nonaction." In the West the term is usually interpreted as referring to passivity. This is quite wrong. What the Chinese mean by *wu wei* is not abstaining from activity but abstaining from a certain *kind* of activity, activity that is out of harmony with the ongoing cosmic process. The distinguished sinologist Joseph Needham defines *wu wei* as "refraining from action contrary to nature" and justifies his translation with a quotation from Chuang Tzu: "Nonaction does not mean doing nothing and keeping silent. Let everything be allowed to do what it naturally does, so that its nature will be satisfied."[32] If one refrains from acting contrary to nature or, as Needham says, from "going against the grain of things," one is in harmony with the Tao and thus one's actions will be successful. This is the meaning of Lao Tzu's seemingly puzzling statement: "By nonaction everything can be done."[33]

In the Chinese view, then, there seem to be two kinds of activity—activity in harmony with nature and activity against the natural flow of things. The idea of passivity, the complete absence of any action, is not entertained. Therefore the frequent Western association of yin and yang with passive and active behavior, respectively, does not seem to be consistent with Chinese thought. In view of the original imagery associated with the two archetypal poles, it would seem that yin can be interpreted as corresponding to responsive, consolidating, cooperative activity; yang as referring to aggressive, expanding, competitive activity. Yin action is conscious of the environment, yang action is conscious of the self. In modern terminology one could call the former "eco-action" and the latter "ego-action."

These two kinds of activity are closely related to two kinds of knowledge, or two modes of consciousness, which have been recognized as characteristic properties of the human mind throughout the ages. They are usually called the intuitive and the rational and have traditionally been associated with religion or mysticism and with science. Although the association of yin and yang with these two modes of consciousness is not part of the original Chinese terminology, it seems to be a natural extension of the ancient imagery and will be so regarded in our discussion.

The rational and the intuitive are complementary modes of functioning of the human mind. Rational thinking is linear, focused, and analytic. It belongs to the realm of the intellect, whose function it is to discriminate, measure, and categorize. Thus rational knowledge tends to be fragmented. Intuitive knowledge, on the other hand, is based on a direct, nonintellectual experience of reality arising in an expanded state of awareness. It tends to be synthesizing, holistic,[34] and nonlinear. From this it is apparent that rational knowledge is likely to generate self-centered, or yang, activity, whereas intuitive wisdom is the basis of ecological, or yin, activity.

This, then, is the framework for our exploration of cultural values and attitudes. For our purposes these associations of yin and yang will be most useful:

YIN	YANG
FEMININE	MASCULINE
CONTRACTIVE	EXPANSIVE
CONSERVATIVE	DEMANDING
RESPONSIVE	AGGRESSIVE
COOPERATIVE	COMPETITIVE
INTUITIVE	RATIONAL
SYNTHESIZING	ANALYTIC

Looking at this list of opposites, it is easy to see that our society has consistently favored the yang over the yin—rational knowledge over intuitive wisdom, science over religion, competition over cooperation, exploitation of natural resources over conservation, and so on. This emphasis, supported by the patriarchal system and further encouraged by the dominance of sensate culture during the past three centuries, has led to a profound cultural imbalance which lies at the very root of our current crisis—an imbalance in our thoughts and feelings, our values and attitudes, and our social and political structures. In describing the various manifestations of this cultural imbalance, I shall pay particular attention to their effects on health, and want to use the concept of health in a very broad sense, including in it not only individual health but also social and ecological health. These three levels of health are closely interrelated and our current crisis constitutes a serious threat to all three of them. It threatens the health of individuals, of the society, and of the ecosystems of which we are a part.

Throughout this book I will attempt to show how the strikingly consistent preference for yang values, attitudes, and behavior patterns has resulted in a system of academic, political, and economic institutions that are mutually supportive and have become all but blind to the dangerous imbalance of the value system that motivates their activities. According to Chinese wisdom, none of the values pursued by our culture is intrinsically bad, but by isolating them from their polar opposites, by focusing on the yang and investing it with moral virtue and political power, we have brought about the current sad state of affairs. Our culture takes pride in being scientific; our time is referred to as the Scientific Age. It is dominated by rational thought, and scientific knowledge is often considered the only acceptable kind of knowledge. That there can be intuitive knowledge, or awareness, which is just as valid and reliable, is generally not recognized. This attitude, known as scientism, is widespread, pervading our educational system and all other social and political institutions. When President Lyndon Johnson needed advice about warfare in Vietnam, his administration turned to theoretical physicists—not because they were specialists in the methods of electronic warfare, but because they were considered the high priests of science, guardians of supreme knowledge. We can now say, with hindsight, that Johnson might have been much better served had he sought his advice from some of the poets. But that, of course, was—and still is—unthinkable.

The emphasis on rational thought in our culture is epitomized in Descartes' celebrated statement *"Cogito, ergo sum"*—"I think, therefore I exist"—which forcefully encouraged Western individuals to equate their identity with their rational mind rather than with their whole organism. We shall see that the effects of this division between mind and body are felt throughout our culture. Retreating into our minds, we have forgotten how to "think" with our bodies, how to use them as agents of knowing. In doing so we have also cut ourselves off from our natural environment and have forgotten how to commune and cooperate with its rich variety of living organisms.

The division between mind and matter led to a view of the universe as a mechanical system consisting of separate objects, which in turn were reduced to fundamental material building blocks whose properties and interactions were thought to completely determine all natural phenomena. This Cartesian view of nature was further extended to living organisms, which were regarded as machines constructed from separate parts. We shall see that such a mechanistic conception of the world is still at the basis of most of our sciences and continues to have a tremendous influence on many aspects of our lives. It has led to the well-known fragmentation in our academic disciplines and government agencies and has served as a rationale for treating the natural environment as if it consisted of separate parts, to be exploited by different interest groups.

Exploitation of nature has gone hand in hand with that of women, who have been identified with nature throughout the ages. From the earliest times, nature—and especially the earth—was seen as a kind and nurturing mother, but also as a wild and uncontrollable female. In prepatriarchal eras her many aspects were identified with the numerous manifestations of the Goddess. Under patriarchy the benign image of nature changed into one of passivity, whereas the view of nature as wild and dangerous gave rise to the idea that she was to be dominated by man. At the same time women were portrayed as passive and subservient to men. With the rise of Newtonian science, finally, nature became a mechanical system that could be manipulated and exploited, together with the manipulation and exploitation of women. The ancient association of woman and nature thus interlinks women's history and the history of the environment, and is the source of a natural kinship between feminism and ecology which is manifesting itself increasingly. In the words of Carolyn Merchant, historian of science at the University of California, Berkeley:

> In investigating the roots of our current environmental dilemma and its connections to science, technology and the economy, we must re-examine the formation of a world-view and a science which, by reconceptualizing reality as a machine rather than a living organism, sanctioned the domination of both nature and women. The contributions of such founding "fathers" of modern science as Francis Bacon, William Harvey, René Descartes, Thomas Hobbes and Isaac Newton must be reevaluated.[35]

The view of man as dominating nature and woman, and the belief in the superior role of the rational mind, have been supported and encouraged by the Judeo-Christian tradition, which adheres to the image of a male god, personification of supreme reason and source of ultimate power, who rules the world from above by imposing his divine law on it. The laws of nature searched for by the scientists were seen as reflections of this divine law, originating in the mind of God.

It is now becoming apparent that overemphasis on the scientific method and on rational, analytic thinking has led to attitudes that are profoundly antiecological. In truth, the understanding of ecosystems is hindered by the very nature of the rational mind. Rational thinking is linear, whereas ecological awareness arises from an intuition of nonlinear systems. One of the most difficult things for people in our culture to understand is the fact that if you do something that is good, then more of the same will not necessarily be better. This, to me, is the essence of ecological thinking. Ecosystems sustain themselves in a dynamic balance based on cycles and fluctuations, which are nonlinear processes. Linear enterprises, such as indefinite economic and technological growth—or, to give a more specific example, the storage of radioactive waste over enormous time spans—will necessarily interfere with the natural balance and, sooner or later, will cause severe damage.

Ecological awareness, then, will arise only when we combine our rational knowledge with an intuition for the nonlinear nature of our environment. Such intuitive wisdom is characteristic of traditional, nonliterate cultures, especially of American Indian cultures, in which life was organized around a highly refined awareness of the environment. In the mainstream of our culture, on the other hand, the cultivation of intuitive wisdom has been neglected. This may be related to the fact that, in our evolution, there has been an increasing separation between the biological and cultural aspects of human nature. Biological evolution of the human species stopped some fifty thousand years ago. From then on, evolution proceeded no longer genetically but socially and culturally, while the human body and brain remained essentially the same in structure and size.[36] In our civilization we have modified our environment to such an extent during this cultural evolution that we have lost touch with our biological and ecological base more than any other culture and any other civilization in the past. This separation manifests itself in a striking disparity between the development of intellectual power, scientific knowledge, and technological skills, on the one hand,

and of wisdom, spirituality, and ethics on the other. Scientific and technological knowledge has grown enormously since the Greeks embarked on the scientific venture in the sixth century B.C. But during these twenty-five centuries there has been hardly any progress in the conduct of social affairs. The spirituality and moral standards of Lao Tzu and Buddha, who also lived in the sixth century B.C., were clearly not inferior to ours.

Our progress, then, has been largely a rational and intellectual affair, and this one-sided evolution has now reached a highly alarming stage, a situation so paradoxical that it borders insanity. We can control the soft landings of space craft on distant planets, but we are unable to control the polluting fumes emanating from our cars and factories. We propose Utopian communities in gigantic space colonies, but cannot manage our cities. The business world makes us believe that huge industries producing pet foods and cosmetics are a sign of our high standard of living, while economists try to tell us that we cannot "afford" adequate health care, education, or public transport. Medical science and pharmacology are endangering our health, and the Defense Department has become the greatest threat to our national security. Those are the results of overemphasizing our yang, or masculine side—rational knowledge, analysis, expansion—and neglecting our yin, or feminine side—intuitive wisdom, synthesis, and ecological awareness.

The yin/yang terminology is especially useful in an analysis of cultural imbalance that adopts a broad ecological view, a view that could also be called a systems view, in the sense of general systems theory.[37] Systems theory looks at the world in terms of the interrelatedness and interdependence of all phenomena, and in this framework an integrated whole whose properties cannot be reduced to those of its parts is called a system. Living organisms, societies, and ecosystems are all systems. It is fascinating to see that the ancient Chinese idea of yin and yang is related to an essential property of natural systems that has only recently been studied in Western science.

Living systems are organized in such a way that they form multi-leveled structures, each level consisting of subsystems which are wholes in regard to their parts, and parts with respect to the larger wholes. Thus molecules combine to form organelles, which in turn combine to form cells. The cells form tissues and organs, which themselves form larger systems, like the digestive system or the nervous system. These, finally, combine to form the living woman or man; and the "stratified order" does not end there. People form families, tribes, societies, nations. All these entities—from molecules to human beings, and on to social systems—can be regarded as wholes in the sense of being integrated structures, and also as parts of larger wholes at higher levels of complexity. In fact, we shall see that parts and wholes in an absolute sense do not exist at all.

Arthur Koestler has coined the word "holons" for these subsystems which are both wholes and parts, and he has emphasized that each holon has two opposite tendencies: an integrative tendency to function as part of the larger whole, and a self-assertive tendency to preserve its individual autonomy.[38] In a biological or social system each holon must assert its individuality in order to maintain the system's stratified order, but it must also submit to the demands of the whole in order to make the system viable. These two tendencies are opposite but complementary. In a healthy system—an individual, a society, or an ecosystem—there is a balance between integration and self-assertion. This balance is not static but consists of a dynamic interplay between the two complementary tendencies, which makes the whole system flexible and open to change.

The relation between modern systems theory and ancient Chinese thought now becomes apparent. The Chinese sages seem to have recognized the basic polarity that is characteristic of living systems. Self-assertion is achieved by displaying yang behavior; by being demanding, aggressive, competitive, expanding, and—as far as human behavior is concerned—by using linear, analytic thinking. Integration is furthered by yin behavior; by being responsive, cooperative, intuitive, and aware of one's environment. Both yin and yang, integrative and self-assertive tendencies, are necessary for harmonious social and ecological relationships.

Excessive self-assertion manifests itself as power, control, and domination of others by force; and these are, indeed, the patterns prevalent in our society. Political and economic power is exerted by a dominant corporate class; social hierarchies are maintained along racist and sexist lines, and rape has become a central metaphor of our culture—rape of women, of minority groups, and of the earth herself. Our science and technology are based on the seventeenth-century belief that an understanding of nature implies domination of nature by "man." Combined with the mechanistic model of the universe, which also originated in the seventeenth century, and with excessive emphasis on linear thinking, this attitude has produced a technology that is unhealthy and inhuman; a technology in which the natural, organic habitat of complex human beings is replaced by a simplified, synthetic, and prefabricated environment.[39]

This technology is aimed at control, mass production, and standardization, and is subjected, most of the time, to centralized management that pursues the illusion of indefinite growth. Thus the self-assertive tendency keeps increasing, and with it the requirement of submission, which is not the complement to self-assertion but the reverse side of the same phenomenon. While self-assertive behavior is presented as the ideal for men, submissive behavior is expected from women, but also from employees and executives who are required to deny their personal identities and to adopt the corporate identity and behavior patterns. A similar situation exists in our educational system, in which self-assertiveness is rewarded as far as competitive behavior is concerned, but is discouraged when expressed in terms of original ideas and questioning of authority.

Promotion of competitive behavior over cooperation is one of the principal manifestations of the self-assertive tendency in our society. It is rooted in the erroneous view of nature held by the Social Darwinists of the nineteenth century, who believed that all life in society had to be a struggle for existence ruled by "survival of the fittest." Accordingly, competition has been seen as the driving force of the economy, the "aggressive approach" has become the ideal of the business world, and this behavior has been combined with the exploitation of natural resources to create patterns of competitive consumption.

Aggressive, competitive behavior alone, of course, would make life impossible. Even the most ambitious, goal-oriented individuals need sympathetic support, human contact, and times of carefree spontaneity and relaxation. In our culture women are expected, and often forced, to fulfill these needs. They are the secretaries, receptionists, hostesses, nurses, and homemakers who perform the services that make life more comfortable and create the atmosphere in which the competitors can succeed. They cheer up their bosses and make coffee for them; they help smooth out conflicts in the office; they are the first to receive visitors and entertain them with small talk. In doctors' offices and hospitals women provide most of the human contact with patients that initiates the healing process. In physics departments women make the tea and serve the cookies over which the men discuss their theories. All these services involve yin, or integrative, activities, and since they rank lower in our value system than the yang, or self-assertive, activities, those who perform them get paid less. Indeed, many of them, such as mothers and housewives, are not paid at all.

From this short survey of cultural attitudes and values we can see that our culture has consistently promoted and rewarded the yang, the masculine or self-assertive elements of human nature, and has disregarded its yin, the feminine or intuitive aspects. Today, however, we are witnessing the beginning of a tremendous evolutionary movement. The turning point we are about to reach marks, among many other things, a reversal in the fluctuation between yin and yang. As the Chinese text says, "The yang, having reached its climax, retreats in favor of the yin." Our 1960s and 1970s have generated a whole series of philosophical, spiritual, and political movements that seem to go in the same direction. They all counteract the overemphasis on yang attitudes and values, and try to reestablish a balance between the masculine and feminine sides of human nature.

There is a rising concern with ecology, expressed by citizen movements that are forming around social and environmental issues, pointing out the limits to growth, advocating a new ecological ethic, and developing appropriate "soft" technologies. In the political arena the antinuclear movement is fighting the most extreme outgrowth of our self-assertive "macho" technology and, in doing so, is likely to become one of the most powerful political forces of this decade. At the same time there is the beginning of a significant shift in values—from the admiration of large-scale enterprises and institutions to the notion of "small is beautiful," from material consumption to voluntary simplicity, from economic and technological growth to inner growth and development. These new values are being promoted by the "human potential" movement, the "holistic-health" movement, and various spiritual movements. Perhaps most important, the old value system is being challenged and profoundly changed by the rise of feminist awareness originating in the women's movement.

These various movements form what cultural historian Theodore Roszak has called the counter culture.[40] So far, many of them still operate separately and have not yet seen how much their purposes interrelate. Thus the human potential movement and the holistic health movement often lack ecological awareness, with Eastern gurus displaying Western capitalist status symbols and spending considerable time building their economic empires. However, some movements have recently begun to form coalitions. As would be expected, the ecology movement and the feminist movement are joining forces on several issues, notably nuclear power, and environmental groups, consumer groups, and ethnic liberation movements are beginning to make contacts. We can anticipate that, once they have recognized the commonality of their aims, all these movements will flow together and form a powerful force of social transformation. I shall call this force the rising culture, following Toynbee's persuasive model of cultural dynamics:

During the disintegration of a civilization, two separate plays with different plots are being performed simultaneously side by side. While an unchanging dominant minority is perpetually rehearsing its own defeat, fresh challenges are perpetually evoking fresh creative responses from newly recruited minorities, which proclaim their own creative power by rising, each time, to the occasion. The drama of challenge-and-response continues to be performed, but in new circumstances and with new actors.[41]

From this broad historical perspective cultures are seen to come and go in rhythms, and preserving cultural traditions may not always be the most desirable aim. What we have to do to minimize the hardship of inevitable change is recognize the changing conditions as clearly as possible and transform our lives and our social institutions accordingly. I shall argue that physicists can play an important role in this process. Since the seventeenth century physics has been the shining example of an "exact" science, and has served as the model for all the other sciences. For two and a half centuries physicists have used a mechanistic view of the world to develop and refine the conceptual framework known as classical physics. They have based their ideas on the mathematical theory of Isaac Newton, the philosophy of René Descartes, and the scientific methodology advocated by Francis Bacon, and developed them in accordance with the general conception of reality prevalent during the seventeenth, eighteenth, and nineteenth centuries. Matter was thought to be the basis of all existence, and the material world was seen as a multitude of separate objects assembled into a huge machine. Like human-made machines, the cosmic machine was thought to consist of elementary parts. Consequently it was believed that complex phenomena could always be understood by reducing them to their basic building blocks and by looking for mechanisms through which these interacted. This attitude, known as reductionism, has become so deeply ingrained in our culture that it has often been identified with the scientific method. The other sciences accepted the mechanistic and reductionistic views of classical physics as the correct description of reality and modeled their own theories accordingly. Whenever psychologists, sociologists, or economists wanted to be scientific, they naturally turned toward the basic concepts of Newtonian physics.

In the twentieth century, however, physics has gone through several conceptual revolutions that clearly reveal the limitations of the mechanistic world view and lead to an organic, ecological view of the world which shows great similarities to the views of mystics of all ages and traditions. The universe is no longer seen as a machine, made up of a multitude of separate objects, but appears as a harmonious indivisible whole; a network of dynamic relationships that include the human observer and his or her consciousness in an essential way. The fact that modern physics, the manifestation of an extreme specialization of the rational mind, is now making contact with mysticism, the essence of religion and manifestation of an extreme specialization of the intuitive mind, shows very beautifully the unity and complementary nature of the rational and intuitive modes of consciousness; of the yang and the yin. Physicists, therefore, can provide the scientific background to the changes in attitudes and values that our society so urgently needs. In a culture dominated by science, it will be much easier to convince our social institutions that fundamental changes are necessary if we can give our arguments a scientific basis. This is what physicists can now provide. Modern physics can show the other sciences that scientific thinking does not necessarily have to be reductionist and mechanistic, that holistic and ecological views are also scientifically sound.

One of the main lessons that physicists have had to learn in this century has been the fact that all the concepts and theories we use to describe nature are limited. Because of the essential limitations of the rational mind, we have to accept the fact that, as Werner Heisenberg phrases it, "every word or concept, clear as it may seem to be, has only a limited range of applicability."[42] Scientific theories can never provide a complete and definitive description of reality. They will always be approximations to the true nature of things. To put it bluntly, scientists do not deal with the truth; they deal with limited and approximate descriptions of reality.

At the beginning of the century, when physicists extended the range of their investigations into the realms of atomic and subatomic phenomena, they suddenly became aware of the limitations of their classical ideas and had to radically revise many of their basic concepts about reality. The experience of questioning the very basis of their conceptual framework and of being forced to accept profound modifications of their most cherished ideas was dramatic and often painful for those scientists, especially during the first three decades of the century, but it was rewarded by deep insights into the nature of matter and the human mind.

I believe this experience can serve as a useful lesson for other scientists, many of whom have now reached the limits of the Cartesian world view in their fields. Like the physicists, they will have to accept the fact that we must modify or even abandon some of our concepts when we expand the realm of our experience or field of study. The following chapters will show how the natural sciences, as well as the humanities and social sciences, have modeled themselves after classical Newtonian physics. Now that physicsts have gone far beyond this model, it is time for the other sciences to expand their underlying philosophies.

Among the sciences that have been influenced by the Cartesian world view and by Newtonian physics, and will have to change to be consistent with the views of modern physics, I shall concentrate on those dealing with health in the broadest ecological sense: from biology and medical science to psychology and psychotherapy, sociology, economics, and political science. In all these fields the limitations of the classical, Cartesian world view are now becoming apparent. To transcend the classical models scientists will have to go beyond the mechanistic and reductionist approach as we have done in physics, and develop holistic and ecological views. Although their theories will need to be consistent with those of modern physics, the concepts of physics will generally not be appropriate as a model for the other sciences. However, they may still be very helpful. Scientists will not need to be reluctant to adopt a holistic framework, as they often are today, for fear of being unscientific. Modern physics can show them that such a framework is not only scientific but is in agreement with the most advanced scientific theories of physical reality.

NOTES

10. See Harman, Willis W. 1977. "The Coming Transformation." *The Futurist*, April.
11. This graph is not meant to give an exact representation of the civilizations shown, but has been drawn merely to illustrate their general pattern of development. Approximate dates

for the beginning, culmination, and end of each civilization have been used, but the individual curves have been given equal and arbitrary height. They have been displaced vertically for the sake of clarity.

12. Toynbee, Arnold. 1972. *A Study of History*. New York: Oxford University Press.
13. For references, see ibid., p. 89.
14. See Henderson, Hazel. 1981. *The Politics of the Solar Age*. New York: Doubleday/Anchor.
15. For a comprehensive discussion of the multiple facets of patriarchy, see Rich, Adrienne. 1977. *Of Woman Born*. New York: Bantam.
16. Ibid., p. 40.
17. Fossil fuels are residues of fossilized plants, plants that were buried in the earth's crust and transformed into their present state by chemical reactions over long periods of time.
18. From the Greek *paradeigma* ("pattern").
19. For an extensive discussion of paradigms and paradigm shifts, see Kuhn, Thomas S. 1970. *The Structure of Scientific Revolutions*. Chicago: University of Chicago Press.
20. Sorokin, Pitirim A. 1937–41. *Social and Cultural Dynamics*, 4 vols. New York: American Book Company.
21. Ibid., vol. 4, pp. 774 ff.
22. Mumford, Lewis. 1956. *The Transformations of Man*. New York: Harper.
23. *I Ching*, comments on the hexagram "The Turning Point," Wilhelm, Richard (*The I Ching*. London: Routledge & Kegan Paul, 1985), p. 97.
24. For an extremely lucid analysis of materialist dialectics that shows striking similarities with ancient Chinese thought, without ever acknowledging them, see Mao Zedong's famous essay "On Contradiction"; Mao Zedong. 1988. *Four Essays on Philosophy*. Beijing: Foreign Languages Press.
25. See Barzun, Jacques. 1958. *Darwin, Marx, Wagner*. New York: Doubleday/Anchor.
26. Wang Ch'ung, quoted in Capra, Fritjof (Berkeley: Shambhala, 1975), p. 106.
27. Porkert, Manfred. 1974. *The Theoretical Foundations of Chinese Medicine* (Cambridge, Mass: MIT Press) pp. 9 ff. For a good introduction, see Porkett. 1979. "Chinese Medicine, a Traditional Healing Science." In Sobel, David, ed. *Ways of Health*. New York: Harcourt Brace Jovanovich.
28. See Goleman, Daniel. 1978. "Special Abilities of the Sexes: Do They Begin in the Brain?" *Psychology Today*, November, for a review of recent research on sex differences.
29. See Merchant, Carolyn. 1980. *The Death of Nature*. New York: Harper & Row, p. 13.
30. Quoted in Capra (1975), p. 114.
31. Wilhelm, Hellmut. 1960. *Change*. New York: Harper Torchbooks.
32. Quoted in Capra (1975), p. 117.
33. Quoted ibid.
34. The term "holistic," from the Greek *holos* ("whole"), refers to an understanding of reality in terms of integrated wholes whose properties cannot be reduced to those of smaller units.
35. Merchant (1980), p. xvii.
36. See Dubos, Rene. 1985. *Man, Medicine and Environment*. New York: Praeger.
37. See Chapter 9, Capra, *The Turning Point*.
38. Koestler, Arthur. 1978, *Janus*. London: Hutchinson.
39. See Mumford, Lewis. 1970. "Closing Statement." In Disch, Robert, ed. *The Ecological Conscience*. New York: Prentice-Hall.
40. Roszak, Theodore. 1969. *The Making of a Counter Culture*. New York: Doubleday/Anchor.
41. Toynbee (1972), p. 228.
42. Quoted in Capra (1975), p. 28.

Liberation from the Affluent Society

Herbert Marcuse

I am very happy to see so many flowers here and that is why I want to remind you that flowers, by themselves, have no power whatsoever, other than the power of men and women who protect them and take care of them against aggression and destruction.

As a hopeless philosopher for whom philosophy has become inseparable from politics, I am afraid I have to give here today a rather philosophical speech, and I must ask your indulgence. We are dealing with the dialectics of liberation (actually a redundant phrase, because I believe that all dialectic is liberation) and not only liberation in an intellectual sense, but liberation involving the mind and the body, liberation involving entire human existence. Think of Plato: the liberation from the existence in the cave. Think of Hegel: liberation in the sense of progress and freedom on the historical scale. Think of Marx. Now in what sense is all dialectic liberation? It is liberation from the repressive, from a bad, a false system—be it an organic system, be it a social system, be it a mental or intellectual system: liberation by forces developing within such a system. That is a decisive point. And liberation by virtue of the contradiction generated by the system, precisely because it is a bad, a false system.

I am intentionally using here moral, philosophical terms, values: 'bad', 'false'. For without an objectively justifiable goal of a better, a free human existence, all liberation must remain meaningless—at best, progress in servitude. I believe that in Marx too socialism *ought* to be. This 'ought' belongs to the very essence of scientific socialism. It *ought* to be; it is, we may almost say, a biological, sociological and political necessity. It is a biological necessity in as much as a socialist society, according to Marx, would conform with the very *logos* of life, with the essential possibilities of a human existence, not only mentally, not only intellectually, but also organically.

Now as to today and our own situation. I think we are faced with a novel

From *The Dialectics of Liberation* by David Cooper (ed.). Middlesex, England: Penguin/Pelican (1968).

situation in history, because today we have to be liberated from a relatively well-functioning, rich, powerful society. I am speaking here about liberation from the affluent society, that is to say, the advanced industrial societies. The problem we are facing is the need for liberation not from a poor society, not from a disintegrating society, not even in most cases from a terroristic society, but from a society which develops to a great extent the material and even cultural needs of man—a society which, to use a slogan, delivers the goods to an ever larger part of the population. And that implies, we are facing liberation from a society where liberation is apparently without a mass basis. We know very well the social mechanisms of manipulation, indoctrination, repression which are responsible for this lack of a mass basis, for the integration of the majority of the oppositional forces into the established social system. But I must emphasize again that this is not merely an ideological integration; that it is not merely a social integration; that it takes place precisely on the strong and rich basis which enables the society to develop and satisfy material and cultural needs better than before.

But knowledge of the mechanisms of manipulation or repression, which go down into the very unconscious of man, is not the whole story. I believe that we (and I will use 'we' throughout my talk) have been too hesitant, that we have been too ashamed, understandably ashamed, to insist on the integral, radical features of a socialist society, its qualitative difference from all the established societies: the qualitative difference by virtue of which socialism is indeed the negation of the established systems, no matter how productive, no matter how powerful they are or they may appear. In other words—and this is one of the many points where I disagree with Paul Goodman—our fault was not that we have been too immodest, but that we have been too modest. We have, as it were, repressed a great deal of what or should have said and what we should have emphasized.

If today these integral features, these truly radical features which make a socialist society a definite negation of the existing societies, if this qualitative difference today appears as Utopian, as idealistic, as metaphysical, this is precisely the form in which these radical features must appear if they are really to be a definite negation of the established society: if socialism is indeed the rupture of history, the radical break, the leap into the realm of freedom—a total rupture.

Let us give one illustration of how this awareness, or half-awareness, of the need for such a total rupture was present in some of the great social struggles of our period. Walter Benjamin quotes reports that during the Paris Commune, in all corners of the city of Paris there were people shooting at the clocks on the towers of the churches, palaces and so on, thereby consciously or half-consciously expressing the need that somehow time has to be arrested; that at least the prevailing, the established time continuum has to be arrested, and that a new time has to begin—a very strong emphasis on the qualitative difference and on the totality of the rupture between the new society and the old.

In this sense, I should like to discuss here with you the repressed prerequisites of qualitative change. I say intentionally 'of qualitative change', not 'of revolution', because we know of too many revolutions through which the continuum of repression has been sustained, revolutions which have replaced one system of domination by another. We must become aware of the essentially new features which distinguish a free society as a definite negation of the established societies, and we must begin formulating these features, no matter how metaphysical, no matter how Utopian, I would even say no matter how ridiculous we may appear to the normal people in all camps, on the right as well as on the left.

What is the dialectic of liberation with which we here are concerned? It is the construction of a free society, a construction which depends in the first place on the prevalence of the vital need for abolishing the established systems of servitude; and secondly, and this is decisive, it depends on the vital commitment, the striving, conscious as well as sub- and un-conscious, for the qualitatively different values of a free human existence. Without the emergence of such new needs and satisfactions, the needs and satisfactions of free men, all change in the social institutions, no matter how great, would only replace one system of servitude by another system of servitude. Nor can the emergence—and I should like to emphasize this—nor can the emergence of such new needs and satisfactions be envisaged as a mere by-product, the mere result, of changed social institutions. We have seen this, it is a fact of experience. The development of the new institutions must already be carried out and carried through by men with the new needs. That, by the way, is the basic idea underlying Marx's own concept of the proletariat as the historical agent of revolution. He saw the industrial proletariat as the historical agent of revolution, not only because it was the basic class in the material process of production, not only because it was at that time the majority of the population, but also because this class was 'free' from the repressive and aggressive competitive needs of capitalist society and therefore, at least potentially, the carrier of essentially new needs, goals and satisfactions.

We can formulate this dialectic of liberation also in a more brutal way, as a vicious circle. The transition from voluntary servitude (as it exists to a great extent in the affluent society) to freedom presupposes the abolition of the institutions and mechanism of repression. And the abolition of the institutions and mechanisms of repression already presupposes liberation from servitude, prevalence of the need for liberation. As to needs, I think we have to distinguish between the need for changing intolerable conditions of existence, and the need for changing the society as a whole. The two are by no means identical, they are by no means in harmony. *If* the need is for changing intolerable conditions of existence, with at least a reasonable chance that this can be achieved within the established society, with the growth and progress of the established society, then this is merely quantitative change. Qualitative change is a change of the very system as a whole.

I would like to point out that the distinction between quantitative and qualitative change is not identical with the distinction between reform and revolution. Quantitative change can mean and can lead to revolution. Only the conjunction, I suggest, of these two is revolution in the essential sense of the leap from pre-history into the history of man. In other words, the problem with which we are faced is the point where quantity can turn into quality, where the quantitative change in the conditions and institutions can become a qualitative change affecting all human existence.

Today the two potential factors of revolution which I have just mentioned are disjointed. The first is most prevalent in the underdeveloped countries, where quantitative change—that is to say, the creation of human living conditions—is in itself qualitative change, but is not yet freedom. The second potential factor of revolution, the prerequisites of liberation, are potentially there in the advanced industrial countries, but are contained and perverted by the capitalist organization of society.

I think we are faced with a situation in which this advanced capitalist society has reached a point where quantitative change can technically be turned into qualitative change, into authentic liberation. And it is precisely against this truly fatal possibility that the affluent society, advanced capitalism, is mobilized and organized on all fronts, at home as well as abroad.

Before I go on, let me give a brief definition of what I mean by an affluent society. A model, of course, is American society today, although even in the US it is more a tendency, not yet entirely translated into reality. In the first place, it is a capitalist society. It seems to be necessary to remind ourselves of this because there are some people, even on the left, who believe that American society is no longer a class society. I can assure you that it is a class society. It is a capitalist society with a high concentration of economic and political power; with an enlarged and enlarging sector of automation and coordination of production, distribution and communication; with private ownership in the means of production, which however depends increasingly on ever more active and wide intervention by the government. It is a society in which, as I mentioned, the material as well as cultural needs of the underlying population are satisfied on a scale larger than ever before—but they are satisfied in line with the requirements and interests of the apparatus and of the powers which control the apparatus. And it is a society growing on the condition of accelerating waste, planned obsolescence and destruction, while the substratum of the population continues to live in poverty and misery.

I believe that these factors are internally interrelated, that they constitute the syndrome of late capitalism: namely, the apparently inseparable unity—inseparable for the system—of productivity and destruction, of satisfaction of needs and repression, of liberty within a system of servitude—that is to say, the subjugation of man to the apparatus, and the inseparable unity of rational and irrational. We can say that the rationality of the society lies in its very insanity, and that the insanity of the society is rational to the degree to which it is efficient, to the degree to which it delivers the goods.

Now the question we must raise is: why do we need liberation from such a society if it is capable—perhaps in the distant future, but apparently capable—of conquering poverty to a greater degree than ever before, of reducing the toil of labour and the time of labour, and of raising the standard of living? If the price for all goods delivered, the price for this comfortable servitude, for all these achievements, is exacted from people far away from the metropolis and far away from its affluence? If the affluent society itself hardly notices what it is doing, how it is spreading terror and enslavement, how it is fighting liberation in all corners of the globe?

We know the traditional weakness of emotional, moral and humanitarian arguments in the face of such technological achievement, in the face of the irrational rationality of such a power. These arguments do not seem to carry any weight against the brute facts—we might say brutal facts—of the society and its productivity. And yet, it is only the insistence on the real possibilities of a free society, which is blocked by the affluent society—it is only this insistence in practice as well as in theory, in demonstration as well as in discussion, which still stands in the way of the complete degradation of man to an object, or rather subject/object, of total administration. It is only this insistence which still stands in the way of the progressive brutalization and moronization of man. For—and I should like to emphasize this—the capitalist Welfare State is a Warfare State. It must have an Enemy, with a capital E, a total Enemy; because the perpetuation of servitude, the perpetuation of the miserable struggle for existence in the very face of the new possibilities of freedom, activates and intensifies in this society a primary aggressiveness to a degree, I think, hitherto unknown in history. And this primary aggressiveness must be mobilized in socially useful ways, lest it explode the system itself. Therefore the need for an Enemy, who must be there, and who must be created if he does not exist. Fortunately, I dare say, the Enemy does exist. But his image and his power must, in this society, be inflated beyond all proportions in order to be able to mobilize this aggressiveness of the affluent society in socially useful ways.

The result is a mutilated, crippled and frustrated human existence: a human existence that is violently defending its own servitude.

We can sum up the fatal situation with which we are confronted. Radical social change is objectively necessary, in the dual sense that it is the only chance to save the possibilities of human freedom and, furthermore, in the sense that the technical and material resources for the realization of freedom are available. But while this objective need is demonstrably there, the subjective need for such a change does not prevail. It does not prevail precisely among those parts of the population that are traditionally considered the agents of historical change. The subjective need is repressed, again on a dual ground: firstly, by virtue of the actual satisfaction of needs, and secondly, by a massive scientific manipulation and administration of needs—that is, by a systematic social control not only of the consciousness, but also of the unconscious of man. This control has been made possible by the very achievements of the greatest liberating sciences of our time, in psychology, mainly psychoanalysis and psychiatry. That they could become and have become at the same time powerful instruments of suppression, one of the most effective engines of suppression, is again one of the terrible aspects of the dialectic of liberation.

This divergence between the objective and the subjective need changes completely, I suggest, the basis, the prospects and the strategy of liberation. This situation presupposes the emergence of new needs, qualitatively different and even opposed to the prevailing aggressive and repressive needs: the emergence of a new type of man, with a vital, biological drive for liberation, and with a consciousness capable of breaking through the material as well as ideological veil of the affluent society. In other words, liberation seems to be predicated upon the opening and the activation of a depth dimension of human existence, this side of and underneath the traditional material base: not an idealistic dimension, over and above the material base, but a dimension even more material than the material base, a dimension underneath the material base. I will illustrate presently what I mean.

The emphasis on this new dimension does not mean replacing politics by psychology, but rather the other way around. It means finally taking account of the fact that society has invaded even the deepest roots of individual existence, even the unconscious of man. *We* must get at the roots of society in the individuals themselves, the individuals who, because of social engineering, constantly reproduce the continuum of repression even through the great revolution.

This change is, I suggest, not an ideological change. It is dictated by the actual development of an industrial society, which has introduced factors which our theory could formerly correctly neglect. It is dictated by the actual development of industrial society, by the tremendous growth of its material and technical productivity, which has surpassed and rendered obsolete the traditional goals and preconditions of liberation.

Here we are faced with the question: is liberation from the affluent society identical with the transition from capitalism to socialism? The answer I suggest is: It is not identical, if socialism is defined merely as the planned development of the productive forces, and the rationalization of resources (although this remains a precondition for all liberation). It is identical with the transition from capitalism to socialism, if socialism is defined in its most Utopian terms: namely, among others, the abolition of labour, the termination of the struggle for existence—that is to say, life as an end in itself and no longer as a means to an end—and the liberation of human sensibility and sensitivity, not as a private factor, but as a force for transformation of human existence and of its environment. To give sensitivity and sensibility their own right is, I think, one of the basic goals of integral socialism. These are the qualitatively different features of a free society. They presuppose, as you may already have seen, a total trans-valuation of values, a new anthropology. They presuppose a type of man who rejects the performance principles governing the established societies; a type of man who has rid himself of the aggressiveness and brutality that are inherent in the organization of established society, and in their hypocritical, puritan morality; a type of man who is biologically incapable of fighting wars and creating suffering; a type of man who has a good conscience of joy and pleasure, and who works, collectively and individually, for a social and natural environment in which such an existence becomes possible.

The dialectic of liberation, as turned from quantity into quality, thus involves, I repeat, a break in the continuum of repression which reaches into the depth dimension of the organism itself. Or, we may say that today qualitative change, liberation, involves organic, instinctual, biological changes at the same time as political and social changes.

The new needs and satisfactions have a very material basis, as I have indicated. They are not thought out but are the logical derivation from the technical, material and intellectual possibilities of advanced, industrial society. They are inherent in, and the expression of, the productivity of advanced industrial society, which has long since made obsolete all kinds of inner-worldly asceticism, the entire work discipline on which Judaeo-Christian morality has been based.

Why is this society surpassing and negating this type of man, the traditional type of man, and the forms of his existence, as well as the morality to which it owes much of its origins and foundations? This new, unheard-of and not anticipated productivity allows the concept of a technology of liberation. Here I can only briefly indicate what I have in mind: such amazing and indeed apparently Utopian tendencies as the convergence of technique and art, the convergence of work and play, the convergence of the realm of necessity and the realm of freedom. How? No longer subjected to the dictates of capitalist profitability and of efficiency, no longer to the dictates of scarcity, which today are perpetuated by the capitalist organization of society; socially necessary labour, material production, would and could become (we see the tendency already) increasingly scientific. Technical experimentation, science and technology would and could become a play with the hitherto hidden—methodically hidden and blocked—potentialities of men and things, of society and nature.

This means one of the oldest dreams of all radical theory and practice. It means that the creative imagination, and not only the rationality of the performance principle, would become a productive force applied to the transformation of the social and natural universe. It would mean the emergence of a form of reality which is the work and the medium of the developing sensibility and sensitivity of man.

And now I throw in the terrible concept: it would mean an 'aesthetic' reality— society as a work of art. This is the most Utopian, the most radical possibility of liberation today.

What does this mean, in concrete terms? I said, we are not concerned here with private sensitivity and sensibility, but with sensitivity and sensibility, creative imagination and play, becoming forces of transformation. As such they would guide, for example, the total reconstruction of our cities and of the countryside; the restoration of nature after the elimination of the violence and destruction of capitalist industrialization; the creation of internal and external space for privacy, individual autonomy, tranquillity; the elimination of noise, of captive audiences, of enforced togetherness, of pollution, of ugliness. These are not—and I cannot emphasize this strongly enough—snobbish and romantic demands. Biologists today have emphasized that these are organic needs for the human organism, and that their arrest, their perversion and destruction by capitalist society, actually mutilates the human organism, not only in a figurative way but in a very real and literal sense.

I believe that it is only in such a universe that man can be truly free, and truly human relationships between free beings can be established. I believe that the idea of such a universe guided also Marx's concept of socialism, and that these aesthetic needs and goals must from the beginning be present in the reconstruction of society, and not only at the end or in the far future. Otherwise, the needs and satisfactions which reproduce a repressive society would be carried over into the new society. Repressive men would carry over their repression into the new society.

Now, at this farthest point, the question is: how can we possibly envisage the emergence of such qualitatively different needs and goals as organic, biological needs and goals and not as superimposed values? How can we envisage the emergence of these needs and satisfactions within and against the established society—that is to say, prior to liberation? That was the dialectic with which I started, that in a very definite sense we have to be free from in order to create a free society.

Needless to say, the dissolution of the existing system is the precondition for such qualitative change. And the more efficiently the repressive apparatus of the affluent societies operates, the less likely is a gradual transition from servitude to freedom. The fact that today we cannot identify any specific class or any specific group as a revolutionary force, this fact is no excuse for not using any and every possibility and method to arrest the engines of repression in the individual. The diffusion of potential opposition among the entire underlying population corresponds precisely to the total character of our advanced capitalist society. The internal contradictions of the system are as grave as ever before and likely to be aggravated by the violent expansion of capitalist imperialism. Not only the most general contradictions between the tremendous social wealth on the one hand, and the destructive, aggressive and wasteful use of this wealth on the other; but far more concrete contradictions such as the necessity for the system to automate, the continued reduction of the human base in physical labour-power in the material reproduction of society and thereby the tendency towards the draining of the sources of surplus profit. Finally, there is the threat of technological unemployment which even the most affluent society may no longer be capable of compensating by the creation of ever more parasitic and unproductive labour: all these contradictions exist. In reaction to them suppression, manipulation and integration are likely to increase.

But fulfillment is there, the ground can and must be prepared. The mutilated consciousness and the mutilated instincts must be broken. The sensitivity and the awareness of the new transcending, antagonistic values—they are there. And they are there, they are here, precisely among the still non-integrated social groups and among those who, by virtue of their privileged position, can pierce the ideological and material veil of mass communication and indoctrination—namely, the intelligentsia.

We all know the fatal prejudice, practically from the beginning, in the Labour Movement against the intelligentsia as catalyst of historical change. It is time to ask whether this prejudice against the intellectuals, and the inferiority complex of the intellectuals resulting from it, was not an essential factor in the development of the capitalist as well as the socialist societies: in the development and weakening of the opposition. The intellectuals usually went out to organize the others, to organize in the communities. They certainly did not use the potentiality they had to organize themselves, to organize among themselves not only on a regional, not only on a national, but on an international level. That is, in my view, today one of the most urgent tasks. Can we say that the intelligentsia is the agent of historical change? Can we say that the intelligentsia today is a revolutionary class? The answer I would give is: No, we cannot say that. But we can say, and I think we must say, that the intelligentsia has a decisive preparatory function, not more; and I suggest that this is plenty. By itself it is not and cannot be a revolutionary class, but it can become the catalyst, and it has a preparatory function—certainly not for the first time, that is in fact the way all revolution starts—but more, perhaps, today than ever before. Because—and for this too we have a very material and very concrete basis—it is from this group that the holders of decisive positions in the productive process will be recruited, in the future even more than hitherto. I refer to what we may call the increasingly scientific character of the material process of production, by virtue of which the role of the intelligentsia changes. It is the group from which the decisive holders of decisive positions will be recruited: scientists, researchers, technicians, engineers, even psychologists—because psychology will continue to be a socially necessary instrument, either of servitude or of liberation.

This class, this intelligentsia has been called the new working class. I believe this term is at best premature. They are—and this we should not forget—today the pet beneficiaries of the established system. But they are also at the very source of the glaring contradictions between the liberating capacity of science and its repressive and enslaving use. To activate the repressed and manipulated contradiction, to make it operate as a catalyst of change, that is one of the main tasks of the opposition today. It remains and must remain a political task.

Education is our job, but education in a new sense. Being theory as well as practice, political practice, education today is more than discussion, more than teaching and learning and writing. Unless and until it goes beyond the classroom, until and unless it goes beyond the college, the school, the university, it will remain powerless. Education today must involve the mind *and* the body, reason *and* imagination, the intellectual *and* the instinctual needs, because our entire existence has become the subject/object of politics, of social engineering. I emphasize, it is not a question of making the schools and universities, of making the educational system political. The educational system is political already. I need only remind you of the incredible degree to which (I am speaking of the US) universities are involved in huge research grants (the nature of which you know in many cases) by the government and the various quasi-governmental agencies.

The educational system *is* political, so it is not we who want to politicize the educational system. What we want is a counter-policy against the established policy. And in this sense we must meet this society on its own ground of total mobilization. We must confront indoctrination in servitude with indoctrination in freedom. We must each of us generate in ourselves, and try to generate in others, the instinctual need for a life without fear, without brutality, and without stupidity. And we must see that we can generate the instinctual and intellectual revulsion against the values of an affluence which spreads aggressiveness and suppression throughout the world.

Before I conclude I would like to say my bit about the Hippies. It seems to me a serious phenomenon. If we are talking of the emergence of an instinctual revulsion against the values of the affluent society, I think here is a place where we should look for it. It seems to me that the Hippies, like any non-conformist movement on the left, are split. That there are two parts, or parties, or tendencies. Much of it is mere masquerade and clownery on the private level, and therefore indeed, as Gerassi suggested, completely harmless, very nice and charming in many cases, but that is all there is to it. But that is not the whole story. There is in the Hippies, and especially in such tendencies in the Hippies as the Diggers and the Provos, an inherent political element—perhaps even more so in the US than here. It is the appearance indeed of new instinctual needs and values. This experience is there. There is a new sensibility against efficient and insane reasonableness. There is the refusal to play the rules of a rigid game, a game which one knows is rigid from the beginning, and the revolt against the compulsive cleanliness of puritan morality and the aggression bred by this puritan morality as we see it today in Vietnam among other things.

At least this part of the Hippies, in which sexual, moral and political rebellion are somehow united, is indeed a nonaggressive form of life: a demonstration of an aggressive non-aggressiveness which achieves, at least potentially, the demonstration of qualitatively different values, a transvaluation of values.

All education today is therapy: therapy in the sense of liberating man by all available means from a society in which, sooner or later, he is going to be transformed into a brute, even if he doesn't notice it any more. Education in this sense is therapy, and all therapy today is political theory and practice. What kind of political practice? That depends entirely on the situation. It is hardly imaginable that we should discuss this here in detail. I will only remind you of the various possibilities of demonstrations, of finding out flexible modes of demonstration which can cope with the use of institutionalized violence, of boycott, many other things—anything goes which is such that it indeed has a reasonable chance of strengthening the forces of the opposition.

We can prepare for it as educators, as students. Again I say, our role is limited. We are no mass movement. I do not believe that in the near future we will see such a mass movement.

I want to add one word about the so-called Third World. I have not spoken of the Third World because my topic was strictly liberation from the affluent society. I agree entirely with Paul Sweezy, that without putting the affluent society in the framework of the Third World it is not understandable. I also believe that here and now our emphasis must be on the advanced industrial societies—not forgetting to do whatever we can and in whatever way we can to support, theoretically and practically, the struggle for liberation in the neo-colonial countries which, if again they are not the final force of liberation, at least contribute their share—and it is a considerable share—to the potential weakening and disintegration of the imperialist world system.

Our role as intellectuals is a limited role. On no account should we succumb to any illusions. But even worse than this is to succumb to the wide-spread defeatism which we witness. The preparatory role today is an indispensable role. I believe I am not being too optimistic—I have not in general the reputation of being too optimistic—when I say that we can already see the signs, not only that *They* are getting frightened and worried but that there are far more concrete, far more tangible manifestations of the essential weakness of the system. Therefore, let us continue with what ever we can—no illusions, but even more, no defeatism.

Implications of Bioregionalism for a Radical Theory of Education

C. A. Bowers

Over the last decade we have witnessed a variety of radical models for thinking about education; but in the diversity that ranged from the free classroom of the neoromantics to the engineered classroom of the behaviorists (not to mention the more purely ideological proposals of the neo-Marxists that were never tested in the classroom), there was a common thread of understanding that betrayed what has been traditionally meant by the term "radical." The original meaning of the word *radicalis* involved going back to the most basic and fundamental source. When used in this way, radical thought means going beyond the view of reality framed by an ideological position. Thus, in a very real sense it means going beyond the ideological formulations of the various streams of liberalism and conservatism in order to get at the root issues. It does not mean, as interpreted by recent educational theorists, developing a complicated rationale for addressing the problem of individual freedom and empowerment. This view of radicalism simply involved working out the programmatic implications of the modern mind-set that was already taken for granted. A radical thinker, by way of contrast, pushes the starting point back to the most basic issues; and in today's world the maximizing of individual freedom is not the most basic issue we face.

Just as it can be argued, to paraphrase Gary Synder, that photosynthesis rather than labor is the true origin of wealth, there are a deeper set of issues that make problematic the very foundations of the bourgeois consciousness that characterizes current radical educational theory. These issues have to do with the destruction of our habitat and with the hubris of modern consciousness that rejects the possibility that we might learn from the wisdom of preliterate societies. Thus, the genuinely radical thinker is more likely to be considering the implications of Eric Havelock's *Preface to Plato* and Herbert Schneidau's *Sacred Discontent* than a revisionist interpretation of Marxism. The problems of inequality and restricted individual empowerment are not

Reprinted by permission of the publisher from Bowers, C. A., *Elements of a Post-Liberal Theory of Education*. (New York: Teachers College Press, © 1987 by Teachers College, Columbia University. All rights reserved.), pp. 158–172.

nearly as important as the cultural roots of our alienation from nature. Regardless of how our agenda for social reform is framed, the bottom line has to do with reversing the global ecological deterioration we are now witnessing.

The ecology movement of the sixties and early seventies helped to awaken many from the cultural myth that held out the promise of unending growth, but it lacked the conceptual sophistication necessary for a radical rethinking of the cultural roots of the problem. Pollution controls, recycling of materials, and campaigns to save endangered species were a few of the genuine achievements. Conservation seemed to be the key metaphor that designated the thrust of this political movement. Recently, a more radical movement made up of loosely affiliated groups in Europe, Great Britain, and North America has emerged. Known as die Grünen in the Federal Republic of Germany, the Ecology Party in Great Britain, the bioregionalists in North America, these groups are concerned with alleviating the danger of nuclear war, the ravaging effects of an industrial social order on the environment, and exploitative relationships between First and Third World countries. For our purposes, however, what is most important about this emergent movement are the conceptual foundations it is helping to lay for a genuinely radical critique of our culture and thus of our approach to education. The bioregionalists in North America seem to be the least controlled by assumptions of modernization and thus are able to ask the most probing questions about the belief systems that underlie our social practices. To accord them the serious attention they deserve, readers must be able to free themselves from the control of the mental habits reinforced by the language of the liberal paradigm.

The following resolution passed unanimously at a cattleman's meeting in Texas (1898) epitomizes the modern mind-set that the bioregionalists view as a form of cultural neurosis:

> *Resolved*, that none of us know, or care to know, anything about grasses, native or otherwise, outside the fact that for the present there are lots of them, the best on record, and we are after getting the most out of them while they last. (cited in Shepard 1982, p. 2)

This mind-set represents in its worst form the attitude of the invader who exploits the resources and moves on; when expressed in its most constructive form, it represents the attitude of the experimenter-explorer who turns inquiry into technology and moves on to the next intellectual quest without being concerned with the ensuing disruptions in either the cultural or physical environment. Both the invader and experimenter-explorer are driven by an inner quest: the one for profits and the other for truth and power. In both cases, the interdependencies that characterize the biotic community are put out of focus.

Echoing the warnings of earlier environmentalists about depleting resources faster than they can be replaced locally and then drawing down the resource base of distant habitats, the bioregionalists have directed their attention to the development of a culture that is rooted in the natural world. As Kirkpatrick Sale put it, a sustainable culture is "in harmony with natural systems and rhythms, constrained by natural limits and capacities and developed according to the natural configurations of the earth and its inherent life forms" (Sale 1985, p. 24). The model for a culture that involves participation of responsible ecological citizens rather than mastery over nature through rational control is not, according to the bioregionalists, to be found in futuristic thinking that seeks power through science and technology. The genuine radicalness of their thinking is clearly reflected in Sale's observation that, if we are to become dwellers within rather than masters over the biotic community, "we must try to regain the spirit of the ancient Greeks, who considered the earth as a living creature, which they worshiped with the name Gaea. We must try to learn that she is, in every real sense, *sacred*, and that there is therefore a holy way to confront her and her works, a way of awe and admiration and respect and veneration that simply will not permit despoliation or abuse" (Sale, p. 24). The suggestion that preliterate ancient societies possessed a form of wisdom that we must recover as part of our living traditions and that we must include the non-human in our sense of community, as well as develop a "sacramental food-chain mutual sharing consciousness"—to quote Gary Snyder, presents a real challenge to the assumptions upon which modern consciousness is based. Yet there is more to the bioregional position that we will touch on briefly before turning to educational implications.

The bioregionalists also take a strong stand against the current organization of society into nation states. Existing political boundaries that influence economic and social practices, as well as the manner in which citizens think about themselves, reflect the historical outcome of political struggles for power and administrative control. The bioregional view is that politics should be attuned to the requirements of a life-territory, which must take account of the life-sustaining characteristics of a habitat—the watershed, soils, and renewable and non-renewable resources that make up the biotic community. The word "place" is often used by bioregionalists as a way of designating a form of politics attuned to nature rather than the dictates of ideology. Thus they reject the current view of the nation state and suggest that a new basis for political units might be found in the way North American Indian tribes occupied distinct bioregions.

In place of the major activities that occupy a modern society—internationalization of economic activity (both in terms of production and mass markets), advancement of scientific forms of knowledge, and a continual quest for more efficient and rationally controlled technologies—the bioregionalists offer an alternative vision that is likely to have little appeal to anomic individuals who are habituated to the fast and flashy pace of modern consumerism. In place of hi-tech and the impersonality of the market place, they urge a rediscovery of how to use our hands and bodies in dealing with the fundamentals of life-cultivating activities, such as growing and preparing food, and in sharing the common tasks of the community as it adjusts to the cycles of the seasons. Their view involves a more communal life style, the use of intermediate, less energy-intensive technologies, and the recovery of the symbolic richness of oral traditions. This is not a vision that will have immediate appeal to many people; in fact, it is likely to be viewed as a backward step from the conveniences associated with modern society.

Judgments about a life style that involve a completely different set of criteria for determining the meaning of human fulfillment will in part be distorted by the ideological conditioning of the existing culture. Yet at a deeper level, the question of whether the views of the bioregionalists should be taken seriously will *not* turn on whether a society organized according to the principles of self-sufficiency and ecological balance will provide as much personal pleasure, leisure, and freedom as some of us now enjoy. We will have to take them seriously, I suspect, because their arguments about what happens when a dominant species within an ecosystem depletes the life-sustaining resources have been thoroughly documented. In the terminology of the bioregionalists, the draw-down of the resource base is followed by an overshoot stage in which severe disruptions and conflicts over increasingly limited resources occur, followed by a crash where the population is reduced to a level where the resources can recover. It occurs in all species, and the historical record indicates that human cultures are not exempt from the fate of exceeding environmental equilibrium. In *Always Coming Home*, which Ursula Le Guin referred to as an "archeology of the future," a group of people, the Kesh, choose to remain behind in a devastated environment from which everyone else has escaped in a galactic spaceship that is no longer dependent upon minerals, plants, and soil (a common escape scenario for technicists who believe meaningful life can be sustained in a totally artificial environment). Instead, the Kesh, the people of the future Le Guin projects as inhabiting a valley in North California, live in small clans as hunters and gatherers. Their technology, form of education, ceremonies, and customs do not represent a progression beyond what we have today; they are instead remarkably similar to premodern cultures that were attuned to the rhythms of the environment. Equally missing from their mythology is our own belief that purposive rationality is an ultimate source of power, allowing us to escape the laws that require other species to live within ecological balance. I suspect that Le Guin, raised in a family that was sensitive to the wisdom of subsistence cultures toward their habitats, represents the more prophetic bioregionalist voice.

Regardless of the questions we may have about the implications of the bioregionalists' argument (Do we have to abandon our credit cards and cities? Do we really have to give up our fossil fuel addiction?), we cannot ignore the evidence that we are now nearing "overshoot" where the demands of an increasingly world-wide consumer culture will exhaust essential resources. The main issue facing educators now is to decide whether to wait for more definitive evidence that we have exceeded ecological limits or to take the threat seriously by beginning to rethink those aspects of our belief system that do not take into account our ecological interdependence. The first approach would involve thinking about the relationship between education and society within the current conceptual framework that associates empowerment with continued progress in the areas of individualism and rationality. In effect, the current cultural trajectory would be supported by a form of education based on any one of the four archetypal models of educational liberalism discussed in the earlier sections of this book—neoromantic free classrooms, the engineered classroom in the Skinner-Taylor mold, the Deweyian classroom that teaches the method of scientific problem-solving, and the emancipatory, consciousness-raising pedagogy of Freire.

A second approach for educational theorists is to give serious attention to some of the basic concepts of bioregional thinking, partly because the concepts are fundamentally sound in their own right and partly because they take into account the forms of understanding we must possess as ecological limits force us to modify our cultural beliefs and practices. This is where educational theorists must be able to free themselves from a restrictive discourse where the vocabulary and conceptual categories force thought into predetermined directions. The basic concepts essential to the biore-gionalist position, as stated earlier, represent a radical turning away from the assump-tions that underlie the ideological positions that evolved out of the Enlightenment, including Marxism (Bookchin 1971).

Alienation, a key concept in the thinking of bioregionalists, is one of those powerful images that can be given a substantially different meaning by changing the root metaphor. Existentialist literature, for example, often started with assumptions that the individual is basically alone and that through an act of will individual life could be given authentic meaning and a sense of purpose. Those who could not find the authority for giving their own life a sense of direction escaped by living an inauthentic life dictated by group norms. Thus, for the existentialists, social conform-ity led to self-alienation. From a more Durkheimian perspective, alienation results from a breakdown in a shared normative framework, with the result being an anomic individual who experiences a loss of meaning. By contrast, the bioregionalist's under-standing of alienation does not start with either the image of the authentic, self-sufficient individual or a concern with the social defenses against individual malaise. The root metaphor of the bioregionalists is the interdependency of all life forms. Consequently, for them, alienation is expressed in the illusion of being free to choose one's place, to be self-accountable for one's actions, and to be oriented toward fulfilling personal wants and goals (values highly regarded within some streams of liberalism). This is really to be rootless and to confuse real power with a cultural myth that equates happiness with freedom.

For the bioregionalists, overcoming alienation is knowing and being responsible for your place—which involves coming to terms with the most fundamental aspects of the spatial and temporal aspects of existence. In the words of Wendell Berry:

> From the perspective of the environmental crisis of our time I think we have to add . . . a further realization: if the land is made fit for human habitation by memory and "old association," it is also true that by memory and association men are made fit to inhabit the land. At present our society is almost entirely nomadic, without the comfort or discipline of such memories, and it is moving about on the face of the continent with a mindless destructiveness, of substance and of meaning and of value, that makes Sherman's march to the sea look like a prank. Without a complex knowledge of one's place, and without the faithfulness to one's place on which such knowledge depends, it is inevitable that the place will be used carelessly, and eventually destroyed. (1972, pp. 68–69)

Gary Snyder put it more succinctly: "You know whether or not a person knows where he is by whether or not he knows the plants. By whether or not he knows what the soils and waters do" (1980, p. 69). Stated somewhat differently, modern interpreta-tions of alienation involve foregrounding the individual by putting out of focus the background (place or context). For the bioregionalist both are integral to each other.

Yet there is more to the bioregionalist position that has direct implications for thinking about the purpose of education, as well as for rethinking certain prejudices that have long held a privileged position in educational circles. A knowledge of place and a concern with rootedness is not the expression of a nostalgic desire to return to the simplicity of a more primitive past. The bioregionalists are really concerned with the problem of empowerment—and their way of understanding the process of empowerment leads them to deviate significantly from how it is conceptualized by the different interpreters of educational liberalism.

In contrast to the anthropocentrism that characterizes the four archetypal interpretations of educational liberalism, the bioregionalist views empowerment in terms of living in harmony with the rhythms of the environment. In more concrete terms, this means learning "how to give full rein to those cooperative and communal and participatory selves, those symbiotic and responsible and multi-dimensional selves that have been blunted and confined" by the binary pattern of thinking that has contributed to the cultural forms of alienation associated with modern consciousness (Sale 1985, p. 33). A brief overview of what has been lost through the long march to achieve the current individualistic and rationalistic mode of consciousness can be seen in how binary thinking progressed by declaring the absolute supremacy of one aspect of experience and denying its supposed opposite qualities. What was lost through this binary process of selection and rejection represents essential elements that must be recovered if we are to overcome the alienation that separates us from our environment.

The following overview of these areas of human experience that have become a casualty of binary thinking is really intended to identify issues that must become part of the discussion of educational reform; if you will, it will help to recover part of the language that will enable us to think about aspects of the educational process that the more restrictive discourses of educational liberalism put out of focus. The overview touches on exceedingly complicated cultural developments, many of which are still being argued, and it is in no way intended as a list of prescriptions for reforming public education. But it does suggest a sense of direction that deserves serious consideration.

The sense of estrangement from the environment that characterizes the modern attitude toward exploitation of resources and ownership is fundamentally different from the way in which many traditional cultures view the earth as alive and sacred. In a fascinating study of how monotheistic religions or the West introduced a binary separation in how the sacred was experienced, Herbert Schneidau (1976) makes the point that belief in a God that could not be located within the environment represented a radical and, in terms of its recent introduction, novel departure from the "animal-man-god interpretation" that is essential to mythological consciousness. By investing the abstract Yahweh with absolute power, the cosmic continuum was disrupted; ancient religion, as a form of geography that "organized space into sacred configurations," to quote Schneidau (p. 71), was now viewed as paganism. The binary logic that made the sacred a transaction between man and God, rather than seeing all forms of giving and taking of life as bound up together, thus separated (alienated) humans from a religious sense of the interdependence of all life forms. Without this sense of interdependence, based on awe, reverence, and respect rather than self-interest and cost effectiveness, there are no limits on how far we can go in exploiting the animal, plant, and mineral resources.

The bioregionalists are very much aware that a culture living in harmony with the environmnt must recover this part of ancient memory that was so attuned to the sacred, as opposed to taking the modern approach of legislating limits and using expert-technicist studies as the basis of authority. In contrast to the natural attitude of those of us who operate within one or more of the conceptual configurations of educational liberalism (some of us are given to syncretistic tendencies where we borrow willy-nilly from all four streams), Native Americans such as the Navajos experience the sacred as a basic part of their sense of empowerment; and basic to their understanding of the alienation of the dominant Western culture. Part of the declaration signed by 64 elders of the Independent Dine' (Navajo) Nation at Big Mountain clearly puts in focus how different views of empowerment relate not only to spiritual but ecological survival: "Our sacred shrines have been destroyed. . . . Our Mother Earth is raped by the exploitation of coal, uranium, oil, natural gas, and helium. . . . We speak for the winged beings, the four-legged beings, and those gone before us and the coming generation. We seek no changes in our livelihood because this Natural life is our only known survival and it's our sacred law" (Mandler 1981, p. 1).

The binary thinking that separates rationalism and mythological consciousness, which many will see as the contending paradigms represented in this quotation, can also be seen in the way modern consciousness has privileged literacy over oral traditions. For the last one hundred and fifty years, literacy has been so closely intertwined with the idea of empowerment that it has become almost the chief criteria for determinating whether people are to be considered as progressive and civilized or backward and primitive. The deeper connections between literacy and the rise of the public school are important both in terms of the social stratification that resulted from the stratification of knowledge and in terms of how schooled literacy contributed to the loss of localized cultural identities (Cook-Gumperz 1986, p. 36). Although the contribution of schooled literacy to the creation of a mass, rootless society is important to the bioregionalist's analysis of the ecological instability of modern society, our main concern is to clarify how the form of empowerment that we automatically associate with literacy contributes to alienation in the bioregional sense of the term. This part of the argument, in turn, puts in focus additional issues that need to be addressed as we move into a post-liberal era of thinking about how education, culture, and the environment interrelate. In looking at the dark side of literacy, it is important to remember the dangers of continuing to be caught up in the categories dictated by a binary form of thinking; thus our brief analysis of literacy is not meant to be interpreted as a total rejection of literacy in favor of an uncritical acceptance of orality as the chief means of sharing knowledge with others.

The work of Walter Ong, Eric Havelock, and others has largely overturned the long-held view that the introduction of the alphabet that made modern writing possible was primarily a technological advance in enabling us to be more rational and objective in our thinking and in contributing to the upward spiral of knowledge (civilization) through a more effective means of sharing knowledge with other rational individuals. Their contribution was in clarifying how literacy differs from oral communication, particularly in how the two modes of communication influence consciousness as well as patterns of social interaction. In contrast to the ideology that now privileges literacy as culturally superior to orality, they found that the transmission process of reading and writing amplifies certain human attributes and patterns and reduces others. Literacy, in brief, amplifies the sense of individualism (writing and reading are highly privatized experiences); an abstract form of thought that allows for a careful editorial refinement of text; a text that is divorced from the living person who produced it and thus fixed in time—allowing for analysis and comparison with other fixed texts; and impersonal communication where the writer has to imagine the reading public (Ong 1982). In addition to empowering the analytical mind, literacy contributes to the reification of the word and thus to the decontextualization of knowledge. Contrary to popular thinking, empowerment is not the binary opposite of alienation; in the case of literacy, it contributes to a form or consciousness that is alienated by virtue of what is reduced or eliminated in communicating knowledge to others.

Ong points out that in contrast to the printed word the spoken word is always a social event, an ongoing action, that allows intuition, context, non-verbal communication, memory, intonations, character of participants, and all the senses to be fully involved (1977, pp. 12–49). As a living event, oral communication involves adjusting the messages to the nuance of the social context and thus serves to renew the shared definitions of reality that underpin communal life. It is, in effect, more dialectical in that both the memory and perspective of the participants remodel what has become irrelevant in the collective experience, rather than, as with abstract thought, creating a disjuncture. As Havelock put it: "New information and new experience are continually grafted on to inherited models" (1963, p. 122). As the text, so to speak, is always updated in the oral tradition, education does not involve absorbing abstract and thus possibly irrelevant or destructive forms of knowledge. But this form of empowerment—in terms of communicating about what is lived—reduces those mental qualities associated with analysis, independent perspective, and the abstract accumulation of knowledge that can be later drawn upon.

Clearly both oral and literate cultures provide for their members different forms of empowerment and alienation. Yet this is not recognized by an ideology that represents literacy as the primary form of empowerment and the key for becoming a modern individual. For instance, Freire's arguments for literacy represent a belief that is so strong and unqualified that he fails to recognize that his educational reforms would contribute to structuring consciousness in a manner that supports the very form of society he wants to overthrow. Our real purpose here, however, is not to engage the blind spots in the thinking of liberal theorists of education; it is to understand how the alienating characteristics of literacy contribute to a form of culture that is out of harmony with its habitat.

Ron and Suzanne Scollon, two linguists who have thought a great deal about how orality and literacy relate to the problem of alienation in the modern world, go to the heart of the matter by reminding us that language is primarily about relationships and only secondarily about ideas (1985, p. 15). We have tended to emphasize the latter, which is really the signifying function of language or what could be called, in terms of the sociology of knowledge, the constituting function of language. But naming "What Is" also involves establishing how the relationships among the different entities named are to be understood, as well as the relationship between the speaker (writer) and that part of the world that is being symbolically represented. It is this latter function of language that the Scollons draw our attention to, particularly how orality and literacy constitute fundamentally different relationships.

The relationships that are reinforced through literacy are in part a function of what is amplified and reduced through the use of print technology; they also reflect our deepest metaphysical assumptions about the world and our place in it. In terms of print technology, the symbolic representation of ideas is amplified, but the relationship between the ideas and their phenomenological origins is reduced. Our cultural orientation of emphasizing writing in the third person and of representing our knowledge as objective (actually an orientation dictated by a class set of epistemological assumptions) fosters a relationship of separation between the word and the person. This separation, where the word takes on an independent, reified existence, creates a reversal in which abstract and fixed symbolic representations are taken to be real, while the life world of the writer (and reader) are put out of focus. The Scollons observed that as a language form, literacy alters our sense of relationship in the most fundamental way by shifting our "focus from what is primary to what is secondary." The primary is actually our embeddedness as sensory and cognitive beings in an interdependent biocommunity; the secondary is what we are able to represent in symbolic form about our existence. The reversal makes the abstract more real than what is experienced, which exceeds in richness, complexity, and depth what can be communicated through the technology of language—especially the printed word. For the Scollons the primacy given to literacy strengthens the kinds of relationships that are alienating, with abstractions being substituted for living relationships between people and between people and the biotic community. They also point out that literacy involves an asymmetry of power, in which the writer and reader relate to each other as sender and receiver (p. 19).

The consequences of the domination of literacy over orality can be seen in how we view knowledge and where it is to be located. As literacy de-emphasizes context as part of the message system, it has led to the distorted view that only the explicit forms of understanding capable of being represented in symbolic form can be viewed as valid knowledge. Tacit understanding of the cultural codes that regulate most aspects of social life thus tend to be ignored or downgraded in importance. The emphasis on literacy also privileges the analytical mind over the body, with the consequence that we fail to recognize the importance of embodied forms of knowledge to our sense of empowerment. David M. Levin makes the point that

> the body is, or is at, the source of all our knowledge. . . . As an ancestral body, an "ancient" body of genetically encoded reproduction, for example, it is the biophysical element which binds our existence to that of our mortal ancestors, even the earliest; as a cultural body, it transcends the chains of nature, participates in the shaping of history, and serves, whether we will it or not—though our willingness makes a difference—as an impressionable medium for the transmission and sedimentation of cultural norms, values, and meanings. (1985, p. 171)

In addition to the attunements, dispositions and preestablished understandings of the body, knowledge can be understood as embodied in our technologies. Becoming sensitive to these embodied forms of knowledge as the foundations of our empowerment also requires that we recognize the environment as a sustaining and shaping force.

In order to overcome the alienation that separates "the word from the body, the society from the earth, and our reason from our spirituality," the Scollons suggest an approach to education that addresses the problems of relationships and empowerment—which they view as intertwined with each other (p. 32). Their educational proposals are grounded in the Confucian idea that the problems of the world, including the fate of the environment, cannot be separated from self-understanding. But most importantly, self-understanding involves getting in touch with the basic organic categories of existence—past, place, relationships, and future possibilities. These are the most fundamental of human relations that are put out of focus by the rationalistic, anthropocentric view of the universe that comes down from the Enlightenment and is currently reinforced in the four interpretations of educational liberalism that continue to serve as our primary models for thinking about education. Their educational proposal addresses the connection between the problem of empowerment and the need for a culture that is in ecological balance—two issues that should be a central concern to educational theorists.

A curriculum guided by a concern with helping students get in touch with the organic categories of their existence must begin with learning about the past. For the Scollons this should include, in addition to the past preserved as part of the Western literate tradition, the legacy of the oral traditions: e.g., the *Iliad* and the *Odyssey* of Homer, the Bible, the Koran, as well as the wisdom given us by the great thinkers of India and China. Learning the oral traditions of the past, as well as the present, provides insight into the archetypal models of how people have confronted and resolved the deepest existential questions. It also involves acquiring the conceptual basis necessary for recognizing the past in the present, including those aspects of earlier forms of consciousness that were more attuned to the cycles of life. By viewing the self (as a carrier of language) as part of a symbolic continuum that stretches back to the earliest formation of our conceptual maps, learning the past is really a way of learning about the self. Yet just as there needs to be a balance between the oral and literate traditions of the past, there also needs to be a balance between being immersed in the oral patterns of retelling important stories and the individualizing analytical form of thought that is associated with literacy. Learning the past through the spoken word helps to attune the student to relationships with others that are grounded in a shared context. The power of this form of learning can be seen in how individuals, in learning their native language, acquire efficacy while at the same time being bonded to the patterns of community life.

That all forms of life can only be understood as they are situated in their place or context suggests the importance of the second organic category. In contrast to the various expressions of educational liberalism that foreground the virtue of self-directing individuals by putting the background (place) out of focus, the Scollons echo the bioregional concern with understanding the life-sustaining processes and resources of one's place. In the past the more explicit part of the school socialization process took the students' relationship to place for granted, with the result that, later as adults, they were caught up in culturally prescribed routines that were largely carried out without adequate awareness of their disruptive effects on other forms of life that shared the same place. A curriculum that takes the life-place seriously as one of the organic categories of existence would focus on the relationship between the cultural life style of students and the resource base of the region: soil, mineral, water, plant, and animal life. Yet learning about the relationship between self and place would not properly clarify the nature of the interdependencies if current cultural lenses were used. Studying the nature of soils (and which cultural practices deplete them) and the characteristics of animal and plant life as though they were being inventoried for future exploitation would simply exacerbate the problem. Learning about place really involves, as Berry, Snyder, and the Scollons remind us, developing a spiritual understanding of the earth as a reference point for understanding self.

This may sound strange to the ear attuned to a language that represents our relationship to the earth in terms of I-It rather than I-Thou. Nevertheless, the capacity to have an I-Thou relationship that is confirming, open, and transforming provides a way of recognizing that we do not have to live entirely by cultural models that involve exploitive and calculating relationships. In terms of curriculum, understanding place does not involve bringing religion, in the usual sense of the term, into the classroom. But it does provide a point of departure for examining the environmental consequences of cultural beliefs and patterns of action. This would involve examining the cultural beliefs that influence the sense of commitment (or lack of it) to place, as well as recognizing what human actions toward the environment are proscribed (and why). In terms of the Scollon's curricular recommendations, this would involve examining how bioregions are intersected by political-cultural lines, and how the bioregion has fared on both sides of the dividing line (p. 33). Comparisons between modern and transitional cultures (e.g., Hopi and Navajo) in terms of their respective impact on the environment would yield useful insights into how the spiritual aspects of culture influence our relationship to place.

The study of place should also involve examining the political and economic implications of how resources are utilized. This part of the curriculum would help students understand the problems connected with living within the resource base of a bioregion, the forms of dependencies that result from misuse of resources, the application of destructive technologies, and the political and economic relationships that do not represent the interests of the people living in a bioregion.

The two other organic categories, cultivating relationships and enlarging the future, have curricular implications that relate directly to learning past and place. Cultivating relationships, in curricular terms, requires an understanding of the models of good and evil that are exhibited in the world's great literature and oral traditions. Understanding what is right and wrong in others and how context may blur these categories is essential to being able to correct within oneself those personal characteristics that undermine mutually empowering relationships with others. The Scollons put in sharper focus the relationship between a curriculum that provides insight into the human character and the student's self-understanding and ability to cultivate relationships by using a quotation from Confucius: "If you hate something in your superiors, do not practice it on those below you; if you hate a thing in those below you, do not do it when working for those over you" (p. 35). Cultivating good relationships with others thus involves understanding self, and this is aided by studying the cultural models and values that both serve as reference points and have been internalized as part of self.

Enlarging the future, according to the Scollons, follows from the study of the past and place. One of the purposes of the latter is to help prepare for the future. The

Scollons want to distinguish between planning for the future, which involves the purposive rational mind that often takes a Maginot Line approach to dealing with a changing environment, and preparing for the future. In curricular terms, enlarging (or preparing) for the future involves learning how to be open to new relationships and how to develop the capacities for negotiation and cooperation. It also involves developing as part of one's self, and encouraging in others, a vision of a shared future. Awareness of a future that is organized around an image of self-fulfillment or what one will do as an isolated individual is not as enlarging as a sense of future that includes relationships with others. This should also involve, as the Scollons remind us, a sense of the future that takes account of the characteristics of the bioregion. Thus, enlarging the individual's sense of future becomes tied to preserving the life sustaining characteristics of the larger biocommunity.

These general guidelines for organizing curricula allow for the specific content to be adjusted to the uniqueness of cultural groups and characteristics of the bioregion. The guiding questions—What soil series are you standing on? What species of animals and plants are on the verge of extinction in your area? and so forth—can be asked of each region, but the answers and thus curriculum content will reflect the diversity of regional characteristics and the teacher's imagination and resourcefulness. The important consideration here does not have so much to do with the fact that a bioregional approach to thinking about education leaves us without a fully fleshed out curriculum or set of pedagogical practices; rather it has to do with identifying a set of priorities that challenge in the most fundamental way the conceptual underpinnings of the liberal paradigm. The argument that literacy is the key to enlightened thinking, that locating authority in the rational judgment or emotive response of the individual, and that because of the progressive nature of change we should emancipate people from the authority of traditional beliefs and practices are all characteristic of the discourse of educational liberalism. The bioregional concern with understanding empowerment in terms of a culture that enables its members to live in harmony with the rhythms and resources of the natural environment introduces a new metaphorical language that makes sense only if we substantially revise the paradigm that has turned such words as progress, emancipation, individualism, critical rationality, and literacy into educational ideals that support an ecologically destructive ideology. By introducing into the discourse of educational and social reform the metaphorical language of cultural practices attuned to long-term survival, both in a spiritual and ecological sense, the bioregionalists are challenging us to reshape the language that will guide how we perceive the world. The task for educational theorists will be to reconcile Black Elk with John Dewey, Confucius with Skinner. This will involve a far more radical discourse than the one now driven by the variant forms of educational emancipation.

REFERENCES

Berry, Wendell. 1983. "Standing By Words." In *Standing By Words*. San Francisco: North Point Press.

———. 1972. *A Continuous Harmony: Essays Cultural and Agricultural*. New York: Harcourt Brace Jovanovich, Harvest Books.

Bookchin, Murray. 1971. *Post-Scarcity Anarchism*. Berkeley, Calif.: Ramparts Press.

Cook-Gumperz, Jenny. 1986. *The Social Construction of Literacy*. Cambridge: Cambridge University Press.

Havelock, Eric. 1963. *Preface to Plato*. Cambridge: Harvard University Press.

———. 1982. *The Literate Revolution in Greece and Its Cultural Consequences*. Princeton: Princeton University Press.

Le Guin, Ursula K. 1985. *Always Coming Home*. New York: Harper & Row.

Levin, David Michael. 1985. *The Body's Recollection of Being*. London: Routledge & Kegan Paul.

Mandler, Jerry. 1981. "Kit Carson in a Three Piece Suit." *The CoEvoluton Quarterly* (Winter).

Ong, Walter. 1977. *Interfaces of the Word*. Ithaca, N.Y.: Cornell University Press.

———. 1982. *Orality and Literacy: The Technologizing of the Word*. London: Methuen.

Sale, Kirkpatrick. 1985. *Dwellers in the Land: The Bioregional Vision*. San Francisco: Sierra Club Books.

Schneidau, Herbert N. 1976. *Sacred Discontent: The Bible and Western Tradition*. Baton Rouge: Louisiana State University Press.

Scollon, Ron, and Scollon, Suzanne. 1985. "The Problem of Power" (monograph). Haines, Ala.: The Gutenberg Dump.

Shepard, Paul, 1982. *Nature and Madness*. San Francisco: Sierra Club Books.

Synder, Gary, 1980. *The Real Work: Interviews and Talks, 1964–1979*. New York: New Directions.

A New Sensibility

Sallie McFague

"Sticks and stones may break my bones, but names can never hurt me." This taunt from childhood is haunting in its lying bravado. It *is* the "names" that hurt; one would prefer the sticks and stones. Names matter because what we call something, how we name it, is to a great extent what it is to us. We are the preeminent creatures of language, and though language does not exhaust human reality, it qualifies it in profound ways. It follows, then, that naming can be hurtful, and that it can also be healing or helpful. The ways we name ourselves, one another, and the world cannot be taken for granted; we must look at them carefully to see if they heal or hurt.

How are we naming reality in the twilight years of the twentieth century? I would suggest that we live most of the time and in most ways by outmoded, anachronistic names. We are not naming ourselves, one another, and our earth in ways commensurate *with our own times* but are using names from a bygone time. However helpful and healing these names may have been once upon a time, they are hurtful now. And Christian theology that is done on the basis of anachronistic naming is also hurtful.

We live in our imaginations and our feelings in a bygone world, one under the guidance of a benevolent but absolute deity, a world that is populated by independent individuals (mainly human beings) who relate to one another and to other forms of life in hierarchical patterns. But this is not *our* world, and to continue doing theology on its assumptions is hurtful, for it undermines our ability to accept the new sensibility of our time, one that is holistic and responsible, that is inclusive of all forms of life, and that acknowledges the interdependence of all life.

We can approach the issue of the difference between the bygone world and our world by evoking some images that may help us feel our world from the inside. The first is a passage from an early essay by Pierre Teilhard de Chardin called "Cosmic

Life," which, despite being more lyrical than his later writings, is characteristic of his mature position. The essay, as he himself says, presents the "fire in his vision." In the passage he is attempting to *feel* "matter."

> . . . and I allowed my consciousness to sweep back to the farthest limit of my body, to ascertain whether I might not extend outside myself. I stepped down into the most hidden depths of my being, lamp in hand and ears alert, to discover whether, in the deepest recesses of the blackness within me, I might not see the glint of the waters of the current that flows on, whether I might not hear the murmur of their mysterious waters that rise from the uttermost depths and will burst forth no man knows where. With terror and intoxicating emotion, I realized that my own poor trifling existence was one with the immensity of all that is and all that is still in process of becoming.[1]

He takes a journey into the unknown, the mystery of his own body, and with lamp in hand tries to see and hear what he is not usually aware of: his connection with everything else that has been, is, and will be. The atoms, molecules, and cells that constitute his organic structure connect him in profound ways to everything else in the universe. As he remarks, "My life is not my own," for although he appears to be an individual to his own consciousness, there lies hidden within him the dense multitude of beings "whose infinitely patient and lengthy labour" has resulted in "the *phylum*" of which, as he put it, he is "for the moment the extreme bud."[2]

The world that Teilhard helps us to feel is one whose heartbeat is relationship and interdependence. The poet Wallace Stevens expresses it precisely: "Nothing is itself taken alone. Things are because of interrelations or interconnections."[3] Moreover, in this world the absolute divisions between human beings and other beings and even between the organic and the inorganic are softened, as are many of the hierarchical dualisms that have accompanied those divisions: spirit/flesh, subject/object, male/female, mind/body. The holistic paradigm suggested in place of the atomistic paradigm has, I believe, revolutionary consequences for Christian theology. Not simply to accept this paradigm but to feel it, to incorporate it into our imaginations, is a necessary dimension of the new sensibility required of Christian theology in our time.

The second image I would like to evoke comes from Jonathan Schell's book *The Fate of the Earth*. In this passage he speaks of extinction—the power to extinguish ourselves and perhaps all life—that is the consequence of nuclear knowledge.

> Death cuts off life; extinction cuts off birth. Death dispatches into the nothingness after life each person who has been born; extinction in one stroke locks up in the nothingness before life all the people who have not yet been born. For we are finite beings at both ends of our existence—natal as well as mortal—and it is the natality of our kind that extinction threatens. We have always been able to send people to their death, but only now has it become possible to prevent all birth and so doom all future human beings to un-creation.[4]

We have never before been in the position of potential "uncreators" of life, of being able to prohibit birth, but it is precisely imagining the extent of this power and feeling deeply what it means to live in a world where this is possible that is part of the new sensibility required for Christian theology. In such a world the future is not simply given to us, as it has always been, but must be achieved.[5] Humanity cannot assume that benevolent forces will take care of the future, for we know—and shall always know—that we have the power to extinguish it. The permanence of this knowledge means that disarmament alone is not sufficient; we must, as Schell says, "learn to live politically in the world in which we already live scientifically."[6] It is also true, I believe, that we must learn to live theologically in the world in which nuclear knowledge is a permanent possession and responsibility.

The third image for a new sensibility comes from a famous passage by Nietzsche:

> What then is truth? A mobile army of metaphors, metonymics, anthropomorphisms: in short, a sum of human relations which become poetically and rhetorically intensi- fied, metamorphosed, adorned, and after long usage, seem to a nation fixed, canonic and binding; truths are illusions of which one has forgotten that they *are* illusions; worn-out metaphors which have become powerless to affect the senses, coins which have their obverse effaced and now are no longer of account as coins but merely as metal.[7]

Nietzsche is saying not only that we construct the worlds we inhabit but also that we forget we have done so. The works of the imagination, the world views in which we live, were once valuable currency for the conduct of life. But what we call truth, says Nietzsche, are worn-out metaphors, coins that have their stated value erased and hence are worthless metal. He presents a challenge—a double-edged one—that Chris- tian theology must take seriously. No longer is it possible to insist without question on the "fixed, canonic and binding" character of metaphors and the concepts built upon them that have come to us "after long usage." The constructive character of theology must be acknowledged, and this becomes of critical importance when the world in which we live is profoundly different from the world in which many of the traditional metaphors and concepts gained currency. Theologians must think experimentally, must risk novel constructions in order to be theologians *for our time.*

The other challenge raised by Nietzsche involves the question whether, if theol- ogy (as well as all other constructive thought) is profoundly metaphorical, it is only "illusion." Is it only the play of fantasy, with one construction as good (or as bad) as another? Nietzsche does not in this passage explicitly address the question of the status of metaphor; he addresses only the status of worn-out metaphor. Yet he raises the former question implicitly with his contrast between metaphors that once were powerful and those which have lost their currency. The question of truth with which Nietzsche sharply challenges us cannot be avoided, for the metaphors, the construc- tions, we accept and live by may well control the future—may help determine both whether we have one and what it will be.

We need to look carefully at each of the aspects of our world suggested by Teilhard de Chardin, Schell, and Nietzsche, and at the implications of those aspects for Christian theology.

A HOLISTIC VIEW OF REALITY

During the last twenty years, feminist Christian theologians have made a strong case against the androcentric, hierarchical character of the Western religious tradition. They have insisted that the humanity of women be given equal status and that the divisions that separate people—male/female, rich/poor, old/young, white/colored, straight/gay, Christian/non-Christian—be minimized in order to create an inclusive vision. As Elisabeth Schüssler Fiorenza puts it, "Not the holiness of the elect but the wholeness *of all* is the central vision of Jesus."[8] But only in a few instances has this vision been extended to the nonhuman world.[9] The feminist theologians who have given attention to the nonhuman world have been, for the most part, those involved in Goddess traditions and witchcraft, for whom the body, the earth, and nature's cycles are of critical importance.[10] Those of us within the Christian tradition have much to learn from these sources,[11] but even these feminists have not, I believe, focused primarily on the intrinsic value of the nonhuman in a way sufficient to bring about the needed change of consciousness. Nor have other forms of liberation theology, which generally speaking are more anthropocentric than is feminist theology. All forms of liberation theology insist on the "deprivatizing" of theology,[12] but to date this has been for the most part limited to human beings and has not included the destiny of the cosmos. The principal insight of liberation theologies—that redemption is not the rescue of certain individuals for eternal life in another world but the fulfillment of all humanity in the political and social realities of this world—must be further deprivatized to include the well-being of all life. This is the case not only because unless we adopt an ecological perspective recognizing human dependence on its environment, we may well not survive, but also, of equal theological if not pragmatic importance, because such a perspective is the dominant paradigm of our time and theology that is not done in conversation with this paradigm is not theology *for our time.*

What is at stake here is not a sentimental love of nature or a leveling of all distinctions between human beings and other forms of life but the realization, as Teilhard de Chardin says, that his and everyone else's "poor trifling existence" is "one with the immensity of all that is and all that is still in the process of becoming." We are not separate, static, substantial individuals relating in external ways—and in ways of our choice—to other individuals, mainly human ones, and in minor ways to other forms of life. On the contrary, the evolutionary, ecological perspective insists that we are, in the most profound ways, "not our own": we belong from the cells of our bodies to the finest creations of our minds, to the intricate, constantly changing cosmos. The ecosystem of which we are part is a whole: the rocks and waters, atmosphere and soil, plants, animals, and human beings interact in dynamic, mutually supportive ways that make all talk of atomistic individualism indefensible. Relationship and interdependence, change and transformation, not substance, changelessness, and perfection, are the categories within which a theology for our day must function.

To appreciate the extent to which we are embedded in the evolutionary ecosystem requires an act of imagination, since the Western sensibility has traditionally been nurtured by an atomistic, reductionistic perspective that separates human beings from other beings and reduces all that is not human to objects for human use. But the example of the human mind shows that human development is both culture- and nature-dependent. Infants have brains, but the human mind depends not only on other human beings in order to develop the distinctive characteristics of human existence but also on the stimuli of nature such as light, sound, smell, and heat: without the "warbling birds, blossoming cherry trees, sighing wind, and speaking humans, there would be no sources of signals—and thus no intellects."[13] We do not ordinarily feel indebted to birds and trees for our minds, but recognizing and appreciating that debt is an aspect of the new sensibility necessary for today's theology.

All of this is a poetic way of expressing the most fundamental tenet of the evolutionary, ecological perspective: that the question of what an entity is most basically is answered in terms of its relationships.[14] Thus, for instance, electrons, protons, and neutrons are viewed not as substantial entities but on the models of waves and particles. It is how they behave within the system of which they are a part that determines, on any particular occasion, which model will be used to describe them. What is the case at the subatomic level becomes even clearer at the level of life: each living organism is part of a system, a system with levels.

> The life of the cell is best understood in terms of ecological relationships among molecules. The living organism is best seen in terms of its ecological relationship with its environment. The interdependence of each living organism with other living organisms and with other components of its environment is the principle of population ecology.[15]

To feel in the depths of our being that we are part and parcel of the evolutionary ecosystem of our cosmos is a prerequisite for contemporary Christian theology. It is the beginning of a turn from the anthropocentrism and individualism so deeply embedded in the Western religious tradition, which is nowhere more precisely put than in Augustine's statement in the *Confessions*: "God and the soul, nothing more, nothing at all." That tradition, with its stress on the human individual, continued in much of Protestantism, flowering in the existentialism of the twentieth century. To be sure, another more political context for theology, with deep roots in the Hebrew Scriptures and certainly also in Augustine's two cities, as well as in Calvin's insistence that God is sovereign over the secular state, emerges in our time in the liberation theologies. But what has received less attention—and that largely from the Greek cosmological rather than the Hebraic historical tradition—is the creation which also "groans" for fulfillment.[16] Such lack of attention leads at the very least to an attitudes of unconcern for the earth that is not only our home but, if we accept the evolutionary, ecological paradigm, also the giver and sustainer of our lives in basic and concrete ways. It has created a mentality of human domination and ruthlessness aptly captured in a remark by Huston Smith contrasting Western and Eastern attitudes toward nature:

> When Mount Everest was scaled the phrase commonly used in the West to describe the feat was "the conquest of Everest." An Oriental whose writings have been deeply influenced by Taoism remarked, "We would put the matter differently. We would speak of 'the befriending of Everest.' "[17]

One is reminded of Oriental nature paintings, in which human beings are often depicted not only as diminutive in comparison with the surrounding water and trees but also in a pose of mutual deference with a mountain—each bent, as it were, toward the other.

The evolutionary, ecological perspective perhaps comes across most clearly by contrast with the picture of the world it is replacing: the mechanical model. The mechanical model, bequeathed to us by Newtonian physics and Leibnizian philosophy, informs not only our daily common-sense assumptions and values in the West but also much of traditional Christian theology. Darwin, in the life sciences, and Einstein, in physics, were to overturn this model, but many of its characteristics, sketched here by A. R. Peacocke, remain part of our sensibility:

> By the end of the nineteenth century the absolutes of space, time, object, and determinism were apparently securely enthroned in an unmysterious, mechanically determined world, basically simple in structure at the atomic level and, statistically at least, unchanging in form—for even geological and biological transformations operated under fixed laws.[18]

This picture, though based in the physical rather than the biological sciences, was assumed to cover both, so that life—and not only the most fundamental physical processes of the universe—was understood on the model of a machine. In the early years of the twentieth century there was a movement toward a model more aptly described as organic, even for the constituents with which physics deals, for there occurred a profound realization of the deep relations between space, time, and matter, which relativized them all. In other words, relationships and relativity, as well as process and openness, characterize reality as it is understood at present in all branches of science. It is a considerably more complex picture than the old view, with a hierarchy of levels of organization from the microworld of the subatomic through the macroworld of the biosphere to the megaworld of intergalactic space.[19] But the characteristics of all levels of reality in this picture are similar: the play of chance and necessity replaces determinism; events appear to be more basic than substances, or to phrase it differently, individuals or entities always exist within structures of relationship; process, change, transformation, and openness replace stasis, changelessness, and completeness as basic descriptive concepts. Whereas with the model of the machine, life is patterned on the nonliving, with the organic model the nonliving takes on characteristics of life. The model is most appropriate to life, and hence the qualities of life—openness, relationship, interdependence, change, novelty, and even mystery—become the basic ones for interpreting all reality.

It is obvious how this perspective breaks through the old dualisms generated by the mechanical model—spirit/flesh, human/nonhuman, objective/subjective, reason/passion, supernatural/natural—for in the organic model hard lines cannot be drawn between matter and energy, the organic and the inorganic, the mind and the body, human beings and other forms of life.[20] In addition, the organic or evolutionary, ecological model is one that unites entities in a way basically different from the mechanistic model: instead of bringing entities together by means of common laws that govern all, creating a pattern of external relations, it unites by symbiotic, mutual interdependencies, creating a pattern of internal relations. In the organic model, one does not "enter into relations" with others but finds oneself in such relationships as the most basic given of existence. What separates entities differs as well: whereas in the mechanistic model entities are separated dualistically and hierarchically, in the organic model (or "mutualistic" model—a term that avoids the suggestion of reducing life to bodies which is implied in "organic") all entities are considered to be subjects as well as objects, to have intrinsic value as well as instrumental worth. "The ecological model is a model of living things which are acted upon and which respond by acting in their turn. They are patients and agents. In short they are subjects."[21] To take this perspective does not mean granting consciousness to amoebas, let alone to rocks, but it is to relativize the differences that have in the past been viewed as absolutes. It is to adopt the view toward the world so well captured in Martin Buber's famous distinction between I-Thou and I-It. It is the difference between an aesthetic and a utilitarian perspective, between one that appreciates the other (*all* others) and one that merely uses the other. An aesthetic sensibility toward the cosmos is one that values what is unselfishly, with a sense of delight in others for their own sakes. Such appreciation and delight are a necessary step in turning from an anthropocentric to an ecological sensibility. Thus, in the evolutionary, mutualistic model, all entities are united symbiotically and internally in levels of interdependence but are also separated as centers of action and response, each valuable in its own "beingness," however minimal or momentary that may appear to us. The symbol of the mountain and the human being bent toward each other, if allowing more agency and response to the mountain than can be empirically defended, does express an attitude of respect for otherness rare in the traditional Western sensibility.

Moreover, such an attitude is a basic ingredient in the development of the kind of global consciousness and conscience in relation to human solidarity and solidarity with other levels of life which is the required sensibility for the twenty-first century. Although it is manifestly utopian to imagine that the appreciation of otherness, whether human or nonhuman, will revolutionize our national and international behavior, it is surely folly to continue to encourage in ourselves and those whom we influence individualistic, hierarchical, dualistic, and utilitarian ways of thinking that are outmoded and have proved to be destructive of life at all levels.

The evolutionary, ecological, mutualistic model suggests an ethic toward others, both human and nonhuman, characterized by both justice and care. Carol Gilligan in her work on male- and female-oriented studies of moral development contrasts the pattern of "competing rights," in which one assumes that self and other should be treated fairly in spite of differences in power, and that of "responsibility and care," in which one assumes that everyone will be responded to and included.[22] The first pattern, characteristic of Western male development, begins from a position of separation and works toward connection; the second, characteristic of Western female development, begins from a position of relationship and works toward independence. The ethical pattern of the West has been principally the first, a logic of justice with emphasis on rights and rules and respect for the other. It is a noble ethic in many ways and underlies both the Western regard for the individual and the democratic form of government. But it is an "unfair" ethic, for it has been applied only to human beings—and even here, selectively. An ethic of justice in the evolutionary, ecological, mutualistic model would include the competing rights of other levels of life and would insist on these rights not simply from a utilitarian but also from an aesthetic point of view. That is to say, other levels of life deserve just treatment because of their intrinsic worth. Sorting out the rights of competing levels of life is, needless to say, a complex task, but to include the cosmos in the justice enterprise is essential. The second ethical pattern, that of care, has had a much slighter impact on Western thought. It has, as Gilligan points out, been seen as a weakness when individuals, usually women, understand moral response to focus on sensitivity to the needs of others, responsibility for including and caring for others, rather than on autonomous thinking and clear decision making in regard to the conflicting rights of separate parties.[23] But the model of reality we have sketched clearly demands not only the logic of justice but also the ethic of care. In fact, when the logic of justice is extended to include the nonhuman world, it moves naturally into such a mode, for appreciation for the cosmos *in our time* means responsibility for what is weaker and more vulnerable than human beings.

This is an important point and signals a significant change from the past. Until a few generations ago, nature appeared more powerful than we are. But this is no longer the case. Our ability to diminish if not destroy life through nuclear energy is perhaps the clearest proof of our power, but damage to other species and the eco-sphere through a variety of pollutants and practices makes the point as well. In other words, the logic of justice, the acceptance of the rights of others, if applied (with meaningful distinctions and relativities) in our time to all others, does inevitably move into an ethic of care, for there is no way that such justice can be accorded except through care. It is for this reason that we need to imagine new models for the relationship between ourselves and our earth. We can no longer see ourselves as namers of and rulers over nature but must think of ourselves as gardeners, caretakers, mothers and fathers, stewards, trustees, lovers, priests, co-creators, and friends of a world that, while giving us life and sustenance, also depends increasingly on us in order to continue both for itself and for us.

If one were to do Christian theology from the holistic perspective, it is evident that some significant changes from traditional models and concepts would be neces-sary for expressing the relationships between God and the world and between ourselves and the world. Language that supports hierarchical, dualistic, external, unchanging, atomistic, anthropocentric, and deterministic ways of understanding these relationships is not appropriate *for our time*, whatever its appropriateness might have been for other times. It would appear that the appropriate language for our time, in the sense of being true to the paradigm of reality in which we actually live, would support ways of understanding the God-world and human-world relationships as open, caring, inclusive, interdependent, changing, mutual, and creative.

Needless to say, I am not proposing that the only criterion for theology is its fit with the reigning understanding of reality. But for theology to do *less* than fit our present understanding—for it to accept basic assumptions about reality from a very different time—seems blatantly wrongheaded. Nor am I suggesting that the holistic perspective and the guidelines it suggests for interpreting the relationships between God and the world and between ourselves and the world will necessarily be more permanent than earlier paradigms and guidelines. The evolutionary, ecological model insists above all else that the only permanence is change and hence that a theology appropriate to the holistic model will, at the very least, have to overcome what Rosemary Radford Ruether calls the "tyranny of the absolutizing imagination," which supposes that revolutions, theological or any other kind, are for all time.[24] What is needed is attention to the needs of one's own time. It is my contention that a theology that does not work within the context of the holistic view of reality cannot address the needs of our time.

THE NUCLEAR NIGHTMARE

"The question now before the human species . . . is whether life or death will prevail on the earth. This is not metaphorical language but a literal description of the present state of affairs."[25] But Jonathan Schell's statement has not sunk in. It has not sunk in because we do not want it to, because we do not want to live in the nuclear age, an age in which we must exist with the knowledge that we can destroy ourselves and other forms of life. We prefer to live in the bygone prenuclear age, when God, the mighty King and benevolent Father, was in charge of the world. The thought that we are in charge is too terrifying to contemplate, for we know the evil in our own hearts and in the hearts of others. The thought threatens us with despair for the future: it raises doubts about whether there will be one and about what it will be. So the nuclear issue becomes the unspoken, unacknowledged terror that shadows all we do. Like sex in the Victorian era, it is the unmentionable of our time. Strategies for avoiding it are many: nuclear protesters are characterized as crazy peaceniks with apocalyptic imaginations; the commercial and other benefits of nuclear energy are expounded; the nuclear issue is accused of diverting concern from political and social forms of oppression. And yet scientists on both sides of the East-West divide concur on the likelihood of a "nuclear winter," and a high percentage of young people in study after study believe there will be a nuclear holocaust in their lifetime.

Why is the nuclear issue, which is certainly a strong candidate to be *the* issue of our time, ignored, ridiculed, and repressed? The reasons undoubtedly lie deep within us and are beyond easy understanding, but surely one reason is that as a threat rather than a reality, nuclear doom requires an act of the imagination if it is to become part of our reality, part of our "world." Nuclear consciousness, an essential part of the sensibility needed in our time, must come about as an act of consciousness-raising. This is the case because the world that we could destroy is not destroyed. What we see when we look about us is not postholocaust wreckage but preholocaust order and beauty. The aftermath of Hiroshima and Nagasaki is our principal aid to imagining postholocaust destruction, but even that picture does not help a great deal since there are approximately twenty thousand megatons of nuclear explosives now in existence and one megaton equals the explosive yield of eighty Hiroshimas.[26] A lesser leap of the imagination is needed in regard to many of the other pressing issues of our time, or rather, more ready means are available to raise consciousness on the issues of starvation, sexism, political oppression, poverty, and racism.[27] But nuclear war has not happened, and in this sense it will always be an "unreality" (so long as it does not happen), in contrast to the other terrible, oppressive realities of our time.

What is real, however, as Schell and others have pointed out, is *the knowledge that we have the power to destroy ourselves and other forms of life.* And it is the acceptance of this knowledge and of the responsibilities that come with it which is essential, I believe, to a new sensibility. Accepting this knowledge and understanding the changes it implies for our ways of thinking about the world and for relating to others in the world do not, however, involve seeing the nuclear nightmare as the issue that dwarfs or eliminates all others. On the contrary, the nuclear issue and issues of political and social oppression are intrinsically related, for at the heart of all these issues is the question of power: who wields it and what sort it is. It is, nonetheless, more immediately clear how the ecological and nuclear issues are related, for since the ecosystem is a whole of which we are a part, a major disturbance such as a nuclear war would undermine the entire system. Thus, the holistic vision and the nuclear nightmare are tightly knit: the former is a prerequisite for avoiding the latter. The awareness of our power over the ecosystem implies, as I suggested, the necessity for changing our images of our relationship to it from ones of domination to ones of care and nurture. But the nuclear issue is also intrinsically related to other issues of domination: of rich over poor, white over black, men over women. For the pattern in each case involves *an understanding of power as domination.* The question posed in each case is whether the only kind of pertinent relations between beings is of domination? Is power always domination? Is there another way to effect change, to bring something about, apart from domination?

The answer that immediately comes to mind invokes of course the "power of love." But one is reluctant to move too quickly in that direction, fearing sentimentality, or worse, ineffectiveness. If the issue is power, the power to destroy life, how dare one speak of "mere" love? Let us keep the answer to that question in abeyance while we look more closely at the nuclear issue and current understandings of power.

If our situation is one in which we know that we have the power to destroy ourselves and other forms of life, then power understood as domination and control, as absolute mastery and sovereignty, is counterproductive. For the political realities are such that the exercise of that kind of power raises rather than lowers international tensions and thus contributes to the likelihood of a nuclear holocaust. If in a nuclear age war is outmoded as a form of settling disputes, because there can be no victors, only losers, then the understanding of power which accompanies nationalism and military solutions is not only anachronistic but harmful.

But—and here Christian theology must take its part in the discussion—power as domination has been and still is a central feature of the Western view of God. One of the most distinctive adjectives describing the Judeo-Christian view of God is "almighty": this God is the creator, redeemer, and sustainer of all that is, the high and holy One who is in control, who is to be worshiped and glorified as the sole power in the universe. Such a view of God does not necessarily move in the direction of domination: the almighty can be seen as providential and loving. But whether the understanding of "almighty" moves in the direction of domination or providence, the power is still all God's—it is not shared. As Gordon Kaufman points out in *Theology for a Nuclear Age,* divine sovereignty is the issue with which theologians in the nuclear age must deal.[28] In cruder versions of the traditional view, God is the king who fights on the side of his chosen ones to bring their enemies down; in more refined versions, God is the father who will not let his children suffer.[29] The first way of thinking supports militarism; the second, escapism. As Kaufman states, two groups of American Christians currently rely on these images of God in their responses to the nuclear situation: one group claims that if a nuclear holocaust comes, it will be God's will—the Armageddon—and America should arm itself to fight the devil's agent, communist Russia; the other group passively relies on the all-powerful father to take care of the situation.[30] What neither version supports is *human* responsibility for the world, nor does the tradition supply us with much material for envisioning what power that is not domination or providence might be. If power as domination supports militarism and thus feeds the tensions that could lead to a nuclear holocaust, and power as providence supports escapism and thus lulls us into passivity, what kind of power does the situation call for? Quite obviously it calls, at the outset, for acceptance of our power, the power of human beings, over life and death. We have become, willy-nilly, co-creators in the sense that we have the power to "let life continue." But the acceptance of that power involves a radical change in the very understanding of power, for in order to exercise that power, power must be conceived differently than in the past. Kaufman makes a very important proposal at this juncture when he says that the relationship between God and the world—in other words, between God's power and ours—has in the past been "dualistic" and "asymmetrical" and now needs to become "unified" and "interdependent."[31] The evolutionary, ecological perspective, the holistic vision that is basic to a new sensibility, renders untenable any understanding of the God-world relationship in which God is viewed as a being externally related to the world as the power that totally controls it. It is, for those who accept the basic assumptions of our world (and not a bygone one), incredible. And yet this view of the God-world relationship still largely dominates the common understanding as well as our liturgies—and often even theology. As Langdon Gilkey writes, attempting to sum up the "classic formulation" of God in Western culture,

> . . . the word or symbol "God" has generally referred to one, supreme, or holy being, the unity of ultimate reality and ultimate goodness. So conceived, God is believed to have created the entire universe, to rule over it, and to intend to bring it to its fulfillment or realization, to "save" it.[32]

The relationship between God and the world envisioned in this passage is neither unified nor interdependent. On the contrary, the stress is on the separation of God from the world and on God's control of it: God is the supreme and holy being who rules and saves the world.

The question arises whether the problem lies with the *personal* God of this tradition. Does a view of God as personal entail the ideas of separation, dualism, and control? Sometimes the attempt to relate God and the world in more unified, interdependent ways is thought to require a sacrifice of the personal dimension of the divine. Kaufman, for instance, questions the viability of the personalistic tradition of the West, opting to understand God as the "unifying symbol of those powers and dimensions of the ecological and historical feedback network which create and sustain and work to further enhance life."[33] One of the most distinctive aspects of the Judeo-Christian tradition is that in its kind of theism the deity is appropriately addressed as Thou, not It. One could credit this to the strongly agential Hebraic roots of the tradition—to the understanding of God as one who wills, loves, acts, and responds.

But this conception of God has persisted as highly characteristic of the Judeo-Christian tradition in spite of the contributions of Platonic and Aristotelian views of the divine which are more impersonal and abstract. The stress on the dynamic, loving action of God is clearly seen in liberation theologies today, especially black and Third World theologies. God is the liberator who will free the oppressed. God as Thou also figures in various kinds of process theologies, which, by taking the relationship of the self to the body as the analogy for understanding the relationship between God and the world, have a basis for underscoring both the personal and the radically interdependent character of the divine in relation to the world. Process theologies, however, have not focused much attention on the kind of personal metaphors and models most appropriate *for our time*; or to put it differently, in criticizing (as Kaufman also does) the monarchical, triumphalist models that support asymmetrical dualism, process theologians have not moved boldly to suggest other models more suited to a view of God as intrinsically and radically relational. And though black and Third World theologies fully retain the agential aspects of the Western concept, they do so in a way that limits God to the realm of persons and history, leaving much of the cosmos unaddressed. Too, they have not experimented with new models, apart from that of liberator, which has been limited to freeing oppressed humanity.

The question, then, is this: In what metaphors and models should we conceive of God as Thou who is related to the world in a unified and interdependent way? To understand God as Thou, it seems to me, is basic for our relating to all reality in the mode of mutuality, respect, care, and responsibility. The qualities of personal relationship are needed in our time not only in the God-world relation but in the human-world relation as well. The problem, I believe, is not that personal metaphors and concepts have been used for God; it is not the personal aspect that has brought about the asymmetrical dualism. The problem lies, rather, in the particular metaphors and concepts chosen. The primary metaphors in the tradition are hierarchical, imperialistic, and dualistic, stressing the distance between God and the world and the total reliance of the world on God. Thus, the metaphors of God as king, ruler, lord, master, and governor, and the concepts that accompany them of God as absolute, complete, transcendent, and omnipotent permit no sense of mutuality, shared responsibility, reciprocity, and love (except in the sense of gratitude). Even the one primary metaphor for God that would allow for a more unified, interdependent view, that of father, has been so qualified by being associated with the metaphors of king and lord (as, for instance, in the phrase, "almighty Father") that its potential as an expression of a unified, interdependent view of God and the world is undercut.

It has become increasingly and painfully evident to many Westerners, both those within the Judeo-Christian tradition and those outside who nonetheless are influenced by its imagery, values, and concepts, that the language used to express the relationship between God and the world needs revision. It is my contention that this revision must begin at the level of the imagination, in a "thought experiment" with metaphors and their accompanying concepts that, unlike the principal ones in the tradition, express a unified, interdependent framework for understanding God-world and human-world relations. I see this experiment in part as a response to Kaufman's call to students of religion to combat the ways the traditional imagery for God supports either militarism or escapism in this nuclear age, by entering "into the most radical kind of deconstruction and reconstruction of the traditions they have inherited, including especially the most central and precious symbols of these traditions, *God and Jesus Christ* and *Torah*."[34] There are, undoubtedly, many ways to respond to this call, but *one* critical aspect of the deconstruction and reconstruction of religious symbols involves both a critique of the triumphalist, imperialistic, patriarchal model and a "thought experiment" with some alternative models that are, I believe, commensurate with the evolutionary, ecological sensibility and with the Christian faith. No one, of course, can create images of God; religious symbols are born and die in a culture for complex reasons. At most, one can try to attend carefully to the images in the culture and church which appear to be emerging and to experiment imaginatively with them, reflecting on their implications for life with God and with others.

The models of God as mother, lover, and friend offer possibilities for envisioning power in unified, interdependent ways quite different from the view of power as either domination or benevolence. I believe these models are uniquely suited for theology in a nuclear age and could serve as well to recontextualize the present dominant metaphor of father in a parental rather than patriarchal direction. We asked earlier about power that is not domination or benevolence and suggested that we hold in abeyance a consideration of the "power of love." The kind of power associated with the models of mother (and father), lover, and friend is indeed love, and love that is unified and interdependent. That is, if one reflects on the characteristics of the love shown by parents, lovers, and friends the words that come to mind include "fidelity," "nurture," "attraction," "self sacrifice," "passion," "responsibility," "care," "affection," "respect," and "mutuality." In fact, all the qualities of love so neatly demarcated in the ancient divisions of agape, eros, and philia come into play. These words suggest power but a very different kind of power from that associated with the models of lord, king, and patriarch.

If theologians and students of religion are to be part of the solution to the problem posed by the unprecedented nuclear knowledge that human beings now possess, they must, I believe, answer the call to deconstruct and reconstruct the traditional symbols of Christian faith. This task suggests that Christian theology, in our time at least, cannot be merely or mainly hermeneutics, that is, interpretation of the tradition, a translation of ancient creeds and concepts to make them relevant for contemporary culture. Rather, theology must be self-consciously constructive, willing to think differently than in the past. If one reflects on the contrasts between the theologies of Paul, Augustine, Luther, Schleiermacher, and Barth (just to take a sampling of the tradition) as to their basic images, root metaphors, concepts, and assumptions about reality, one has to acknowledge an enormous variety, all of it, however, capable of being accommodated within the Christian paradigm. Theology in our day needs to be self-consciously constructive in order to free itself from traditional notions of divine sovereignty sufficiently to be able to experiment with other and more appropriate metaphors and models that may help us cope with the "question now before the human species . . . whether life or death will prevail on earth."

THEOLOGICAL CONSTRUCTION

In addition to the holistic vision and acceptance of responsibility for nuclear knowledge, a third aspect of the new sensibility for doing theology in our time is consciousness of the constructive character of all human activities, especially of those within which we live and therefore of which we are least aware: our world views, including our religions. One of the distinctive features of the twentieth century, evident in all fields including science, is increasing awareness of the creative, interpretive character of human existence. But it is important that our interpretive creations not be reified or petrified. Paul de Man, the deconstructionist literary critic, makes the point vividly with his comment that the story of language is "like the plot of a Gothic novel in which someone compulsively manufactures a monster" on which one "then becomes totally dependent" and which one "does not have the power to kill."[35] We are reminded of Nietzsche's description of truth as worn-out metaphors that have become "fixed, canonic and binding" so that we forget that they are "illusions." The double-edged allegation of Nietzsche concerning the constructive as well as the illusory character of human language—in our case, the language of theology—must be squarely faced. I do not believe that recognition of, even celebration of, the constructive character of theology necessarily involves the admission that all construction is merely play and that hence one construction is no better than another. At this point, the absolutism of fundamentalism and the absolutism of deconstruction are similar: the first insists that only one construction (which is not admitted to be a construction) is true, right, and good, and the second insists that all constructions (which are solely the products of aesthetic playfulness) are equally illusory, with none more true, more right, or better than any of the others.[36] What links these positions, in my view, is related to metaphor: fundamentalism fails to appreciate that the language of theology is metaphorical, and deconstruction refuses to acknowledge that there is anything but metaphor.

It is evident that fundamentalism does not accept the metaphorical character of religious and theological language, for its basic tenet is the identification of the Word of God with human words, notably those human words in the canonical Scriptures of the church. The essence of metaphorical theology, however, is precisely the refusal to identify human constructions with divine reality.[37] Since a metaphor is a word or phrase appropriate to one context but used in another, no metaphorical construction can be univocally applied, that is, applied in the form of identity. To say that "God is mother" is not to identify God with mother, but to understand God in light of some of the characteristics associated with mothering. It is, then, also to say, "God is not mother," or, to combine the positive and negative aspects of metaphorical assertion, "God is/is not mother," or yet again, "God *as* mother" (which underscores the comparative nature of metaphor: God viewed in the capacity, character, or role of mother). In other words, the constructive character of metaphor is self-evident, since the appropriate, literal, or conventional context for applying the title of mother is obviously not the divine. Yet much if not all religious language and a great deal of theological language is of this type; that is, language that is literally appropriate to personal, social, or political human relationships or to the natural world is applied metaphorically to God. Thus, the fundamentalist's assertion of univocity between human language about God and God or "God's Word" fails to appreciate the most basic characteristic of religious and theological language: its iconoclastic character, what the tradition calls the *via negativa*. All language about God is human construction and as such perforce "misses the mark."

On the other hand, deconstruction, in many ways a highly perceptive critique of Western metaphysics, focuses on metaphor, for one way of describing deconstruction is as an insistence that there is nothing but metaphor.[38] As the latest stage of a journey beginning with Nietzsche—who saw how language deceives us into believing it is fixed and definite, referring to something outside ourselves, when in fact it is nothing but the play of metaphors—deconstruction concludes that the root metaphor of human existence is writing and interprets writing literally as metaphoricity itself.[39] The increasing realization of the power of language as the most distinctive attribute of human existence, and the realization of the ways in which we construct the worlds we inhabit through it, have during this century come to the point of claiming with the French deconstructionist Jacques Derrida that "there is nothing outside the text"—and this statement includes author and referent.[40] If there is only text, or writing, this means there is only the play of words, interpretation upon interpretation, referring to nothing but other words, an endless spiral with no beginning or end. This is language as "metaphoricity itself." There is nothing but metaphor; metaphor is the ultimate metaphor, for all words miss the mark, are inappropriate, and out of context, because there is no mark, there is no way to judge appropriateness, there is no conventional or literal context for a word or phrase.

I disagree with this understanding of metaphor, but before going into that, I would first underscore the value of deconstruction's critique of Western metaphysics for the new sensibility needed to do Christian theology in our time. Its extreme position gives it a base for launching a full-scale attack on what it calls the "metaphysics of presence" in Western thought. This metaphysics takes many forms, but in essence it is an attempt to cover up the absence, emptiness, and uncertainty we sense (and fear) may be at the heart of things. What metaphor does, say the deconstructionists, is to insist on absence, for if metaphor is a word or sign standing for another word or sign in endless repetition with no reference outside itself, then there is no possibility of words conveying "presence": not our presence to one another, or the world's presence to us, or God's to us. The metaphysics of presence is most evident in the desire for completeness and totality, full presence, in the Judeo-Christian tradition, and especially in the orthodox christological assertion that God is present, fully and completely, in one human being. Jesus Christ, fully God and fully man, is the ultimate assurance that the universe is not blank emptiness: on the contrary, full and unmediated presence, not just of other selves or the reality of the world but of Presence itself is ours in the Christ, and, through him we are assured of the return of what we have lost, the garden of Eden, as well as of even greater fulfillment in the paradise to come.[41] And, says deconstruction, Western theology claims also to have assurance of this Presence in the Book, the Text of texts, in which human words truly refer to the Word itself. Hence, in our language about this Presence we need not take *aporia,* absence, seriously into account nor acknowledge the uncertainty, incompleteness, or relativity of our interpretations so long as we stay close to the Book. But, deconstruction continues, the history of Western metaphysics is one of massive forgetfulness, forgetfulness that metaphor lies at the base of all our constructions, including that most sacred Text: it too is but the play of words, interpretation upon interpretation, creating a shimmering surface that has no author and no referent

One need not agree with all this to see its value for informing the sensibility of late twentieth-century theology. Deconstruction is not a new method or theory; rather, as its name itself suggests, it is a calling to attention of what could be called the underside of all our constructions, the "is not," the incompleteness, the partiality, the uncertainty, that must accompany all our creations lest we reify them into absolutes. Deconstruction cautions us against trying to save ourselves through our constructions. The temptation is to seek security, in a vast number of complex ways, against the abyss, the chaos, the different, the other, the unknown—whatever threatens us. By seeking security through our constructions, we refuse to step outside the houses of language we have erected to protect us from the emptiness and the terror we cannot control. Our safe havens, called dogmas and orthodoxy, become absolutes, giving the illusion of being certain, being "on the inside," having the truth.

Deconstruction criticizes as childish our nostalgia for Presence. It calls Christian theology (and all other constructions or world views) to adulthood. In this it makes a major contribution to adjusting the sensibility of our time. The desire for full presence, whether in the form of nostalgia for the garden of Eden, or the quest for the historical Jesus, or the myth of God incarnate, is a denial of what we know as adults to be the case in human existence: such innocence, certainty, and absoluteness are not possible. What deconstruction, with its denial of all presence, brings out powerfully even for nondeconstructionists is that absence is at least more prevalent than presence: the world in which we live is one in which we create structures to protect us against the chaos, absence, death, oppression, and exclusion that surround us—a negativity symbolized by the ultimate absence, a nuclear holocaust. It is by no means a completely new insight when deconstruction speaks of the absence of presence, for a long tradition of negative theology has accompanied the tradition of presence and is vividly encapsulated in H. Richard Niebuhr's statement that faith as the attitude of fundamental trust in being itself comes about only when one becomes "suspicious" of one's own "deep suspicion of the Determiner of Destiny."[42] But deconstruction's critique makes clear the necessity of developing "negative capability"—the ability to endure absence, uncertainty, partiality, relativity, and to hold at bay the desire for closure, coherence, identity, totality. It is a call "to put away childish things" and grow up.

What deconstruction does not do, however, is offer any assistance on the question of *which* constructions are better than others. It deals eloquently with the "is not" of metaphor, but it refuses to deal with the "is." I agree with the deconstructionists that all constructions are metaphorical and hence miss the mark; I nevertheless disagree with them when they say that language (writing) is about only itself and that no construction is any better than any other. To claim that all constructions are metaphorical is to insist that one never experiences reality "raw"; it does not follow from this, however, that there is nothing outside language. All that follows is that our access to reality is in every case mediated and hence partial and relative. Nor is the admission of the metaphoricity of our constructions a denial that interpretations can genuinely conflict. In fact, the opposite is the case, for the presence of many constructions, many metaphors, assumes conflict and the need for criteria.

There is indeed no way behind our constructions to test them for their correspondence with the reality they presume to represent, but the constructions do, I believe, have a twofold relationship with reality which deconstruction ignores. First, they are productive of reality; that is, our metaphorical constructions are redescriptions or new readings of what lies outside them, in place of old or conventional descriptions or readings. All renderings of reality are metaphorical (that is, none is literal), but in our novel constructions we offer new possibilities in place of others. In this sense we create the reality in which we live; we do not copy it, or to put it more pointedly, there are no copies, only creations. The assumption here, however, is that there is a reality to which our constructions refer, even though the only way we have of reaching it is by creating versions of it.[43] This is altogether different from the deconstructionist's position that there is nothing to which the text refers.

Second, our constructions are intended to be better than the ones they refute or replace. This is of course a very difficult issue, because if one admits that all are readings, with the new replacing the old, on what basis can some be better than others? They certainly cannot claim to be better absolutely, or from all perspectives, or for all time.[44] At the most, they might be better relatively (to other constructions) from a particular perspective, and for a particular time. And this is the claim I would make: that a construction of the Christian faith in the context of a holistic vision and the nuclear threat is from our particular perspective and for our particular time relatively better than constructions that ignore these issues. It is relatively better in part because of what Christian faith at base is about. The claim is that to understand the Christian faith in terms of the holistic vision and in response to the nuclear threat is in continuity with the basic Christian paradigm as well as being an appropriate construction of that faith for our time. I will attempt to make that case, but it cannot be proved. As with any construction, the most one can do is to "live within" it, testing it for its disclosive power, its ability to address and cope with the most pressing issues of one's day, its comprehensiveness and coherence, its potential for dealing with anomalies, and so forth. Theological constructions are "houses" to live in for a while, with windows partly open and doors ajar; they become prisons when they no longer allow us to come and go, to add a room or take one away—or if necessary, to move out and build a new house.

In this chapter, I have been searching for a standpoint from which to do Christian theology in our time. I have suggested that a new sensibility is required, one characterized by the felt awareness of our intrinsic interdependence with all that lives, a holistic, evolutionary, ecological vision that overcomes ancient and oppressive dualisms and hierarchies, that encourages change and novelty, and that promotes an ethic of justice and care; one characterized as well by a profound acceptance of human responsibility for the fate of the earth, especially in view of a possible nuclear holocaust, and therefore by the willingness to think differently, to think in metaphors and models that support a unified, interdependent understanding of God-world and human-world relationships; and finally, one characterized by the recognition that although all constructive thought is metaphorical and hence necessarily risky, partial, and uncertain, implying an end to dogmatism and absolutism, it is not thereby fantasy, illusion, or play.

I believe that the supposition that theology is a verbal game is as dangerous as the refusal to admit the role of imagination in theology. There is something outside language, or to phrase it differently, the "games" we play with language make a difference in what we understand reality to be and how we conduct our lives in relation to other beings, both human and nonhuman. A person who is starving, imprisoned, discriminated against, tortured, or homeless can scarcely be expected to believe that the ideology that permits such oppression is a mere game, no worse than any other. Nor would such a person believe that language is the totality of reality: hunger, fear, and suffering unite beings, both human and nonhuman, in a wordless community where a cry of pain is the universal word. Language is nonetheless a serious matter; it is our window, albeit not a transparent one, onto the world. We live our lives according to our constructions of the world; as Erich Heller said, "Be careful how you interpret the world; it *is* like that." There is no retreat from the conflict of interpretations, because life is not a game—or if one chooses to think that it is, then it should be said that the game may be up unless the rules by which we have been playing are changed.

NOTES

1. Pierre Teilhard de Chardin, *Writings in Time of War*, trans. René Hague (London: William Collins Sons, 1968), 25.
2. Ibid., 26.
3. Wallace Stevens, *Opus Posthumous*, ed. S.F. Morris (New York: Alfred A. Knopf, 1957), 163.
4. Jonathan Schell, *The Fate of the Earth* (New York: Avon Books, 1982), 117.
5. Ibid., 174.
6. Ibid., 108.
7. Friedrich Nietzsche, "On Truth and Falsity in Their Ultramoral Sense" (1873), in *Works* 2:180.
8. Elisabeth Schüssler Fiorenza, *In Memory of Her: A Feminist Theological Reconstruction of Christian Origins* (New York: Crossroad, 1983), 121.
9. A well-known exception is Rosemary Radford Ruether, who when stating her understanding of the biblical critical principle of renewal, invariably extends it to include a critique of "humanocentrism." "The 'brotherhood' of man needs to be widened to embrace not only women but also the whole community of life" (*Sexism and God-Talk: Toward a Feminist Theology* [Boston: Beacon Press, 1983], 87).
10. See, e.g., Ynestra King, "Making the World Live: Feminism and the Domination of Nature," in *Women's Spirit Bonding*, ed. Janet Kalven and Mary I. Buckley (New York: Pilgrim Press, 1984); Susan Griffin, *Woman and Nature: The Roaring inside Her* (New York: Harper & Row, 1978); Mary Daly, *Pure Lust: Elemental Feminist Theology* (Boston: Beacon Press, 1984); Starhawk, *Dreaming the Dark: Magic, Sex, and Politics* (Boston: Beacon Press, 1982); and idem, *The Spiral Dance: A Rebirth of the Ancient Religion of the Great Goddess* (San Francisco: Harper & Row, 1979).
11. See chap. 4, pp. 99–100.
12. The phrase "the deprivatising of theology" comes from "Editorial Reflections," in *Cosmology and Theology*, ed. David Tracy and Nicholas Lash (New York: Seabury Press; Edinburgh: T. & T. Clark, 1983), 89.
13. Harold K. Schilling, "The Whole Earth Is the Lord's: Toward a Holistic Ethic," in *Earth Might Be Fair: Reflections on Ethics, Religion, and Ecology*, ed. Ian Barbour (Englewood Cliffs, N.J.: Prentice-Hall, 1972), 102. Schilling makes the further and related point that almost everything we value is of a social, relational sort: not only the obvious communities in which we exist, such as family, city, and country, but also education, politics, the arts, science, and language. Moreover, the most basic, precious things we value are profoundly social and relational: friendship, love, parenthood, loyalty, wisdom.
14. Two recent sources (among the many available) that flesh out the implications of this statement for theology are Charles Birch and John B. Cobb, Jr., *The Liberation of Life: From the Cell to the Community* (Cambridge: At the Univ. Press, 1981), and A. R. Peacocke, *Creation and the World of Science* (Oxford: At the Clarendon Press, 1979). Another very interesting treatment by Stephen Toulmin depicts a postmodern cosmology in

which human beings, in order to be "at home" in the world, must adopt not just a utilitarian but an appreciative attitude toward the other forms of life with which we are in relationship: "We can do our best to build up a conception of 'the overall scheme of things' which draws as heavily as it can on the results of scientific study, informed by a genuine piety in all its attitudes toward creatures of other kinds: a piety that goes beyond the consideration of their usefulness to Humanity as instruments for the fulfillment of human ends. That is an alternative within which human beings can both *feel,* and also *be,* at home. For to be at home in the world of nature does not just mean finding out how to utilize nature economically and efficiently—home is not a hotel! It means making sense of the relations that human beings and other living things have toward the overall patterns of nature in ways that give us some sense of their proper relations to one another, to ourselves, and to the whole" (*The Return to Cosmology: Postmodern Science and the Theology of Nature* [Berkeley and Los Angeles: Univ. of California Press, 1982], 272). Toulmin claims that postmodern science has more in common with the classical theory of "correspondences" among all aspects of the natural world—the various interlocking relations in creation—than it does with modern (Newtonian) science.

15. Birch and Cobb, *The Liberation of Life,* 42.
16. See George S. Hendry, *Theology of Nature* (Philadelphia: Westminster Press, 1980), for a treatment of what he calls the cosmological, political, and psychological contexts for presenting the saving activity of God.
17. Huston Smith, *The Religions of Man* (New York: Harper & Row, 1965), 209.
18. Peacocke, *Creation and the World of Science,* 54.
19. Ibid., 61–62.
20. One illustration of this point is found in a number of studies with higher mammals, such as apes and dolphins, that reveal complex problem-solving abilities; other studies among a broad range of animals underscore that what could be called "spirit"—experiences of vitality, joy, and grief—is not limited to human beings. Anyone who has been in a "symbiotic relationship" with a pet for any length of time knows that there is communication across the dividing line of species.
21. Birch and Cobb, *The Liberation of Life,* 123.
22. Carol Gilligan, *In a Different Voice: Psychological Theory and Women's Development* (Cambridge: Harvard Univ. Press, 1982).
23. Ibid., chap. 1.
24. Rosemary Radford Ruether, "Envisioning Our Hopes: Some Models of the Future," in *Women's Spirit Bonding,* ed. Kalven and Buckley, 335.
25. Schell, *The Fate of the Earth,* 113.
26. Ibid., 67.
27. The role of reporters and especially of television in raising consciousness—and in producing subsequent action—in such events as the Vietnam war and more recently the anti-apartheid struggle in South Africa is well known.
28. Gordon Kaufman, *Theology for a Nuclear Age* (Philadelphia: Westminster Press, 1985). Kaufman's fine study is almost alone in attempting a serious revision of theology, especially the image-concept of God, for a nuclear age.
29. For an interesting study of the use of political discourse for images of God, see David Nicholls, "Images of God and the State: Political Analogy and Religious Discourse," *Theological Studies* 42 (1981): 195–215. Elsewhere he writes that "our legitimate political concerns should . . . be reflected in the liturgy" but are not; on the contrary, "they [the liturgies] reveal a picture of God as an all-powerful but benevolent administrator whose principal role is to ensure the stability of the *status quo* and in particular to guarantee a quiet life for the church. . . . Almost entirely absent is the idea that Christians are called

by God to be 'workers together with him' in the building of his kingdom (or commonwealth) of justice on earth" *(Times* [London], August 16, 1980, p. 14).

30. "Nuclear Eschatology and the Study of Religion," *Journal of the American Academy of Religion* 51 (1983): 7–8.
31. Kaufman, *Theology for a Nuclear Age,* 42.
32. Langdon Gilkey, "God," in *Christian Theology: An Introduction to Its Traditions and Tasks,* rev. ed., ed. Peter C. Hodgson and Robert H. King (Philadelphia: Fortress Press, 1985), 89–90.
33. Kaufman, *Theology for a Nuclear Age,* 56. The closest Kaufman comes to an agential view is in phrases such as "unpredictable grace" and "hidden creativity" as designations for the symbol "God."
34. Ibid., 13.
35. Paul de Man, "The Epistemology of Metaphor," in *On Metaphor,* ed. Sheldon Sacks (Chicago: Univ. of Chicago Press, 1979), 23.
36. The literature on deconstruction and theology is now extensive. The work of Mark Taylor, esp. his *Erring: A Postmodern A/theology* (Chicago: Univ. of Chicago Press, 1984) is one of the most ambitious works to date. See also Thomas J. J. Altizer et al., *Deconstruction and Theology* (New York: Crossroad, 1982), and Charles E. Winquist, *Epiphanies of Darkness: Deconstruction in Theology* (Philadelphia: Fortress Press, 1986).
37. For a fuller treatment of the relationship between models and their referents, see my book *Metaphorical Theology: Models of God in Religious Language* (Philadelphia: Fortress Press, 1982; 2d printing with new preface, 1985), esp. chaps. 1, 2, and 4. I will, however, attempt a brief reply here. What prevents models of God, such as mother, lover, and friend, from being arbitrary? The most direct answer to that question is that they are not arbitrary, because, along with the father model, they are the deepest and most important expressions of love known to us, rather than because they are necessarily descriptive of the nature of God. But, pressing the ontological issue more sharply, are these loves descriptive of God *as God is?* As I say several times in this essay, it seems to me that to be a Christian is to be persuaded that there is a personal, gracious power who is on the side of life and its fulfillment, a power whom the paradigmatic figure Jesus of Nazareth expresses and illuminates; but when we try to say something more, we turn, necessarily, to the "loves" we know (unless one is a Barthian and believes that God defines love and that all human love only conforms to the divine pattern). That is to say, I do not know whether God (the inner being of God) can be described by the models of mother, lover, and friend; but the only kind of love I know anything about and that matters most to me is the love of these basic relationships, so I have to use these loves to speak of divine love. The metaphors do not illustrate a concept of love (that is basically an allegorical direction); rather, they *project a possibility:* that God's love can be seen through the screen of these human loves. Metaphors and models relate to reality not in imitating it but in being productive of it. There are only versions, hypotheses, or models of reality (or God): the most that one can say of any construct, then, is that it is illuminating, fruitful, can deal with anomalies, has relatively comprehensive explanatory ability, is relatively consistent, has humane consequences, etc. This is largely a functional, pragmatic view of truth, with heavy stress on what the implications of certain ways of seeing things (certain models) are for the quality of both human and nonhuman life (since the initial assumption or belief is that God is on the side of life and its fulfillment). This is obviously something of a circular argument, but I do not see any way out of it: I do not *know* who God is, but I find some models better than others for constructing an image of God commensurate with my trust in a God as on the side of life. God is and remains a mystery. We really do not know: the hints and clues we have of the way things are—whether we call them experi-

ences, revelation, or whatever—are too fragile, too little (and more often than not, too negative) for much more than a hypothesis, a guess, a projection of a possibility that, although it can be comprehensive and illuminating, may not be true. We can believe it is and act as if it were, but it is, to use Ricoeur's term, a "wager." At the most, I find I can make what Philip Wheelwright calls a "shy ontological claim" with the metaphors and models we use to speak of divine reality (see *Metaphor and Reality* [Bloomington: Indiana Univ. Press, 1971], 162).

38. An excellent entrée into deconstruction and its nineteenth-century background is Christopher Norris, *Deconstruction: Theory and Practice* (London: Methuen & Co., 1982). Another fine essay appears as chap. 5 in Frank Lentricchia, *After the New Criticism* (Chicago: Univ. of Chicago Press, 1980), which traces two directions from the key work of Jacques Derrida, one toward the literary criticism of the "Yale school" and the other toward the social-political historiography of Michel Foucault.

39. See Norris, *Deconstruction,* 64ff., for a discussion of this point

40. See Derrida's critical essay on metaphor, "White Mythology: Metaphor in the Text of Philosophy," *New Literary History* 6 (1974): 5–74.

41. For two different treatments of this point, see Louis Mackey, "Slouching toward Bethlehem: Deconstructive Strategies in Theology," *Anglican Theological Review* 65 (1983): 255-72; and Carl A. Raschke, "The Deconstruction of God," in Altizer et al., *Deconstruction and Theology,* 1–33.

42. H. Richard Niebuhr, *The Responsible Self: An Essay in Christian Moral Philosophy* (New York: Harper & Row, 1963), 175.

43. This is of course what has been called critical realism, and from some contemporary perspectives it is not fashionable. See, e.g., George Lindbeck's espousal of what he calls a "cultural-linguistic" position, which stresses language over "reality reference." In speaking of Scripture, he writes, "It is the text, so to speak, which absorbs the world, rather than the world the text" (*The Nature of Doctrine: Religion and Theology in a Postliberal Age* [Philadelphia: Westminster Press, 1984], 118). This position gives up the issue of the conflict of interpretations, opting for formation of its own adherents within particular linguistic communities.

44. Michel Foucault's contribution to the demise of the metaphysics of presence is his critique of the illusion of the myth of selves as objective and value-free centers in control of history. He insists that, on the contrary, discourse formation is the product of dominant social and political forces, creating "insiders" and "outsiders." This is a point echoed in the liberation theologies' position on the social context of theology. See esp. "The Discourse on Language," in Foucault's *The Archeology of Knowledge,* trans. A. M. Sheridan Smith (New York: Pantheon Books, 1972), 215–37.

Index